# A RABBINIC COMMENTARY ON THE NEW TESTAMENT

## THE GOSPELS OF

## MATTHEW, MARK, and LUKE

*Samuel Tobias Lachs*

KTAV PUBLISHING HOUSE, INC.
HOBOKEN, NEW JERSEY

ANTI-DEFAMATION LEAGUE
OF B'NAI B'RITH
NEW YORK

The Scripture quotations in this publication are from the Revised Standard Version of the Bible, copyrighted 1946, 1952 © 1971, 1973 by the Division of Christian Education of the National Council of the Churches of Christ in the U.S.A., and used by permission.

**Library of Congress Cataloging-in-Publication Data**

Lachs, Samuel Tobias.
   A rabbinic commentary on the New Testament.

   Bibliography: p.
   Includes index.
   1. Bible. N.T. Matthew—commentaries. 2. Bible.
N.T. Mark—Commentaries. 3. Bible. N.T. Luke—
Commentaries. 4. Rabbinical literature—Relation to
the New Testament. I. Title.
BS2555.3.L33  1987     226'.07     87-3895
ISBN 0-88125-089-9

Printed in the United States of America

*To my wife*

# CONTENTS

xiii • *Contents*

## THE SYNOPTIC APOCALYPSE (Matt. 24.14–36, Mark 13.5–37, Luke 21.8–36)

# Abbreviations of
# Works Frequently Cited

| | |
|---|---|
| *AJTh* | *American Journal of Theology* |
| *Ant.* | Josephus, *Antiquities* |
| *APB* | Singer, Authorized Prayer Book |
| *BA* | Biblical Archaeologist |
| *BAG* | Bauer-Arndt-Gingrich, *Greek–English Lexicon of the New Testament and Other Early Christian Literature* (Chicago: University of Chicago Press, 1957) |
| *BHM* | A. Jellinek, *Bet Hamidrasch*, 6 vols. (Jerusalem, 1938). |
| *BJ* | Josephus, *Wars of the Jews* |
| *CD* | Cairo Genizah Text of the Damascus Document |
| *CTM* | R. Travers Herford, *Christianity in Talmud and Midrash* (1903; reprint ed., New York: Ktav). |
| *D* | Codex Bezae |
| *DJD* | *Discoveries in the Judaean Desert* (Oxford: Clarendon Press, 1955–) |
| *ESBNT* | J. A. Fitzmyer, *Essays on the Semitic Background of the New Testament* (London: Chapman, 1951) |
| *EWJ* | J. Jeremias, *The Eucharistic Words of Jesus* (Philadelphia: Fortress Press, 1977) |
| *Expos. T.* | *Expository Times* |
| *FTG* | M. Dibelius, *From Tradition to Gospel* (New York: Scribner's, 1938) |
| *GJV* | E. Schürer, *Geschichte des jüdischen Volkes im Zeitalter Jesu Christi*, 4th ed. (Leipzig, 1901) |
| *GLL* | S. Krauss, *Griechishe und lateinische Lehnwörter in Talmud, Midrasch und Targum* (Berlin, 1898) |
| *GV* | L. Zunz, *Die gottesdiestlichen Vorträge der Juden*, 2nd ed. (Frankfurt am Main, 1892) |
| *HALAT* | W. Baumgartner, *Hebräisches und aramäisches Lexikon zum Alten Testament* (Leiden: Brill, 1967–) |
| *HST* | R. Bultmann, *History of the Synoptic Tradition* (Oxford: Blackwell, 1968) |

| | |
|---|---|
| *HTR* | *Harvard Theological Review* |
| *HUCA* | *Hebrew Union College Annual* |
| ICC | International Critical Commentary |
| *IDB* | *Interpreter's Dictionary of the Bible* (4 vols; Nashville: Abingdon, 1962) |
| *IEJ* | *Israel Exploration Journal* |
| *JBL* | *Journal of Biblical Literature* |
| *JBR* | *Journal of Bible and Religion* |
| *JE* | *Jewish Encyclopedia*, ed. I. Singer (New York: Funk & Wagnalls, 1902) |
| *JJS* | *Journal of Jewish Studies* |
| *JN* | J. Klausner, *Jesus of Nazareth: His Life, Times and Teaching* (New York: Macmillan, 1946) |
| *JNES* | *Journal of Near Eastern Studies* |
| *JPOS* | *Journal of the Palestine Oriental Society* |
| *JQR* | *Jewish Quarterly Review* |
| *JSNT* | *Journal for the Study of the New Testament* |
| *JTS* | *Journal of Theological Studies* |
| *LNT* | J. D. M. Derrett, *Law in the New Testament* |
| *MGWJ* | *Monatsschrift für Geschichte und Wissenschaft des Judentums* |
| *MT* | Massoretic Text |
| *NEB* | New English Bible |
| *NH* | Pliny, *Natural History* |
| *NT* | *Novum Testamentum* |
| *NTS* | *New Testament Studies* |
| *NTsup.* | Supplement to *Novum Testamentum* |
| *NTRJ* | D. Daube, *New Testament and Rabbinic Judaism* (London: Athlone, 1956) |
| *PAAJR* | *Proceedings of the American Academy for Jewish Research* |
| *Oxy.P.* | Oxyrhynchus Papyri |
| *PJ* | J. Jeremias, *The Parables of Jesus*, 6th ed. S. H. Hooke (New York: Scribners, 1963) |
| *QDAP* | *Quarterly Department of Antiquities in Palestine* |
| *RB* | *Revue Biblique* |
| *REJ* | *Revue des Études Juives* |
| *RFJS* | S. Zeitlin, *The Rise and Fall of the Judaean State*, 3 vols. (Philadelphia: Jewish Publication Society, 1962–78) |
| *RLGT* | C. G. Montefiore, *Rabbinic Literature and Gospel Teachings* (New York: Ktav, 1970) |
| *RSV* | Revised Standard Version |
| *S* | Codex Sinaiticus |

| | |
|---|---|
| *SB* | H. L. Strack and P. Billerbeck, *Kommentar zum Neuen Testament aus Talmud und Midrasch*, 6 vols. (Munich, 1956) |
| *SBL* | Society of Biblical Literature |
| *SG* | Claude G. Montefiore, *The Synoptic Gospels*, 2 vols. (1927; reprint ed., New York: Ktav, 1968) |
| *SJ* | T. A. Manson, *The Sayings of Jesus* (London, 1961) |
| *SJLA* | *Studies in Judaism in Late Antiquity* |
| *SNT* | J. D. M. Derrett, *Studies in the New Testament*, 3 vols. (Leiden: Brill, 1977) |
| *SNTSMS* | *Studiorum Novi Testamenti Societas*, Monograph Series |
| Sonc. Tal. | Soncino Talmud |
| *SSM* | W. D. Davies, *The Setting of the Sermon on the Mount* (Cambridge: Cambridge University Press, 1966) |
| *SSMUOT* | K. Stendahl, *The School of St. Matthew and Its Use of the Old Testament* (Philadelphia: Fortress Press, 1968) |
| *Studies I, II* | I. Abrahams, *Studies in Pharisaism and the Gospels*, reprint of 1917 & 1924 eds. of First and Second Series (New York: Ktav, 1967) |
| TA | S. Krauss, *Talmudische Archäologie*, 3 vols. (Leipzig, 1910) |
| *TDNT* | G. Kittel, *Theological Dictionary of the New Testament*, ed. and trans. G. W. Bromiley, 10 vols. (Grand Rapids, Mich.: Eerdmans, 1981) |
| *TJ* | T. S. Mason, *The Teachings of Jesus*, 2d ed. (Cambridge: Cambridge University Press, 1935) |
| *ZAW* | *Zeitschrift für die alttestamentliche Wissenschaft* |
| *ZDMG* | *Zeitschrift der Deutschen Morgenländischen Gesellschaft* |
| *ZNW* | *Zeitschrift für die neutestamentliche Wissenschaft* |

# Abbreviations of Rabbinic Works

| | |
|---|---|
| M. | Mishnah |
| T. | Tosefta, ed. M. S. Zuckermandel (Jerusalem, 1937) |
| B. | Babylonian Talmud |
| TJ | Palestinian Talmud |
| R. | Rabba Gen. R., Exod. R., etc. |
| Targ. | Targum; J. (Yerushalmi), O. (Onqelos) |

*Tractates*

| | |
|---|---|
| Ar. | Arakhin |
| AZ | Avodah Zarah |
| BB | Baba Batra |
| Bekh. | Bekhorot |
| Ber. | Berakhot |
| Beẓ. | Beẓa (Yom Tov) |
| BM | Baba Meẓi'a |
| BQ | Baba Qamma |
| Dem. | Demai |
| Eduy. | Eduyot |
| Er. | Eruvin |
| Git. | Gittin |
| Ḥag. | Ḥagigah |
| Hor. | Horayot |
| Ḥul. | Ḥullin |
| Kel. | Kelim |
| Ker. | Keritot |
| Ket. | Ketubot |
| Mak. | Makkot |
| Meg. | Megillah |
| Men. | Menaḥot |
| Mid. | Middot |
| Miq. | Miqvaot |
| MQ | Mo'ed Qatan |
| M.Sh. | Ma'aser Sheni |
| Naz. | Nazir |
| Ned. | Nedarim |
| Neg. | Nega'im |
| Nid. | Niddah |
| Ohol. | Oholot |
| Pes. | Pesaḥim |
| Qid. | Qiddushin |
| RH | Rosh Hashanah |
| Sanh. | Sanhedrin |
| Sem. | Semaḥot |
| Shab. | Shabbat |
| Shev. | Shevuot |
| Sheq. | Sheqalim |
| Sof. | Soferim |
| Sot. | Sota |
| Suk. | Sukkah |
| Tam. | Tamid |
| Ta'an | Ta'anit |

| | |
|---|---|
| Tem. | Temurah |
| Ter. | Terumot |
| Yev. | Yevamot |
| Yom. | Yoma |
| Zev. | Zevaḥim |
| | |
| *Aggad. Ber.* | Aggadat Bereshit, ed. S. Buber (Krakow, 1903) |
| *ARN* | Avot de R. Nathan |
| *ARN II* | Avot de R. Nathan, ed. S. Schechter (New York, 1945) |
| *DE* | Derekh Ereẓ |
| *DER* | Derekh Ereẓ Rabba |
| *DEZ* | Derekh Ereẓ Zutta |
| *Mek.* | Mekilta de R. Ishmael |
| *MHG* | Midrash Hagadol, Genesis, ed. M. Margulies (Jerusalem, 1947) |
| *Mid. Pr.* | Midrash Proverbs |
| *Mid. Ps.* | Midrash Psalms, ed. S. Buber (Vilna, 1891) |
| *Mid. Sam.* | Midrash Samuel, ed. S. Buber (Cracow, 1893) |
| *Mid. Tan.* | Midrash Tannaim |
| *MRS* | Mekilta de R. Shimon b. Yoḥai |
| *PR* | Pesikta Rabbati, ed. M. Friedmann (Vienna, 1880) |
| *PRE* | Pirqe de R. Eliezer (Warsaw, 1832) |
| *PRK* | Pesikta de Rav Kahana, ed. S. Buber (Lyck, 1868) |
| *SER* | Seder Eliyahu Rabba |
| *SOR* | Seder Olam Rabba |
| *Tan.* | Tanḥuma |
| *Tan.B.* | Tanḥuma, ed. S. Buber (New York, 1946) |
| *Yal.* | Yalqut Shimoni |

# Dead Sea Scrolls

| | |
|---|---|
| 1QApoc. | Genesis Apocryphon from Cave 1 |
| 4QEn | Enoch texts from Cave 4 |
| 1QM | *Milḥamah*, The War Scroll |
| 4QFlor. | Florilegium from Cave 4 |
| 4QP.Bless. | Patriarchal Blessings from Cave 4 |
| 1QH. | *Hodayot*, Thanksgiving Hymns from Cave 1 |
| 1Q. 2Q, *etc.* | Numbered caves of Qumran |

# PREFACE

Any new commentary to the New Testament requires a justification and explanation. Many of the recent commentaries have added little to our knowledge of the text. They have, for the most part, relied upon their predecessors, repeating their findings and with them their errors. Among serious and creative scholars of the past twenty-five years we find that most have concentrated their efforts on the Qumran discoveries in explaining early Christian literature. Others have been occupied with the development and application of Form and Redaction Criticism. There are, of course, the many theologically oriented writers on the New Testament who seek in the text support for their established religious convictions and as a result lack the objectivity and independence of mind that are essential to sound and disinterested scholarship. But few, if any, have turned to rabbinic literature to write a commentary which would explain the text, and place it in the historical setting in which it was produced.

The German scholar Hermann Reimarus (1694–1768) was one of the first to set forth the idea that to understand the life of Jesus and the Gospel narrative one had to examine Jewish post-biblical literature, which to him was more important in this regard than the Hebrew Bible, which serves only as background to Jesus' times and culture. In the two centuries following Reimarus, many articles and monographs appeared which utilized rabbinic sources in New Testament studies, but almost no one wrote a running commentary to the Synoptics from this point of view. The notable exception was the publication of Strack-Billerbeck's monumental work, *Kommentar zum Neuen Testament aus Talmud und Midrasch*[1] (see below). Many of these studies have been flawed because their authors did not have sufficient grasp of the languages and/or of the rabbinic sources in context to appreciate their meaning. More often than not, these researchers relied upon dictionaries and lexicons and on anthologies of rabbinic materials in translation, which in the hands of the uninitiated can and have produced errors of the most egregious variety. Others, aware of the Semitic background of the Synoptic material, sought parallels and sources only in the Hebrew Bible and in the intertestamental literature and treated them as a monolith rather than appreciating their anthological character, each with its own individuality and dating. These writers preferred to cite biblical passages, no matter how old and remote from the first Christian century, than to turn to contemporary sources or those which are of a slightly later period. They do this either because of their unfamiliarity with rabbinic literature or from purposeful avoidance.[2] Others have restricted their use of rabbinic sources to the contemporary literature, labeling all other material as "late" and not worthy of consideration. This they explain and support in the name of scholarship and sound methodology. Sandmel's popularization of the term "parallelomania" was a warning to scholars to be circumspect in using rabbinic literature with abandon regardless of date and regardless of the precise content of the passage in their study of the New Testament.[3] The import of this warning was with great merit because of widespread abuse in this area, but it must not be followed so restrictively as to exclude *all* material of a late date. There has always been an unbroken transmission of rabbinic traditions. Amoraic passages citing the names of tannaitic authorities should be respected and accepted as valid unless there is a cogent textual reason to suspect the correctness of the passage. Late compilations of midrashim have preserved early traditions, some of which reflect the thinking of early rabbinic times in Palestine. Even late material can often be instructive as an explicit parallel to an early and sometimes difficult and confusing source.

In addition to these factors which have influenced New Testament scholarship in general and the study of rabbinic materials in particular, there is another which is both disturbing and pernicious—that is scholarship which is permeated by religious bigotry. Writers of this ilk feel compelled, when citing rabbinic passages, to show the superiority of New Testament teachings over those of the Rabbis. When not engaging in this type of invidious comparison they continue to characterize Pharisaic Judaism as a dry, sterile, casuistic system of legalism devoid of any human feeling and compassion. One would think that this characterization of Pharisaic Judaism had been put to rest after the appearance of the writings of enlightened men of letters such as George Foot Moore[4] and R. Travers Herford,[5] who saw the beauty and true worth of early rabbinic thought and institutions and sought to expunge the opprobrious connotations attached to the term "Pharisaism." But prejudice long held is slow to disappear, and we find some modern writers continuing to use "Pharisaic" in an insulting fashion.

Sadly, both of these self-serving attitudes characterize two works upon which most twentieth-century scholars of the New Testament have relied, viz., Gerhard Kittel's multivolume work *Theologisches Wörterbuch zum Neuen Testament*,[6] and Strack-Billerbeck's *Kommentar zum Neuen Testament*. The former abounds in anti-Jewish comments, and Kittel himself acted on his prejudices and became a Nazi. The latter work is a testimony to Billerbeck's diligence in amassing and arranging thousands of passages from the intertestamental literature, the Mishnah, Tosefta, Talmudim, and Midrashim. Unfortunately, however, this herculean task, as impressive as it might appear to some, is disappointing to the careful scholar. The overwhelming majority of the passages adduced are not relevant to the study of the New Testament. Added to this is the fact that the interpretive comments of the editor are often wrong and misleading. They likewise never miss an opportunity to denigrate rabbinic Judaism through gratuitous comparisons with New Testament teachings. The scholar untrained in rabbinics is misled by the material proffered, and the religiously unenlightened will have his prejudices reinforced by their seemingly authoritative criticism and evaluation.

A lack of competent and objective scholarship is not restricted to Christians. Jews who have dealt with the New Testament have frequently exhibited a lack of critical expertise in handling the Synoptic texts. Others have engaged in comparative study of Christian and Jewish sources, but have used them indiscriminately by thinking that superficial similarity is sufficient reason to cite a passage as a parallel. Under proper scientific scrutiny their findings are frequently found wanting. Much of this genre of scholarship is the result of academic dilettantism.

What motivated some Jews in the nineteenth and twentieth centuries to turn their attention to the New Testament, particularly to the Synoptic Gospels, was a desire to formulate a Jewish position about the person of Jesus.[7] Many engaged in this quest, but no one wrote a running commentary utilizing rabbinic sources. Claude G. Montefiore is an exception. He wrote a running commentary to the Gospels, *The Synoptic Gospels*,[8] but this work contains little rabbinic material. In a separate volume, *Rabbinic Literature and Gospel Teachings*,[9] he gathered and commented on rabbinic sources. This book, however, is a misguided commentary. It is dedicated more to the cause of Liberal Judaism, to which Montefiore was passionately committed, than to the explication of the Synoptic Gospels.[10] His rejection of traditional Judaism with its emphasis on ethnicity and halakhah finds expression in his condemnation of the Rabbis and the Talmud, which he contrasts with the beauty of the Gospel teachings. This partisan stance, intended to promote and justify a religious position, seriously weakens the credibility of his scholarly objectivity.

Montefiore does not stand alone as one who let religiously motivated emotionalism color his scholarship. There were those who took the opposite position; i.e., they set out to prove that rabbinic Judaism was superior to Christian teachings. Some wrote in reaction to Montefiore's approach. Friedländer is one example. In his *The Jewish Sources of the Sermon on the Mount*,[11] he takes Montefiore to task for his pro-Christian attitudes and comments. He becomes the champion defending Jewish honor, and he does this by declaring: "Four-fifths of the Sermon on the Mount is exclusively Jewish" (p. 266) and "In our opinion this Pharisaic teaching is infinitely superior to that of the Gospel" (p. 214). Clearly polemics, apologetics, and the misuse of historical texts to justify a religious position are unwelcome in the area of disinterested scholarship.

Because all or most of the factors mentioned above are still with us today, I have written a limited commentary to the Synoptic Gospels to present to the open-minded reader insights into the text through an examination of rabbinic traditions from the close of the Bible through the Mishnah, Targum,

Talmud, and classical midrashim. I have not restricted myself to an arbitrary *terminus ad quem* in citing instructive parallels. My position is *caveat lector*, for in the final analysis it is the reader who will decide whether the passage adduced is appropriate or relevant. I have taken pains to make no judgmental comments about the text of the Synoptics and no comparisons between the ethical value systems of the two religious cultures. I am not intent on defending or attacking any theological position. I leave theology to the theologian. To be sure, I have used many commentaries and anthologies, including those works which I have roundly criticized. I have culled from them what I feel is correct and germane to the inquiry, and at the same time I have shown where they were in error. In addition, I have included some of my own insights into the Synoptic literature. Most of these result from retroverting the Greek into Hebrew and/or Aramaic, for by positing a Semitic original and retroverting the passages textual difficulties can often be solved. Most of these suggestions are included in the notes; in all cases the traditional readings are preserved and explicated.

In the commentary I have concentrated the rabbinic material on the Matthean text, and only secondarily do I comment on Mark and Luke when the text is found in all three Gospels. It is not that I accept the priority of Matthew to Mark, but I have done so for two practical reasons: first, Matthew traditionally occupies first position in the order of the Synoptics, and second, there are more rabbinic parallels to Matthew than to either of the other two Evangelists.

It was my good fortune to have Dr. Richard T. White read the manuscript. His comments, corrections, and suggestions were enormously helpful, and I wish to express my thanks to him. I, of course, take full responsibility for all errors. My thanks also go to Bernard Scharfstein of KTAV Publishing House, Inc. who proposed this project, encouraged me to undertake it, and painstakingly saw it through the press. I also wish to express my appreciation for the secretarial assistance afforded me at Bryn Mawr College. I am especially indebted to Ms. Eileen Pisciella and Ms. Christine McFarland, who were so helpful and cooperative in typing the manuscript. Finally, my thanks go to the American Bible Society for their permission to use the Revised Standard Version of the New Testament text.

Bryn Mawr College                                        December 21, 1984

## NOTES

1. Munich, 1922–26.
2. I have dealt with this problem in an article "Rabbinic Sources for New Testament Studies, Use and Misuse," *JQR* 74 (1983): 159-173
3. S. Sandmel, "Parallelomania," *JBL* 81 (1962): 1 ff.
4. G. F. Moore, "Christian Writers on Judaism," *HTR* 14 (1921): 187-254; *Judaism in the First Centuries of the Christian Era: The Age of the Tannaim*, 2 vols. (Cambridge: Harvard University Press, 1927), vol. 3, Notes (1930).

5. R. T. Herford, *Pharisaism: Its Aim and Its Method* (1912), revised and enlarged under the name *The Pharisees* (New York, 1924).

6. Eng. trans., 10 vols., ed. G. W. Bromiley (Grand Rapids, Mich., 1964–76).

7. For a discussion of this subject, see S. Sandmel, *We Jews and Jesus* (New York: Oxford University Press, 1965), pp. 51 ff.

8. 2 vols., 1927; reprint ed., New York: Ktav, 1968.

9. 1930; reprint ed., New York: Ktav, 1970.

10. See E. Mihaly, Prolegomenon to the Ktav edition, p. xxi.

11. 1911; reprint ed., New York: Ktav, 1969.

# THE INFANCY NARRATIVES

## A. The Matthean Infancy Narrative

### MATTHEW 1—2

## The Genealogy of Jesus

### MATT. 1.1–7

1 The book of the genealogy of Jesus Christ, the son of David, the son of Abraham. 2 Abraham was the father of Isaac, and Isaac the father of Jacob, and Jacob the father of Judah and his brothers, 3 and Judah the father of Perez and Zerah by Tamar, and Perez the father of Hezron, and Hezron the father of Ram,[a] 4 and Ram[a] the father of Amminadab, and Amminadab the father of Nahshon, and Nahshon the father of Salmon, 5 and Salmon the father of Boaz by Rahab, and Boaz the father of Obed by Ruth, and Obed the father of Jesse, 6 and Jesse the father of David the king. And David was the father of Solomon by the wife of Uriah, 7 and Solomon the father of Rehoboam, and Rehoboam the father of Abijah, and Abijah the father of Asa,[b] 8 and Asa[b] the father of Jehoshaphat, and Jehoshaphat the father of Joram, and Joram the father of Uzziah, 9 and Uzziah the father of Jotham, and Jotham the father of Ahaz, and Ahaz the father of Hezekiah, 10 and Hezekiah the father of Manasseh, and Manasseh the father of Amos,[c] and Amos[c] the father of Josiah, 11 and Josiah the father of Jechoniah and his brothers, at the time of the deportation to Babylon. 12 And after the deportation to Babylon: Jechoniah was the father of Shealtiel,[d] and Shealtiel[d] the father of Zerubbabel, 13 and Zerubbabel the father of Abiud, and Abiud the father of Eliakim, and Eliakim the father of Azor, 14 and Azor the father of Zadok, and Zadok the father of Achim, 15 and Achim the father of Eliud, and Eliud the father of Eleazar, and Eleazar the father of Matthan, and Matthan the father of Jacob, 16 and Jacob the father of Joseph the husband of Mary, of whom Jesus was born, who is called Christ.[e] 17 So all the generations from Abraham to David were fourteen generations, and from David to the deportation to Babylon fourteen generations, and from the deportation to Babylon to the Christ fourteen generations.

a  Greek *Aram*.
b  Greek *Asaph*.
c  Other authorities read *Amon*.
d  Greek *Salathiel*.
e  Some texts read *Joseph, to whom was betrothed the virgin Mary, was the father of Jesus who is called Christ*. Others read *Joseph, to whom was betrothed the virgin Mary, who (fem.) bore Jesus the Christ*.

1

## COMMENTARY

The purpose of this genealogy is threefold: The first is to prove that Jesus is the legitimate Messiah, a descendant of the royal Davidic family. Second, is to trace his descent back to the patriarch Abraham, with whom God made a covenant which culminated with Jesus. The third is to refute slanderous accusations, apparently widespread, to the effect that Jesus was of illegitimate birth due to his mother's improper behavior. This slander is presumably very old, perhaps first century, for it is already refuted in the Gospel of John, "We were not born of fornication" (8:41). One version of the slander is that Jesus was born of a Roman soldier named Pantheras and Mary, who had been divorced from her husband after having been found an adulteress. Origen indicates that Celsus (ca. 170–180) knew of slander relating to Jesus' birth, including the one about Pantheras.[1] It is against this type of slander that the genealogy evidences a polemical approach. It includes four women in addition to Mary. Each one, despite having lived a morally questionable life or being possessed of a disqualifying family background, was part of the legitimate and noble line of David. Tamar, daughter-in-law of Judah, played the harlot and bore twins sired by her father-in-law (Gen. 38:1 ff.). One of the twins, Perez, nevertheless, was part of the Davidic ancestry. Rahab, a prostitute by profession, according to this genealogy, becomes the mother of Boaz, ancestor of King David (see Josh. 2:1 ff., Ruth 4:21–22). Ruth, the Moabite, whose own background disqualified her from membership in the Jewish community according to the deuteronomic law (Deut. 23:4), was an ancestress of David (Ruth 4:21–22), and there is a reasonable assumption of a questionable sexual escapade involving Ruth (see ibid. 3:7 ff.), and finally Bathsheba, who committed adultery with David (2 Sam. 11), bore him the legitimate heir to the throne, Solomon. All of them are cited presumably as a protest against the vilification of Mary and the cloud over the birth of Jesus.[2]

The genealogy is divided into three sections, each containing fourteen generations. The first is from Abraham to David, the second from Solomon to Jechoniah, and the third from Shealtiel to Jesus. The last section, however, is lacking one name. The first two sections are dependent on the genealogical material in 1 Chron. 1.34–3.19 according to the LXX. The second section differs from the Lucan genealogy (3.23–38), where the line is traced not through Solomon but through Nathan, a younger son of David. This two-line descent of the Davidic kings is not unknown to Jewish tradition. The Targum to Zech. 1.12 implies this, "and the descendants of the house of David mourn [presumably from Solomon] . . . and the descendants of the house of Nathan."[3] The two genealogies agree with Shealtiel and Zerubbabel but diverge again until Matthan. (See below pp. 47 ff.)

The division of the genealogy into three groups of fourteen generations each is clearly artificial, and this intentional structure could account for several of the historical lacunae. Since the purpose was to emphasize the Davidic ancestry of Jesus, the author worked this into the very form of the genealogy. The numerical value of דוד, David, in *gematria* is 14 — 4 plus 6 plus 4.[4] Another explanation is that the author intended that this fourteen-generation pattern in the genealogy imitate the fourteen generations from Moses to the rabbinic period recorded both in *Mishnah Avot* and in the *Avot de Rabbi Nathan*. In both texts the number fourteen is clearly stylized, for some generations are omitted in each so that the number fourteen is maintained, and it is against this background of rabbinic tradition of fourteen generations that Matthew constructed his genealogy of Jesus. It is as if to say to the Pharisees, "You think that the tradition has been transmitted to you from Moses by way of fourteen generations in your literature; I say to you, on the contrary, the founder of our religion received the tradition from Abraham, and this genealogy has three times fourteen generations going back to the patriarch!"[5]

1 *The book of the genealogy of Jesus Christ* This superscription is formed on the analogy of Gen. 5.1, *This is the book of the generations of Man* (cf. also *the book of the genealogy* of Neh. 7.5). Genealogical tables were considered extremely important documents by Jews, particularly after the Babylonian Exile, for they relied heavily upon them to ensure family purity, keeping them unsullied by intermarriage with the pagan world and by other prohibited marriages. This concern for genealogies was especially marked in reference to the priesthood.[6]

*son of David* Emphasizing his messianic role. The expression "Son of David" is used as a messianic title in all of the Synoptics (Matt. 9.27, 15.22, 20.30; Mark 10.47-9; Luke 18.38). The promise that a scion of David is to be the legitimate ruler of the people goes back to Jewish sources, e.g., 2 Sam. 7.16. "Son of David" as a title appears for the first time in Pss. Sol. 17.23. In the Talmud, we find it in the phrase "the son of David comes."[7]

2 *Judah and his brothers* Judah is dominant in the monarchal line, cf. Gen. 49.10. The inclusion of *and his brothers* is strange. Perhaps it is because Judah was not the firstborn and this was an exception to the rule of primogeniture or because the brothers were the ancestors of the entire people of Israel.[8]

5 *Salmon the father of Boaz by Rahab.* In Jewish sources, Rahab is the wife of Joshua.[9] The rabbinic solution to the problem of Ruth's legitimacy in light of the prohibition of accepting converts from the tribe of Moab is "a Moabite male [*moabi*] but not a Moabite female [*moabit*] shall not enter the congregation."[10] Josephus' comment on Ruth as part of David's ancestry is of note: "Of Obed was born Jesse, and of him David, who became king and bequeathed his dominion to his posterity for one and twenty generations. This story of Ruth I have been constrained to relate, being desirous to show the power of God and how easy it is for Him to promote even ordinary folk

to rank so illustrious as that to which He raised David, sprung from such ancestors."[11]

6 *the wife of Uriah* Bathsheba, who is significantly referred to by her husband's name. This is perhaps to emphasize her adulterous relationship with David. Was she, like other women named in the genealogy, non-Jewish? This is a possibility, since she was thought to be the granddaughter of Ahitophel, who probably was not of Israelite stock.[12]

8–9 *Asa . . . Hezekiah* There is an omission here of three generations, i.e., Ahaziah, Joash, and Amaziah (see 1 Chron. 3.11–12). Some have suggested that the evangelist follows the LXX of 1 Chron., which states (3.11) that Joram was the father of Uzziah. Matt. reads that Uzziah was the father of Jotham, and the LXX has Joash his son, Amaziah his son, Azariah his son, Jotham his son. The result is that Matt. did not omit Ahaziah (LXX Ozeias) but Joash, Amaziah, and Azariah (Uzziah). The reason is that in LXX 1 Chron. 3.11 the son of Joram is called Ozeia. The LXX generally reads Ochozeias for Ahaziah and Ozeia for Uzziah, therefore Ozeia in 1 Chron. 3.11 is a mistake, and the copyist thought that Ozeia meant Uzziah and so omitted the three kings. For Asa the Greek reads Asaph, a variant of the same name.

10 *Amos* The Heb. of 1 Chron. 3.14 reads Amon. MSS of the LXX vary between the two names. It has nothing to do with the prophet by the same name.

11 *Jechoniah was the father of Shealtiel* In 1 Chron. 3.17 the name Asir comes between Jechoniah and Shealtiel. The Hebrew *asir* should probably be read *ha'asir*, "the captive," not as a proper name, *Asir*. Shaltiel is the father of Zerubbabel in Hag. 1.1 and in some MSS of 1 Chron. 3.19. In the MT Zerubbabel is the son of Jehoniah's other son, Pediah.

13 *Zerubbabel the father of Abihud* Not in MT.

16 *Joseph the husband of Mary* Gr. *ton andra Marias*. Some MSS read "who was the betrothed of." Perhaps the original was "Joseph, אָרֵשׂ [the fiancé] of Mary," and it was misread as "Joseph אִישׁ [the husband] of Mary.[13]

## NOTES

1. Origen, *Contra Celsum* I.28, 32, 33, 39. On the Pantheras tradition in particular and the Hebrew sources in general about Jesus, see S. Krauss, *Das Leben Jesu nach jüdischen Quellen* (Berlin, 1902), pp. 181–194; Herford, *CTM*, pp. 35 ff., 103 ff., 138, 344 ff.; Klausner, *JN*, pp. 20, 23–24, 38, 40, 48, 232.

2. On the theory of slander as the reason for the inclusion of the women in this genealogy, see J. Weiss, *Die Schriften des Neuen Testaments überzetzt und . . . erklärt*, vol. 1, *Die Drei Ältern Evangelien*, 3d ed. (1917), *ad loc.*

3. McNeile, *The Gospel according to St. Matthew*, p. 2, is in error in his reading of the Targum. The Targum does not mention Solomon by name but contrasts the House of David (Solomon) and the House of Nathan.

4. G. H. Box, *Interpreter*, January 1906, p. 199; idem, "The Gospel Narrative of the Nativity and the Alleged Influence of Heathen Ideas," *ZNW* 6 (1905): 80. *Gematria*

is a cryptograph which is the numerical value of the letters of the Hebrew language or a cipher produced by a permutation of letters.

5. L. Finkelstein, *Mabo le-Massekhtot Abot ve-Abot D'Rabbi Natan* (New York, 1950), pp. 6–8. For "Son of David" as a messianic title, see G. Dalman, *The Words of Jesus: Considered in the Light of Post-Biblical Jewish Writings and the Aramaic Language* (Edinburgh, 1909), pp. 316 ff.

6. Cf. M. Qid. 4.1–4; B. ibid. 71a, 75a; M. Yev 4.13; Josephus, *Contra Ap.* 1.7. On this genealogy of Jesus, see M. Johnson, *The Purpose of the Biblical Genealogies* (Cambridge, 1969), particularly pp. 139 ff. On the term "Christ," see below p. 6.

7. Cf. B. Sanh. 97a, 98a; TJ. Ta'an. 4.8, 68d (44).

8. H. B. Green, *The Gospel According to Matthew* (Oxford, 1975), p. 52.

9. See Sifre Num. 78, Sifre Zutta 75.

10. TJ. Yev. 8.3 (9c) and parallels.

11. Josephus, *Ant.* V.9.4.

12. See B. Sanh. 101b, Ps. Jerome, 2 Sam. 11.3.

13. See Johnson, op. cit., pp. 182–184.

14. See S. T. Lachs, "Studies in the Semitic Background to the Gospel of Matthew," *JQR* 67 (1977): 195–197. Montefiore, *SG* 2:3, suggests that "the 16th verse must . . . have run originally: 'And Joseph begat Jesus.' For if he did not, the whole genealogy would be valueless." He then cites as textual evidence the Sinaitic Syriac, which reads, "Joseph to whom the Virgin Mary was betrothed, begat Jesus Christ."

# The Virgin Birth

## MATT. 1.18–25

18 Now the birth of Jesus Christ[f] took place in this way. When his mother Mary had been betrothed to Joseph, before they came together she was found to be with child of the Holy Spirit; 19 and her husband Joseph, being a just man and unwilling to put her to shame, resolved to divorce her quietly. 20 But as he considered this, behold, an angel of the Lord appeared to him in a dream, saying, "Joseph, son of David, do not fear to take Mary your wife, for that which is conceived in her is of the Holy Spirit; 21 she will bear a son, and you shall call his name Jesus, for he will save his people from their sins." 22 All this took place to fulfill what the Lord had spoken by the prophet: 23 "Behold, a virgin shall conceive and bear a son, and his name shall be called Emmanuel" (which means, God with us). 24 When Joseph woke from sleep, he did as the angel of the Lord commanded him; he took his wife, 25 but knew her not until she had borne a son;[g] and he called his name Jesus.

---

f Other ancient authorities read *of the Christ*; some omit *Christ*.
g Some texts read *her firstborn son*.

## COMMENTARY

The contradiction between the genealogy and the Virgin Birth story has given rise to many attempts at reconciliation, none of them with satisfactory results. The genealogy was intended for Jews, emphasizing the Davidic lineage of Jesus, while the Virgin Birth story was intended for the Greco-

Roman world, where virgin birth stories or tales of divine impregnation of mortal women were well known.[1] The original Virgin Birth story probably contained no Davidic messianic elements. What we have here is an adaptation of this separate tradition. Once the two separate documents were placed in juxtaposition to each other the contradictions between them appeared.[2] Eusebius states that the Jews (presumably Judeo-Christians) regarded Jesus as a man of perfect moral character. If so, then the Virgin Birth story was not intended for them.[3]

18 *Now the birth of Jesus Christ took place in this way* The fact that the Gr. *genesis* is used here, as in Matt. 1.1, indicates that this section is completely separate in origin from the genealogy which precedes it.

*Christ* Gr. *christos*, Heb. *mashiaḥ*, "the anointed." Some texts read "the Christ." This title is basically one of the king of the house of David (cf. Ps. 2.2, 18.50; 1 Sam. 2.10) who will arise and save his people from the hands of their enemies and oppressors. He is also called *meshi'aḥ adonai*, the Anointed of the Lord (Pss. Sol. 17.36, cf. Luke 2.26), or simply *mashi'aḥ* (2 Ezra 7.28–29, 2 Bar. 29.3).

*When his mother Mary had been betrothed to Joseph* The betrothal, Heb. *erusin*, at the beginning of the Christian era generally took place about a year before the marriage ceremony when the bride came to the groom's house.[4] The betrothal carried with it binding commitments; it could be dissolved only by divorce even though the marriage had not been consummated. During the period of the *erusin* the bride remained with her family.

*before they came together* The traditional explanation is before they had sexual relations, i.e. during *erusin*. Although this is implicit, the Greek does not yield only this meaning, it could also refer to the act of taking the bride to the groom's house.[5]

19 *being a just man* The Gr. *dikaios*, "just," is used for one who is observant of the *mizvot*, "commandments," of the Torah. It does not refer to the way he treated Mary, but what he had to do according to the Law. Since she was presumed to have committed adultery, he had no choice but to divorce her, but he wanted to spare her embarrassment and punishment, and hence he decided to divorce her without a public hearing.

20 *behold, an angel of the Lord*, etc. Biblical examples of prediction of birth by an angel: Sarah (Gen. 18.10); the mother of Samson (Judg. 13.3 ff.).

*Joseph, son of David* This is probably from the editor's hand, for the original Virgin Birth story most likely did not contain any Davidic elements.

*Mary your wife* Already your wife by virtue of the *erusin*.

21 *and you shall call his name Jesus* Heb. *Yashu'a* or *Yehoshu'a*, traditionally, "God is salvation." The unborn child will become the nation's deliverer, a Hebrew wordplay—*yoshi'a*, "he shall save." It follows the biblical practice explaining the significance of proper names.[6]

22 *to fulfill what the Lord had spoken by the prophet* A Heb. technical phrase, *leqayem*, employed when citing a scriptural proof.[7]

23 *Behold, a virgin . . . Emmanuel* Isa. (LXX) 7.14 except for *v'qarat*, for which the LXX reads *kaleseis*. "This is an intentional change, dependent upon the fact that Immanuel was not the name which the parents gave their child. Instead it is interpreted as one of the messianic titles symbolically ascribed to Jesus: 'they (*i.e.* one) will call him Immanuel.' In Lk. 1.31 the language is colored by Is. 7.14, but the explicit reference to the virgin is not given and Luke merges the O.T. command to name the child Immanuel with the order in the N.T. to name him Jesus. In Matt. the two are kept distinct, 1.23 and 1.21."[8] The Heb. *almah* means a young woman of marriageable age (masc: *elem*).[9] The reason for the choice of *parthenos* in the LXX is not known; later Greek versions read *neanis*, "a young person." Isa. 7.14 has nothing whatever to do with birth by a virgin. The LXX even uses *parthenos* for one who is not a virgin, cf. Gen. 34.3.

*Emmanuel* I.e., "God is with us."

## NOTES

1. R. E. Brown, *The Birth of the Messiah*, pp. 104–121, good bibliography. Against this view, see W. L. Knox, *Some Hellenistic Elements in Primitive Christianity* (London: British Academy, 1944), pp. 22–23; M. S. Enslin, "The Christian Stories of the Nativity," *JBL* 54 (1940): 317–38.

2. Daube's suggestion, *NTRJ*, pp. 5–9, that a Jewish source preserves a tradition that Moses was born of a virgin birth is without foundation.

3. Eusebius, *Eccl. Hist.* I.3.

4. M. Ket. 5.2 In tannatic literature the betrothed woman was called *arusah*, "betrothed," not *isha*, "wife." On the misinterpretation of *erusin* by NT scholars, see S. T. Lachs, "Rabbinic Sources for New Testament Studies—Use and Misuse," 166–68.

5. See preceding note and Liddell and Scott, *Greek-English Lexicon*, s.v. *sunerchomai* (I.b).

6. M. Noth, *Die israelitischen Personennamen* (Stuttgart, 1928), pp. 101–110, 154. J. Fitzmyer, *Luke*, p. 347. See Brown, op. cit., pp. 96–104.

7. W. Bacher, *Die exegetische Terminologie der jüdischen Traditionsliteratur* (Leipzig, 1899), p. 171.

8. K. Stendahl, *SSMUOT*, p. 98. Brown, op. cit., pp. 143–153.

9. On the meaning of *almah*, see C. H. Gordon, "Almah in Is. 7.14," *JBR* 21 (1954): 106; E. R. Lacheman, "Apropos Is. 7.14," ibid. 22 (1954): 43.

# The Visitation of the Magi

## MATT. 2.1–12

1 Now when Jesus was born in Bethlehem of Judea in the days of Herod the king, behold, wise men from the East came to Jerusalem, saying, 2 "Where is he who has been born king of the Jews? For we have seen his star in the East, and have come to worship him." 3 When Herod the king heard this, he was troubled, and all Jerusalem with him; 4 and assembling all the chief priests and scribes of the people, he inquired of them where the Christ was to be born. 5 They told him, "In Bethlehem of Judea; for so it is written by the prophet:

6 'And thou Bethlehem, in the land of Judah,
art by no means least among the rulers of
Judah;
for from thee shall come a ruler
who will govern my people
Israel.' "

7 Then Herod summoned the wise men secretly and ascertained from them what time the star appeared; 8 and he sent them to Bethlehem, saying, "Go and search diligently for the child, and when you have found him bring me word, that I too may come and worship him." 9 When they had heard the king they went their way; and lo, the star which they had seen in the East went before them, till it came to rest over the place where the child was. 10 When they saw the star, they rejoiced exceedingly with great joy; 11 and going into the house they saw the child with Mary his mother, and they fell down and worshiped him. Then, opening their treasures, they offered him gifts, gold and frankincense and myrrh. 12 And being warned in a dream not to return to Herod, they departed to their own country by another way.

## COMMENTARY

Both Matt. and Luke record the birth of Jesus in Bethlehem, but in all else the two narratives differ. In Matt., he is born in Joseph's house (2.11), while in Luke he is born in a manger because there was no room at the inn (2.7). Luke has the visitation of the shepherds, Matthew the visitation of the Magi. Matt. tells of the flight into Egypt, Luke recounts the birth rites of circumcision (2.21) and the purification of Mary (2.22–24), and then the return of Joseph and Mary to Nazareth (2.39).

The choice of Bethlehem, common to both, as the place of Jesus' birth is more theological than historical. It is closely connected with David and the messianic claim, and Mic. 5.2 is cited to support this claim. Most likely he was born in Nazareth in Galilee. He is called the Nazarene, his followers, Nazarenes, and the Roman inscription on his cross stated that he was of Nazareth. Jesus is said to refer to the town as his *patris*, his place of birth or ancestral home.[1]

1 *Bethlehem of Judah* Emphasizing the city of David's birth, an appropriate place for the birth of the Messiah.[2]

*Herod the king* Herod the Great, an Idumaean by ancestry, a friend of Julius Caesar. He became governor of Galilee in 47 B.C.E. and was given the title of king of Judea in 40 B.CE. by Antony and Octavius. He died in 4 B.C.E. The cruelty of Herod's reign is well attested in antiquity.[3]

*the wise men* The magi, wise men from the East. The magi originally were priests of Persia, noted as astrologers and masters of divination. "Magi" later became a general term for magicians and sorcerers. The magus appears not infrequently in Jewish sources as *magush* or *am'gusha*.[4] The magi here represent the nations of the world who come to proclaim the birth of the savior.

2 *king of the Jews* I.e., the Messiah of the royal family. The king was anointed originally by a prophet (I Sam. 1.10; 1 Kings 19.16; 2 Kings 9.6) and was called "God's anointed" (I Sam. 24.6, 10; 26.16), later shortened to "the anointed," Heb. *mashiaḥ*, Gr. *christos*. See above p. 6.

*We have seen his star in the East* More properly "we saw his star at its rising," cf. Ps. 113.3. The appearance of a star or of a phenomenon of light accompanying the birth of a hero or a worthy is commonplace in legend.[5] For example, it was predicted that Alexander the Great was destined to conquer all of Asia from the appearance of a bright constellation on the night of his birth.[6] In late Jewish sources, too, one finds this motif:

> "When our father Abraham was born, one star from the east came and swallowed up four stars of the four corners of the heavens. The wise men said to Nimrod: 'At this hour a son is born to Terah and a nation will issue forth from him and will inherit this world and the world-to-come . . .' "[7]

> "When the patriarch Isaac was born, God intensified the light of the sun forty-eight times its normal brilliance."[8]

> "When Moses was born the house was filled with light: *And when she saw him that he was good*, and it is written elsewhere, *And God saw the light that it was good* [Gen. 1.4]."[9]

The star also symbolizes the Messiah. The classic passage which is used to support this is Num. 24.17, *A star rises from Jacob, a meteor [shevet] comes forth from Israel.*[10] This verse is frequently interpreted as referring to Simeon bar Koziba (Kokhba), who led an unsuccessful rebellion against Rome in 132 C.E. "R. Simon bar Yoḥai taught: 'My teacher Akiba would expound, *A star rises from Jacob*, Koziba rises from Jacob. R. Akiba when he would see Bar Koziba he would recite, 'This is the Messiah King.' "[11]

*to worship him* The Gr. *proskunēin* is regularly used to translate Heb. *lehishtaḥavot*, "to prostrate oneself," especially before a king; cf., e.g., Ps. 72.11.

4 *chief priests* The term "chief priests" in the plural is relatively rare in rabbinic sources.[12] There was, of course, only one high priest at a time. The term "chief priests" probably refers to the priestly families from whom the high priests were selected, or those who served a term as high priest.[13]

*the scribes of the people* "The learned," Heb. *soferim*, a term used synono-mously with *ḥakhamim*, the learned class of the Pharisaic party.[14]

5 *for so it is written by the prophet* See above to Matt. 1.22 (p. 6). The verse here differs from the MT and from the LXX. It is a combination of Mic. 5.1 with the last clause assimilated from 2 Sam. 5.2.[15]

9 *When they had heard the king* Perhaps in the Semitic sense of "and obeying the king."

*the star . . . went before them* A star standing over a spot indicates a momentous occasion; e.g., a star stood over Jerusalem shortly before the destruction of the city.[16]

11 *they offered him gifts, gold and frankincense and myrrh*  Gifts for the Messiah offered both by Jews and non-Jews is well attested to in rabbinic literature.[17] Gold and frankincense were costly gifts worthy of a king; cf. Isa. 60.6, *they shall bring gold and frankincense.*

15 *frankincense and myrrh*  See Cant. 3.6.

## NOTES

1. Cf. Matt. 13.57. See also *Coptic Gospel of Thomas* and Oxy. P. 1.11, 31–36.
2. Cf. Targ. Mic. 5.1; TJ. Ber. 2.4, 5a (12); also John 7.41 ff., Test., Judah 24.
3. See Josephus, *Ant.* XVII, 6, 5; 8.1, 13.2; *BJ* I.33.1 ff.; II.6.2; B.BB 3b; cf. A. H. M. Jones, *The Herods of Judaea* (Oxford, 1939); S. Perowne, *The Life and Times of Herod the Great* (London, 1956); Zeitlin, *RFJS*, 1:371 ff.
4. E.g. Targ. J. 1 Exod. 7.15; 8.16; B. Shab. 45a, 75a; B. Sot. 22a; B. Yom. 35a; B. Sanh. 30a, 98a.
5. See Stith Thompson, *Motif-Index of Folk-Literature* (Bloomington: University of Indiana Press, 1958), D. 1314.13, a star indicates the location of a newborn hero; F. 961.2.1, a bright star indicates the birth of a holy person.
6. Cf. Cicero, *De Divinatione* I.47. See a good bibliography in Derrett, *SNT*, 2:21 n. 71. On the messianic hopes at the time of Virgil, see *Eclogue* IV.
7. *Ma'ase Avraham*, ed. Horwitz, 43; *Ma'ase Avraham* in Jellinek's *BHM*, II, 18ff.; *Midrash Decalogue* ibid. III; p. 203; *Sefer HaYashar* 18a–19a. See Brown, *Birth of the Messiah*, pp. 170–173 for other passages.
8. *PR* 42 (p. 177a–b).
9. B. Sota 12a. Cf. also Exod. R. 1.25, B. Meg. 14a, *Mid. Prov.* 14.1 (37b–38a).
10. E.g., Test. Judah 24.1 ff. Stendahl, *SSMUOT*, p. 136, comments: "The term *anatole* is natural in the text (in Matt.) without allusion. There is, however, the startling fact that the verse in Numbers 24.17 is the only one in the *LXX* where *darakh* is translated by *anatellein* in forming the translation."
11. TJ. Ta'an. 4.9, 68d (44). Lam. R. 2. 2 (51a).
12. Cf., however, M. Ket. 13.1–2, M. Ohol. 17.5. Josephus, *BJ* II 12.6; IV.4.4.
13. Cf. Josephus, *BJ* VI.2.2 On the priesthood in the days of the Second Temple, see Schürer, *GJV*, 2: 267–277. All three Gospel writers are generally inaccurate as to the titles of Jewish leaders. See M. J. Cook, *Mark's Treatment of the Jewish Leaders*, Supplements to *NT* 51 (Leiden: E. J. Brill, 1978).
14. Against this view see Daube, *NTRJ*, pp. 210 ff.
15. See Stendahl op. cit., p. 101. For a messianic interpretation of Mic. 5.1 see *PRE* 3. and Targ. Mic. 5.2.
16. Josephus, *BJ* VI.5.3. Cf. Virgil, *Aeneid* II.691, a star shows Aeneas where Rome is to be founded.
17. Cf. B. Pes. 118b and parallels; See Esther R. 1.1 *Tan. Shoftim* 19; *Mid. Ps.* 87.6 (189b), Gen. R. 78.16; Exod. R. 35.5.

# The Flight into Egypt

## MATT. 2.13–15

13 Now when they had departed, behold, an angel of the Lord appeared to Joseph in a dream and said, "Rise, take the child and his mother, and flee to Egypt, and remain there till I tell you; for Herod is about to search for the child, to destroy him." 14 And

he rose and took the child and his mother by night, and departed to Egypt, 15 and remained there until the death of Herod. This was to fulfill what the Lord had spoken by the prophet.

"Out of Egypt have I called my son."

## COMMENTARY

The Flight into Egypt appears to be an attempt to refute the libel which places Jesus in Egypt, where he is said to have become a magician. Matt. clearly states that Joseph is told by the angel of God to take Mary and the child down to Egypt, not to learn magical procedures, but to escape the wrath of Herod. One such libel is recorded by Celsus to the effect that Jesus worked as a laborer in Egypt, where he learned magic which he subsequently employed when he returned to Judea and proclaimed himself a god.[1]

Jesus' Egyptian sojourn associated with the study of magical arts is also found in Jewish sources.

> "R. Eliezer [ben Hyrcanus] said to the Sages: 'Did not Ben Stada [i.e., Jesus] bring spells from Egypt in a cut which was on his flesh?' They said to him: 'He was a fool, and they do not bring proof from a fool.' "[2]

> "When Yannai the king killed our Rabbis, R. Joshua b. Peraḥyah [and Jesus] fled to Alexandria of Egypt. One day R. Joshua intended to accept him [previously he had excommunicated him] and made a sign to him. Jesus thought that he repelled him. He went and put up a brick and worshiped it. R. Joshua said to him: 'Repent!' He replied: 'Thus I have received from you, that everyone who sins and causes the multitude to sin, is not given the opportunity to repent.' And a teacher said: 'Jesus the Nazarene practiced magic, and led astray and deceived Israel.' "[3]

15 *death of Herod*    Shortly before Passover 4 B.C.E.[4]

*Out of Egypt, etc.*    Hos. 11.1 The literal meaning of the verse cannot apply here, for it describes an event in the past, not a prediction of one in the future. Most commentators see in the Matthean use of this verse the theme of the New Exodus.[5] It is, however, not convincing. Although there are obvious motifs, especially in the Prologue material, which are fashioned after the Egyptian sojourn and the life of Moses, there is not enough evidence to create a thesis of a New Exodus. It is true that there is a connection between the redemption from Egypt, often called the "first redemption," and the messianic redemption, called the "final redemption," but the connection of these two in Matthew is at best tenuous. This verse does not, except in a very nebulous way, bring the two together.[6]

## NOTES

1. Origen. *Contra Celsum* I.28, 38. Montefiore, *SG*, 2:10, see another reason for the Flight into Egypt. "It is possible that the story of the Flight into Egypt arose

independently, but it is, perhaps, more probable that it was invented on the basis of the passage in Hosea and on the general idea that Jesus, the Son of God, the incarnation of the true Israel, must also be called out of Egypt like Israel of old." This is unlikely, for there is no evidence in the literature that Jesus was viewed as the "incarnation of true Israel."

2. B. Shab. 104b On this passage see Herford, *CTM*, pp. 355 ff., which includes a discussion of the name Ben Stada. Cf. also T. Shab. II.15 (p.126). See M. Smith, *Jesus the Magician* (San Francisco: Harper & Row, 1978), pp. 59 ff.

3. B. Sanh. 107b, B. Sot. 47a; also see TJ. Ḥag. 2.2 (77d), and TJ. Sanh. 6.9 (23c). This passage has a glaring historical anachronism—Joshua b. Peraḥyah lived more than two generations before Jesus. See Herford, *CTM*, pp. 50 ff. On the "setting up of the brick," see S. T. Lachs, "A Jesus Passage in the Talmud Re-examined," *JQR* 59 (1969): 244–247.

4. See Zeitlin, *RFJS*, 2:95. Schürer, *GJV*,1:464 ff., relied on the unhistorical date of the 7th of Kislev as found in the *Megillat Ta'anit*. On the problem of the date of Jesus' birth, see S. Zeitlin, "The Date of the Birth and Crucifixion of Jesus," *JQR* 55 (1964): 1 ff.

5. Most fully discussed by Davies, *SSM*, pp. 25 ff.

6. For the passages connecting the two redemptions in rabbinic literature, see *SB*, 1:85–88.

# Herod's Massacre of the Babies

## MATT. 2.16–18

16 Then Herod, when he saw that he had been tricked by the wise men, was in a furious rage, and he sent and killed all the male children in Bethlehem and in all that region who were two years old or under, according to the time which he had ascertained from the wise men. 17 Then was fulfilled what was spoken by the prophet Jeremiah:

> 18 "A voice was heard in Ramah,
> wailing and loud lamentation,
> Rachel weeping for her children;
> she refused to be consoled,
> because they were no more."

### COMMENTARY

16 *Then Herod . . . killed all the male children*, etc.   The model for this act of Herod is the Pharaoh of the enslavement (Exod. 1.16).[1] The comparison is strengthened when rabbinic sources are examined. Pharaoh's desire to remove the threat of a newborn pretender was so intense that he was willing to kill even the children of his own people.

> "*And Pharaoh charged all his people* [Exod. 1.22]. R. Jose b. Ḥanina said: 'He imposed the same decree upon his own people' [to kill the male children because the astrologers warned him that a boy was soon to be born who

would overthrow him]. R. Jose b. Ḥanina also said: 'He made three decrees: first if it be a son, then you shall kill him; then, every son that is born you shall cast into the Nile, and finally he imposed the same decree upon his own people.' "[2]

18 *A voice was heard*, etc. The verse is Jer. 31.14 (LXX 15). It follows the LXX more than the MT but also differs from it. Rachel's mourning is interpreted as being for the massacre of the children, not for the historical scene of the captives going into exile and passing Ramah on their way.[3]

## NOTES

1. Daube, *NTRJ*, p. 189, however, sees a parallel between Herod's persecution of Jesus and Laban's persecution of Jacob as recounted in the Passover Haggadah.
2. B. Sota 12a; see also Exod. R. 1.18.
3. On the verse see Stendahl, *SSMUOT*, p. 102.

## *The Return from Egypt*

### MATT. 2.19–23

19 But when Herod died, behold, an angel of the Lord appeared in a dream to Joseph in Egypt, saying, 20 "Rise, take the child and his mother, and go to the land of Israel, for those who sought the child's life are dead." 21 And he rose and took the child and his mother, and went to the land of Israel. 22 But when he heard that Archelaus reigned over Judea in place of his father Herod, he was afraid to go there, and being warned in a dream he withdrew to the district of Galilee. 23 And he went and dwelt in a city called Nazareth, that what was spoken by the prophets might be fulfilled, "He shall be called a Nazarene."

## COMMENTARY

20 *Rise, take the child*, etc. This is reminiscent of the Moses story and of his return to Egypt from Midian. Note the phrase "for those who sought the child's life are dead" here and Exod. 4.19, *And the Lord said to Moses, "Go, return into Egypt; for all the men are dead that sought your life."*

*the land of Israel* I.e. Judea.[1]

22 *Archelaus* The eldest son of Herod. Upon the death of Herod his estate was divided as follows: The eldest, Archelaus, received a double portion, including the province of Judea, and was called ethnarch, not king. The other two sons, Antipas and Philip, each received one portion with the title of tetrarch; Antipas received Galilee and Perea (district east of the Jordan), and Philip ruled over Gaulonitis and Trachonitis, Batanaea and Paneas. He gave Jabneh, Azotus, and Phasaelis to Salome.[2]

*Galilee* See on Matt. 4.12 (below p. 53).

23 *Nazareth . . . He shall be called a Nazarene* This verse remains a *crux*

*interpretum*. Linguistically, there is no relationship with the word "watch-tower" (from *n-ẓ-r*) because the city is situated on a hill.[3] Furthermore, the Heb. letter *ẓadi* is not transliterated by the Gr. *zeta*. It is also doubtful that the play involves *nazir*, "a nazirite." More likely the evangelist is playing on the Heb. *neẓer*. "a branch," as in Isa. 11.1, *and there shall come forth a shoot out of the stem of Jesse and a branch [neẓer] shall grow out of his roots*, with messianic implications.[4] Cf. also Jer. 23.5, 33.15, where the Davidic Messiah is also described as a branch but by a different term, *ẓemaḥ*.[5] "R. Joshua b. Levi said: *ẓemaḥ* [branch, shoot] is the name of the Messiah."[6] Nazareth in Lower Galilee is 15 miles SW of Tiberias, a little N of the Great Plain of Esdraelon. It is not mentioned in the MT, Apocrypha, Josephus, or in the talmudic literature. See, however, the fragmentary Hebrew inscription discovered at Caesarea Maritima which lists the twenty-four *mishmarot* (priestly courses) and the places from which they came. According to this inscription, the eighteenth *mishmar*, Happizzez (1 Chron. 24.15), came from *nẓrt*, Nazareth. This inscription is dated end of 3rd–beg. 4th cent.[7]

## NOTES

1. On the use of "land of Israel," see M. Ḥul. 4.8; T. ibid. 2.11 (p. 99).
2. Josephus, *Ant.* XVII.8.1; cf. Luke 3.1.
3. See Dalman, *Grammatik des jüdisch-palästinischen Aramäisch* (Leipzig, 1905), p. 119.
4. Cf. also Targ. Isa. 11.1; Zech. 3.8, 6.12.
5. Zech., loc. cit.
6. TJ. Ber. 2, 5a (12), Lam. R. 1.16 (p. 66).
7. See M. Avi-Yonah, "A List of Priestly Courses from Caesarea," *IEJ* 12 (1962): 137–139; idem, "The Caesarea Inscription of the Twenty-Four Priestly Courses," in *The Teacher's Yoke: Studies in Memory of Henry Trantham*, ed. E. J. Vardaman and J. L. Garrett, Jr. (Waco Texas: Baylor University Press, 1964), pp. 46–57.

# B. The Lucan Infancy Narrative

## LUKE 1–2

# The Prologue to the Gospel

## LUKE 1.1–4

1 Inasmuch as many have undertaken to compile a narrative of the things which have been accomplished among us, 2 just as they were delivered to us by those who from the beginning were eyewitnesses and ministers of the word, 3 it seemed good to me also, having followed all things closely[h] for some time past, to write an orderly

account for you, most excellent Theophilus, 4 that you may know the truth concerning the things of which you have been informed.

---

h Or *accurately.*

## COMMENTARY

This prologue is written in the classical style of Greek historical writings and has often been compared to those of Herodotus and Polybius. In Jewish Hellenistic literature it can be compared to the prologues in the *Letter of Aristeas* and the *Contra Apionem* of Josephus.

> Inasmuch as the account of our deputation to Eleazar, the High Priest of the Jews, is worth narrating, Philocrates, and because you set a high value, as you constantly remind me, on hearing the motives and purposes of our mission, I have endeavored to set the matter forth clearly. I appreciate your characteristic love of learning, for it is indeed men's highest function "ever to add knowledge, ever to acquire it," either through researches or by actual experience of affairs.[1]

> In my history of our Antiquities, most excellent Epaphroditus, I have, I think, made sufficiently clear to any who may pursue that work the extreme antiquity of our Jewish race, the purity of the original stock, and the manner in which it established itself in the country which we occupy today. That history embraces a period of five thousand years, and was written by me in Greek on the basis of our sacred books. Since, however, I observe that a considerable number of persons, influenced by the malicious calumnies of certain individuals, discredit the statements in my history concerning our antiquity, and adduce as proof of the comparative modernity of our race the fact that it has not been thought worthy of mention by the best-known Greek historians, I consider it my duty to devote a brief treatise to all these points; in order at once to convict our detractors of malignity and deliberate falsehood, to correct the ignorance of others, and to instruct all who desire to know the truth concerning the antiquity of our race.[2]

> In the first volume of this work, my most esteemed Epaphroditus, I demonstrated the antiquity of our race, corroborating my statements by the writings of Phoenicians, Chaldaeans, and Egyptians, besides citing as witnesses numerous Greek historians; I also challenged the statements of Manetho, Chaeremon, and some others. I shall now proceed to refute the rest of the authors who have attacked us.[3]

## NOTES

1. *Aristeas to Philocrates* 1.1–12, trans. M. Hadas (New York, 1951), p. 93.
2. Josephus, *Contra Ap.* I.1–3.
3. Ibid. II.1.

# The Prediction of the Baptist's Birth

## LUKE 1.5–25

5 In the days of Herod, king of Judea, there was a priest named Zechariah,[i] of the division of Abijah; and he had a wife of the daughters of Aaron, and her name was Elizabeth. 6 And they were both righteous before God, walking in all the commandments and ordinances of the Lord blameless. 7 But they had no child, because Elizabeth was barren, and both were advanced in years. 8 Now while he was serving as priest before God when his division was on duty, 9 according to the custom of the priesthood, it fell to him by lot to enter the temple of the Lord and burn incense. 10 And the whole multitude of the people were praying outside at the hour of incense. 11 And there appeared to him an angel of the Lord standing on the right side of the altar of incense. 12 And Zechariah was troubled when he saw him, and fear fell upon him. 13 But the angel said to him, "Do not be afraid, Zechariah, for your prayer is heard, and your wife Elizabeth will bear you a son, and you shall call his name John. 14 And you will have joy and gladness, and many will rejoice at his birth; 15 for he will be great before the Lord, and he shall drink no wine nor strong drink, and he will be filled with the Holy Spirit, even from his mother's womb. 16 And he will turn many of the sons of Israel to the Lord their God, 17 and he will go before him in the spirit and power of Elijah, to turn the hearts of the fathers to the children, and the disobedient to the wisdom of the just, to make ready for the Lord a people prepared." 18 And Zechariah said to the angel, "How shall I know this? For I am an old man, and my wife is advanced in years." 19 And the angel answered him, "I am Gabriel, who stand in the presence of God; and I was sent to speak to you, and to bring you this good news. 20 And behold, you will be silent and unable to speak until the day that these things come to pass, because you did not believe my words, which will be fulfilled in their time." 21 And the people were waiting for Zechariah, and they wondered at his delay in the temple. 22 And when he came out, he could not speak to them, and they perceived that he had seen a vision in the temple; and he made signs to them and remained dumb. 23 And when his time of service was ended, he went to his home. 24 After these days his wife Elizabeth conceived, and for five months she hid herself, saying, 25 "Thus the Lord has done to me in the days when he looked on me, to take away my reproach among men."

---

[i] Greek *Zacharias.*

## COMMENTARY

5 *Zechariah* Lit. "God has remembered," i.e., in granting them a child in their old age. The MT records other priests with the same name.[1]

*the division of Abijah* Gr. *ephēmeria* refers to the daily duties performed by the priests.[2] The priesthood was divided into twenty-four divisions called *mishmarot*, lit. "watches"; each watch or division was to serve in the Temple twice each year for one week at a time, from Sabbath to Sabbath.[3] Their times of service were determined by lot.[4] According to the Bible it was David who instituted this order of service, and Abijah was the head of the eighth division.[5] After the Babylonian Captivity only four divisions returned to Judaea, viz., Jedaiah, Immer, Pashhur, and Harim,[6] but subsequently we hear of twenty-four divisions under the old names.[7] Josephus speaks of twenty-four divisions[8] and of four.[9] The head of each priestly division was called *rosh hamishmar;* each section was divided so that on a given day a select number of priests served in the Temple, each group called *bet av* and the head of that group called *rosh bet av.*[10]

*of the daughters of Aaron*    On this phrase see 2 Chron. 2.14. Although it was not obligatory for a priest to marry a woman of priestly descent, frequently it was the case.[11]

*Elizabeth*    Heb. Elisheva. Elizabeth was also the name of the wife of Aaron, and perhaps this was the reason for the choice here.[12]

6 *they were both righteous before God*    "This description is added by Luke to make sure that the couple's childlessness is not understood by the reader as resulting from any wickedness or unworthiness in the sight of God."[13] The expression "before God" most likely is a translation of the Heb. *lifnē adonai* and is better translated "in the opinion of God."[14]

7 *But they had no child*    John's birth is patterned after MT stories of barren women—Sarah (Gen. 16.1), Rebecca (ibid. 25.21), Rachel (ibid. 30.1), the mother of Samson (Judg. 13.2), Hannah (1 Sam. 1.2). The rabbinic comment on Gen. 16.1 is interesting: *"Sarah was barren, she had no child.* R. Levi said, 'Wherever it is written, *she had no* [child] means that she would bear one.' "[15]

*both were advanced in years*    Lit. "in their days," Heb. *ba'im bayamim.*[16]

9 *it fell to him by lot . . . incense*    This procedure of choosing by lot is described in detail in the Mishnah: "He, the officer, said to them, 'You that are new to the incense preparation, come and cast lots,' and they cast lots and the lot fell upon whom it fell."[17]

*to enter the temple of the Lord*    Gr. *naos,* as in 1.21–22, a holy place, here the front part of the Temple where the altar of incense stood together with the menorah and the showbread.[18] The term *naos* could also mean the Holy of Holies, which was at the back of the inner court and separated by a curtain (cf. Luke 23.45), but only the high priest entered the Holy of Holies, once a year on Yom Kippur.[19] Zechariah was not a high priest, although a Christian tradition makes him one.[20] The term *naos* is different from *hieron,* used by Luke for the Temple in general.[21]

10 *And the whole multitude of the people were praying outside at the hour of incense*    This was not a normal occurrence; people did not pray there at the times of sacrifice or at the offering of the incense, no reference to this is to be found in any Jewish source.[22] It is an indication of Luke's unfamiliarity with Temple service and procedure.

*at the hour of incense*    Offered morning and at twilight. Cf. *And Aaron shall burn fragrant incense on it; every morning when he dresses the lamps he shall burn it, and when Aaron sets the lamps at twilight he shall burn it, a perpetual incense before the Lord throughout your generations.*[23]

11 *And there appeared* Lit. "there was seen to him," Aram. *ithazē*.[24]

*an angel of the Lord* Reminiscent of the angel appearing to the wife of Manoah.[25]

*the right side of the altar* For a description of the altar, see Exod. 30.1–10, 37.25–29. Perhaps "right" is to indicate favorable circumstances.[26]

13 *Do not be afraid* Because of divine appearance, as was Manoah the father of Samson. Cf. also Gen. 15.1, Dan. 10.12, 19.

*you shall call his name John* Heb. *Yoḥanan*, "God has shown favor." For commands in the MT to give a child a specific name, see Isa. 9.5, Jer. 11.16; Apoc.: Tob. 1.9; NT: Matt. 1.21, 25; Luke 1.31.

15 *for he will be great before the Lord* I.e., by God's determination.[27]

*and he shall drink no wine nor strong drink* I.e., he shall be a Nazirite (Num. 6.3). It seems to be patterned on the Samson story (Judg. 13.4), where his mother is told not to drink "wine or strong drink," for her child will be a *nazir*, consecrated by a vow. The same is recorded about Samuel (1 Sam. [LXX] 1.11), "he shall not drink wine or strong drink."[28] This seems to be Luke's way of indicating that John is to be a Nazirite prophet.

*wine nor strong drink* Heb. *yayin v'shekhar*, Num. (LXX) 6.3 *oinos kai sikera*. Targ. O. and Targ. J. I ad loc., *ḥadat v'atiq*, "new and old wine." Rashi ad loc. follows the Targum. A midrashic passage reads, "R. Eleazar ha-Kappar said: *yayin* [wine] is mixed wine; *shekhar* [strong drink] is unmixed wine."[29] In the Talmud *shekhar* is understood as a type of beer or a drink made from grain.[30]

*filled with the Holy Spirit* This is an expression not regularly found in rabbinic sources. Note, however, in a late source: "Moses and the seventy elders were filled with the Holy Spirit."[31]

*even from his mother's womb* Lit. "still from the womb of his mother." In the MT "from his mother's womb" is ambiguous, it can mean from birth, e.g., Isa. 48.8, Ps. 22.11; or while in the womb, e.g., Judg. 13.5, 7; 16.17; Isa. 44.2. See also Gal. 1.15.

16 *he will turn many*, etc. Cf. Mal. 2.6, referring to a priest; perhaps the phrase was chosen because of John's priestly descent, although the general tone of this section is more similar to the traditions about the prophet Elijah.[32]

17 *in the spirit and power of Elijah* Reminiscent of Elijah's promise to his disciple Elisha that he would receive a double portion of his spirit.[33]

*to turn the hearts of the fathers to the children* Mal. 3.24 (RSV 4.6).[34]

*to make ready for the Lord a people prepared* Cf. 2 Sam. 7.24, Exod. 19.10–11, and perhaps Sira 48.10, "you who are ready at the appointed time."

18 *How shall I know this?* Similar question asked by Abraham (Gen. 15.8). Zechariah, by this question, is asking for a sign, as did Gideon (Judg. 6.37–40) and Hezekiah (2 Kings 20.8–11, Isa. 7.11).

19 *I am Gabriel* One of the two angels along with Michael who are named in the MT.[35] Gabriel came to Daniel at the time of the evening sacrifice.[36] Lit. "man of God" or "God has shown himself strong."[37] Angelology is of post-

Exilic period. "Resh Laqish said, '. . . Also the names of angels [as well as the names of the months] came with us from Babylonia.' "[38]

*Who stand in the presence of God*   Heb. *malakhē hasharet* or *malakhē hapanim.* There were, according to most accounts, seven of this group.[39]

20 *you will be silent and unable to speak.*   I.e., You will become a deaf-mute, Heb. *ḥeresh.* See below Luke 1.62 (p. 28 n.5), where the people have to make signs to him.[40]

21 *And the people were waiting for Zechariah*   Again Luke shows that he does not know the Temple ritual. Several priests would enter the holy place to perform the task assigned to Zechariah.[41] It was only on the Day of Atonement that the high priest entered the Holy of Holies, and then he did so alone, and was not to tarry "lest he put Israel to terror."[42] This is not applicable here unless Luke has confused this tradition and applied it to the incense service.[43]

22 *And when he came out, he could not speak to them*   After the offering of the *tamid* the priest(s) were expected to bless the people with the priestly blessing (Num. 6.24–26).[44]

*he had seen a vision*   The literature records several passages in which a priest had seen a vision in the Temple, e.g., "Then it was that the Lord of spirits and of all authority caused a great apparition to appear, so that all who had been bold enough to accompany him were struck with panic at the power of God, and were faint with wretched fear."[45]

23 *And when his time of service was ended, he went to his home.*   Where it was is not specified, although 1.39 indicates that it was in the "hill country" (see below ad loc.).

25 *to take away my reproach*   Cf. Gen. 30.23.

*among men*   Perhaps this is a translation of *anashim*, meaning "people," both men and women.

## NOTES

1. Cf. 1 Chron. 15.24, Neh. 11.12. On various Christian confusions concerning Zechariah, see Brown, *Birth of the Messiah,* p. 258.
2. Cf. Neh. 13.30.
3. M. Ta'an. 4.2; T. ibid. 2.1 (p. 216), M. Tam. 5.1. See Schürer, *GJV,* 2:286 ff.
4. See below n. 17.
5. See 1. Chron. 24.10.
6. Ezra 2.36–39, 2 Chron. 10.18–22.
7. Cf. Neh. 12.1–7.
8. *Vita* I.2, *Ant.* VII.14.7.
9. *Contra Ap.* II.8. Schürer, loc. cit., suggests that it is an error for twenty-four.
10. T. Zev. 11.16 (p. 497).
11. See TJ. Ta'an. 4.11, 69c (29, 49).
12. Exod. 6.23. Cf. Gen. (LXX) 17.15 On the meaning of the name, see Koehler-Baumgartner, *HALAT,* p. 55; L. Koehler, "Hebräische Vokabeln II," *ZAW* 55 (1937): 165–166.
13. Fitzmyer, *Luke,* p. 323 See however, Susanna, v. 3.

14. See Koehler-Baumgartner, *HALAT*, s.v לִפְנֵי .
15. *PRK* 20 (141b), *PR* 32 (148a).
16. See Gen. 18.11; 24.1; 1 Kings 1.1. See also below Luke 2.36 (p. 31).
17. M. Tam. 5.2.
18. See 1 Macc. 1.21–22.
19. M. Yom. 5.1, Heb. 9.6–7.
20. See *Protevangelium of James* 8.1–3.
21. See, e.g., Luke 2.27, 37, 46; 4.9; 18.10; 19.45, 47; 20.1.
22. See, however, Jth. 9.1, but this was not at the Temple.
23. Exod. 30.7–8. Cf. Sira (Heb.) 50.11 ff., M. Tam. 6.1–3.
24. Cf. 1QApoc. 22.27.
25. Judg. 13.3. The Greek, omitting the definite article, shows it to be a direct translation of *malakh adonai*.
26. Cf. B. Yom. 33b, Targ. Cant. 4.16.
27. See above n. 14. On *meglas* see Fitzmyer, loc. cit.
28. See also 4QSam. 1. 3.
29. Sifre Num. 23, Num. R. 10.16.
30. The Gr. *sikra* is a transliteration of the Aramaic *shikhra*, Heb. *shekhar*. See M. Pes. 3.1. B. ibid. 42b.
31. Num. R. 13.
32. See also Sira 48.12.
33. 2 Kings 2.9–10.
34. See P. Winter, "Lukanische Miszellen," *ZNW* 49 (1958): 65–66.
35. Dan. 8.16, 9.21; Michael, see ibid. 10.13; 12.1. Equally familiar to early Christians would be Raphael (Tob. 3.17; En. 9.1; 20.7, 40.9; 1QM 9.26); Uriel (En. 9.1, 19.1, 20.2, cf. 1QS 3.20), Phanuel (En. 40.9). According to En. 40.2–9 there were "four presences" including Gabriel.
36. Dan. 9.21.
37. On the name, see Dan. 8.15, En. 40.9. Traditionally, "strength of God." See, however, Brown, op. cit., p. 262; Fitzmyer, *CBQ* 39 (1977): 438, "God is my hero/warrior."
38. Cf. TJ. RH 1.56d (56).
39. Cf., e.g., Tob. 12.15, 1 En. 20, Rev. 8.6 ff.
40. In rabbinic usage *ḥeresh* is a technical term for one who can neither speak nor hear.
41. See M. Tam. 5.4–6; 6.1–3; 7.1–2.
42. M. Yoma 5.1. Cf. TJ. ibid. 5.42c (17).
43. See Fitzmyer, *Luke*, p. 328 who suggests it might have been the *tamid* offering.
44. See M. Tam. 7.2.
45. See M. Yoma 5.1; Josephus, *Ant.* XII.10.3; 2 Macc. 3.24 ff.; T. Sot. 21.8 (p. 319); B. ibid. 33a.

# The Annunciation

## LUKE 1.26–38

26 In the sixth month the angel Gabriel was sent from God to a city of Galilee named Nazareth, 27 to a virgin betrothed to a man whose name was Joseph, of the house of David; and the virgin's name was Mary. 28 And he came to her and said, "Hail, O favored one, the Lord is with you."ⁱ 29 But she was greatly troubled at the saying, and

considered in her mind what sort of greeting this might be. 30 And the angel said to her, "Do not be afraid, Mary, for you have found favor with God. 31 And behold, you will conceive in your womb and bear a son, and you shall call his name Jesus. 32 He will be great, and will be called the Son of the Most High; and the Lord God will give to him the throne of his father David, 33 and he will reign over the house of Jacob forever; and of his kingdom there will be no end." 34 And Mary said to the angel, "How can this be, since I have no husband?" 35 And the angel said to her, "The Holy Spirit will come upon you, and the power of the Most High will overshadow you; therefore the child to be born[k] will be called holy, the Son of God. 36 And behold, your kinswoman Elizabeth in her old age has also conceived a son; and this is the sixth month with her who was called barren. 37 For with God nothing will be impossible." 38 And Mary said, "Behold I am the handmaid of the Lord; let it be to me according to your word." And the angel departed from her.

---

j   Some texts add *Blessed are you among women!*
k   Some texts add *of you.*

## COMMENTARY

26 *In the sixth month*   I.e., of Elizabeth's pregnancy. It seems that this phrase is to connect the two birth stories which are juxtaposed here.[1]

*Nazareth*   See above pp. 13f.

27 *betrothed*   See above p. 6.

28 *the Lord is with you*   See Judg. 6.12, where the angel of God greets Gideon with *The Lord is with you, you mighty man of valor*, and Ruth 2.4, where Boaz greets his reapers with *The Lord be with you*, and they reply, *The Lord bless you*. Since there is no verb in Hebrew nor one in the Greek, in both MT passages, it may mean, "May the Lord be with you" rather than "The Lord is with you." Here in Luke it perhaps has, by design, a *double entendre.*[2]

29 *she was greatly troubled at the saying*, etc.   Why was she perplexed? Some suggest that it was on seeing him, relying on some MSS, C TH and Koine Text tradition which add *idousa*, "seeing [him]." This is not satisfactory, since it is the greeting, not the sight of him, which caused her perplexity. Others explain that she was troubled because she was greeted by a strange male, which was not proper.[3] This, too, is unacceptable. It was the *greeting* which upset her. In the biblical period, the accepted way of greeting another was by using the name of God, always rendered in the LXX by *kurios*. In the period of the Second Temple, the Jews used substitute names for God in order to protect the sanctity of the Divine Name, names such as *Hamaqom*, "the Omnipresent," *Haqadosh barukh hu*, "the Holy One, blessed be He," *Hagevurah*, "the Power." With the rise of sectarian groups *(minim)*, and among them Judeo-Christians, the Jews reverted to the use of the name of God when greeting someone. "And it was ordained that a man should salute his fellow with the use of the name of God, for it is written, *And behold, Boaz came from Jerusalem and said to the reapers, "The Lord is with you, mighty men of*

*valor.*" And it is written, *And despise not your mother when she is old.* And it is written, *It is time to work for the Lord; they have made void your Law.* R. Nathan says: 'They have made void your Law because it was a time to work for the Lord.' "[4] The thrust of this mishnah is that with the increase of the sectarians, including the Judeo-Christians, the Jews, for the purpose of identifying themselves to others and to discover the identity of others, reinstituted the custom of using the Divine Name in greetings. This was to determine who was and who was not a Jew, for the one greeted was expected to return the greeting using the same formula and name employed by the one who initiated the greeting. A Judeo-Christian presumably would be required to greet (bless) in the name of Jesus and not employ the traditional Divine Name. It is possible that this custom was known to Luke and was inserted here into the Annunciation although clearly anachronistic, but Luke's narratives have many examples of anachronistic material. He was also sensitive to the exclusion of the Judeo-Christians by the Jewish community.[5] Since the angel used the Divine Name *kurios* instead of *theos* or a substitute name which was in vogue, Mary was perplexed by the language of the angel's greeting.[7]

*you have found favor with God*   Cf. Gen. 6.8, 18.3; 1 Sam. 2.26.

*Jesus*   See above p. 6.

32 *He will be called the Son of the Most High*   This phrase appears in an Aramaic text from Qumran: "he shall be called [son of] the [g]reat [God], and by his name shall he be named. He shall be hailed [as] the Son of God, and they shall call him Son of the Most High."[7] Ultimately the term "Most High" goes back to the MT, e.g., Gen. 14.18, Ps. 78.35.[8] In the NT, outside of Luke 1.35, only Mark 5.7, Heb. 7.1.

*the throne of his father David.*   Cf. 2 Sam. 7.12–13.

35 *and the power of the Most High will overshadow you.*   Daube sees in this an analogue to Ruth 3.9, *I am Ruth thine handmaid, spread therefore thy wing over thine handmaid, for thou art a redeemer.* "It is the power of the Most High which is to overshadow Mary so that she shall bear a son, Jesus."[9] Perhaps it is significant that Ruth, ancestress of David the king, like Sarah and Rebecca, is said to have no womb.[10]

*For with God nothing will be impossible*   Cf. Gen. (LXX) 18.14, Job 42.2, Zech. 8.6.

*I am the handmaid of the Lord.*   Similar to Hannah's statement, 1 Sam. 1.11.

### NOTES

1. On the juxtaposition, similarity, and comparison between the stories about the births of John and Jesus, see Brown, *Birth*, pp. 294–307; Fitzmyer, *Luke*, pp. 313 ff.

2. See below n. 4.

3. See Fitzmyer, op. cit., p. 346, citing B. Qid. 20a, which is neither tannaitic nor Palestinian. It should also be noted that the Amora Samuel is never called "Rabbi" as Fitzmyer.

4. M. Ber. 9.5, B. Mak. 23b.

5. See, e.g., Luke 6.22 and below pp. 77f.

6. See S. T. Lachs, "Some Synoptic Passages and their Jewish Background" (forthcoming).

7. Cited by Fitzmyer, op. cit. p. 347.

8. For other examples of *Elyon* used for God, see Ps. 7.18; 57.3; 78.56; Num. 24.16; Deut. 32.8; Pss. 9.3, 21.8.

9. Daube, *NTRJ*, p. 27. Cf. Ruth R. 4.13, where *tallit* is related to *talal*, "to shadow."

10. Ruth R., loc. cit., cited by Daube, loc. cit.

# Mary's Visit to Elizabeth

## LUKE 1.39–56

39 In those days Mary arose and went with haste into the hill country, to a city of Judah, 40 and she entered the house of Zechariah and greeted Elizabeth. 41 And when Elizabeth heard the greeting of Mary, the babe leaped in her womb; and Elizabeth was filled with the Holy Spirit 42 and she exclaimed with a loud cry, "Blessed are you among women, and blessed is the fruit of your womb! 43 And why is this granted me, that the mother of my Lord should come to me? 44 For behold, when the voice of your greeting came to my ears, the babe in my womb leaped for joy. 45 And blessed is she who believed that there would be a fulfillment[l] of what was spoken to her from the Lord." 46 And Mary[m] said,

"My soul magnifies the Lord,
47 and my spirit rejoices in God my Savior,
48 for he has regarded the low estate of his handmaiden.
For behold, henceforth all generations will call me blessed;
49 for he who is mighty has done great things for me,
and holy is his name.
50 And his mercy is on those who fear him
from generation to generation.
51 He has shown strength with his arm,
he has scattered the proud in the imagination of their hearts,
52 he has put down the mighty from their thrones,
and exalted those of low degree;
53 he has filled the hungry with good things,
and the rich he has sent empty away.
54 He has helped his servant Israel,
in remembrance of his mercy,
55 as he spoke to our fathers,
to Abraham and to his posterity forever."

56 And Mary remained with her about three months, and returned to her home.

---

l Or *believed, for there will be a fulfillment*.
m *Elizabeth* instead of Mary in Origen, some of the Itala.

## COMMENTARY

**39** *Mary arose*, etc.  This is a transitional verse, connecting Gabriel's announcement of the conception of Mary with the conception of Elizabeth. The Annunciation and the narratives of the births of Jesus and John the Baptist in Luke are rooted in and are in imitation of the stories of the birth of Isaac, Samson, and especially of Samuel.[1] Despite the similarity of language and motif there is one strange omission. In each of these three birth stories in the MT and in that of John the Baptist, after the prediction of the woman's conception, the text records that each did indeed conceive or give birth, fulfilling that prediction.[2] The only exception is Mary, where there is no mention that she conceived. Verse 39 might contain such a reference but concealed through an error in the transmission of a Semitic original.[3]

*went with haste*  Gr. *meta spoudēs*, perhaps "with eagerness."[4]

*to a city of Judah*  Better "to the province or country of Judah." Heb. *medinah* or Aram. *medinta*.[5]

**41** *leaped*  The Gr. verb *eskirtēsen* used for *vayitrozezu* of Gen. 25.22 (LXX *eskirton*).

**42** *Blessed are you among women*  I.e., the most blessed. Cf. *Most blessed of women be Jael, the wife of Heber the Kenite;*[6] "O daughter, you are blessed by the Most High God above all women on earth."[7]

*fruit of your womb*  An Heb. idiom, and it indicates that Jesus was already conceived.[8] The origin of vv. 46–55, the Magnificat, is obscure. "It is not a reply to Elizabeth nor an address to God. It is rather a meditation, an expression of personal emotions and experience."[9] There are those who argue that it was originally said by Elizabeth, not Mary. Many of the phrases are taken from the MT but, according to some, through Greek not Hebrew. The strongest similarity is to Hannah's prayer, 1 Sam. 2.1–10.

**46** *My soul magnifies the Lord*  Cf. 1 Sam. 2.1; Ps. 69.31; 34.3; Sira 43.31.

**48** *for he had regarded . . . handmaiden*  Cf. 1 Sam. 1.11. Also Gen. 16.11, 29.32.

*all generations will call me blessed*  Cf. Gen. 30.13.  ˙

**49** *for he who is mighty*  Yahweh. Gr. *ho dunatos*. See Zeph. (LXX) 3.17, Ps. (LXX) 89.9.

*has done great things for me*  Cf. Deut. 10.21.

*and holy is his name*  Cf. Ps. 111.9.

**50** *his mercy is on those who fear him*  Cf. Ps. 103.17.

**51** *He has shown strength with his arm*  Cf. Ps. 89.11.

*he has put down the mighty from their thrones*  Job 12.19, 1 Sam. 2.7.[10]

**53** *he has filled the hungry with good things*  Ps. 107.9, 1 Sam. 2.5.[11]

*and the rich he has sent empty away*  1 Sam. 2.7.[12]

**54** *He has helped his servant Israel,*  Isa. 41.8–9.

*in remembrance of his mercy*  Ps. 98.3.

**55** *as he spoke to our fathers*  Mic. 7.20.

**56** *and returned to her home*  As with Hannah, 1 Sam. 1.19.

## NOTES

1. See Gen. 17.16 ff.; 18.11–13; Judg. 13.2 ff.; 1 Sam. 1.11 ff.
2. Gen. 21.1, Judg. 13.24, 1 Sam. 1.20.
3. Cf. Lachs, "Some Synoptic Passages." If one were to retrovert this text into Hebrew it might have read ביׄמים ההם ותמהר מרים ותלך ההרה למדינת יהודה
or ומרים מהרה וקמה והלכה ההרה.למדינת יהודה
There are several possibilities from this retroverted text to find a reference to Mary's conception: (1) For ותמהר, "and she hastened," it could have read ותהר, "and she conceived." (2) ומרים מהרה, "and Mary hastened," might have read ומרים הרה "and Mary conceived." (3) Possibly ההרה, "to the hill country," might have been הרה, i.e., that Mary (although) pregnant arose and went, etc.
4. Cf. 3 Macc. 5.24–27; Josephus, *Contra Ap.* II.4.
5. See C. C. Torrey, "Medina and Polis and Luke 1.39," *HTR* 17 (1924): 83–91. For a discussion of this suggestion, see Fitzmyer, *Luke*, p. 363. On rabbinic usage of *medinah*, see below, p. 180.
6. Judg. 5.24.
7. Jth. 13.18.
8. See Gen. 30.21; Deut. 7.13; 28.4; Lam. 2.20.
9. See B. Metzger, *A Textual Commentary*, pp. 130–131; Fitzmyer, *Luke*. See especially S. Benko, "The Magnificat: A History of the Controversy," *JBL* 86 (1967): 263–275.
10. Plummer, *Luke*, p. 30.
11. See also En. 46.4 ff.
12. See B. Shab. 151b and parallels, Exod. R. 31.3, *Tan. Mishpatim*, *Tan. B.* ibid. 8 (43a), Lev. R. 34.

# The Birth of John the Baptist

## LUKE 1.57–80

57 Now the time came for Elizabeth to be delivered, and she gave birth to a son. 58 And her neighbors and kinsfolk heard that the Lord had shown great mercy to her, and they rejoiced with her. 59 And on the eighth day they came to circumcise the child; and they would have named him Zechariah after his father, 60 but his mother said, "Not so; he shall be called John." 61 And they said to her, "None of your kindred is called by this name." 62 And they made signs to his father, inquiring what he would have him called. 63 And he asked for a writing tablet, and wrote, "His name is John." And they all marveled. 64 And immediately his mouth was opened and his tongue loosed, and he spoke, blessing God. 65 And fear came on all their neighbors. And all these things were talked about through all the hill country of Judea; 66 and all who heard them laid them up in their hearts, saying, "What then will this child be?" For the hand of the Lord was with him. 67 And his father Zechariah was filled with the Holy Spirit, and prophesied, saying,

68 "Blessed be the Lord God of Israel,
for he has visited and redeemed his people,
69 and has raised up a horn of salvation for us
in the house of his servant David,
70 as he spoke by the mouth of his holy prophets from of old,

71 that we should be saved from our enemies,
and from the hand of all who hate us;
72 to perform the mercy promised to our fathers,
and to remember his holy covenant,
73 the oath which he swore to our father Abraham,
74 to grant us
that we, being delivered from the hand of our enemies,
might serve him without fear,
75 in holiness and righteousness before him all the days of our life.
76 And thou, child, shalt be called the prophet of the Most High;
for thou shalt go before the Lord to prepare his ways,
77 to give knowledge of salvation to his people
in the forgiveness of their sins,
78 through the tender mercy of our God,
when the day shall dawn upon[n] us from on high
79 to give light to those who sit in darkness and in the shadow of death,
to guide our feet into the way of peace."

80 And the child grew and became strong in spirit, and he was in the wilderness till the day of his manifestation to Israel.

---

n Or *whereby the dayspring will visit*; others *since the dayspring has visited*.

## COMMENTARY

57 *Now the time . . . delivered* Lit. "for Elizabeth the time of her giving birth was filled up," cf. Gen. 25.24.

59 *on the eighth day* The day of circumcision, cf. Gen. 17.21; 21.4; Lev. 12.3. Circumcision supersedes all the laws of date even the Sabbath.[1]

*and they would have named him Zechariah* There is no contemporaneous evidence from the first century which unequivocally proves that a male child was named at the time of his circumcision. This was, however, the practice a few centuries later, and more than likely reflects a continuum which may well include the first century.[2] There is an old *baraita* which records the benediction of the father at the circumcision, "Blessed art Thou . . . who has sanctified us by Thy commandments, and has commanded us to make him enter into the covenant of Abraham our father." The congregation then responds, "As he has been made to enter the covenant so may he also be made to enter into the study of the Torah, the *ḥuppah* [bridal canopy], and the performance of good deeds."[3] The use of the pronoun "him" in the benediction of the father and the response of the congregation seems to indicate that originally the child was named immediately after the circumcision.

*after his father* There is evidence that at this period children were indeed named after the father, but more common appears to be the custom of naming after the grandfather.[4]

60 *John*   Heb. Yoḥanan, a priestly name. See Neh. 12.13, 42; 1 Macc. 2.1-2.

62 *And they made signs*   Lit. "nodded."[5]

63 *writing tablet*   Gr. *pinakidion*, Heb. *lu'aḥ, tavla, pinqas*.[6]

66 *laid them up in their hearts*   Cf. 1 Sam. 21.13, Mal. (LXX) 2.2.

68 *Blessed be the Lord God of Israel*   Ps. 41.14, 72.18, 106.48. Also variant 1 Chron. 16.36; 1 Kings 1.48.

*he has visited his people*   Gr. *epeskepsato*, Heb. *paqad*.[8]

*and redeemed his people*   Ps. 111.9.

69 *horn of salvation*   Ps. 18.3 = 2 Sam. 22.3; Ps. 132.17; Ezek. 29.21.

*house of . . . David*   2 Sam. 7.12–13.

*his servant*   Gr. *paidos autou*, Ps. 18.1, Isa. 37.35.[9]

70 *by the mouth of his holy prophets from of old*.   This expression is not in the MT; however, it does occur in the Qumran 1QS 1.3, "as he commanded through [lit. by the hand of Heb., *al yedē*] Moses and through all his servants the prophets."[10]

71 *that we should be saved from our enemies*   Reminiscent of Ps. 18.18 = 2 Sam. 22.18. Cf. Ps. 106.10.

72 *to perform the mercy*   Lit. "to do [mercy]," Heb. *la'asot*.[11]

*our fathers*   Cf. e.g., Mic. 7.20.

73 *the oath*   Gen. 22.16–17.

74 *being delivered from the hand of our enemies*   Cf. Ps. 97.10.

76 *prophet of the Most High*   Cf. Test. Levi 8.15. It is moot whether this is a messianic title.[12]

*go before the Lord to prepare his ways*   Cf. Mal. 3.1, Isa. 40.3.

78 *when the day shall dawn upon us from on high*   An exceedingly difficult verse and has remained a *crux interpretum*. The Gr. *anatolē* has been understood metaphorically as "the rising of the sun, stars, etc." as in Mal. (LXX) 3.20, *for you who fear My name the sun of righteousness shall rise [anatolai] with healing in its wings*.[13] Another explanation is that it renders the Heb. *ẓemaḥ*, "a sprout, a shoot, a scion,"[14] which, as Isa. 11.1, *There shall come forth a shoot [ḥoter] from the stump of Jesse, and a branch [neẓer] shall grow out of his roots*, has been interpreted with messianic connotation.[15]

## NOTES

1. See M. Shab. 18.3, 19.1–4.

2. Fitzmyer, *Luke*, p. 380, comments, "Such a custom of naming children at circumcision is not otherwise attested among Palestinian Jews until several centuries later. . . . Among Palestinian Jews it had been the practice to name a child at birth (See Gen. 4.1; 21.3; 25.26)." It is far more reasonable to cite as evidence a Palestinian practice, albeit later in terms of a few centuries, than to adduce as evidence that which is a millennium old, citing no proof that this practice was ongoing. Cf. *PRE* 48, where Moses is said to have been given the name of Yekutiel on the day of his circumcision, also *Leqaḥ Tov, Ḥayyē Sarah* 25.1.

3. B. Shab. 137b.

4. The practice of naming after relatives is rare in the MT; with the exception of Gen. 11.24, 26, and 1 Chron. 7.20–21; 5.35, 36, there are no examples of a grandfather and grandson with the same name. Other examples of kinsmen bearing a common name are: 2 Sam. 21.7; 13.1; 14.27; 3.3; 1 Kings 15.2; 22.26, 40; 2 Kings 8.16–18, 26; 11.2; 8.26; (undoubtedly some are mere coincidences). Cf. also 1 Chron. 6.2–14; 3.5; 6.7. The practice of naming members of the family goes back to the 6th cent. B.C.E. Egyptian Jews did this, as evidenced by the Elephantine Papryi. I. Löw places this practice one century later (*Lebensalter*, pp. 92–109; *Orient. Lit.* 6, pp. 129–241; 7, pp. 42, 620). L. Zunz, "Namen der Juden," in *Gesammelte Schriften* (Berlin, 1876), 3:19, points out that naming a boy after his father or a relative stems from the Seleucid period. For naming after the father, see Tob. 1.9; Josephus, *Ant.* XIV. 1.3, XX.9.1; *BJ* V.13.2. This apparently, however, was not a common practice. See S. Krauss, *TA*, 2:440 n. 131. It was more common to name after the grandfather, for which see 1 Macc. 2.1–2, Jub. 11.15., Josephus, *Vita* I.1. Cf. E. Sukenik, *JPOS* 8 (1928): 119.

5. On communicating with a deaf mute, see M. Git. 5.7.

6. See, e.g., T. Shab. 17.5 (p. 137), B. Git. 20a, B. Shab. 149a.

7. IQM 14.4; cf. 13.2, "Blessed be the God of Israel who preserves mercy for His covenant and periods of salvation for the people He redeems."

8. Cf. Exod. 4.31, Ruth 1.6, Ps. 80.15; 106.4.

9. Cf. Jeremias, *Son of God*, *TDNT* 5:681.

10. Cf. 4Qp Hos.ᵃ 2.5 (*DJD* 5.31), cited by Fitzmyer, op cit., p. 384.

11. See Gen. (LXX) 24.12; Judg. 1.24; 8.35; Ruth 1.8.

12. See A. R. C. Leaney, "Birth Narratives in St. Luke and St. Matthew," *NTS* 8 (1961–62): 161. Against this, Fitzmyer, op. cit., p. 385.

13. Cf. also Test. Levi 18.3; Matt. 2.2–3.

14. Cf. Jer. 23.5, *zedeq*, LXX *anatolēn dikaian*; Zech. 3.8, *avdi zemaḥ*, LXX *ton doūlon mou Anatolēn*; ibid. 6.12, *ish zemaḥ shemo*, LXX *Anatolē onoma autō*.

15. In rabbinic literature see TJ. Ber. 2, 5a (12); Lam. R. 1.16 (58b); Targ. Jer. 23.5, 33.15; Targ. Zech. 3.8; 6.16. *Shemoneh Esreh: et zemaḥ david*; Num. R. 18; *Mid. Ps.* 19.21 (44a). Qumran: 4Q Bless 3; J. M. Allegro, "Further Messianic References in Qumran Literature," *JBL* 75 (1956): 175; "until the coming of the Righteous Messiah, the Shoot (*zemaḥ*) of David"; 4QFlor, 1.11 = 4Q 174.1–2 i 11; *DJD*, 5.53–54, "He is the Shoot (*zemaḥ*) of David who will arise with the interpreter of the Law." Note the verb *anatellein* in Test. Naph. 8.2, Test. Gad. 8.1.

# The Birth of Jesus

## LUKE 2.1–20

1 In those days a decree went out from Caesar Augustus that all the world should be enrolled. 2 This was the first enrollment, when Quirinius was governor of Syria. 3 And all went to be enrolled, each to his own city. 4 And Joseph also went up from Galilee, from the city of Nazareth, to Judea, to the city of David, which is called Bethlehem, because he was of the house and lineage of David, 5 to be enrolled with Mary, his betrothed, who was with child. 6 And while they were there, the time came for her to be delivered. 7 And she gave birth to her first-born son and wrapped him in swaddling cloths and laid him in a manger, because there was no place for them in the inn. 8 And in that region there were shepherds out in the field, keeping

watch over their flock by night. 9 And an angel of the Lord appeared to them, and the glory of the Lord shone around them, and they were filled with fear. 10 And the angel said to them, "Be not afraid; for behold, I bring you good news of a great joy which will come to all the people; 11 for to you is born this day in the city of David a Savior, who is Christ the Lord.⁰ 12 And this will be a sign for you: you will find a babe wrapped in swaddling cloths and lying in a manger." 13 And suddenly there was with the angel a multitude of the heavenly host praising God and saying,

> 14 "Glory to God in the highest,
> and on earth peace among men with whom he is pleased!"ᴾ

15 When the angels went away from them into heaven, the shepherds said to one another, "Let us go over to Bethlehem and see this thing that has happened, which the Lord has made known to us." 16 And they went with haste, and found Mary and Joseph, and the babe lying in a manger. 17 And when they saw it they made known the saying which had been told them concerning this child; 18 and all who heard it wondered at what the shepherds told them. 19 But Mary kept all these things, pondering them in her heart. 20 And the shepherds returned, glorifying and praising God for all they had heard and seen, as it had been told them.

---

o Others *Christ of the Lord.*
p Others *peace, goodwill among men;* others *peace and goodwill among men.*

## COMMENTARY

1 *Caesar Augustus* Born Gaius Octavius 63 B.C.E.; died 14 C.E. In 29 his earlier title, Imperator, was ratified, and in 27 the Senate gave him the title of Augustus.

*all the world should be enrolled* There is no evidence of a universal census during this period. Some census did take place, however, and perhaps Luke adjusted it for his purpose.[1]

2 *first enrollment* Or the first time a census took place in Judea, or an enrollment before he became governor.[2] There was a census in Judea in 6 C.E.,[3] and Luke knew of this (cf. Act 5.37), but this was not during the days of Quirinius.[4]

*Quirinius* Augustus appointed him to be the adviser of Gaius Caesar, the adopted son of the emperor, who was given proconsular power and made vice-regent of the eastern provinces, including Syria, ca. 1 B.C.E.–4 C.E. When Augustus annexed Archelaus' territory, i.e., Judaea, Samaria, and Idumea, to the Roman province of Syria,[5] Quirinius was sent as legatus by the emperor to take a census of property in Syria and to sell the estate of Archelaus in Palestine.[6]

4 *the city of David which is called Bethlehem* In MT the city of David was Jerusalem.[7] but David is called son of Jesse the Bethlehemite.[8]

*swaddling clothes* See Ezek. 16.4, Wisd. 7.4.

9 *the glory of the Lord* Heb. *kevod adonai.* Cf. Exod. 16.7, 10; 24.17; 40.34; Ps. 6.3; cf. Num. 12.8. This appears to be identical with "light" in Matt. 2.2.

12 *a sign for you* MT parallels: Exod. 3.12; 2 Kings 19.29, Isa. 37.30; cf. 1Q 27.1.5, "This is for you to sign that this will take place."

13 *multitude of the heavenly host* Heb. *zeva shamayim, zava shel ma'alah,istaritia shel ma'alah.* In the LXX *bē stratia toū ouranoū:* I Kings 22.19, Jer. 19.13, Hos. 13.4, 2 Chron. 33.3, 5.

*praising God* Cf. Ps. 147.12, 148.2: Jth. 13.14

14 *Glory to God in the highest* Not in the MT, but see Bar. 2.17, 18; 1 Esd. 9.8; 4 Macc. 1.12; cf. Rom. 11.36, Heb. 13.21.

*among men with whom he is pleased* Gr. *eudokia = razon;* cf. Ps. 51.18. Qumran: 1QH 4.32.33, *benē rezono*," sons of his good will; 1QH 11.9, *lekhol benē rezonekha*," for all the sons of your good pleasure"; 4QH 'A' 18, *be'enosh re'ut[eh]*], "among men of [his] good pleasure."[9]

19 *But Mary kept all these things pondering them in her heart* Cf. Gen. 37.11.

## NOTES

1. See Suetonius, *Augustus* 27.5.
2. See Fitzmyer, *Luke*, p. 401.
3. Josephus, *Ant.* XVIII.1.1.
4. Cf. also ibid. XVIII.1.6.
5. *BJ* II.8.1.
6. *Ant.* XVII.18.5, XVII.1.1 In 6–7 c.e.
7. E.g., 2 Sam. 5.7, 9; 1 Chron. 11.5, 7; 2 Sam. 6.10.12, 16; 2 Kings 9.28; 12.22.
8. 1 Sam. 12.58; 20.6
9. As cited by Fitzmyer, op. cit., pp. 411–12.

# The Circumcision of Jesus and the Presentation in the Temple

## LUKE 2.21–40

21 And at the end of eight days, when he was circumcised, he was called Jesus, the name given by the angel before he was conceived in the womb. 22 And when the time came for their purification according to the law of Moses, they brought him up to Jerusalem to present him to the Lord. 23 (as it is written in the law of the Lord, "Every male that opens the womb shall be called holy to the Lord") 24 and to offer a sacrifice according to what is said in the law of the Lord, "a pair of turtle-doves, or two young pigeons." 25 Now there was a man in Jerusalem, whose name was Simeon, and this man was righteous and devout looking for the consolation of Israel, and the Holy Spirit was upon him. 26 And it had been revealed to him by the Holy Spirit that he should not see death before he had seen the Lord's Christ. 27 And inspired by the Spirit he came into the temple; and when the parents brought in the child Jesus, to do for him according to the custom of the Law, 28 he took him up in his arms and blessed God and said,

> 29 "Lord, now lettest thou thy servant depart in peace
> according to thy word;

30 for mine eyes have seen thy salvation
31 which thou hast prepared in the presence of all peoples,
32 a light for revelation to the Gentiles,
and for glory to thy people Israel."

33 And his father and his mother marveled at what was said about him; 34 and Simeon blessed them and said to Mary his mother,

"Behold, this child is set for the fall and rising of many in Israel,
and for a sign that is spoken against
35 (and a sword will pierce through your own soul also),
that thoughts out of many hearts may be revealed."

36 And there was a prophetess, Anna, the daughter of Phanuel, of the tribe of Asher; she was of a great age, having lived with her husband seven years from her virginity, 37 and as a widow till[r] she was eighty-four. She did not depart from the temple, worshiping with fasting and prayer night and day. 38 And coming up at that very hour she gave thanks to God, and spoke of him to all who were looking for the redemption of Jerusalem.

39 And when they had performed everything according to the law of the Lord, they returned into Galilee, to their own city, Nazareth. 40 And the child grew and became strong,[s] filled with wisdom; and the favor of God was upon him.

---

q  Or *And in the Spirit*.
r  Some texts omit *till*.
s  Some add *in spirit*.

## COMMENTARY

21 *At the end of eight days, etc.*    As with John, both the circumcision and the naming took place on the eighth day. See above pp. 26f.

22 *their purification*   The problem here is with Gr. *auton*, "their," which does not apply, since the purification ceremony was only for a woman *post partem* (see below, next note). "What has to be recognized is that Luke, not being a Palestinian Jewish Christian, is not accurately informed about this custom of the purification of a woman after childbirth."[1]

*according to the law of Moses*   Lev. 12.2–8. A woman who gave birth to a male child was unclean for seven days. On the eighth, the child was circumcised. The mother was confined for thirty-three days "until the days of her purification were completed" (Lev. 12.14), only then could she touch anything sacred or enter the Temple precincts. Numbers double for a female child 14/66. After her confinement she was to bring a sacrifice in the Temple of a one-year-old lamb for a burnt offering (*olah*) and a young pigeon or turtle-dove for a sin offering (*ḥattat*). If she could not afford a lamb she brought two turtle-doves or two young pigeons.

*they brought him up to Jerusalem to present him to the Lord*   This parallels the presentation of Samuel by his mother Hannah at Shiloh (1 Sam. 1.22–24). Luke again errs as to Jewish practice by connecting this presentation at the Temple with the law of the redemption of the firstborn. The essential element of the redemption ceremony was the payment of five shekels to a priest (Num. 3.47–48, 18.15–16), which could be done anywhere. Luke is silent on this point. Taking a child up to Jerusalem for redemption is found nowhere in the MT, the intertestamental literature, or the Mishnah.[2]

23 *as it is written*   See above p. 7. Cf. 2 Kings. (LXX) 14.6. Qumran: *ka'asher katuv*, e.g., 1QS 8.14, 5.17.[3]

*Every male*, etc.   Luke's paraphrase of Exod. 13.2

24 *and to offer a sacrifice*   Not for the redemption but for the purification. Presumably these birds were offered and not a lamb because Mary and Joseph could not afford it. This offering is called *qorban ani*, "the poor sacrifice," Lev. 5.7.[4]

25 *Simeon*   On the name see below p. 58. This incident is otherwise unknown.[5]

*looking for the consolation of Israel*   Cf. also Luke 2.38, *redemption of Jerusalem*; looking for the kingdom of God. Said of Joseph of Arimathea, *ibid.* 23.50, 51. This is an anachronism, for the term is applicable only *after* the destruction of the Second Temple.[6] It appears also as "day of consolation"; "May I see the consolation"; "May he see the consolation of the community,"[7]

26 *should not see death*   Cf. Ps. 89.49.

*Lord's Christ*   The Lord's anointed, e.g., 1 Sam. 24.7, 11; 26.9, 11, 16, 23.

29 *lettest thou thy servant depart in peace*   I.e., die peacefully.[8]

30 *for mine eyes have seen thy salvation*   Isa. 40.5; cf. also Luke 3.6.

31 *in the presence of all peoples*   Cf. Isa. 52.10.

32 *a light for revelation to the Gentiles*   Isa. 42.6, 49.6.[9]

*glory to your people*   Isa. (LXX) 46.13, *I shall set salvation in Zion for glory to Israel*.

35 *(a sword will pierce through you own soul)*   "As if he takes a sword and pierces it through his heart."[10]

36 *Anna*   Same name as the mother of Samuel (1 Sam. 1.2), Hannah, a Greek form of the name and apparently not by accident. The biblical Hannah is sometimes referred to as a prophetess: "Forty-eight prophets and seven prophetesses prophesied in Israel . . . seven prophetesses Sarah, Miriam, Deborah, Hannah, Abigail, Hulda, and Esther."[11]

*Phanuel*   Gr. of Heb. *penu'el*. In 1 Chron. 4.4 name of a man; in Gen. 32.32, Judg. 8.8., name of a place.[12]

*Asher*   What significance there is in this name is hard to say, particularly since there was no tribal indentification during Second Temple days.[13]

37 *worshiping . . . night and day*   It would seem that Luke has Anna participating in the prayers of the people attending the daily sacrifices; see Luke 1.10.

38 *redemption of Jerusalem*   See above to v. 25.

## NOTES

1. Fitzmyer, *Luke*, p. 424.
2. On the *pidyon ha-ben* (redemption of the firstborn), see M. Bekh. 8.1, 7; Num. R. 4; Sifre Num. 118; B. Bekh. 12b; T. Qid. 1.11 (p. 336); T. Bekh. 6.3 (p. 540).
3. See Fitzmyer, *ESBNT*, pp. 8–9.
4. See Lev. R. 3.5.
5. It is not reasonable to assume that he is the son of Hillel, father of R. Gamaliel the Elder, as suggested by A. Cutler, "Does the Simeon of Luke 2 Refer to Simeon the Son of Hillel?" *JBR* 34 (1966): 29–35.
6. Fitzmyer, *Luke*, p. 427, states, "Luke does not further explain the 'consolation of Israel,' but it is to be understood as the post-exilic hope for God's eschatological restoration of the Theocracy to Israel." There is no support for this in the literature. This and similar phrases refer only to the restoration of the Second Temple.
7. See below p. 73.
8. Cf., e.g., B. Ber 64a; Gen. R. 63.16.
9. This is a messianic function. Note Targum to Isa. 42.1, where the servant of the Lord is identified with the Messiah.
10. Note similar expression TJ. Ned. 9, 41b (48).
11. B. Meg. 14a.
12. Cf. B. Git. 58a.
13. Fitzmyer *Luke*, p. 43, connects it with "fortunate am I," Gen. 20.3 and Luke 1.42b, 48b. And then comments, "This identifies Anna as a member of an outlying Northern tribe. What a prophetess from a tribe like Asher would be doing in the Jerusalem Temple is a bit puzzling; Luke is probably little interested in the geographical location of Asher, as his attempt to describe Anna in the following phrases would suggest."

# The Precocious Jesus

## LUKE 2.41–52

41 Now his parents went to Jerusalem every year at the feast of the Passover. 42 And when he was twelve years old, they went up according to custom; 43 and when the feast was ended, as they were returning, the boy Jesus stayed behind in Jerusalem. His parents did not know it, 44 but supposing him to be in the company they went a day's journey, and they sought him among their kinsfolk and acquaintances; 45 and when they did not find him, they returned to Jerusalem, seeking him. 46 After three days they found him in the temple, sitting among the teachers, listening to them and asking him questions; 47 and all who heard him were amazed at his understanding and his answers. 48 And when they saw him they were astonished; and his mother said to him, "Son, why have you treated us so? Behold, your father and I have been looking for you anxiously." 49 And he said to them, "How is it that you sought me? Did you not know that I must be in my Father's house?" 50 And they did not understand the saying which he spoke to them. 51 And he went down with them and came to Nazareth, and was obedient to them, and his mother kept all these things in her heart. 52 And Jesus increased in wisdom and in stature,ᵗ and in favor with God and man.

---

t  Or *years.*

## COMMENTARY

**41** *every year at the feast of the Passover*   Every Jewish male was obligated to go up to the Temple at the three pilgrim festivals, i.e., Passover, Shavuot, and Sukkot.[1] "Feast of the Passover" is not found in the LXX; in the NT only here and John 13.1. Luke does not identify Passover here with the Festival of Unleavened Bread as he does in 22.1, 7. The Feast of Passover, Heb. *ḥag hapesaḥ* falls on the fourteenth of Nisan.[2] Starting on the evening of the fifteenth of Nisan and lasting for seven days is the Festival of Unleavened Bread, *ḥag ḥamaẓot*.[3] In the course of time "Passover" became the name for all seven days.[4] The two are mentioned together in 2 Chron. 35.17. Though Josephus still distinguishes the two,[5] he sometimes refers to the whole period as the Feast of Unleavened Bread.[6]

**42** *when he was twelve years old*   This mention of the twelfth year is a bit strange, since a male attained his religious majority at thirteen, when he had to observe the *miẓvot* of the Torah.[7] However, a child who did not need the ministration of his mother could be obligated to observe the Law at an earlier age.[8] Furthermore, since there is such a dependency here and in the birth story of John the Baptist on the birth story of Samuel, it is significant that Josephus states that the beginning of Samuel's prophetic period started during his twelfth year.[9]

*went up according to custom*   Cf. 1 Sam. 1.3, 21; 2.19.

**43** *and when the feast was ended*   I.e., after the first day or after the seven days. The latter is more likely,[10] since pilgrims who had made the journey generally stayed the entire period in Jerusalem.

**49** *How is it that you sought me?*[11]

**52** *And Jesus increased*, etc.   Cf. 1 Sam. 2.21, 26.[12]

## NOTES

1. Exod. 23.17; 34.23 ff.; Deut. 16.16.
2. Deut. 16.4; Exod. 12.6 ff.
3. Exod. 12.15 ff.; 23.15; 34.18.
4. Deut. 16.1–4, Ezek. 45.21–25, Josephus, *Ant.* VI.9.3, XX.5.3.
5. *Ant.* III.10.5.
6. *BJ* II.14.3, *Ant.* XVII.8.3.
7. M. Nid. 5.6. Cf. M. Avot 5.21. See also *Tan.B.*, *Toledot* 2 (p. 63a); Gen. R. 63.14; M. Ḥag. 1.1.
8. See T. Ḥag. 1.2 (p. 232). This is particularly important since it applies to the rule requiring all adult males to make the pilgrimage to Jerusalem on the three Festivals.
9. *Ant.* V.10.4.
10. See Sifre Deut. 134.
11. See P. Winter, "Luke 2.49 and Targum Yerushalmi," *ZNW* 45 (1954): 145–149; idem, "Luke 2.49 and Targum Yerushalmi Again," ibid. 46 (1955): 140–144.
12. Of Moses see Josephus, *Ant.* II.9.6. Note the expression in Prov. (LXX) 3.5 and M. Avot 3.10.

# THE GALILEAN SECTION

MATT. 3–18 = MARK 1–9 = LUKE 3.1–9.50

## 1. John the Baptist

### MATT. 3.1–6

1 In those days came John the Baptist, preaching in the wilderness of Judea, 2 "Repent, for the kingdom of heaven is at hand." 3 For this is he who was spoken of by the prophet Isaiah when he said,

> "The voice of one crying in the wilderness:
> Prepare the way of the Lord, make his paths
> straight."

4 Now John wore a garment of camel's hair, and a leather girdle around his waist; and his food was locusts and wild honey. 5 Then went out to him Jerusalem and all Judea and all the region about the Jordan, 6 and they were baptized by him in the river Jordan, confessing their sins.

### MARK 1.1–6

1 The beginning of the gospel of Jesus Christ, the Son of God.ᵘ 2 As it is written in Isaiah the prophet,ᵛ

> "Behold, I send my messenger before thy face,
> who shall prepare thy way;
> 3 the voice of one crying in the wilderness:
> Prepare the way of the Lord,
> make his paths straight."

4 John the baptizer appearedʷ in the wilderness, preaching a baptism of repentance for the forgiveness of sins. 5 And there went out to him all the country of Judea, and all the people of Jerusalem; and they were baptized by him in the river Jordan, confessing their sins. 6 Now John was clothed with camel's hair, and had a leather girdle around his waist,ˣ and ate locusts and wild honey.

### LUKE 3.1–6

1 In the fifteenth year of the reign of Tiberius Caesar, Pontius Pilate being governor of Judea, and Herod being tetrarch of Galilee, and his brother Philip tetrarch of the region of Ituraea and Trachonitis, and Lysanias tetrarch of Abilene, 2 in the high-priesthood of Annas and Caiaphas, the word of God came to John the son of Zechariah in the wilderness; 3 and he went into all the region about the Jordan, preaching a baptism of repentance for the forgiveness of sins. 4 As it is written in the book of the words of Isaiah the prophet,

"The voice of one crying in the wilderness;
Prepare the way of the Lord,
make his paths straight.
5 Every valley shall be filled,
and every mountain and hill shall be brought low,
and the crooked shall be made straight,
and the rough ways shall be made smooth;
6 and all flesh shall see the salvation of God."

---

u  Some texts omit *the Son of God.*
v  Some texts read *the prophets* (minus *Isaiah*).
w  Some texts read *was baptizing in.*
x  D.It. omits *and had a leather girdle around his waist.*

## COMMENTARY

This section marks the beginning of Jesus' ministry in which John the Baptist is presented as the forerunner of the Messiah, heralding the coming of Jesus.[1] This is based on the tradition that Elijah the prophet will announce the "coming of the great and terrible day of the Lord," and that he is the messenger whom God will send, as predicted by the prophet Malachi.[2] John has been cast into this Elijah figure both as to his function as a messianic herald and as to his description. Luke, in omitting the description of the Baptist, bypasses the Elijah theme.

Josephus is the only available authority outside of the NT who furnishes independent information about John.

> "But to some of the Jews the destruction of Herod's army seemed to be divine vengeance, and certainly a just vengeance, for his treatment of John, surnamed the Baptist. For Herod had put him to death, though he was a good man and had exhorted the Jews to lead righteous lives, to practice justice towards their fellows and piety towards God, and so doing to join in baptism. In his view this was a necessary preliminary if baptism was to be acceptable to God. They must not employ it to gain pardon for whatever sins they committed, but as a consecration of the body implying that the soul was already thoroughly cleansed by right behavior. When others, too, joined the crowds about him, because they were aroused to the highest degree by his sermons, Herod became alarmed. Eloquence that had so great an effect on mankind might lead to some form of sedition, for it looked as if they would be guided by John in everything they did. Herod decided therefore that it would be much better to strike first and be rid of him before his work led to an uprising, than to wait for an upheaval, get involved in a difficult situation and see his mistake. Though John, because of Herod's suspicions, was brought in chains to Machaerus, the stronghold that we have previously mentioned, and there put to death, yet the verdict of the Jews was that the destruction visited upon Herod's army was a vindication of John, since God saw fit to inflict such a blow on Herod."[3]

From an independent historical personage he was cast into the role of the precursor of the Messiah.

2 *Repent, for the kindgom of heaven is at hand*   John is preaching the advent of a new era or a new kingdom, entrance into which requires the removal of sin through repentance and good deeds. These prerequisites are widely attested to in Jewish sources, e.g., "Great is repentance, which hastens [lit. brings near] redemption."[4] John's warning is a continuation of the prophetic admonition that "the day of the Lord" will be a day of punishment for all nations, including Israel.[5] The term "repent," in Heb. is *shuvu*, "return," i.e., return to God and to the covenant which you have broken.

3 *the voice of one crying in the wilderness*   A quotation from Isa. 40.3, following the LXX, in which the Gr. *en tē erēmō*, "in the wilderness," is connected with *phōnē boōntos*, "a voice crying"; whereas in the MT "in the wilderness" is connected with "prepare the way of the Lord." In Mark 1.2–3 the prophecy is a combination of Isa. 40.3 and Mal. 3.1. The meaning here is that John is the voice heralding the future age.

4 *a garment of camel's hair, etc.*   This is an outer garment and is in contrast with "soft raiment of courtiers" of Matt. 11.8.[6] The hairy mantle was the sign of the prophetic office,[7] and Elijah, the prototype of John, is described as "a hairy man, and girt with a girdle of leather about his loins."[8]

*locusts and wild honey*   Locust was a popular food, even considered a dainty of kings.[9] There were many varieties of locust, some clean, others unclean. According to one account there were eight hundred species of clean locust.[10] Klausner suggested that wild honey, Gr. *meli agrion*, Heb. *devash haya'ar*, originally was *ya'arat devash*, the honeycomb.[11]

5 *Jerusalem and all Judea*   Jerusalem is not mentioned here together with Judea because it was its most important city. Jerusalem, going back to the days of David and continuing through Israelite history, was a separate political entity, neither part of Judah nor of the Northern Kingdom of Israel. This distinction as a political entity continued after the Return, as evidenced by the genealogies in Ezra, where those of Jerusalem are listed separately from those of Judah (Ezra 10.7, Neh. 7.6). Here it is a continuation of this traditional expression, although it is no longer applied politically.[12]

6 *they were baptized by him in the river Jordan*   This "baptism of repentance" has remained an enigma. Neither biblical nor rabbinic Judaism knows of this type of baptism, nor is it similar to the later Christian rite. In Jewish sources there are only two kinds of immersion—for purification from ritual uncleanness and proselyte baptism.[13] It is possible that it represents some sectarian ritual, such as immersion among the Essenes, the Morning Bathers, and others.[14]

*confessing their sins*   It is not clear whether there was a confessional formula to be recited or one composed by the individual penitent. The confession of the high priest on Yom Kippur, suggested by some, has no relevance here.[15] The following are several examples of personal confessions:

How should one confess? R. Berekhya in the name of R. Ba b. Bina: "My Lord: I have sinned and have walked in a far-off path. I will no longer do what I have done. May it be Thy will, O Lord my God, that You grant me atonement and forgive all my sins and pardon all my sins."[16]

R. Hamemuna said, "Confession on Yom Kippur: O God, before I was created I was worthless, and now that I have been formed, I am as if I were not formed. I am dust in my life, how much more in my death. Behold, I am before Thee as a vessel filled with shame and reproach. Now may it be Thy will before Thee that I sin no more, and that which I have sinned, cast out in Thy mercy but not through painful troubles."[17]

R. Bibi[ai] bar Abaye said: "How shall a man confess on Yom Kippur? He should say: 'I confess [admit] all the evil I have done before Thee in the evil way in which I have been standing. What I have done I shall not do like it again. May it be for Thee, O Lord my God, that You forgive me of all my sins, and pardon all my transgressions and grant me atonement for all my sins."[18]

Mark, v. 1 *in Isaiah the prophet* As the text stands it is incorrect, since verses are taken from Mal. 3.1 and Isa. 40.3. "The mistake may have arisen because the Malachi quotation was added later, or possibly St. Mark took the texts, already combined, from a testimony-book i.e. a collection of passages from the Old Testament put together by the early Church as throwing light on the life and work of Christ."[19] The variant reading "the prophets" if not original was substituted to solve the problem.

Luke, v. 1 *In the fifteenth year of the reign of Tiberius Caesar* Luke is the only one of the evangelists who relates the call of John the Baptist to Roman as well as to Jewish chronology. This was probably due to the universal goal of his message. The problem with this date is, when does one reckon the beginning of his reign? Most count from the death of Augustus, making the fifteenth year August–September 28–29 C.E.[20]

*Pontius Pilate being governor of Judea* On Pontius Pilate see below p. 422.

*Herod being tetrarch of Galilee* I.e., Herod Antipas, younger son of Herod the Great and Malthace. His rule began in 4 B.C.E. and it ended in 39 C.E., when Caligula exiled him.[21]

*and his brother Philip tetrarch of the region of Ituraea and Trachonitis* Philip, the son of Herod the Great and Cleopatra of Jerusalem, ruled from 4 B.C.E. to 34 C.E., when his tetrarchy became part of the Roman province of Syria. He died without issue.[22]

*Lysanias tetrarch of Abilene* Abilene is a well-known area NW of Damascus around the town of Abila at the southern end of the Anti-Lebanon range; but Lysanias seems to defy identification. He could not have been the Lysanias who was the son of Ptolemaeus of Chaleis in Coele-Syria, for he was put to death by M. Antony in 36 B.C.E.[23] Several times Josephus mentions the area and the man, but this does not help in identifying him.[24]

Luke, v. 2 *in the high priesthood of Annas and Caiaphas*  Luke's reference to high priesthood here is vague. No two priests were high priests concurrently. Most probably he was not intending historical precision but a general period of time. On these priests see below pp. 398, 419.

*as it is written* Heb. *kemo shekatuv*, a technical term introducing a biblical proof-text.[25]

Luke, v. 5 *Every valley . . . salvation of God.*  Only Luke adds these verses from Isa. 40.4 ff. Have they been added because of their universal import, which is characteristic of Luke's approach to the gospel?

## NOTES

1. Cf. Acts 10.37, "beginning from Galilee after the baptism which John preached." See also ibid. 1.22.

2. Mal. 3.23; 3.1. See below p. 261.

3. Josephus, *Ant.* XVIII.5.2. There is no reason to suspect the genuineness of this passage, although there have been those who have considered it to be spurious. Cf. Krauss, *Das Leben Jesu,*p. 275. H. Graetz, in the first edition of his *Geschichte der Juden*, accepted Josephus' account of John the Baptist as authentic, but in later editions he changed his mind. S. Zeitlin, *RFJS*, 2:148, accepts its authenticity but argues that as it stands there are some interpolations, for example, "John that was called the baptist," since as he points out in n. 116 ad loc., the term *hamatbil*, "the baptizer," does not appear in the Hebrew literature of that period. The authenticity is supported by the fact that the Josephus text does not connect John with Jesus. Furthermore, Origen, *Contra Celsum* I.48, states that the Jews did not associate John with Jesus. Cf. also ibid. 47. This passage in Josephus about John the Baptist should not be put together with the Josephus "Jesus passage" which stems from the Slavonic Josephus, and is surely a forgery. See S. Zeitlin, "The Christ Passage in Josephus," *JQR* 17 (1928): 230–255; idem, *Josephus on Jesus* (1931), pp. 61–70. See also Appendix IV. On the differences between the Gospel account of John and that of Josephus, see Zeitlin, *RFJS*, 2:149 ff.; Abrahams, *Studies I*, pp. 30 ff.

4. B. Yoma 86b.

5. E.g. Amos 5.18. On the kingdom of heaven, see below p. 72.

6. Cf. also Josephus, *BJ* I.24.3.

7. Zech. 13.4; 1 Kings 19.13.

8. 2 Kings 1.8.

9. See Gen. R. 67.2; Pliny, *NH* VI.35, VII.2.

10. See Lam. R., Intro. 34 (p. 20a). See also M. Ter. 10.9, M. Ḥul. 3.7; B. ibid. 65a–66b. On wild honey see Judg. 14.8–9.

11. Klausner, *JN*, p. 243.

12. See J. Bright, *A History of Israel* (Philadelphia: Westminister Press, 1952), pp. 178–179.

13. See B. Pes. 41a; *PR* 14 (66a); *Tan.B. Hukkat* 28 (51a/b), *Mezora* 9 (24b), 10 (27a). Some have suggested that John's baptism harks back to Ezek. 36.25 or Isa. 1.16–18.

14. On these sects see M. Simon, *Jewish Sects at the Time of Jesus* (Philadelphia, 1973).

15. M. Yom. 3.8.

16. TJ. Yom. 8.9, 45c (34).

17. B. Yom. 87.

18. Lev. R. 3.3.

19. Nineham, *St. Mark*, p. 60.

20. On the background of this problem and suggested solutions, see J. Finegan, *Handbook of Biblical Chronology*, pp. 259–280; H. W. Hoehner, *Chronological Aspects of the Life of Christ*, pp. 29–44.

21. See Josephus, *Ant.* XVII.1.4; cf. *BJ* I.33.8. H. W. Hoehner, *Herod Antipas*, SNTSMS 17 (Cambridge University Press, 1972).

22. Josephus, *Ant.* XVII.11.4, mentions Batanaea, Trachonitis, Aurantis, and part of the realm of Zenodorus; in ibid. XVII.8.1 Gaulonitis, Trachonitis, Batanaes, and Paneas. All, however, were E. of the Jordan.

23. Josephus, *Ant.* XV.4.1.

24. See ibid. XIX.5.1, Abila which belongs to Lysanias; ibid. XX.7.1, "Abila which had been the Lysanian tetrarchy; *BJ* II.12.8, "Kingdom of Lysanias."

25. *See* Bacher, *Terminologie*, 1:90.

# 2. John's Preaching of Repentance

## MATT. 3.7–10

7 But when he saw many of the Pharisees and Sadducees coming for baptism, he said to them, "You brood of vipers! Who warned you to flee from the wrath to come? 8 Bear fruit that befits repentance, 9 and do not presume to say to yourselves, 'We have Abraham as our father'; for I tell you, God is able from these stones to raise up children to Abraham. 10 Even now the axe is laid to the root of the trees; every tree therefore that does not bear good fruit is cut down and thrown into the fire."[y]

## LUKE 3.7–9

7 He said therefore to the multitudes that came to be baptized by him, "You brood of vipers! Who warned you to flee from the wrath to come? 8 Bear fruits that befit repentance, and do not begin to say to yourselves, 'We have Abraham as our father'; for I tell you, God is able from these stones to raise up children to Abraham. 9 Even now the axe is laid to the root of the trees; every tree therefore that does not bear good fruit is cut down and thrown into the fire."[y]

---

y Cf. Matt. 7.19 (Sec. 41, below p. 147).

## COMMENTARY

7 *Pharisees and Sadducees* Two of the major divisions of the Jews of the Second Temple period; their respective doctrinal positions are set forth in Josephus:

> "The Jews from the most ancient times, had thorough philosophies pertaining to their traditions, that of the Essenes, that of the Sadducees, and, thirdly, that of the group called the Pharisees. To be sure, I have spoken about them in the second book of the Jewish War but nevertheless I shall here too dwell on them for a moment.

The Pharisees simplify their standard of living, making no concession to luxury. They follow the guidance of that which their doctrine has selected and transmitted as good, attaching the chief importance to the observance of those commandments which it has seen fit to dictate to them. They show respect and deference to their elders, nor do they rashly presume to contradict their proposals. Though they postulate that everything is brought about by fate, still they do not deprive the human will of the pursuit of what is in man's power, since it was God's good pleasure that there should be a fusion and that the will of man with his virtue and vice should be admitted to the council-chamber of fate. They believe that souls have power to survive death and that there are rewards and punishments under the earth for those who have led lives of virtue or vice: eternal imprisonment is the lot of evil souls, while the good souls receive an easy passage to a new life. Because of these views they are, as a matter of fact, extremely influential among the townsfolk; and all prayers and sacred rites of divine worship are performed according to their exposition. This is the great tribute that the inhabitants of the cities, by practicing the highest ideals both in their way of living and in their discourse, have paid to the excellence of the Pharisees.

The Sadducees hold that the soul perishes along with the body. They own no observance of any sort apart from the laws; in fact they reckon it a virtue to dispute with the teachers of the path of wisdom that they pursue. There are but few men to whom this doctrine has been made known, but these are men of the highest standing. They accomplish practically nothing, however. For whenever they assume some office, though they submit unwillingly and perforce, yet submit they to the formulas of the Pharisees, since otherwise the masses would not tolerate them."[1]

"Of the two first-named schools, the Pharisees, who are considered the most accurate interpreters of the laws, and hold the position of the leading sect, attribute everything to Fate and to God; they hold that to act rightly or otherwise rests, indeed, for the most part with men, but that in each action Fate cooperates. Every soul, they maintain, is imperishable, but the soul of the good alone passes into another body, while the souls of the wicked suffer eternal punishment.

The Sadducees, the second of the orders, do away with Fate altogether, and remove God beyond, not merely the commission, but the very sight of evil. They maintain that the man has the free choice of good or evil, and that it rests with each man's will whether he follows the one or the other. As for the persistence of the soul after death, penalties in the underworld and rewards, they will have none of them.

The Pharisees are affectionate to each other and cultivate harmonious relations with the community. The Sadducees, on the contrary, are, even among themselves, rather boorish in their behavior, and in their intercourse with their peers are as rude as to aliens."[2]

The vituperation directed against the Pharisees and Sadducees by the Baptist is consistent with the "anti-Jewish polemic which runs through the whole Gospel."[3] The Pharisees and the Sadducees did not come to be baptized, but to witness the proceedings.[4]

*you brood of vipers* This expression is found neither in Heb. nor in Aram. In the NT it is used both by John and by Jesus and has the meaning of hypocrites.[5] The serpent, however, does not symbolize hypocrisy. The Gr. *echidna* is probably a mistranslation of an Aram. original, *af'a*, which denotes a spotted cat, a leopard, or possibly a hyena. The translator read the word *effe*, "a viper" or "an adder," instead of *af'a*, "a spotted cat." The meaning therefore is one of hypocrisy—you are attractive on the outside but inwardly you are vicious and rapacious.[6]

*the wrath to come* I.e., the day of judgment and the punishment of Gehinom. This expression is common in the intertestamental literature, e.g., "The Holy Lord will come forth with wrath";[7] "The staff of His wrath";[8] "nor one that shall be saved on the day of the wrath of judgment."[9]

8 *fruit that befits repentance* I.e., good deeds. Heb. *ma'asim tovim*. Cf. "R. Eliezer b. Jacob said: 'Repentance and good works are a shield against punishment.' "[10]

9 *and do not presume to say*, etc. John warns the Pharisees and the Sadducees not to rely on the principle of *zekhut avot*, "the merit of the fathers," believing that this would protect them, arguing that they will escape punishment by virtue of the fact that they are the descendants of the patriarch Abraham, to whom God promised that his progeny would prosper, grow, and continue forever. No one escapes deserved punishment, neither Jew nor non-Jew—the day of judgment is for all.[11]

*Abraham as our father* Abraham is cited not only because he was the first patriarch but because he is the father of proselytes, for a proselyte becomes a "son of our father Abraham."[12]

*God is able from these stones*, etc. This verse is generally explained as representing a wordplay between *avanim*, "stones," and *banim*, "sons," connected by the verb *benot*, "to build." It is possible that a wordplay does indeed exist but that the original of Gr. *lithoi*, "stones," was not *avanim* but *evyonim*, "the poor," the outcasts of society, referring to the soldiers, tax collectors, and harlots who came to be baptized.[13]

10 *Even now the axe is laid to the root of the trees*, etc. Perhaps an echo of Isa. 10.33–34.

Luke, v. 7 *to be baptized by him* MS D reads "to be baptized before him." "This would suggest that John did not do all the baptizing himself."[14] If this be the correct reading it might well stem from the Heb. *lifanav*, meaning by the "authority of" or "by the direction of" John.[15]

## NOTES

1. Josephus, *Ant.* XVIII.1.2–4.
2. *BJ* II.8.14. For modern studies on the Pharisees and Sadducees, see L.

Finkelstein, *The Pharisees*, 2 vols. (Philadelphia, 1940); S. Zeitlin, *RFJS*, 1: 175 ff.; E. Rivkin, *A Hidden Revolution* (Nashville: Abingdon, 1978); J. Neusner, *The Rabbinic Traditions about the Pharisees before 70*. (Leiden: E. J. Brill, 1971).

3. Allen, *Matt.*, p. 24.
4. See below p. 353.
5. Cf. Matt. 12.34, 23.33; Luke 3.7. M. Avot 2.10 is not applicable.
6. For the linguistic evidence for this emendation, see S. T. Lachs, "Studies in the Semitic Background to the Gospel of Matthew," *JQR* 67 (1977): 197–199.
7. En. 91.7. Cf. B. BB. 10a, B. AZ. 18b.
8. En. 90.18.
9. Jub. 24.30. In the NT cf. Rom. 1.18, 2.5; Rev. 6.17.
10. M. Avot 4.13. See Taylor's notes ad loc. Cf. also Gen. R. 39.3; TJ Ta'an. 2.1, 65b (27).
11. For exemplary acts performed by Abraham and recounted by Israel before God, see *SB*, 1: 117 ff. Cf. also Gal. 3.6–7 and Test. Levi 15.4. On the concept of *zekhut avot* see S. Schechter, *Some Aspects of Rabbinic Theology* (New York and London, 1910), pp. 170 ff.
12. Cf. TJ. BQ 1.4, 64a (15). See also L. Ginzberg, *Legends*, 5: 233, n. 122.
13. For the development of this explanation, see S. T. Lachs, "John the Baptist and His Audience," *Gratz College Annual of Jewish Studies*, 4 (1975): 28 ff.
14. Fitzmyer, *Luke*, p. 468.
15. See above p. 17.

## 3. *The Soldiers and the Tax Collectors and John*

### LUKE 3.10–14

10 And the multitudes asked him, "What then shall we do?" 11 And he answered them, "He who has two coats, let him share with him who has none; and he who has food, let him do likewise." 12 Tax collectors also came to be baptized, and said to him, "Teacher, what shall we do?" 13 And he said to them, "Collect no more than is appointed you." 14 Soldiers also asked him, "And we, what shall we do?" And he said to them, "Rob no one by violence or by false accusation, and be content with your wages."

### COMMENTARY

10 *What then shall we do?* I.e., to enter the kingdom. John's answer involves neither belief nor ascetic behavior. He follows the traditional view that repentance must be coupled with the performance of good deeds, as here, sharing with the needy, not taking advantage in collecting taxes nor abusing military authority by robbing the populace. It does not reflect the philosophy of the Essenes or the Qumran covenanters, who advocated communal ownership of property, hence this weakens an identification of John with these sects.

12 *tax collectors* Gr. *telōnai;* Heb. *mokhsim*, a lower echelon of tax (toll) collectors but part of the tax-farming system. Most were Jews. There was

the chief tax collector, *architelōnēs* (cf. Luke 19.2), who farmed out the territory to the *telōnai*, who, in order to make a profit, inflated the amount to be collected. On the status of these tax collectors in society, see below p. 109.

*Teacher* Gr. *didaskalos*. On this term and the title Rabbi, see below pp. 367f, 373 n.24.

*Soldiers* Probably not Romans, since there were no Roman legions in Judea at this time.[1]

14 *Rob no one . . . content with your wages* This is similar to Josephus' advice to his men, "I thanked them and advised them neither to attack anyone nor to sully their hands with rapine, but to encamp in the plain and be content with their rations, as my desire was to quell these disturbances without bloodshed."[2]

## NOTES

1. See Josephus, *Ant.* XVIII.5.1.
2. Josephus, *Vita* 47.244. See also *BJ* II.20.7.

# 4. John Predicts the Coming of the Messiah

## MATT. 3.11–12

11 "I baptize you with water for repentance, but he who is coming after me is mightier than I, whose sandals I am not worthy to carry; he will baptize you with the Holy Spirit and with fire. 12 His winnowing fork is in his hand, and he will clear his threshing floor, and gather his wheat into the granary, but the chaff he will burn with unquenchable fire."

## MARK 1.7–8

7 And he preached, saying, "After me comes he who is mightier than I, the thong of whose sandals I am not worthy to stoop down and untie. 8 I have baptized you with water; but he will baptize you with the Holy Spirit."

## LUKE 3.15–18

15 As the people were in expectation, and all men questioned in their hearts concerning John, whether perhaps he were the Christ, 16 John answered them all, "I baptize you with water; but he who is mightier than I is coming, the thong of whose sandals I am not worthy to untie; he will baptize you with the Holy Spirit and with fire. 17 His winnowing fork is in his hand, to clear his threshing floor, and to gather the wheat into his granary; but the chaff he will burn with unquenchable fire." 18 So, with many other exhortations, he preached good news to the people.

## COMMENTARY

11 *I baptize you with water for repentance* Mark reads "for forgiveness of sin." Matt. deletes this to show that Jesus is superior to John, in that he alone can forgive sin.[1]

*whose sandals I am not worthy to carry* The carrying of the shoes, especially to the bath, was a function of a slave and was a symbol of subservience and servility. This was particularly true in Roman society. In Jewish sources the following are significant:

> "Our Rabbis taught: How is a non-Jewish slave acquired by *ḥazaqah* [presumption]? If he unlooses his shoes for him [the purchaser] or carries his baggage to the bath. If he undresses, washes him, anoints him, scrapes him, dresses him, puts on his shoes, or lifts him, he acquires him."[2]

> "R. Joshua b. Levi said: 'All manner of service that a slave must render to his master, a student must render to his teacher, except that of taking off his shoes'."[3]

*he will baptize you with the Holy Spirit and with fire* Many argue that the original text dealt only with baptism by fire and only later was "baptism by the Holy Spirit" added. A clear reference to baptism by fire is found but once in rabbinic literature and it is significant that it appears in a polemical passage.

> A certain *min* [sectarian] said to R. Abbahu: "Your God is a priest, for it is written, *that they take for Me terumah* [Exod. 25.2]. When they buried Moses wherewith did he purify himself? Should you say with water, is it not written, *who has measured the waters in the hollow of His hands* [Isa. 40.12]?" He said to him: "With fire did He purify Himself, for it is written, *Behold the Lord will come in fire* [Ibid. 66.15]." "Does then purification by fire avail?" he said. "On the contrary," he replied, "essentially purification is in fire, as it is written, *all that abideth not the fire, shalt thou make pass through water* [Num. 31.23]."[4]

## NOTES

1. M. Dibelius, *Die urchristliche Ueberlieferung von Johannes dem Täufer* (Göttingen, 1911), p. 55.

2. B. Qid. 22b, B. BB 53b.

3. B. Ket. 96a, *Mek.* Exod. 21.2, and B. Er. 27b; B. BM 41a, TJ. ibid. 7.9 (11c). See, however, *PRK* 10 (84b).

4. B. Sanh. 39a. On this passage see Herford, *CTM*, p. 276; S. T. Lachs, "Rabbi Abbahu and the Minim," *JQR* 60 (1970): 210. Klausner, *JN*, p. 247, stated: "should baptize with fire not with the Holy Spirit which is not a Hebrew form of expression." S. Schechter, *Studies in Judaism*, Second Series (Philadelphia, 1908), pp. 102–110, supports the reading of "the Holy Spirit" by citing TJ. Suk., 5.1 (55a), *sho'avin ru'aḥ haqodesh*. Cf. Ezek. 39.29, Joel 3.2, Gen. R. 90.4.

# 5. *John's Imprisonment*

## LUKE 3.19–20

19 But Herod the tetrarch, who had been reproved by him for Herodias, his brother's wife, and for all the evil things that Herod had done, 20 added this to them all, that he shut up John in prison.
See below Sec. 111 (p. 238).

# 6. *The Baptism of Jesus*

## MATT. 3.13–17

13 Then Jesus came from Galilee to the Jordan to John, to be baptized by him. 14 John would have prevented him, saying, "I need to be baptized by you, and do you come to me?" 15 But Jesus answered him, "Let it be so now; for thus it is fitting for us to fulfill all righteousness." Then he consented. 16 And when Jesus was baptized, he went up immediately from the water, and behold, the heavens were opened[z] and he saw the Spirit of God descending like a dove, and alighting on him; 17 and lo, a voice from heaven, saying, "This is my beloved Son,[a] with whom I am well pleased."

## MARK 1.9–11

9 In those days Jesus came from Nazareth of Galilee and was baptized by John in the Jordan. 10 And when he came up out of the water, immediately he saw the heavens opened and the Spirit descending upon him like a dove; 11 and a voice came from heaven, "Thou art my beloved Son;[a] with thee I am well pleased."

## LUKE 3.21–22

21 Now when all the people were baptized and when Jesus also had been baptized and was praying, the heaven was opened, 22 and the Holy Spirit descended upon him in bodily form, as a dove, and a voice came from heaven, "Thou art my beloved Son;[a] with thee I am well pleased."[b]

---

z  Other ancient authorities add *to him.*
a  Or *my Son, my* (or *the*) *Beloved.*
b  Other ancient authorities read *today I have begotten thee.*

### COMMENTARY

16 *the heavens were opened*  Cf. Ezek. 1.1; and "The heavens shall be opened and from the Temple of Glory shall come upon him with sanctification with the Father's voice [*phone - bat qol*] from Abraham to Isaac."[1]

*the spirit of God descending like a dove*  In Jewish sources the dove is the symbol of the Holy Spirit or it is used metaphorically as the Holy Spirit.[2] Note the following:

"*And the spirit of God hovered over the waters* [Gen. 1.2] like a dove which hovers over her young without touching them."[3]

"It has been taught: R. Jose says: 'I was once traveling on the road and I entered into one of the ruins of Jerusalem in order to pray. Elijah of blessed memory appeared and waited for me at the entrance until I had finished my prayer. After I finished my prayer he said to me, 'My son, what sound did you hear in this ruin?' 'I heard a divine voice [*bat qol*] cooing like a dove and saying, "Woe to the children on account of whose sins I destroyed My house and burnt My Temple and exiled them among the nations of the world!" ' And he said to me: 'By your life and by your head! Not in this moment alone does it so exclaim, but thrice each day does it proclaim thus . . .' "[4]

Although the Holy Spirit is frequently compared to a dove, it is also compared with other birds, e.g., "The Holy Spirit hovers over the waters as an eagle over its young in the nest."[5]

17 *Heavenly voice* Heb. *bat qol*, lit., "a daughter of a voice," explained as an echo, uttered in heaven and heard on earth.[6]

*beloved son* "Beloved" is frequently used for the Messiah.[7]

*with whom I am well pleased* Likely a combination of Ps. 2.7 and Isa. 42.1. Klausner understands this as "in whom I shall be blessed."[8]

## NOTES

1. Test. Levi 18, which might be a Christian interpolation.
2. F. Zimmermann, *The Aramaic Origin of the Four Gospels*, p. 71, argues that the Aramaic of the passage was misread by the Greek translator, reading *kayona*, "like a dove," instead of *kiwanna*, "directly, straightaway."
3. B. Ḥag. 15a. Fitzmyer, *Luke*, p. 484, who comments, "Gen. 1.2 does not speak of a 'dove,' and no rabbinical literature has ever interpreted it so," has overlooked this passage. Cf. also Gen. R. 42.4, where it is not a dove but a bird.
4. B. Ber. 3b.
5. T. Ḥag. 2.5 (p. 234); cf. also TJ. ibid. 2.1, 77a (61).
6. The *bat qol* was the substitute for the Holy Spirit of the prophets. Cf. T. Sot. 13.2 (p. 318), B. Sanh. 11a. It was considered to be a form of divine communication with men, cf. B. Meg. 32a, Gen. R. 37.7. See S. Lieberman, *Hellenism in Jewish Palestine* (New York, 1950), Appendix I, pp. 149 ff.; A. Marmorstein, *Studies in Jewish Theology* (New York: Oxford University Press 1950), pp. 122 f.; A. Finkel, *The Pharisees and the Teacher of Nazareth* (Leiden: E. J. Brill, 1964), p. 106.
7. E. g., Eph. 1.6; Ascen. Isa. 1.4, see Charles' note ad loc. Klausner, *JN*, p. 251. Cf. also Koh. R. 9.7 On the text see Stendahl, *SSMUOT*, pp. 107–115.

# 7. *The Genealogy of Jesus*

## LUKE 3.23–38

23 Jesus, when he began his ministry, was about thirty years of age, being the son (as was supposed) of Joseph, the son of Heli, 24 the son of Matthat, the son of Levi, the son of Melchi, the son of Jannai, the son of Joseph, 25 the son of Mattathias, the son

of Amos, the son of Nahum, the son of Esli, the son of Naggai, 26 the son of Maath, the son of Mattathias, the son of Semein, the son of Joseph, the son of Joda, 27 the son of Joanan, the son of Rhesa, the son of Zerubbabel, the son of Shealtiel,$^c$ the son of Neri, 28 the son of Melchi, the son of Addi, the son of Cosam, the son of Elmadam, the son of Er, 29 the son of Jesus, the son of Eliezer, the son of Jorim, the son of Matthat, the son of Levi, 30 the son of Symeon, the son of Judas, the son of Joseph, the son of Jonam, the son of Eliakim, 31 the son of Melea, the son of Menna, the son of Mattatha, the son of Nathan, the son of David, 32 the son of Jesse, the son of Obed, the son of Boaz, the son of Sala, the son of Nahshon, 33 the son of Amminadab, the son of Admin, the son of Arni, the son of Hezron, the son of Perez, the son of Judah, 34 the son of Jacob, the son of Isaac, the son of Abraham, the son of Terah, the son of Nahor, 35 the son of Serug, the son of Reu, the son of Peleg, the son of Eber, the son of Shelah, 36 the son of Cainan, the son of Arphaxad, the son of Shem, the son of Noah, the son of Lamech, 37 the son of Methuselah, the son of Enoch, the son of Jared, the son of Mahalaleel, the son of Cainan, 38 the son of Enos, the son of Seth, the son of Adam, the son of God.

---

c  Greek: Salathiel

## COMMENTARY

The Lucan genealogy indicates marked differences when compared with the Matthean account.[1] First, there does not seem to be an artificial pattern here as there is in Matthew.[2] Unlike, Matthew, it goes backwards from Jesus to Adam rather than to Abraham. Although the genealogy goes through David, the Davidic element is not emphasized as in Matt. The fact that it goes back to Adam may be indicative that Luke had the *Adam Qadmon* concept in mind, i.e., that Jesus is the reappearance of primordial man, *Adam Qadmon;*[3] it also gives the presentation a greater universal appeal, transcending ethnic limitations. Just why the Lucan genealogy is inserted here is not at all clear. Perhaps if the Infancy material is of a later period this might have been the beginning of the Gospel. Some see a parallel to the Moses' birth and infancy narrative, which is followed by a genealogy (Exod. 6.14–20).

23 *as was supposed*  Perhaps the Gr. *hōs enomizeto* = Heb. *kemo shehuḥzaq*, "a presumption."[4] This phrase seems to be an addition to harmonize the genealogy with the virgin birth.

*the son of Heli*  Heli most likely is the Heb. Eli.[5]

24 *son of Matthat . . . Rhesa*  These seven names are unknown and no identification with any MT personalities is possible.

27 *Rhesa*  Some do not take this as a proper name but as a title; the Gr. *Resa* transliterated *resha*, "a prince," and read it with the preceding verse: (Prince) Joanan, son of Zerubbabel, i.e., Hananiah son of Zerubbabel of 1 Chron. 3.19.[6]

*Shealtiel the son of Neri*  In Matt. Shealtiel is the son of Jechoniah.

28 *Melchi*, etc., to *Mattatha*    All are unknown.

31 *Nathan*    The third son of David born in Jerusalem.[7] From David to Abraham the Lucan list agrees with the Matthean except for Amminadab and Admin in v. 32.

## NOTES

1. See above p. 1.
2. See, however, Fitzmyer, *Luke*, pp. 76–77.
3. On *Adam Qadmon* see Jeremias, *Adam* in *TDNT*, I: 141–143.
4. TJ. Qid. 4.66a (45).
5. Cf. 1 Sam. (LXX) 1.3. Codex Bezae contains a genealogy that is quite different from vv. 23–31.
6. See Plummer, *Luke*, p. 104; Jeremias, *Jerusalem*, p. 296.
7. 2 Sam. 5.14; 1 Chron. 3.5, 14.4.

# 8. *The Temptation*

## MATT. 4.1–11

1 Then Jesus was led up by the Spirit into the wilderness to be tempted by the devil. 2 And he fasted forty days and forty nights, and afterward he was hungry. 3 And the tempter came and said to him, "If you are the Son of God, command these stones to become loaves of bread." 4 But he answered, "It is written,
    'Man shall not live by bread alone,
    but by every word that proceeds from the mouth of God.' "
5 Then the devil took him to the holy city, and set him on the pinnacle of the temple, 6 and said to him, "If you are the Son of God, throw yourself down; for it is written,
    'He will give his angels charge of you,' and
    'On their hands they will bear you up,
    lest you strike your foot against a stone.' "
7 Jesus said to him, "Again it is written, 'You shall not tempt the Lord your God.' " 8 Again, the devil took him to a very high mountain, and showed him all the kingdoms of the world and the glory of them; 9 and he said to him, "all these I will give you if you will fall down and worship me." 10 Then Jesus said to him, "Begone, Satan! for it is written, 'You shall worship the Lord your God and him only shall you serve.' " 11 Then the devil left him, and behold, angels came and ministered to him.

## MARK 1.12–13

12 The Spirit immediately drove him out into the wilderness. 13 And he was in the wilderness forty days, tempted by Satan; and he was with the wild beasts; and the angels ministered to him.

## LUKE 4.1–13

1 And Jesus, full of the Holy Spirit, returned from the Jordan, and was led by the Spirit 2 for forty days in the wilderness, tempted by the devil. And he ate nothing in

those days; and when they were ended, he was hungry. 3 The devil said to him, "If you are the Son of God, command this stone to become bread." 4 And Jesus answered him, "It is written, 'Man shall not live by bread alone.' " 5 And the devil took him up, and showed him all the kingdoms of the world in a moment of time, 6 and said to him, "To you I will give all this authority and their glory; for it has been delivered to me, and I give it to whom I will. 7 If you, then, will worship me, it shall all be yours." 8 And Jesus answered him, "It is written, 'You shall worship the Lord your God, and him only shall you serve.' " 9 And he took him to Jerusalem, and set him on the pinnacle of the temple, and said to him, "If you are the Son of God, throw yourself down from here; 10 for it is written 'He will give his angels charge of you, to guard you,' 11 and 'On their hands they will bear you up, lest you strike your foot against the stone.' " 12 And Jesus answered him, "It is said, 'You shall not tempt the Lord your God.' " 13 And when the devil had ended every temptation, he departed from him until an opportune time.

## COMMENTARY

The theme that a hero or holy man was to be tested before his career began or before his mission was undertaken is commonplace in the literature of antiquity.[1] Rabbinic homilies on this theme are often based on Ps. 11.5, *The Lord tests the righteous, not the wicked.*[2] The most notable example of this testing in Jewish tradition is Abraham, of whom it is stated, "With ten trials our father Abraham was tried, and he withstood them all to make known how great was the love of Abrahan our father."[3] One can legitimately explain the temptation at the beginning of the gospel in several ways: One is that it is to indicate that Jesus is the Messiah who will overpower the forces of evil as represented by the Satan, a motif amply attested to in rabbinic sources.[4] Second, the confrontation with Satan could be seen as Jesus' struggle with himself and overcoming the *yezer hara*, the evil inclination, part of all men, and which is externalized in the literature by the figure of Satan.[5] Finally, the struggle sets up a model for the Church or individuals who, too, must struggle with temptation and overcome it.

1 *wilderness*  It was a common belief that desolate places were the haunts of demons. This is found in the Bible, in rabbinic literature, and in Greco-Roman sources.[6]

*devil*  Gr. *diabolos*, Heb. *satan*, Satan, the obstructionist, adversary, accuser. The root *s-t-n*, cog. *s-t-m*, indicates hostility and hatred. He is also called Samael.[7] In the MT the Satan opposes man but remains God's messenger, in the intertestamental literature he evolves as the opponent of God as well.[8]

2 *fasted forty days and forty nights*  This is on the model of Moses, *And he was with the Lord forty days and forty nights, he neither ate bread nor drank water* (Exod. 34.28),[9] and Elijah, who also fasted forty days, *And he arose, and ate and drank and went in the strength of that food forty days and forty nights to Horeb the Mount of God* (1 Kings 19.8).

3 *Son of God*  Here "the Son of God" seems to indicate his role as Messiah.

Cf. "He professes to have knowledge of God, and calls himself a child of God."[10]

4 *Man shall not live by bread alone*, etc.  Deut. (LXX) 8.3. Cf. Targ. O. and Targ. J. ad loc. Is there an allusion here to the miracle of the manna produced by divine fiat and to the children of Israel who tested God in the wilderness (Exod. 16.4)?

*then the devil took him*  Similar to Ezekiel, who was lifted by the Spirit and brought to Jerusalem (Ezek. 8.3).

5 *holy city*  I.e., Jerusalem, a popular term for the city in the Bible, in the intertestamental literature, and in rabbinic sources.[11]

*pinnacle of the temple*  Probably something which projected out sideways— a wing, for in the LXX the Gr. *pterugion* stands for the Heb. *kanaf*, "wing," or Heb. *senapir*, "a fin." This "refers not to the top of the Temple proper but probably to the SE corner of the outer court, high above the Kidron Valley, very much as is the situation today."[12] There is possibly a messianic element in this part of the Temptation, i.e., that Jesus is atop the Temple. A comparatively late rabbinic source records: "When the King Messiah reveals himself he will come and stand on the roof of the Temple!"[13]

6 *throw yourself down*  In this second trial, in Matt., third in Luke, Jesus should prove his status by performing a daring test involving the danger of bodily harm and perhaps death. This is the type of act performed to amaze the onlooker and was said to have been attempted by Simon Magus.[14]

*He will give his angels*, etc.  Ps. 91.11–12.[15]

7 *You shall not tempt the Lord your God*  Deut. 6.16. "Jesus means to say that he had no right to throw himself into uncommanded danger, and then expect God to deliver him."[16] Cf. "R. Yannai said: 'A man should never stand in place of danger [purposely] saying that God will perform a miracle for him, for perchance no miracle will be performed for him.' "[17]

8 *the devil took him to a very high mountain*  Viewing all of the kingdoms of the world from atop a mountain is reminiscent of the following: "Go up therefore to the top of that mountain, and there shall pass before thee all the regions of that land, and the figure of the inhabited world and the top[s] of the mountains and the depths of the seas, and the waves . . ."[18] The Satan is often identified in rabbinic literature, among others, with the angel of death, and is also known as *cosmocrator*, a title of the Roman emperor—"Lord of the world," a motif which perhaps lies behind the Temptation. "R. Johanan said in the name of R. Eliezer b. R. Jose ha-Galili: When the Israelites stood at Mount Sinai and said, *all that the Lord has spoken we will do and be obedient* [Exod. 24.7], the Holy One, blessed be He, called to the Angel of Death and said to him, 'Although I have made you *cosmocrator* over all creatures, you have nothing to do with this nation, for they are My children.' "[19]

10 *You shall worship*, etc.  Deut. 6.13.

11 *and behold, angels came*, etc.  This appears to be the Marcan conclusion of the Temptation.[20]

Mk. 13 *wild beasts and the angels ministered to him*  Why wild beasts? One suggestion is to emphasize the loneliness of the desert;[21] another is that the wild beast in the MT is associated with evil and the triumph of righteousness.[22] It is significant that in the Test. Naph. 8.4 the flight of the devil, the fear of wild beasts, and the support of angels are mentioned together, and in Ps. 91.11–13 dominion over wild beasts is coupled with the protective support of angels. Furthermore there is the motif that wild beasts are under the control of the righteous and they do not harm him.[23]

## NOTES

1. For the literature see H. P. Houghton, "On the Temptation of Christ and Zarathustra," *Anglican Review* 26 (1944): 166–175; M. E. Andrews, "Pierasmos: A Study in Form Criticism," ibid. 24 (1942): 229–244.

2. Reading the verse against the MT. Cf. Gen. R. 55.2, Cant. R. 2.16, Num. R. 15.9.

3. M. Avot. 5.4.

4. Montefiore, *SG*, pp. 19, 21. On the fall of Satan and his hosts, see En. 67.6, Test. Dan 5.10–11, Test. Judah 25.3, Sib. Or. 3.7 ff.

5. Cf. B. BB 16a, "Satan, the *yezer hara*, and the Angel of Death are one. The Satan stirs up the *yezer hara*, reduces him to sin, denounces him before God, and then punishes him with death." See also Gen. R. 22.6. Cf. Luke 22.3, 31; John 13.27, when Satan tempts Judas and Simon Peter; Acts 5.3, when he influences Ananias to withhold his contribution; and in 1 Cor. 7.5, where he incites incontinence, and Mark 4.15, where he shuts men's hearts and ears to the message of God.

6. Note *Se'irim* of Lev. 17.7; Isa. 13.21; 34.14; Azazel of Lev. 16.10, Tob. 8.3. On the literature of the haunts of the demonic, see *IDB*, s.v. "demon," bibliography #21.

7. Cf. Gen. R. 77, 78; Cant. R. 3.6.

8. On the development of the Satan figure, see B. J. Bamberger, *Fallen Angels* (Philadelphia, 1952); W. Foerster, *Diabolos TDNT*, 2:74–80.

9. Exod. R. 47.8–9.

10. Wisd. 2.13. The term *pais* means both "child" and "servant." Cf. ibid., v. 16, "and vaunts that God is his father," and ibid., v. 18, "if the righteous be God's son He will uphold him" The expression "Sons of God" (Heb. *benē elohim*), although used for angels (Gen. 6.2, Job 38.7), for Israel (Hos. 11.1), also for the king (Ps. 2.7), is rarely applied to the Messiah. However, see En. 105.2; 2 Ezra 7.28–29, 13.32, 37, 52.

11. Isa. 52.1; Dan. 3.28; 9.24; Neh. (Theod.) 11.1, 18; Tob. 13.9; 2 Macc. 3.1, 9.14; 15.14; Sira 36.18; 49.6. Josephus, *Ant.* XX.20.1; idem, *Cont. Ap.* I.31; B. BQ 97b; B. Sanh. 107b.

12. *IDB* s.v. "Pinnacle."

13. *PR* 36 (p. 162a).

14. Cf. Acts 6.35–37; Josephus, *Ant.* XX.51. The earliest account of this legend about Simon Magus is in Arnobius, *Adv. Gent.* II.12.

15. Ps. 91.11–12 Cf. B. Ta'an. 11a, Gen. R. 78.8.

16. Toy, *Quotations in the New Testament* (New York, 1884), p. 22.

17. B. Shab. 32a, B. Ta'an. 20a. Cf. also Rav's statement, "A man should never bring himself to temptation" (B. Sanh. 107a).

18. Apoc. Bar. 76.3.

19. Lev. R. 18.3.

20. Is there a connection with Ps. 91.11–14?

21. Swete, *The Gospel according to St. Mark*, p. 11.

22. Cf. Ps. 22.11–21; Ezek. 34.5; 8.25; Isa. 11.6–9.

23. E. g., Adam, Gen. 1.26, 28; 2.19; cf. also Job 5.22 ff.; Test. Benj. 5.2.

# 9. First Preaching in Galilee

## MATT. 4.12–17

12 Now when he heard that John had been arrested, he withdrew into Galilee; 13 and leaving Nazareth he went and dwelt in Capernaum by the sea, in the territory of Zebulun and Naphtali, 14 that what was spoken by the prophet Isaiah might be fulfilled: 15 "The land of Zebulun and the land of Naphtali, toward the sea, across the Jordan, Galilee of the Gentile—16 the people who sat in darkness have seen a great light, and for those who sat in the region of the shadow of death light has dawned." 17 From that time Jesus began to preach, saying, "Repent, for the kingdom of heaven is at hand."

## MARK 1.14–15

14 Now after John was arrested, Jesus came into Galilee, preaching the gospel[d] of God, 15 and saying, "The time is fulfilled, and the kingdom of God is at hand; repent, and believe in the gospel."

## LUKE 4.14–15

14 And Jesus returned in the power of the Spirit into Galilee, and a report concerning him went out through all the surrounding country. 15 And he taught in their synagogues, being glorified by all.

---

d  Some texts read *gospel of the kingdom of God*.

## COMMENTARY

12 *he withdrew*  "The verb *anechōrēsen*, withdrew, seems to show that Matthew thought that Jesus went to Galilee from fear of Antipas. Matthew did not remember, however, that the territory of Antipas included Galilee."[1]

*Galilee*  Region in N. Palestine, an administrative district under the Romans. When the kingdom of Herod the Great was split into three parts in 4 B.C.E., Galilee was one of them, with its capital at Sepphoris, until it was replaced by Tiberias, ca. 25 C.E. In 44 C.E., Herod Agrippa I, last of the Jewish rulers of Palestine, died after a six-year rule over Galilee, and all Palestine was then formed into a province and governed by procurators.[2]

13 *Capernaum*  Heb. *K'far Nahum*, "the village of Nahum," a town on the NW shore of the Sea of Galilee; not in MT; mentioned, however, in rabbinic literature[3] and by Josephus.[4] The exact site is unknown; most probably it is the Arabic *Tell Hum*—probably a corruption of *Tanhum*, a variant of the word *Nahum*, 2½ miles farther NE than Khirbet (or Khan) Minyeh, which was formerly thought to be the site of Capernaum.[5]

*the land of Zebulun*, etc.   Isa. 8.23. There are major variants between this text and the MT, and seems to be independent of the LXX.[6]

16 *the people who sat in darkness* Isa. 9.1 reads, *The people who walked in darkness have seen a great light; those who dwelt in a land of deep darkness, on them has light shined.* Light is a symbol of the Messiah and is one of his names—*Nehora*, or *Nehira*, "light."[7]

17 *repent*, etc. This is the same call as John's, see above 3.2 (p. 35). Some texts omit the word "repent."

## NOTES

1. Montefiore, *SG*, 2:24.
2. In MT see 2 Kings 15.29, Isa. 8.23; in Apoc.: 1 Macc. 5.15. Cf. Josephus, *BJ* III.3.1. On the three regions, Judea, Beyond the Jordan, and Galilee, see M. Ket. 13.10.
3. E.g., Koh. R. 1.8; 7.26.
4. *BJ* III.10.8, *Vita* 403.
5. See *IDB*, s.v. "Capernaum."
6. See Stendhal, *SSMUOT*, pp. 104 ff.
7. Cf. *PR* 36 (162a, b). For other passages see *SB*, ad loc. (1:161–162).

# 10. *Jesus Rejected in Nazareth*

### Matt. 13.53–58

53 And when Jesus had finished these parables, he went away from there, 54 and coming to his own country he taught them in their synagogue, so that they were astonished, and said, "Where did this man get this wisdom and these mighty works? 55 Is not this the carpenter's son? Is not his mother called Mary? Are not his brothers James and Joseph and Simon and Judas? 56 And are not all his sisters with us? Where then did this man get all this?" 57 And they took offense[e] at him. But Jesus said to them, "A prophet is not without honor except in his own country and in his own house." 58 And he did not do many mighty works there, because of their unbelief.

### Mark 6.1–6

1 He went away from there and came to his own country; and his disciples followed him. 2 And on the sabbath he began to teach in the synagogue; and many who heard him were astonished, saying, "Where did this man get all this? What is the wisdom given to him? What mighty works are wrought by his hands! 3 Is not this the carpenter, the son of Mary and brother of James and Joses and Judas and Simon, and are not his sisters here with us?" And they took offense[e] at him. 4 And Jesus said to them, "A prophet is not without honor, except in his own country, and among his own kin, and in his own house." 5 And he could do no mighty work there, except that he laid his hands upon a few sick people and healed them. 6 And he marveled because of their unbelief.

---

e Or *stumbled*.

## LUKE 4.16–30

16 And he came to Nazareth, where he had been brought up; and he went to the synagogue, as his custom was, on the sabbath day. And he stood up to read; 17 and there was given to him the book of the prophet Isaiah. He opened the book, and found the place where it was written, 18 "The Spirit of the Lord is upon me, because he has anointed me to preach good news to the poor. He has sent me to proclaim release to the captives and recovering of sight to the blind, to set at liberty those who are oppressed, 19 to proclaim the acceptable year of the Lord." 20 And he closed the book, and gave it back to the attendant, and sat down; and the eyes of all in the synagogue were fixed on him. 21 And he began to say to them, "Today this scripture has been fulfilled in your hearing." 22 And all spoke well of him, and wondered at the gracious words which proceeded out of his mouth; and they said, "Is not this Joseph's son?" 23 And he said to them, "Doubtless you quote to me this proverb, 'Physician, heal yourself; what we have heard you did at Capernaum, do here also in your own country.' " 24 And he said, "Truly, I say to you, no prophet is acceptable in his own country. 25 But in truth, I tell you, there were many widows in Israel in the days of Elijah, when the heaven was shut up three years and six months, when there came a great famine over all the land; 26 and Elijah was sent to none of them but only to Zarephath, in the land of Sidon, to a woman who was a widow. 27 And there were many lepers in Israel in the time of the prophet Elisha; and none of them was cleansed but only Naaman the Syrian." 28 When they heard this, all in the synagogue were filled with wrath. 29 And they rose up and put him out of the city, and led him to the brow of the hill on which the city was built, that they might throw him down headlong. 30 But passing through the midst of them he went away.

## COMMENTARY

54 *his own country* Gr. *patris* = Heb. *medinah*, Aram. *medinta*, which means "country, province, or city." See below p. 180.

55 *Is this not the carpenter's son?* Mark 6.3 calls Jesus "the carpenter." Perhaps the original was *bar nagara*, which can mean either "the son of a carpenter" or simply "the carpenter."[1] The Gr. *tektōn* = Heb. *ḥarash*, means "an artisan in stone, wood, or metal." Mark 6.3 is a more difficult reading: "Is this the carpenter, the son of Mary, etc." It is highly unlikely that he would be described through his mother rather than through his father unless it is meant as an insult.[2] Perhaps the best reading is the variant "the son of the carpenter and Mary." Luke omits Mary as well as the siblings and reads, "Is this not Joseph's son?"

*Is not his mother called Mary? Are not his brothers*, etc. This indicates that the concept of the Perpetual Virginity of Mary was unknown to the Evangelists.[3]

57 *A prophet is not without honor except in his own country* A variant: "No prophet is accepted in his own town."[4] This statement does not stem from any known Jewish source, but in a similar form it is frequently quoted by Jews.

Luke, 16 *And he went to the synagogue*, etc.   Jesus was a frequent worshiper in the synagogue, see Luke 4.15.

*And he stood up to read*   It was a Jewish custom at the beginning of the Christian era for the worshipers to stand during the reading of the Torah and the reading of the *haphtarah*.[5] In addition to these two readings the synagogal service most likely included a variety of prayers and recitations. It is, however, nearly impossible to ascertain with any authority exactly which were included during the days of Jesus because of the lack of contemporary evidence. At the end of the century we do know that the *Shema* (Deut. 6.4–9, 11.13–21; Num. 15.37–41) and the accompanying blessings, the *Shemoneh Esreh*, the daily psalm, and the priestly blessing (Num. 6.24–26) were recited daily.[6] The Gospels do not make mention of the Torah reading or of the other passages, since they concentrate only on the Isaiah passage, which was presumably the *haphtarah* of that Sabbath.

Luke 17 *and there was given to him the book of the prophet Isaiah*   This presumably was done by the *archisynagogos*, the president of the synagogue, who had the authority to choose those who would read from the Torah and recite the *haphtarah*.[7] The book here was in all likelihood a scroll; Heb. *megillah*, "scroll," and *sefer*, "a book," were used synonymously.[8]

*and found the place where it was written*, etc.   This is subject to two interpretations: either Jesus was looking for the assigned passage or he was looking for this passage, which was his choice for the reading and his subsequent comments. The former is more likely.

Luke, 18 *The Spirit of the Lord*, etc.   From Isa. 61.1–2; 58.6, following the LXX, which agrees with the MT except for Isa. 61.1d.[9]

Luke, 20 *and gave it back to the attendant*   Probably the *ḥazzan hakenesset*. See Acts 13.5.[10]

*and sat down*   On teaching from a sitting position, see below p. 67.

Luke, 21 *in your hearing*   Lit. "in your ears," Heb. *be'oznekhem*; cf. Deut. 5.1, 2 Sam. 3.19.

Luke, 23 *Physician, heal yourself*   Apparently a well-known saying. In a rabbinic source "Physician heal your own lameness";[11] in Greek "a physician for others, but himself teaming with sores."[12] A variant in the Gospel of Thomas: "A physician does not heal those who know him."[13]

Luke, 24 *country,*   Better "city," see below p. 180.

Luke, 25 *many widows in the days of Elijah*   See 1 Kings 18.1, where the rains came in the third year. This Lucan tradition is paralleled by James 5.17.[14]

Luke, 26 *Zarephath . . . a widow*   Cf. 1 Kings 17.9 she was a Gentile. The name Zarephath is Heb. *ẓarphat*, cf. Obad. 20.[15]

Luke 27 *many lepers in Israel*   See 2 Kings 7.3–10, 2 Chron. 26.19–21.

*Naaman the Syrian*   See 2 Kings 5.1–19. Note that he, too, like the widow above, was a Gentile.

Luke, 29 *put him out of the city*   Perhaps an example of excommunication.

*brow of the city*  This cannot be identified and may be an indication of Luke's poor knowledge of Palestinian geography.

## NOTES

1. Cf., e.g., B. AZ 50b; B. BB 73b; B. Sanh. 106b; TJ Qid. 4.6, 65d (bot.); Origen, *Contra Celsum* I.28.

2. Cf. Judg. 11.1, 1 Sam. 26.6; 2 Sam. 23.18. See Nineham, *St. Mark*, p. 166.

3. The Church Father Basil (d. 377) held that belief in the Virginity was not necessary as an article of faith but a pious opinion (*Hom. in Sanct. Christ.*, Gen. ii). The idea that the brothers and sisters were either children of Joseph by a former marriage or cousins is traceable no earlier than the middle of the second century.

4. Oxy. P. I continues, "neither does a physician cure those who know him" (see below). Cf. also John 4.44.

5. On the *haphtarah* and its reading, see J. Heinemann, "The Triennial Lectionary Cycle," *JJS* 19 (1968): 41–48.

6. See Moore, *Judaism*, 1:291 ff.

7. He was also responsible for maintaining order and removing disturbances from the synagogue (Luke 13.14). Other examples that he was involved in giving out honors as here, cf. Acts 13.15, M. Sot. 7.7–8. It appears that he kept the reading of the Torah as his personal right, against which we find the *halakhah* that the *archisynagogos* was forbidden to read from the Torah unless he was granted such permission by the congregation T. Meg. 4.21 (p. 227). See S. Krauss, *Synagogale Altertümer* (Berlin and Vienna, 1922), pp. 112 ff.

8. Cf., e.g., Jer. 36.2, 4, Ezek. 2.9; Cf. also B. Sanh. 68a.

9. On this verse see J. A. Sanders, "From Isaiah 61 to Luke 4," in *Christianity, Judaism and Other Graeco-Roman Cults*, SJLA 2, ed. J. Neusner (Leiden: Brill, 1975), 1:75–106.

10. Gr. *hupēretēs*, generally the assistant to the *archisynagogos*, who in turn gave it to the prefect of the high priest or king (M. Sota 7.7–8) In the synagogue proper he handed the scroll of the Torah and/or the *haphtarot* to the reader (M. Sof. 14.3).

11. Gen. R. 23.5. See also Lev. R. 5.6, B. BM 107b for other similar sayings.

12. Euripides, *Frag.* 1086.

13. *Gospel of Thomas* logion 31. See Fitzmyer, *ESBNT*, pp. 401–402; Bultmann, *HST*, p. 31.

14. Fitzmyer, *Luke*, pp. 537–538, suggests "The duration was equated with the stereotyped length of the period of distress in apocalyptic literature (apparently derived from the length of persecution under Antiochus IV Epiphanes; see Dan. 7.25; 12.7; Rev. 11.2; 12.6, 14."

15. See also Josephus, *Ant.* VIII.13.2. "Sarephtha."

# 11. The Call of the First Disciples

## MATT. 4.18–22

18 As he walked by the Sea of Galilee, he saw two brothers, Simon who is called Peter and Andrew his brother, casting a net into the sea; for they were fishermen. 19 And he said to them, "Follow me, and I will make you fishers of men." 20 Immediately they left their nets and followed him. 21 And going on from there he saw two other brothers, James the son of Zebedee and John his brother, in the boat

with Zebedee their father, mending their nets, and he called them. 22 Immediately they left the boat and their father and followed him.

## MARK 1.16–20

16 And passing along by the Sea of Galilee he saw Simon and Andrew the brother of Simon casting a net into the sea; for they were fishermen. 17 And Jesus said to them, "Follow me and I will make you become fishers of men." 18 And immediately they left their nets and followed him. 19 And going on a little farther, he saw James the son of Zebedee and John his brother, who were in their boat mending the nets. 20 And immediately he called them, and they left their father Zebedee in the boat with the hired servants, and followed him.

## COMMENTARY

This call of the disciples is modeled after the call of Elisha by Elijah (1 Kings 19.19 ff.). Unlike the scribe in Matt. 8.19, these disciples left both property and family, as did Elisha, who left his father and mother and gave away his property. The renunciation of the things of this world, including livelihood and family relationships, is a dominant theme in the Gospels.

18 *Sea of Galilee*   Called by various names in the MT and postbiblical source: Sea of Chinnereth (Num. 34.11, Josh. 13.27) or Chennoroth (Josh. 12.3), also Genneseret (1 Macc. 11.67; Jos. *Ant.* XIII.5, X.2.1; *Vita* 65; Targ. O., Num. 34.11),[1] also Sea of Tiberias (John 21.1, Jos. *BJ* III.3.5): and often in rabbinic literature, (e.g., TJ. Sheq. 6.2, 50a [23]). The term "Sea of Galilee" is found only in the NT.

*Simon who is called Peter*   His original name was Simon, Heb. *Shimon*, Gr. *Simon*. In double names the first is always the older one. The name Peter came later and has the same meaning as Cephas, "rock," Aram. *kepha*. If *Simon* is not just a Gr. substitute for the Heb. *Shimon* but originally Greek, it may indicate that he came from a Hellenistic background.

*Andrew*   A Greek name, but one used by Jews. In the Talmud it appears as Andrai or Andre'i.[2]

*for they were fishermen*   The fishermen on the Sea of Galilee were well-known throughout the land.[3]

19 *fishers of men*   Most commentators seeking a biblical parallel or source for this expression have opted for the Heb. *dug*, as in Jer. 16.16, Ezek. 47.10. This, however, is not satisfactory, for the verb *dug* is used only in the sense of to catch men for the purpose of punishment, and that is hardly the meaning here in this verse.[4] Furthermore, *dug* is replaced in the later literature by the Heb. *zud*, Aram. *zadē*, which carries with it a variety of meanings, viz., to hunt animals, birds, and fish. It is likewise used for men—i.e., to catch them physically, and used metaphorically to catch them by words, or by argu-

ment, sometimes by deception, other times by convincing them through argumentation or by dialectics.[5] For example, one could be "armed to hunt souls"[6] or described as one who "catches men with his mouth,"[7] or who "catches people through their own mouths,"[8] or as a "hunter catching in the house or catching in the field,"[9] or used of a scholar.[10] It is this root *zud* which is behind the expression "fishers of men."[11] It should be noted that this root meaning "fishing" is found in the NT in the proper name Beth Saida.[12] The import of Jesus' words is that "in this particular case the special vocation to which the converts were called was that of assisting Jesus in catching men, i.e., drawing them out of the waters of this world into the net of the eschatological life of the age to come, even if all are not called, as these four were, to devote themselves exclusively and professionally to it."[13] One might, in questioning the suggestion of *zud* as the original, point up the fact that in general this expression, as applied to the catching of men, is less than attractive in its application. This can be countered by citing the fact that the disciples, in performing their mission, were called upon to be "as innocent as doves and as shrewd as foxes."[14] "This promise to make them 'fishers of men' at least in its formulation, may be traced to the early church and therefore reflects the persuasive activity of the adherents in gaining converts which was often more shrewd than innocent."[15]

21 *James the son of Zebedee and John his brother*   There was a fourth-century rabbi named Jacob (James) son of Zabdi. Zebedee = Zabdi, which is a shortened form of Zebida, which goes back to Zabdi.[16]

Mark, 20 *and followed him* I.e., became his disciples. See below p. 66.

## NOTES

1. B. Er. 30a.
2. Cf., e.g., TJ Meg. 4.5, 75b (36).
3. Cf. M. MQ. 2.5; B. ibid. 18b; TJ. Pes. 4, 30d.
4. This is noted by most commentators but they offer no suggestion for an alternative reading. See, e.g., Green, *Matthew*, p. 74.
5. See Jastrow, *Dictionary*, s.v. צוד   .
6. Gen. R. 66.6.
7. Ibid. 63.15.
8. Ibid.
9. Ibid. The idea here is that Esau, in order to gain a favorable opinion from his father, asked the right questions which would appeal to his father, e.g., "How does one tithe salt?"
10. Cf. B. Er. 54b.
11. See Lachs, "Some Synoptic Passages and Their Jewish Background." (forthcoming).
12. The house of the fisherman. Cf. Luke. 9.10; John 1.44, Mark 8.22.
13. Nineham, *St. Mark*, p. 71.
14. See Matt. 10.16 and comments ad loc. (below p. 181).
15. Nineham, op. cit., p. 72.
16. Cf. Josh. 7.1, 1 Chron. 8.19, et al.

# 12. *Jesus in the Synagogue at Capernaum*

### MATT. 7.28–29

28 And when Jesus finished these sayings, the crowds were astonished at his teaching, 29 for he taught them as one who had authority, and not as their scribes.

### MARK 1.21–28

21 And they went into Capernaum; and immediately on the sabbath he entered the synagogue and taught. 22 And they were astonished at his teaching, for he taught them as one who had authority, and not as the scribes. 23 And immediately there was in their synagogue a man with an unclean spirit; 24 and he cried out, "What have you to do with us, Jesus of Nazareth? Have you come to destroy us? I know who you are, the Holy One of God." 25 But Jesus rebuked him, saying "Be silent, and come out of him!" 26 And the unclean spirit, convulsing him and crying with a loud voice, came out of him. 27 And they were all amazed, so that they questioned among themselves, saying, "What is this? A new teaching! With authority he commands even the unclean spirits, and they obey him." 28 And at once his fame spread everywhere throughout all the surrounding region of Galilee.

### LUKE 4.31–37

31 And he went down to Capernaum, a city of Galilee. And he was teaching them on the sabbath; 32 and they were astonished at his teaching, for his word was with authority. 33 And in the synagogue there was a man who had the spirit of an unclean demon; and he cried out with a loud voice, 34 "Ah!f What have you to do with us, Jesus of Nazareth? Have you come to destroy us? I know who you are, the Holy One of God." 35 But Jesus rebuked him, saying, "Be silent, and come out of him!" And when the demon had thrown him down in the midst, he came out of him, having done him no harm. 36 And they were all amazed and said to one another, "What is this word? For with authority and power he commands the unclean spirits, and they come out." 37 And reports of him went out into every place in the surrounding region.

---

f  Or *let us alone.*

### COMMENTARY

28 *the crowds were astonished*  What was the cause of the astonishment of the crowds? Was it due to the fact that Jesus spoke as an apostolic prophet or as a messianic figure, or did he appear as a brash young man speaking on his own authority, or was it for another reason? The crowds were used to the type of preaching which characterized the Scribes-Pharisees. Their procedure was to teach the Oral Law by citing the authorities from whom the speaker received the traditions being transmitted. Failure to do so was

considered not only a display of arrogance but destructive of the system, breaking the continuum of the process. This is emphasized in the statement "Anyone who says a thing in the name of one who said it brings deliverance to the world, as it is said, *And Esther told it in the name of Mordecai* [Esther 2.22]."[1] Jesus' presentation appeared strange to the people, who were accustomed to hearing the citations together with the tradition taught. Jesus appealed to no such authority in his teaching, neither by name nor by inference.

*authority* Gr. *exousia*   The precise meaning of the term is not clear. Daube notes, "the contrast between 'to teach with authority' and to teach like the scribes is a crux to this day. The scribes—if we identify them with the leading Rabbis of the time—were held in the highest esteem. *Reshut* or *reshuta* means Rabbinic authority *inter alia*. We may assume that originally 'authority' had this meaning. The people were surprised that Jesus should teach like one ordained."[2]

## NOTES

1. B. Meg. 15a. See also M. Avot 6.
2. Daube, *NTRJ*, p. 206; idem, "Echousia in Mark 2 and 27," *JTS* 39 (1938): 45–59.

## 13. *The Healing of Peter's Mother-in-Law*

### MATT. 8.14–15

14 And when Jesus entered Peter's house, he saw his mother-in-law lying sick with a fever; 15 and he touched her hand, and the fever left her, and she rose and served him.

### MARK 1.29–31

29 And immediately he[g] left the synagogue, and entered the house of Simon and Andrew, with James and John. 30 Now Simon's mother-in-law lay sick with a fever, and immediately they told him of her. 31 And he came and took her by the hand and lifted her up, and the fever left her; and she served them.

### LUKE 4.38–39

38 And he arose and left the synagogue, and entered Simon's house. Now Simon's mother-in-law was ill with a high fever, and they besought him for her. 39 And he stood over her; and he rebuked the fever and it left her and immediately she rose and served them.

---

g  Some texts read *they*.

## COMMENTARY

14 *Peter's house* Presumably in Capernaum, but see John 1.44, which mentions Bethsaida as "the town of Simon and Andrew."

*his mother-in-law* That Simon was married see 1 Cor. 9.5.

15 *and he touched her hand* Curing illness by touching is well known. In rabbinic literature it is recorded that R. Johanan had such power.[1]

*and she served him* Some see in this act a departure from or a violation of a rabbinic prohibition for a woman to serve men at table, citing "Samuel said: 'One must not be waited on by a woman.' "[2] Montefiore, citing another passage, comments: "But certainly the relations of Jesus towards women, and of them towards him, seem to strike a new note, and a higher note, and to be off the line of rabbinic tradition."[3] These citations and comments are unwarranted and misleading. They are from the Babylonian tradition and from the 3rd/4th centuries. H. Loewe, cited by Montefiore, is on point: "We hear of no attack upon Jesus on the part of the Scribes and Rabbis because of his consorting so much with, or being so much waited on by women. If what is indicated in viii.15 has so violated the Jewish habits of the times, should we not have been told something of the criticism of Jesus from the Rabbis in this regard?"[4]

## NOTES

1. See B. Ber 5b.
2. B.Qid. 70a.
3. Montefiore, *RLGT*, p. 218.
4. Ibid. See *DE* 6, ed. M. Higger, p. 200.

# 14. Healing the Sick at Evening

## MATT. 8.16–17

16 That evening they brought to him many who were possessed with demons; and he cast out the spirits with a word, and healed all who were sick. 17 This was to fulfill what was spoken by the prophet Isaiah, "He took our infirmities and bore our diseases."

## MARK 1.32–34

32 That evening at sundown, they brought to him all who were sick or possessed with demons. 33 And the whole city was gathered together about the door. 34 And he healed many who were sick with various diseases, and cast out many demons; and he would not permit the demons to speak, because they knew him.

## LUKE 4.40–41

40 Now when the sun was setting, all those who had any that were sick with various diseases brought them to him; and he laid his hands on every one of them and healed them. 41 And demons also came out of many, crying, "You are the Son of God!" But he rebuked them, and would not allow them to speak, because they knew that he was the Christ.

### COMMENTARY

16 *That evening* I.e., after the Sabbath. Mark and Luke both emphasize this by adding "at sundown," when the sun was setting. The people waited until evening to carry their sick to him and thus avoid desecrating the Sabbath by carrying them, an act which was forbidden.[1]

*many who were possessed with demons . . . all who were sick* Mark and Luke place the sick before the demoniacs. Matt. apparently changed the order so that the former become directly connected with the quotation from Isaiah which only he cites.

*cast out the spirits*, etc. Since it was the common belief that sickness of all kinds was the result of demonic activities, the verse might well mean that there were those mentally afflicted by the demonic, i.e., possessed by demons, and those physically afflicted as a result of demonic attack.[2]

17 *this was to fulfill*, etc. On this introductory formula, see above to Matt. 1.22 (p. 6).

*He took our infirmities*, etc. Isa. 53.4.[3] Chapter 53 of Isaiah is one of the Suffering Servant chapters widely cited by the Church Fathers as predictions of the Coming of Jesus and His Passion. Chapter 53 and the others are also cited in Jewish sources referring to messianic times.[4]

### NOTES

1. See M. Shab. 7.2.
2. For the literature on demons causing illness, see *IDB*, s.v. "Demons," and T. H. Gaster's extensive bibliography there. See below pp. 161 f.
3. On this verse and the disagreement among scholars as to the original text, see Stendahl, *SSMUOT*, pp. 106–107.
4. See S. R. Driver and A. Neubauer, *The 53rd Chapter of Isaiah According to the Jewish Interpretation: Texts and Translations*, 2 vols. (Oxford, 1876). Cf., e.g., B. Sanh. 98a, B. BM 85a; *SB*, 1:481–482.

## 15. Jesus' Departure from Capernaum

### MARK 1.35–38

35 And in the morning, a great while before day, he rose and went out to a lonely place, and there he prayed. 36 And Simon and those who were with him followed him, 37 and they found him and said to him, "Everyone is searching for you." 38 And

he said to them, "Let us go on to the next towns, that I may preach there also; for that is why I came out."

## LUKE 4.42–43

42 And when it was day he departed and went into a lonely place. And the people sought him and came to him, and would have kept him from leaving them; 43 but he said to them, "I must preach the good news of the kingdom of God to the other cities also; for I was sent for this purpose."

## COMMENTARY

35 *a great while before day . . . and there he prayed*   Early morning prayer is known in the MT, e.g., Ps. 5.4; 88.14; 119.147. It is strange that Luke, who frequently mentions Jews at prayer, omits it here. Perhaps his text of Mark did not have it. Also, there is a question whether this refers to a personal, spontaneous prayer, or the recitation of the *Shema* or the *Shemoneh Esreh*; if the latter, then this is a later addition, since the recitation of the *Shemoneh Esreh* did not become obligatory until the end of the first century.[1]

## NOTES

1. See M. Ber. 4.3.

# 16. *A Preaching Journey in Galilee*

## MATT 4.23–25

23 And he went about all Galilee teaching in their synagogues and preaching the gospel of the kingdom and healing every disease and every infirmity among the people. 24 So his fame spread throughout all Syria, and they brought him all the sick, those afflicted with various diseases and pains, demoniacs, epileptics and paralytics, and he healed them. 25 And great crowds followed him from Galilee and the Decapolis and Jerusalem and Judea and from beyond the Jordan.

## MARK 1.39

And he went throughout all Galilee, preaching in their synagogues and casting out demons.

## IBID. 3.10

for he had healed many, so that all who had diseases pressed upon him to touch him;

## Ibid. 3.7–8

7 and a great multitude from Galilee followed; also from Judea 8 and Jerusalem and Idumea and from beyond the Jordan and from Tyre and Sidon a great multitude, hearing all that he did, came to him.

## Luke 4.44

And he was preaching in the synagogues of Judea.[h]

## Ibid. 6.18, 19, 17

18 and those who were troubled with unclean spirits were cured. 19 And all the crowd sought to touch him, for power came forth from him and healed them all. 17 And he came down with them and stood on a level place, with a great crowd of his diciples and a great multitude of people from all Judea and Jerusalem and the seacoast of Tyre and Sidon, who came to hear him and to be healed of their diseases.

---

h Some texts read *Galilee;* others *synagogues of the Jews*

## Ibid. 3.7–8

## COMMENTARY

23 *All Galilee . . . all Syria*  There is a contrast here—all of Galilee with all of (Gentile) Syria. "Syria, seems not to denote the whole Roman province which included Palestine, but that part to the N and NE for which the Jews of Palestine employed the name."[1]

24 *epileptics*  Moonstruck, i.e., lunatics, cf. Ps. 121.6

25 *Decapolis*  A federation of ten Greek cities in Palestine mentioned in the NT only here and in Mark 5.20; 7.31. All of them were situated E of the Jordan except for Scythopolis (Beth Shan). Josephus shows that it indicated a specific region and that the term was well known in the days of Jesus.[2]

*Idumea*  In the MT Edom; a country conquered by John Hyrcanus ca. 128 b.c.e., its inhabitants forceably converted, and was incorporated to the Hasmonean kingdom.

*beyond the Jordan*  I.e., Perea between the Arnon and the Jabbok.

Luke, 8 *Tyre and Sidon*  Non-Jewish area but with a large Jewish population.

## NOTES

1. Mc Neile, *Matt.*, p. 47. Cf. Acts 15.23, 41; Gal. 1.21. Josephus *BJ* VII. 3.3: Cf. also M. AZ 1.8.

2. *BJ* III.9.7. The ten are listed in Pliny *NH* XVIII.74. See F. Abel, *Géographie de la Palestine*, II (1938), pp. 145 ff., 234 ff. Also Schürer, *GJV*, 2:148 ff.

# 17. *The Miraculous Catch of Fish*

## LUKE 5.1–11

1 While the people pressed upon him to hear the word of God, he was standing by the lake of Gennesaret. 2 And he saw two boats by the lake; but the fisherman had gone out of them and were washing their nets. 3 Getting into one of the boats, which was Simon's, he asked him to put out a little from the land. And he sat down and taught the people from the boat. 4 And when he had ceased speaking, he said to Simon, "Put out into the deep and let down your nets for a catch." 5 And Simon answered, "Master, we toiled all night and took nothing! But at your word I will let down the nets." 6 And when they had done this, they enclosed a great shoal of fish; and as their nets were breaking, 7 they beckoned to their partners in the other boat to come and help them. And they came and filled both boats, so that they began to sink. 8 But when Simon Peter saw it, he fell down at Jesus' knees, saying, "Depart from me, for I am a sinful man, O Lord." 9 For he was astonished, and all that were with him at the catch of fish which they had taken; 10 and so also were James and John, sons of Zebedee, who were partners with Simon. And Jesus said to Simon, "Do not be afraid; henceforth you will be catching men." 11 And when they had brought their boats to land, they left everything and followed him.

### COMMENTARY

3 *he sat down and taught the people from the boat*   See Matt. 13.1–2, Mark 4.1. For the posture of the teacher and teaching outside of the academy or synagogues, see below pp. 67ff.

*you will be catching men*   Gr. *zogron*, lit. "to capture alive." In Matt. and Mark it is "fishers of men." See above pp. 58f. Luke, recognizing that "fishers of men" is singularly inappropriate when applied to saving men for salvation, and not aware of the Semitic metaphorical usage, changes it to *zogron*, "to take alive."[1]

*and followed him*   I.e., became his disciple, from the Heb. *lalekhet aḥarē*, following a Rabbi.[2]

### NOTES

1. See Fitzmyer, *Luke*, p. 563.
2. See above p. 59. Also, Josephus, *Ant.* VIII. 13.8 uses *akolouthein* of Elisha becoming a disciple of Elijah, cf. 1 Kings (LXX) 19.21.

# THE SERMON ON THE MOUNT

MATTHEW 5–7

---

## 18. Introduction

MATT. 5.1–2

1 Seeing the crowds, he went up on the mountain, and when he sat down his disciples came to him. 2 And he opened his mouth and taught them saying:

LUKE 6.12, 20

12 In these days he went out into the hills to pray; and all night he continued in prayer to God. 20 And he lifted up his eyes on his disciples and said:

COMMENTARY

1 *Seeing the crowds*, etc.   This verse is a literary link with the foregoing 4.25, "*and great crowds followed him*, etc." for the Sermon was apparently intended only for the disciples.

*he went up on the mountain*   Matt.'s setting for the Sermon on a mountain is intended to parallel the Giving of the Law at Mount Sinai (Exod. 19.1 ff.).[1]

*and when he sat down*   Ordinarily in the first Christian century teaching took place indoors in the *bet ha-midrash*, the academy, or in the synagogue (cf. Luke 4.44), but there were frequent exceptions to this general rule (cf. Luke 5.3). In rabbinic literature the following are of note: "It was related of R. Johanan ben Zakkai that he was sitting in the shadow of the Temple and teaching all day."[2] He lectured outside since he was addressing the masses on the laws of the festival and the crowds were very large. "Again, on one occasion, Rabbi [Judah the Prince] issued an order that they should not teach disciples in the public marketplace. . . . R. Ḥiyya went out and taught."[3]

Davies is correct, that "Matthew has transformed what we may loosely call a 'sermonic scene' to a didactic one, in which Jesus suggests a rabbi giving his Torah to his *talmidim*."[4] He is in error, however, when he states that "these references to sitting are not accidental but probably a memory of the way in which Jesus actually taught."[5] From the middle of the first century the traditional position of the teacher, while discoursing, was sitting, and the expression "he sat and discoursed" is commonplace.[6] Early in that century this was not the case. "Our Rabbis taught: From the days of Moses up to Rabban Gamaliel, the Torah was learned only standing. When Rabban Gamaliel died, feebleness [lit. sickness] descended upon the world, and they

67

learned the Torah sitting."[7] In using the phrase *"and when he sat down,* etc.*,"* Matt. was describing a *late*-first-century practice of teaching from a sitting position.[8]

2 *And he opened his mouth* This is a Semitic idiom meaning "to speak" and does not describe the physical act of opening the mouth; cf. Ps. 38.14, *But I am like a deaf man, I do not hear; I am like a dumb man who does not open his mouth.*[9]

## NOTES

1. Luke 6.17 reads *"And he came down with them, and stood upon a level place,"* hence the Lucan version of the Sermon is called the Sermon on the Plain. Davies (*SSM*, p. 99) argues "that the Lucan account is, if anything, more reminiscent of Exod. xix where Moses descended from the Mount to give the commandments he had received upon it." This is not convincing, for in its scrupulous adherence to the particulars of the event at Sinai the parallel would have been lost on the hearer or the reader.

2. B. Pes. 26a.

3. B. MQ 16a–b. Cf. also B. Er. 29a, "Raba once said, 'I am today in the condition of Ben Azzai in the markets of Tiberias.' " Ben Azzai regularly discoursed in those marketplaces.

4. Davies, *SSM*, p. 8.

5. Ibid.

6. Cf. TJ Sheq. 2.5 (46d); B. Bez. 15b; B. Sanh. 99b; B. Pes. 26b.

7. B. Meg. 21a. This Rabban Gamaliel is undoubtedly Rabban Gamaliel the Elder, the reputed teacher of Paul (cf. Acts 22.3) because Rabban Gamaliel II of Yavneh "remained seated and expounded the Law." B. Ber. 27b.

8. See S. T. Lachs, "Some Textual Observations on the Sermon on the Mount," *JQR* 69 (1978): 99–101; M. Aberbach, "The Change from a Standing to a Sitting Posture by Students after the Death of Rabban Gamaliel," ibid. 52 (1960): 168–174.

9. See also Job 3.1, Dan. 10.16, et al. In the NT cf. Luke 1.64, Acts 8.35; 10.34; 18.14. Luke 6.20 does not employ this idiom, but reads, "And he lifted up his eyes on his disciples and said:"

# 19. *The Beatitudes*

## MATT. 5.3–12

3 "Blessed are the poor in spirit, for theirs is the kingdom of heaven. 4 "Blessed are those who mourn, for they shall be comforted. 5 "Blessed are the meek, for they shall inherit the earth. 6 "Blessed are those who hunger and thirst for righteousness, for they shall be satisfied. 7 "Blessed are the merciful, for they shall obtain mercy. 8 "Blessed are the pure in heart, for they shall see God. 9 "Blessed are the peacemakers, for they shall be called the sons of God. 10 "Blessed are those who are persecuted for righteousness' sake, for theirs is the kingdom of heaven. 11 "Blessed are you when men revile you and persecute you and utter all kinds of evil against you falsely on my account. 12 "Rejoice and be glad, for your reward is great in heaven, for so men persecuted the prophets who were before you."

LUKE 6.20–23

20 "Blessed are you poor, for yours is the kingdom of God. 21 "Blessed are you that hunger now, for you shall be satisfied. 22 "Blessed are that weep now, for you shall laugh. 22 "Blessed are you when men hate you and when they exclude you and revile you and cast out your name as evil, on account of the Son of man! 23 Rejoice in that day, and leap for joy, for behold, your reward is great in heaven; for so their fathers did to the prophets."

# The Woes

LUKE 6.24–26

24 "But woe to you that are rich, for you have received your consolation. 25 Woe to you that are full now, for you shall hunger. Woe to you that laugh now, for you shall mourn and weep. 26 Woe to you, when all men speak well of you, for so their fathers did to the false prophets."

## COMMENTARY

"The beatitudes serve as an introduction to the Sermon. They serve to set up the requirements for true Christian living. These do not purport to be the ideals of Jewish living. On the contrary. In addition to the explicit or nearly explicit references to the encounter with Judaism, throughout the Gospel, Christians emerge as a very markedly set over against the Jewish community. Within the Sermon itself, the Beatitudes suggest this."[1]

Although the Beatitudes represent an epitome of the message of the Sermon, it is without foundation to assert that "The Sermon in Matt. V–VII is modelled on Exod. XX–XXIV, where the Decalogue of chapter XX finds an exposition in the Covenant Laws given in the rest of the section, Exod. XX–XXIII. The Beatitudes occupy a place in the Sermon corresponding to that of the Decalogue in Exod. XX–XXIV, the rest of the Sermon being an orderly exposition or application of the Beatitudes."[2] This is entirely homiletic. First, there are not ten beatitudes (the number of the original beatitudes is in doubt, but ten is certainly out of the question). Second, the Torah does not begin with Exod. 20. Even were one to argue that the legal material follows chap. 20, there is legal material starting with Exod. 12.2. Furthermore, Exod. 20.18–26 intrudes and negates the argument.[3]

The Beatitudes in their Matthean setting appear to be a recast of a former version intended to express Matthew's own theological position and to reflect the attitudes of his community.[4] The Lucan Beatitudes, 6.20–23, seem closer to an original than the Matthean version. First, speaking to his disciples, Jesus addresses them directly, using the second-person plural; Matt. uses the third-person except in v. 11. Second, Matthew joins the crowds with the disciples in his version. Third, the setting on the mountain is artificial and clearly the invention of the author. Fourth, the Lucan material speaks of the current vital matters affecting the daily lives of the audience, note the use of "*now*" (6.21, 6.25), albeit with eschatological implications and promises, while the Beatitudes in Matthew are more studied, theologically worked out, but with stronger eschatological overtones.

The arrangement of the Beatitudes in Luke in contrasting verses, i.e., 6.20–23 and 24–26 with the contrast of *makarioi* and *ouai* is reminiscent of several biblical passages (cf. Deut. 27.1 ff. et al.). Beatitudes, as a literary form, are found frequently in the intertestamental literature.[5] In rabbinic literature the following are representative:

". . . and R. Johanan b. Zakkai said . . . 'Happy are you, our father Abraham, that Eleazar b. Arakh came forth from your loins'."[6]

"R. Jose the priest went and told what had happened before R. Johanan b. Zakkai, and the latter said, 'Happy are you, happy is she who bore you, happy are my eyes that I have seen this'."[7]

"Happy is the king who is praised in his house! Woe to the father who had to banish his children, and woe to the children who had to be banished from the table of their father."[8]

3 *Blessed* The Gr. *makarioi* should not be translated "blessed," but rather "happy" or "fortunate." The Hebrew original is *ashre;* the opposite *ouai*, as in Luke 6.24–26, is the Hebrew *oi*. In the MT the term *ashre* occurs 44 times, 26 in Psalms, and 30 verses begin with it. It is always rendered *makarioi* in the LXX.

*the poor in spirit* Luke omits "*in spirit*." Matthew, in adding "*in spirit*," seems to have spiritualized the message so as not to offend the affluent of his community. Allen argues that "the Semitic *'ani* with its implication of down trodden and oppressed lives despite their endeavour of living pious lives would be misunderstood by Greek readers."[9] This is not convincing, for Matthew, unlike Luke, did not change Semitic idioms such as "Kingdom of heaven" to "Kingdom of God." Davies hedges: "thus the Lucan 'poor' need not be regarded as necessarily more primitive than the Matthean 'poor in spirit.' But it is still more likely that Matthew made the term 'the poor' more precise by the addition of 'in spirit'; than that Luke deleted the latter, although, as we indicate in the text, 'the poor' and 'the poor in spirit' have the same connotation."[10]

The expression "poor in spirit," which would be *aniyē ru'ah*, is not found either in the MT or in rabbinic literature. The Qumran War Scroll, 1QM XIV, however, has the reading *v'aniyē ru'ah* in the statement, "blessed be the Lord God of Israel . . . giving . . . vigor to the shoulders of the bowed . . . And [. . .] to the lowly spirits, firmness to the melting heart."[11] The poor, Gr. *hoi ptochoi*, is either the Hebrew *aniyim* or Aramaic *anaya*. The Hebrew *ani* is represented 38 times in the LXX by *ptochos*. There is a third possibility—that it is *anav*, "humble," for in the MT there is great confusion between *ani* and *anav*.[12]

Who are the poor? In light of the Semitic antecedents and the two different readings in Matt. and Luke, the term is certainly ambiguous. It could surely mean the poor in the sense of those who are without property or wealth, and this seems to require no proof.[13] Another suggestion is that the *ptochoi* are the *Am ha-Arez*.[14] This is out of the question, since many of the *Am ha-Arez* were quite wealthy.[15]

Manson suggests that "the use of the word 'poor' in this way goes back to the days of the Seleucid rule in Palestine. Then it was the poor above all who remained faithful to their religion and the Law. The well-to-do upper classes in Jerusalem allowed themselves to be tainted with heathenism. Hence 'rich' tends to mean 'worldly' and 'irreligious' and 'poor' the opposite. In this specialized sense the word is used here. In Matt. the paraphrase 'poor in spirit' is an attempt to make this fact clear. In Judaism of the last two centuries BCE the term was practically a synonym for *hasid*, 'pious' or 'saintly' in the best senses. So, for example, Pss. Sol. 10.7 'The saints also shall give thanks in the assembly of the people and God will have mercy on the poor in the (days of) gladness of Israel.' Here 'the saints' and the 'poor' stand in synonomous parallelism. Again in the Talmud they are treated as synonyms (Ber. 6b)."[16]

Identification of the poor with the Essenes simply because members of that community were called "poor" is weak; nor is the suggestion that "poor in spirit" means "poor in will," i.e., voluntary poor, appealing.[17]

Since both *ani*, "poor," and *anav*, "humble," are in the category of the unfortunates of the society, there are many biblical verses which Matthew might have had in mind when he composed this version. Isa. 61.1 appears to be a likely choice, *The Spirit of the Lord God is upon me, because the Lord has anointed me to bring good tidings to the afflicted* (poor: Heb. *anavim*). It is significant that while the LXX renders *anavim* by *ptocoi*, the Targum sometimes reads *mekhikhē ruḥa*, "afflicted in spirit."[18]

Poverty in Jewish thinking is not in itself a virtue or a virtuous state, nor is the poor man considered to be happy or fortunate because of his poverty. Here, too, in Matthew, the poor are not happy because they are poor but because the Kingdom of Heaven awaits them (see below). Poverty, however, can be instructive, challenging, and sobering as a test of character: "Elijah said to Bar He-He and others say to R. Eliezer, 'What is meant by the verse, *Behold, I have refined you, but not like silver; I have tried you in the furnace of affliction [oni]* [to be the best]. Samuel said, and others say R. Judah: 'This agrees with the popular saying, Poverty befits Israel like red trappings to a white horse,' "[19] In this context the thought is that through the experience of poverty the Jew will be moved to repentance, not that poverty itself is a desirable condition.

*kingdom of heaven* Heb. *malkhut shamayim*, Aram. *malkhuta dishmaya*. "Heaven" is a standard substitute for "God" to protect the sanctity of the divine name. These substitutes for the divine name are numerous in rabbinic literature, viz., Heaven, Merciful One, *Ha-Maqom* (the Omnipresent), the Power, the Holy One, blessed be He. Matthew is the only NT writer who employs this term. "Kingdom of heaven" here in Matt. is paralleled in Luke 6.22 by "kingdom of God." Luke uses "God" for "heaven" because his Greek-speaking audience would not have understood the point of "heaven" in this context. Dalman[20] is undoubtedly correct in pointing out that *malkhut* here means "sovereignty," not "kingdom," as in Ps. 103.19, *The Lord has established His throne in the heavens, and His kingdom rules over all.* Cf. also Dan. 4.31, *For His dominion is an everlasting dominion, and His kingdom endures from generation to generation;* En. 84.2, "and Thy power and kingship and greatness abide for ever and ever"; Jub. 12.19, "and Thee and Thy dominion have I chosen."[21]

In rabbinic literature the idea of sovereignty is best illustrated by the expression *'ol malkhut shamayim*, "[the acceptance of] the yoke of the kingdom of Heaven."[22]

The kingdom of heaven likewise has an eschatological meaning, first used in Zech. 14.9, *And the Lord will become king over all the earth; on that day the Lord will be one and His name one.* ". . . and then God will be recognized throughout the world as one, and His kingdom will be established for all eternity";[23] "then His kingdom shall appear throughout all His creation."[24] An expanded expression of the eschatological meaning is in the *'Alenu* prayer.

> We therefore hope in Thee, O Lord our God, that we may speedily behold the glory of Thy might, when Thou wilt remove the abominations from the earth and the idols will be utterly cut off. When the world will be perfected under the kingdom of the Almighty [*malkhut shaddai*], and all the children of the flesh will call upon Thy name. When Thou wilt turn unto Thyself all the wicked on the earth. Let all the inhabitants of the world perceive and know that unto Thee every knee must bend, every tongue must swear. Before Thee, O Lord our God, let them bow and fall; and unto Thy glorious name let them give honor; let them all accept the yoke of Thy kingdom, and do Thou reign over them speedily and forever and ever. For the kingdom is Thine, and to all eternity Thou wilt reign in glory; as it is written in Thy Law, *The Lord shall reign forever and ever.* And it is said, *And the Lord shall be king over all the earth, on that day shall the Lord be One and His name One.* [25]

4 *Blessed are those who mourn, for they shall be comforted* Who are these mourners, and why are they mourning? Allen (and others following him, including Albright-Mann) misses the point when he explains this, "for the sin in Israel, which checks and thwarts God's purposes for His people, and delays the coming of the kingdom."[26] This comment lacks historical perspective and should be rejected out of hand. These mourners should be identified

with the *avēlē zion*, the Mourners for Zion, a well-known group among the Jews who were so deeply affected by the destruction of the Temple that they lived their lives amidst grief and mourning because of the national tragedy. Matt.'s language indicates that he drew upon Isa. 61. 2–3 when framing this beatitude, *to comfort all who mourn; to grant to those who mourn in Zion—to give them a garland instead of ashes, the oil of gladness instead of mourning.* Who according to the Gospel was to comfort these mourners? Jesus is represented as the comforter, and it is of note that the Messiah is called *Menaḥem*, the Comforter.[27]

Following the destruction, the Mourners for Zion carried this mourning into all aspects of their daily living. The destruction of the Temple even created a form of an oath, *er'eh beneḥamah*, "may I live to see the consolation."[28]

The following are two rabbinic passages dealing with mourning over the destruction of the Temple.

"From the time the Temple was destroyed, ascetics, [*perushim*] increased in Israel who refrained from eating meat and drinking wine. R. Joshua joined them and said, 'My children, Why do you not eat meat?' 'Shall we eat meat,' they said to him, 'When every day the *tamid* sacrifice was offered on the altar and now it is gone?' 'And why,' he asked them, 'do you not drink wine?' 'Shall we drink wine,' they responded, 'when of it libations were made upon the altar and now it is gone?' He said to them, 'We should, then, not eat figs and grapes, for of them they would bring first fruits on Shavuot. We should not eat bread, for of it they would bring the two [new] loaves and the showbread. We should not drink water, for of it they would pour it out as a libation on Sukkot.' They were silent. He said to them, 'Not to mourn at all is unthinkable, for it has been decreed, but yet to mourn excessively is likewise unthinkable. But this is what our Sages said: 'When a man whitewashes his house he should leave a small place [unwhitewashed] as a reminder of Jerusalem; a woman who adorns herself should leave some small spot unadorned as a reminder of Jerusalem, as it is written, *If I forget you, O Jerusalem, let my right hand wither! If I do not remember you, let my tongue cleave to the roof of my mouth. If I do not set Jerusalem above my highest joy* [Ps. 137.5–6]. All who mourn over Jerusalem merit its [ultimate] joy, as it is written, *Rejoice with Jerusalem, and be glad with her, all you who mourn over her* [Isa. 66.10].' "[29]

"R. Ishmael b. Elisha said: 'Since the days of the destruction of the Temple we should by rights bind ourselves not to eat meat, nor to drink wine, only we do not lay a hardship on the community unless the majority can endure it.' "[30]

*for they shall be comforted* The passive here and also in vv.6, 7, 9 is a reverential circumlocution for the action of God.[31] The Lucan parallel (6.21), *Blessed are you that weep now, for you shall laugh*, seems to indicate that the underprivileged poor and needy shall have their condition changed and those who are presently enjoying life to the fullest will change places with those unfortunate poor (cf. the Woes, Luke 6.24–25). It is also possible that the Lucan version might be related to the destruction of the Temple. Two words in the verse, "now" and "laugh," bring to mind an interpretation of Ps. 126.2 in the Talmud:

> "R. Johanan said in the name of R. Simeon b. Yohai: 'It is forbidden that a man's mouth be filled with laugher in this world because it is written, *then will our mouths be filled with laughter and our tongues with singing* [Ps. 126.2]. When? At the time when they will say among the nations, *the Lord has done great things for them* [ibid].' It was said of R. Simeon b. Laqish that never again was his mouth full of laughter in this world after hearing this teaching from his master R. Johanan."[32]

5 *Blessed are the meek, for they shall inherit the earth* The order of vv. 4 and 5 varies. In some MSS and early texts v. 5 precedes v. 4. This is significant and probably correct since v. 5 appears to be a gloss of v. 3 or a variant of *aniyim*.[33] It seems reasonable that v. 5 is indeed a marginal note to 5.3. A scribe presumably recalled Ps. 37.11, *the meek shall possess the land*, because of its similarity to 5.3, and because of the confusion between *ani* and *anav*, he wrote it on the side of the MS, from which place it subsequently became part of the text as a separate beatitude. Not only are *ani* and *anav* interchangeable, but the phrase "to inherit the earth" is synonymous with "*theirs is the kingdom of heaven*"; "All Israelites have a share in the world-to-come, for it is written, *Your people shall all be righteous; they shall possess the land forever* [Isa. 60.21]"[34] In addition to Ps. 37.11 mentioning "inheriting the land," the following should be noted:

> "And after that they shall get possession of the whole earth and inherit it forever."[35]

> "The elect shall possess light, joy, peace, and they shall inherit the earth."[36]

> "Be meek, since the meek shall inherit the earth [citing Ps. 37.11]."[37]

6 *Blessed are those who hunger and thirst for righteousness, for they shall be satisfied.* The Lucan parallel, 6.21, "*Blessed are you that hunger now, for you shall be satisfied,*" deals only with physical hunger; the "now," however, strengthens the eschatological aspect of "*shall be satisfied,*" perhaps implying a messianic banquet.[38] Matthew has reworded the original, adding "*thirst*," possibly influenced by Isa. 55.1, Amos 8.11, or Sira 24.21; Ps. 42.3, 107.9, all of which take "hunger" and "thirst" metaphorically, the object of which is *righteousness*, Matthew's second addition. Clearly "*thirst*" is an addition.[39]

*righteousness* Matt. probably added this, again, as not to offend the more affluent of his community. Montefiore suggests that the Matthean verse, as it now stands, means that he who wishes to do *ḥesed* (an act of kindness) is helped by God to do so.[40]

It is possible that there is a connection between those who mourn, i.e., the Mourners for Zion, and those referred to in this verse, since the former engaged in voluntary abstinence and regular fasts (see above).

This is no rabbinic parallel to this beatitude but the following seems to be of the same genre: "R. Tanḥum b. R. Ḥanilai said: 'Whoever starves himself for the sake of the words of Torah in this world, the Holy One, blessed be He, satisfies him in the world-to-come, as it is written, *they feast on the abundance of thy house, and thou givest them drink from the rivers of thy delight* [Ps. 36.9].' "[41]

7 *Blessed are the merciful, for they shall obtain mercy* This beatitude and the two following are missing in Luke. Just why they are included by Matt. is not at all clear. All the beatitudes, except for these three, deal with the unfortunates of society. These, on the other hand, are to be rewarded for some meritorious act performed. One suggestion for the inclusion of this verse is that "it is possible that 'righteousness' in the previous verse v. 6 suggested 'mercy' in this. The Hebrew *zedaqah* means righteousness as well as charity (mercy). And, the LXX frequently translates the Hebrew by either term."[42]

A rabbinic comment directly on point here is "He who shows mercy to his fellow creature obtains mercy from Heaven."[43]

This explanation of the inclusion of this verse on the basis of juxtaposition is not truly satisfactory, and an acceptable reason as to why the meritorius are cited in the Beatitudes has yet to be provided. We suggest that all or at least two of these three verses have suffered in translation from a Semitic original. It is always risky to change a *textus receptus*, especially when no linguistic difficulty is present. But this caveat notwithstanding, we offer some radical suggestions. Here in 5.7 we may have a problem stemming from a misreading of a Heb. original which might have read *ashrē hamuḥramin ki hemah yeruḥamu*, "Happy are they who are excommunicated (i.e., excluded), for they shall receive mercy (i.e., merciful treatment in their new belief)." The error in transmission was with the word *hamuḥramim*, "those who are excommunicated," which was transmitted *hameraḥamim*, "those who show mercy." In support of the emendation cf. Luke 6.22, ". . . *revile you and exclude you*," which is precisely what *ḥerem*, "excommunication," means.[44]

8 *pure in heart* Heb. *barē levav*. Ps. 24.4; 73.1; cf. ibid. 51.12, *tehor lev*, the meaning is "sincere one(s)."

In view of the fact that v. 7–9 are not in harmony with the other Beatitudes, some have emended the text. Albright-Mann have advanced the idea that the original Aramaic word here would have been *dakhim*, "broken" (-hearted)," in the sense of contrite. Presumably what they had in mind was that there was a confusion of *dakhē* and *barē lev*. Asher Finkel has correctly noted that "pure in heart," *bar lev*, goes back to Isa. 61.1, *nishbarē lev*, "broken-hearted."[45] We retrovert the text of Matt. 5.8 to be, through haplography of the first two words, *ashrē [nish]barē lev*, what remained was *ashrē barē lev*, "blessed are the pure in heart."

*for they shall see God*   We suggest that this phrase, "they shall see God," is a midrash on the text *v'la'asurim peqaḥ qo'aḥ* of Isa. 61.1, rendered in the LXX by *kai turphlois anablepsin*," and sight to the blind.[46] To see God is expressed in rabbinic sources as "to see the Shekhinah" and is employed as a reward for the performance of a meritorious act. "He who does such-and-so is worthy that the Shekhinah dwell with him." "Shekhinah" is not simply a substitute term for the Divine Name but most often used as a technical term of God's immanence.[47] Some examples of the use of Shekhinah as a reward for the performance of a *mizvah* are:

"R. Dostai b. R. Jannai expounded: 'Observe that the ways of God are not like the ways of flesh and blood. How does flesh and blood act? If a man brings a present to a king, it may be accepted or it may not be accepted, even if it is accepted it is still doubtful whether he will be admitted to the presence of the king or not. Not so with God. If a man gives a coin to a beggar he is deemed worthy to receive the Divine Presence, as it is written, *I shall behold Thy face in righteousness, I shall be satisfied when I awake with Thy likeness* [Ps. 17.15]' "[48]

"R. Menasyah the grandson R. Joshua b. Levi said: 'We find that if a person happens to see a naked part of the body and does not feed his eyes upon it, he is worthy of giving welcome to the Shekhinah. What is his reason? It says, *and shuts his eyes from looking upon evil* [Isa. 33.15]. What is written after this? *Thine eyes shall see the king in His beauty, they shall behold a land stretching afar.* [ibid. 17].' "[48]

"R. Simeon b. Yoḥai says: 'Whoever is scrupulous in the observance of this *mizvah* is worthy to receive the Divine Presence, for it written, *that you may look upon it* [Num. 15.39], and it is written, *thou shalt fear the Lord thy God, Him shalt thou serve* [Deut. 6.13].' "[50]

9 *peacemakers*   Gr. *eirēnopoioi* is read as an adjective and its meaning is not clear. Does it mean those who are peaceable, i.e., conciliatory and inclined to peaceful existence, even loving peace, or does it mean those who make peace either between two others or between themselves and others? The Heb. would be either *shelemim* or *osē shalom*. The former is preferable.[51] Peacemakers, however, are nowhere in rabbinic literature called "the children of God." Hillel called the peacemakers "disciples of Aaron." "Hillel said: 'Be of the disciples of Aaron, loving peace, and pursuing peace, loving your fellow creatures and bringing them near to the Torah."[52]

The peacemaker is, however, called blessed: "Blessed is he who established peace and love."[53] "Blessed is he who goes [sc. one that has] and brings [sc. others] together in peace."[54] "Cursed is he who disturbs what is in peace. Blessed is he who speaks peace and has peace."[55]

It may be significant that God is called "Peace,"[56] hence peacemakers are called "sons of Peace" (God).

As stated above v. 7–9 are not in harmony with the other Beatitudes, which deal with the unfortunates of society. Here it is more difficult to suggest an emendation to harmonize this verse with the others. We offer a suggestion with only a modicum of conviction, and that is the original might have been *ashrē hanikhshalim ki hemah yiqar'u benē ha'elohim*, "Happy are they who stumble, for they shall be called the children of God." We read *hanikhshalim* for *hashlemim*. The imagery possibly can be supplied by Deut. 1.30–31: *The Lord your God who goes before you will Himself fight for you, just as He did for you in Egypt before your eyes, and in the wilderness where you have seen how the Lord your God bore you, as a man bears his own son, in all the way you went until you came to this place.* They that stumble shall be lifted up by God the Father.

Verse 10 is found only in Matt. and concludes the basic list of the Beatitudes, which begins with the same phrase as here in v. 10, *for theirs is the kingdom of heaven.* This is a literary device called *inclusio* frequently used by Matthew the evangelist.[57] Verse 10 also contains the use of the third-person plural, whereas vv. 11–12 employ the second-person plural. The connection between v. 10 and vv. 11–12 has been the subject of much discussion and conjecture.[58] Is v. 10 a shortened form of vv. 11–12, or are vv. 11–12 an extension of v. 10? They both treat one and the same subject—the promise to the faithful that their suffering will be rewarded because of their commitment to and belief in Jesus as the Christ. The Lucan parallel 6.22–23, *Blessed are you when men hate you, and when they shall separate you from their company and shall reproach you, and cast out your name as evil, for the Son of man,* appears to have been an independent tradition and is perhaps closer to the original. Matthew's version reflects the experience of his community, i.e., persecution or social rejection.[59]

10 *persecuted for righteousness' sake*   Gr. *hoi dediōgmenoi heneken dikaiosunēs.* Early followers of Jesus were often persecuted for a variety of reasons both by the Romans and by the Jewish community but certainly not for righteousness' sake.[60] It is stretching the meaning of *ẓedeq,* "righteousness," to include commitment to a person (Jesus) or to a creed (his teaching). The concept of *ẓedeq,* which is probably the original of *dikaiosunēs,*[61] presupposes an act or series of acts. It is noteworthy that in Matt. 6.33 "kingdom" and "righteousness" are likewise linked—*but seek first his kingdom* [*tēn basileian*], *and his righteousness* [*kai tēn dikaiosunēn autou*], *and all these things shall be yours as well.* In the Lucan parallel to Matt. 6.33 "*righteousness*" is omitted: "*Instead seek his* [others: God's] *kingdom and these things shall be yours as well.*" We suggest that the original reading for *dikaiosunēs* both in Matt. 5.10 and 5.30 was *ẓ-d-q* but should have been read *ẓadiq,* "Righteous One," not "righteousness," and it refers to Jesus himself, who often is called by this title.[61]

If one sees the teacher of righteousness (*moreh ẓedeq*) of the Dead Sea Scrolls as a parallel to the Jesus figure, then *dikaios* = *ẓadiq* is a most appropriate title.[63]

*Revile . . . persecute . . . utter all manner of evil*   Parallel: Luke 6.2b; *hate . . . separate, reproach and cast out your name as evil.* The last phrase is probably an awkward translation of the Heb. *lehozi shem ra,* "to issue an evil report" about someone. All of these terms indicate that the persecution is the rejection of the new Christians (Judeo-Christians) by the Jewish community. If we take "persecute" in the sense of "drive away" (cf. Matt. 1.23, 23.34), it would be comparable to "separate" or "exclude" in Luke.[64]

The Jewish community through the Patriarch did take steps to exclude the *minim,* the sectarians, many of whom were Judeo-Christians, from the Synagogue, and from the community itself. The most well known act in this regard was the composition of the *birkat haminim,* the malediction against sectarians, and its inclusion in the *Shemoneh Esreh* prayer so that no Judeo-Christian could serve as a *sheliah zibbur,* precentor. The text of the *birkat haminim* reads: "As for the apostates let there be no hope and in judgment cause the arrogant soon to be destroyed. Blessed art Thou, O Lord, who humbles the proud." This was composed by Samuel the Less at the request of the Patriarch R. Gamaliel II ca. 90 in Yavneh.[65] It was also the same R. Gamaliel who disapproved of the practice of "dipping" at the Passover Seder since it was symbolically connected with the blood of the paschal lamb and with the blood of circumcision. The reason for his objection to this practice was that blood imagery was transferred by the Judeo-Christians to the redemptive power of the Savior who was identified with the paschal lamb.[66]

There are numerous passages involving the *minim* in the Talmud and Midrash but it is not always easy to establish whether the *min* was a Judeo-Christian or another sectarian.[67]

There is no rabbinic parallel to vv. 10–12, but the spirit of these verses is contained in the passage: "They that are reviled but do not revile, they that hear themselves being put to shame but do not answer back, they act out of love and are happy with affliction, concerning them Scripture says, *But they that love him shall be as the sun when he goes forth in his might* (Jud. 5.31).[68]

12 *for so men persecuted the prophets* This is to be understood in terms of a well-established tradition that the prophets had been persecuted.[69] The reference could have been to the persecution of the prophets by Ahab and Jezebel,[70] or to the persecutions of Jeremiah.[71] Amos, Jeremiah, and Isaiah are said to have been martyred.[72]

## NOTES

1. Davies, *SSM,* p. 288.

2. Austin Farrer, *St. Matthew and St. Mark* (1954); also argued by Green, *Matthew,* p. 15.

3. For criticism of this suggestion, see Davies, *SSM,* pp. 9 ff.

4. In this recast one of the sources used by the evangelist or by a glossator was Isa. 61.1f (see above pp. 71, 75, 76).

5. Pss. Sol. 5.18, 6.1, 10.1; En. 52 (with curse), 114.4, 48.9, 62.1, 66.7; Sira 14.1, 25.8, 9, 28.19, 31.8, 48.11, 50.28.

6. T. Hag. 2.1 (p. 234).

7, B. Hag. 14b.

8. B. Ber. 3a.

9. Allen, *Matt.*, p. 39.

10. Davies, *SSM*, p. 251 n. 2. For a full discussion of the problem see J. Dupont, *Les Béatitudes* (1958), pp. 209–217. On the "poor" see E. Bammel, *ptochos TDNT*, 6.881–915.

11. Translation, Albright-Mann ad loc., p. 46, cf. also 1QS IV.3.

12. Sifre Num. 101 reflects this confusion between *ani* and *anav*. Further on the *anav*, see above p. 74.

13. McNeile, *Matt.*, ad loc., p. 50, erred when he wrote that "*ptochos* represents '*ani* (Aram. *anaya*), which does not mean 'lacking wealth' *(rash, 'ebyon)* or 'humble' *('anaw)*, but describes the *pious* in Israel, for the most part literally poor, whom the worldly rich despised and persecuted," for *ebyon* does not necessarily mean one who is materially poor. See Lachs, "John the Baptist," p. 32.

14. *SB* ad loc. (1:190).

15. See Montefiore, *RLGT*, p. 3; Abrahams, *Studies I*, p. 50; S. Zeitlin, "The Am Ha-Aretz," *JQR* 23 (1932–33): 45 ff.

16. Manson, *SJ*, p. 47.

17. Cf. Shubert, *SNT*, p. 122, quoted by Davies (*SSM*, p. 251), who properly refutes this identification; nor is Brown's suggestion (*Birth*, pp. 350–355) that the *anawim* were a Jewish Christian circle convincing.

18. For further indication that Isa. 61.1 ff. influenced the Matthean version of the Beatitudes, see below pp. 73, 75 f.

19. B. Hag. 9b; also see Lev. R. 13.4.

20. Dalman, *Words*, pp. 91 ff.

21. See also Dan. 2.44; 7.14, and cf. Josephus, *Contra Ap.* II.16 and his use of "theocracy."

22. E.g., Sifre, Deut. 916.

23. *Mek.* Exod. 17.14.

24. *Asmp. M.* 10.1.

25. Singer, *APB*, p. 95. On the kingdom of God in Jewish sources, see S. Schechter, *Some Aspects of Rabbinic Theology* (London and New York, 1910), pp. 65–115. On the kingdom in the NT, see N. Perrins, *The Kingdom of God in the Teaching of Jesus* (London, 1963); R. Schnakenburg, *God's Rule and the Kingdom* [Eng. trans.] (London, 1963); G. E. Ladel, *Jesus and the Kingdom* (London, 1966).

26. Allen, *Matt.* p. 41. Albright-Mann, p. 46.

27. Cf. B. Sanh. 98b; TJ Ber. 2.4, 5a. Cf. also Qalir, in *Midreshē Ge'ullah* (Heb.), ed. J. Even Shemu'el [J. Kaufman] (Jerusalem, 1953/54), pp. 113–116.

28. E.g., B. Mak. 5b; B. Sanh. 37b; TJ Ket. 5.13, 30c (1); B. Ket. 66b; 104a. See above p. 32.

29. T. Sota 15.11 (p. 322). See S. Lieberman, *Tosefta Kifshuta, Seder Nashim*, Sota, pp. 772 f. Also *Mid. Ps.* 137.6 (pp. 262–263); cf. B. Ta'an. 30b; B. BQ 57a.

30. B. BB 60b. Cf. also B. Git. 57a; Meg. Ta'an. 13 and *Didache* 8.1.

31. Green, *Matt.*, p. 77.

32. B. Ber. 31a.

33. Wellhausen, *Das Evangelium Matthäii* (Berlin, 1904), ad loc. Allen and McNeile support the traditional order of the verses without convincing argument, maintaining that the 'poor" and "meek" are unrelated and should be understood as separate entities. Green's argument for Matthean originality (p. 77) is likewise unconvincing. He argues that "the beatitude is nevertheless Mt's own, and not as some have suggested a late interpolation since it seems certain from the importance he attaches to humility elsewhere in the gospel."

34. M. Sanh. 10.1

35. Jub. 32.19.

36. En. 5.7.

37. *Didache* 3.

38. Cf. M. Avot 3.16; En. 60.7; Syr. Apoc. Bar. 29.4; 2 Esd. 6.52; Targ. J. Num. 11.16; B.BB 74b; Rev. 19.9; Luke 13.28–29; 22.30 et al.

39. For linguistic evidence, see McNeile, *Matt.*, ad loc. (p. 51).

40. Montefiore, op. cit., pp. 17–23. Cf. B. Shab. 104a; B. Mak. 10b; B. Yoma 38b/49a; et al. The idea of physical hunger in Luke is supported by the negative woe in 6.25.

41. Friedländer, *Sermon*, pp. 21–22. Cf. Ps. 41.1 and Prov. 14.21.

43. Sifre Deut. 36 (end); B. Shab. 151b; cf. T. BQ 9.30 (p. 366); B. Bez. 32b. Other exhortations to be merciful: TJ BQ 8.5, 6c (5); TJ Meg. 4.9, 59c (11); TJ Ber. 5.3, 9c (21).

44. On the hostile attitude of the Jewish community toward the Judeo-Christians *(minim)*, see Herford, *CTM*, pp. 97 ff. On this suggestion and emendation, see S. T. Lachs, "Hebrew Elements in the Gospels and Acts" *JQR* 71 (1980): 37–38.

45. A. Finkel, *The Pharisees and the Teacher of Nazareth* (Leiden, 1964), p. 157.

46. Note a similar passage in Isa. 35.4–5.

47. McNeile, *Matt.* p. 52, comments that "to possess the kingdom will be to see God," is without foundation, especially if *Shekhinah* were part of the original reading of this verse. On *Shekhinah* see J. Abelson, *The Immanence of God in Rabbinical Literature* (London, 1912).

47. B. BB 10b.

48. Lev. R. 23.13.

50. B. Men. 43b.

51. Cf. Prov. (LXX) 10.10 and Targ. ad loc.

52. M. Avot 1.12.

53. Slav. En. 52.11.

54. Ibid. 52.13.

55. Ibid. 12–13.

56. E.g., Lev. R. 9.9.

57. Cf. J. C. Fenton, "Inclusio and Chiasmus in Matthew," *Studia Evangelica* 3 (1964).

58. See D. R. A. Hare, *The Theme of Jewish Persecution of Christians in the Gospel of St. Matthew*, SNTSM 6 (Cambridge, 1967), pp. 118 ff., 130 ff.

59. Davies, *SSM*, pp. 297 ff.

60. Burney, *The Poetry of Our Lord*, p. 168, retroverts the text *tubehon d'rad'phin l'sidka*, "Blessed are those who pursue righteousness," assuming that the translator read *r'diphin*, "persecuted, lit. pursued," for *rad'phin*, "pursuing," and he relies on Deut. 16.20, *Righteousness, righteousness shall you pursue.*

61. Cf. Ps. (LXX) 54.8.

62. Cf. En. 58.6, the son of Man is called the Righteous and Elect (Messiah). Note the parallel between 5.11, reading "the Righteous one, and 5.10, "on my account"; Luke 6.22 = Matt. 5.11, which reads "on account of the Son of man." Cf. Matt. 27.18, 24, where Jesus is called "righteous," but here it is notable, but means that he is innocent; cf. also Acts 7.52, 22.14, 1 John 2.1, 3.7.

63. See A. Dupont Sommer, *The Essene Writings from Qumran* (Cleveland and New York: Meridian Books, 1961), pp. 358–378. On this emendation see Lachs, "Some Textual Observations on the Sermon on the Mount," 101–103.

64. Davies, *SSM*, pp. 279 ff. Manson, *TJ*, p. 34, disagrees. On the abandoned Christians, see C. H. Hunzinger, "Die jüdische Bannpraxis im neutestamentlichen Zeitalter," *Theologische Literaturzeitung* 80 (1955): 144 f., cited by Davies, *SSM*, p. 244 n. 1.

65. B. Ber. 28b.

66. See S. Zeitlin, "The Liturgy of the First Night of Passover," *JQR* 38 (1948): 434 ff.

67. See S. T. Lachs, "Rabbi Abbahu and the Minim," *JQR* 61 (1970): 197 ff. On this beatitude cf. D. Daube, "Three Questions of Form in Matthew V." *JTS* 45 (1944): 21–24.

68. B. Shab. 88b.

69. Davies, *SSM*, p. 252. Cf. Matt. 23.35. See A. Decamps, *Les justes et la justice* (1950), pp. 47–53; F. Gils, *Jésus prophète d'apres les évangiles synoptiques* (Louvain, 1957), p. 19. Shubert, *The Scrolls and the New Testament*, ed. K. Stendahl, pp. 122 ff., forces this verse into a reference to an Essene background. On this attempt see Davies, *SSM*, loc. cit.

70. 1 Kings 19.10.

71. Jer. 26.20–24, 38.6–13.

72. See Heb. 11.37; Ascen. Isa. 5; C. C. Torrey, *The Lives of the Prophets* (Philadelphia: Society of Biblical Literature, 1964), pp. 34–35; Ginzberg, *Legends of the Jews*, 4:262 (Amos); 4:279, 6.371, 374–375, 396 (Isaiah); 4.399–400 (Jeremiah).

# 20. *The Parables of Salt and Light*

## Matt. 5.13–16

### Matt. 5.13

"You are the salt of the earth; but if salt has lost its taste, how can its saltness be restored? It is no longer good for anything to be thrown out and trodden under foot by men."

### Mark 9.50

"Salt is good; but if the salt has lost its saltness, how will you season it?"

### Luke 14.34–35

34 "Salt is good; but if salt has lost its taste, how shall saltness be restored? 35 It is fit neither for the land nor for the dunghill; men throw it away. He who has ears to hear, let him hear."

### Matt. 5.14–16

14 "You are the light of the world. A city set on a hill cannot be hid. 15 Nor do men light a lamp and put it under a bushel, but on a stand, and it gives light to all in the house. 16 Let your light so shine before men, that they may see your good works and give glory to your father who is in heaven."

### Mark 4.21

And he said to them, "Is a lamp brought in to be put under a bushel, or under a bed, and not on a stand?"

### LUKE 8.16

"No one after lighting a lamp covers it with a vessel, or puts it under a bed, but puts it on a stand, that those who enter may see the light."

### LUKE 11.33

"No one after lighting a lamp puts it in a cellar or under a bushel, but on a stand, that those who enter may see the light."

### COMMENTARY

13 *You are the salt of the earth*    Undoubtedly this was a popular proverb; its language is a bit confused and its moral is not clear. It is addressed to the disciples, and in calling them "salt," Jesus is using a term with positive meaning. In Matt., vv. 14–16, Jesus calls them "light of the world" with similar implication. The disciples are called "salt" presumably because they, like salt itself, are considered to be essential for the well-being of the world. Cf. "The world cannot exist without salt."[1] The disciples are not only essential to the world, but having been granted "authority" they cannot lost it. The phrase *it is no longer good for anything*, etc. should be understood as, "were it to have lost its saltiness, it would then be good for nothing." The implication as to the disciples is, saltness is your very quality, Heb. *ta'am*, *raison d'etre*, the essence of your discipleship. Allen suggests, "the idea underlying 'salt' here is probably to its use as a preservative. The disciples are the element in the world which keep it wholesome, and delays the day of decay and of consequent judgment."[2]

Many have seen in this proverb an Aramaic original. Bischoff suggested that there is a wordplay here, *tabla de'tebel*, "salt of the world."[3] The word "earth" means world.[4] F. Perles reads it *la letabla wela lezable khasher*, "fit neither as a spice (*tabla*, confused with *tebel*, which is rendered in the Gr. by *ge*) nor as fertilizer (*zabla*).[5] M. Black reconstructs the Aramaic in a most convincing fashion:

"Ye are the salt of the earth ('attun me'lah 'ar'a). But if the salt has lost its savour wherewith shall it be salted ('m taphel me'lah le'ma tabbe'lunnah).

"It is neither fit for the ground, not yet for dung (la le'ara, 'aph la lere'a kashar), (but) men throw it out (and) trample it down."[6]

The question "how shall it be restored?" is purely rhetorical. Salt cannot lose its saltiness. All attempts to prove that it can are unconvincing.[7] Understood rhetorically, it is admirably illustrated by a rabbinic passage in the same vein: "They asked [R. Joshua]: 'When salt became unsavory wherewith is it to be salted?' He replied, 'With the afterbirth of a mule!' 'And is there an afterbirth of a mule?' 'And can it become unsavory?' "[8]

14 *You are the light of the world*    Probably goes back to Isa. 49.6, *I have given you a covenant to the people, a light to the nations.*[9] Similarly, "You are the

light of Israel."[10] "Thou only art left . . . as a lamp in a dark place."[11] In the NT, *and if you are sure that you are a guide to the blind, a light to these who see in darkness,*[12] *That you may be blameless and innocent children of God without blemish in the midst of a crooked and perverse generation; among whom you shine as the light of this world.*[13] Israel is called light,[14] and individuals called light of the world, e.g., Adam,[15] and R. Johanan b. Zakkai.[16]

*a city*, etc. This phrase has prompted some rather strange and forced explanations. For example, "a city set on a hill, perhaps proverbial, but especially appropriate to Jerusalem on account both of its situation and of its symbolic importance for Judaism. Jerusalem and its Temple are both called 'the light of the world' in late Jewish writing."[17] There are several objections to this explanation. The city imagery disturbs the light theme which characterizes vv. 14–16. Second, Jerusalem is built on hills, not a hill, and finally neither Jerusalem nor its Temple is aggrandized in the Gospels. It is likewise forced and grasping at straws to cite, in this connection, a "combination of light and city" from Cicero.[18] The problem with the reading "city" can be solved and harmonized with the light motif of vv. 14–16 if we assume a Semitic original of the passage, which appears to be certain here. What is it which if set on a hill cannot be hid? One possible answer could be fire. The text here could have been נור , "fire," and it was misread as ע ר ,"city," for the letters נ and ו could have been misread as ע. This reading, now consistent with the other components, would be, "a fire set on a hill cannot be hid."[19] This might refer to the practice of lighting flares on mountaintops to announce the New Month (Rosh Hodesh): "And from what place did they kindle the flares? From the Mount of Olives [they signaled] to Sarteba, and from Sarteba to Agrippina, and from Agrippina to Hauran and from Hauran to Beth Baltin. They did not go beyond Beth Baltin, but the flare was waved to and fro and up and down until a man could see the whole exile [in Babylon] before him like a sea of fire."[20]

15 *nor do men light a lamp*, etc. Note the other readings: Mark 4.21, *Is a lamp brought in to be put under a bushel, or under a bed and not on a stand?* Luke 8.16, *No one after lighting a lamp covers it with a vessel, or puts it under a bed, but puts it on a stand that those who enter may see the light*; ibid. 11.33, *No one after lighting a lamp puts it in a cellar or under a bushel but on a stand that those who enter may see the light.* This aphorism is based on observation of a purely domestic character.[21]

It appears that the Marcan version is probably the earliest, since Mark uses the metaphor of light for the teaching of Jesus, while both Matt. and Luke use it in reference to the disciples and their mission.[22] Matthew alone gives an explicit application of the parable in the words, *In the same way let your light shine before men in order that they may see your good works and glorify your Father in Heaven.* It is clear that each Gospel writer used the material to fit his individual outlook. In Matt., for example, the lamp is placed on the stand to give light to those *in* the house, the parable aimed at the Jewish community.

Luke, on the other hand, sees the lamp giving light to those who *enter* the house, aimed at the Gentile world.[23]

The basic difference among the four passages is where one does *not* place the lamp, viz., under a bushel, Gr. *modios*, in all but Luke 8.16; under a bed, Gr. *klinē*, in Mark and Luke 8.16; in a cellar, Gr. *kruptē*, only in Luke 11.33; or under a vessel, Gr. *skeuei*, only in Luke 8.16. To trace the process of divergence in the various passages one should start with Mark's version, which is in the form of a question, Does a man light a lamp and put it down below? (No!) He places it on a stand (high up). The Hebrew for "down below" is *lematah*, the purpose of the lighting of the lamp is to place it in the most advantageous position in the house to give the most light to the largest area. This is reminiscent of a discussion between Rabbi Judah the Prince and the Emperor Antoninus. "Antoninus asked Rabbi [Judah the Prince], 'If a man has a dwelling which is ten cubits square, where does he set his lamp?' He answered, 'In the middle of the dining room' [the main room of the house]."[24] The key point in the NT is exactly the same, the lamp is to be set high up, visible to all and in a place where it would cast the most light. It should therefore not be hidden, not set in a low position, but on a stand, high up. From an original reading, *lematah*, "down low," as we reconstruct the process, the first change which took place was that the translator misread the word "down low" as *lemitah*, "a bed," and adjusted the Greek to this figure. Second, the term *modios* here might go back to the Hebrew *middah*, "a measure," an error for *mitah*. Finally, the two Lucan passages, from two different sources, are paraphrastic, Luke 8.16 has *skeuei*, "a vessel," for *modios*. This is perhaps due to the fact that *modion* was a bit ambiguous, since it was the measure, not the container (*skeuei* is a common noun and used regularly in the LXX for the Heb. *keli*; the term *modios*, Lat. *modius*, a dry measure holding 16 sextarii or 1/6 of an Attic *medimnus*), and by using *skeuei* this ambiguity is clarified. The reading *kruptē*, which is translated as "cellar" by RSV and others, rather than "a secret place," is an explicit paraphrastic interpretation of *lematah*, "down low" or "below."[25]

16 *let your light so shine*, etc. "This verse takes up the words 'shine,' 'light' and 'men' in the three preceding verses and is therefore probably Matthew's comment on them as a whole."[26]

*good works* Heb. *ma'asim tovim*, not found elsewhere in the NT. H. Schlatter points out that the thrust of this comment is that the disciples are to impress men by their good works in contrast to the sects commonly labeled gnostic, who do not emphasize works but ideas.[27]

*your father who is in heaven* This expression, "Father in heaven," is characteristic of Matt. and does not occur elsewhere in the NT except in Mark 11.25 and Luke 25.15 but was in general use by the Jews in the first Christian century.[28] It is of interest that Gr. *ouranoi* in the plural is not at all common in Greek, and the strong likelihood is that *ouranoi* has been influenced by the Heb. *shamayim* or Aram. *shemaya*, always in the plural.

What is particularly striking about this verse is that there is an apparent non sequitur—If people see your good works they should praise you, not your Father in heaven. But this transference of praise from man to God, already present in the interestamental writings, is a common motif in rabbinic literature.

"God shall be glorified among the Gentiles through you, but through him that doeth not that which is good, God shall be dishonored."[29]

"R. Simon b. Eleazar said: 'When the Israelites do God's will, His name is exalted in the world. When they do not do His will, His name is, as it were, profaned in the world, as it says, *And they profaned My holy name* [Ezek. 36.20]'."

"There is a story about R. Simon b. Shetaḥ who bought a donkey from an Ishmaelite. His students went and discovered a precious stone hanging from its neck. They said to him, 'Rabbi, *the blessing of the Lord makes rich*' [Prov. 10.22]. R. Simon b. Shetaḥ said to them, 'I bought a donkey, I did not buy a precious stone.' He went and returned the stone to the Ishmaelite, who said to him, 'Blessed be the God of Simon b. Shetaḥ'."[30]

## NOTES

1. M. Sof. 15.8.
2. Allen, p. 43. The rest of his comment is valueless. Note that both Matt. and Luke use *moranthē* for *analos* of Mark 9.50, showing that there was an adaptation of the proverb to the disciples.
3. Bischoff *Jesus u.d. Rabb.*, p. 21 cited by McNeile, *Matt.*, p. 55.
4. Cf. Matt. 10.34, Apoc. Bar. 8.12, Gen. 18.25, the world of man.
5. F. Perles, "La parabole du sel sourd," *REJ* 82 (1926): 122 ff. Cf. Abrahams, *Studies II*, pp. 183–184.
6. Black, *Aramaic Approach*, p. 25.
7. E.g., Jeremias, *PJ*, pp. 168 ff., quoted by Green. "Salt cannot strictly speaking lose its salinity but Palestine Jews normally gathered it in an impure form combined with other matter which would remain after the salt proper had been dissolved by water, and be useless without it. The original form of the saying was probably a warning not to the disciples but to a hostile audience." See also attempts by Carlston, p. 176; Jülicher, *Die Gleichnisreden Jesu*, 2:68; Schmid, *Markus*, p. 183; Lohmeyer, *Markus*, p. 98; Johnson, *Mark*, p. 167.
8. B. Bekh. 8b.
9. Cf. also Isa. 60.3.
10. Test. Levi 14.3.
11. 2 Esd. 12.42.
12. Rom. 2.19.
13. Philem. 2.15.
14. Cant. R. 1.3, Exod. R. 36.2; *Tan.B. Tezaveh* 6 (50a).
15. TJ Shab. 2, 5b. (46).
16. *ARN* 25. B. Ber. 28b. For other rabbinic parallels see Abrahams, *Studies II*, pp. 14–15; *SB*, 1:237.
17. Green, *Matt.*, p. 79.
18. *Videor enim mihi hanc urbem videre, lucem orbis terrarum atque arcem omnium gentium*, cited by Allen, p. 43.

19. See Lachs, "Studies in the Semitic Background to the Gospel of Matthew," 200–201.

20. M. RH 2.4.

21. Jeremias, *PJ*, pp. 120 ff. Similarly unconvincing is Jeremias's suggestion, "Die Lampe unter dem Scheffel," *ZNW* 39 (1941), "Dann aber ist vollends deutlich, dass wir Mt. 5.15 sinngemäss zu übersetzen haben. Mann zündet eine Lampe doch nicht an, um sie gleich wieder auszulöschen! Nein! Auf den Leuchter gehört sie." It is unnecessary, as Derrett, *LNT*, pp. 189 ff., to argue "that the lamp lit in the house is for a festival in particular for that of Dedication (cf. I Macc. 4.49 f.) and the bushel (i.e. the bushel measure) would be turned over the lamp, not to be extinguished but to hide it. But its proper place is the lamp-stand (a link with the Temple and this with v. 14)." This is totally unnecessary and farfetched. First, if it does involve the lighting of a menorah for Hanukkah, the connection with the menorah of the Temple would be meaningless. Second, what this involves is both silly and ludicrous. One just does not put an exposed flame under a bushel or anything which could ignite. C. H. Dodd, *Parables of the Kingdom*, p. 142, takes an amusing position about this verse in the following comment, amusing since we are dealing with a lighted lamp. ". . . he [Luke] conceives the lamp as standing in the vestibule of a house of the Graeco-Roman type; as such houses at Pompeii show a niche for a lamp in the vestibule. Matthew has in view a Galilean 'but and ben' where there is no living room so that a single lamp suffices for the whole family. No doubt the 'cellar' is also a feature of the more pretentious house which Luke has in view, whereas in the cottage, if you want to hide a lamp there is no place for it but under the meal-tub or perhaps under the bed.'

22. Ibid., p. 143. It is possible that the original *Q* form was closely similar to this (Matthean version).

23. Manson, *SJ*, p. 385.

24. Midrash Hallel to Ps. 113 in A. Jellinek's *BHM*, 5:89.

25. For *kruptē* in the sense of cellar, see J. H. Moulton and G. Milligan, *Vocabulary of the Greek New Testament* (London, 1949), s.v. *kruptē*. On this reconstruction of the verse, see Lachs, op. cit., p. 201.

26. Green, *Matt.*, p. 79.

27. Schlatter, *Der Evangelist Matthäus* (Stuttgart, 1963) ad loc. Contra: Davies, *SSM*, p. 196.

28. Further on this expression, see below to Matt. 6.9 (p. 119).

29. Test. Naph. 8.4.

30. Deut. R. 3. Cf. also Sifra, Lev. 19.1; Sifre, Deut. 319; B. MQ 16b; Lam. R. 1 (70a), *PRK* 26 (p. 166 a/b).

# 21. Jesus on the Law

## MATT. 5.17–20

17 "Think not that I have come to abolish the law and the prophets; I have come not to abolish them but to fulfill them. 18 For truly, I say to you, till heaven and earth pass away, not an iota, not a dot, will pass from the law until all is accomplished. 19 Whoever then relaxes one of the least of these commandments and teaches men so, shall be called least in the kingdom of heaven; but he who does them and teaches them shall be called great in the kingdom of heaven. 20 For I tell you, unless your righteousness exceeds that of the scribes and Pharisees, you will never enter the kingdom of heaven."

## COMMENTARY

17 *Think not* etc. This and the following three verses form the introduction to a section of the Sermon called by many, "The Antitheses." ". . . although there can be little doubt that the Antitheses of v. 22 ff. are the formulation of Matthew, there can be equally little doubt that Jesus himself set his own teaching in relation to the Law of his people."[1] Note that Jesus refers to the "Law and the Prophets," two sections of the Hebrew Canon, omitting the third, the *Ketuvim*. This seems to reflect a period prior to the time when Matthew was active, i.e., after 70. According to the best evidence the first stage of the canonization of the *Ketuvim* took place in 65 C.E. and was not completed until about 140 C.E.[2] The purpose of this declaration is to introduce Jesus' singular interpretation of various biblical laws in 5.21 ff. His intention is not to abolish the Law but to give it what he considered to be its true import and application.

A portion of this verse is cited in a talmudic passage but in an entirely different context.

> Imma Shalom, R. Eliezer's wife, was the sister of Rabban Gamaliel. A certain philospher [*min*, sectarian] lived in the vicinity. He was reported as never accepting bribes [he was a judge]. They wished to expose him [lit. to make sport], so she brought him a golden lamp, went before him, and said to him, "I wish that a share of my father's estate be given to me." He ordered, "Divide." R. Gamaliel said to him, "It is decreed for us where there is a son, a daughter does not inherit." [He replied] "Since the day that you were exiled from your land the Law of Moses has been superseded [lit. taken away] and another book given, wherein a son and a daughter inherit equally." The next day he [R. Gamaliel] brought him a Libyan ass. He said to him, "Look [descend] to the end of the book wherein it is written, 'I came not to destroy the Law of Moses nor to add to the Law of Moses,' and it is written therein, 'a daughter does not inherit where there is a son.' " She said to him, "Let your light shine forth like a lamp." Said R. Gamaliel to him, "An ass came and knocked the lamp over."[3]

18 *For, truly I say to you, till heaven and earth pass away*, etc. The Lucan parallel (16.17), *It is easier for the heaven and earth to pass away than for one dot of the Law to fall*, is closer to the rabbinic parallels (see below). Allen's comment is cogent, "The attitude of the Law here described (5.17–20) is inconsistent with the general tenor of the Sermon. Vv. 21–48 are clearly intended to explain and illustrate the way in which Christ fulfilled the Law. . . . It seems probable, therefore, that vv. 18–19 did not originally belong to the Sermon."[4]

*for truly* Lit. "amen." This is the first time "amen" is used as a participle not confirming a previous statement, and there is no rabbinic analogy. Dalman explains that since Jesus was opposed to swearing, consequently he put "amen" in place of an oath.[5] The term "amen" is used in the NT only by Jesus himself, and mostly, if not exclusively, where the advent of the true kingdom is concerned.

*till heaven and earth pass away* The use of "heaven and earth" for permanence is common and often applied to the Law: e.g., "The Law is immortal as long as the sun and moon and the whole heaven and universe exist;"[6] "everything has its end, the heavens and earth have their end; only one thing is excepted which has no end, and that is the Law."[7]

*an iota* The Greek *iota* represents the Hebrew letter *yod* to the Greek-speaking audience.[8] Note: "Not a letter shall be abolished from the Law forever";[9] "R. Alexander the Reader: 'If all the world were gathered together to destroy the *yod*, which is the smallest letter in the Law, they would not succeed' ";[10] "The guilt of one who destroys one [letter] is so great that if it were done the world would be destroyed."[11] The reference is made presumably because of the fact that the *yod* is the smallest letter of the Hebrew alphabet. This could mean only the *yod* of the square script, since in the old Hebrew script the *yod* was no smaller than any other letter. In the Nash MS (beg. of the 1st cent.), the oldest Hebrew document in Aramaic script in Palestine, the square script is already definitely established.[12] The translations "dot" of RSV and "tittle" of AV are too vague. As for *kereia* in classical Greek, it is a projection, hook or stroke of the letter. The Vulgate reads *apex* for *kereia*.[13] Assuming that the original of *kereia* is Semitic, there are several possibilities to be noted. Does *kereia* represent *keter*, "a crown," an ornament atop several letters of the Hebrew alphabet in Torah scrolls?[14] This ornamentation is also called *taga* when adorning other letters.[15] If so, the meaning would be that although these strokes or ornaments do not affect the meaning of the words which they decorate, they nevertheless will not pass away. As simple as this explanation is, there remains a serious problem. "The *iota* (Heb. *yod*) was certainly employed at the time of Jesus but *kereia* (small horns) attached to some letters to guard against confusion with others is another matter. So far as is known at present the device came into use in the Herodian phase of Hebrew script. To determine what meaning the word might have had at the time of Jesus we cannot know whether the Greek *kereia* referred to the small horns with any real certainty."[16] Others have argued that the *iota* represents the *yod*, while *kereia*, a stroke, stands for the Hebrew letter *vav*. Since both of these letters are used as *matres lectionis*, and they do not affect the meaning of the word, nevertheless they shall not pass away.[17] This is not acceptable, since both letters also have a consonental function aside from serving as a *matres lectionis*. The *iota* and *kereia* are not to be misunderstood as a separate entities but as parts of a hendiadys meaning the smallest part of the smallest letter, as in the Hebrew expression *qozo shel yod*, e.g., "The Law had to be taught in respect to the tittle of the letter *yod [qozo shel yod]*."[18]

19 *least of these commandments* In rabbinic sources the differentiation among the commandments is between light and grave, as in the statement of R. Judah the Prince, "Be heedful of a light commandment as of a grave one, for you do not know the grant of reward for each commandment,"[19] and "Ben Azzai said, 'Run to do a light command.' "[20]

*Whoever then relaxes . . . great in the kingdom of heaven*  There are no rabbinic sources or parallels, but it does appear that M. Avot 2.2 (see above) could be behind it. Perhaps there is a connection between "length of days" and "kingdom of heaven." If so, Deut. 5.16 (honoring one's parents) and Deut. 22.6–7 (the law of the mother bird and her young) are examples of grave and light commandments respectively, and both possess the identical reward, i.e., length of days.

20 *For I tell you, unless your righteousness exceeds that of the scribes and the Pharisees, you will never enter the kingdom of heaven.*  Friedländer[21] argues that this verse is an interpolation; it does not appear in the other Gospels, it contradicts the preceding verses as well as Matt. 23.33, "the scribes and the Pharisees sit on Moses' seat, all things therefore whatsoever they tell you, those do and observe," and finally v. 20 is lacking in the Beza Codex (4th cent.). Daube[22] understands this verse in connection with the antithesis which follow, "Your righteousness shall exceed that of the Scribes (How?) Heb. *kezad*, then follows the ways; this illustrating the principle of *kelal* and *peshat*, the general and the specific."

## NOTES

1. Davies, *SSM*, pp. 430–431, 100, 334 ff.
2. See S. Zeitlin, "An Historical Study of the Canonization of Hebrew Scriptures," *PAAJR* 2 (1932): 129 ff.
3. B. Shab. 116b. On the story see Sifre, Num. 131. On the ass and the lamp, see *PRK* (122b ff.) B. Yoma 38; Lev. R. 21. Cf. W. Bacher, *Die Agada der palästinischen Amoräer* 2:42 n. 5. Herford, *CTM*, pp. 146–147; Leveroff, *Rel. Denk. d. Hasidim*, p. 126; E. B. Nicholson, *Gospel According to the Hebrews*, p. 146; Klausner, *JN*, pp. 44 ff.; Güdemann, *Religionsgeschichtliche Studien*, pp. 65 ff.; *SB* 1:20. Is it happenstance that Imma Shalom brought a lamp as a bribe and that the preceding verses in Matthew deal with a lamp?
4. Allen, *Matt.*, p. 45. For the role of Torah in the messianic period, see Davies, *SSM*, pp. 156 ff., 447 ff.
5. Dalman, *Words*, p. 226. See below pp. 100f. Daube, *NTRJ*, p. 388, sees the background of "amen" in Isa. 65.16.
6. Philo, *The Life of Moses* 2.3.
7. Gen. R. 10.1.
8. E.g., B. Sanh. 107a. On the perpetuity of the Law, see Allen, *Matt.*, p. 45; A. Honeyman, "Matthew 5.18 and the Validity of the Law," *NTS* 1 (1954): 141–142.
9. Exod. R. 6.1.
10. Cant. R. 5.11; cf. Lev. R. 19.
11. Lev. R. 19.1.
12. W. Chomsky, *Hebrew the Eternal Language* (Philadelphia, 1957), p. 86.
13. For the literature, see *BAG*, s.v. *kereia*; M. Lidzbarski, *Hand. d. nord. sem. Epig.* (1898), p. 190.
14. Allen, *Matt.*, p. 47.
15. On *tagin* and *ketarim*, see C. D. Ginsburg, *The Massorah* (London, 1880–1905), 2:680–701.
16. Albright-Mann, pp. 58–59. See also M. Grintz, "Hebrew as Spoken and Written Language in the Last Days of the Second Temple," *JBL* 79 (1960): 32–47.
17. McNeile, *Matt.*, p. 59.
18. B. Men. 34b Cf. also ibid. 29a. Rashi, Tos., and Munich MS read *qoza shel yod;*

Exod. R. 6.1. Cf. Zimmermann, *Aramaic Origin of the Four Gospels*, p. 81, who suggests reading "neither the yod or a particle of it." Also Lachs, "Some Textual Observations," 106–108.
19. M. Avot. 2.1.
20. Ibid. 4.2. Cf. Matt. 23.23. Also Sifre, Deut. 76; B. AZ 3b.
21. *Sermon*, pp. 35–36.
·22. Daube, *NTRJ*, p. 6.

# 22. On Murder

## MATT. 5.21-26

21 "You have heard that it was said to the men of old, 'You shall not kill; and whoever kills shall be liable to judgment.' 22 But I say to you that every one who is angry with his brother[i] shall be liable to judgment; whoever insults[j] his brother shall be liable to the council, and whoever says, 'You fool!' shall be liable to the hell[k] of fire. 23 So if you are offering your gift at the altar, and there remember that your brother has something against you, 24 leave your gift there before the altar and go; first be reconciled to your brother, and then come and offer your gift. 25 Make friends quickly with your accuser, while you are going with him to court, lest your accuser hand you over to the judge, and the judge to the guard, and you be put in prison; 26 truly, I say to you, you will never get out till you have paid the last penny."

## LUKE 12.57-59

57 "And why do you not judge for yourselves what is right? 58 As you go with your accuser before the magistrate, make an effort to settle with him on the way, lest he drag you to the judge, and the judge hand you over to the officer, and the officer put you in prison. 59 I tell you, you will never get out till you have paid the very last copper."

---

i  Some add *without cause.*

j  Greek *says Raca to.*

k  Greek *Gehenna.*

## COMMENTARY

This is the first of several passages in Matthew in which Jesus states the traditional law followed by an antithesis, his individual interpretation and/or application. Davies borders on sophistry when he comments, "Matthew indeed, seems pointedly to have avoided the use of the phrase 'new teaching' to describe the words of Jesus and presents them as the true interpretation of the Law of Judaism. Not antithesis but completion expresses the relationship between the Law of Moses and the teaching of Jesus."[1] Davies also sees in "six antitheses" an analogy to the Six Orders of the Mishnah but recognizes the difficulty in this observation, that five antitheses is arrived at by taking the antithesis on divorce as subordinate to that on adultery.[2] Manson may well be correct in stating that this antithesis originally concluded with "shall be liable to judgment,"[3] the rest being a later expansion of it. It includes the traditional law against killing (murder), followed by Jesus' inclusion of anger against one's brother as being equal to the taking of a life. Anger, however, is not an offense at law; one who is overcome with anger toward another may be morally culpable but he cannot be tried because of it by a human tribunal. He is answerable before a heavenly court and is judged by the "laws of Heaven," a rabbinic term for moral culpability for acts not covered by the laws of man,[4] and this appears to be the meaning of "liable to judgment" in v. 22.[5]

21 *You have heard*  Not simply an act of hearing but a translation of *shamata, lit.* "you have heard," with the meaning "you have received a tradition," *shemu'ah.*[6]

Daube comments,[7] "This falls into two parts: The first gives a Scriptural rule narrowly interpreted, the second a wider demand made by Jesus. . . . Rabbinic discussion *shome'a 'ani,* 'I hear,' 'understand,' or rather, 'I might understand,' introduces an interpretation of Scripture which, though conceivable, yet must be rejected," (citing Ex. 20.12). . . . Quite often, as in this instance, the interpretation introduced by 'I heard,' 'I might understand,' is primitive, narrow, literal, compared with that accepted in its stead." Daube then suggests that the translation of "the first part of the Matthean form by Ye have literally understood, or Ye might understand literally, Ye have literally understood what was said by them or olden times thou shalt not kill." It is precisely here that Daube's argument weakens. Did they learn it *literally?* Probably not, since the Pharisees emphasized the Oral Law and were not restricted to the literal meaning of the text.[8]

21 *It was said*  Gr. *errethē,* Heb. *ne'emar,* a common technical term employed when citing scriptural verses.[9]

*to the men of old*  Gr. *tois archaiois,* "the men of past ages."[10] There are several possibilities as to the Semitic original: Heb. *dorot rishonim,* "former generations," as in "so in former generations [*dorot rishonim*] the men of the Great Synagogue, Hillel and Shammai, and R. Gamliel the Elder in the later generation";[11] the early Sages, *zeqenim harishonim, lit.* "the early Elders,"[12] simply the former *harishonim.*[13]

*you shall not kill*  Gr. *ou phoneuseis* Exod. (LXX) 20.15 (13), Heb. *lo tirzah.* There are no rabbinic parallels to this antithesis but the following are of note:

> R. Eliezer said: "He who hates his brother belongs to the shedders of blood!"[14]

> A tanna recited before R. Naḥman b. Isaac: "He who publicly shames his neighbor is as though he shed blood."[15]

> All who descend into Gehinom [subsequently reascend] except those who do not reascend, viz., he who commits adultery, publicly shames his neighbor, fastens an evil epithet [nickname upon his neighbor].[16]

The last passage is particularly instructive since it mentions Gehinom as a punishment for one who employs an insulting term for his neighbor, possibly *raka* and/or *mōre*.

**22** *every one who is angry with his brother.* On murder and anger cf. Lev. 19.17; Sira 10.6, 28.7. *"brother"* here in Matt. is used in the sense of neighbor; cf. Lev. 19.17, Deut. 15.2. Matthew seems to turn the Jewish brother into a Christian brother, i.e., fellow disciple.[17]

*liable (to judgment)* Gr. *enochos*, Heb. *hayyav*, i.e., punishment by a proper authority.

*he who insults* Lit., "calls him a *raqa*," an Aram. term, רקא an insulting epithet meaning "empty-headed, a fool, empty of knowledge," used frequently in rabbinic literature.[18]

*liable to the council* Gr. *enochos estai tō sunedriō*. The term *tō sunedriō* could not mean a human tribunal here, for calling another fool is not an actionable offense. As a matter of fact there is a reference which actually treats this type of insult in a light-hearted way, "If your neighbor calls you an ass, put a saddle on."[19] Calling one a name was not subsumed under the category of *boshet* "shame" involved in payment for injury.[20] It was likewise ruled out in the offense of *mozi shem ra*, giving a person an evil name, which was actionable. What is meant here is liability before a heavenly court, *bet din shel ma'alah*, "the court on high," *bet din shel haqadosh barukh hu*, "the court of the Holy One, blessed be He"; sanhedrin, which is used interchangeably with *bet din*, "court," and is used specifically for the celestial court: "R. Meir said: '*These are the ordinances*. God gave the Law to the elders of Israel just as a sanhedrin sits on high before the Lord.' "[21] Admittedly the use of *sunedrion* is a bit strange; in Matt. 5.21 the evangelist employs *krisei* in citing murder, in 5.22a the same term is used for anger, but for calling one *more* the punishment is hell's fire. *Krisei* in v. 21 probably means "judgment" or "court." In v. 22 we see three parts: 22a anger, 22b calling one *raka*, and 22c calling one *more*, and we maintain that 22c is a gloss of 22b, i.e., *mōre* stands for the aramaic *raka*, and *tēn geennan toū puros* stands for *tō sunedriō*.[22] The purpose of the gloss is clear: the audience or the readership might not have understood the Aramaic *raka*, transliterated in the Greek, hence the Greek equivalent *more* was substituted, and to emphasize that the punishment will be divine, not human, and will occur elsewhere, not here on earth, Gehinom was substituted for *sunedrion*, which most surely would have been misunderstood by an unlettered audience.[23]

*fool* Gr. *mōre*, found frequently in rabbinic literature as a synonym for "fool," *shoteh*, *tipesh*. It is not the Heb. *moreh*, "rebel." Note the following: "With whom may Moses be compared? With [a tutor in the employ of] a king. When the king turned over his son to the tutor, the king said, 'Whatever you do, do not call my son *more*.' 'It is the same,' said R. Reuben, 'as *moros*, the epithet that Greeks used for moron . . .' "[24]

*Gehenna* Heb. *gehinom*. A place of punishment of the dead. The name is derived from the notorious valley of Ben Hinom, SW of Jerusalem, cf. Jer. 19.2, and paralleled by the Garden of Eden of Gen. 2.8, the place of reward and serenity for the departed pious.[25] Verses 23–24 are not part of the original material of the Sermon. They were inserted here because of the idea of reconciliation between men suggested by the previous verse. Because of the mention of the altar it most probably was composed before 70 c.e. The main point is that before a man can propitiate God to forgive him of his sins, he must first be reconciled with his fellow man, repair the wrong done, ask his pardon, and only then ask God for His forgiveness. All of this procedure must take place before an offering is made at the altar. Reconciliation is more important than sacrifice, cf. Hos. 6.6. There are no direct rabbinic parallels but the following are of the same genre.

It is necessary for those who are about to go to the Temple to partake in the Sacrifice to be pure in body and soul and also to be adorned with virtues expressed by praiseworthy actions. But let him whose head harbors covetousness and desire of unjust things cover his head in shame and be silent. Truly the Temple of the living God may not be approached by unholy sacrifices.[26]

For transgressions that are between man and God the Day of Atonement affects atonement, but for those transgressions that are between man and his fellowman the Day of Atonement affects atonement only if he has appeased his fellowman.[27]

If you wish to offer a sacrifice rob nothing from any man. Why? *For I the Lord love justice, I hate robbery and wrong* [Isa. 61.8]. And when do you offer up the *olah* [burnt offering] and I receive it? When your hands are clean of robbery. David said, *Who shall ascend into the mountain of the Lord? He who has clean hands and a pure heart* [Ps. 24.3–4].[28]

. . . for if a man has brought what he has stolen before he offered his guilt offering, he has fulfilled his obligation, but if he brought his guilt offering before he brought what he had stolen, he has not fulfilled his obligation.[29]

23 *gift (at the altar)* Gr. *dōron*, Heb. *qorban* or *minhah; dōron* is used for both *qorban* and *minhah* in the LXX, and frequently in rabbinic literature for any gift.[30]

Verses 25–26 represent the second "reconciliation passage," and here it involves one's adversary at law. Cf. Luke 12.57–59. The setting seems to indicate arrest for debt,[31] but if so, the background of the passage is not Jewish but probably Greco-Roman. There are two reasons which militate against a Jewish setting. First, there is mention of one judge, not judges, for according to the accepted practice at the time, the minimum number of judges was three.[32] Second, the penalty of imprisonment is virtually foreign to Jewish usage and certainly was not the penalty for debt.

The moral of this verse seems to be obvious—men even now are on their way to the celestial court, where they must give account of their lives. For the comparison of a sinner to an insolvent debtor, see Matt. 18.23–25, Luke 7.41–45, "the only hope for man is to come to terms by repentance while there is still time."[33]

25 *make friends* Gr. *isthi eunoōn*, "agree, be favorably minded." Luke 12.58 reads "to be quit of him." The reading "make friends" may have arisen from a mistranslation of the Heb. *leshalem*, "to pay back," as it also means "to make peace."[34]

*accuser* Gr. *antidikos*, "the injured party," Heb. *antidigos*.[35]

*guard* Gr. *hupēretēs*, Heb. *hazzan*; it is used for a synagogue official,[36] but that is doubtful here, since the passage does not seem to reflect Jewish practice. Jeremias, however, argues that the use of *hupēretēs* provides the original setting for the parable, i.e., the synagogue.[37]

26 *penny* Gr. *kodrantes*, *quadron*, late Heb. *qurdintis*, ¼ as, ⅙ denarius, smallest coin of the Roman currency.[38]

## NOTES

1. Davies, *SSM*, p. 107.
2. Ibid., p. 300. See below pp. 98f.
3. Manson, *SJ*, p. 155.
4. E.g., M. BQ 5.2.
5. On the expansion of the original, see below p. 93.
6. M. Eduy, 5.7, M. Sanh. 11.2. Cf. Bacher, *Die exegetische Terminologie der jüdischen Traditionsliteratur*, s.v.שמע(p. 187),שמועה,ת(p. 192).
7. Daube, *NTRJ*, p. 55.
8. The gist of Daube's statement was originally suggested by S. Schechter, *JQR*, o.s. 10 (1898): 11, and rightly rejected by Bacher, op. cit., p. 190 n. 3.
9. Cf. Bacher, op. cit. s.v.אמר (p. 6). *SB* ad loc. suggest Aram. *itmar* as the original reading. This is possible, but in a later period it was used as a technical term when citing tannaitic, not biblical, material. Allen, *Matt.*, p. 96, is mistaken in stating that the thrust of "You have heard" is to an unlearned audience, i.e., they have heard rather than read.
10. Cf. Arist., *Eq.* 507; idem, *Metaph.* XI.1.2.
11. Cant. R. 5.14.
12. B. Shab. 64b.
13. B. Yoma 9b; Aram. *deqadmonin*, TJ ibid., 38c; *Mid. Ps.* 137.4 (263); Jos. *Ant.* XIII.10.5, "we have heard from our elders *para ton presbuteron*." See A. Büchler, *Types of Jewish Palestinian Piety from 70 C.E.: The Ancient Pious Men* (New York: Ktav, 1968), p. 78 n. 2 et passim.
14. *DER* XI. Cf. also Sifre, Deut. 186–187.
15. B. BM 58b.
16. Ibid.
17. Friedlander, *Sermon*, p. 42.
18. E.g., Targ. O. Gen. 37.14; B. Ta'an 20b; B. Ber. 32a; B. Ned. 65a; B. Sanh.

100a. In the NT only here and John 2.21. Origen, *Our Lord's Sermon on the Mount* 1.9.23 stated that he was told by a Jew that it had no meaning but was an angry interjection; Chrysostom, *Homily on Matt.* XIV.10 explained it as a haughty way of addressing inferiors. On *raqa* and *morē*, see Davies, *SSM*, pp. 235 ff.; C. F. D. Moule, *Expos. T.* 81 (1969/70): 10 ff.

19. B. BQ 92b.

20. M. BQ 8.6. and B. ibid 86a–87a.

21. Exod. R. 30.18. Cf. also ibid. 5.12, Lev. R. 24.2.

22. Friedlander, *Sermon*, loc. cit.

23. See K. Kohler, "Zu Mat. 5.22," *ZNW* 19 (1920): 91–95, who sees *morē* as the translation of *raqa*. McNeile, *Matt.*, p. 62, is in error in his understanding of this antithesis: "The Rabbis say that murder is liable to judgment but I say that anger, its equivalent, is liable to (divine) judgment and (the Rabbis say that) abusive language such as *raka* is punishable by the fire of Gehenna." The first part of his reasoning is correct; the second is totally wrong.

Allen, *Matt.*, p. 48, is likewise wrong when citing "parallels" to this passage, for he did not understand the citations which he adduced vis-à-vis the NT text. He cited "He that calleth his neighbor a slave, let him be excommunicated" (B. Qid. 28a); "he that calleth him a bastard, let him be punishable with forty stripes" (B. BM 58b). These are quite different from calling him a fool, for calling one a slave or a bastard is actionable, since this damages his reputation and standing in the community and he suffers thereby.

24. *PRK* 14 (118b), *Mid. Ps.* 9 (46b). Cf. also Sifre, Deut. 218, where *shoteh* is equated with *morē*. See also *REJ* 22.

25. See *IDB*, s.v. "Gehinom."

26. Philo, *On Those Who Sacrifice* 3.

27. M. Yoma 8.9.

28. *Tan.B. Zav* 3 (p. 7a).

29. M. BQ 9.12.

30. E.g., Targ. Ps. 20.4, B. Zev. 7b, B. Pes. 18b.

31. See Jeremias, *PJ*, p. 181.

32. Cf. M. Sanh. 1 and Talmud ad loc.

33. Manson, *SJ*, p. 414.

34. McNeile, *Matt.*, p. 63, Cf. B. Sanh. 95b.

35. E.g., Gen. R. 82.9, 100.10; *PRK* 16 (126a); Deut. R. 5.5, also called *ba'al din*, M. Avot 4.22.

36. Cf. T. Mak. 5.12 (p. 444), where the *ḥazzan* inflicts lashes. Cf. also B. Mak. 23a; also called *shoter* as an officer of the court (Deut 16.18), B. Sanh. 16b, et al. Josephus, *Ant.* IV.8.14, in an unique passage, states that "to each magistracy let there be assigned two subordinate officers [*hupēretoi*] of the tribe of Levi." Cf. Deut. 21.5.

37. Jeremias, *PJ*, p. 27 n.

38. E.g., TJ Qid. 1.1, 58d (34).

# 23. On Adultery

## MATT. 5.27–30

27 "You have heard that it was said, 'You shall not commit adultery.' 28 But I say to you that every one who looks at a woman lustfully has already committed adultery with her in her heart. 29 If your right eye causes you to sin, pluck it out and throw it

away; it is better that you lose one of your members than that your whole body be thrown into hell.[k] 30 And if your right hand causes you to sin, cut it off and throw it away; it is better that you lose one of your members than that your whole body go into hell."[k]

## MATT. 18.8-9

8 "And if your hand or your foot causes you to sin, cut it off and throw it from you; it is better for you to enter life maimed or lame than with two hands or two feet to be thrown into the eternal fire. 9 And if your eye causes you to sin, pluck it out and throw it from you; it is better for you to enter life with one eye than with two eyes to be thrown into the hell of fire."

## MARK 9.43, 45, 47-48

43 "And if your hand causes you to sin, cut it off; it is better for you to enter life maimed than with two hands to go to hell, to the unquenchable fire. 45 And if your foot causes you to sin, cut it off; it is better for you to enter life lame than with two feet to be thrown into hell. 47 And if your eye causes you to sin, pluck it out; it is better for you to enter the kingdom of God with one eye than with two eyes to be thrown into hell, 48 where their worm does not die, and the fire is not quenched."

---

k  Gr. *Gehenna*.

## COMMENTARY

This is the second antithesis in Matthew. The commandment is Exod. 20.14 and Deut. 5.18. "Jewish moral teaching in the time of Jesus already extended the scope of the seventh commandment (apart from strictly legal contexts) to cover any sexual activity outside of the married state."[1] It included lustful thoughts as well as deeds.[2]

28  *every one who looks*, etc.   In rabbinic literature, as here, there is a desire to emphasize the danger inherent in sinful thoughts.[3] This is often expressed by hyperbole, equating the thought with the act, and even on occasion deeming it to be more reprehensible. E.g.:

> Unchaste imagination is more injurious than the sin itself.[4]

> *Shall commit* [Num. 5.6]. The future indicates that they have only intended to commit a sin, but have not yet done so. This is to teach you that the moment a man contemplates sin, it is as though he has committed a trespass against the Omnipresent.[5]

On lustful thoughts of adultery and the act itself:

> He who has a pure heart in love, looks not on a woman with thoughts of fornication.[6]

*The eye of the adulterer waits for the twilight saying, "No eye shall see me," etc.* [Job. 24.15]. Resh Laqish expounded: "You must not suppose that only he who had committed the crime with his body is called an adulterer, if he commits adultery with his eyes he is also called an adulterer, for it says, *the eye of the adulterer, etc.*"[7]

He who looks at a woman with desire is as one who had illicit intercourse with her.[8]

When a man has the intention to sin, it is as though he has already sinned against God.[9]

Verses 29–30 have been introduced because of the lustful eye and the subject of adultery in 27–28. They are paralleled by Mark 9.43–48, where hand, foot, and eye are mentioned. In D and S[1] v. 30 is lacking.

29 *right eye* The right eye is presumably the more valuable of the two.[10] The eye is the bodily member most often blamed for leading men astray, especially to sexual sin.[11]

*to sin* Gr. *skandalizein*, probably "to stumble," Heb. *lehikashel*.[12]
*into hell* See above p. 93.

30 *and if your right hand*, etc. In addition to the eye leading men astray, the heart runs a close second;[13] even the feet are occasionally held to be culpable.[14] Nowhere, however, in biblical or in rabbinic literature do we find the hand among the offenders.[15] The right hand here, as opposed to the left, has no particular significance, it is only in imitation of the "right eye" of v. 29. We explain the phrase *if your (right) hand causes you to sin*, etc., with a rather radical suggestion. This verse should be connected with the subject of adultery. One therefore would expect not the "hand" to be cut off, but the *membrum virile*. At first reading this might seem far-fetched. On second thought, however, it seems less startling when one considers that it is Matthew who records the verse, *For there are eunuchs who have been so from birth, and there are eunuchs who have been made eunuchs by men, and there are eunuchs who have made themselves eunuchs for the sake of heaven* (Matt. 19.12). There is an apparent example of the Hebrew *yad* (hand) used euphemistically for the *membrum virile*. It is the difficult expression *yad ḥazit* of Isa. 57.8 but understood by many in this sense since it appears in a passage with clear sexual overtones.[16]

## NOTES

1. Cf. Derrett, *LNT*, pp. 370 ff.
2. See B. Ber. 24a; generally called *hirhurē averah*, e.g., ibid. 12b.
3. See B. S. Jackson, "Liability for Mere Intention in Early Jewish Law," *HUCA* 42 (1971): 192–255; J. J. Rabinowitz, "The Sermon on the Mount and the School of Shammai," *HTR* 49 (1956): 79.
4. B. Yoma 29a.
5. Num. R. 8.5, cf. also B. Ned. 13b.
6. Test. Benj. 8.2.

7. Lev. R. 23.12. Also see *PR* 24 (124b/125a); Num. R. 9.1; *Tan.B.*, *Naso* 3 (p. 13b), *Tan.* ibid. 7; *MHG*, Exod. 20.14.

8. Mas. Kalla 1.

9. Num. R. 8.5.

10. Cf. 1 Sam. 11.2. The significance of the right over the left is well known in folk traditions, the former used in a positive sense, the latter almost always in a negative one. Cf. B. Ber. 62a.

11. Cf. Num. 15.39; Prov. 21.4; Ezek. 6.9, 18.6, 20.8, 23.27; Koh. 11.9. In rabbinic sources see *Sifre*, Num. 115; B. Ber. 12b; TJ Ber. 9.2 13c (4); Num. R. 17; *Tan. Shelaḥ* 15; B. Sot. 8a; B. Sanh. 45a; *DER* 1; B. Shab. 108b.

12. E.g., Dan. (LXX) 11.41; Sira. 8.5, 23.8, 34.5, 34.15; Targ. Mal. 2.8. Aquila: Ps. 63.9; Isa. 40.30, 63.13; Prov. 4.12, Dan. 11.35.

13. E.g., Koh. 11.9, Prov. 23.26, Num. 15.39.

14. Prov. 1.15, 3.26, 4.27.

15. Cf., however, Deut. 25.11–12, where a woman's hand is to be cut off as a punishment for an obscene act; cf. also B. Nid. 13b, B. Shab. 88b, neither of which contradicts this statement.

16. See Brown, Driver and Briggs, *Hebrew and English Lexicon of the Old Testament*, s.v. יד . For further use of "hand" in a sexual sense in the literature of the Near East, see M. Pope, *The Song of Songs* (Anchor Bible), on Cant. 5.4 (p. 517). Also Lachs, "Some Textual Observations," pp. 108–109.

# 24. On Divorce

## Matt. 5.31–32

31 "It was also said, 'Whoever divorces his wife, let him give her a certificate of divorce.' 32 but I say to you that every one who divorces his wife, except on the ground of unchastity, makes her an adulteress; and whoever marries a divorced woman commits adultery."

## Ibid. 19.9

"And I say to you: whoever divorces his wife, except for unchastity[1] and marries another, commits adultery."[m]

## Mark 10.11–12

11 And he said to them, "Whoever divorces his wife and marries another, commits adultery against her; 12 and if she divorces her husband and marries another, she commits adultery."

## Luke 16.18

"Everyone who divorces his wife and marries another commits adultery, and he who marries a woman divorced from her husband commits adultery."

---

l Some texts add *against her*, others add *makes her commit adultery*.

m Some texts add *and whoever marries a divorced woman commits adultery*.

COMMENTARY

Matt. 5.31–32 is stylistically different from the other antitheses, note the use of *errethē*, "it was said." It was presumably introduced because of the preceding antithesis on adultery. Allen sees it as "a special application to divorce, cf. Isa. 50.1; Jer. 3.8."[1] The text itself seems to have been altered. The original of this passage appears to be Luke 16.18, *Whoever divorces his wife and marries another commits adultery.* Cf. parallel Mark 10.12 and the preceding vv. in which Jesus explains his completely negative position on divorce to the Pharisees. *And Jesus answered them, 'For the hardness of your heart he wrote you this precept, But from the beginning of the creation God made them male and female. For this cause shall a man leave his father and his mother and cleave to his wife. And they two shall be one flesh so then they are no more two but one flesh. What God has joined together let no man put asunder.'*[2] By assuming that the phrase *except on grounds of unchastity* is a later addition, the passage is harmonized with the divorce passages in the other gospels which more accurately reflect the earlier view. Now the awkward phrase *and whoever marries a divorced woman commits adultery* is no longer a non-sequitur of the first part of the passage. It is unnecessary to delete the phrase (although lacking in several MSS) or to explain that it refers to any circumstance "save for adultery." Green is completely in error in stating, "A woman sent away by her husband would normally (unless it was still possible for her to return to her father's house) be forced to cohabit with another man or else starve. Jesus puts this responsibility for this situation squarely on the husband."[3] Green, obviously not aware of the socio-economic life of the Jews in the rabbinic period, has made his case on an inference from early biblical material. There is no Jewish source or parallel to this antithesis, since divorce is both prescribed in the Bible (Deut. 24 1 f., Jer. 3.8, Mal. 2.14–16) and continued as a legal remedy throughout the post-biblical period. Many, erroneously say that Jesus followed the Shammaitic view in regard to divorce. Not so. Manson is quite correct when he states that Jesus agrees with neither the School of Shammai nor with the School of Hillel about the matters of divorce.[4] The mishnah in question reads: "The School of Shammai says: 'A man may not divorce his wife unless he has found unchastity in her, for it is written, *Because he finds something obnoxious in her* [Deut. 24.1].' And the School of Hillel says: "He may divorce her even if she spoils a dish for him, for it is written, *Because he finds something obnoxious in her.*' R. Akiba says, 'Even if he found another more beautiful than she, for it is written, *she fails to please him* [ibid.].' "[5] Both schools interpret the phrase *ervat davar*, "something obnoxious," the former as adultery, the latter either as a general expression of something displeasing or odious, or this enigmatic phrase might mean that she does not please him sexually.

31 *It was also said . . . let him give her a certificate of divorce*   Referring to Deut. 24.1, but it is not a literal quotation.

*a certificate of divorce*   A written document, in the Bible *sefer keritut* (Deut.

24.1, Jer. 3.8); in rabbinic literature *get*. The laws of divorce are found in M. Gittin and the Talmud thereto.[6]

32 *except on ground of unchastity* Gr. *parektos logou porneias*, "a matter of unchastity," Heb. *devar ervah* (Deut. [LXX] 24.1).[7]

## NOTES

1. Allen, *Matt.*, p. 51.
2. Mark 10.5–9. For the Pauline view on divorce, see 1 Cor. 7.10 ff.
3. Green, *Matt.*, p. 83.
4. Manson, *SJ*, p. 440.
5. M. Git. 9.10, cf. B. ibid. 90a; also Matt. 19.9, Mark 10.11, Luke 16.18, 1 Cor. 7.10, 11.
6. For a discussion of this passage, see D. W. Amram, *Jewish Law of Divorce* (Philadelphia, 1886); G. D. Kilpatrick, *The Church and the Law of the Nullity of Marriage* (London, 1955), Appendix 7, pp. 61 ff.; Derrett, *LNT*, 363 ff., J. Dupont, *Mariage et divorce dans l'évangile* (Bruges, 1959); A. Isaksson, *Marriage and the Ministry in the New Temple* (Lund, 1965); V. N. Olsen, *The New Testament Logic on Divorce* (Tübingen, 1971).
7. The term *porneia* rather than the expected *morcheia* is the sin of a married woman. See Hos. 2.2 (4), 4(6); Amos 7.17; Sira 23.23. See IDB, s.v. "Divorce." Daube, *NTRJ*, pp. 71 ff.; Zeitlin, "The Pharisees and the Gospels," *Essays and Studies in Memory of Linda R. Miller* (New York, 1938), pp. 247–249.

# 25. On Swearing

## MATT. 5.33–37

33 "Again you have heard that it was said to the men of old, 'You shall not swear falsely, but shall perform to the Lord what you have sworn.' 34 But I say to you, Do not swear at all, either by heaven, for it is the throne of God, 35 or by the earth, for it is his footstool, or by Jerusalem, for it is the city of the great King. 36 And do not swear by your head, for you cannot make one hair white or black. 37 Let what you say be simply 'Yes' or 'No'; anything more than this comes from evil."[n]

n Or *the evil one*.

## COMMENTARY

Most commentators have difficulty with this antithesis, noting that there is a confusion between swearing and vows, particularly in v. 33b, "but shall perform to the Lord what you have sworn." They have, therefore, explained this phrase as an interpolation which disturbs the continuity of the passage.[1] Some see it as a mistaken translation from an Aramaic original. Neither is satisfactory. S. Lieberman[2] has shown that "vow," Heb. *neder*, and "oath," Heb. *shevu'ah*, were used interchangeably in the tannaitic literature: "Although there is a difference between *neder*, a vow, and *shevu'ah*, an oath, the differences are theoretical (M. Ned. II.2; Tos. *ibid.* I.5) an oath is a personal obligation to do or not to do something (swear I shall not do something, shall abstain from something) whereas a vow makes an item forbidden to the person (See TB.Ned. 2b, This shall be forbidden to me). The vow is a development of the original vow, *neder, votum,* when the man dedicated an object to God, which he could not subsequently enjoy anymore. In practice the people seem not to have discriminated between these two terms. In the Mishnah we read, 'if a man was under obligation of an oath to his fellow and the latter said to him, Vow by the life of thy head, vow is used here in the sense of swear.' "[3]

An earlier version of this passage in Matt., according to Manson, is James 5.12, *But above all, my brethren, do not swear either by heaven or by earth, or by any other oath, but let your yes be yes and your no be no, that you may not fall under condemnation.*[4]

33 *You shall not swear falsely*   No direct biblical source; the closest is Lev. 19.12, *And you shall not swear by My name falsely, so that you do not profane the name of your God.* This verse contains "swearing falsely" and "by the name of your God." This latter phrase is the key to the understanding of "by heaven, etc.," which are substitutes for the divine name in oaths (vows).[5]

*but shall perform to the Lord,* etc.   Cf. *If a man makes a vow to the Lord or takes an oath imposing an obligation on himself, he shall not break his pledge, he must carry out all that has crossed his lips.*[6] *When you vow a vow to God, defer not to pay it, for He has no pleasure in fools, pay that which you vow. Better is it that you should not vow than that you should vow and not pay.*[7]

34 *Do not swear at all*   The following are of the same genre:

"For I swear to you my children, but I will not swear by a single oath neither by heaven or by earth nor by anything made by God. God said, 'There is no swearing in Me nor injustice but truth.' If there is no truth in men let thou swear by a word yea yea, nay nay. But I swear to you yea yea."[8]

"Accustom not your mouth to swearing, neither use thyself to the naming of the Holy One."[9]

"To swear not at all is the best course and most profitable to life, well suited to a rational nature which has been taught to speak the truth so well on each occasion that its words are regarded as oaths; to swear truly is only, as people say, a second-best voyage, for the mere fact of his swearing casts suspicion on the trustworthiness of the man. Let him, then, lag and linger in the hope that by repeated postponement he may avoid the oath altogether."[10]

"The Holy One, blessed be He, said to Israel, 'Do not imagine that you are permitted to swear by My name even in truth . . .' "[11]

"Right or wrong, do not involve yourself in an oath."[12]

Although the rabbinic point of view, represented by these quotations, indicates that they wished to limit the oath and/or swearing, they did not as a matter of law prohibit it. The Essenes, on the other hand, were well known for their refusal to take an oath as being contrary to their belief.[13]

*neither by heaven*, etc. This refers to oaths and vows which do not contain the name of God but do contain substitutes; accepted formulas, "handles" (abbreviation of vows).[14] Note the following:

> . . . or if one should swear by earth, sun, stars, heaven, the whole universe . . .[15]

> I adjure you, O daughters of Jerusalem [Cant. 2.7]. By what did he adjure them? By heaven and earth.[16]

*it is the throne of God* Cf. Isa. 66.1, *the heaven is My throne, and the earth is My footstool.*[17]

35 *Jerusalem, for it is the city of the great king* Jerusalem as city of God, see Ps. 48.3, Ps. 47.3, Mal. (LXX) 1.14. Jews frequently used to swear by Jerusalem—"If one says Jerusalem or by Jerusalem . . ."[18]

36 *And do not swear by your head* The Heb. expression is *ḥayye roshkha*, lit., "by the life of your head." The Greek translator apparently shortened it for clarity.[19]

*you cannot make one hair white or black* No rabbinic parallels, but in a similar vein note the following: "R. Alexandri b. Haggai and R. Alexandri Karota said: 'If all the nations of the world should gather together to make white one wing of a raven they would not be able to accomplish it' "[20]

37 *Let what you say*, etc. "R. Huna said, 'The yeas of the righteous are a yea, their nos are a no!' "[21] "Let your no and your yes be correct [lit. righteous]."[22] It should be noted that yes and no in rabbinic literature could be regarded as an oath, for example: "R. Eleazar said, 'Yes is an oath, no is an oath.' Raba said, 'But only if he said no no twice or if he says yes yes twice,' "[23] (but this is not intended here).

## NOTES

1. Manson, *SJ*, p. 40, and others.
2. S. Lieberman, *Greek in Jewish Palestine* (New York, 1942), p. 117.
3. Cf. also TJ Ber. 5, 29a (bot.). We find the same meaning of *neder* in *Mek.* Exod. 13.2.
4. Manson, *SJ*, p. 451.
5. Cf. also Exod. 20.7; Deut. 5.11; Philo, *De Spec. Leg.* 1; *Mek.* Exod. 20.7; *PR* 22 (111a–112b); B. Ber. 33a.
6. Num. 30.3.
7. Koh. 5.3–4. Also cf. Deut. 23.2–3, Ps. 50.14. Cf. also Sifre, Deut. 265; T. Ḥul. 2.17 (p. 503); B.ibid. 2a; B. Ned. 9a; TJ ibid 1, 30d (38); Koh. R. 5.4; Lev. R. 37.
8. Slav. Enoch 49.1–2.
9. Sira 23.9–11.

10. Philo, *On the Decalogue* 17; On Philo's view of oaths, see S. Belkin *Philo and the Oral Law* (Cambridge, Mass., 1940), pp. 140–178.

11. Num. R. 22.1; *Tan.B.*, *Mattot; Tan.* ibid.

12. Lev. 6.3. Cf. also TJ Shev. 6.6, 37a. See *Bet Talmud*, 1:245 ff.; L. Ginzberg, *Eine unbekannte jüdische Sekte* p. 130 n. 3.

13. Cf. Josephus, *BJ* II.8.6 ff.

14. Cf. M. Ned. 1.1, TJ ibid. 2b. For a discussion of these substitutes, see Lieberman, loc. cit.

15. Philo, *De. Spec. Leg.* II.5. Cf. M. Shev. 4.13, where it is stated that to swear by heaven and earth is not an oath which is binding on witnesses. See above. M. Shev. 20.17; B. ibid. 35a; Cant. R. 4.2.

16. Cant. R. 2.7.

17. Two passages cited by McNeile, p. 68, are not applicable, Lam. 2.1 and Sifre Deut. 43, for they both refer to the "footstool" as God's Temple not the earth.

18. See T. Ned. 1.3 (p. 276); TJ ibid. 1, 37a (23); cf. M. Ket. 9.14. On the use of the prepositional prefixes and indiscriminately and the relationship between *eis* and *en* in *koine* Greek, see Lieberman, op. cit., p. 132 n. 129. Cf. TB Sanh. 36a; Lev. R. 18; Lam. R. 5.11; Sifre Deut. 32; TJ Sanh. 7, 25d (48); Gen. R. 39, 84; Cant. R. 1.3; *PR* 44 (101a); B. BM 49a; Sifra 18.6, 19.36; TB Shev. 36a; *Mek.* 20.1, *Mid. Prov.* 8.4; B. Meg. 32a.

19. Cf. M. Sanh. 3.12.

20. Lev. R. 19.2; Cant R. 5.8.

21. Ruth R. 3.18.

22. B. BM 49a; *DE* 5.1.

23. B. Shev. 36a.

# 26. *On Retaliation*

## MATT. 5.38–42

38 "You have heard that it was said, 'An eye for an eye and a tooth for a tooth.' 39 But I say to you, Do not resist one who is evil. But if anyone strikes you on the right cheek, turn to him the other also; 40 and if anyone would sue you and take your coat, let him have your cloak as well; 41 and if anyone forces you to go one mile, go with him two miles. 42 Give to him who begs from you, and do not refuse him who would borrow from you."

## LUKE 6.29–30

29 "To him who strikes you on the cheek, offer the other also; and from him who takes away your cloak do not withhold your coat as well. 30 Give to everyone who begs from you; and of him who takes away your goods, do not ask them again."

## COMMENTARY

38 *An eye for an eye* Exod. 21.25, Lev. 24.19 ff., Deut. 19.21. The antithesis of this law is contained in Matt. 39b, 40, and 42, and paralleled by Luke 2.29 ff. Luke 6.25 omits *eye for an eye* and reads only *and to him that smites you on one cheek offer also the other*. By the time of Jesus the *lex talionis* was no

longer practiced and the biblical text was interpreted to mean that a money payment was to be paid to the injured party, as prescribed by the then current law. The comment that the Pharisees were against, and the Sadducees for, the *lex talionis* is found only in the scholion of *Megillat Ta'anit*, composed at the end of the amoraic period. Zeitlin argues that there never was such a controversy between them.[1] As to Josephus, *Ant.* IV.8.3–5 280, which seems to contradict Zeitlin's contention, Daube points out that this is from Roman law, not Jewish.[2] "The Pharisees avoided the talion by legal fiction (cf. BQ 81–83b) making it impossible for the plaintiff to demand an eye for an eye and not to assist any evil by repaying evil."[3] He goes on to say, "From the choice of this example it is evident that he meant to pronounce immoral not the law concerning mutilation but that concerning insult. A man should be meek under insult, this was his teaching, and not to insist on such redress as the maxim an eye for an eye would give him which was such a sum of money for this kind of insult such a sum for another kind."[4]

The rabbinic interpretation of the biblical law is, "If a man wound his fellow man, he thereby becomes liable on five counts: for injury, for pain, for healing, for loss of time, and for indignity afflicted."[5] During this entire period it remained a private wrong, and it was up to the injured party whether or not he would press his claim and demand judgment in the form of a money payment. Jesus advises against exercising this prerogative and suggests taking a position described by the Rabbis as "passing over one's rights" or "He who is yielding, who ignores a slight or a wrong, has all his sins forgiven."[6]

*one who is evil* Gr. *tō ponērō.* The Heb. perhaps *rasha,* "the culprit, the instigator of the wrong." Allen translates "resist not the malicious," others, "the evil one."[7]

*if anyone strikes you*, etc. The subject here seems to be the insult (shame), not the physical injury."[8]

*strike you* A slap, which was considered more insulting than a punch. "If a man cuffed his fellow-man he must pay him a *sela* [four *zuz*]. R. Judah says in the name of R. Jose the Galilean. 'One hundred *zuz*.' If he slapped him he must pay two hundred *zuz*. If he struck him with the back of his hand he must pay him four hundred *zuz*."[9]

39 *right cheek* Luke omits "right." An appealing explanation of "right cheek" is that "with a right handed assailant the first blow would normally be on the left cheek of the victim. What is probably meant is a buffet with the back of the hand."[10] Jeremias suggests that the allusion here is to the insult offered one adjudicated to be a heretic.[11] Also note: "If you are struck you must forgive the offender even though he does not ask for your forgiveness";[12] and "My God, unto those who curse me may my soul be dumb, yea, may my soul be dust unto all.[13]

40 *if anyone would sue you* Here it is clearly a legal action in tort or contract which is described; in Luke it is a matter of robbery. The difference

is further reflected in the reversal of the order of the garments. In Luke, which deals with robbery, the thief takes the outer garment, Gr. *himation*, and the victim is to give him his coat, Gr. *chiton*, as well; and in Matthew, which involves a civil court case, the coat is claimed and the cloak is to be proffered. Jesus, in the Matthean version, says that if he demands your coat do not refute his claim and give him your cloak also, which according to Deut. 24.10–17, he cannot legally take and retain.[14]

*coat*  Gr. *chitōn*, Heb. *kutonet*, Aram. *ketunta*.[15]

*cloak*  Gr. *himation*, Heb. *beged, salmah, simlah*, rabbinic, *tallit.*[16]

**41** *if anyone forces you*  Gr. *aggareusei*, Vulgate *angariaverit*, a term of Persian origin used for the mounted messengers of the Persian kings.[17] In the NT (Matt. 27.23-Mark 15.1), any impressed service. In rabbinic literature it appears as a noun, *angaria*, e.g., "I was impressed into service to carry myrtles,"[18] "The donkey was seized for public services."[19] Manson's understanding of this passage is sensible: "It is natural to suppose that Matt. 1.41 is concerned with the situation which would arise if a Jewish civilian is impressed as baggage-carrier by a Roman soldier of the army of occupation. If the victim is a follower of Jesus, he will give double what is demanded. The first mile renders to Caesar the things that are Caesar's, the second mile, by meeting oppression with kindness, renders to God the things that are God's."[20]

*mile*  Gr. *milion*, Lat. *milium*, Heb. *mil*. Frequently as a measure of distance in rabbinic literature.[21]

**42** *Give to him who begs from you*  As part of the originial antithesis or even as an addition to it, this verse is difficult. Both Matthew and Luke agree on the reading of the first half, i.e., *Give to him* (Luke: *everyone*) *that begs from you*, which probably means even though you might not be repaid. It could conceivably refer to requests for loans just before the Sabbatical Year, when all loans were automatically canceled (see below to Matt. 6.12). The second part can be understood simply as part of a Semitic parallelism to "give him"—"do not refuse." Manson, on the basis of the Lucan reading, suggests that "when someone has borrowed your property, do not be constantly dunning him to let you have it back. In all these transactions delicacy and consideration of the feelings of the other man are essential."[12] He cites Sira 20.15, "Today he lendeth, tomorrow he will demand it back; hateful is such a one."[23]

## NOTES

1. Zeitlin, "The Pharisees and the Gospels." pp. 235–236.
2. Daube, *NTRJ*, p. 255.
3. Ibid., p. 257.
4. Ibid.
5. M. BQ 8.1; T. ibid. 1.1 ff. (p. 363); B. ibid. 83a ff; 84a; Sifre, Deut. 190; M. Mak. 1.1; B. ibid. 5b; *Mek.* Exod. 21.23.

6. B. Yom. 23a. On avoiding the talion, *lifnim mishurat hadin* or *leha'avir al midotav*, see B. Ta'an. 25b; B. Meg. 28a; B. BQ 92b; Gen. R. 45, 93; B. Shab. 88b; B. Ber. 17a; *Mid. Ps.* 56.1 (147). On the *lex talionis*, see Zeitlin, op. cit., pp. 240–247.

7. See below to Matt. 6.13 (p. 122).

8. See B. Sanh. 58b, B. BM 59b; M. BQ 8.7; T. ibid. 9.29 (p. 336); Sifra, Lev. 24.19.

9. M. BQ 8.6.

10. Manson, *SJ*, p. 343. Another explanation, see *Expos. T.*, January 1914, p. 89.

11. Jeremias, *Sermon on the Mount*, p. 27.

12. T. BQ 9.29 (p. 366).

13. Singer, *APB*, pp. 5, 119, 142, 166.

14. See Schlatter ad loc. Cf. also Exod. 22.25–26, Amos. 2.8.

15. E.g., B. Shab. 140b.

16. E.g., Exod. 22.25, *Mek.* ad loc., B. BM 114b; TJ ibid. 9, 12b (20).

17. Cf. Herodotus VIII.9.8, Xen. *Cyp.* VIII.VI.17; Josephus, *Ant.* XIII.11 uses it of animals impressed into service by the government. On this verb see Adolph Deissmann, *Biblical Studies* (Edinburgh, 1903), pp. 88 ff.

18. TJ Ber. 1, 2d (bot.).

19. M. BM 6.3, B. ibid, 78a. Cf. Lev. R. 12.23; *PR* 21 (99b); *Mid. Ps.* 112 (234b); B. Sanh. 96a, 101b; B. Yom. 67a.

20. Manson, *SJ*, p. 160.

21. E.g., M. BM 6.3, 4; T. ibid. 4 (3).13 (p. 188).

22. Manson, *SJ*, pp. 343–44.

23. Albright-Mann, p. 69, emend the text unnecessarily to *toneme thelonta* and argue that *daziein* means to lend on interest and then translate, "and do not refuse one who is unable to pay interest." Cf. also Luke 6.35, "and lend never despairing," which fits the structure of the Sabbatical Year and the remission of debts (Deut. 15.7–11).

# 27. On Love of One's Enemies

## MATT. 5.43–48

43 "You have heard that it was said, 'You shall love your neighbor and hate your enemy.' 44 But I say to you, Love your enemies and pray for those who persecute you, 45 so that you may be sons of your Father who is in heaven; for he makes his sun rise on the evil and on the good, and sends rain on the just and on the unjust. 46 For if you love those who love you, what reward have you? Do not even the tax collectors do the same? 47 And if you salute only your brethren, what more are you doing than others? Do not even the Gentiles do the same? 48 You, therefore, must be perfect, as your heavenly Father is perfect."

## LUKE 6.27–28, 32–36

27 "But I say to you that hear, Love your enemies, do good to those who hate you, 28 bless those who curse you, pray for those who abuse you. 32 If you love those who love you, what credit is that to you? For even sinners love those who love them. 33 And if you do good to those who do good to you, what credit is that to you? For even sinners do the same. 34 And if you lend to those from whom you hope to receive, what credit is that to you? Even sinners lend to sinners, to receive as much again. 35

But love your enemies, and do good and lend, expecting nothing in return;ᵒ and your reward will be great, and you will be sons of the Most High; for he is kind to the ungrateful and the selfish. 36 Be merciful, even as your Father is merciful."

---

o Some texts *despairing of no man*.

## COMMENTARY

43 *You shall love your neighbor*   Lev. 19.18, where the verse does not have a universal meaning. Note that it is parallel there to *the sons of your people*. Furthermore, the same chapter has the command that *you shall love the stranger*.[1] In rabbinic literature, in the haggadah, universal application prevails. In halakhic exegesis, however, Heb. *re'a*, "neighbor," is used in a narrow restrictive sense to exclude the non-Jew.[2] The statement that this is the greatest principle in the Torah is echoed throughout the literature.[3]

> When you might have revenge do not repay either your neighbor or your enemy.[4]

> Rabbi Simeon ben Eleazar says: "Under solemn oath was this pronounced, *but thou shalt love thy neighbor as thyself*; 'for I the Lord have created him [cf. Isa. 45.8]. If thou lovest him, I am faithful to reward thee in goodly measure; but if not, I am judge to punish.' "[5]

> R. Ḥanina, the deputy high priest, said of neighborly love that it is a thing on which the whole world depends. This command was given with an oath at Mount Sinai, "If thou hate thy neighbor who is as bad as thyself, I will exact payment from thee. If thou love thy neighbor who is as good as thyself, I will have mercy on thee."[6]

*and hate your enemy*   This part of the verse is nowhere to be found in the Bible. The closest to it would be Ps. 139.21, where hatred is directed against God's enemies, not those of the psalmist, *Do I not hate them, O Lord, that hate Thee? And do I not strive with those who rise up against Thee? I hate them with utmost hatred; I count them mine enemies*. Allen suggests that this "is an inference from the distinction drawn in the OT between the conduct towards Israelites and conduct towards Gentiles."[7] Green sees this as "the typically Semitic opposite of love . . . hate (meaning in effect to love A more than B *cf.* 6.24) accurately conveys its original scope through the O.T. (despite Ps. 26.5; 139.21) contains no explicit parallel to the language."[8] He has, however, overlooked Deut. 21.15[9] In the Qumran literature there is a command "to love all the sons of light and hate all the sons of darkness" (1QS 1.9, v. p. 72, cf. 9.2 of v. p. 80), but Matthew's gloss more probably reflects the sense in which Lev. 19.18 was regularly taken by his Jewish contemporaries (i.e., the Tradition).[10] Allen is correct that the background is Lev. 19.18, but his inference that the phrase *hate your enemy* was part of that interpretation is not supported by the tradition. The only passage which condones hatred of enemies in rabbinic literature and which cites verses from the psalm cited above is the following:

> What is meant by "and the hatred of mankind"? [cf. M. Avot 2.16]. This teaches that no man should think of saying, "Love the Sages but hate the disciples," or "Love the disciples but hate the *am ha-arez.*" On the contrary, love all of these, but hate the sectarians, apostates, and the informers. And so David said: *Do I not hate them, O Lord, that hate Thee? And do I not strive with those that rise up against Thee? I hate them with utmost hatred, I count them mine enemies* [Ps. 139.21–22].[11]

Is it possible that *and hate your enemies* was added by a Judeo-Christian aware of this attitude and some similar teaching directed against the new sect?

44  *love your enemies*   It has been suggested that this a midrash on "and you shall love your neighbor as yourself," reading *ra'akha*, "your enemy." This is unlikely since *ra* ("enemy") is not used in Heb. in the singular, substantively as a noun. Nowhere in biblical or rabbinic Judaism is one called upon to transcend human nature and to love one's enemies. This does not, however, preclude positive moral actions toward those who are your enemies. Typical of this position are: *When you encounter your enemy's ox or ass wandering, you must take it back to him. When you see the ass of your enemy prostrate under its burden and would refrain from raising it, you must nevertheless raise it with him.*[12] *If your enemy be hungry give him bread to eat, and if he be thirsty give him water to drink.*[13] *Do not say I will requite evil; wait for the Lord and He will save you.*[14] [You shall see] *your brother's ass or his ox fallen by the way* [Deut. 22.4]. From this I know only about your brother, Whence do I know about your enemy's ox? Scriptures states *the ox of your enemy* [Exod. 23.4–5]. Why then does it say *your brother?* This teaches that the Torah speaks against man's evil inclination."[15]

*pray for those who persecute you*   "There were once some lawless men in the neighborhood of R. Meir who caused him a great deal of trouble. R. Meir accordingly prayed that they should die. His wife Beruria said to him, 'How do you justify that such a prayer be permitted? Because it is written, "let *ḥaṭṭa'im* cease"? Is it written, *ḥoṭ'im* [sinners]? It is written, *ḥaṭṭa'im* [sins]. Further, look at the end of the verse *and let the wicked be no more*. Since sins will cease there will be no more wicked men. Rather pray for them that they should repent, and these will be no more wicked.' He did pray for them and they repented."[16]

45  *sons of your father*, etc.   Unique in NT, but see: Deut. 14.1, *You are sons of the Lord your God*. "Be as a father unto the fatherless and instead of a husband unto their mother, so shalt thou be as the son of the Most High, and He shall love thee more than thy mother doth."[17]

*he makes his sun to rise*, etc.   In most passages sun and rain are sent by virtue of the righteous; some passages speak of sending rain to be merciful to the wicked.[18] There are no direct parallels, but the following is instructive:

Alexander of Macedon marched away to another province named Africa [Africa Propria of the Romans, cf. Jastrow]. . . . as they were sitting, two men came before the king for judgment.

One said, "Your Majesty! I bought a carob tree from this man and in scooping it out I found a treasure therein, so I said to him, 'Take your treasure, for I bought the carob tree, not the treasure.' " The other argued, 'Just as you are afraid of risking punishment for robbery so am I. When I effected the sale I sold you the carob tree and all that is therein. The king called one of them and said to him: 'Have you a son?' 'Yes,' he replied. He called the other and asked him, 'Have you a daughter?' 'Yes,' he replied. 'Go,' said the king to them, 'and let them get married to one another and let them both enjoy the treasure.' Alexander of Macedon began to show surprise. 'Why,' the king asked him, 'are you surprised? Have I not judged well?' 'Yes,' he assured him. 'If this case had arisen in your country,' he asked him, 'what would have been done?' He replied, 'We should have removed this man's head and that one's and the treasure would have gone to the king.' 'Does the sun,' he asked Alexander, 'shine in your country?' 'Yes,' he answered. 'And does rain fall in your country?' 'Yes,' he answered. 'Perhaps,' said the other, 'there are small cattle in your country?' 'Yes,' he said. He exclaimed, 'O woe to that man! It is because of the merit of the small cattle that the sun shines upon you and the rain falls upon you. For the sake of the small cattle you are saved."[19]

46 *tax collectors*   Gr. *telōnai*, Heb. *mokhsin*. Often used as an example of the despised of society because of their oppressive and cruel activity. More than likely they were Jews employed by the government. The tax collector is coupled here and in Matt. 18.17 with the Gentiles; they are connected also with sinners, 9.10 and with harlots, 21.31 ff. Luke 6.32 reads *sinners* for both tax collectors and Gentiles. It is clear that they have been chosen to represent examples of the antithesis of correct behavior. In rabbinic literature, too, the tax collector is a person rejected and despised.[20]

47 *And if you salute*, etc.   Great importance was attached to the greeting of one's fellowman, and being the first to offer the greeting was considered praiseworthy. "R. Ḥelbo said in the name of R. Huna: 'If one knows that his fellow is used to greet him, greet him first, for it is said, *seek peace and pursue it* [Ps. 34.15].' " It is likewise praiseworthy to initiate this greeting to all regardless of difference in social status: ". . . and one should always strive to be on the best terms with his brethren, and his relatives and with all men and even with the heathen in the street, in order that he may be beloved and well-liked below and be acceptable to his fellow creatures. It was related of R. Joḥanan b. Zakkai that no man ever gave him greeting first, even a heathen in the street."[22]

*Gentiles*   Gr. *ethnikoi*. The term occurs only five times in the NT, three in Matt. (5.47, 6.7, 18.17), once in Gal. (2.14), and once in 3 John (7). It has been variously translated as "gentiles," "pagans," and "heathens." This is strange, since Matthew, when referring to the non-Jewish world, would always employ *ethnos*.[23] It is likewise significant that Jerome, when translating the Matthean passages where *ethnikoi* appears, renders it by *ethnici*, while in Gal. 2.14 and in 3 John 7, he translated it by *gentibus*. Presumably Jerome realized that *ethnikoi* was not employed by Matthew as a general term for the non-Jew, rather it designated a specific group within the Jewish people. Here in Matt. 5.47 and in 18.17 *ethnikoi* are coupled with the tax collector or the tax farmer, who represent the antithesis of correct behavior. Matthew also emphasizes that the faithful should do more than the Scribes and the Pharisees, whom he calls the hypocrites, a favorite epithet for this group.[24] Presumably all of these are Jews, i.e., the tax collectors, the Scribes, the Pharisees, and the *ethnikoi*. Furthermore, the *adelphoi* of Matt. 5.47 means "one's fellow disciples"; those who act properly and in conformity with religious principles, while the *ethnikoi* are those who do not observe the religious traditions of the people. We suggest that the term *ethnikoi* refers to the *am ha-arez*, lit. "the people of the land." Originally it meant only the farming population. Subsequently it came to connote those who were lax in the taking of the tithe from the produce of the field, thus causing the unsuspecting purchaser to eat untithed food and thereby to violate a biblical law. Finally, *am ha-arez* became a term for the ignoramus, the unlettered, and the boor. It is of interest and perhaps of significance that there is a parallel development in the word "pagan." Originally he was one who came from the *pagus*, a rustic, but later it came to mean the superstitious and from that the idolater. The same is true of the word "heathen," one from the heath, hence a countryman, a peasant, a rustic, which took on the meaning of an illiterate. In support of our identification of the *ethnikoi* with the *am ha-arez*, note that Justinian employed *ethnikos* to designate the "provincial."[25] The *am-ha-arez* was looked down upon by all members of the Pharisaic community and was charged with many counts of reprehensible behavior. The *adelphos* as a member of the group of disciples is perhaps a translation of *haver*, which would be a perfect parallel to *am-ha-arez*.[26]

48 *you, therefore, must be perfect*, etc. Luke 6.36, *merciful*, Gr. *oiktirmon*, which is preferable, since in the NT "merciful" is regularly used of God, rarely of men.[27] It is therefore more appropriate to a passage enjoining the imitation of God than "perfect," which is always used of men, never of God.[28]

This verse is the rabbinic expression of the principle of *imitatio dei*, "just as He is, so should you [strive] to be."[29]

## NOTES

1. Lev. 19.34.
2. Cf. *Mek.* Exod. 21.14, 22.8; Sifre Deut. 112, 266. On this verse see Abrahams, *Studies II*, pp. 206–220; Montefiore, *RLGT*, pp. 59–104; Friedländer, *Sermon*, pp. 69–75; idem, *The Law of Love in the Old and New Testaments* (1909).

3. Sifra, Lev. 19.18, TJ Ned. 9, 41c (31).
4. Slav. Enoch 50.1–4.
5. *ARN* 1.16.
6. *ARN II*, 26.
7. Allen, *Matt.*, p. 55.
8. Green, *Matt.*, p. 86.
9. M. Smith, "Mt. 5.43 Hate Thine Enemy," *HTR* 45 (1952): 75 ff., thinks that there may have been a targum to this effect.
10. Green, loc. cit.
11. *ARN* 1.16.
12. Exod. 23.4–5, Deut. 22.4.
13. Prov. 25.21.
14. Ibid.
15. Sifre Deut. 22; cf. B. BM 32b; T. ibid. 2.26 (p. 275); Sifre Deut. 225.
16. B. Ber. 10a; and parallels. Cf. also B. San 37a; *Mid. Ps.* 41.8 (131a).
17. Sira 4.10.
18. B. Sanh. 95a, B. Ḥul. 91b; Gen. R. 68; Targ. Koh. 11.3.
19. B. Tamid 32a–b; Lev. R. 27.1; *Tan. B. Emor* 9 (44b) and parallels.
20. M. BQ 10.2, B. ibid. 113a, B. Sanh. 25b, Shev. 39a. On the tax collector see Schürer, *GJV*, 1:478 ff.; IDB, s.v. "tax collector"; Jeremias, "Zöllner und Sünder," *ZNW* 30 (1931): 292–300; Lachs, "John the Baptist and His Audience," *Gratz College Annual of Jewish Studies* 4 (1975); idem, "Studies in the Semitic Background," 203, 206.
21. Cf. B. Ber. 6b.
22. Ibid. 17a. For other passages on greetings, see *SB* ad loc.
23. Cf. 10.5, 18.20, 19.25.
24. 15.7; 23.13, 15, 23, 25, 27, 29.
25. *Cod. Just.* 12.63, 2.6.
26. On the *am ha-areẓ* see above to Matt. 5. and Lachs, "Studies in the Semitic Background," 203, 206.
27. On *raḥum*, as a name of God, see Dalman, *Words*, p. 204.
28. See of Noah, Gen. 6.9; cf. Job 1.1.
29. Cf. Gen. R. 46; B. Ned. 32a; *Tan B.* Gen. (40a); TJ Meg. 4.10, 75c (14); Targ. J. I Lev. 22.18.

## 28. *On Almsgiving*

### MATT. 6.1–4

1 "Beware of practicing your piety[p] before men in order to be seen by them; for then you will have no reward from your Father who is in heaven. 2. Thus, when you give alms, sound no trumpet before you, as the hypocrites do in the synagogues and in the streets, that they may be praised by men. Truly, I say to you, they have their reward. 3 But when you give alms, do not let your left hand know what your right hand is doing, 4 so that your alms may be in secret; and your Father who sees in secret will reward you."[q]

---

p Some texts *charity*.
q Some texts add *openly*.

## COMMENTARY

At the beginning of this chapter three duties are listed: almsgiving, prayer, and fasting. This triad appears in the statement, "R. Eleazar said: Three things annul the severe decree and these are they: prayer, charity, and repentance."[1]

1 *piety* Gr. *dikaiosunē*, which in Hebrew is *ẓedaqah*, an act of righteousness involving the giving of money; best given in secret, *matan beseter*. There is a plethora of materials on *ẓedaqah* but only those which emphasize the giving in secret are relevant.[2]

2 *Thus, when you give alms, sound no trumpet before you.* The knotty problem here in this verse is the phrase *sound no trumpet before you.* Nowhere in rabbinic literature is there even one statement connecting the sounding of the trumpet with the giving of *ẓedaqah.* Cyril of Alexandria and others simply assumed that it was a Jewish custom to summon the poor to receive their *ẓedaqah* by sounding the trumpet.[3] This simply is not the case. It is also not feasible to accept the suggestion, long advocated, that it is to be understood metaphorically,[4] for this metaphorical use of trumpet is found neither in Greek nor in Hebrew nor in Aramaic. It is equally unconvincing to cite *foedae bucina famae* in order to explain *trumpet* here in Matthew.[5] A. Büchler suggested that the sounding of the trumpet was an allusion to the public fasts which were accompanied by the sounding of trumpets when prayers for rain were recited outside in the streets.[6] There is unfortunately a flaw in this suggestion. The giving of *ẓedaqah*, it is true, is sometimes connected with the recitation of prayers and with the ensuring efficacy of fasting,[7] and the blowing of trumpets is connected with the observance of fasts,[8] but these two observations do not connect the giving of *ẓedaqah* with the blowing of the trumpet in the context of the Matthean statement. The problem can be solved if we assume that the origin of the passage was either Hebrew or Aramaic. In Hebrew it would read *al ta'aviru shofar lifnekhem* and in Aramaic *la ta'avrun shufra qadmekhon.* In the Bible *shofar* is always a wind instrument, a horn, or a trumpet, and the verbs employed with *shofar* are either *litqo'a*, "to blow," or *leha'avir*, "to cause to pass"; an example of the latter is Lev. 25.9, *then shall you send abroad the proud trumpet on the tenth day of the seventh month, on the Day of Atonement shall you send abroad the trumpet throughout all your land.* In rabbinic literature the primary meaning of *shofar* remained "a horn" but it took on yet another meaning. The Mishnah states that there were thirteen *shofarot* in the Temple.[9] Here *shofar* is a term for a container shaped in the form of a horn, hence its name, narrow at the top and wide at the bottom, and it was used as a receptacle for money given for various charitable purposes. This shape was apparently chosen to prevent the unscrupulous from taking out instead of putting in a donation.[10] But it was not only in the Temple that this *shofar* container was to be found. After the destruction of the

Temple it was used outside of the Temple precincts, and we know that it was portable.[11] We suggest that it was in this sense that the trumpet *(shofar)* is to be understood in this Matthean verse. We further suggest that the verb employed in the original was *leha'avir*, "to cause to pass." The meaning, therefore, of the phrase is, "don't cause the *shofar* [*zedaqah* box] to be passed before you," similar to the modern expression "to pass the [collection] plate." The translator thought not of this rabbinic usage of *shofar* but of a *shofar* as a wind instrument, hence a trumpet. The passing of the *zedaqah* box was considered an ostentatious show of charity and Jesus decried this practice. He advised instead that the *zedaqah* be given in secret, hidden from public view.[12] Understanding *shofar* as a *zedaqah* box also helps in the understanding of "*hypocrite*." What is hypocritical about sounding a trumpet? It is vulgar and ostentatious but not hypocritical. The hypocrite in Greek usage was an actor and a showman. If one pretended to drop money into the *zedaqah* box or claimed that he gave more than he actually did, then this would fit the role of the hypocrite and make other explanations of the term superfluous.[13]

The following are illustrative passages on giving *zedaqah* in secret.

> He who gives *zedaqah* in secret is greater than Moses.[14]

> *God will bring every work into judgment, with every secret thing whether it be good or whether it be evil* [Koh. 12.14]. What is the meaning of *whether it be good or evil?* R. Yannai said: "It is he who gives money to the poor publicly!" For R. Yannai once saw a man give money to a poor man publicly. He said: "It had been better that you gave him nothing than you should have given him and put him to shame."[15]

> There were two vestries in the Temple, one called the Vestry of the Secret Ones, the other the Vestry of the Utensils. In the former the sin-fearing men used to put their gifts secretly, and the poor of gentle birth were supported from them secretly.[16]

> Just as there was a Vestry of Secret Givers in the Temple, so was there one in every city, for the sake of respectable people who had come down in life, so that they might be helped in secret.[17]

*hypocrites* An epithet especially favored by Matt. in describing the Pharisees.[18] "The accusation of hypocrisy should not be pressed theologically. In the first place it is the accusation which the Christian congregation of Matthew's time has taken over from a time of embittered struggle in which the Jews were known only as fanatical enemies. Thus Haenchen: 'Here all is at stake; and so arise those black and white colours which can no longer see any good in the enemy (p. 59). In such situations it is generally found that the enemy is accused of hypocrisy. Thus for Did. 8.1 the heretics are called hypocrites. The same applies to the gnostic heretics in I Tim. 4.2 and Josephus denoted his enemies by the same term (Bell, 2.587). For Judaism Christians were generally styled as the hypocrites (Gen. R. 48) Cf. A.

Schlatter, *Die Kirche Jerusalems von Jahr 70–130*, 1898, p. 20. The accusation of hypocrisy must not on that account be dismissed. Matthew is able to make so much more room for it here because it suits his major concern. It should also not be exaggerated.' "[19]

This explanation is appealing, but one must not accept the passage from Gen. R. as necessarily referring to Christians, since *minut* could refer to all sorts of sectarianism and/or heresies. What is more important is that the word *minut* can mean, in addition to "hypocrisy," and more often did mean, "godlessness" or "faithlessness."

*they have their reward.* "For they who give, hoping to receive a requital such as praise or honor and seeking for a return of the favor which they are conferring under the specious name of a gift are really making a bargain."[20]

**4** *in secret* Some MSS add, after "you," "openly." Note the following passages where secret acts are destined to come to light, especially meritorious acts which will receive public recognition and/or reward.

> You call in secret and I answer you and thunder at the whole world for your sake.[21]

> R. Meir says: "A man transgresses in secret and the Holy One, blessed be He, proclaims it against him in public, as it is said, *And the spirit of jealousy comes upon him* [Num. 5.14], *and comes upon* means publicizes, as it is written, *So Moses gave command and the word was proclaimed throughout the camp* [Exod. 3.6]."[22]

> R. Johanan ben Beroqah said: "Whoever profanes the Name of Heaven in secret will suffer for it in public, and this whether the Heavenly Name be profaned in ignorance or in willfulness."[23]

*and your Father who sees in secret* "Concerning the suspected adulteress [*sota*] it is said, *She does it in secret*, but He who sits in the secret place, the Most High, looks on her."[24]

## NOTES

1. Koh. R. 5.6. Cf. B. RH 16b. Repentance is often equated with and symbolized by fasting; cf. 1 Kgs 21.27; Joel 2.12; Jonah 3.5; Neh. 9.1. See also Sira 7.8–10, "Be not faint-hearted when you make your prayer and neglect not to give alms."

2. See *SB*, 1: 387 ff. Cf. Prov. (LXX) 10.2; Tob. 4.10, 12.8–9, 14.11 ff.; Sira 16.14; Deut. (LXX) 4.24.

3. Cyril, cited by McNeile, *Matt.*, p. 74.

4. E.g., Chrysostom, *Homily XIX* on Matt. 6.1

5. Juvenal, *Satire* XIV. 152.

6. A. Büchler, 'St. Matthew VI. 1–6 and other Allied Passages," *JTS* 26 (1909): 266–270.

7. Cf. B. Sanh. 35a; TJ Ta'an. 2.6; B. Ber. 6b.

8. See M. Ta'an. 2.5 et al.

9. M. Sheq. 5.1.

10. TJ Sheq. 6.1 49a (12f); Bartinoro to M. Sheq., loc. cit.

11. Cf. B. Git. 60b. Rashi ad loc.; cf. also B. Er. 32a.

12. On this interpretation of *shofar*, see Lachs, "Some Observations on the Semitic Background," pp. 103–105.

13. Cf. Albright-Mann, Appendix to pt. IX of Introduction, pp. 115 ff.; D. E. Garland *The Intention of Matthew 23* (Leiden, 1979), pp. 91 ff. On the hypocrite in rabbinic literature, see B. Yom. 86a; B. Sot. 42a, *DE* 1 (beg.); Koh. R. 4.11, 5.5.

14. B. BB 9b.

15. Koh. R. 12.14; cf. B. Ḥag. 5a.

16. M. Sheq. 5.6. Further on the Vestry of the Secret Ones, see T. Pe'a 4.19–21 (p. 24), B. Suk. 49b; B. Men. 17a; B. Ḥag. 5a, B. Ket. 67b, also the Test. Zeb. 4.6–7, Test. Iss. 38.1.

17. T. Sheq. 2.16 (p. 177).

18. Matt. 6.5, 16; 7.5; 15.7; 16.3, 22, 18; 23.13–15, 23, 25, 27, 29; 24.51.

19. G. Bornkamm, G. Barth and H. J. Held, *Tradition and Interpretation in Matthew* (Philadelphia, 1963), pp. 61–62.

20. Philo, *On Cherubim* 34. See Gen. R. 44.1; 33.3; Num. R. 10; B. Sanh. 70a, 101a; Lev. R. 27; *Mid. Ps.* 103 (p. 218b); B. Er. 65a; Koh. R. 9.7.

21. *Mek.* Exod. 19.2.

22. B. Sot. 3a.

23. M. Avot 4.5.

24. B. Sot. 9a. On acts in secret and reward given openly, see B. Ber. 15b; B. Sanh. 92a.

## 29.   On Prayer

### MATT. 6.5–8

5 "And when you pray, you must not be like the hypocrites; for they love to stand and pray in the synagogues and at the street corners, that they may be seen by men. Truly, I say to you, they have their reward. 6 But when you pray, go into your room and shut the door and pray to your Father who is in secret; and your Father who sees in secret will reward your[r] 7 And in praying do not heap up empty phrases as the Gentiles do; for they think that they will be heard for their many words. 8 Do not be like them, for your Father knows what you need before you ask him."

---

r   Some texts add *openly*.

### COMMENTARY

5 *the hypocrites*   See above to Matt. 6.2 (p. 113).

*they love to stand and pray*   The standing posture was the required position when reciting the prayer par excellence, the *Shemoneh Esreh*, which is also called the *Amidah*, i.e., the prayer recited while standing.[1]

*in the synagogues and at the street corners*   The usual place for communal prayer was the synagogue. On fast-days prayers were recited outside in the open. Individuals also prayed wherever they happened to be when the time of prayer was at hand, whether at work, while traveling, or under other conditions.[2]

*that they may be seen by men*  It is doubtful that the point here is of one standing either in the synagogue or on the street corner as an individual worshiper but rather of one who seeks to be the *sheliah zibbur*, the precentor, who in leading the congregation in prayer is in a position of prominence and is seen by all assembled.

6 *go into your room*  Cf. Luke 12.3; Matt. 10.27. The Gr. *tamieion* is used for a room without windows and which can be locked, a closet, a room which provides maximum privacy, also used of a storeroom. Cf. Isa. (LXX 26.20). For praying inside a room, cf. Dan. 6.11, *When Daniel knew that the document had been signed, he went to his house where he had windows in his upper chamber toward Jerusalem, and he got down upon his knees three times a day and prayed and gave thanks before his God, as he had done previously.* It is of some interest that this verse is cited in the Talmud as a proof for the statement that one should always pray in a house which has windows.[3] Is it possible that this is a polemic against the NT passage, which advises against public exposure in prayer and suggests the *tameion* as the proper place for worship? The rabbinic equivalent for *tamieion* may well be *hadar hadarim*, lit. "room of rooms."[4]

7 *do not heap up empty phrases*  Gr. *battalogein*. The meaning of this term is obscure.[5] The sense of the verse is to avoid verbosity and/or repetitions; either is possible. The following should be noted:

> Repeat not thy words in prayer. Be not rash with thy mouth and let not thy heart be hasty to utter anything before God, for God is in heaven and you are upon the earth, therefore, let your words be few.[6]

> The righteous has only to say one word and it is accepted by God, and therefore it was not necessary for him [Moses] to pray long.[7]

> God said to Moses, "My children are in distress and you are making long prayers!"[8]

*Gentiles*  Gr. *ethnikoi*. See above to Matt. 5.47 (pp. 109ff). There is no indication that the Gentiles were more verbose or repetitious in prayer than the Jews. The *ethnikoi* were the *am ha-arez*, the ignorant, who because of their ignorance, think "that they will be heard for their many words."

## NOTES

1. On this posture in prayer see Luke 18.11; B. Ber. 10b, 26b; TJ ibid. 4.1, 7a (58); B. Ber. 30a; M. Ber. 4.5; *Mid Ps.* 4.9 (p. 23b); Targ. J. Num. 10.35; Targ. Esther 4.1; T. Ber. 3.5 (p. 6).
2. McNeile, *Matt.*, ad loc. is in error when he said, "For the picture of praying in the street there is no Jewish evidence except on the occasion of public fast." Against this note *inter alia* B. Ber. 3a, B. Meg. 26a.
3. B. Ber. 31a.
4. M. BB 4.1, B. Shab. 64b. See also ibid. 146a; B. Bez. 9a; B. AZ 12a; also Test. Joseph 3.
5. Green, *Matt.*, p. 89. Except for those writers dependent on Matthew the term is

unknown earlier than Simplicius (ca. 530). Among the suggestions as to the origin and meaning of the term are the following: (1) It is connected with *baparizein*, Lev. (LXX) 5.4, meaning "to speak thoughtlessly." Cf. Heb. נבטא. (2) A fanciful derivation from Bapos, a Lybian king who stammered. (3) Perhaps connected with the Aramaic *b-ṭ-l*, "idle" or "useless," hence "babble." (4) Onomatopoeic for "babble." (5) Related to *battalos*, "gabbler," the nickname bestowed on Demosthenes for his astonishing fluency.

6. Sira 7.14; B. Ber. 61a.

7. Sifre Num. 105.

8. *Mek.* Exod. 15.25. Other passages on brevity in prayer, B. Ber. 34a, 5b, 61a; B. Shab. 10a; M. Yom. 5.1; B. ibid. 53b; B. Sot. 37a; T. Ber. 3.5(6) (p. 6); TJ Ber. 4, 7b (62); TJ Ta'an 4, 67c (11); *Mid. Sam.* (pp. 25b, 26b); TJ RH 2, 58b (7); for examples of tannaitic prayers, see B. Ber. 32b–54b; TJ Ber. 1, 8d (52).

# 30. *The Lord's Prayer*

## MATT. 6.9–15

9 "Pray then like this:

> Our Father who are in heaven,
> Hallowed be thy name.
> 10Thy kingdom come,
> Thy will be done,
> On earth as it is in heaven.
> 11Give us this day our daily bread;[s]
> 12And forgive us our debts,
> As we also have forgiven our debtors;
> 13And lead us not into temptation,
> But deliver us from evil.[t,u]

14 For if you forgive men their trespasses, your heavenly Father also will forgive you; 15 but if you do not forgive men their trepasses,[v] neither will your Father forgive your trespasses."

## LUKE 11.2–4

2 And he said to them, "When you pray, say: Father, hallowed be thy name. Thy kingdom come. 3 Give us each day our daily bread[s] 4 and forgive us our sins, for we ourselves forgive everyone who is indebted to us; and lead us not into temptation."

## MARK 11.25

25 "And whenever you stand praying, forgive, if you have anything against anyone; so that your Father also who is in heaven may forgive you your trespasses."[w]

---

s Or *our bread for the morrow.*

t Or *the evil one.*

u Some texts add *for thine is the kingdom and the power and the glory, forever, Amen.*
v Some texts omit *their trespasses.*
w Some texts add v. 26, *But if you do not forgive, neither will your Father who is in heaven forgive your trespasses.*

## COMMENTARY

The Lord's Prayer exists in two versions, a shorter one in Luke 11.2–4 and a longer one in Matt. 6.9–13. The Lucan version is probably closer to the original, but both texts were undoubtedly influenced by liturgical use. As to the model or prototype for the Lord's Prayer, most scholars look to the *Shemoneh Esreh*, or prayer of the Eighteen Benedictions, which forms the basis of each Jewish worship service.[1] Others, fewer in number, see the prototype in the *Kaddish*, a doxology used frequently in the synagogal service.[2] Neither of these theories is satisfactory, and both are highly tenuous. It is appealing at first blush to see the Lord's Prayer as a miniature *Shemoneh Esreh*. Both were to be recited three times daily by the faithful.[3] Furthermore, the structure of the *Shemoneh Esreh* is tripartite, consisting of three benedictions of praise, twelve (thirteen) benedictions of petition, and three concluding benedictions of thanksgiving. One can easily discern the same tripartite division in the Matthean version of the *Paternoster*. Most New Testament scholars recognize that the *Paternoster* in its original form goes back to earlier times and is not the invention of the evangelists. The *Shemoneh Esreh*, however, emerges as the prayer par excellence only at the *end* of the first Christian century during the patriarchate of Rabban Gamaliel II.[4] Furthermore, the Lord's Prayer is so scant, that to see in it a mini–*Shemoneh Esreh* is imaginative. Finally, the observation of the tripartite division fails, since in the best MSS of the NT the last line, i.e., a liturgical ending of the Lord's Prayer, is lacking.[5]

The *Kaddish*, too, fails as a model for the Lord's Prayer, for the similarity of a few phrases is hardly enough to warrant this hypothesis.[6]

The key to the understanding of the Lord's Prayer is its simplicity and its brevity, as evidenced by the warning against verbosity and repetitions in prayer which precedes it in Matt. 6.7–8 (note also the substance of v. 8 in 5.32). It belongs to a genre of prayer called in Hebrew *tephillah qezarah*, "short prayer," which, in tannaitic sources, designated a prayer to be recited in a place of danger.[7] Unlike the *Shemoneh Esreh*, which is a set liturgical form, the "short prayer" has individuality and variety. The following are several examples of the genre.

> Rabbi Joshua says: "He who is traveling in a place of danger should pray a short prayer, saying, 'Save, O Lord, the remnant of Your people at every crossroad [others: whenever they transgress], let their needs be before You. Blessed are You who hears prayer.' "[8]

If one is traveling in a place of danger or of robbers, he should pray a short prayer. What is a short prayer? Rabbi Eleazar says: "Perform Your will in heaven and bestow satisfaction on earth upon those who revere You, and do that which is good in Your sight. Blessed are You who hears prayer."[9]

Rabbi Eleazar bar Ẓadok says: "Hear the sound of the cry of Your people Israel and speedily grant their petition. Blessed are You who hears prayer."[10]

9 *Pray then like this*    This advice, a Matthean addition, indicates that the *Paternoster* is to be a paradigm for prayer, not the prayer itself. The thrust is that one should pray briefly and with similar content.[11]

*Our father who art in heaven*    Heb. *avinu shebashamayim*. In the NT only here in Matt., in Mark 11.25, and in Luke 11.13[12] God as father appears in the NT,[13] and in the apocryphal sources;[14] and in rabbinic literature, often in dicta and prayers.[15]

*hallowed be thy name*    Considered by some as paralleling the third blessing of the *Shemoneh Esreh;*[16] by others as the opening formula of the *Kaddish*, "Let Thy great name be magnified and hallowed,"[17] and by others as a blessing *(berakhah)* for His acts already performed.[18]

10 *Thy kingdom come*    The mention of "kingdom," Heb. *malkhut*, Aram. *malkhuta*, is an essential part of a benediction (prayer): "Any benediction in which there is no [mention of] *malkhut* is no benediction."[19]

*Thy will be done*, etc.    This phrase appears in "short prayers."[20] For example, "Do Thy will in heaven above and give rest of spirit to them that fear beneath. May it be Thy will, O Lord our God, to establish peace in the upper family and in the lower family."[21] "If a man sanctifies himself below, they [God] sanctify him above."[22]

11 *daily bread*    Gr. *epiousios*, a rare word, and in the NT it is a hapax legomenon. Outside of the Lord's Prayer it has also remained a problem.[23] Suggestions as to its meaning are numerous. E. Nestle, for example, has listed thirteen, and others have augmented this list.[24] Modern translators render *epiousios* either as "daily" (bread) or (bread) "sufficient for tomorrow."[25] Even the ancients were confused as to its meaning. Origen stated that as an adjective it was rare in his day and that in his opinion it was invented by the evangelists.[26] Jerome apparently was not sure of the meaning and has left us perplexing translations: Matt. 6.11 reads *panum nostrum supersubstantialem da nobis hodie*, while in Luke 11.2 we find *panem nostrum quotidianum da nobis hodie*. Even more confusing is his statement that he found in the *Gospel According to the Hebrews* the word *maḥar*, "tomorrow," in this Matthean passage—*panem nostrum crastinum id est futurum*, which gives preference to "sufficient for tomorrow."[27] This third alternative of Jerome raises the problem of a contradiction between this meaning, i.e., "bread of tomorrow," and the warning to those of little faith: *therefore do not be anxious saying, What shall we eat? . . . therefore do not be anxious about tomorrow, for tomorrow will be*

*anxious for itself. Let the day's own trouble be sufficient for the day* (Matt. 6.31–34). Jerome, recognizing this contradiction, cleverly offers an eschatological explanation, *panem quem daturus es nobis in regno tuo.*[28]

The meaning of *epiousios* here can be established by examining one of the "short prayers" discussed above. "Others say [that a short prayer is], 'The needs of your people are many but they are impatient [others: Rashi, B. Ber. 29b; 'but they do not know how to express their wishes'], may it be Your will, O Lord, that You fulfill everyone's needs and supply each person's want. Blessed are You who hears prayer.' "[29] In this passage the two terms *zarakhav*, "his needs," and *dē maḥsarav*, "enough for that which he lacks," represent the idea behind *epiousios*, and the phrase *dē maḥsarav*, supplies the linguistic evidence. We suggest that the original reading of which *epiousios* is a translation was *dē maḥsarenu*, "sufficient for what we lack" (for our needs).[30] This expression is also biblical and connects sufficiency with need: *but you shall open your hand to him, and lend him sufficient for his need, whatever it may be.*[31]

The temporal translations of *epiousios* can be explained if we assume that *dē maḥsorenu* was the original reading. It is possible that a confusion arose between *dē maḥsarenu*, "sufficient for our needs," and *dē maḥarenu*, "sufficient for our tomorrow." This explanation holds as well in understanding Jerome's reading *maḥar*; it was probably a mistaken reading for *maḥsor* in that the letter *sameq* dropped out in transcription. In this way, by positing a Heb. original, one can account for the two categories of explanation for *epiousios*, "sufficiency" and "temporality."

Many maintain that the primary and true meaning of *epiousios* is not "sufficient for our needs" but "sufficient for tomorrow," and even seek to avoid the contradiction mentioned above by stating that "tomorrow" means the ensuing day, i.e., the same day on which the prayer is recited, in the evening and/or in the morning. This explanation is difficult on several counts. If, in fact, the Lord's Prayer was patterned after the *Shemoneh Esreh*, then the times of its recitation were also influenced by the times of the recitation of this latter prayer. If the ensuing day is meant, then the most important time of its recitation must be the evening, when the day begins according to Jewish usage. This is highly unlikely, first because we have no evidence that the *Shemoneh Esreh* was indeed recited by Jews at the time of Jesus (see above n. 4). Some, it is true, maintain that it is much older, going back to the time of the "Men of the Great Synagogue." This fanciful exaggeration was intended to give to the *Shemoneh Esreh* an established antiquity so that it might be more readily accepted by the masses. Of the three times daily that the *Shemoneh Esreh* was to be recited, certainly by 90 C.E. the one time which was the subject of a long, protracted discussion and controversy was the evening recitation (cf. B. Ber 27b). Furthermore, if the meaning "the ensuing day" were correct, we have a difficulty arising from a Christian source. At a very early period the *Paternoster* was used liturgically by the church. The *Didache* VIII, 2.3 presents the Lord's Prayer as a substitute for "praying as the hypocrites," and it was to be recited three times daily. If "ensuing day" is meant, i.e, the same day on which the prayer is recited, the afternoon recitation would present no small difficulty.[32]

12 *And forgive us our debts, as we also have forgiven our debtors* In Luke 11.4: *and forgive us our sins, for we ourselves forgive every one who is indebted to us.* The difference between the two versions is easily explained by the fact that Luke spoke to a Gentile audience and his phrase *forgive us our sins* would have been more readily understood by them. The original was undoubtedly the Aram. word *ḥova*, "debt," "obligation", "sin," or "guilt."[33] Matthew uses only the notion of debt in both parts of the verse, i.e., *forgive us our debts*, and *as we also have forgiven our debtors*. Luke, when referring to man's relationship to God, uses "sins," and to fellowman, "those who owe us something" in the second clause. The basis of the petition is that because we forgive the debts owed to us, may God forgive the obligations we owe Him or the sins for which we have incurred guilt before Him.

There is, however, a fundamental question which one must ask: Does a man normally forgive debts owed to him? The answer is no. The giving of charity is one thing, extending of a loan another. In the former, the donor does not look forward to repayment; in the latter, he expects the return of the loan. "If you have borrowed, you have borrowed to repay."[34] Since the charging of interest was forbidden, the loan itself was regarded as an act of kindness, but the lender did expect repayment.[35] What, then, would have been the circumstances under which the creditor would forgive a debt and that act be considered the fulfillment of a religious duty and meritorious? The answer to this question can be found in the pentateuchal law of the Seventh Year. *At the end of every seven years you shall grant a release. And this is the manner of the release: every creditor shall release what he has lent to his neighbor, he shall not exact it of his neighbor, his brother, because the Lord's release has been proclaimed.*[36] The background of the NT verse therefore can well be the law of release of the Seventh Year. As the pious individual observes "the Lord's release" of the debts owed to him, so may God forgive the individual his debts owed Him.

This argument can be carried even further by placing it in the historical setting of NT times. During the early rabbinic period the law of release was modified, primarily by Hillel the Elder. He instituted the *prosbul*, a "declaration" or "application" before the court. This was a legal fiction whereby a creditor could collect his debt at any time, even after the seventh year.[37] The formula of the *prosbul* went as follows: "I declare before you, judges in this place, that I shall collect my debt that I have outstanding with . . . whenever I desire."[38] The *prosbul* protected the creditor from losing his loan: first, when the creditor received a note which he did not deposit with the court, second, when the loan was transacted without witnesses.[39] The motivation, however, behind this enactment was to protect the needy, for if the lender could not collect his loan because of the automatic release of the law of the seventh year, he would be loath to lend money to anyone during the sixth year. To ensure the uninterrupted flow of money, especially in the sixth year, the *prosbul* was introduced.

In light of this legal fiction one can reconstruct the background of this passage even more precisely. The author might well have rejected the concept of the *prosbul*, seeing in it only the recovery of the loan by the creditor and ignoring the original intent which was to help those in need of assistance. He appears to argue that although lenders in his day had the option to recover their loans despite the pentateuchal laws of release through the application of the *prosbul*, he eschews this option and advocates the remission of debts according to the law of the Torah. In opting to forgive these debts, he calls upon God to do the same.[40]

13 *Lead us not into temptation*, etc. Reminiscent of the prayer: "Blessed is He who causes the bands of sleep to fall upon my eyes and slumber on my eyelids, and gives light to the apple of the eye. May it be Thy will, O Lord my God, to make me lie down in peace, and set my portion in Thy Law, and accustom me to the performance of religious duties, but do not accustom me to transgression, and bring me not into sin, or into iniquity, or into temptation, or into contempt. And may the good inclination have sway over me. And deliver me from evil hap and sore diseases, and let not evil dreams and evil thoughts disturb me, and may my couch be flawless before Thee, and enlighten mine eyes lest I sleep the sleep of death. Blessed are Thou, O Lord, who givest light to the whole world in Thy glory."[41] Note also: "Rab Judah said in the name of Rav: 'One should never [intentionally] bring himself to the test, since David King of Israel did so and fell.' "[42]

*Deliver us from evil* In light of the prayer just cited it is probable that this refers to the evil inclination, the propensity to sin possessed by each individual, according to the rabbinic definition of man. It is significant that in some MSS the text reads "from the evil [one]," which refers to Satan, who is in reality the externalization by the Rabbis of the *yezer hara*, the evil inclination, which is internal in man.[43]

*For thine is the kingdom . . . Amen* This liturgical conclusion to the Lord's Prayer is missing in the best MSS of the NT. It apparently goes back to 1 Chron. 29.11, *Thine, O Lord, is the greatness and the power, the glory and the victory, and the majesty; for all that is in the heavens and in the earth is Thine; Thine is the kingdom, O Lord, and Thou art exalted and head above all.* Cf. also Ps. 145.11, *They shall speak of the glory of Thy kingdom and tell of Thy power.*[44]

14 *For if you forgive men their trespasses*, etc. Verses 14–15 are significantly missing in Luke. They were probably added in Matthew as a marginal note to 12b, which the Gr. *gar* ("for") connects. It is important to note that it is "trespasses," not "debts," as above. The form of these verses, i.e., the positive and negative presentation, is typically Hebraic. Similar dicta in Jewish sources are:

He who takes vengeance shall find vengeance from the Lord.[45]

As you withhold mercy, so they [God] withhold mercy from you.[46]

Even though a man pays [him that suffers indignity], it is not forgiven him [by God] until he seeks forgiveness from him, for it is written, *Now, therefore, restore the man's wife . . . and he shall pray for you.*[47]

Forgive your neighbor the hurt that he has done to you, so shall your sins also be forgiven when you pray.[48]

## NOTES

1. On the Lord's Prayer as a reshaped *Shemoneh Esreh*, see Davies, *SSM*, pp. 309 ff. On the interpretation of the Lord's Prayer, see C. F. Evans, *The Lord's Prayer* (London, 1963); Jeremias, *PJ*, p. 82; E. Lohmeyer, *The Lord's Prayer*, (Eng. trans., London, 1965), R. E. Brown, "The Paternoster as an Eschatological Prayer," *NT Essays* pp. 217 ff. J. J. Petuchowski and M. Brocke, eds., *The Lord's Prayer and the Jewish Liturgy* (New York, 1978).

2. McNeile, *,Matt.*, p. 77; Montefiore, *RLGT*, pp. 127, 129, 132.

3. M. Ber. 12. 13. On the three-times-a-day recitation of the Lord's Prayer, see *Didache* 8.3.

4. B. Ber. 28b, "Our Rabbis taught: Simeon ha-Paquli arranged the eighteen benedictions before Rabban Gamaliel in Yavne."

5. McNeile, Matt., p. 82.

6. Cf. Montefiore, *RLGT*, pp. 127, 129, 133.

7. See L. Ginzberg, *A Commentary on the Palestinian Talmud*, vol. 3 [Hebrew] (New York, 1941), p. 355. Lachs, "Epiousios: Another Suggestion," *Jewish Civilization: Essays and Studies II* (Philadelphia, 1978), pp. 65–71. On the nature of the *tefillah qezarah* and its possible relationship to *me'ain shemoneh esreh*, see S. Lieberman, *Tosefta Kifshuta, Seder Zeraim*, I (New York, 1955), p. 33.

8. M. Ber. 4.4.

9. T. Ber. 3.2 (pp. 5–6).

10. Ibid.

11. See *Didache* 8.

12. Jeremias, *PJ*, pp. 32 ff., suggests that the Lucan *Abba* was the original. See H. F. D. Sparks in *Studies in the Gospels*, ed. D. Nineham (Oxford, 1955).

13. E.g., Isa. 63.16; Mal. 1.6, 2.10.

14. E.g., Tob. 13.4; 3 Macc 5.7; Jub. 1.25; Sira 23.1, 4; Wisd. 2.16.

15. E.g., *Mek.* to Exod. 15.2; M. Sot. 9.5; M. Yom. 8.9; M. Avot 5.22.

16. See Friedlander, *Sermon*, p. 134.

17. See Ezek. 38.23, 31.4 Singer, *APB*, p. 30.

18. See Luke 1.47–49. Also Ps. 111.9; Isa. 29.23; 1 Cor. 16.22; Rev. 22.20; B. Ber. 3a; Sifre Deut. 306; Zunz, *GV*, p. 385.

19. B. Ber. 40b. Cf. also Asmp. Moses 10.1; M. Cant. R. 2.13; Targ. Isa. 31.4, 40.9; Targ. Zech. 14.9; TJ Ber. 9, 12d (30). On the kingdom of God, see Friedlander, *Sermon*, pp. 38–141.

20. E.g., TJ Ber. 4, 7a (48); B. Ber. 29b. On "short prayers," see above p. 118f.

21. B. Ber. 17a.

22. B. Yom. 39a.

23. It appears in three late MSS of 1 Macc. 1.8 after *tous artous*. It is also to be found in a fifth-cent. papyrus (Sammelbuch 5224.20), cf. *JTS* 35 (1934): 377, but its

meaning there is not clear. See B. M. Metzger, "How Many Times Does Epiousios Occur Outside the Lord's Prayer?" *Expos. T.* 69, no. 2 (November 1957).

24. E. Nestle, "Epiousios in Hebrew and Aramaic," *Expos. T.* 21, no. 43. Cf. also McNeile, *Matt.*, pp. 79–80.

25. Suggested Greek etymologies are mostly forced, see McNeile, *Matt.*, pp. 79–80, and the following note.

26. *De Orat.* 27.7. He derives it from *epi* and *ousia*, meaning "essential." So too Peshitta and Arabic. Cf. Prov. (LXX) 30.8. but *epi* and *ousia* are unlikely.

27. Jerome, *Commentary to Matthew*. Cf. also Prov. (LXX) 27.1.

28. Jerome, loc. cit. This eschatological explanation of the elements of the Lord's Prayer is held by many modern scholars. see J. Jeremias, "The Lord's Prayer in Modern Research," *Expos. T.* 71, no. 5 (February 1960).

29. T. Ber. 3.11 (pp. 6–7).

30. Need and sufficiency are connected, see next note.

31. Deut. 15.18. Black, *Aramaic Approach*, p. 150, commented, "But even if this abstract meaning of the Greek adjective could be conceded, the two ideas 'our sufficient bread' and 'our needful bread,' however closely associated, are by no means equivalent, and *epiousios* cannot be made to mean 'sufficient.' " In light of *dē maḥsaro* this comment must be discounted.

32. For a criticism of Black's reconstruction of this verse from the Aramaic, see Lachs, "Epiousios", pp. 68–69.

33. For *ḥova* as debt, see Targ. J. Deut. 19.15; as sin or guilt, see Targ. Gen. 20.9; TJ Ḥag. 2.2 77d (47); TJ Sanh. 6.9 23c (35). Note the similar double meaning of *Schuld* in German.

34. Cf. *DEZ* 3: "If you have borrowed, you have borrowed to repay."

35. Cf. Ps. 37.21 and M. Avot 2.9.

36. Deut. 15.1–2. It is noteworthy that the LXX reads "that which he has lent," paralleling *tois opheiletais* of Matt.

37. M. Shev. 10.2, M. Git. 4.3.

38. M. Shev., loc. cit.

39. Zeitlin, "Prosbul, A Study in Tannaitic Jurisprudence," *JQR* 37 (1947): 347–348.

40. On this suggestion see S. T. Lachs, "On Matthew VI.12," *NT* 17 (1975): 6–8.

41. B. Ber. 60b.

42. B. Sanh. 107a. Cf. Exod. R. 31, B. Men. 99b.

43. Cf. B. Ber. 16b, 17b; B. Ḥag. 16a; B. BB 16a.

44. Cf. B. Ber. 58a; Num. R. 18; TJ Ber. 9.5, 14c (10); B. Sot. 40b; Sifre Deut. 31; Gen. R. 98. On the doxology, see Davies, *SSM*, pp. 451 ff.

45. Sira 28.1.

46. *Mid. Tan.* 15.11 p. 85.

47. M. BQ 8.7.

48. Sira 28.2.

# 31. On Fasting

## MATT. 6.16–18

16 "And when you fast, do not look dismal, like the hypocrites, for they disfigure their faces that their fasting may be seen by men. Truly, I say to you, they have their reward. 17 But when you fast, anoint your head and wash your face, 18 that your fasting may not be seen by men but by your Father who is in secret; and your Father who sees in secret will reward you."

## COMMENTARY

This third antithesis is on religious observance. Fasting is a part of Jewish ritual, Yom Kippur, the Day of Atonement, and the days commemorating national disasters.[1] The Jews also held public fasts in times of emergency, especially in times of drought.[2] There were also private fasts observed by individuals, cf. Luke 18.12, Mark 2.18. These private fasts were customarily observed on Mondays and Thursdays,[3] but not exclusively.

The verse here deals with private fasts, and the observant is advised not to publicize the fact of his fasting. It is interesting that this probably was not directed to the disciples, for they were not known to engage in fasting, compared to the disciples of John the Baptist, who were given to regular fasting.[4] Except for the Day of Atonement, prior to the destruction of the Second Temple, only food was forbidden on fast-days, not liquids.[5]

16 *they disfigure their faces* Friedländer sees this in Test. Zeb. 8.6, "make the face unsightly," and cites Test. Joseph 3.4, "And I fasted in those seven years, and I appeared to the Egyptians as one living delicately. For they that fast for God's sake receive beauty of face."[6]

*anoint your head.* Anointing was not ordinarily practiced in time of mourning or fasting.[7]

*who is in secret* Probably should be deleted as a dittography of this phrase at the end of the verse.

## NOTES

1. Not New Years, as Manson, *TJ*, p. 171.
2. On the fasts see Moore, *Judaism*, 2:55–69.
3. Cf. *Didache* 8.11, where the advice is given to fast on Wednesdays and Fridays, not as the hypocrites who fast on Mondays and Thursdays. On these private fasts see Moore, op. cit., 2:257–266; Abrahams, *Studies I*, pp. 121–128; SB, Excursus "Fasting."
4. See below p. 168f.
5. Cf. B. Yom. 73b, TJ Ta'an. 1.4 (64b); Friedlander, *Sermon* p. 120.
6. See Friedlander *Sermon* p. 121.
7. See 2 Sam. 12.20; cf. Ps. 23.5, TJ Shab. 9, 12a (56), M. Yom. 8.1, TJ Ta'an. 1, 64c (42).

# 32. *On Treasures*

## MATT. 6.19–21

19 "Do not lay up for yourselves treasures on earth, where moth and rust[x] consume and where thieves break in and steal, 20 but lay up for yourselves treasures in heaven, where neither moth nor rust[x] consumes and where thieves do not break in and steal. 21 For where your treasure is, there will your heart be also."

## LUKE 12.33-34

33 "Sell your possessions and give alms; provide yourselves with purses that do not grow old, with a treasure in the heavens that does not fail, where no thief approaches and no moth destroys. 34 For where your treasure is, there will your heart be also."

---

x Or *worm*

## COMMENTARY

19 *Do not lay up for yourselves treasures on earth*   "It is not a question of contrasting earthly with heavenly treasure, but where the treasure is stored."[1] Wealth given away is wealth stored away; it actually ensures its existence. This idea is best illustrated in the following passages:

> As thy substance is, give alms of it according to thine abundance; if thou hast much, according to the abundance thereof give alms, if thou hast little bestow it, and be not afraid to give alms according to that little, for thou layest up a good treasure for thyself against the day of necessity because alms delivereth from death and suffereth not to come unto darkness.[2]

> Do righteousness, My sons upon earth, that you may have treasure in heaven.[3]

> Monobaz arose and distributed all his treasure to the poor in a year of famine. His brothers sent to him and said, "Your fathers gathered treasures and added to those of their fathers, and you have dispersed yours and theirs." He said to them, "My fathers gathered treasures for below, I have gathered treasures for above. . . . they stored treasures in a place over which the hand of man can rule but I have stored treasures in a place over which the hand of man cannot rule. . . . my fathers collected treasures which bear no fruit [interest]. I have gathered treasures which do bear fruit. . . . my fathers gathered treasures of money [mammon], I have gathered treasures in souls . . . my fathers gathered treasures for others, I have gathered treasures for myself . . . my fathers gathered treasure in this world, I have gathered treasures for the world to come."[4]

> Is there not a proverb current in Jerusalem: The salt [the safeguard] of money is diminution? Others read "benevolence."[5]

> For thou hast treasures of works laid up with the Most High.[6]

*moth . . . rust*   Reminiscent of *and I will banish the 'devourer'* [Heb. *okhel*] *from you so that they will not destroy the yield of your soil;*[7] and *For the moth shall eat them up like a garment, the worm* [Heb. *ash*] *shall eat them up like wool.*[8]

## NOTES

1. Jeremias, *PJ*, p. 202n.
2. Tob. 4.8.
3. Test. Levi 13.5.

4. T. Pe'ah 4.18 (p. 24); TJ ibid 1.1, 15b (53); B. BB 11a; *PR* 25 (126b). Monobaz was converted to Judaism ca. 36 c.e.

5. The difference is only in one Hebrew letter, either ḥaser, "diminish," or ḥesed, "kindness." B. Ket. 66b.

6. Cf. 2 Bar. 14.12; 4 Ezra 7.77, 8.33 (8.36); Apoc. Bar. 24.1; Slav. En. 50.5; I En. 38.12.

7. Mal. 3.11.

8. Isa. (LXX) 51.8. Cf. Zimmermann, *Aramaic Origin of the Four Gospels*, p. 71, who would translate "as a weevil." In Greek *ses* is "a bookworm." Cf. Gospel of Thomas 76: "worm/mice." Green, p. 92, notes: "the saying presupposes (cf. v. 26 & Luke 12.13 ff) Palestinian conditions with the storing of goods in kind in barns (cf. v. 26 & Luke 12.13 ff.) not money in coin."

## 33. *The Sound Eye*

### M A T T .  6 . 2 2 – 2 3

22 "The eye is the lamp of the body. So if your eye is sound, your whole body will be full of light; 23 but if your eye is not sound, your whole body will be full of darkness. If then the light in you is darkness, how great is the darkness!"

### L U K E  1 1 . 3 4 – 3 6

34 "Your eye is the lamp of your body; when your eye is sound, your whole body is full of light; but when it is not sound, your body is full of darkness. 35 Therefore be careful lest the light in you be darkness. 36 If then your whole body is full of light, having no part dark, it will be wholly bright, as when a lamp, with its rays gives you light."

### COMMENTARY

This section is best understood in relationship to the performance of acts of mercy, kindness, and generosity noted in Matt. 6.19–21.[1] The key to its understanding is the meaning of the "sound eye" and its opposite, "the unsound eye." This translation tends to obscure its real meaning. It should be understood against the background of the Heb. idioms for "generosity" and "niggardliness," i.e., lit. *aiyin tovah*, "the good eye," and *aiyin ra'ah*, "the evil eye." One who gives with or who possesses a "good eye" is generous in his acts and thoughts."[2] There is by no means unanimity among scholars as to the meaning of this passage. Manson, for example, rejects the idea of the eye representing generosity and states: "As this is a parable based on physical facts, the description of the fact must not be mixed up with other consider- ations. It is not relevant to the interpretation of the saying that 'a good eye' is used in Jewish teaching as a synonym for a generous disposition and 'an evil eye' for a covetous disposition. We are not here concerned with the business of the moralist, but with that of the oculist. The saying then comes to this: The lamp of the body is the eye (or your lamp is your eye). If your eye is healthy you yourself will see. If your eye is diseased you yourself will be blind."[3]

There are several passages in the MT where the eye connotes generosity or lack thereof.

> Beware that . . . thine eye be evil against thy poor brother, and thou give him naught.[4]

> his eye shall be evil against his brother . . . her eye shall be evil against her husband of her bosom, etc.[5]

> Eat not the bread of him that has an evil eye.[6]

> He that hath an evil eye hastens after riches.[7]

In the intertestamental literature note the following:

> An evil eye is grudging of bread and he is miserly at his table.[8]

> I never slandered anyone, nor did I censure the life of any man, walking as I did in singleness of eye.[9]

> For the good man hath not a dark eye; for he showeth mercy to all men, even though they be sinners. And though they devise with evil intent considering him, by doing good he overcometh evil, being shielded by God, and he loveth the righteous as his own soul. If anyone is glorified, he envieth him not; if anyone is enriched, he is not jealous; if anyone is valiant he praiseth him, the virtuous man he laudeth, on the poor man he hath mercy, on the weak he hath compassion; unto God he singeth praise.[10]

In the NT note Matt. 20.15, where "eye" is used for the envious; Mark 7.22, the evil eye is listed with theft, covetousness, wickedness, lasciviousness, blasphemy, pride, and foolishness.

In rabbinic literature, the following are illustrative:

> A good eye and a humble spirit and a lowly soul, they in whom are these are of the disciples of Abraham our father.[11]

> He who is willing to give but not that others should give, his eye is evil toward the others [i.e., he wishes to have a monopoly on liberality for himself].[12]

> R. Joshua said: "The evil eye and the evil nature and the hatred of mankind put a man out of the world."[13]

*Your whole body*   Dalman suggests that body is a translation of an Aram. expression meaning "you yourself."[14]

## NOTES

1. See Jeremias, *PJ*, p. 163.
2. See Jülicher, *Gleichnisreden Jesu*, pp. 98 ff.; W. Brandt, "Der Spruch von lumen

internum: exegetische Studie," *ZNW* 44 (1913): 97–116, 177–201, esp. 189 ff.; H. J. Cadbury, "The Single Eye," *HTR* 45 (1954): 69–74.

3. Manson, *SJ*, p. 385.
4. Deut. 15.9.
5. Ibid. 28.54–56.
6. Prov. 23.6.
7. Ibid. 28.22.
8. Sira 14.10.
9. Test. Iss. 3.4; cf. ibid. 4.6.
10. Test. Benj. 4.2–4.
11. M. Avot. 5.19.
12. Ibid. 5.15, cf. Exod. R. 31.
13. Ibid. 2.11.
14. Dalman, *Gramm.* p. 115; Zimmermann, *Aramaic Origin of the Four Gospels*, p. 36, would read Heb. *nefesh* for Gr. *soma*; cf. Prov. 20.27.

## 34. On Serving Two Masters

### MATT. 6.24

"No one can serve two masters; for either he will hate the one and love the other, or he will be devoted to the one and despise the other. You cannot serve God and mammon."

### LUKE 16.13

"No servant can serve two masters; for either he will hate the one and love the other, or he will be devoted to the one and despise the other. You cannot serve God and mammon."

### COMMENTARY

**24** *No one can serve two masters*, etc.   Note Luke 16.13 has "servant," missing in Matt. If the background of this parabolic statement involved a slave who is owned by two masters who are partners or by two brothers, then the following are relevant:

One who is half slave and half free man (as when the slave belonged to two partners and one of them manumitted him) as well as a slave belonging to two partners does not go out free for the mutilation of the principal limbs.[1]

If a man was half slave, he should work one day for his master and one day for himself. So the School of Hillel. The School of Shammai said to them: "You have ordered it well for the master, but you have not ordered it well for him, [thus] he cannot marry a woman slave since he is a half-freed man, and he cannot marry a freed woman since he is half slave. May he never marry? And was not the world created only for fruition and increases, as it is written, *He created it not as waste, He formed it to be inhabited* [Isa. 45.18]. But as a precaution for the general good they should compel his master to set him free, and the slave writes him a bond of indebtedness for half of his value." The School of Hillel changed their opinion and taught according to the opinion of the School of Shammai.[2]

*hate . . . love*   Used as opposites, see Deut. 21.15–17, Exod. R. 51. See above p. 107.

*mammon*   A word of uncertain origin, but surely Semitic, used regularly in both Heb. and Aram. Its meaning is "wealth, money, profit, or property." It occurs in the NT here and in Luke 16.9, 11, 13.[3]

*You cannot serve God and mammon*   There is no rabbinic parallel, but the idea is expressed in the Testament of Judah: "Beware, therefore, my children of fornication and the love of money . . . for these things blind you from the law of God . . . for he is a slave to two contrary passions, and cannot obey God, because they have blinded his soul and he walks in the day as in the night."[4]

## NOTES

1. B. Qid. 90a. On the mutilation of the principal limbs, cf. Exod. 21.26, B Qid. 25a.
2. M. Git. 4.5, M. Eduy. 1.13.
3. Cf. also Sira 31.8, 2 En. 63.10, M. Avot 2.12. On *mammon* see *IDB*, s.v. *mammon*; A. M. Honeyman, "The Etymology of Mammon," *Archivum Linguisticum* IV, fasc. 1 (1953), pp. 60–65. Jeremias, *PJ*, pp. 31–36.
4. 18.1 ff. In Greek sources see Plato, *Republic* VIII.555c: "It is impossible for the citizens of a state to honor wealth, and at the same time acquire a proper amount of temperance; because they cannot avoid neglecting either the one or the other"; Persius, *Sat.* V. 154 ff. to one torn between avarice and extravagance: "You have two hooks pulling you different ways—are you for following this or that? You must need obey your masters by turns and shirk them by turns, by a division of duty." Philo, *Frag.* II.64: "It is not possible for the love of the world to coexist with the love of God" (*SB*, 1:435); Poimandres IV.6: "It is not possible, my son, to attach yourself both to things mortal and to things divine."

## 35. *On Anxiety*

### M A T T.   6 . 2 5 – 3 4

25 "Therefore I tell you, do not be anxious about your life, what you shall eat or what you shall drink,[y] nor about your body, what you shall put on. Is not life more than food, and the body more than clothing? 26 Look at the birds of the air: they neither sow nor reap nor gather into barns, and yet your heavenly Father feeds them. Are you not of more value than they? 27 And which of you by being anxious can add one cubit to his span of life?[z] 28 And why are you anxious about clothing? Consider the lilies of the field, how they grow; they neither toil nor spin; 29 yet I tell you, even Solomon in all his glory was not arrayed like one of these. 30 But if God so clothes the grass of the field, which today is alive and tomorrow is thrown into the oven, will he not much more clothe you, O men of little faith? 31 Therefore do not be anxious,

saying, 'What shall we eat?' or 'What shall we drink?' or 'What shall we wear?' 32 For the Gentiles seek all these things; and your heavenly Father knows that you need them all. 33 But seek first his kingdom and his righteousness, and all these things shall be yours as well. 34 Therefore do not be anxious about tomorrow, for tomorrow will be anxious for itself. Let the day's own trouble be sufficient for the day."

## LUKE 12.22–31

22 And he said to his disciples, "Therefore I tell you, do not be anxious about your life, what you shall eat, nor about your body, what you shall put on. 23 For life is more than food, and the body more than clothing. 24 Consider the ravens: they neither sow nor reap, they have neither storehouse nor barn, and yet God feeds them. Of how much more value are you than the birds! 25 And which of you by being anxious can add a cubit to his span of life?ᶻ 26 If then you are not able to do as small a thing as that, why are you anxious about the rest? 27 Consider the lilies, how they grow; they neither toil nor spin;ᵃ yet I tell you, even Solomon in all his glory was not arrayed like one of these. 28 But if God so clothes the grass which is alive in the field today and tomorrow is thrown into the oven, how much more will he clothe you, O men of little faith? 29 And do not seek what you are to eat and what you are to drink, nor be of anxious mind. 30 For all of the nations of the world seek these things; and your Father knows that you need them. 31 Instead, seek his ᵇ kingdom, and these things shall be yours as well."

---

y  Some texts read *what you shall eat and what you shall drink;* others omit *what you shall drink.*

z  Or *stature.*

a  Some texts read *lilies, they neither spin nor weave.*

b  Or *God's.*

## COMMENTARY

25 *Therefore I tell you.*   Although Luke 12.22 seems to introduce a new section, evidenced by, "And he said to his disciples," Matt. clearly intends this section to be a continuation of the preceding, hence the use of "therefore." Luke undoutedly had "therefore" in his source, but the point of reference is obscured. If the preceding parable is meant, which is a distinct possibility, the intrusion of "and he said to his disciples" is difficult. Matt. seems to have in mind a house slave who is preoccupied with matters of mammon, i.e., the physical necessities of life which are provided by his master, hence the admonition of Jesus not to take this attitude but to rely on God. This is reflected in the following: "Antignos of Soho received the Law from Simon the Just. He used to say, 'Be not like the slaves who minister to the master for the sake of receiving a reward [Heb. *peras*, bounty, compensation], but be like slaves who minister to the master not for the sake of the bounty and let the fear of Heaven be upon you!'"[1]

*do not be anxious about your life.* For "life" the Greek reads *psuche*, which is probably the Heb. *nefesh*.[2]

26 *Look at*/Gr. *katamathete*, a rare word, but see Gen. (LXX) 24.21.

*birds of the air* A Hebraism, cf., e.g., Gen. 2.19 et al. Luke 12.24, perhaps the original, reads "consider the ravens." He probably had in mind Ps. 147.9, *He gives the beast his food, and to the young ravens which cry.* Green suggests that the raven, being an unclean bird, may sharpen the point.[3]

The birds of the air as well as other creatures of nature are a source of instruction for man:

> But ask now the beast and they shall teach thee and the fowls of the air and they shall teach thee.[4]

> Who teaches us more than the beasts of the earth and makes us wiser than the fowls of heaven?[5]

> Simeon b. Eleazar says: "Have you ever seen an animal or bird practicing a craft? Yet they have their sustenance without care and were not created to serve my Maker. How much more then ought not I to have my sustenance without care. But I have wrought evil and so forfeited my right to sustenance without care.[6]

27 *add one cubit to his open span of life* The Gr. *helikia* can mean "stature" as well as "span of life."[7] To add a cubit to one's stature is no small feat, and one would expect a much lesser amount to fit the meaning of the passage. Adding a cubit to one's span of life mixes measure of space with measure of time, although metaphorically it is acceptable, as in the translation of "span" of life. Commentators are divided as to their preference. Those who take it as "stature" connect it with the height of growth of the crops in the preceding comment. In the LXX and Sym. of Ezek. 13.18, *helikia* is the translation of the Heb. *qomah*, and perhaps here there is a confusion between *qomah*, "stature" or "height," and *qamah*, meaning "standing corn" and the meaning that no one could, without God, add to the height of his crops.

28 *lilies of the field* Gr. *ta krina tou agrou*, parallel to "the birds of the air." It is difficult to say whether they are flowers in general, Gr. *krina* = Heb. *perahim*, flowers,"[8] or a specific flower, such as *shoshana*, "the rose."[9] Man is compared to the flowers of the field. Ps. 103.15, *As for man, his days are as grass; as the flower of the field so shall he flourish.* That these flowers are fit for burning, to be thrown into an oven, suggests to some the possibility of gladioli or irises.[10]

*they neither toil nor spin*, etc. The point of this statement about the flowers is quite clear. One expression, however, does disturb this clarity, that is the term *kopiosin*, "toil." This seems to be entirely too general for the specific verbs employed throughout. In comparing man to the birds of the air we find three specific acts connected with producing food, *viz.*, sow, reap, gather into barns. As to the making of clothing we would expect the same specificity, not a verb of general meaning. To explain this verse by the remark "the flowers perform neither men's work in the field *kopiosin* nor woman's work at home *methounsin*," is wholly absurd.[11] It is significant that the tradition is not clear as to the authenticity of *kopiosin*. For Matt. 6.25 the Oxy.P. reads, "you are far better than the lilies which grow but do not spin," omitting *kopiosin*. One Lucan text is even more instructive. "Consider the lilies they neither spin nor weave" (Luke 12.27). We would emend the text and read *kopanizousin*, "beat" (flax), for *kopiosin*, "toil," making a suitable mate to *methousin*, "spin." Perhaps the original had beat, spin, weave paralleling the three stages of agricultural labor, viz., sow, reap, and gather into barns. Is, however, the verb *kopiosin* used for the beating of flax? We have not been able to find a passage in Greek literature to prove the point. There is a reference in the Palestinian Talmud to the flail used for the beating of flax called *qofana*, derived from the Greek *kopanon*, giving support for the emendation *kopani-zousin*.[12]

29 *Solomon in all his glory*   Solomon's wealth is legendary; he is the exemplar of opulence.[13]

> "It once happened that R. Johanan b. Matthias said to his son, 'Go and hire laborers for us.' He went and undertook to give them their food. When he came to his father his father said to him, 'My son, even if you prepare for them a banquet like Solomon's in his time, you will not have fulfilled your duty toward them, for they are sons of Abraham, Isaac, and Jacob.' "[14]

> "Should the ninth of Ab fall on the Sabbath, one may eat and drink as much as he needs and he may load his table with [as much food] as at a Solomonic feast . . ."[15]

30 *the grass of the field, which today is alive, and tomorrow is thrown into the oven.*   Cf. Isa. 40.6–8. Heb. expression is "here today and tomorrow in the grave."[16]

*O men of little faith*   Gr. *oligopistoi*, Heb. *qetanē emunah* or *mehusarē emunah*.

Note the following:

> "Whoever has a morsel of bread in a basket and says, 'What shall I eat tomorrow' is one of those who has little faith."[17]

> "He who has what he will eat today and says, 'What shall I eat tomorrow,' behold, this man lacks faith."[18]

> "And Moses said to him, 'Let no man leave of it till the morning.' Notwithstanding they hearkened not unto Moses, these were those of little faith among the Israelites."[19]

32 *and your heavenly Father knows*, etc.   See above p. 124.
33 *His righteousness*   See above p. 77.

*all of these things*, etc.   The form of this presentation is similar to the one in God's promise to Solomon.[20]

**34** *Therefore be not anxious about tomorrow*   Missing in Luke. This is a well-known aphorism; e.g., "Fret not over tomorrow's trouble, for you do not know what a day may bring forth,"[21] and "peradventure tomorrow he is no more, thus he shall be found grieving over a world that is not his."[22]

*Let the day's own troubles be sufficient for the day*   A well-known proverb, contained in the following passage: . . . *I am that I am* [Exod. 3.14]. The Holy One, blessed be He, said to Moses, 'Go and say to Israel, I was with you in this servitude of the other kingdoms [i.e., Babylonia and Rome].' He said to Him, "Lord of the universe, sufficient is the evil in the time thereof.' Thereupon the Holy One, blessed be He, said to him, 'Go and tell them, *I am has sent me unto you* [ibid.].'."[23]

## NOTES

1. M. Avot. 1.3. On *peras* in the sense of rations, see E. J. Bickerman, "The Maxim of Antigonus of Socho," *HTR* 44 (1951): 153 ff.

2. Zimmermann, *Aramaic Origin of the Four Gospels*, p. 107, suggests that *psuche* goes back to the Aram. *ḥiyyuta*, which is highly unlikely.

3. Green, *Matt.*, p. 93.

4. Job 12.7.

5. Ibid. 35.11.

6. M. Qid. 4.4; B. ibid. 82b; T. Ibid. 5.15 (p. 343), TJ ibid. 4, 66b (38).

7. This is so understood by Old Syr., Pesh., Old Latin, Vulg., Tertullian and Hilary. Cf. also Luke 19.3, Cant. 7.7 (Sym).

8. Cf. Exod. 30.31 (30).

9. Cf. Cant. (LXX) 2.16, *tois krinous* for Heb. *bashoshanim*; also cf. Cant. 4.5, 6.2, 3. Luke omits *ta agrou*.

10. Cf. I. Löw, *Die Flora der Juden* (Vienna, 1924–28), pp. 1–28.

11. McNeile, *Matt.*, p. 88.

12. Jastrow, *Dictionary*, s.v.קוֹפַנָה, incorrectly connects *qofana* with the word *qofa*, "a bent stick." Krauss, *GLL*, s.v.קוֹפְנָה, however, points out that it is indeed derived from *kopanon*. On this emendation see Lachs, "Some Textual Observations," 110–111.

13. E.g., 2 Chron. 9.15. Note that the Gr. reads *doxe*, "glory." It is most likely that this is a translation of the Heb. *kavod*, which is regularly translated as *doxe* in the LXX, and one of the meanings of *kavod* is "wealth," cf. Gen. 31.3, Isa. 10.3, 61.6, 66.11, 12, which fits the context here.

14. M. BM. 7.1.

15. T. Ta'an. 4.13 (p. 221) cf. also B. Er. 40b–41a, B. Ta'an. 29b.

16. Cf. B. Ber. 32b, where it is applied to man, not to grass. On grass (flowers) used as fuel for the oven, see T. Shev. 5.19 (p. 68); M. Ter. 10.4; M. Shab. 3.1.

17. B. Sot. 48b.

18. *Mek.* Exod. 16.4; *MRS*, ed. J. N. Epstein, E. Z. Melamed, ibid., p. 106.

19. *Mek.* Exod. 16.9 for those who gathered manna and worried what they would eat. Cf. also *Mek.* Exod. 16.27, B. Pes. 118b, B. Ar. 15a.

20. Cf. 1. Kings 3.11 ff.

21. Prov. 27.1.

22. B. Sanh. 100b. Cf. also B. Yev. 63b, attributed to Ben Sira.

23. B. Ber. 9b. See also Exod. R. 3, B. Beẓ. 16a, B. Yev. 63b. In the NT, cf., James 4.14, "whereas you do not know tomorrow."

# 36. *On Judging*

## MATT. 7.1–5

1 "Judge not, that you be not judged. 2 For with the judgment you pronounce you will be judged, and the measure you give will be the measure you get. 3 Why do you see the speck that is in your brother's eye, but do not notice the log that is in your own eye? 4 Or how can you say to your brother, 'Let me take the speck out of your eye,' when there is the log in your own eye? 5 You hypocrite, first take the log out of your own eye, and then take the speck out of your brother's eye."

## LUKE 6.37–38, 41–42

37 "Judge not, and you will not be judged; condemn not, and you will not be condemned; forgive, and you will be forgiven; 38 give, and it will be given to you; good measure, pressed down, shaken together, running over, will be put into your lap. For the measure you give will be the measure you get back. 41 Why do you see the speck that is in your brother's eye, but do not notice the log that is in your own eye? 42 Or how can you say to your brother, 'Brother, let me take out the speck that is in your eye,' when you yourself do not see the log that is in your own eye? You hypocrite, first take the log out of your own eye, and then you will see clearly to take out the speck that is in your brother's eye."

## COMMENTARY

1 *Judge not, that you be not judged*   The parallelism in Luke 6.37–38 is much longer and indicates poetic form; in all probability it is the original, and the Matthean verses are a shortened version.[1] Luke 6.37 concludes with *forgive and you shall be forgiven*, which is natural and logical. Matt. 7.1 should be compared with James 4.11 ff.

No direct rabbinic parallels, but note the following:

Joshua B. Peraḥyah said: ". . . judge all men in the scale of merit."[2]

Hillel said, "Judge not thy fellowman until thou are come into his place."[3]

Isaac said: "Three things call a man's iniquities to mind . . . and calling for divine judgment on one's fellowman. For R. Abin said: 'He who calls down divine judgment on his neighbor is himself punished first for his own sins, as it says, *And Sarah said unto Abraham, My wrong be upon thee* [Gen. 16.5], and it is written later, *And Abraham came to mourn for Sarah and to weep for her* [ibid. 23.2].' "[4]

Thus a story is told of a certain man who descended from Upper Galilee and was engaged by an individual in the South for three years. On the eve of the Day of Atonement he requested him, "Give me my wages that I may go and support my wife and children." "I have no money," he answered. "Give me land." "I have none." "Give me cattle." "I have none." "Give me pillows and bedding!" "I have none." So he slung his things behind him and went home with a sorrowful heart. After the Festival his employer took his wages in his hand together with three laden asses, one bearing food, another drink, and the third various sweetmeats, and went to his house. After they had eaten and drunk, he gave him his wages. Said he to him, "When you asked me, 'Give me my wages,' and I answered you, 'I have no money,' of what did you suspect me?" "I thought perhaps you came across cheap merchandise and had purchased it therewith." "And when you requested me, 'Give me cattle,' and I answered, 'I have no cattle,' of what did you suspect me?" "I thought they might be hired to others." "When you asked me, 'Give me land,' and I told you, 'I have no land,' of what did you suspect me?" "I thought, Perhaps they are not tithed." "And when I told you I have no pillows or bedding, of what did you suspect me?" "I thought, Perhaps he has sanctified all his property to Heaven." "By the Temple service," he exclaimed, "it was even so; I vowed away all my property because of my son Hyrcanus, who would not occupy himself with the Torah, but when I went to my companions in the South they absolved me of all my vows. And as for you, just as you judged me favorably, so may the Omnipresent judge you favorably."[5]

2 *For with the judgment you pronounce you will be judged*, etc.   "Raba said, 'He who waives his right to retribution [lit. passes by his measure] is forgiven all his sins, as it is said, *that pardoneth iniquity and passeth by transgression* [Mic. 7.81]. Whose iniquity is forgiven? The iniquity of him who passes by transgression.' "[6]
   *and the measure of*, etc.

In the measure with which a man measures it is meted out to him. She [the suspected adulteress] adorned herself for a transgression, the Holy One, blessed be He, made her repulsive [cf. Num. 5.18]. She exposed herself for a transgression, the Holy One, blessed be He, held her up for exposure [ibid. 5.21 ff.].[7]

Samson went after the desire of his eyes, therefore the Philistines put out his eyes, as it is said, *And the Philistines laid hold of him, and put out his eyes* [Judg. 16.21]. Absalom gloried in his hair, therefore he was hanged by his hair. And because he slept with the ten concubines of his father, therefore he was stabbed with ten lances, as it is written, *And ten young men that bare Joab's armor compassed about* [2 Sam. 18.15]. And because he stole three hearts, the heart of his father, the heart of the court of justice, and the hearts of the men of Israel, as it is said, *So Absalom stole the hearts of the men of Israel* [ibid. 15.6], therefore three darts were thrust through him, as it is said, *And he took three darts in his hand and thrust them through the heart of Absalom* [ibid. 18.14]. It is the same in connection with the good. Miriam waited a short while for Moses, as it is said, *And his sister stood afar off* [Exod. 2.4], therefore Israel was delayed for her seven days in the wilderness, as it is said, *And the people journeyed not until Miriam was brought in again* [Num. 12.15]. Joseph earned merit by burying his father and there was none among his brothers greater than he, as it is said, *And Joseph went up to bury his father*, etc. [Gen. 50.7), *and there went up with him both chariots and horsemen.* [ibid. 9]. Whom have we greater than Joseph, since none other than Moses occupied himself with his burial? Moses earned merit through the bones of Joseph, and there was none in Israel greater than he, as it is said, *and Moses took the bones of Joseph with him* [Exod. 13.19]. Whom have we greater than Moses, since none other than the Omnipresent occupied himself with his burial, as it is said, *And he buried him in the valley* [Deut. 34.6]. Not only concerning Moses did they say this but concerning all the righteous, as it is said, *And the righteous shall go before thee, the glory of the Lord shall be thy reward* [Isa. 58.8].[8]

R. Simeon b. Abba said: "All the measures have ceased [presumably four modes of execution], yet the rule of measure for measure has not ceased.[9]

A similar idea is expressed in the phrase, "in the pot in which they cooked they were cooked."[10]

3 *Why do you see the speck that is in your brother's eye, but do not notice the log that is in your own eye?* This passage contains a popular Palestinian folk saying about individuals who refuse to take criticism or to see faults in themselves but who are quick to notice them in others.[11]

R. Tarfon said, "I wonder whether there is anyone in this generation who accepts reproof, for if one say to him, 'Remove the mote from between your eyes,' he would answer, 'Remove the beam from between your eyes.' "[12]

R. Johanan said, "What is the meaning of *In the days of the judging of judges* [Ruth 1.1]? It was a generation which judged its judges. If the judge said to a man, 'Take the splinter from between your teeth [text of *Ein Yaaqov*; text of the Talmud: 'between your eyes'], he would retort, 'Take the beam from between your eyes.' "[13]

Do not taunt your neighbor with the blemish which you have.[14]

He who accuses another of fault, has it himself.[15]

In interpreting Zeph. 2.1 Resh Laqish interpreted, "Adorn thyself [correct thyself] and then adorn others [correct others]."[16]

## NOTES

1. See Burney, *The Poetry of Our Lord*, pp. 114, 123.
2. M. Avot 1.6; cf. also *DEZ* 3, B. Shab. 127a.
3. M. Avot 2.5.
4. B. RH 16b; cf. B. BQ 93a. See also Gen. R. 45 for a similar statement.
5. B. Shab. 127a.
6. B. Meg. 28a, B. RH 17a, and B. Yom. 23a.
7. M. Sot. 1.7. See also Wisd. of Sol. 11.15 ff., 12.23, 18.4–11; Sira 16.12, 14. H. P. Ruger, "Mit welchem Mass ihr messt, wird euch gemessen werden," *ZNW* 60 (1969): 174–183, points out that "measure for measure" is used in the Targumim eschatalogically.
8. M. Sot. 1.8. Also *Mek.* Exod. 13.19. The principle of "measure for measure" as exemplified by the *sota*, see T. Sot. 3.2 ff. (p. 295). B. Sot. 8b, Num. R. 9, Sifre Num. 106.

9. Gen. R. 9.13.

10. Exod. R. 1. See also *Mek.* Exod. 18.11.

11. Davies, *SSM*, p. 98, is correct when stating that "in Matt. a 'brother' except when blood brother is meant, means a Christian."

12. B. Ar. 16b. See also Sifre Deut. 1.1, Sifra Lev. 19.17. In citing this passage McNeile suggests that R. Tarfon's words were possibly an attack on the NT words. This is highly unlikely, for the mote/beam comment is not restricted to "those of this generation" but has other applications of a moral nature (see below) and hence would hardly have been used by the Rabbis had it been taken from the NT.

13. B. BB 16b. The reading "from between your teeth" has a logical appeal and the two readings "eyes" and "teeth" involve only one letter in Hebrew, *enaiyim* and *shinayim*.

14. B. BM 59b.

15. B. Qid. 20b, *Mek.* Exod. 22.20. Cf. Rom. 2.1, *when you judge another, for in passing judgments upon him you condemn yourself, because you the judge are doing the very same thing.* Cf. also Plutarch, *De Cur.* 515d; Horace, *Sat.* I.iii.25.

16. B. Sanh. 18a, 19a; B. BB 60b; B. BM 107b and Yal. Jer. 302. See also Gospel of Thomas, logion 26.

# 37. On Profaning the Holy

## MATT. 7.6

"Do not give dogs what is holy; and do not throw your pearls before swine, lest they trample them underfoot and turn to attack you."

## COMMENTARY

This verse has three parts, the first two preserve a parellelism, characteristic of Semitic poetry, and might well be a translation from the Hebrew or Aramaic.[1] The third part is not a translation but an addition to the Greek text.[2]

6 *Do not give dogs what is holy*  This verse is to be understood figuratively, not literally.[3] Perles, suggested that the first two parts are a translation from the Aramaic, which he reconstructs as: "Do not hang (precious) rings on dogs and do not adorn the snout with pearls."[4] The meaning is, do not teach Torah, i.e., that which is holy, to the non-Jew, who on occasion is called disparagingly a dog (see below).

R. Ammi said: "The teachings of the Torah are not to be transmitted to a non-Jew, for it is said, *He hath not dealt so with any nation, and as for His ordinances they have not known them* [Ps. 147.20]."[5]

R. Ḥelbo said: "Four adjurations are mentioned [in Cant. 2.7, 3.5, 5.8, 8.4]. God adjured Israel that they should not rebel against governments, that they should not seek to hasten the end, that they should not reveal their mysteries to the other nations [presumably the Oral Law], and that they should not attempt to go up from the Diaspora by force [simultaneously]."[6]

R. Judah ha-Levi b. Shalom said: "Moses wanted that the Mishnah [traditional learning], too, be given in writing. God, however, foresaw that the nations of the world [i.e., the Christians] would translate the Torah and read it in Greek and say, 'We are the true Israel, etc.' "[7]

*and do not throw your pearls before swine*   This is the second part of the parallelism. The only difficulty in the passage is the word "throw," Gr. *ballō*, which is parallel to "do not give" of the first stich. The Semitic original of *ballō* is *toru*, from the root *yaro*, which means "to teach" and also "to throw." The translator, not realizing that "pearls" was used here in a metaphorical sense for biblical verses, naturally chose the meaning "to throw," for to his mind to translate "to teach" would have been absurd. The meaning of the passage then is, "Do not present that which is holy, i.e., scriptural verses, before the dogs, and do not teach 'pearls,' i.e., biblical passages or any nuggets of 'wisdom,' before swine."[8]

Who are the dogs and the swine in this passage? It is well known that they are both used as derogatory terms for the Gentiles.[9] Within the context of the passage we can be more specific. We suggest that "dogs" refers to the Samaritans, who are similarly compared to dogs in an early rabbinic source.[10] As to "swine," although it too is used for Gentiles, again we can be quite specific. It probably refers to the Romans, for Esau-Edom in rabbinic literature stands for Rome—and he is compared to a dog.[11] We suggest that *choiros*, Heb. *ḥazir*, is not to be taken as domestic swine but as the "wild boar," as in Ps. 81, and which, in later literature, stands for the enemies of Israel.[12] The figure of the wild boar adorned the banners of the Roman legions then stationed in Palestine.[13] Some New Testament scholars are disturbed by the identification of these animals with the Gentiles and by the idea that Jesus advised the disciples not to bring the gospel to them. In their view this does not fit the character and mission of Jesus.[14] Whether this passage is one which goes back to Jesus is a moot point. One thing is, however, clear, it is found only in Matt. This fact is instructive, for whatever was the personal outlook of the evangelist, he did use the *logia* which have a narrowly Jewish intent.[15] One cannot ignore the Matthean passages which indicate that the message of Jesus was directed to the members of the Jewish people: *I was sent only to the lost sheep of the house of Israel* (Matt. 15.24); *Go nowhere among the Gentiles and enter no town of the Samaritans, but go rather to the lost sheep of the house of Israel* (ibid. 10.6); *You will not have gone through all the towns of Israel before the Son of man comes* (ibid. 10.23); *You who have followed me will also sit on twelve thrones, judging the twelve tribes of Israel* (ibid. 19.28).[16] Luke probably has omitted this passage, i.e., Matt. 7.6, as being offensive to his Greek audience.[17]

The last phrase, "lest they trample," is not part of the Semitic original, and it clearly presupposes the Greek translation of *ballō* as "throw."[18]

## NOTES

1. See Black, *Aramaic Origin*, pp. 147–148. Cf. Gospel of Thomas, logion 93.

2. On this verse see S. T. Lachs, "Semitic Background," 209–211.

3. There are several passages which treat this literally and we do not think that they are applicable here, e.g., ". . . hence we infer that we do not redeem dedicated sacrifices to give food to the dogs" (B. Bekh. 15a); "All animal offerings that have been rendered *terefah* may not be redeemed, since animal offerings may not be redeemed in order to give them as food to the dogs" (M. Tem. 6.5); cf. also B. ibid. 117a, B. Shev. 11b, B. Pes. 29a.

4. F. Perles, "Zur Erklärung von Mt. 7.6," ZNW 25 (1926), pp. 163–164.

5. B. Hag. 13a, the texts read "Cuthean-Samaritan." Sonc. Tal. ad loc., "this and not Cuthean (substituted on account of the censorship) is undoubtedly the correct reading (i.e. idolator). Dicta of this kind were directed against heathens and were inspired by the fear lest the knowledge of the Torah be unscrupulously used against the Jews." Cf. the story of the Roman commissioners referred to in BQ 38a; also R. Johanan's statement in B. Sanh. 59a and Num. R. 13. On Gentiles and Oral Law, see Exod. R. 47.

6. Cant. R. 2.17.

7. *PR* 5 (14b) cf. also *Tan. B. Ki Tisa* 17 (58b); Ex. R. 47.1.

8. For pearls used in a figurative sense for bon mots, adages, or clever teaching, cf., e.g., Cant. R. 1.10, B. Hag. 3a, *ARN* 18, T. Sot. 7 (p. 307), *Mek.* Exod. 13.2.

9. Cf. B. Shab. 188a, B. Yom. 29a, *Panim Aherim* 71.

10. Cf. Gen. R. 81.3, "to what are you compared [addressed to the Samaritans], to dogs . . ."

11. Gen. R. 65.1.Cf. also Lev. R. 13.5 and A. Epstein, *Miqadmoniyot Ha-Yehudim* (Vienna, 1887), p. 35, who gives several reasons for this identification.

12. *Mid. Ps.*, ed. prin., 80.14; *ibid.*, ed. S. Buber, p. 182a; *Yal. Ps.* ad loc.

13. Ginzberg, *Legends*, 5:284, where he cites the literature.

14. Several such views are cited by Montefiore, *RLGT*, p. 117.

15. Allen, *Matt.* p. 67.

16. Against this line of reasoning, see W. D. Davies, "Knowledge in the Dead Sea Scrolls and Matthew 11.25–30," HTR 46 (July 1953): 117; *SSM* p. 526.

17. McNeile, *Matt.*, p. 91.

18. Perles, loc. cit.

# 38. *God Answers Prayer*

## MATT. 7.7–11

7 "Ask, and it will be given you; seek, and you will find; knock and it will be opened to you. 8 For everyone who asks receives, and he who seeks find, and to him who knocks it will be opened. 9 Or what man of you, if his son asks him for a loaf, will give him a stone? 10 Or if he asks for a fish, will give him a serpent? 11 If you, then, who are evil, know how to give good gifts to your children, how much more will your Father who is in heaven give good things to those who ask him?"

## LUKE 11.9-13

9 "And I tell you, Ask, and it will be given to you; seek, and you will find; knock, and it will be opened to you. 10 For everyone who asks receives, and he who seeks finds, and to him who knocks it will be opened. 11 What father among you, if his son asks for a[c] fish, will instead of a fish give him a serpent; 12 or if he asks for an egg, will give him a scorpion? 13 If you then, who are evil, know how to give good gifts to your children, how much more will the heavenly Father give the Holy Spirit to those who ask him?

---

c   Some texts add *a loaf, will give him a stone; or if he asks for.*

## COMMENTARY

The emphasis here is on the efficacy of earnest petition and of God's goodness expressed in three pithy phrases.[1]

7 *Ask, and it will be given you*   Friedländer suggests Ps. 2.8, *Ask of me and I will give.* What is significant as to Semitic background is that "ask," Heb. *sha'al,* is a technical expression for prayer.[2] There are no rabbinic parallels per se. The idea that God answers sincere prayer is, of course, commonplace.[3]

*seek, and you will find*   Cf. Prov. 8.17, *And those that seek me and find me;* Isa. 60.6, *Seek you the Lord while He may be found."*[4] Note the rabbinic comment:

R. Isaac said: "If a man says to you I have labored and not found," do not believe him. If he says, "I have labored and found, "you may believe him. This is true in respect of words of Torah, but in respect to business, all depends on the assistance of Heaven, and even for words of Torah this is true only of penetrating the meaning, but for remembering what one has learned all depends on the assistance of Heaven.[5]

*knock, and it will be opened*   Note the following:

[Mordecai] the son of Kish indicates that he knocked at the gates of mercy and they were opened to him.[6]

R. Benna's said: "A man should always immerse himself in Mishnayot, for if he knows, it will be opened for him, and if in Talmud, Talmud, if in Aggadah, Aggadah."[7]

R. Ammi said, "Anyone who does not conclude *Ge'ulah* [concluding blessing after the *Shema*] with the *Shemoneh Esreh,* to whom is he compared? To a friend of a king who came and knocked on the king's door. He came out to find out what he wanted, and finding that he, the friend that had knocked at the door, had withdrawn, he too withdrew."[8]

9 *Or what man of you, if his son asks for a loaf, will give him a stone?* 10 *Or if he asks for a fish, will give him a serpent?* Note Luke 11.11–12, where after fish/serpent there is the addition, *or if he asks for an egg, will give him a scorpion?* There are no rabbinic sources for these verses and they do not readily yield wordplays either in Hebrew or in Aramaic.[9]

11 *If you, then, who are evil, know how to give good gifts to your children, how much more will your Father who is in heaven give good things to those who ask him* The only variant, in Luke 11.13, is "Holy Spirit" for "good things." In this instance the Matthean version is to be preferred for originality.

This verse contrasts the reactions of man and God to the needs and requests of their children, and we find the typical rabbinic *qal v'homer* argument *(a minori ad maius);* "If you . . . know, how much more, etc." The only problem in this contrast is the characterization of men as evil. This is not in keeping with what we might call "gospel theology." The emphasis on the concept that man is evil from birth, born in sin, and the like, is of a later theological development. The idea that "in comparison with God, all men, even parents, are evil" is unconvincing.[10] In rabbinic parables of comparison between man and God the points of difference are that man is human, limited, and created, while God is divine, eternal, and the Creator of all. One would expect therefore that this passage conform with some aspect of the rabbinic paradigm. We think that this verse had a very close, almost literal parallel in rabbinic literature: "If a member of a man's household is well treated, *a fortiori* a member of the household of Him who spoke and the world was" (Sifre Num. 88, p. 76). The point of comparison is between man, lit. "flesh and blood," *basar vadam,* and God. It is possible that the original of the Matthean verse contained the expression "flesh and blood," *basar vadam,* instead of "evil," but it was in the form of a scribal abbreviation, ו"ב or בש"ו for *basar vadam,* and it was misread by the translator as *bisha,* "evil." Another passage of interest is ". . . thereupon R. Tanhuma raised his face to heaven and said to the Holy One, blessed be He: 'Sovereign of the Universe: If this man, who is flesh and blood, cruel and not responsible for her [his divorced wife's] maintenance, was filled with compassion for her and gave her, how much more should You be filled with compassion for us who are the children of Your children Abraham, Isaac, and Jacob, and are dependent on You for our maintenance.'"[11]

12 *know how* Gr. *oidate,* Aram. *hakham.*[12]

## NOTES

1. On the poetry of these verses, see Burney, *Poetry of Our Lord,* pp. 67, 82, 114.
2. Cf., e.g., M. Ta'an. 1.2.
3. For these passages see *SB,* 1:450 ff.
4. Cf. also 1 Chron. 29.9; 2 Chron. 15.2.
5. B. Meg. 6b.
6. B. Meg. 12b Note the passive construction as in Matt. 7.7a.
7. *PRK* 27 (176a). Cf. also Lev. R. 21.5.

8. TJ Ber. 1, 2d (62).

9. Zimmermann, *Aramaic Origin of the Four Gospels*, p. 78, sees a wordplay between "bread" and "stone" from the Aramaic ריפתא, "bread," and כיפתא, "stone," and between "fish" and "serpent" likewise from Aramaic נונא, "fish," and תנינא, "serpent," citing B. Shab. 150a. Commenting on the Lucan parallel he sees a wordplay between the verbs and the nouns: "ask," בעי; "egg," ביעא; "scorpion," עקרב, "and offer," אקרב. What is really required is a wordplay on the nouns. Furthermore אקרב in this context seems forced. Matthew's "fish and serpent" and Luke's "egg and scorpion" were probably derived from the current Greek proverb "for a perch a scorpion"; see Friedlander, *Sermon*, p. 229, citing Jülicher, op. cit., 2:39. The "bread/stone" phrase might well be paralleled by a passage in Seneca, *De Beneficiis* II.7, "Fabius Verrucosus used to compare a benefit conferred by a harsh man in an offensive manner to a stone loaf [*panem lapidosum*] which a hungry man is forced to receive, but which he cannot eat." Cited by Friedlander, loc. cit.

10. See McNeile, *Matt.*, p. 92.

11. Lev. R. 34.14 Cf. also Gen. R. 33.3. On the problem of the term "evil," see Lachs, "Some Textual Observations," 109–110.

12. E.g. Lev. R. 5.

# 39. *The Golden Rule*

## MATT. 7.12

"So whatever you wish that men would do to you, do so to them; for this is the law and the prophets."

## LUKE 6.31

"And as you wish that men do to you, do so to them."

## COMMENTARY

This verse, often called the Golden Rule, appears both in a positive and in a negative formulation, the former more common in Christian texts, the latter in Jewish sources.[1]

You shall love your neighbor as yourself.[2]

And that which you hate, do to no man.[3]

Just as a man asks something for his own soul from God, so let him do to every living soul.[4]

What is the teaching of wisdom? And the other [the one to whom the king directed the question] replied: "As you wish that no evil should befall you, but to be a partaker of all good things, so you should act on the same principle toward your subjects and offenders."[5]

The way of life is this: First thou shalt love the God who made thee, secondly thy neighbor as thyself; and whatsoever thou wouldst not have done to thyself, do not thou to another.[6]

He hath also not created the world for naught, but that His creatures should fear Him, and that none should do to his neighbor what he does not like for himself.[7]

Be considerate to thy companion as thyself, and be mindful of all thou detesteth.[8]

On another occasion it happened that a certain heathen came before Shammai and said to him: "Make me a proselyte on condition that you teach me the whole Torah while I stand on one foot." Thereupon he repulsed him with a builder's cubit which was in his hand. When he went before Hillel, he said to him: "What is hateful to you do not to your neighbor, that is the whole Torah, while the rest is commentary thereof; go and learn it."[9]

The following are examples of passages which embody the principle of the Golden Rule.

R. Eliezer says: "Let the honor of thy fellow be as dear to thee as thy own."[10] How so? This teaches that even as one looks out for his own honor, so should he look out for his fellow's honor; and even as no man wishes that his own honor be held in ill repute, so should he wish that the honor of his fellow shall not be held in ill repute.[11]

R. Joshua says: "A grudging eye . . . put[s] a man out of the world.[12] What is this? This teaches that even as a man looks out for his own home, so should he look out for the home of his fellow. And even as no man wishes that his wife and children be held in ill repute, so should no man wish that his fellow's wife and children be held in ill repute."[13]

12 *the law and the prophets* See above p. 87. Luke omits this. He places the Golden Rule at the end of Jesus' teaching about love of enemies and gifts.

## NOTES

1. In addition to Jewish and Christian versions of the Rule, it also appears in Greek literature, e.g., Isocrates, *Nicocles* 61, "Do not do unto others that which angers you when others do it to you." Cf. also Herodotus 3.142.
2. Lev. 19.18.
3. Tob. 4.15.
4. Slav. En. 61.1.
5. Aristeas 207; cf. Philo. *Hypothetica;* Eusebius, *Prae. Evang.* 8.7.
6. *Didache* 1.2 Note that this has a negative form of the Golden Rule. It is also found in some MSS, e.g., ms. D of Acts 15.29, "Whatever you do not wish to happen to you, do not do to another."
7. Test. Naph. (Heb.) 1.6.
8. Sira 31.15.
9. B. Shab. 31a. Cf. Targ. JI Lev. 19.18. On this passage see Herford, *Talmud and Apocrypha,* p. 148.
10. M. Avot 2.10
11. *ARN* 1.15.
12. M. Avot 2.11.

13. *ARN* 1.16. On the Golden Rule see: Abrahams, *Studies I*, pp. 18–29; G. B. King, "The Negative Golden Rule," *JR* 8 (1928): 268–279; L. Philippides, *Die "Goldene Regel" religionsgeschichtlich untersucht* (1929); G. Friedlander, *Sermon*, pp. 226–238.

# 40. *The Narrow Gate*

## MATT. 7.13–14

13 "Enter by the narrow gate; for the gate is wide and the way is easy,[d] that leads to destruction, and those who enter by it are many. 14 For the gate is narrow and the way is hard, that leads to life, and those who find it are few."

## LUKE 13.23–24

23 And some one said to him, "Lord, will those who are saved be few?" And he said to them, 24 "Strive to enter by the narrow door; for many, I tell you, will seek to enter and will not be able."

---

d Some texts read *for the way is wide and easy.*

### COMMENTARY

13 *Enter by the narrow gate,* etc. Note that Luke 13.23–24 is quite different from Matt., citing only the *narrow door*; for Matt. has both the door/gate of the Lucan version conflated with "the way" of another source.[1] The "two ways" have many antecedents in biblical sources: Deut. 11.26, *Behold, I set before you this day a blessing and a curse*; ibid. 39.19, *I call heaven and earth to witness against you this day that I have set before you life and death are blessing and the curse*; ibid. 30.15, *I have set before you this day life and good, and death and evil.*[2]

In the intertestamental literature:

> The way of sinners is made plain with stones but at the end thereof is the pit of hell.[3]

> And he said unto me: "There is a sea lying in a wide expanse so that it is broad and vast; but the entrance thereto lies in a narrow space so as to be like a river. He then that really desireth to go upon the sea to behold it or to navigate it, if he pass not through the narrow part, how shall he be able to come into the broad? Again, another [illustration]. There is a builded city which lies on level ground, and it is full of all good things; but its entrance is narrow and lies on a steep having fire to the right hand and deep water on the left; and there is one path lying between the fire and the water, [and so small] is this path, that it can contain only one man's footstep at once. If, now, this city is given to a man for an inheritance, unless the heir pass through the danger set for him, how shall he receive his inheritance?" And I

said: "It is so, Lord!" Then said He unto me: "Even also is Israel's portion, for it was for their sakes I made the world; but when Adam transgressed my statutes, then that which had been made was judged, and then the ways of this world become narrow and sorrowful and painful [few and evil] and full of perils coupled with great toils. But the ways of the future world are broad and safe and yield the fruit of immortality."[4]

In rabbinic literature there are numerous passages involving choice and in the spirit of "the ways," but no real parallel. Two, however, deserve attention, one is early, the other is very late.

> *Behold I have set before you a blessing and a curse.*[5] Why is this stated? For it had been said, *I have set before you . . . the blessing and the curse.*[6] Perhaps Israel will say: "Since God has set before us two paths, the path of life and the path of death, we shall go in which ever one we choose." The text says, *choose life that you may live, you and your seed* [ibid.]. It is like one who sat by a crossroad and before him were two paths of which one was smooth to start with, and ended in thorns, and the other was thorny to start with but became smooth. And he told the passers-by, "You see this path which at the outset is smooth, yet for only a few paces will you walk on the smooth, after that it is thorny. And as to the path which begins with thorns it soon becomes smooth." So Moses said to Israel, "The wicked whom you see prosperous have prosperity but for a brief space in this world, but their end is to fall. And you see the righteous who suffer torments in this world, it is for a short time that they suffer, but their end is rejoicing."[7]

> Rabbi Eliezer says: "I have heard in my ears the Lord of Hosts speaking. What did he say? *See, I have set before you this day life and good and death and evil.*[8] The Holy One, blessed be He, said: "Behold, I have given two things to Israel, one of good and the other of evil. That of good is of life, that of evil is of death. That of good has two paths, one of *zedaqah* [righteousness], by the other of *ḥesed* [an act of kindness]. And Elijah of blessed memory stands between them, and when a man comes to enter he proclaims saying, *Open ye the gates that the righteous nation that keepeth faithfulness may enter,*[9] and the one of evil has in it four entrances, and at each entrance there are seven angelic guards seated there, four on the outside and three within. Those on the outside are compassionate, but those who are within are cruel."[10]

## NOTES

1. See Green, *Matt.*, p. 96.

2. Cf. also Jer. 21.8, *Behold, I set before you the way of life and the way of death.* Also Prov. 28.6, 18. Cf. *Didache* 1.1 ff. In classical literature cf. Hesiod, *Works and Days*, pp. 287–292; Cebes, *Tabula* 15; Maximus of Tyre, *Diss.* 39.3; Virgil, *Aeneid* 6.540–543 et al.

3. Sira 21.10.

4. 4 Ezra 7.3–15. N.B., in vv. 12 and 13 trans. from the Gr. and so in the Ethiopic. The Latin and Syriac have "entrances," an interesting variant similar to the conflated reading in Matt.

5. Deut. 11.26.
6. Ibid. 30.19.
7. Sifre Deut. 53.
8. Deut. 30.15.
9. Isa. 26.2.
10. *PRE* 15.

# 41. *The Test of a Good Man*

## MATT. 7.15–20

15 "Beware of false prophets, who come to you in sheep's clothing but inwardly are ravenous wolves. 16 You will know them by their fruits. Are grapes gathered from thorns, or figs from thistles? 17 So, every sound tree bears good fruit, but the bad tree bears evil fruit. 18 A sound tree cannot bear evil fruit, nor can a bad tree bear good fruit. 19 Every tree that does not bear good fruit is cut down and thrown into the fire. 20 Thus you will know them by their fruits."

## IBID. 12.33–35

33 "Either make the tree good, and its fruit good; or make the tree bad, and its fruit bad; for the tree is known by its fruit. 34 You brood of vipers! how can you speak good, when you are evil? For out of the abundance of the heart the mouth speaks. 35 The good man out of his good treasure brings forth good, and the evil man out of his evil treasure brings forth evil."

## LUKE 6.43–45

43 "For no good tree bears bad fruit, nor again does a bad tree bear good fruit; 44 for each tree is known by its own fruit. For figs are not gathered from thorns, nor are grapes picked from a bramble bush. 45 The good man out of the good treasure of his heart produces good, and the evil man out of his evil treasure produces evil; for out of the abundance of the heart his mouth speaks."

## COMMENTARY

15 *false prophets* The meaning is bogus prophets, not that their prophecy is false. Cf. Mark 13.22 ff., Matt. 24.11. It is clear that Christian literature does not reflect the rabbinic dicta concerning the cessation of prophecy. "With the death of the last of the prophets, Haggai, Zechariah, and Malachi, the Holy Spirit departed from Israel."[1] "R. Abdimi of Haifa said: 'From the day that the Temple was destroyed, prophecy was removed from the prophets and given to the sages.' R. Joḥanan said: 'From the day the Temple was destroyed, prophecy was removed from the prophets and given to fools and children.' "[2] These, in part, were probably uttered as a polemic against Christianity, which maintained that prophecy did not indeed cease.[3]

*in sheep's clothing . . . ravenous wolves* I.e., within the Christian fold, as confirmed by v. 22. For the imagery of "wolves" see Ezek. 22.27, Zeph. 3.3. Manson is undoubtedly correct in saying, "the figure of the wolf disguised as a sheep goes with the thought of the disciples as the flock of Jesus as their shepherd."[4] This imagery is similar to other examples of hypocrisy employed by Matthew, e.g., "the whitened sepulchers" and "the generation of vipers."[5]

16 *you will know them by their fruits* This is clearly a Semitic espression, probably *peri ma'asekhem*," by the fruit of their deeds," Cf. James 3.12. This is an example of *inclusio* characteristic of Mathew.[6]

*Are grapes gathered from thorns* Luke reverses the fruit, i.e., "figs from thorns" and "grapes from thistles." Matthew is to be preferred.[7] These are two of the fruits for which the Land of Israel is famous, among those of the expression "the seven species," viz., wheat, barley, grapes, figs, pomegranates, olive oil, and date (honey), mentioned in Deut. 8.8. Cf. M. Ber. 6.4. The imagery of fruit is common in the Bible. The vineyard of Isa. 5.2 ff., Joel 2.22, *for the tree beareth her fruit, the fig tree and the vine do yield their strength.*[8]

17 *bears* "The words 'bringeth forth' in Mat. and Lk. represent two different Greek words, which themselves are alternate translations of a single Aramaic word, which in this context can best be rendered by 'utters.' The utterances of a man express his character, for speech is the outpouring of what is in the heart. So that Rabbis use the expression, 'What is in the heart is in the heart, and 'What is in the heart is in the mouth' (for feelings repressed and feelings expressed respectively."[9]

18 *bad tree* The Greek describes something which is unfit for eating, not rotten, as in some of the older translations. It may be influenced by the fact that the Aram. word "to be evil," *ba'ash*, is etymologically identical with the Heb. *ba'ash*, "to stink." The wild grapes in Isa. 5.2, 4 have a name in Hebrew which means literally "stinking things," *be'ushim*. This bad tree, then, is a wild tree producing fruit but unsuitable for eating because of its harsh or bitter taste.[10] The rabbinic term would be *ilan seraq*, which in addition to its meaning of a tree which does not produce any fruit, means a tree which produces inedible fruit.[11]

19 *Thus you will know them by their fruit* Note the following in the same vein:

> The fruit of a tree declares the husbandry thereof, so is the utterance of the thought of a man's heart.[12]

> Blessed is he who understands every work of the Lord and glorifies the Lord God, for the works of the Lord are just; and of the works of man some are good and others evil, and by their works those who have wrought them are known.[13]

> God judges by the fruit of a tree, not by the roots.[14]

> or fruit testify against us.[15]

> The fruit of a righteous man is his good conduct.[16]

## NOTES

1. B. Sanh. 11a.
2. B. BB 12b.
3. Cf. concerning Christian prophets Acts 13.2, 1 Cor. 12.28, Eph. 4.11 in the NT. Cf. also *Didache* 10. It is difficult to identify these false prophets. Schlatter's identification with the gnostics, *Der Evangelist Matthäus* (Stuttgart, 1948), p. 797, is not convincing. We are inclined to agree with Davies, *SSM*, p. 200, "that they were Christian prophets whose outward conduct belies their nature, which is one of lawlessness and unrighteousness. This appears still more likely if we identify the false prophets of 7.15 with those who cry Lord, Lord in 7.21 ff."
4. Cf. Luke 10.3, Matt. 10.16.
5. On these two examples see S.T. Lachs, "On Matthew 23.27–28," *HTR* 68 (1975): 385–388; idem, "Studies in the Semitic Background," 197–199.
6. See above p. 77 and Matt. 3.10, 12.33.
7. The Gr. for "thorn," *akantha*, is the same as is used in the LXX for *be'ushim* of Isa. 5.2, 4, and "the fruit of the thistle bears at least a faint resemblance to a fig" (Manson, *SJ*, p. 60). Both thorns and thistles are weeds, cf. Gen. 3.18, Hos. 10.8. On gathering grapes from thorns, see Cant. R. 1.1.
8. Cf. also Jer. 17.8, Prov. 11.30.
9. Manson, *SJ*, p. 60.
10. Ibid.
11. E.g., B. BQ 91b.
12. Sira 27.6.
13. Slav. En. 42.14.
14. Philo, *On Curses* 6.
15. Gen. R. 16.3.
16. Ibid. 30.6.

# 42. *Warning Against Self-Deception*

### MATT. 7.21–23

21 "Not every one who says to me, 'Lord, Lord,' shall enter the kingdom of heaven, but he who does the will of my Father who is in heaven. 22 On that day many will say to me, 'Lord, Lord, did we not prophesy in your name, and cast out demons in your name, and do many mighty works in your name?' 23 And then will I declare to them, 'I never knew you; depart from me, you evildoers.' "

### LUKE 6.46

"Why do you call me 'Lord, Lord, and not do what I tell you?"

### IBID 13.26–27

26 "Then you will begin to say, 'We ate and drank in your presence, and you taught in our streets.' 27 But he will say, 'I tell you, I do not know where you come from; depart from me, all you workers of iniquity.' "

## COMMENTARY

21 *Not every one who says*, etc.   I.e., deeds, not words, are the important things. The better reading is Luke: "you *call* me but do not *do*."

*to do the will of my Father*   A common expression in rabbinic literature.[1]

22 *On that day*   I.e., the Day of Judgment. Cf. Isa. 2.16, 17; Zech. 14.6.

23 *Did we not prophesy in your name*, etc.   Note that the expression "in your name," Heb. *beshimkha*, occurs three times in this verse for emphasis. The name possesses the power of the one named. For examples of exorcism in the name of Jesus in Jewish sources, see below p. 178).

*I never knew you*   An expression of rejection used by the Rabbis, often as a form of a ban.[2]

*Depart from me, you evildoers* Ps. (LXX) 6.9.

### NOTES

1. E.g., B. Ket. 66b, B. BB 146b.
2. See B. MQ 16a, B. Er. 53a, TJ MQ 3.8, 83d (56).

# 43. Hearers and Doers of the Word

## MATT. 7.24–27

24 "Everyone then who hears these words of mine and does them will be like a wise man who built his house upon the rock; 25 and the rain fell, and the floods came, and the winds blew and beat upon that house, but it did not fall, because it had been founded on the rock. 26 And everyone who hears these words of mine and does not do them will be like a foolish man who built his house upon the sand; 27 and the rain fell, and the floods came, and the winds blew and beat against the house, and it fell; and great was the fall of it."

## LUKE 6.47–49

47 "Everyone who comes to me and hears my words and does them, I will show you what he is like: 48 he is like a man building a house, who dug deep, and laid the foundation upon rock; and when a flood arose, the stream broke against that house, and could not shake it, because it had been well built. 49 But he who hears and does not do them is like a man who built a house on the ground without a foundation; against which the stream broke, and immediately it fell, and the ruin of that house was great."

---

e  Some texts read *because it had been founded on the rock.*

## COMMENTARY

There is no direct rabbinic parallel to this parable, but it is undoubtedly in the rabbinic style and should be compared to the following:

Elisha ben Abuyah says: "One in whom there are good works, who has studied much Torah, to what may he be likened? To a person who builds first with stones and afterward with brick: even when much water comes and collects by their side, it does not dislodge them. But one in whom there are no good works, though he studied Torah, to what may he be likened? To a person who builds first with bricks and afterward with stones: even when a little water gathers, it overthrows them immediately."[1]

He used to say: "One in whom there are good works, who has studied much Torah, to what may he be likened? To lime poured over stones: even when any number of rains fall on it, they cannot push it out of place. One in whom there are no good works, though he studied much Torah, is like lime poured over bricks: even when a little rain falls on it, it softens immediately and is washed away."[2]

Eleazar b. Azariah said: ". . . He whose wisdom is more abundant than his works, to what is he like? To a tree whose branches are abundant but whose roots are few: and the wind comes and uproots it and overturns it, as it is written, *He shall be like a tamerisk in the desert and shall not see when good cometh; but shall inhabit the parched places in the wilderness* [Jer. 17.6]. But he whose works are more abundant than his wisdom, to what is he like? To a tree whose branches are few but whose roots are many; so that even if all the winds in the world come and blow against it, it cannot be stirred from its place, as it is written, *He shall be as a tree planted by the waters, and that spreadeth out his roots by the river, and shall not fear when heat cometh, and his leaf shall be green; and shall not be careful in the year of the drought, neither shall cease from yielding fruit* [ibid. 17.8]."[3]

### NOTES

1. *ARN* 24.
2. Ibid.
3. M. Avot 3.18.

# 44. *The End of the Sermon*

## MATT. 7.28–29

28 And when Jesus finished these sayings, the crowds were astonished at his teaching, 29 for he taught them as one who had authority, and not as their scribes.

## MARK 1.21–22

21 And they went into Capernaum; and immediately on the sabbath he entered the synagogue and taught. 22 And they were astonished at his teaching, for he taught them as one who had authority, and not as the scribes.

## LUKE 4.31–32

31 And he went down to Capernaum, a city of Galilee. And he was teaching them on the sabbath; 32 and they were astonished at his teaching, for his word was with authority.
See above Sec. 12 (p. 60)

# 45. *The Healing of a Leper*

## MATT. 8.1–4

1 When he came down from the mountain great crowds followed him; 2 and behold, a leper came to him and knelt before him, saying, "Lord, if you will, you can make me clean." 3 And he stretched out his hand and touched him, saying, "I will; be clean." And immediately his leprosy was cleansed. 4 And Jesus said to him, "See that you say nothing to anyone; but go, show yourself to the priest, and offer the gift that Moses commanded for a proof to the people."[f]

## MARK 1.40–45

40 And a leper came to him beseeching him, and kneeling said to him, "If you will, you can make me clean." 41 And being moved with pity, he stretched out his hand and touched him, and said to him, "I will; be clean." 42 And immediately the leprosy left him, and he was made clean. 43 And he sternly charged him, and sent him away at once, 44 and said to him, "See that you say nothing to anyone; but go, show yourself to the priest, and offer for your cleansing what Moses commanded for a proof to the people."[f] 45 But he went out and began to talk freely about it, and to spread the news, so that Jesus[g] could no longer openly enter a town, but was out in the country; and people came to him from every quarter.

## LUKE 5.12–16

12 While he was in one of the cities, there came a man a men full of leprosy; and when he saw Jesus, he fell on his face and besought him, "Lord, if you will, you can make me clean." 13 And he stretched out his hand, and touched him, saying, "I will; be clean." And immediately the leprosy left him. 14 And he charged him to tell no one; but "go and show yourself to the priest, and make an offering for your cleansing, as Moses commanded for a proof to the people."[f] 15 But so much the more the report went abroad concerning him; and great multitudes gathered to hear and to be healed of their infirmities. 16 But he withdrew to the wilderness and prayed.*

---

f Greek *to them*.
g Greek *he*.
* Cf. Mark 1.35, Luke 4.42.

## COMMENTARY

This is the first of the miracle stories which form a literary unit in Matthew (8.1–9.34). Presumably they are placed in this position immediately after the Sermon in Matthew to illustrate the great acts of Jesus following his great teachings. The author-editor was apparently unaware of the problem which has resulted by placing this first miracle story here. The connecting literary link between the Sermon and the miracle stories is v. 1, which relates that "great crowds followed him." In the leper story, however, Jesus tells the leper not to tell it to anyone, an act witnessed by the great crowds. Perhaps the reason the leper story was chosen to lead the list of miracle stories was that the leper, according to a rabbinic tradition, was considered as dead,[1] and restoring the dead to life was the greatest of all feats.[2] Weiss suggested that the leper asked Jesus to pronounce him clean, but Jesus, loyal to the Law, told him to go to the priest, and subsequently this case was expanded into a miracle story.[3]

2 *leper* Heb. *meẓora* or *mukhē shekhin*, cf. Lev. 13.1–59, is one suffering a skin disorder. The leprosy in antiquity covered a variety of skin ailments, among them one which we identify today as the disease. Lev. 13, where it is said to be curable, seems to rule out leprosy as we know it. The leper was segregated from society, and only when pronounced clean by the priest could he return.[4]

*and knelt before him* Gr. *prosekunei autō*.  Better "prostrated himself before him." See above on Matt. 2.2 (p. 9)

*make me clean*  In the LXX *katharizein*. translates the Hebrew *letaher*, "to pronounce one clean."[5]

4 *show yourself to the priest*  See Lev. 14.1 ff. This might well suggest that the incident took place near Jerusalem.[6]

*for a proof to the people*  "The clause can only refer to the supposed hostility of Jesus to the Law already implied in 5.17–20, the fact that Christ bade His patient present himself to the priests, and offer the usual sacrifices, should convince them that He did not seek to undermine the Mosaic ritual. The illustration here given Christ's attitude toward legal ceremonies, may be one reason why the editor places this incident immediately after the Sermon on the Mount."[7] The proof is Jesus' loyalty to the Law, not proof of cure, which would be completely unnecessary before the priestly experts.[8]

## NOTES

1. B. Ned. 64b.
2. See B. Sanh. 47a.
3. J. Weiss, *Die Schriften des Neuen Testaments übersetzt und . . . erklärt.* Vol. I. *Die drei ältern Evangelien,* 3rd ed. 1917, p. 152.
4. On leprosy, see J. Preuss, *Biblisch-talmudische Medizin* (Berlin, 1923), pp. 369 ff.

5. Cf. Lev. 18.6, 23, 34, 37. It is rare, outside of the NT and the LXX; it is found only once in Josephus, *Ant.* XI.5.4.
6. Cf. Luke 2.44.
7. Allen, *Matt.*, pp. 75–76.
8. McNeile, *Matt.*, p. 103.

# 46. *The Centurion's Servant*

## MATT. 8.5–13

5 As he entered Capernaum, a centurion came forward to him, beseeching him 6 and saying, "Lord, my servant is lying paralyzed at home, in terrible distress." 7 And he said to him, "I will come and heal him." 8 But the centurion answered him, "Lord, I am not worthy to have you come under my roof; but only say the word, and my servant will be healed. 9 For I am a man under authority, with soldiers under me; and I say to one, 'Go,' and he goes, and to another, 'Come,' and he comes, and to my slave, 'Do this,' and he does it." 10 When Jesus heard him, he marveled, and said to those who followed him, "Truly, I say to you, not even[h] in Israel have I found such faith. 11 I tell you, many will come from east and west and sit at table with Abraham, Isaac, and Jacob in the kingdom of heaven, 12 while the sons of the kingdom will be thrown into the outer darkness; there men will weep and gnash their teeth." 13 And to the centurion Jesus said, "Go; be it done for you as you have believed." And the servant was healed at that very moment.[i]

## LUKE 7.1–10; 13.28–30

1 After he had ended all his sayings in the hearing of the people he entered Capernaum. 2 Now a centurion had a slave who was dear to him, who was sick and at the point of death. 3 When he heard of Jesus, he sent to him elders of the Jews, asking him to come and heal his slave. 4 And when they came to Jesus, they besought him earnestly, saying, "He is worthy to have you do this for him, 5 for he loves our nation, and he built us our synagogue." 6 And Jesus went with them. When he was not far from the house, the centurion sent friends to him, saying to him, "Lord do not trouble yourself, for I am not worthy to have you come under my roof; 7 therefore I did not presume to come to you. But say the word, and let my servant be healed. 8 For I am a man set under authority, with soldiers under me: and I say to one, 'Go,' and he goes; and to another, 'Come,' and he comes; and to my slave, 'Do this,' and he does it." 9 When Jesus heard this he marveled at him, and turned and said to the multitude that followed him, 'I tell you, not even in Israel have I found such faith." 13.28 "There you will weep and gnash your teeth, when you see Abraham and Isaac and Jacob and all the prophets in the kingdom of God and you yourselves thrust out. 29 And men will come from east and west, and from north and south, and sit at table in the kingdom of God. 30 And behold, some are last who will be first, and some are first who will be last." 7.10 And when those who had been sent returned to the house they found the slave well.

---

h Some texts read *with no one.*
i Some texts read *and when the centurion returned to his house in that hour he found the servant well.*

## COMMENTARY

The key to the understanding of this second miracle story is that the centurion is a Gentile who exhibits a faith in Jesus' power which the latter has not found in Israel. In Luke it comes first after the Sermon. The motif of the story is similar to that of the Syro-Phoenician Woman.[1] The custom of going to a holy man or a miracle worker seeking a cure is widespread. In the Bible the most famous are the Elijah-Elisha stories.[2] The theme is quite common in rabbinic sources; e.g., "R. Phinḥas b. Ḥama expounded: 'Anyone who has a sick person in his home should go to a scholar [sage] and have him seek mercy for him, as it is written, *A king's wrath is a messenger of death, and a wise man will appease it* [Prov. 16.14].' "[3]

6 *my servant* Gr. *ho pais mou*, better "my boy" or "my lad," the Gr. bearing both meanings, and in light of v. 9 (cf. Luke 7.7) "boy" is preferred.
*I am not worthy* Perhaps orginal Heb. *ayni khedai.*
5 *a man under authority* A difficult phrase. Torrey tries to get over the difficulty by supposing that the word "set" (in Luke 7.8) is a misreading of an Aram. original and that the true rendering would be something like "exercising authority."[4] This is not convincing because the word "set" occurs *only* in Luke. A more likely explanation is that there has been a confusion of the two senses of the Aram. preposition *teḥot*, which means both "under" and "in place of." What the centurion was really saying was, "I am the representative of the governor or of the deputy, of the commander-in-chief, i.e., in his stead." This makes sense with what follows and also makes clear the analogy between the centurion's position and that of Jesus. Both are representatives of the king, the centurion of Antipas (probably) and Jesus of God, and both have such authority as belongs to their respective offices.[5] To this should be added that the centurion has only to bid something to be done and it is, without him actually being there, so by comparison he believes that Jesus can heal without actually going to his house.
11 *many will come from east and west* A Semitism using the opposites to include everything. Cf. Ps. 106.3; cf. Mark 1.11. Most likely the centurion is referring to Gentiles, not to Jews (see below).
*to sit at table* Actually "to recline at table." Gr. *anaklithēsontai* = Heb. *hasev.* The meal in the NT symbolizes the joys of the kingdom,[6] and this idea goes back to Jewish sources about the messianic banquet, which included among other dainties Leviathan and Behemoth. "At the last coming they will lead forth Adam with our forefathers and lead them there, that they may rejoice as a man calls those whom he loves to feast with him.[7]
12 *sons of the kingdom* In the NT only here and in Matt. 13.38. This

phrase is not found in rabbinic sources, but in the same vein are the phrases "Who is the son of the world-to-come?"[8] and "son of the covenant."[9] This phrase is most difficult. The "son of the kingdom" or the rabbinic "son of the world-to-come" refers to one who *inherits* his portion because of merit or by faith and is used in a positive not in a negative sense. Dalman, however, states: "The sons of the theocracy are these who belong to it in virtue of their birth, who thereby have a natural right to possession of it."[10] Also Allen: " 'Sons of the kingdom' is a Semitic idiom equivalent to those who should inherit it, its rightful heirs."[11] Abrahams' comments "No doubt this under-lies" Matthew viii.12, especially in the light of the illustration quoted from Philo. Nevertheless, though 'son' and 'heir' are naturally associated, this is by no means regularly the case with the Rabbinic 'son of the world to come.' In a very large number of passages a 'son of the world to come' does something to deserve it and does not acquire it by privilege of birth."[12] The "sons of the kingdom" in this passage "no doubt, signifies the Jewish nation or people. Such of them as are lacking in the faith which the centurion possessed will be cast out of the kingdom, whilst Gentiles sit down with the righteous patriarchs at the banquet."[13]

*into outer darkness* Darkness as punishment is met with frequently in Jewish sources: "Into darkness will your spirits enter";[14] "Those who were born in darkness will be cast into darkness";[15] "their inheritance is dark-ness";[16] "the inheritance of the sinner is darkness";[17] "He will send back the ungodly into darkness."[18] In rabbinic literature these are also of note: "God calls Gehenna darkness";[19] "The sinner in Gehinom will be covered with darkness."[20]

*men will weep and gnash their teeth* A common phrase in Matt., cf. 13.42, 50; 22.13; 24.51; 25.30; and only once in Luke, 13.28. That the sinners in Gehinom will weep is well known, e.g., "the transgressors will cry and make lamentation,"[21] "the voice of crying and weeping and lamenting and strong pain,"[22] "the mighty hell–full of lamentation."[23]

13 *And the servant was healed at that very moment* A striking parallel of curing the sick from a distance is the following story:

> Our Rabbis taught: "Once the son of Rabban Gamaliel fell ill. He sent two scholars to R. Ḥanina b. Dosa to ask him to pray for him. When he saw them he went to an upper room and prayed for him. When he came down he said to them, 'Go, the fever has left him.' They said to him, 'Are you a prophet?' He replied, 'I am neither a prophet nor the son of a prophet, but I have learned from experience that if my prayer is fluent in my mouth, I know that he is accepted, but if not I know that he is rejected.' They sat down and made a note of the exact moment. When they came to R. Gamaliel, he said to them, 'By the Temple Service [oath], you have not been a moment too soon or too late, but so it happened at that very moment the fever left him and he asked for water to drink.' "[24]

## NOTES

1. Mark 7.24–30, Matt. 15.21, 28.
2. See 1 Kings 17.17, 2 Kings 4.22 ff., 5.1 ff.
3. B. BB 116a. See below for another example, and cf. John 4.47 ff.
4. C. C. Torrey, *The Four Gospels*, p. 292.
5. Manson, *SJ*, p. 65.
6. Cf. Matt. 26.29; Luke, 14.15–24; Rev. 3.20, 19.9.
7. En. 42.5. Cf. also ibid. 62.14, Apoc. Bar. 29.4, *PRK* 29(188b).
8. E.g., B. Pes. 8a, B. Shab. 153a. Cf. Matt. 13.38.
9. B. Ber. 16b.
10. Dalman, *Words*, p. 115.
11. Allen, *Matt.*, p. 78.
12. Abrahams, *Studies II*, p. 187. Cf. B. Ber 4a, B. Shab. 153a, B. Meg. 28b, B. Ta'an. 22a.
13. Allen, loc. cit.
14. En. 103.8.
15. Ibid. 108.14.
16. Ps. Sol. 14.6.
17. Ibid. 15.11.
18. Sib. Or. 4.43.
19. Lev. R. 27.
20. Exod. R. 14.2. Cf. also En. 42.12; TJ Sanh. 10, 29b; Koh. R. 1.15. On the symbolic use of light and darkness, see John 1.5 and 1QM passim.
21. En. 108.3.
22. Ibid. 108.5.
23. Ibid. 40.12.
24. B. Ber. 34b. Cf. John 4.46–54. Cf. B. Ned. 41a.

## 47. *The Healing of Peter's Mother-in-Law*

### MATT. 8.14–15

14 And when Jesus entered Peter's house, he saw his mother-in-law lying sick with a fever; 15 he touched her hand, and the fever left her and she rose and served him.
See above Sec 13 (p. 61)

## 48. *Healing the Sick at Evening*

### MATT. 8.16–17

16 That evening they brought to him many who were possessed with demons; and he cast out the spirits with a word, and healed all who were sick. 17 This was to fulfill what was spoken by the prophet Isaiah, "He took our infirmities and bore our diseases."
See above Sec. 14 (p. 62).

# 49. *The Nature of Discipleship*

## MATT. 8.18–22

18 Now when Jesus saw great crowds around him, he gave orders to go over to the other side. 19 And a scribe came up and said to him, "Teacher, I will follow you wherever you go." 20 And Jesus said to him, "Foxes have holes, and birds of the air have nests; but the Son of man has nowhere to lay his head." 21 Another of his disciples said to him, "Lord, let me first go and bury my father." 22 But Jesus said to him, "Follow me, and leave the dead to bury their own dead."

## LUKE 9.57–60

57 And as they were going along the road, a man said to him, "I will follow you wherever you go." 58 And Jesus said to him, "Foxes have holes, and birds of the air have nests; but the Son of man has nowhere to lay his head." 59 "To another he said, "Follow me," But he said, "Lord, let me first go and bury my father." 60 But he said to him, "Leave the dead to bury their own dead; but for you, go and proclaim the kingdom of God."

## COMMENTARY

18 *he gave orders to go over to the other side*   This is to introduce the story of the calming of the storm, which is the very next miracle, but he interjects this passage about discipleship, which is better placed in Luke.[1]

19 *a scribe*   Heb. *sofer*, learned member of the Pharisees. Luke has "a certain man," typical in rabbinic stories. It is significant that the scribe calls Jesus "teacher."[2]

*teacher* Gr. *didaskalos*   Is this a translation of Heb. *rabbi?* If so this passage is late, for the title of rabbi was not used until the end of the first Christian century.[3]

*I will follow you*   I.e., become your disciple. See above pp. 59, 66. Manson has an unusual explanation of this passage: "Now as an apocalyptic symbol the birds of the air stand for the Gentile nations, and the phrase is used again in this sense by Jesus in the parable of the Mustard Seed . . . In *Enoch* (89) 'foxes' is a symbol for Ammonites, a people racially akin to, but politically enemies of Israel. Jesus Himself uses the epithet 'fox' of Herod (Lk. 13.22). Then the sense of the saying may be: everyone is at home in Israel's land except the true Israel. The birds of the air—the Roman overlords, the foxes—the Edomite interlopers, have made their position secure. The true Israel is disinherited by them: and if you cast your lot with me and mine you join the ranks of the dispossessed, and you must be prepared to serve God under those conditons."[4]

20 *Son of man*   Here, Jesus himself. "Son of man" is perhaps the most enigmatic expression in the NT. Of all the explanations offered so far, perhaps the most likely is that it is a euphemism for "Son of God."[5]

*Foxes have their holes* This appears to have been a popular proverb placed in the mouth of Jesus by the evangelist.[6] If this encounter took place *late* in the ministry of Jesus, as in Luke, it may be authentic. Klausner argues for the period of the Northern travels (Mark 7.24–34) when Jesus was escaping from his enemies, and was pursued by both the civil and the religious authorities.[7]

21 *another of the disciples* *of the disciples* found only here in Matt. is difficult and has remained a *crux interpretum*. If he had been a disciple, what is the meaning of *first* and *follow you?* Luke's reading is much smoother, i.e., that the speaker was not yet a disciple. An appealing solution to the Matthean reading has been advanced by Albright-Mann: "At present the text reads *heteros de tōn mathētōn eipen autō* another of the disciples said to him. Now *de* is a particle which is so frequent in the N.T. (nearly 400 times, 55 of them in Matt.) that it is difficult to decide on occasion whether it is to be ignored or taken note of. But it is also frequently joined to the negative as *oude* (26 times in Matt. out of a total of 137 in the N.T.). We conclude that the Greek must originally have read *heteros oude tōn mathētōn* on the grounds of haplography between the final syllable of *heteros* and the first of *oude* another (not one) of the disciples."[8]

*let me first bury my father* Reminiscent of the call of Elisha, 1 Kings 19.19–21.

22 *leave the dead to bury their own dead* Although the burial of the dead is meritorious, especially for a child to bury a parent, the work of the Kingdom had absolute priority. The explanation that those who are spiritually dead should bury the deceased among their number is not satisfactory.[9] It is best explained by going back to the Aram. original, which suffered in translation. The translator read *le'meqbar*, "to bury," instead of *lemeqaber*, "to the burier, to the undertaker!"[10]

# NOTES

1. Montefiore, *SG*, 2:32.
2. See Fitzmyer, *Luke*, p. 833.
3. See Zeitlin, *Who Crucified Jesus?* pp. 39–40, 221–222. See below p. 000.
4. Manson, *SJ*, p. 72.
5. See J. Massingberg Ford, "The Son of Man a Euphemism?" *JBL* 87 (1968): 257–267, Colpe, *ho nios toū anthrōpou*, *TDNT*, 8:400–477.
6. Manson, *SJ*, 72 notwithstanding (see above).
7. Klausner, *JN*, p. 296. See H. Conzelmann, *The Theology of St. Luke*.
8. Albright-Mann, p. 96.
9. *SB*, 1 ad loc. cite, in support of this interpretation, TJ Ber. 24c (21) and parallels "that the wicked are called in their lifetime dead and the righteous in their death are called alive." This is not applicable to this passage.
10. F. Perles, "Zwei Übersetzungsfehler im Text der Evangelien. 1. Mt 8.22 (= Lc 9.60) 2. Lc 14.35," *ZNW* 19 (1919–20): 96, and I. Abrahams, *Studies II*, pp. 183 ff.

## 50. *Calming the Storm*

### MATT. 8.23–27

23 And when he got into the boat, his disciples followed him. 24 And behold, there arose a great storm on the sea, so that the boat was being swamped by the waves; but he was asleep. 25 And they went and woke him, saying, "Save, Lord; we are perishing." 26 And he said to them, "Why are you afraid, O men of little faith?" Then he rose and rebuked the winds and the sea; and there was a great calm. 27 And the men marveled, saying, "What sort of man is this, that even the winds and sea obey him?"

### MARK 4.35–41

35 On that day, when evening had come, he said to them, "Let us go across to the other side." 36 And leaving the crowd, they took him with them, just as he was, in the boat. And other boats were with him. 37 And a great storm of wind arose, and the waves beat into the boat, so that the boat was already filling. 38 But he was in the stern, asleep on the cushion; and they woke him and said to him, "Teacher, do you not care if we perish?" 39 And he awoke and rebuked the wind, and said to the sea, "Peace! Be still!" And the wind ceased, and there was a great calm. 40 He said to them, "Why are you afraid? Have you no faith?"[j] 41 And they were filled with awe, and said to one another, "Who then is this, that even wind and sea obey him?"

### LUKE 8.22–25

22 One day he got into a boat with his disciples, and he said to them, "Let us go across to the other side of the lake." So they set out, 23 and as they sailed he fell asleep. And a storm of wind came down on the lake, and they were filling with water, and were in danger. 24 And they went and woke him, saying, "Master, Master, we are perishing!" And he awoke and rebuked the wind and the raging waves; and they ceased, and there was a calm. 25 He said to them, "Where is your faith? And they were afraid, and they marveled, saying to one another, "Who then is this, that he commands even the wind and water, and they obey him?"

---

j  Some texts read *Why are you so very afraid? Why have you no faith?* Others *Why are you so very afraid? Have you no faith?*

### COMMENTARY

24 *And behold, there arose a great storm . . . but he was asleep.*  The setting harks back to Jon. 1.4–5, but here the similarity ends.

25 *O men of little faith.*  This phrase is used four times in Matt. See above p. 133.

26 *rebuked the winds*  A sign of divine power, and has several analogues in the MT, especially in Pss.[1] Gr. *epitimaō*, "rebuke" = Heb. *ga'ar*, is a technical term for a command to the demon.[2] Jesus "rebuked the winds and the lake as though they were conscious beings possessed with demons (cf. xvii 18) . . .

The incident is related, not primarily for the sake of recording a miracle, but as an instance of the subduing of the powers of evil, which was one of the signs of the nearness of the Kingdom."[3] We suggest, in addition, that the winds as well as the sea were said to be represented by a *sar*, as in the expression *sar shel yam*, "a prince, angel, or *demon* of the sea."[4]

There are no direct rabbinic parallels to this story but there are several passages about the calming of the sea and winds; among them the following is typical:

> R. Gamaliel was returning by boat and a wild sea was about to drown him. He said: "It appears to me that this situation is only because of R. Eliezer b. Hyrcanus." He stood up and said: "Ruler of the universe! It is known and revealed before You that it was not for my honor that I did this and not for the honor of my father's house, but for Your honor, so that dissenters should not multiply in Israel." And the sea calmed from its ragings![5]

### NOTES

1. Cf. Ps. 89.10–11, 93.3–4, 104.6–7, 106.8–9; Isa. 51.9–10.
2. See H. C. Kee, "The Terminology of Mark's Exorcism Stories," *NTS* 14 (1967–68): 232–246. Mark 4.39 has an additional phrase, "Peace! Be still." The Greek *phimoō*, which may be translated "to be muzzled," is a term used in exorcism—i.e., to silence or make the demon ineffective. See Mark 1.25, Luke 4.35.
3. McNeile, p. 111.
4. Note that in Mark 3.9 Jesus "rebukes the wind" (sing.) and "says to the sea." On the expression *sar shel yam* see, e.g., TJ Sanh. 7.19, 25d, where he is mentioned twice. Also note B. BB 73a, where specific mention is made of the spirit or demon of the sea. Cf. also B. Ḥul. 7a; TJ Ber. 9, 13b (p. 22). The chief of the Sea is sometimes called Rahab; cf. B. BB 74b, Exod. R. 15.22, Num. R. 18.22
5. B. BM 59b.

## 51. *The Gadarene Demoniac(s)*

### MATT. 8.28–34

28 And when he came to the other side, to the country of the Gadarenes,[k] two demoniacs met him, coming out of the tombs, so fierce that no one could pass that way. 29 And behold, they cried out, "What have you to do with us, O Son of God? Have you come here to torment us before the time?" 30 Now a herd of many swine was feeding at some distance from them. 31 And the demons begged him, "If you cast us out, send us away into the herd of swine." 32 And he said to them, "Go!" So they came out and went into the swine; and behold, the whole herd rushed down the steep bank into the sea, and perished in the waters. 33 The herdsmen fled, and going into the city they told everything, and what had happened to the demoniacs. 34 And behold, all the city came out to meet Jesus; and when they saw him, they begged him to leave their neighborhood.

## MARK 5.1–20

1 They came to the other side of the sea, to the country of the Gerasenes.<sup>k</sup> 2 And when he had come out of the boat, there met him out of the tombs a man with an unclean spirit, 3 who lived among the tombs; and no one could bind him any more, even with a chain; 4 for he had often been bound with fetters and chains, but the chains he wrenched apart, and the fetters he broke in pieces; and no one had the strength to subdue him. 5 Night and day among the tombs and on the mountains he was always crying out, and bruising himself with stones. 6 And when he saw Jesus from afar, he ran and worshiped him; 7 and crying out with a loud voice, he said, "What have you to do with me, Jesus, Son of the Most High God? I adjure you by God, do not torment me." 8 For he had said to him, "Come out of the man, you unclean spirit!" 9 And Jesus asked him, "What is your name?" He replied, "My name is Legion, for we are many." 10 And he begged him eagerly not to send them out of the country. 11 Now a great herd of swine was feeding there on the hillside; 12 and they begged him, "Send us to the swine, let us enter them." 13 So he gave them leave. And the unclean spirits came out, and entered the swine; and the herd, numbering about two thousand, rushed down the steep bank into the sea, and were drowned in the sea. 14 The herdsmen fled and told it in the city and in the country. And the people came to see what it was that had happened. 15 And they came to Jesus, and saw the demoniac sitting there, clothed and in his right mind, the man who had had the legion; and they were afraid. 16 And those who had seen it told what had happened to the demoniac and to the swine. 17 And they began to beg Jesus<sup>l</sup> to depart from their neighborhood. 18 And as he was getting into the boat, the man who had been possessed with demons begged him that he might be with him. 19 But he refused, and said to him, "Go home to your friends, and tell them how much the Lord has done for you, and how he had mercy on you." 20 And he went away and began to proclaim in the Decapolis how much Jesus had done for him; and all men marveled.

## LUKE 8.26–39

26 Then they arrived at the country of the Gerasenes,<sup>k</sup> which is opposite Galilee. 27 And as he stepped out on land, there met him a man from the city who had demons; for a long time he had worn no clothes, and he lived not in a house but among the tombs. 28 When he saw Jesus, he cried out and fell down before him, and said with a loud voice, "What have you to do with me, Jesus, Son of the Most High God? I beseech you, do not torment me." 29 For he had commanded the unclean spirit to come out of the man. (For many a time it had seized him; he was kept under guard, and bound with chains and fetters, but he broke the bonds and was driven by the demon into the desert.) 30 Jesus then asked him, "What is your name?" And he said, "Legion," for many demons had entered him. 31 And they begged him not to command them to depart into the abyss. 32 Now a large herd of swine was feeding there on the hillside; and they begged him to let them enter these. So he gave them leave. 33 Then the demons came out of the man and entered the swine, and the herd rushed down the steep bank into the lake and were drowned. 34 When the herdsmen saw what had happened, they fled, and told it in the city and in the country. 35 Then the people went out to see what had happened, and they came to Jesus, and found the man from whom the demons had gone, sitting at the feet of Jesus, clothed and in his

right mind; and they were afraid. 36 And those who had seen it told them how he who had been possessed with demons was healed. 37 Then all the people of the surrounding country of the Gerasenes[k] asked him to depart from them; for they were seized with great fear; so he got into the boat and returned. 38 The man from whom the demons had gone begged that he might be with him; but he sent him away, saying, 39 "Return to your home, and declare how much God has done for you." And he went away, proclaiming throughout the whole city how much Jesus had done for him.

---

k  Some texts read *Gergesenes*, others *Gadarenes*.
l  *him*.

## COMMENTARY

28 *Gaderenes*  Gadera, a city of the Decapolis 5 miles SE of the sea of Galilee; its territory extended to and included the hot spring of Hamon, north of the Yarmuk. Variants to Gadarenes are Gerasenes and Gergesenes; today Gadera is the modern Um Qeis. According to Josephus (*Ant.* XVII.11.4 and *BJ* II.VI.3) it was predominately Greek in its population, and this may account for swine breeding in the area. Gadera is mentioned frequently in rabbinic sources.[1]

*tombs*  An area ritually unclean (cf. Matt. 23.21) and hence a suitable location for the demons and the demoniacs. See below in this section on Luke 8.27.

29 *What have you to do with us?*  Cf. Judg. 11.12, 2 Kings 16.10, 1 Kings 17.18.

*Son of God*  The demons, recognize his true identity, even though, as yet, humans do not. Apparently "Son of God" is a messianic title, cf. Rom. 1.3. It is the Messiah who will break the power. I of the demons.[2]

*before the time*  I.e., before the Final Judgment, when the demonic forces will be punished. "From the days of the slaughter and destruction and death [of the giants] from the souls of whose flesh the spirits, having gone forth, shall destroy without incurring judgment—thus shall they destroy until the day of consummation, the great judgment in which age shall be consummated over the Watchers and the godless, ye shall be wholly consummated."[3]

32 *"Go!" So they came out*  Of interest are the following two exorcism passages from the first century:

> And God granted him [Solomon] knowledge of the art used against demons for the benefit and healing of men. He also composed incantations by which illnesses are relieved and left behind forms of exorcisms with which those possessed by demons drive them out, never to return. And this kind of cure is of very great power among us to this day, for I have seen a certain Eleazar, a countryman of mine, in the presence of Vespasian, his sons, tribunes, and a number of other soldiers, free men possessed by demons, and this was the manner of the cure: he put to the nose of the possessed man a ring which had

under its seal one of the roots prescribed by Solomon, and then, as the man smelled it, drew out the demon through his nostrils, and when the man at once fell down, adjured the demon never to come back to him, speaking Solomon's name and reciting the incantations which he had composed. Then, wishing to convince the bystanders and prove to them that he had this power, Eleazar placed a cup or a foot-basin full of water a little way off and commanded the demon, as it went out of the man, to overturn it and make it known to the spectators that he had left the man.[4]

Then Ben Temalion [a demon or a goblin] came to meet them. He said: "Is it your wish that I accompany you?" Thereupon R. Simeon wept and said: "The handmaid of my ancestor's house was found worthy of meeting an angel three times, and I not even to meet him once. However, let the miracle be performed, no matter how." Thereupon he [Ben Temalion] advanced and entered into the Emperor's daughter. When R. Simeon arrived there he called out: "Ben Temalion leave her, Ben Temalion, leave her"; and as he proclaimed this he left her.[5]

32 *the whole herd . . . into the sea* Gadera must have been near the Sea of Galilee.

33 *the herdsmen,* etc. More than likely they were Gentiles, since it was forbidden by law for Jews to raise swine.[6]

Luke 8.27 *there met a man,* etc. Only Luke and Mark describe the actions of the demoniac, and this description is closely paralleled by the rabbinic definition of an imbecile: "Our Rabbis taught: 'Who is considered to be an imbecile? He who goes out alone at night, and he who spends the night on a cemetery, and he that tears his garments.' "[7]

## NOTES

1. See *SB*, 1:490–491.
2. Cf. Josephus. *Ant.* VIII.46–47. See also E. Best, *The Temptation and the Passion: The Markan Soteriology* (Cambridge, 1965).
3. En. 16.1, Jub. 10.5–11, Test. Sim. 6, Test. Jud. 2.5.
4. Josephus, *Ant.* VIII.2.5.
5. B. Me'ila 17b.
6. M. BQ 7.7; B. ibid. 82b. See also B. Men. 64b; B. Sot. 49b; Josephus, *Ant.* XIV.2.2; TJ Ber. 4, 7b (22); B. Ned. 49b.
7. B. Ḥag. See also T. Ter. 1.3 (p. 25); TJ Ter. 1.1 (40b); TJ Git. 7.1 (48c).

# 52. The Healing of the Paralytic

## MATT. 9.1–8

1 And getting into a boat he crossed over and came to his own city. 2 And behold, they brought to him a paralytic, lying on his bed; and when Jesus saw their faith he said to the paralytic, "Take heart, my son; your sins are forgiven." 3 And behold,

some of the scribes said to themselves, "This man is blaspheming." 4 But Jesus, knowing,ᵐ their thoughts, said, "Why do you think evil in your hearts? 5 For which is easier, to say, 'Your sins are forgiven,'ⁿ or to say, 'Rise and walk'? 6 But that you may know that the Son of man has authority on earth to forgive sins."—he then said to the paralytic—"Rise, take up your bed and go home." 7 And he rose and went home. 8 When the crowds saw it, they were afraid, and they glorified God, who had given such authority to men.

## Mark 2.1–12

1 And when he returned to Capernaum after some days, it was reported that he was at home. 2 And many were gathered together, so that there was no longer room for them, not even about the door; and he was preaching the word to them. 3 And they came, bringing to him a paralytic carried by four men. 4 And when they could not get near him because of the crowd, they removed the roof above him; and when they had made an opening, they let down the pallet on which the paralytic lay. 5 And when Jesus saw their faith, he said to the paralytic, "My son, your sins are forgiven." 6 Now some of the scribes were sitting there, questioning in their hearts, 7 "Why does this man speak thus? It is blasphemy! Who can forgive sins but God alone?" 8 And immediately Jesus, perceiving in his spirit that they thus questioned within themselves, said to them, "Why do you question thus in your hearts? 9 Which is easier, to say to the paralytic, 'Your sins are forgiven'; or to say, 'Rise, take up your pallet and walk'? 10 But that you may know that the Son of man has authority on earth to forgive sins"—he said to the paralytic—11 "I say to you, rise, take up your pallet and go home." 12 And he rose, and immediately took up the pallet and went out before them all; so that they were all amazed and glorified God, saying, "We never saw anything like this!"

## Luke 5.17–26

17 On one of those days, as he was teaching, there were Pharisees and teachers of the law sitting by, who had come from every town of Galilee and Judea and from Jerusalem; and the power of the Lord was with him to heal.º 18 And behold, men were bringing on a bed a man who was paralyzed, and they sought to bring him in and lay him before Jesus;ᵖ but finding no way to bring him in, because of the crowd, they went up on the roof and let him down with his bed through the tiles into the midst before Jesus. 20 And when he saw their faith he said, "Man, your sins are forgiven you." 21 And the scribes and the Pharisees began to question, saying, "Who is this that speaks blasphemies? Who can forgive sins but God only?" 22 When Jesus perceived their questionings, he answered them, "Why do you question in your hearts? 23 Which is easier, to say, 'Your sins are forgiven you,' or to say, 'Rise and walk'? 24 But that you may know that the Son of man has authority on earth to forgive sins"—he said to the man who was paralyzed—"I say to you, rise, take up your bed and go home." 25 And immediately he rose before them, and took up that on which he lay, and went home, glorifying God. 26 And amazement seized them all, and they glorified God and were filled with awe, saying "We have seen strange things today."

m Other ancient authorities read *seeing.*
n Some read *have been forgiven.*
o Some read *was present to heal them.*
p Greek *him.*

## COMMENTARY

In this miracle story, the new theme introduced here is the forgiveness of sin by Jesus, adumbrating the essential function of the Christ figure. Here in this miracle story, sin is the cause of illness, which, when forgiven, causes the illness to disappear.

1 *to his own city*   I.e., Capernaum; see Mark 2.1.
*lying on his bed*   A stretcher, or portable bed.[1]
2 *your sins are forgiven*   This notion that sickness is the result of sin is well attested to in rabbinic sources. E.g., "R. Hiyya stated: 'The patient is not healed of his sickness until his sins are forgiven' "[2] "R. Ammi: 'There are no sufferings without sin.' "[3] The prayer for forgiveness (in the *Shemoneh Esreh*) precedes the prayer for healing.[4] In rabbinic Judaism, man could forgive a sin, and it was a moral imperative so to do when the sin committed was against himself, but not for others; for forgiveness is from God, through direct access and not through an intermediary.
6 *But that you may know that the Son of man has authority*, etc.   This verse and v. 8 seem to be contradictory. Is "Son of man" here a messianic title, or is it the Aram. for "human being," *bar nesha?* If it means "human being," then what is the miracle of Jesus?
8 *When the crowds saw it*   Seeing the healing, the crowds were afraid and glorified God, who had given the power to heal to a human being, and perhaps recited the blessing for such an occasion, "Who has apportioned from His wisdom to those who fear Him."[5]

## NOTES

1. For an example of a portable bed, see M. RH 2.9.
2. B. Ned. 41a.
3. B. Shab. 55a. Cf. Büchler, *Types of Jewish Palestinian Piety*, pp. 328, 329, 340. On the forgiveness of sins, see Abrahams, *Studies I*, chaps. IX and XX.
4. That sin causes sickness, see B. Meg. 17b; Singer, *APB*, pp. 456–457.
5. B. Ber. 58a.

# 53. The Call of Levi

## MATT. 9.9–13

9 As Jesus passed on from there, he saw a man called Matthew sitting at the tax office; and he said to him, "Follow me." And he rose and followed him. 10 And as he sat at table⁹ in the house, behold, many tax collectors and sinners came and sat down with

Jesus and his disciples. 11 And when the Pharisees saw this, they said to his disciples, "Why does your teacher eat with tax collectors and sinners?" 12 But when he heard it, he said, "Those who are well have no need of a physician, but those who are sick. 13 Go and learn what this means, 'I desire mercy, and not sacrifice.' For I came not to call the righteous but sinners."

## MARK 2.13–17

13 He went out again beside the sea; and all the crowd gathered about him, and he taught them. 14 And as he passed on, he saw Levi[r] the son of Alphaeus sitting at the tax office, and he said to him, "Follow me." And he rose and followed him. 15 And as he sat at table in his house, many tax collectors and sinners were sitting with Jesus and his disciples; for there were many who followed him. 16 And the scribes of[s] the Pharisees, when they saw that he was eating with sinners and tax collectors, said to his disciples, "Why does he eat[t] with tax collectors and sinners?" 17 And when Jesus heard it, he said to them, "Those who are well have no need of a physician, but those who are sick; I came not to call the righteous, but sinners."

## LUKE 5.27–32

27 After this he went out, and saw a tax collector, named Levi, sitting at the tax office; and he said to him, "Follow me." 28 And he left everything, and rose and followed him. 29 And Levi made him a great feast in his house and there was a large company of tax collectors and others sitting at table[q] with him. 30 And the Pharisees and their scribes murmured again[s] his disciples, saying, "Why do you eat and drink with tax collectors and sinners?" 31 And Jesus answered them, "Those who are well have no need of a physician but those who are sick; 32 I have come not to call the righteous, but sinners to repentance."

---

q  Greek *reclined*.
r  Some read *James*.
s  Other ancient authorities read *and*.
t  Other ancient authorities add *and drink*.

## COMMENTARY

9 *a man called Matthew*  In Mark he is called Levi the son of Alphaeus; perhaps both were tax collectors.

*sitting at the tax office*  On the tax collector as an undesirable of society, see above p. 109. He was most likely in the service of Antipas. "The custom officer would sit by the landing stage to collect custom dues on exports carried across the lake to territory outside of Herod's rule."[1]

10 *as he sat at table*  I.e., reclining at table. "It is clear from the reaction of the Pharisees and from rabbinic sources, that one should avoid the company of the undesirable of society. The reason why the Pharisees did not want to break bread with the sinners was not due to pride or to exclusiveness. For the Pharisees, the table was not merely a place for eating and drinking and

satisfying their human needs, but it was as well a place for learned discussion and prayers. Again, it was very hard for the Pharisees, who observed the laws of purity and impurity to eat with sinners who were neither versed in the laws of purity and impurity, nor observed them."[2]

11 *tax collectors and sinners* "The association in the Gospels of the two expressions, Publicans and Sinners, is parallel to the combination of 'publicans and robbers' in Rabbinic literature. The 'sinners' were thus not those who neglected the rules of ritual piety, but were persons of immoral life, men of proved dishonesty or followers of suspected and degrading occupations."[3]

12 *Those who are well have no need of a physician* This "is probably a secular *mashal* of uncertain application."[4]

13 *go and learn* A frequent expression both in Heb., *zē u'lemad*, and in Aram., *zil gemor*, and is the language of debate or challenge.[5]

*I desire mercy and not sacrifice* Hos. 6.6.[6]

## NOTES

1. McNeile, *Matt.*, p. 117.
2. Zeitlin, *Who Crucified Jesus*, p. 135. On avoiding the company of sinners, especially avoiding eating with them, see B. Ber. 43b; T. Demai 3.6 f. (p. 49); TJ ibid. 2, 22d (53); Sifre Deut. 1.
3. Abrahams, *Studies I*, p. 55. On suspected and degrading occupations, see M. Qid. 4.14. Cf. also B. ibid. 82b
4. C. E. Carlston, *The Parables of the Triple Tradition* (Philadelphia, 1975), p. 110, citing Schmid, *Markus*, p. 65. For the philosophers' justification for consorting with the sick, see Pausanias and Aristippus in Plutarch, *Moralia* 230F (Loeb 3:382).
5. *SER* 18 Num. R. 8, M. Avot 2.9. See Bacher, *Terminologie*, 1:75.
6. See Stendahl, *SSMUOT*, pp. 128 ff., for the dependency of this citation on the MT or LXX and the possible influence of the Targum upon it.

# 54. *The Question About Fasting*

## MATT. 9.14–17

14 Then the disciples of John came to him, saying, "Why do we and the Pharisees fast,ᵘ but your disciples do not fast?" 15 And Jesus said to them, "Can the wedding guests mourn as long as the bridegroom is with them? The days will come when the bridegroom is taken away from them, and then they will fast. 16 And no one puts a piece of unshrunk cloth on an old garment, for the patch tears away from the garment, and a worse tear is made. 17 Neither is new wine put into old wineskins; if it is, the skins burst, and the wine is spilled, and the skins are destroyed; but new wine is put into fresh wineskins, and so both are preserved."

## MARK 2.18–22

18 Now Johns's disciples and the Pharisees were fasting; and people came and said to him, "Why do John's disciples and the disciples of the Pharisees fast, but your

disciples do not fast?" 19 And Jesus said to them, "Can the wedding guests fast while the bridegroom is with them? As long as they have the bridegroom with them, they cannot fast. 20 The days will come, when the bridegroom is taken away from them, and then they will fast on that day. 21 No one sews a piece of unshrunk cloth on an old garment; if he does the patch tears away from it, the new from the old, and a worse tear is made. 22 And no one puts new wine into old wineskins; if he does, the wine will burst the skins, and the wine is lost, and so are the skins; but new wine is for fresh skins."[v]

### Luke 5.33–39

33 And they said to him, "The disciples of John fast often and offer prayers, and so do the disciples of the Pharisees, but yours eat and drink." 34 And Jesus said to them, "Can you make wedding guests fast while the bridegroom is with them? 35 The days will come, when the bridegroom is taken away from them, and then they will fast in those days." 36 He told them a parable also: "No one tears a piece from a new garment and puts it upon an old garment; if he does, he will tear the new, and the piece from the new will not match the old. 37 And no one puts new wine into old wineskins; if he does the new wine will burst the skins and it will be spilled, and the skins will be destroyed. 38 But new wine must be put into fresh wineskins. 39 And no one after drinking old wine desires new; for he says, 'The old is good.' "[w]

---

u  Other ancient authorities add *much* or *often*.

v  Other ancient authorites omit *but new wine is for fresh skins*.

w  Other ancient authorities read *better*.

### COMMENTARY

14 the disciples of John[1]  Although there is no integral connection between this passage and the one above, one can see why they are juxtaposed—eating-fasting.

*Why do we and the Pharisees fast*, etc.  There were public fasts and private fasts, and it is difficult to ascertain which is meant here. Zeitlin has suggested that the fasting controversy centers "on the point that Jesus claimed to be the Messiah, a scion of the house of David. Hence, his disciples were not supposed to observe the national fast days which were connected with the destruction of the first Temple. From the Bible we learn that upon the restoration of the Jewish State, the people asked the Prophet Zechariah if they should continue to fast on the days that were instituted in commemoration of the destruction of the first Temple. The Prophet Zechariah answered the Jews in the name of God in these words: 'The fast of the Fourth month and the fast of the Fifth and the fast of the Seventh and the fast of the Tenth, shall be to the House of Judah joy and gladness and cheerful feasts (Zec 7.3; 8.19).' "[2]

15 *Can the wedding guests mourn*, etc.  It has been suggested that the wedding setting has as its background the relationship between God and

Israel, his bride.[3] It is more likely that the bridegroom imagery refers to the messianic figure.[4] Note the comment that "the wedding was turned into mourning when Jonathan and Simon killed many of the sons of Jambri."[5]

*the wedding guests*  The expression might well go back to the Heb. *benē ha-ḥuppah*.[6] Since a wedding is time for rejoicing, and it is proper to gladden the bridegroom and the bride, some prescriptions regarding mourning were relaxed or eliminated. The allegory involving the crucifixion is apparent. It has been noted that in antiquity, the guests, not the bridegroom, left when the wedding festivities were over.[7]

16 *And no one puts a piece of unshrunk cloth*, etc.  The idea of this passage seems clear—old institutions vs. new ideas which are incompatible. If indeed this is the meaning, it is unlikely that these are the words of Jesus (cf. 5.17 ff.) but rather the words of the evangelist or of an editor.[8] What is difficult is the abrupt transition from the wedding picture and fasting to this new subject of patches and wineskins. Perhaps there was a sentence or clause which existed in the original which was omitted, to the effect that when the bridegroom is taken away from them, i.e. dies, they will fast and will rend their garments (as a sign of mourning).[9]

## NOTES

1. For a parallel to this passage, see Gospel of Thomas, logion 104. On fasting, see above p. 169.
2. Zeitlin, *Who Crucified Jesus*, p. 131.
3. Hos. 2.16, Isa. 54.5–6, 62.4–5.
4. Cf. Exod. R. 15.30; Lev. R. 11.2; TJ Shev. 4, 35c (25). Carlston (*Parables of the Triple Tradition*, p. 14) comments correctly "that 'fasting is interpreted as *mourning*.' " His statement (loc cit.) "that fasting is a common penitential practice, and the added fasts observed by the Pharisees are primarily of this type," is not accurate.
5. 1 Macc. 9.41.
6. E.g., T. Ber. 2.10 (p. 4), or Aram. *benē genana*, B. Er. 40a, B. BB 145b. Cf. Lagrange, 542. Jülicher, *Gleichnisreden Jesu*, 1:181, suggests *shushbinin*, "groomsmen."
7. Jülicher, op. cit., p. 184.
8. Jeremias, *PJ*, pp. 117 ff. Contra: A. Kee, "The Old Coat and the New Wine: A Parable of Repentance," *NT* 12 (1970): 13–21.
9. M. Avot 4.20, suggested by some, is not applicable here.

# 55. Jairus' Daughter and the Woman with the Hemorrhage

## MATT. 9.18–26

18 While he was thus speaking to them, behold, a ruler came in and knelt before him saying, "My daughter has just died; but come lay your hand on her, and she will live." 19 And Jesus rose and followed him, with his disciples. 20 And behold, a woman who had suffered from a hemorrhage for twelve years came up behind him and touched the fringe of his garment. 21 For she said to herself, "If I only touch his garment, I shall be made well." 22 Jesus turned and seeing her he said, "Take heart,

daughter; your faith has made you well." And instantly the woman was made well. 23 And when when Jesus came to the ruler's house, and saw the flute players, and the crowd making a tumult, 24 he said, "Depart; for the girl is not dead but sleeping." And they laughed at him. 25 But when the crowd had been put outside, he went and took her by the hand, and the girl arose. 26 And the report of this went through all that district.

## MARK 5.21–43

21 And when Jesus had crossed again in the boat to the other side, a great crowd gathered about him; and he was beside the sea. 22 Then came one of the rulers of the synagogue, Jairus by name; and seeing him, he fell at his feet, 23 and besought him, saying, "My little daughter is at the point of death. Come and lay your hands on her, so that she may be made well, and live. 24 And he went with him. And a great crowd followed him and pressed around him. 25 And there was a woman who had had a flow of blood for twelve years, 26 and who had suffered much under many physicians, and had spent all that she had, and was no better but rather grew worse. 27 She had heard the reports about Jesus, and came up behind him in the crowd and touched his garment. 28 For she said, "If I touch even his garments, I shall be made well." 29 And immediately the hemorrhage ceased; and she felt in her body that she was healed of her disease. 30 And Jesus, perceiving in himself that power had gone forth from him, immediately turned about in the crowd, and said, "Who touched my garments?" 31 And his disciples said to him, "You see the crowd pressing around you, and yet you say, 'Who touched me?' " 32 And he looked around to see who had done it. 33 But the woman, knowing what had been done to her, came in fear and trembling and fell down before him, and told him the whole truth. 34 And he said to her, "Daughter, your faith has made you well; go in peace, and be healed of your disease." 35 While he was still speaking, there came from the ruler's house some who said, "Your daughter is dead. Why trouble the Teacher any further? 36 But ignoring^x what they said, Jesus said to the ruler of the synagogue, "Do not fear, only believe." 37 And he allowed no one to follow him except Peter and James and John the brother of James. 38 When they came to the house of the ruler of the synagogue, he saw a tumult, and people weeping and wailing loudly. 39 And when he had entered, he said to them, "Why do you make a tumult and weep? The child is not dead but sleeping." 40 And they laughed at him. But he put them all outside, and took the child's father and mother and those who were with him, and went in where the child was. 41 Taking her by the hand he said to her, "Talitha cumi"; which means "Little girl, I say to you, arise." 42 And immediately the girl got up and walked; for she was twelve years old. And immediately they were overcome with amazement. 43 And he strictly charged them that no one should know this, and told them to give her something to eat.

## LUKE 8.40–56

40 Now when Jesus returned, the crowd welcomed him, for they were all waiting for him. 41 And there came a man named Jairus, who was a ruler of the synagogue; and falling at Jesus' feet he besought him to come to his house, 42 for he had an only daughter, about twelve years of age, and she was dying. As he went, the people

pressed round him. 43 And a woman who had had a flow of blood for twelve years[y] and could not be healed by anyone, 44 came up behind him, and touched the fringe of his garment; and immediately her flow of blood ceased. 45 And Jesus said, "Who was it that touched me?" When all denied it, Peter and those who were with him[z] said, "Master, the multitudes surround you and press upon you!" 46 But Jesus said, "Someone touched me; for I perceive that power has gone forth from me." 47 And when the woman saw that she was not hidden, she came trembling, and falling down before him declared in the presence of all the people why she had touched him, and how she had been immediately healed. 48 And he said to her, "Daughter, your faith has made you well; go in peace." 49 While he was still speaking, a man from the ruler's house came and said, "Your daughter is dead; do not trouble the Teacher any more." 50 But Jesus on hearing this answered him, "Do not fear; only believe, and she shall be well." 51 And when he came to the house, he permitted no one to enter with him, except Peter and John and James, and the father and mother of the maiden. 52 And all were weeping and bewailing her; but he said, "Do not weep; for she is not dead but sleeping." 53 And they laughed at him, knowing that she was dead. 54 But taking her by the hand he called, saying, "Child, arise." 55 And her spirit returned, and she got up at once; and he directed that something should be given her to eat. 56 And her parents were amazed; but he charged them to tell no one what had happened.

---

x  Or *overhearing*. Other ancient authorities read *hearing*.
y  Other ancient authorities add *and had spent all her living upon physicians*.
z  Other ancient authorities add *and those who were with him*.

## COMMENTARY

The seventh and eighth miracles, involving reviving (?) the dead and healing the ill, are similar to the Elijah and Elisha miracle stories.[1]

18 *ruler*  In Mark and Luke he is called Jairus, and more specifically, "head of the synagogue," Gr. *archisynagōgos*, Heb. *rosh keneset*, which could mean any Jewish leader or person of importance.[2]

*lay your hand on*  On healing by the laying on of hands, see above p. 62.

20 *a woman who had suffered from a hemorrhage*  Heb. *zaba*.[4]

*the fringe of his garment*  On the corners of the garments at the time of Jesus were fringes fulfilling the command of Num. 15. 1 ff. The Gr. *kraspedon* is the translation of "fringe," *zizit*. The *zizit* had one fringe of blue (ibid. 15.38). It was believed that the *zizit*, and here the *zizit* of a holy man, possessed some magical power, particularly of healing. Both the color blue as well as the knotting of the fringes, which are prescribed by Jewish law, were looked upon by the superstitious as possessing prophylactic and healing powers.[5]

23 *and saw the flute players*,etc.  There is ample attestation as to the playing of musical instruments at a funeral, particularly the flute. E.g., "R. Judah says: 'Even a poor man in Israel will not have fewer than two flute players and one wailing woman.' "[6]

**24** *the girl is not dead but sleeping:* Is it possible that there is a wordplay here producing a double-entendre, for in Aram. *demakh,* "to sleep," is used euphemistically for "death,"[7] and the crowd laughs because of the meaning that they attach to "asleep"?

## NOTES

1. 2 Kings 4.18 ff.
2. On the *archisynagōgos* see Schürer, *GJV* 2: 509–512. Cf. also John 31, 7.36; Acts 4.5; Luke 14.1, 18.18; Matt. 19.16.
3. On the "laying on of the hands" in the NT, see Daube, *NTRJ*, pp. 224 ff.
4. See M. Zev. 5, and for the cure see B. Shab. 110a.
5. See B. Ta'an. 23b; for a discussion of this passage, see S. T. Lachs, "The End of the Blue Thread," in *Jewish Civilization: Essays and Studies II*, ed. R. Brauner (Philadelphia, 1981), pp. 55 ff.
6. M. Ket. 4.4. Cf. also Josephus, *BJ* III.9.5; B. Ket. 27b; T. ibid. 2.17 (p. 231). Also M. Kelim 15.6, 16.7; T. Yev 14.7 (p. 259).
7. TJ AZ 3.1, 42c; Gen. R. 96. Cf. also 1 Cor. 15.51, 1 Thess. 4.13.

# 56. Two Blind Men Healed

## MATT. 9.27–31

27 And as Jesus passed on from there, two blind men followed him, crying aloud, "Have mercy on us, Son of David." 28 When he entered the house, the blind men came to him; and Jesus said to them, "Do you believe that I am able to do this?" They said to him, "Yes, Lord." 29 Then he touched their eyes, saying, "According to your faith be it done to you." 30 And their eyes were opened. And Jesus sternly charged them, "See that no one knows it." 31 But they went away and spread his fame through all that district.

## IBID. 20.29–34

29 And as they went out of Jericho, a great crowd followed him. 30 And behold, two blind men sitting by the roadside, when they heard that Jesus was passing by cried out, "aHave mercy on us, Son of David!" 31 The crown rebuked them, telling them to be silent; but they cried out the more, "Lord, have mercy on us, Son of David!" 32 And Jesus stopped and called them, saying, "What do you want me to do for you?" 33 They said to him, "Lord, let our eyes be opened." 34 And Jesus in pity touched their eyes, and immediately they received their sight and followed him.

## MARK 10.46–52

46 And they came to Jericho; and as he was leaving Jericho with his disciples and a great multitude, Bartimaeus, a blind beggar, the son of Timaeus, was sitting by the roadside. 47 And when he heard that it was Jesus of Nazareth, he began to cry out and say, "Jesus, Son of David, have mercy on me!" 48 And many rebuked him, telling him to be silent; but he cried out all the more, "Son of David, have mercy on

me!" 49 And Jesus stopped and said, "Call him." And they called the blind man, saying to him, "Take heart; rise, he is calling you." 50 And throwing off his mantle he sprang up and came to Jesus. 51 And Jesus said to him, "What do you want me to do for you?" And the blind man said to him, "Master,b let me receive my sight." 52 And Jesus said to him, "Go your way; your faith has made you well." And immediately he received his sight and followed him on the way.

## Luke 18.35–43

35 As he drew near to Jericho, a blind man was sitting by the roadside begging: 36 and hearing a multitude going by, he inquired what this meant. 37 They told him, "Jesus of Nazareth is passing by." 38 And he cried, "Jesus, Son of David, have mercy on me!" 39 And those who were in front rebuked him, telling him to be silent; but he cried out all the more, "Son of David, have mercy on me!" 40 And Jesus stopped, and commanded him to be brought to him; and when he came near, he asked him, 41 "What do you want me to do for you?" He said, "Lord, let me receive my sight." 42 And Jesus said to him, "Receive your sight; your faith has made you well." 43 And immediately he received his sight and followed him, glorifying God; and all the people, when they saw it, gave praise to God.

------------

a  Other ancient authorities insert *Lord*.
b  Or *Rabbi*.

## COMMENTARY

27  *two blind men followed him*,etc.  The fact that we are not dealing with demonic recognition of Jesus, as above, but recognition by two blind men, seems to indicate that this was a testimony story to the disciples for use as a missionary text—even the blind recognized him, how much more so should the sighted. A similar implication is in the story of Balaam and his ass in Num. 23.22 ff. Only Mark 10.46 names a blind beggar, calling him Bartimaeus, and explains the name as "the son of Timaeus." It is clear that if this is original with Mark and not a scribal addition, it was addressed to an audience not familiar with Aramaie.
*Son of David*  I.e., Messiah.[1]

## NOTES

1.  Cf. above p. 3. Cf. Pss. Sol. 17.21, B. Sanh. 97–98.

# 57. *The Healing of a Dumb Demoniac*

## Matt. 9.32–34

32 As they were going away, behold, a dumb demoniac was brought to him. 33 And when the demon had been cast out, the dumb man spoke; and the crowds marveled, saying, "Never was anything like this seen in Israel." 34 But the Pharisees said, "He casts out demons by the prince of demons."

## Ibid. 12.22–24

22 Then a blind and dumb demoniac was brought to him, and he healed him, so that the dumb man spoke and saw. 23 And all the people were amazed, and said, "Can this be the Son of David?" 24 But when the Pharisees heard it they said, "It is only by Beelzebub, the prince of the demons, that this man casts out demons."

## Mark 3.22

And the scribes who came down from Jerusalem said, "He is possessed by Beelzebub, and by the prince of demons he casts out the demons.

## Luke 11.14–15

14 Now he was casting out a demon that was dumb; when the demon had gone out, the dumb man spoke, and the people marveled. 15 But some of them, said, "He casts out demons by Beelzebub, the prince of demons."

### COMMENTARY

This tenth miracle (Matt.) is one of the healing stories which have survived as a group. Perhaps it is added in Matt. to make up the number ten. Another possibility is that this and the preceding miracle of the healing of the blind have as their background Exod. 4.11.[1]

32 *a dumb demoniac* The Gr. *kōphos*, "blunt" or "dull," can mean "deaf," or "dumb," or both. The Heb. *ḥeresh*, especially in late Heb., means "a deaf mute."[2]

34 *prince of demons* In rabbinic literature generally called Ashmadai, but he is also called by many other names.[3]

### NOTES

1. *Who has made man's mouth? Who makes him dumb, or deaf, or seeing or blind? Is it not I the Lord?*

2. Exod. 4.11 mentions the dumb, the deaf, the blind, and with a slight emendation of *piqe'aḥ*, "sighted," to *pise'aḥ*, "lame." Cf. S. T. Lachs, "Evidence for an Emendation: Exodus 4.11," *Vetus Testamentum* 24 (1976): 249–250. In rabbinic literature *ḥeresh*, "deaf," includes both deafness and muteness; cf., e.g., M. Yev. 14.1, T. Ter. 1.1 (p. 25). The same is true of the Gr. term *kophos*. Cf. Philo, *Spec. Leg.* 4.197, Sib. Or. 4.28, Hab. (LXX) 2.18, 3 Macc. 4.16.

3. Prince of the demons: cf. TJ Pe'ah 8, 21b (23), TJ Sheq. 5, 49b (2). See below Sec. 85 (p. 210).

## 58. *Sending Out of the Twelve*

### Matt. 9.35–10.16

35 And Jesus went about all the cities and villages, teaching in their synagogues and preaching the gospel of the kingdom, and healing every disease and every infirmity. 36 When he saw the crowds, he had compassion for them, because they were

harassed and helpless, like sheep without a shepherd. 37 Then he said to his disciples "The harvest is plentiful, but the laborers are few; 38 pray therefore the Lord of the harvest to send our laborers into his harvest." 10.1 And he called to him his twelve disciples and gave them authority over unclean spirits, to cast them out, and to heal every disease and every infirmity. 2 The names of the twelve apostles are these: first, Simon, who is called Peter, and Andrew his brother; James the son of Zebedee, and John his brother; 3 Philip and Bartholomew; Thomas and Matthew the tax collector; James the son of Alphaeus, and Thaddaeus;<sup>c</sup> 4 Simon the Cananaean, and Judas Iscariot, who betrayed him. 5 These twelve Jesus sent out, charging them, "Go nowhere among the Gentiles, and enter no town of the Samaritans, 6 but go rather to the lost sheep of the house of Israel. 7 And preach as you go, saying, 'The kingdom of heaven is at hand.' 8 Heal the sick, raise the dead, cleanse lepers, cast out demons. You received without pay, give without pay. 9 Take no gold, nor silver, nor copper in your belts, 10 no bag for your journey, nor two tunics, nor sandals, nor a staff; for the laborer deserves his food. 11 And whatever town or village you enter, find out who is worthy in it, and stay with him until you depart. 12 As you enter the house, salute it. 13 And if the house is worthy, let your peace come upon it; but if it is not worthy, let your peace return to you. 14 And if any one will not receive you or listen to your words, shake off the dust from your feet as you leave that house or town. 15 Truly, I say you, it shall be more tolerable on the day of judgment for the land of Sodom and Gomorrah than for that town. 16 Behold, I send you out as sheep in the midst of wolves; so be wise as serpents and innocent as doves."

## MARK 6.6

And he went about among the villages teaching.

## IBID. 6.34

As he landed he saw a great throng, and he had compassion on them, because they were like sheep without a shepherd.

## IBID. 6.7

And he called to him the twelve, and began to send them out two by two, and gave them authority over the unclean spirits.

## IBID. 3.13–19

13 And he went up into the hills and called to him those whom he desired; and they came to him. 14 And he appointed twelve,<sup>d</sup> to be with him, and to be sent out to preach 15 and have authority to cast out demons: 16 Simon whom he surnamed Peter; 17 James the son of Zebedee and John the brother of James, whom he surnamed Boanerges, that is sons of thunder; 18 Andrew, and Philip, and Bartholomew, and Matthew, and Thomas, and James the son of Alphaeus, and Thaddaeus, and Simon the Cananaean, 19 and Judas Iscariot, who betrayed him.

## I B I D . 6 . 8 – 1 1

8 He charged them to take nothing for their journey except a staff; no bread, no bag, no money in their belts; 9 but to wear sandals and not put on two tunics. 10 And he said to them, "Where you enter a house, stay there until you leave the place. 11 And if any place will not receive you and they refuse to hear you, when you leave, shake off the dust that is on your feet for a testimony against them."

## L U K E   1 0 . 1 – 2

1 After this the Lord appointed seventy others, and sent them on ahead of him, two by two, into every town and place where he himself was about to come. 2 And he said to them, "The harvest is plentiful, but the laborers are few; pray therefore the Lord of the harvest to send out laborers into his harvest."

## I B I D .   9 . 1

And he called the twelve together and gave them power and authority over all demons and to cure diseases.

## I B I D .   6 . 1 3 – 1 6

13 and chose from them twelve, whom he named apostles; 14 Simon, whom he named Peter, and Andrew his brother, and James and John, and Philip, and Bartholomew, 15 and Matthew, and Thomas, and James the son of Alphaeus, and Simon who was called the Zealot, 16 and Judas the son of James, and Judas Iscariot, who became a traitor.

## I B I D .   9 . 2 – 5

2 And he sent them out to preach the kingdom of God and to heal. 3 And he said to them, "Take nothing for your journey, no staff, nor bag, nor bread, nor money; and do not have two tunics. 4 And whatever house you enter stay there, and from there depart. 5 And wherever they do not receive you, when you leave that town, shake off the dust from your feet as a testimony against them."

## I B I D .   1 0 . 3 – 1 2

4 "Carry no purse, no bag, no sandals; and salute no one on the road. 5 Whatever house you enter, first say, 'Peace be to this house!' 6 And if a son of peace is there, your peace shall rest upon him; but if not, it shall return to you. 7 And remain in the same house, eating and drinking what they provide, for the laborer deserves his wages; to not go from house to house. 8 Whenever you enter a town and they receive you, eat what is set before you; 9 heal the sick in it and say to them, 'The kingdom of God has come near you.' 10 But whenever you enter a town and they do not receive you, go into its streets and say, 11 'Even the dust of your town that clings to our feet, we wipe off against you; nevertheless know this, that the kingdom of God has come

near.' 12 I tell you it shall be more tolerable on that day for Sodom than for that town. 3 Go your way; behold, I send you out as lambs in the midst of wolves."

---

c  Some read *Lebbaeus*, others *Lebbaeus called Thaddaeus*, others  *Thaddaeus called Lebbaeus*.
d  Some add *whom also he named apostles*.

## COMMENTARY

The choice of twelve as a number is clearly symbolic, representing the twelve tribes of Israel (cf. Rev. 21.12–14). The number was retained even after the betrayal of Jesus by Judas Iscariot, whose place was taken by Matthias (Acts 1.15, 26). There are considerable variations in the lists of the Twelve in the Synoptics and attempts to harmonize them have not been successful.[1]

37  *the harvest is plentiful*, etc.    Note the interesting parallel, "R. Tarfon said: 'The day is short, the work is great, and the laborers are sluggish, and the wages are great and the householder is urgent.' "[2]

10.1  *unclean spirits* Heb. *ruḥot ha-tumah*, "spirits of uncleanness," i.e., spirits which cause uncleanness.[3]

*to heal every disease*, etc.    In Jewish literature these disciples and those who followed them were best known through their healing activity in the name of Jesus. The following is a typical passage:

> The case of R. Eleazar b. Dama whom a snake bit. Jacob a man of Khefar Sama came in to cure him in the name of Joshua ben Pandira, but R. Ishmael did not permit it. He said: "You are not permitted, Ben Dama!" He said: "I will prove to you that he may heal me." But he did not finish bringing proof when he died. R. Ishmael said: "Fortunate are you, Ben Dama, for you have departed in peace, and have not broken through the ordinances of the Sages; for everyone who breaks through the fence of the Sages punishment comes at last, as it is written, *Who breaks through a wall, a serpent will bite him* [Koh. 10.8]."[4]

2  *first* Gr. *photos*,    "first and foremost."
*Simon called Peter*    See above p. 58.[5]
*Andrew-Zebedee*    See above p. 58.

3  *Philip*    The name appears in rabbinic sources as Philipi or Philipai.[6]

*Bartholomew*    A Grecized form of the Aramaic name Bar Talmai in rabbinic sources.

*Thomas* Heb. *Te'om*,    "twin," cf. John 11.16, 20, 24, "Thomas called the twin."[8]

*Matthew*    In rabbinic sources it appears as Mattai or Mattya.[9]

*Alphaeus*    Appears in rabbinic sources as Ilpha or Ilphi or Hilpha.[10]

*Thaddaeus*    Also-called Lebbaeus. Thaddaeus appears in Jewish sources as Tadi or Tedai; Lebbaeus as Libai.[11]

4 *Simon the Cananaean*    Luke reads *zelotes*, which is the correct reading, for the original was *qana'i*, "the zealot." The interpretation that he was from Cana is not acceptable and certainly not that he was a Canaanite. He was presumably a member of a "zealot" group which was actively engaged in violence against Rome.[12]

*Judas Iscariot.*    The word Iscariot has remained a crux to this day. The usual explanation has been *ish Qeriyyot*, "a man of Qeriyyot," identified with Keriot Hezron of Josh. 25.25, 12 miles S of Hebron, or with Keriyyot in Moab (Jer. 48.24, where the LXX reads *Karioth*). The phrase *apo kariotou* appears several times in John indicating a place-name. The objection strongly voiced today against this interpretation is that *ish*, "a man" in Heb., would not have been employed, since the spoken language was Aramaic. But names are not easily changed, and Josephus records *Istobos*, Heb. *Ish Tov* (*Ant.* VV.121, "a man of Tob"), and there are several examples in the Mishnah, e.g., *Ish Yerushala'im*, "a man of Jerusalem," *Ish Zeredah*, "a man of Zeredah" (M. Avot 1.4). The more serious objection is that if Iscariot were one of these place-names, Judas would have been the only Judean among the twelve. Torrey sees in Iscariot *ishgaya*, "a liar, hypocrite."[13] Another suggestion is that it is from the Aram. *sagor* "of red," hence a man of ruddy complexion, red-headed.[14] Other suggestions include "an assassin," from *sikarios*; a member of the *sicarii*; "a man of Sychar," i.e., a Samaritan; "a man of Issachar"; "a man of Jericho"; a carrier of the leather bag *scortea*. Recently A. Ehrman has argued against these suggestions and has offered the theory that the root is *sagor*, which means "to dye or paint," hence "a (red) dyer."[15] The final word has yet to be written on Iscariot.

5 *Go nowhere*, etc.    This verse is in the form of Semitic poetic parallelism. The Gentiles are presumably the Greco-Oriental population and the Samaritans.

*Among the Gentiles*    Gr. *eis hodon ethnōn*    Lit. the way of the Gentiles, i.e., a road leading to a Gentile city, perhaps it refers to one of the Decapolis.[16]

*Samaritans*    This group held to some aspects of Jewish practice and belief. They accepted the Pentateuch. Their Temple was not the one in Jerusalem but one on Mount Gerizim with their own priesthood and ritual. To the Jews they were sectarians and not regarded as full Jews.[17] A similar attitude is reflected in Ben Sira: "For two nations does my soul feel abhorrence, yea and for a third which is not a people. The inhabitants of Seir and Philistia and that foolish nation that dwells in Shechem."[18]

*the lost sheep*, etc.    Cf. Matt. 15.24 (p. 247), where the same is said by Jesus to the Canaanite woman. Note that this is not found in Mark and that these last two verses cannot be reconciled with Matt. 28.19, *Go therefore and make disciples of all nations*; Jesus did minister only to Jews, and this was the attitude of the leaders of the early church in Palestine.[19]

8 *you received without pay*    Gr. *dōrean*,    A translation of Heb. *hinam* in the LXX, "without fee." The meaning is: "I taught you without payment, do it

likewise for others without payment." This is directly paralleled in rabbinic literature: "[God said to Moses,] 'Just as you received it [the Torah] without payment, so teach it without payment.' "[20]

9 *take no gold . . . belts* Coins were regularly carried in a money belt; the Gr. *zōnē* is used in this sense; rabbinic sources have *punda (funda)* and in the expression "between his belt and his undergarment" indicate that it was worn, not carried.[21] The disciples were not to take money with them on their travels.

10 *no bag for your journey* Gr. *pērain*; Heb. probably *tarmil*. Most likely a traveling bag, as "the proselyte who comes with nothing but his staff and traveling bag,"[22] and "as soon as she put his staff and his bag on that animal."[23] It is also used of a shepherd's bag, "neither shall the shepherd go out with his bag [on a holiday]."[24] Others understand it as a beggar's bag, which is not likely.[25]

*nor two tunics* Not only was one not to take a traveling bag but one was not to take a change of garment, i.e., two tunics; the one which he wore was all he was to have. On *chitōn* as a garment worn next to the skin, see above p. 105.

*nor sandals nor a staff* Mark 6.8–9 permits them, while Matt. and Luke forbid sandals; Luke omits staff. "These modifications, if they are not accidental, are probably due to the fact that in the Roman version of the tradition the circumstances of later missionaries were in view."[26] In Luke, since we have the verb *bastazō*, sandals were not to be carried in addition to those worn on the feet. Probably even in Matt. it means "do not take an extra pair of sandals." If the meaning be, however, *no* sandals at all, and this became the mark of an apostle, the following may be applicable: "[If a man, possibly a Judeo-Christian, said,] I will not go before it [the ark] in sandals, he may not even go before it barefoot?[27]

*the laborer deserves his food* Cf. "Every prophet who wishes to settle among you is worthy of his food."[28]

11 *and stay with him until you depart* "R. Judah said in the name of Rav: 'Whence do we know from the Torah that one should not change his lodging place, as it is written, *to the place where he had his tent before . . .*' "[29]

12 *salute it* As in Luke 10.5, "Peace to this house."[30]

12 *let your peace return to you* I.e., the blessing shall not take effect.

14 *shake off the dust* This act of deprecation is known in Jewish sources. The lands of the idolaters, i.e., all lands outside of Palestine, were considered to be unclean, and therefore when a Jew returned to Palestine from foreign lands he would shake off the dust from his feet, representing a rejection of the dust of pagan lands.[31]

15 *the land of Sodom and Gomorrah* These two cities are regularly cited as prime examples of total wickedness and deserving of punishment.[32] The term "land" instead of "city" is probably the result of misunderstanding of the Semitic word *medinah*, which came to be rendered either "city" or "county" (land).[33]

16 *Behold, I send you out as sheep*, etc. "In the Apocalyptic literature (Enoch 90.6–17) the lambs are a symbol for the Hasidim, those in Israel who, in times of persecution and defection had remained loyal to the Faith. . . . The task of the disciples is not going to be easy. The kingdom to which they belong is one to which the kingdoms of the world are hostile, and they must not expect better treatment from the Herods and the Caesars than the Hasidim had from Antiochus."[34] Israel and the nations are compared to sheep and wolves respectively: "Hadrian said to R. Joshua: 'Great is the sheep which stands amidst seventy wolves.' He said to him: 'Great is the shepherd who saves them and who keeps them and breaks them in their presence. This is what is meant by *No weapon that is fashioned against you shall prosper* [Isa. 54.17].' "[35]

16 *be as wise as serpents*, etc. The translation of the Gr. *phronimoi* by AV and RSV as "wise" is too weak; "shrewd," "crafty," or "cunning" is by far a better rendering and fits the imagery of the serpent. The LXX uses *phronimos* when rendering Heb. *arum*, descriptive of the serpent in Gen. 3.1. Furthermore, the serpent and the dove are described in rabbinic literature with precisely the same adjectives as are found in this verse. In commenting on Cant. 2.14, *my dove is in the cleft of the rock*, "R. Judah said in the name of R. Simeon: 'With me they are innocent as doves, but with the nations of the world they are like cunning serpents.' "[36]

## NOTES

1. See E. J. Goodspeed, *The Twelve* (1957), passim.
2. M. Avot 2.15. See Abrahams, *Studies II*, pp. 100–101, where he cites the suggested reading *yom qazir*, i.e., "the day of the harvest," for *yom qazar*, "the day is short."
3. See this use in B. Ḥag. 3b, B. Sanh. 65b.
4. T. Ḥul. 2.22–23 (p. 503). See also TJ Shab. 14, 14d (35); TJ AZ 2, 40d–41a; B. AZ 27b. On this passage see Herford, *CTM*, pp. 103 ff. Cf. also Koh. R. 1.8, B. Sanh. 89a.
5. There are several Peter legends in Jewish sources. See Jellinek, *BHM*, 5:60 ff., 6:9 ff. Also see J. Greenstone, "Jewish Legends About Simon Peter," *Historia Judaica* 12, no. 2 (October 1950): 89–104.
6. See, e.g., TJ Meg. 1, 70b (14); TJ Ta'an. 4, 86b (6).
7. Cf. Num. 13.22; 2 Sam. (LXX) 3.3, *tholmi*. Cf. also F. Delitzsch, *Zeitschrift für Lutheranische Theologie und Kirche*, 1876 p. 597, who cites Gen. 49.5, "Simeon and Levi are brothers rendered *telamin* in Targ. J and means twins." Cf. also *bar talmion*, *PR* 22 (112b), Lev. R. 6; and *ben talmion*, B. Me'ilah 51b.
8. Cf. also Gen. (LXX) 25.24, *didumos*.
9. See, e.g., M. Avot 1.7, Nittai is a variant cf. M. Sheq. 5.1, M. Eduy. 2.2, B. Sanh. 43a.
10. See, e.g., B. RH 17b, T. M.Sh. 4.5 (p. 93), TJ ibid. 49d (41).
11. See Dalman, *Words*, p. 40; B. Qid. 72a; B. MQ 11a.
12. On the Zealots see Schürer, *GJV*, 1:486 ff., 573 ff., 617 ff.; Zeitlin, *RFJS*, passim. On the use of the term *qan'ai*, see *ARN* 6 (3); M. Sanh. 9.1. For the view that there was no Zealot party until 66 C.E., see M. Smith, "Zealots and Sicarii: their Origins and Relations," *HTR* 64 (1971): 1–19; Foakes Jackson and Lake, *Beginnings of Christianity*, pt. I, *The Acts of the Apostles*, 1:425.

13. C. C. Torrey, "The Name Iscariot," *HTR* 36 (1943): 58.

14. H. Ingholt "The Surname of Judas Iscariot," *Studia Orientalia Ioanni Petersen . . . dicata* (Copenhagen, 1953), pp. 159–160.

15. A. Ehrman, "Judas Iscariot and Abba Saqqara," *JBL* 97 (1978): 572–573. He fails, however, to give sufficient evidence that *saqor* indeed means "to dye." Although he relies on L. Ginzberg and his citation of B. Git. 56a of "Aram the Dyer" (Aram. *zabla'a*) in *JE*, 1:35, s.v. "Abba Sakkara," he does not show that *saqqara* and *zabla'a* are used interchangeably, nor does he produce another passage where *saqor* is used unequivocally with the meaning "to dye"; nor does the argument that "the color red was the preeminent color of the dyer's trade is amply documented from both Hebrew Scriptures and Rabbinic literature" sound convincing.

16. Manson, *SJ*, p. 179. See. M. AZ 1.4.

17. See Schürer, *GJV*, 2:19–23. On the area of the Samaritans, see Josephus, *BJ* III.3.4. Cf. 2 Kings 17.24 ff. Moore, *Judaism*, 1:23–27. *SB*, 1:538–560.

18. Sira 50.25 ff.

19. Cf. also Gal. 2.6–10.

20. B. Bekh. 29a, *DE* 2.4 and parallels. TJ Ned. 4.4, 38c (51); B. ibid. 37a; Sifre Deut. 48; Num. R. 1.

21. B. Shab. 120a; TJ RH 2, 57d; M. Shab. 10.3; T. Ber. 7.19 (p. 17). See on the clothing, Y. Yadin, *The Cave of the Letters* (Jerusalem, 1963), 1:204 ff.

22. TJ Shev. 8.1, 38c (bot.).

23. B. Shab. 31a.

24. T. Beẓ. 3.17 (p. 206). Cf. also Josephus, *Ant.* VI.9.4

25. See *Expos. T.* November 1906, p. 62.

26. Rawlinson, *The Gospel according to St. Mark*, 7th ed. (London, 1949), p. 77. Allen, *Matt.*, p. 103, and Manson, *SJ*, pp. 181, following him, are out of line in suggesting that the prototype for these warnings is based on M. Ber. 9.5, which mentions the removal of dust from one's feet and forbids the wearing of shoes and the carrying of a wallet or a staff when entering the Temple precincts.

27. M. Meg. 3.8.

28. *Didache* 13.1.

29. B. Ar. 16b.

30. Cf. also Num. R. 21.1, *Tan. Pinḥas* 1. *she'al shalom.*

31. Cf. T. Miq. 6.1 (p. 657), B. Sanh. 12a, M. Toh. 4.5, B. Git 8a, B. Shab. 15b, M. Ohol. 18.6.

32. Cf. e.g., Isa. 1.9, 10, Gen. R. 41, M. Sanh. 10.3, Luke 17.29, Rom. 9.29, 2 Pet. 2.6, Jude 7, Jub. 36.10.

33. See Lachs, "Studies in the Semitic Background," 213.

34. Manson, *SJ*, p. 75.

35. *Tan. Toledot* 5.

36. Cant. R. 2.14. Cf. also *Mid. Ps.* 28.2 (115a), 119.1 (244b); Lev. R. 33. See Lachs, "Studies in the Semitic Background," 211–213.

# 59. *The Fate of the Disciples*

## MATT. 10.17–25

17 "Beware of men; for they will deliver you up to councils, and flog you in their synagogues, 18 and you will be dragged before governors and kings for my sake, to bear testimony before them and the Gentiles. 19 When they deliver you up, do not be

anxious how you are to speak or what you are to say; for what you are to say will be given to you in that hour; 20 for it is not you who speak, but the Spirit of your Father speaking through you. 21 Brother will deliver up brother to death, and the father his child, and children will rise against parents and have them put to death; 22 and you will be hated by all for my name's sake. But he who endures to the end will be saved. 23 When they persecute you in one town, flee to the next; for truly, I say to you, you will not have gone through all the towns of Israel before the Son of man comes. 24 A disciple is not above his teacher, nor a servant^e above his master; 25 it is enough for the disciple to be like his teacher, and the servant^e like his master; If they have called the master of the house Beelzebub, how much more will they malign those of his household."

---

e  Or *slave*.

## COMMENTARY

17 *Beware of men*  The Gr. may be a misreading of a Heb. original *nesi'im*, "princes," and rendered it "men" (people), *anashim*. A support for this emendation is in Ezek., who employs the symbolism of wolves and their prey representing the princes and the common people. *Her princes in the midst of her are like wolves tearing the prey, shedding blood, destroying lives to get dishonest again.*[1]

*councils . . . and synagogues*  the former is used for one of the courts, presumably the court of three; the latter could mean the institution or simply assemblies.[2]

18 *governors* Gr. *hegemonas*, which in the NT refers to the procurators of Judea, i.e., Pilate (Matt. 27.28, Luke 20.20), Felix (Acts 23.24), Festus (ibid. 26.30).

*princes* Gr. *basileis*, "Kings"; Herodians, i.e., Antipas *(Ant.* XIX 9; Mark 6.14, 22), Agrippa I (Acts 12.1), Agrippa II (ibid. 25.13).

20 *for it is not you*, etc.  This is reminiscent of Exod. 4.15.

21 *Brother will deliver up*, etc.  Family problems were to be characteristic of the Last Days. This may well lie behind Mal. 3.4. Cf. Luke 12.5. It is a very common motif in the apocalyptic literature. E.g., "In that generation the sons will convict their fathers and their elders of sin and unrighteousness . . . and they will strive one with another, the young with the old, the old with the young."[3] "And they shall hate one another, and provoke one another to fight, and the mean shall rule over the honorable, and those of low degree shall be extolled above the famous."[4]

22 *But he who endures to the end*  This presents a difficulty. What about the one who does not "endure to the end"? Some will die before the coming of the kingdom (see Mark 9.1 and parallels). An unorthodox reading of this verse is that he who remains "wholehearted" will be saved. This is based on the Heb. *tom*, which means both "end" and "wholeheartedness."[5]

24 *A disciple is not above his teacher*, etc.  The disciple can expect no better

treatment than accorded the master. A similar statement is found in rabbinic literature, "It is sufficient for the servant to be like his master."[6]

25 *Beelzebub*  See on Matt. 12.24 (below p. 211). The argument here is the Heb. *qal vehomer, a minore ad maius.*

## NOTES

1. Ezek. 22.27. See Lachs, "Studies in the Semitic Background," 212–213.
2. The former means any of the courts of twenty-three (M. Sanh. 1.1) or the court of three (ibid.). The Gr. *sunagōgē* could mean either the institution or simply assembly, or simply a synonym for *sunedrion.* Cf. Eusebius, *HE* V.16.2.
3. Jub. 23.19.
4. 2 Bar. 70.3. Cf. also 2 Esd. 5.9.
5. See Lachs, op. cit. p. 213.
6. Gen. R. 49.2, *Tan. Ki Tisa;* Sifra 25.23, cf. *Mid. Ps.* 27.5 (113b); *Tan.B. Lekh Lekha;* B. Ber. 58b.

# 60. *Exhortation to Fearless Confession*

## MATT. 10.26–33

26 "So have no fear of them; for nothing is covered that will not be revealed, or hidden that will not be known. 27 What I tell you in the dark, utter in the light; and what you hear whispered, proclaim upon the housetops. 28 And do not fear those who kill the body but cannot kill the soul; rather fear him who can destroy both soul and body in hell[f]. 29 Are not two sparrows sold for a penny? And not one of them will fall to the ground without your Father's will. 30 But even the hairs of your head are all numbered. 31 Fear not, therefore; you are of more value than many sparrows. 32 So everyone who acknowledges me before men, I also will acknowledge before my Father who is in heaven; 33 but whoever denies me before men, I also will deny before my Father who is in heaven."

## LUKE 12.2–9

2 "Nothing is covered up that will not be revealed, or hidden that will not be known. 3 Whatever you have said in the dark shall be heard in the light, and what you have whispered in private rooms shall be proclaimed upon the housetops. 4 I tell you, my friends, do not fear those who kill the body and after that have no more that they can do. 5 But I will warn you whom to fear: fear him who, after he has killed, has power to cast into hell[f]; yes, I tell you, fear him! 6 Are not five sparrows sold for two pennies? And not one of them is forgotten before God. 7 Why, even the hairs of your head are all numbered. Fear not; you are of more value than many sparrows. 8 And I tell you, every one who acknowledges me before men, the Son of man also will acknowledge before the angels of God; 9 but he who denies me before men will be denied before the angels of God."

---

f  Greek *Gehenna.*

## COMMENTARY

26 *for nothing is covered that will not be revealed,*etc.   No direct biblical or rabbinic parallels, but there are many statements in the same spirit. E.g., *Even in your thought do not curse the king, nor in your bedchamber curse the rich, for a bird of the air will carry your voice, or some winged creature tell the matter* (Koh. 10.20). "In the end every thing in this world which is done in secret will be publicized and made known to mankind, and for this reason, fear the Lord."[1] "R. Joḥanan b. Beroqa says: 'Anyone who profanes the name of Heaven in secret, they exact the penalty from him openly.' "[2]

28 *And do not fear*   "Let us not fear him who thinks he kills. Great is the trial of soul, and the danger laid up in eternal tribulation, for those who transgress the commandment of God."[3] "The wicked of Israel in their bodies and the wicked of the nations of the world in their bodies go down to hell and are punished in it for twelve months. After twelve months, their souls become extinct and their bodies are burned up and hell casts them out, and they turn to ashes and the wind scatters them and strews them beneath the soles of the feet of the righteous."[4]

29 *Are not two sparrows sold for a penny?*   "At the end of the third century A.D. an edict of the Emperor Diocletian fixed the maximum price of ten sparrows at the sum equivalent to three pence–halfpenny. The sparrow is the cheapest life in the market, but it is not outside of God's care."[5] Note in this spirit, "God sits and feeds the world, from the horns of the *re'em* to the eggs of a louse."[6]

*and not one of them will fall to the ground without your Father's will*   "R. Simon b. Yoḥai said: 'No bird perishes without God, how much less man.' "[7]

30 *But even the hairs of your head are all numbered*   ". . . and he said to him, 'Many hairs have I created in man, and for every hair have I created a separate follicle, so that no two hairs should drink from one follicle, for if they did it would darken the sight of man."[8]

## NOTES

1. Targ. Koh. 12.13.
2. M. Avot 4.4.
3. 4 Macc. 13.14 ff. See Abrahams, *Studies II*, pp. 41–49; cf. Luke 12.5.
4. T. Sanh. 13.4 (p. 434). On this passage, see Moore, *Judaism*, 2:387; cf. also B. Ber. 28b.
5. Manson, *SJ*, p. 108. On two birds see Lev. 14.4 ff., where two birds are designated as a sacrifice for the poor who cannot afford a larger sacrifice. See Matt 12.5. Cf. M. Ḥul. 12.5.
6. B. Shab. 107b and parallels.
7. TJ Shev. 9.1, 38d (22); Gen. R. 79.6; *PRK* 10 (88b); *Mid. Ps.* 17.13 (27b); Esther R. 1.9; Koh. R. 10.9.
8. B. BB 16a. See also Lev. R. 16.3, *Tan.B. Tazria* 8 (18a–b).

# 61. *Division in Households*

## MATT. 10.34–36

34 "Do not think that I have come to bring peace on earth; I have not come to bring peace, but a sword. 35 For I have come to set a man against his father, and a daughter against her mother, and a daughter-in-law against her mother-in-law; 36 and a man's foes will be those of his own household."

## LUKE 12.51–53

51 "Do you think that I have come to give peace on earth? No, I tell you, but rather division; 52 for henceforth in one house there will be five divided, three against two and two against three; 53 they will be divided, father against son and son against father, mother against daughter and daughter against her mother, mother-in-law against her daughter-in-law and daughter-in-law against her mother-in-law."

## COMMENTARY

This is a continuation of the theme of Matt. 10.21, i.e., family disunity, which is a sign of the coming of the messianic age.[1]

**34** *to bring the sword* In Matt. "a sword," while in Luke "division." Most commentators prefer the Lucan reading. A nagging question does remain about the reading "sword": does Matthew use it to represent any *sicarii* background, a prelude to the messianic era?

*for I have come to set*, etc. Based on Mic. 7.6, *for the son treats the father with contempt, the daughter rises up against her mother. The daughter-in-law against her mother-in-law; a man's enemies are the men of his own house.* The spirit of this deterioration of family relationships is reflected in rabbinic treatment of Mic. 7.6, where it is explained as a prelude to the messianic coming: "With the footprints of the Messiah presumption shall increase and death reach its heights . . . children shall shame the elders and the elders shall rise up before the children, for the son treats the father with contempt, the daughter rises up against her mother, the daughter-in-law against her mother-in-law, a man's enemies are the men of his own house. The face of this generation is as the face of a dog, and the son will not be put to shame by his father."[2] Similarly, "And in that generation the sons will convict their fathers and their elders of sin and unrighteousness . . . and they will strive with one another, the young with the old and the old with the young."[3]

## NOTES

1. Plummer (*Luke, ICC*, p. 334) has missed the point: "It was the belief of the Jews that the Messiah would at once introduce a reign of peace and prosperity. Jesus does not wish His followers to live in a fool's paradise. He is no enthusiast making wild and delusive promises. In this world they must expect tribulation."

2. B. Sot. 49b. See also B. Sanh. 97a.
3. Jub. 23.16, 19.

# 62. *Conditions of Discipleship*

### MATT. 10.37–39

37 "He who loves father or mother more than me is not worthy of me; and he who loves son or daughter more than me is not worthy of me; 38 and he who does not take his cross and follow me is not worthy of me. 39 He who finds his life will lose it, and he who loses his life for my sake will find it."

### LUKE 14.26–27

26 "If anyone comes to me and does not hate his own father and mother and wife and children and brothers and sisters, yes, and even his own life, he cannot be my disciple. 27 Whoever does not bear his own cross and come after me, cannot be my disciple."

### IBID. 17.33

"Whoever seeks to gain his life will lose it, but whoever loses his life will preserve it."

### COMMENTARY

37 *He who loves*, etc. "It is true that the honour of God is to be put before obedience to parents so that if a father commands his son to violate an injunction of the Law, the son must disobey his father (Yeb. 5b) but this seems different from what we read in 37."[1] On the greater duty to serve the teacher over a parent, note: "If a man went to seek his own lost property and that of his father, his own has priority; if his own and that of his teacher, his own has priority; if that of his father and that of his teacher, his teacher's has priority, for his father brought him into this world, but his teacher, who has taught him wisdom, brings him into the world-to-come."[2]

38 *and he who does not take*, etc. There are no rabbinic parallels, but this verse and v. 39 clearly refer to the willingness on the part of the faithful to suffer martyrdom for their beliefs. There are many passages in this vein, e.g., "The words of the Law are only established in a man who would die for them."[3]

39 *He who finds his life will lost it* There is a very close parallel to this aphorism: "Alexander of Macedon asked the wise men of the South: 'What shall a man do that he may live?' They answered: 'Let him kill himself.' 'And what should a man do that he may die?' They answered: 'Let him keep himself alive.' "[4] The same thought seems to be contained in the following: "R. Judah the Prince said: 'If you have performed His will as your will, you

have not performed His will as His will; and if you have performed His will against your will, then you have performed His will as His will; if it be your will that you should not die, die that you may not die; if it be your will that you should live, live not, so that you may live; it is better for you to die in this world against your will than to die in the world-to-come.' "⁵

### NOTES

1. Montefiore, *RLGT*, p. 230.
2. M. BM 2.11.
3. B. Ber. 63b. See also Montefiore, op. cit, pp. 233 ff.
4. B. Tam. 32a.
5. *ARN* II (2), p. 36a.

## 63. *End of the Discourse*

### MATT. 10.40–11.1

40 "He who receives you receives me, and he who receives me receives him who sent me. 41 He who receives a prophet because he is a prophet shall receive a prophet's reward, and he who receives a righteous man because he is a righteous man shall receive a righteous man's reward. 42 And whoever gives to one of these little ones even a cup of cold water because he is a disciple, truly, I say to you he shall not lose his reward." 11.1 And when Jesus had finished instructing his disciples, he went on from there to teach and preach in their cities.

### COMMENTARY

40 *He who receives you receives me* A man's agent is like himself; he has the authority of his principal.¹ There are no rabbinic parallels to this or the following three verses, but if one substitutes "learned" or "wise" for "prophet," and "God" for "me", as Montefiore,² then parallels abound: "He who shows hospitality to the wise [*talmid ḥakham*] is as if he brought the first fruits of his produce to God."³ "He who greets the learned is as if he has greeted God [lit. received the *Shekhinah*]."⁴ R. Abin the Levite said: 'He who enjoys a meal at which a learned man is present is as one who enjoys the radiance of the *Shekhinah*.' "⁵ "He who gives a piece of bread to a righteous man, it is as though he has fulfilled the whole Law."⁶

41 *because he is a prophet* Gr. *eis onoma* is the rabb. Heb. *l'shem*, "for the sake of," as in, "Everyone who occupies himself with the Law for its own *sake* [*lishma*], i.e., because it is the Law."⁷

42 *one of these little ones . . . because he is a disciple.* "Little," Gr. *mikros.*, Heb. *qatan*, Aram. *ze'ira*, not the ordinary term for a disciple or even a descriptive term for him, but implies a young, inexperienced scholar, as in the passage "He who learns from the young [*qetanim*] . . ."⁸

## NOTES

1. B. Qid. 41b, M. Ber. 5.5.
2. Montefiore, *RLGT*, p. 235.
3. Lev. R. 34.8.
4. *Mek.* Exod. 18.12.
5. B. Ber. 64a.
6. Gen. R. 58.12. Further on hospitality see B. Shab. 127a.
7. B. Ber. 17a. Cf. M. Avot 5.22.
8. M. Avot 4.20. See also B. Sot. 22a, Gen. R. 42.4.

# 64. *John's Question to Jesus*

## MATT. 11.2–6

2 Now when John heard in prison about the deeds of the Christ, he sent word by his disciples 3 and said to him, "Are you he who is to come, or shall we look for another?" 4 And Jesus answered them, "Go and tell John what you hear and see; 5 the blind receive their sight and the lame walk, lepers are cleansed and the deaf hear, and the dead are raised up, and the poor have good news preached to them. 6 And blessed is he who takes no offense at me."

## LUKE 7.18–23

18 The disciples of John told him of all these things. 19 And John, calling to him two of his disciples, sent them to the Lord, saying, "Are you he who is to come, or shall we look for another?" 20 And when the men had come to him, they said, "John the Baptist has sent us to you, saying, 'Are you he who is to come, or shall we look for another?' " 21 In that hour he cured many of diseases and plagues and evil spirits, and on many that were blind he bestowed sight. 22 And he answered them, "Go and tell John what you have seen and heard: the blind receive their sight, the lame walk, lepers are cleansed, and the deaf hear, the dead are raised up, the poor have good news preached to them. 23 And blessed is he who takes no offense at me."

## COMMENTARY

2 *When John heard in prison*    John was confined in the fortress of Machaerus on the E. of the Dead Sea.[1] The details of the cause of his imprisonment are given in a later chapter.[2] Apparently, John's disciples and/or friends had access to him (cf. Matt. 25.36) and hence he could send his disciples to Jesus.

*the deeds of the Christ*    MS. D reads "the words of Jesus."

3 *Are you he who is to come?*    The thrust of this question is: Are you the Messiah? It is prompted, presumably, because Jesus did not do the things which the expected Messiah was to perform. This verse seems to contradict the accounts of Jesus' baptism by John. Because of his doubts John sends his disciples with this question, which is fully answered by Jesus. John preached

the coming of one who would execute judgments (cf. Matt. 3.11), whereas Jesus speaks of mercy and loving-kindness; he preferred to heal rather than to destroy the wicked.[3]

5 *the blind receive their sight* This seems to be based on Isa. 61.1 and 35.5. The healing of the infirm is one of the signs of the Messiah: " . . . not only this but all who suffer affliction will be cured in the world-to-come, all except for the serpent, who is not cured, as it is written, *cursed are you above all animals*, what is the meaning of 'above all' [Heb. *mikol*]? It means that he is not cured. That humans are to be healed, as it is written, *Then shall the lame man leap like a hart* [Isa. 35.6] *and then shall the eyes of the blind be opened* [ibid. 35.5]."[4]

*the poor have good news preached to them* This phrase, in light of the foregoing, i.e., the blind receive their sight, the lame walk, the lepers are cleansed, and the dead raised up, is most difficult. Some commentators have, therefore, made of this activity on the part of Jesus a spiritual one and see it as a series of metaphors. This is highly unlikely. "What need, moreover, to add the poor have the Good Tidings preached to them if all which precedes refers to the preachment of the Good Tidings? It is unnatural to express the same fact first by a series of metaphors and then literally."[5] But this notwithstanding, the problem remains, *all* have the gospel preached to them, and *all* have benefited in a physical way. What is unique about the poor that the gospel should be preached (only) to them? Furthermore, the suggestion that this phrase goes back to Isa. 61.1, *to bring good tidings to the afflicted*, does not explain this difficulty, and it is meaningful only if we assume that the reference to the poor is a latter addition. We suggest that the text might have been that "the poor are made rich," *ha'anavim mitashrim*, and was read *ha'anavim mitbasrim*, "the poor have the gospel preached to them," as the scribe was thinking of Isa. 61.1. This emendation involves only one letter in Hebrew, a *bet* for an *ayin*. The poor here are identical with the poor in the first beatitude (Matt. 5.3) and/or the humble of 5.5, whose wealth is either the kingdom of heaven for the former, or to inherit the earth as to the latter. Should it be argued that the other gifts were already bestowed, while this one was a promise for the future, it must be remembered that here the disciples of John were told about what they saw and what they heard, hence including a promise for the future as well as miracles already performed.[6]

## NOTES

1. Josephus, *Ant.* XVIII.5.2.
2. See Matt. 14.3–12 (Sec. 111, below p. 238).
3. Manson, *SJ*, p. 66.
4. *Tan.B. Mezora* 7 (24a). See also Gen. R. 20.5.
5. Plummer, *St. Luke*, p. 203.
6. S. T. Lachs, "Hebrew Elements in the Gospels and Acts," *JQR* 71 (1980): 38–39.

# 65. *Jesus Speaks About John*

### MATT. 11.7–19

7 As they went away, Jesus began to speak to the crowds concerning John: "What did you go out into the wilderness to behold? A reed shaken by the wind? 8 Why then did you go out? To see a manᵍ clothed in soft raiment? Behold, those who wear soft raiment are in kings' houses. 9 Why then did you go out? To see a prophet?ʰ Yes, I tell you, and more than a prophet. 10 This is he of whom it is written,

> 'Behold, I send my messenger before thy face,
> who shall prepare thy way before thee.'

11 Truly, I say to you, among those born of women there has risen no one greater than John the Baptist; yet he who is least in the kingdom of heaven is greater then he. 12 From the days of John the Baptist until now the kingdom of heaven has suffered violence,ⁱ and men of violence take it by force. 13 For all the prophets and the law prophesied until John; 14 and if you are willing to accept it, he is Elijah who is to come. 15 He who has ears to hear,ʲ let him hear. 16 But to what shall I compare this generation? It is like children sitting in the market places and calling to their playmates, 17 'We piped to you, and you did not dance; we wailed, and you did not mourn.' 18 For John came neither eating nor drinking, and they say, 'He has a demon'; 19 the Son of man came eating and drinking, and they say, 'Behold, a glutton and a drunkard, a friend of tax collectors and sinners! Yet wisdom is justified by her deeds.'"ᵏ

### LUKE 7.24–30

24 When the messengers of John had gone, he began to speak to the crowds concerning John: "What did you go out into the wilderness to behold? A reed shaken by the wind? 25 What then did you go out to see? A man clothed in soft raiment? Behold, those who are gorgeously appareled and live in luxury are in kings' courts. 26 What then did you go out to see? A prophet? Yes, I tell you, and more than a prophet. 27 This is he of whom it is written,

> 'Behold, I send my messenger before thy face,
> who shall prepare thy way before thee.'

28 I tell you, among those born of women none is greater than John; yet he who is least in the kingdom of God is greater than he." 29 (When they heard this all the people and the tax collectors justified God, having been baptized with the baptism of John; 30 but the Pharisees and the lawyers rejected the purpose of God for themselves, not having been baptized by him.)

### IBID. 16.16

"The law and the prophets were until John; since then the good news of the kingdom of God is preached, and everyone enters it violently."

31 "To what then shall I compare the men of this generation, and what are they like? 32 They are like children sitting in the market place and calling to one another, 'We piped to you, and you did not dance; we wailed, and you did not weep.' 33 For John the Baptist has come eating no bread and drinking no wine; and you say, 'He has a demon.' 34 The Son of man has come eating and drinking; and you say, 'Behold, a glutton and a drunkard, a friend of tax collectors and sinners!' 35 Yet wisdom is justified by all her children."

---

g  Or *What then did you go out to see? A man . . .*
h  Other ancient authorities read *What then did you go out to see? A prophet?*
i  Or *has been coming violently.*
j  Other ancient authorities omit *to hear.*
k  Other ancient authorities read *children* (Luke 7.35).

## COMMENTARY

7  *What did you go out . . . to behold? A reed shaken by the wind?*  "The long cane grass was plentiful in the Arabah by the banks of the Jordan and its tributaries. Did you go out to see the very ordinary sight of cane grass shaken by the wind?"[1] Manson sees the point of this question as pointing up the strictness, even severity, of John's message. It was part of John's "prophetic nature," which was the antithesis of the symbolism of the reed, which bends with the wind.[2]

8  *clothed in soft raiment*  This is meant to contrast with John's hairy mantle (Matt. 3.4).[3]

9  *to see a prophet . . . more than a prophet*  The force of "more than a prophet" seems to be that this prophet is *sui generis* in that he was to be the precursor of the Messiah, as indicated by the following scriptural verses and the subsequent comments.[4] It should be noted that prophets are sometimes called *malakhim* "angels, messengers."[5]

10  *Behold, I send my messenger*, etc.  Exod. 23.20 (MT), *Behold, I send an angel before you to guard you on the way;* Mal. 3.1 (MT), *Behold, I send my messenger to prepare the way before me.*

*born of women*  I.e., a mortal. This expression is found in rabbinic literature but only in the singular, *yelud ishah.*[6]

11  *least in the kingdom of heaven*, etc.  This seems to be a put-down of the Baptist and is one of the passages which indicates some friction or even hostility between the followers of John and the followers of Jesus.[7] There are frequent comparisons between those of this world and those of the world-to-come. The following is a typical example: "R. Jeremiah said to R. Zera: 'What is the meaning of the verse, *The small and the great are there, and the slave is free from his master* [Job 3.19]? Do we not know that the small and the great

are there? But one who humbles himself for the sake of the words of Torah in this world will be made great in the world-to-come.' "[8]

12 *the kingdom . . . has suffered violence* Cf. Luke 16.16. This is a most difficult verse. The problem is the Gr. *biazomai*, "apply violence." Daube sees it as the equivalent of the Heb. *kabash*, as in "a prophet who does violence to his message."[9] Others see in it a reference, albeit forced, to the activity of revolutionaries or zealots who used terrorism and physical violence to bring about the kingdom.[10]

14 *and if you are willing* Clearly a Semitism, *im tirzeh* or *im timza lomar*, "if you wish," or, "may I suggest."[11]

*He is Elijah who is to come* I.e., Elijah redivivus.[12]

16 *But to what shall I compare this generation?* This is the typical rabbinic formula introducing a parable—*lema hadavar domeh.*[13]

### NOTES

1. McNeile, *Matt.*, p. 153.
2. See Manson, *SJ*, p. 70. For this symbolism see B. Ta'an. 20a, 3 Macc. 2.22.
3. Cf. Josephus, *BJ* I.24.3, where *esthetes basilikai* are contrasted with *ek trichon pepoiemenai.* Manson, *SJ*, p. 66, errs in stating that the point is the "wearers of it [soft apparel] are in the king's courts, but John is in the king's prison."
4. N.b., B. BB 12a is not applicable.
5. Here the messenger is the forerunner of God Himself and there is no idea of a Messiah (Manson, *SJ*, p. 69). Cf. also B. MQ 1.2, Luke 7.27. In Mal. 3.23 (RSV 4.5) and Sira 48.10 the messenger is Elijah. On the composition of this verse in Matt. and its sources, see Stendahl *SSMUOT*, pp. 49 ff.
6. See *ARN* 2, B. Shab. 88b, Num. R. 4 et al.
7. See C. H. Kraeling, *John the Baptist* (1951), pp. 138 ff.
8. B. BB 85b. Cf. also *PR* 83 (198b); Koh. R. on 1.17; Exod. R. 23; *Mek.* Exod. 15.2; ibid. 19.11.
9. Daube, *NTRJ*, p. 287, citing M. Sanh. 11.15, correct to 11.5.
10. Allen, *Matt.*, ad loc., cites M. Eduy. 8.7, *berabeq bameqoravim bizro'a.*
11. Cf. Bacher, *Exegetische Terminologie*, s.v. מצא (2:118).
12. On Elijah redivivus, see Ginzberg, *Legends*, passim. See Index, s.v. "Elijah, the Prophet, messianic activity of."
13. Bacher, op. cit., s.v. משל p. 121.

## 66. *Woes on the Cities of Galilee*

### MATT. 11.20–24

20 Then he began to upbraid the cities where most of his mighty works had been done, because they did not repent. 21 "Woe to you, Chorazin! woe to you Bethsaida! for if the mighty works done in you had been done in Tyre and Sidon, they would have repented long ago in sackcloth and ashes. 22 But I tell you, it shall be more tolerable on the day of judgment for Tyre and Sidon than for you, 23 And you, Capernaum, will you be exalted to heaven? You shall be brought down to Hades. For

if the mighty works done in you had been done in Sodom, it would have remained until this day. 24 But I tell you that it shall be more tolerable on the day of judgment for the land of Sodom than for you."

## LUKE 10.13–15

13 "Woe to you, Chorazin! woe to you Bethsaida! for if the mighty works done in you had been done in Tyre and Sidon, they would have repented long ago, sitting in sackcloth and ashes. 14 But it shall be more tolerable in the judgment for Tyre and Sidon than for you. 15 And you, Capernaum, will you be exalted to heaven? You shall be brought down to Hades."

### COMMENTARY

20 *Then he began to upbraid the cities,*etc.   There is no rabbinic parallel to this section, although it may contain some Semitic wordplay. It is reminiscent of the prophet Micah's condemnation of several cities.[1] What seems to form the background of this passage is the repentance of the inhabitants of Nineveh in the Book of Jonah versus the recalcitrance of the Jews (Jewish cities). There is a midrash to the effect that Jonah did not wish to go on his mission to Nineveh for fear that they would, in fact, repent and that this would serve as an embarrassment to Israel, who did not.[2]

21 *Chorazin*   There is no mention of Chorazin either in the Bible or in Josephus. Today it is identified with Khisbet Kerazeh, 2 miles N of Capernaum. In the Talmud we find Kharazim (text uncertain), which was famous for its wheat.[3]

*sackcloth and ashes*   Symbols of mourning, specifically mentioned in Jon. 3.6.

*Bethsaida*   Aram. *bait ẓaida,* "house of the fisher." It is identified with Julias, a village made into a city by Herod Philip, who named it in honor of Julia, daughter of Augustus (Josephus, *Ant.* XVIII.2.2) Bethsaida-Julia is identified with a double city E of the Jordan near the entry into the Sea of Galilee, called el-Tell, 2 miles from the sea, i.e., Julias, while the remains called el'Araj on the shore of the lake are understood as the makeup of the fishers' settlement of Bethsaida.[4]

23 *And you, Capernaum*   An echo of Isa. 14.13–15. The comparison between Capernaum and Sodom might also be on the basis of geography— Capernaum was on comparatively high ground as to the Sea of Galilee, while Sodom is at the lowest point on earth.

24 *land of Sodom*   On this description of Sodom as a "land," see above Matt. 10.15 (p. 180).

### NOTES

1. Mic. 1.10 ff.
2. *Mek.* Exod. 12.1; TJ Sanh. 11.7, 30b (47). Manson, *SJ*, p. 77, suggests: "There

is no account whatsoever in the Gospels, apart from this mention, of any visit of Jesus to Chorazin. Yet activity there must have been, and that of such a sort that it would have brought the heathen cities, Tyre and Sidon to repentance."

3. B. Men. 85a.

4. See *IDB*, s.v. "Bethsaida."

## 67. *Jesus' Thanksgiving to the Father*

### MATT. 11.25–27

25 At that time Jesus declared, "I thank thee Father, Lord of heaven and earth, that thou hast hidden these things from the wise and understanding and revealed them to babes; 26 yea, Father, for such was thy gracious will.[1] 27 All things have been delivered to me by my Father; and no one knows the Son except the Father, and no one knows Father except the Son and any one to whom the Son chooses to reveal him."

### LUKE 10.21–22

21 In that same hour he rejoiced in the Holy Spirit and said, "I thank thee, Father, Lord of heaven and earth, that thou hast hidden these things from the wise and understanding and revealed them to babes; yea, Father, for such was thy gracious will.[1] 22 All things have been delivered to me by my Father, and no one knows who the Son is except the Father, or who the Father is except the Son and anyone to whom the Son chooses to reveal him."

---

1 Or *so it was well-pleasing before thee.*

### COMMENTARY

This thanksgiving passage is clearly written in poetic form with balanced Semitic parallelism. The introduction to it likewise reflects a Hebrew expression, i.e., "at that time," Heb. *ba'et hahi* or *be'otah sha'ah.*

25 *Lord of heaven and earth*   This phrase, although not in MT, is found in the Apocrypha.[1]

*Father* Heb. *Av*, Aram. *Abba*, is not the normal way of addressing God, i.e., without a pronominal suffix, such as "my father" or "our father," etc.[2]

*to babes*   Gr. *auta nēpiois*, which is the translation of the Heb. *peta'im*, "the simple," the inexperienced, which is a better parallel to *apo sophōn*, "from the wise."[3]

26 *for such was thy gracious will*   In Heb. this phrase is always in the future, *yehi razon milfanekha*, and also in Aram., *yehē ra'ava qadamakh*, and found frequently in rabbinic sources.[4]

## NOTES

1. E. g., Tob. 7.17.
2. On the use of Abba, see Jeremias, "Abba," in *PJ*, pp. 11–65.
3. Cf. Ps. (LXX) 23.7, 118(119).130.
4. Cf. B. Ber. 19a; TJ ibid. 4, 7d (28). Cf. also Dalman, *Words*, p. 21. The Aram. *yebē qadam* in Targum—e.g., Targ. O. Gen. 24.42, but not in the past.

# 68. *Comfort for the Heavy-Laden*

## MATT. 11.28–30

28 "Come to me, all who labor and are heavy-laden, and I will give you rest. 29 Take my yoke upon you, and learn from me; for I am gentle and lowly in heart, and you will find rest for your souls. 30 For my yoke is easy, and my burden light."

### COMMENTARY

28 *I will give you rest*   One of the blessings forthcoming in the messianic age will be the giving of rest to the weary pious.[1]

29 *my yoke*   I.e., my authority. "yoke" is used with a variety of meanings in rabbinic literature, e.g., the yoke of the kingdom of heaven,[2] the yoke of the Torah,[3] the yoke of the commandments,[4] and the yoke of repentance.[5]

### NOTES

1. Cf. En. 48.4, *PRK* 27 (163a), *PR* 32 (149a).
2. B. Ber. 10b, *SER* 11.
3. M. Avot 3.5; *Tan. Vezot Haberakbab* 5.
4. M. Ber. 2.2.
5. B. AZ 5a.

# 69. *Plucking Ears of Grain on the Sabbath*

## MATT. 12.1–8

1 At that time Jesus went through the grainfields on the sabbath; his disciples were hungry, and they began to pluck ears of grain and to eat. 2 But when the Pharisees saw it, they said to him, "Look, your disciples are doing what is not lawful to do on the sabbath." 3 He said to them, "Have you not read what David did, when he was hungry, and those who were with him; 4 how he entered the house of God and ate the bread of the Presence, which it was not lawful for him to eat nor for those who were with him, but only for the priests? 5 Or have you not read in the law how on the sabbath the priests in the temple profane the sabbath, and are guiltless? 6 I tell you, something greater than the temple is here. 7 And if you had known what this means, 'I desire mercy, and not sacrifice,' you would not have condemned the guiltless. 8 For the Son of man is lord of the sabbath."

## MARK 2.23–28

23 One sabbath, he was going through the grainfields; and as they made their way his disciples began to pluck ears of grain. 24 And the Pharisees said to him, "Look, why are they doing what is not lawful on the sabbath?" 25 And he said to them, "Have you never read what David did, when he was in need and was hungry, he and those who were with him: 26 how he entered the house of God, when Abiathar was high priest,ᵐ and ate the bread of the Presence, which it was not lawful for any but the priests to eat, and also gave it to those who were with him?" 27 And he said to them, "The sabbath was made for man, not man for the sabbath;º so the Son of man is lord even of the sabbath."

## LUKE 6.1–5

1 On a sabbath,ⁿ while he was going through the grainfields, his disciples plucked and ate some ears of grain, rubbing them in their hands. 2 But some of the Pharisees said, "Why are you doing what is not lawful to do on the sabbath?" 3 And Jesus answered, "Have you not read what David did when he was hungry, he and those who were with him: 4 how he entered the house of God, and took and ate the bread of the Presence, which it is not lawful for any but the priests to eat, and also gave it to those with him?" 5 And he said to them, "The Son of man is lord of the sabbath."

---

m Some texts omit *when Abiathar was high priest.*

n Other ancient authorities read *On the second first sabbath* (on the second sabbath after the first).

o Some omit v. 27. Others omit 27b. For Luke 6.5 D reads *On the same day seeing someone working on the sabbath, he said to him, "Man, if indeed you know what you are doing, you are blessed; but if you do not know, you are cursed and a transgressor of the law."*

## COMMENTARY

1 *his disciples were hungry*, etc.    According to the law in Deut. 23. 25–26, one may enter the vineyard or field of another and eat of the produce as long as one does not take the grapes away or use a sickle on the grain. This earlier law was later modified and applied only to laborers working there for the owner. Since the Pharisees are represented in this passage as rebuking Jesus for allowing his disciples to pluck ears of corn on the Sabbath, which is prohibited since it is equated with reaping,[1] but not as raising any objection to the act of his followers in entering a field that is not theirs, this indicates that the NT writer was familiar with the older tradition.[2] McNeile attempts to place this incident in a particular season—"the ripeness of the corn places the incident in the spring during the few weeks after the Passover."[2] This may well be correct if the incident is genuine.

3 *Have you not read*, etc.    Cf. 1 Sam. 21.1–6. "David is related to have come alone to the priest, but to have told him he had appointed his young

men to such a place; on the basis of this Jesus assumed that 'they that were with him' shared the bread with David; that they hungered is an inference from the facts, added to bring out the parallel."[3] There is, of course, a difference between the two incidents. "The Pharisees . . . believed that David ate the bread in the Temple to save his life, but the disciples of Jesus did not eat the ears of the corn to save their lives."[4]

4 *the house of God.* This is an inference, for actually it was a meeting tent which housed the ark.

*Bread of the Presence* Heb. *leḥem ha-panim* or *leḥem ha-ma'arekhet.*[5]

5 *Or have you not read in the law* There is no specific law in the Torah which authorizes the violation of the Sabbath. There are rules, however, for Temple service which mandate that the priest perform them on the Sabbath, hence the rabbinic statement "Temple service takes precedence over the Sabbath."[6] Positive commandments which are governed by a specific time take precedence over the Sabbath law if the two are in conflict.[7]

7 *I desire mercy,* etc. Hos. 6.6, and this text agrees with the MT against the LXX and the Targum.[8] It is also cited in Mk. 9.13.

*the guiltless* I.e., the disciples.

8 *the Son of man is lord of the sabbath* "Son of man" here is not a title but the Aram. *bar nesha,* i.e., "man," cf. Mk. 2.27–28. This is paralleled by the rabbinic statement "The Sabbath was made for man, not man for the Sabbath, so that man is the lord over the Sabbath."[9] Zeitlin is wrong in stating that "Jesus claimed dispensation from the Pentateuchal law which prohibited work on the Sabbath on the grounds that he was a priest, the son of David, and hence 'Lord of the Sabbath day.' "[10]

## NOTES

1. B. Shab. 73b.
2. B. Cohen, "The Rabbinic Law Presupposed by Matthew XII.1, and Luke VI.1," *HTR* 23 (1930): 91–92.
3. Swete, cited by McNeile. Cf. also M. Men. 11.2, Yal. Sam. 21.5.
4. Zeitlin, *Who Crucified Jesus* (New York, London, 1942), p. 129.
5. Cf. Exod. 40.21.
6. B. Shab. 132b; cf. also B. Yev. 7a.
7. M. Ned. 3.1; M. RH 1.4; TJ Yom. 38d (59); B. Shab. 131a. N.b., showbread changed (Lev. 24.8), burnt offerings doubled (Num. 28.8 ff.). Cf. Jub. 1.10 f., no work done on the Sabbath except for the bringing of frankincense and the bringing of oblations and sacrifices before the Lord. For other Temple duties permitted on the Sabbath, see, e.g., M. Pes. 6.1; B. Er. 12.15.
8. See Stendahl, *SSMUOT*, pp. 128 ff.
9. *Mek.* Exod. 31.13, 31.14; B. Yom. 85b; Apoc. Bar. 14.18; B. Er. 43a. So Torrey, *The Four Gospels; A New Translation.* For a discussion of this passage, see F. W. Beare, "The Sabbath Was Made for Man?" *JBL* 79 (1960): 130–136.
10. Zeitlin, loc. cit.

## 70. *The Healing of the Man with the Withered Hand*

### MATT. 12.9–14

9 And he went on from there and entered their synagogue. 10 And behold, there was a man with a withered hand. And they asked him, "Is it lawful to heal on the sabbath?" so that they might accuse him. 11 He said to them, "What man of you, if he has one sheep and it falls into a pit on the sabbath, will not lay hold of it and lift it out? 12 Of how much more value is a man than a sheep! So it is lawful to do good on the sabbath." 13 Then he said to the man, "Stretch out your hand." And the man stretched it out, and it was restored, whole like the other. 14 But the Pharisees went out and took counsel against him, how to destroy him.

### MARK 3.1–6

1 Again he entered the synagogue, and a man was there who had a withered hand. 2 And they watched him, to see whether he would heal him on the sabbath, so that they might accuse him. 3 And he said to the man who had the withered hand, "Come here," 4 And he said to them, "Is it lawful on the sabbath to do good or to do harm, to save life or to kill?" But they were silent. 5 And he looked around at them with anger, grieved at their hardness of heart, and said to the man, "Stretch out your hand." He stretched it out, and his hand was restored. 6 The Pharisees went out, and immediately held counsel with the Herodians against him, how to destroy him.

### LUKE 6.6–8

6 On another sabbath, when he entered the synagogue and taught, a man was there whose right hand was withered. 7 And the scribes and the Pharisees watched him, to see whether he would heal on the sabbath, so that they might find an accusation against him. 8 But he knew their thoughts, and he said to the man who had the withered hand, "Come and stand here." And he rose and stood there.

### IBID. 14.5

5 And he said to them, "Which of you, having an ass or an ox that has fallen into a well, will not immediately pull him out on a sabbath day?"

### IBID. 6.9–11

9 And Jesus said to them, "I ask you, is it lawful on the sabbath to do good or to do harm, to save life or to destroy it?" 10 And he looked around on them all, and said to him, "Stretch out your hand." And he did so, and his hand was restored. 11 But they were filled with fury and discussed with one another what they might do to Jesus.

### COMMENTARY

10 *Is it lawful to heal on the sabbath?* The answer to this question is a categorical yes, if life is in danger, but no, if it is not in danger—as in the

situation here. The issue is the curing of a withered hand, which neither endangered life nor was a recent illness requiring immediate treatment. The healing could have waited for the following day. The literature is replete with passages reflecting this philosophy: "Every case where life is in danger supersedes the Sabbath."[1] "Rabbi [Judah the Prince] and R. Meir permitted healing on the Sabbath."[2]

11 *What man of you*, etc.   There is sufficient material indicating that one could and should save an animal on the Sabbath or on a Festival.[3] "On the point raised in this verse it is not possible to say with certainty what the scribes would have said in our Lord's day. Opinions were still divided in the Rabbinical schools at a much later time. Some said that if an animal fell into a pit on the Sabbath, it was lawful to bring food to it there. Others held that it was further permissable to place a mattress and cushions under it so that it might get out by its own exertion."[4] The opposite of this approach has come down to us: "And if it [an animal] falls into a pit or a ditch, he shall not raise it on the Sabbath."[5] This regulation, however, does not represent the view of rabbinic Judaism.

*one sheep*   A Semitism meaning "a sheep."

12 *Of how much more*   Another example of the *a fortiore*, the *qal veḥomer*. See above pp. 142, 184.

*to do good*   I.e., to perform *ma'asim tovim*, "good deeds."[6]

## NOTES

1. M. Yom. 8.6.
2. TJ Bez. 63a (34). Cf. also B. ibid. 22b; *Mek.* Exod. 31.13; TJ Shab. 15.16 (134); *Tan.B. Lekh Lekha* 20 (38b), Deut. R. 10.
3. See B. Shab. 128b; M. Beẓ. 5.2, 31.3 (Festival); T. Beẓ. 3.2 (p. 205); cf. B. Beẓ. 37a; B. Shab. 117b; TJ Pes. 3, 30a (59); TJ Beẓ. 3, 62a (38).
4. Manson, *SJ*, p. 188.
5. *A Fragment of a Zadokite Work* 13.22 (Charles).
6. Cf. the usage of Gr. *agathopoieō* in Luke 6.9 = Heb. *ḥetev*, Lev. 5.4, Jer. 12.22, Zech. 8.15. On *ma'asim tovim*, e.g., B. Shab. 12a; TJ ibid. 15, 15b (2); *PR* 23 (116b); T. Shab. 16.22 (p. 136); B. Shab. 30a–b.

# 71. Jesus Heals the Multitudes

## Matt. 12.15

Jesus, aware of this, withdrew from there. And many followed him. . . .

## Ibid. 4.25

And great crowds followed him from Galilee and the Decapolis and Jerusalem and Judea and from beyond the Jordan.

## Ibid. 12.15b–21

15b and he healed them all, 16 and ordered them not to make him known. 17 This was to fulfill what was spoken by the prophet Isaiah: 18 "Behold, my servant whom I have chosen, my beloved with whom my soul is well pleased. I will put my Spirit upon him, and he shall proclaim justice to the Gentiles. 19 He will not wrangle or cry aloud, nor will any one hear his voice in the streets; 20 he will not break a bruised reed or quench a smoldering wick, till he brings justice to victory; 21 and in his name will the Gentiles hope."

## Mark 3.7–12

7 Jesus withdrew with his disciples to the sea, and a great multitude from Galilee followed; also from Judea 8 and Jerusalem and Idumea and from beyond the Jordan and from about Tyre and Sidon a great multitude, hearing all that he did, came to him. 9 And he told his disciples to have a boat ready for him because of the crowd, lest they should crush him; 10 for he had healed many, so that all who had diseases pressed upon him to touch him. 11 And whenever the unclean spirits beheld him, they fell down before him and cried out, "Your are the Son of God." 12 And he strictly ordered them not to make him known.

## Luke 6.17–19

17 And he came down with them and stood on a level place, with a great crowd of his disciples and a great multitude of people from all Judea and Jerusalem and the seacoast of Tyre and Sidon, who came to hear him and to be healed of their diseases; 18 and those who were troubled with unclean spirits were cured. 19 And all the crowd sought to touch him, for power came forth from him and healed them all.

## Ibid. 4.41

And demons also came out of many, crying. "You are the Son of God!" But he rebuked them and would not allow them to speak, because they knew that he was the Christ.

## COMMENTARY

18 *Behold, my servant*, etc.    Isa. 42.1–4. The text sometimes follows the LXX against the MT.[1]

## NOTES

1. See Stendahl, *SSMUOT*, pp. 107 ff.

# 72. *The Call of the Twelve*

## MATT. 10.1–4

1 And he called to him his twelve disciples and gave them authority over unclean spirits, to cast them out, and to heal every disease and every infirmity. 2 The names of the twelve apostles are these: first Simon, who is called Peter, and Andrew his brother; James the son of Zebedee, and John his brother, 3 Philip and Bartholomew; Thomas and Matthew the tax collector; James the son of Alphaeus, and Thaddaeus; 4 Simon the Cananaean, and Judas Iscariot, who betrayed him.

## MARK 3.13–19

13 And he went up into the hills, and called to him those whom he desired; and they came to him. 14 And he appointed twelve[p] to be with him, and to be sent out to preach 15 and to have authority to cast out demons: 16 Simon whom he surnamed Peter; 17 James the son of Zebedee and John the brother of James, whom he surnamed Boanerges, that is, sons of thunder; 18 Andrew, and Philip, and Bartholomew, and Matthew, and Thomas, and Thaddaeus, and Simon the Cananaean, 19 and Judas Iscariot, who betrayed him.

## LUKE 6.12–16

12 In these days he went out into the hills to pray; and all night he continued in prayer to God. 13 And when it was day, he called his disciples, and chose from them twelve, whom he named apostles; 14 Simon, whom he named Peter, and Andrew his brother, and James and John, and Philip, and Bartholomew, 15 and Matthew, and Thomas, and James the son of Alphaeus, and Simon who was called the Zealot, 16 and Judas the son[q] of James, and Judas Iscariot, who became a traitor.

———————————

p Some add *whom also he named apostles* . . .
q Or *brother*.
See above Sec. 58 (p. 175).

# THE SERMON ON THE PLAIN

LUKE 6.20–49

## 73. *The Beatitudes*

### MATT. 5.3, 4, 6, 11, 12

3 "Blessed are the poor in spirit, for theirs is the kingdom of heaven. 4 Blessed are those who mourn, for they shall be comforted. 6 Blessed are those who hunger and thirst for righteousness, for they shall be satisfied. 11 Blessed are you when men revile you and persecute you and utter all kinds of evil against you falsely on my account. 12 Rejoice and be glad, for your reward is great in heaven, for so men persecuted the prophets who were before you."

### LUKE 6.20–23

20 And he lifted up his eyes on his disciples, and said, "Blessed are you poor, for yours is the kingdom of God. 21 Blessed are you that hunger now, for you shall be satisfied. Blessed are you that weep now, for you shall laugh. 22 Blessed are you when men hate you, and when they exclude you and revile you, and cast out your name as evil, on account of the Son of man! 23 Rejoice in that day, and leap for joy, for behold, your reward is great in heaven; for so their fathers did to the prophets."
See above Sec. 19 (p. 68f).

## 74. *The Woes*

### LUKE 6.24–26

24 "But woe to you that are rich, for you have received your consolation. 25 Woe to you that are full now, for you shall hunger. Woe to you that laugh now, for you shall mourn and weep. 26 Woe to you, when all men speak well of you, for so their fathers did to the false prophets."
See above Sec. 19 (p. 69).

## 75. *On Love of One's Enemies*

### MATT. 5.39–42, 44

44 "But I say to you, Love your enemies and pray for those who persecute you. 39 But I say to you, Do not resist one who is evil. But if anyone strikes you on the right cheek, turn to him the other also; 40 and if anyone would sue you and take your coat,

let him have your cloak as well; 41 and if anyone forces you to go one mile, go with him two miles. 42 Give to him who begs from you, and do not refuse him who would borrow from you."

## IBID. 7.12

"So whatever you wish that men would do to you, do so to them; for this is the law and the prophets."

## IBID. 5.46–47

46 "For if you love those who love you, what reward have you? Do not even the tax collectors do the same? 47 And if you salute only your brethren, what more are you doing than others? Do not even the Gentiles do the same?"

## IBID. 5.45, 48

45 ". . . so that you may be sons of your Father who is in heaven; for he makes his sun rise on the evil and on the good, and sends rain on the just and on the unjust. 48 You, therefore, must be perfect, as your heavenly Father is perfect."

## LUKE 6.27–36

27 "But I say to you that hear, Love your enemies, do good to those who hate you, 28 bless those who curse you, pray for those who abuse you. 29 To him who strikes you on the cheek, offer the other also; and from him who takes away your cloak do not withhold you coat as well. 30 Give to everyone who begs from you; and of him who takes away your goods, do not ask them again. 31 And as you wish that men would do to you, do so to them. 32 If you love those who love you, what credit is that to you? For even sinners love those who love them. 33 And if you do good to those who do good to you, what credit is that to you? For even sinners do the same. 34 And if you lend to those from whom you hope to receive, what credit is that to you? Even sinners lend to sinners, to receive as much again. 35 But love your enemies, and do good, and lend, expecting nothing in return;ʳ and your reward will be great, and you will be sons of the Most High; for he is kind to the ungrateful and the selfish. 36 Be merciful, even as your Father is merciful."

---

r  Some read *despairing of no man.*
See above Secs. 26, 27, 39 (pp. 103, 106, 143).

# 76. *On Judging*

## MATT. 7.1–2

1 "Judge not, that you be not judged. 2 For with the judgment you pronounce you will be judged, and the measure you give will be the measure you get."

## IBID. 15.14

"Let them alone; they are blind guides. And if a blind man leads a blind man, both will fall into a pit."

## IBID. 10.24–25

24 "A disciple is not above his teacher, nor a servant above his master; 25 it is enough for the disciple to be like his teacher, and the servant like his master."

## IBID. 7.3–5

3 "Why do you see the speck that is in your brother's eye, but do not notice the log that is in your own eye? 4 Or how can you say to your brother, 'Let me take the speck out of your eye,' when there is the log in your own eye? 5 You hypocrite, first take the log out of your own eye, and then you will see clearly to take the speck out of your brother's eye."

## LUKE 6.37–42

37 "Judge not, and you will not be judged; condemn not, and you will not be condemned; forgive, and you will be forgiven; 38 give, and it will be given to you; good measure, pressed down, shaken together, running over, will be put into your lap. For the measure you give will be the measure you get back. 39 He also told them a parable: Can a blind man lead a blind man? Will they not both fall into a pit? 40 A disciple is not above his teacher, but everyone when he is fully taught will be like his teacher. 41 Why do you see the speck that is in your brother's eye, but do not notice the log that is in your own eye? 42 Or how can you say to your brother, 'Brother, let me take out the speck that is in your eye,' when you yourself do not see the log that is in your own eye? You hypocrite, first take the log out of your own eye, and then you will see clearly to take out the speck that is in your brother's eye."
See above Secs. 36, 59 (pp. 135, 182)

# 77. *A Test of Goodness*

## MATT. 7.16–20

16 "You will know them by their fruits. Are grapes gathered from thorns, or figs from thistles? 17 So, every sound tree bears good fruit, but the bad tree bears evil fruit. 18 A sound tree cannot bear evil fruit, nor can a bad tree bear good fruit. 19 Every tree that does not bear good fruit is cut down and thrown into the fire. 20 Thus you will know them by their fruits."

## IBID. 12.33–35; 7.21

33 "Either make the tree good; and its fruit good; or make the tree bad, and its fruit bad; for the tree is known by its fruit. 34 You brood of vipers! how can you speak good, when you are evil? For out of the abundance of the heart the mouth speaks. 35

The good man out of his good treasure brings forth good, and the evil man out of his evil treasure brings forth evil. 21 Not everyone who says to me, 'Lord Lord,' shall enter the kingdom of heaven but he who does the will of my Father who is in heaven."

### LUKE 6.43–46

43 "For no good tree bears bad fruit, nor again does a bad tree bear good fruit; 44 for each tree is known by its own fruit. For figs are not gathered from thorns, nor are grapes picked from a bramble bush. 45 The good man out of the good treasure of his heart produces good, and the evil man out of his evil treasure produces evil; for out of the abundance of the heart his mouth speaks. 46 Why do you call me 'Lord, Lord,' and not do what I tell you?"
See above Sec 41 (p. 147).

# 78. *Hearers and Doers of the Word*

### MATT. 7.24–27

24 "Every one then who hears these words of mine and does them will be like a wise man who built his house upon the rock; 25 and the rain fell, and the floods came, and the winds blew and beat upon that house but it did not fall, because it had been founded on the rock. 26 And every one who hears these words of mine and does not do them will be like a foolish man who built his house upon the sand; 27 and the rain fell, and the floods came, and the winds blew and beat against that house, and it fell; and great was the fall of it."

### LUKE 6.47–49

47 "Everyone who comes to me and hears my words and does them, I will show you what he is like: 48 he is like a man building a house, who dug deep and laid the foundation upon rock; and when a flood arose, the stream broke against that house, and could not shake it, because it had been well built[s] 49 But he who hears and does not do them is like a man who built a house on the ground without a foundation; against which the stream broke, and immediately it fell, and the ruin of that house was great."

---

s  Others read *founded on the rock.*
See above Sec. 43 (p. 150)

# 79. *The Centurion's Slave*

### LUKE 7.1–10

1 After he had ended all his sayings in the hearing of the people he entered Capernaum. 2 Now a centurion had a slave who was dear[t] to him, who was sick and at the point of death. 3 When he heard of Jesus, he sent to him elders of the Jews,

asking him to come and heal his slave. 4 And when they came to Jesus, they besought him earnestly, saying, "He is worthy to have you do this for him, 5 for he loves our nation, and he built us our synagogue." 6 And Jesus went with them. When he was not far from the house, the centurion sent friends to him, saying to him, "Lord, do not trouble yourself, for I am not worthy to have you come under my roof; 7 therefore I did not presume to come to you. But say the word, and let my servant be healed. 8 For I am a man set under authority, with soldiers under me; and I say to one, 'Go,' and he goes; and to another 'Come,' and he comes; and to my slave, 'Do this,' and he does it." 9 When Jesus heard this he marveled at him, and turned and said to the multitude that followed him, "I tell you, not even in Israel have I found such faith." 10 And when those who had been sent returned to the house, they found the slave well.

---

t  Or *valuable*.
See above Sec. 46 (p. 154).

# 80. *The Widow's Son at Nain*

## LUKE 7.11–17

11 Soon afterward[u] he went to a city called Nain, and his disciples and a great crowd went with him. 12 As he drew near to the gate of the city, behold, a man who had died was being carried out, the only son of his mother, and she was a widow; and a large crowd from the city was with her. 13 And when the Lord saw her, he had compassion on her and said to her, "Do not weep." 14 And he came and touched the bier, and the bearers stood still. And he said "Young man, I say to you, arise." 15 And the dead man sat up, and began to speak. And he gave him to his mother. 16 Fear seized them all; and they glorified God, saying, "A great prophet has arisen among us!" and "God has visited his people!" 17 And this report concerning him spread through the whole of Judea and all the surrounding country.

---

u  Some texts read *next day*.

### COMMENTARY

This is similar to the Elijah-Elisha stories. Cf. 1 Kings 17.17–24, 2 Kings 4.33–37.[1]

11 *Nain* Perhaps from Heb. *na'im*, "pleasant," a town in SW Galilee, modern Arab village Nein. In the midrash the territory of Issachar is called "the land that was pleasant" (Gen. 49.15) and alludes to the town of Nain.[2] It is not the city cited by Josephus, which is on the border of Idumea.[3]

14 *he touched the bier* To make the bearers stop. In an earlier phase of the story did he touch the body?[4]

NOTES

1. If this is a resuscitation story, see Pliny, *NH* XXVI.13; Apuleius, *Florida* 19; and Philostratus, *Vita Apollonii* IV.45.
2. Gen. R. 98.12. See Abel, *Géographie de la Palestine*, 2:394–395.
3. Josephus, *BJ* IV.9.4–5.
4. Montefiore, *SG* II, pp. 425–426.

# 81. *John's Question to Jesus*

## Luke 7.18–23

18 The disciples of John told him of all these things. 19 And John, calling to him two of his disciples, sent them to the Lord, saying, "Are you he who is to come, or shall we look for another?" 20 And when the men had come to him, they said "John the Baptist has sent us to you, saying, 'Are you he who is to come, or shall we look for another?' " 21 In that hour he cured many of diseases and plagues and evil spirits, and on many that were blind he bestowed sight. 22 And he answered them, "Go and tell John what you have seen and heard: the blind receive their sight, the lame walk, lepers are cleansed, and the deaf hear, the dead are raised up, the poor have good news preached to them. 23 And blessed is he who takes no offense at me."
See above Sec. 64 (p. 189).

# 82. *Jesus Speaks About John*

## Luke 7.24–35

24 When the messengers of John had gone, he began to speak to the crowds concerning John: "What did you go out into the wilderness to behold? A reed shaken by the wind? 25 What then did you go out to see? A man clothed in soft raiment? Behold, those who are gorgeously appareled and live in luxury are in kings' courts. 26 What then did you go out to see? A prophet? Yes, I tell you, and more than a prophet. 27 This is he of whom it is written, 'Behold, I send my messenger before thy face, who shall prepare thy way before thee.' 28 I tell you, among those born of women none is greater than John; yet he who is least in the kingdom of God is greater than he." 29 (When they heard this all the people and the tax collectors justified God, having been baptized with the baptism of John; 30 but the Pharisees and the lawyers rejected the purpose of God for themselves, not having been baptized by him.) 31 "To what then shall I compare the men of this generation, and what are they like? 32 They are like children sitting in the marketplace and calling to one another, 'We piped to you, and you did not dance; we wailed, and you did not weep.' 33 For John the Baptist has come eating no bread and drinking no wine; and you say, 'He has a demon.' 34 The Son of man has come eating and drinking; and you say, 'Behold, a glutton and a drunkard, a friend of tax collectors and sinners!' 35 Yet wisdom is justified by all her children."
See above Sec. 65 (p. 191).

# 83. *The Woman with the Ointment*

## LUKE 7.36–50

36 One of the Pharisees asked him to eat with him, and he went into the Pharisee's house, and sat at table. 37 And behold, a woman of the city, who was a sinner, when she learned that he was sitting at table in the Pharisee's house, brought an alabaster flask of ointment, 38 and standing behind him at his feet, weeping, she began to wet his feet with her tears, and wiped them with the hair of her head, and kissed his feet, and anointed them with the ointment. 39 Now when the Pharisee who had invited him saw it, he said to himself, "If this man were a prophet, he would have known who and what sort of woman this is who is touching him, for she is a sinner." 40 And Jesus answering said to him, "Simon, I have something to say to you." And he answered, "What is it, Teacher?" 41 "A certain creditor had two debtors; one owed five hundred denarii, and the other fifty. 42 When they could not pay, he forgave them both. Now which of them will love him more?" 43 Simon answered, "The one, I suppose, to whom he forgave more." And he said to him, "You have judged rightly." 44 Then turning toward the woman he said to Simon, "Do you see this woman? I entered your house, you gave me no water for my feet, but she has wet my feet with her tears and wiped them with her hair. 45 You gave me no kiss, but from the time I came in she has not ceased to kiss my feet. 46 You did not anoint my head with oil, but she has anointed my feet with ointment. 47 Therefore I tell you, her sins, which are many, are forgiven, for she loved much; but he who is forgiven little, loves little." 48 And he said to her, "Your sins are forgiven." 49 Then those who were at table with him, began to say among themselves, "Who is this, who even forgives sins?" 50 And he said to the woman, "Your faith has saved you; go in peace."

## COMMENTARY

36 *one of the Pharisees*   Presumably named Simon (vv. 40, 43, 44); perhaps from Mark 14.3.

*asked him to eat with him*   The reason for the invitation is not clear. It may be that he was extending hospitality to a learned man, which was considered to be a *mizvah*.[1] This conjecture is supported by v. 40, where Simon calls him "Teacher."

37 *a woman of the city, who was a sinner*   Her sin is not stated explicitly, perhaps she was an unchaste woman.[2] Possibly she violated the standards of modest behavior in that she did not keep her hair covered, which was considered an act of immodesty.[3] Black argues that the original for "sinner" was the Aram. *ḥayyabta*, meaning "debtor," and hence the connection between this and the parable of the debtor.[4]

*alabaster flask of ointment*   See Matt. 26.7 (p. 400). "Ointments are very well preserved in alabaster flasks."[5]

## NOTES

1. See, e.g., B. Ber. 10a.
2. See Plummer, "The Woman that was a Sinner," *Expos.T.* 27 (1915–16): 42–43.

3. M. Ket. 8.6, T. ibid. 7.6 (p. 269), TJ Ta'an. 1, 64b (41).
4. Black, *Aramaic Approach*, pp. 181–183.
5. Pliny, *NH* XIII.3.9. On these flasks, see I. Ben Dor, "Palestinian Alabaster Vases," *QDAP* 11 (1945): 93–112.

# 84. *The Ministering Women*

## LUKE 8.1–3

1 Soon thereafter he went on through cities and villages, preaching and bringing the good news of the kingdom of God. And the twelve were with him, 2 and also some women who had been healed of evil spirits and infirmities; Mary, called Magdalene, from whom seven demons had gone out, 3 Joanna, the wife of Chuza, Herod's steward, and Susanna, and many others, who provided for them,ᵛ out of their means.

---

v  Some read *him*.

### COMMENTARY

2 *Mary called Magdalene*  On Magdala see p. 251.

3 *Joanna, the wife of Chuza, Herod's steward*  Joanna is probably Heb. Yoḥanna, the fem. form of Yoḥanan, John, mentioned again only in Luke 24.10 with Mary Magdalene, Mary the mother of James, and the other woman at the empty tomb. The term "steward" probably means manager of an estate.[1]

*Susanna*  As a proper name in the NT only here.

### NOTES

1. See Josephus, *Ant.* XVIII.6.6.

# 85. *Accusations Against Jesus*

## MATT. 12.22–24

22 Then a blind and dumb demoniac was brought to him, and he healed him, so that the dumb man spoke and saw. 23 And all the people were amazed, and said, "Can this be the Son of David?" 24 But when the Pharisees heard it they said, "It is only by Beelzebul, the prince of demons, that this man casts out demons."

## MARK 3.19b–22

19b Then he went home; 20 and the crowd came together again, so that they could not even eat. 21 And when his friends heard it, they went out to seize him, for they said, "He is beside himself." 22 And the scribes who came down from Jerusalem said,

"He is possessed by Beelzebub, and by the prince of demons he casts out the demons."

## LUKE 11.14–16

14 Now he was casting out a demon that was dumb; when the demon had gone out, the dumb man spoke, and the people marveled. 15 But some of them said, "He casts out demons by Beelzebub the prince of demons"; 16 while others, to try him, sought from him a sign from heaven.

## COMMENTARY

24 *It is only by Beelzebul*, etc.  This is the earliest evidence that Jesus was accused of being a magician, which is the most frequent accusation bruited about him in rabbinic literature. For example, a baraita states: "Yeshu [of Nazareth] practiced sorcery and led Israel astray."[1] See above the story of Ben Stada.[2]

*Beelzebul*  "In the MSS there are three forms of this name: Beelzebub; Beelzebul and Beezebul."[3] The meaning of the name is not at all clear. Some suggestions as to its meaning are: (a) *zbl* in Ugaritic means "prince," and *zbl baal* is used for the god Baal and perhaps used for the antagonist of God;[4] (b) *zbl* in rabbinic Heb. means "dung," hence an opprobrious designation of the Evil One; (c) *zbl* in rabbinic sources and in the Dead Sea Scrolls is the name of one of the heavens, Beelzebul may mean the lord of that region;[4] (d) *Baal zevul* a lord of the heavenly abode and a rival of God; (e) perhaps *baal devov*, lord of enmity. No form of the name appears in Jewish literature.

## NOTES

1.  B. Sanh. 107b; B. Sot. 47a; TJ Ḥag. 2.2, 77d. See also T. Shab. 11.15 (p. 126). Cf. in Church Fathers, Justin, *Dial.* 69; Origen, *Contra Celsum* 1.28. See Klausner, *JN*, pp. 18–54.
2.  See above p. 11.
3.  See Foerster, *TDNT*, s.v. "Beelzebul" (1:605); W. E. M. Aitken "Beelzebul," *JBL* 21 (1912): 34–53; B. S. Easton, "The Beelzebul Sections," ibid. 32 (1913): 57–73. T. H. Gaster, *IDB*, s.v. "Beelzebul" (1:374).
4.  See W. F. Albright, "Zabûl Yam and Thâpiṭ Nahar in the Combat between Baal and the Sea," *JPOS* 11 (1936): 17–20.

# 86. *House Divided*

## MATT. 12.25–37

25 Knowing their thoughts, he said to them, "Every kingdom divided against itself is laid waste, and no city or house divided against itself will stand; 26 and if Satan casts out Satan, he is divided against himself; how then will his kingdom stand? 27 And if I cast out demons by Beelzebub,ʷ by whom do your sons cast them out? Therefore they shall be your judges. 28 But if it is by the Spirit of God that I cast out demons,

then the kingdom of God has come upon you. 29 Or how can one enter a strong man's house and plunder his goods unless he first binds the strong man? Then indeed he may plunder his house. 30 He who is not with me is against me, and he who does not gather with me scatters. 31 Therefore I tell you, every sin and blasphemy will be forgiven men, but the blasphemy against the Spirit will not be forgiven. 32 And whoever says a word against the Son of man will be forgiven; but whoever speaks against the Holy Spirit will not be forgiven, either in this age or in the age to come. 33 Either make the tree good, and its fruit good; or make the tree bad and its fruit bad; for the tree is known by its fruit. 34 You brood of vipers! How can you speak good, when you are evil? For out of the abundance of the heart the mouth speaks. 35 The good man out of his good treasure brings forth good, and the evil man out of his evil treasure brings forth the evil. 36 I tell you, on the day of judgment men will render account for every careless word they utter. 37 For by your words you will be justified, and by your words you will be condemned."

## Mark 3.23–30

23 And he called them to him, and said to them in parables, "How can Satan cast out Satan? 24 If a kingdom is divided against itself, that kingdom cannot stand, 25 And if a house is divided against itself, that house will not be able to stand. 26 And if Satan has risen up against himself and is divided, he cannot stand, but is coming to an end. 27 But no one can enter a strong man's house and plunder his goods, unless he first binds the strong man; then indeed he may plunder his house. 28 Truly, I say to you all sins will be forgiven the sons of men, and whatever blasphemies they utter; 29 but whoever blasphemes against the Holy Spirit never[x] has forgiveness, but is guilty of an eternal sin." 30 For they had said, "He has an unclean spirit."

## Luke 11.17–23

17 But he, knowing their thoughts, said to them, "Every kingdom divided against itself is laid waste, and house falls upon house. 18 And if Satan also is divided against himself, how will his kingdom stand? For you say that I cast out demons by Beelzebub.[w] 19 And if I cast out demons by Beelzebub,[w] by whom do your sons cast them out? Therefore they shall be your judges. 20 But if it is by the finger of God that I cast out demons, then the kingdom of God has come upon you. 21 When a strong man, fully armed, guards his own palace, his goods are in peace; 22 but when one stronger than he assails him and overcomes him, he takes away his armor in which he trusted, and divides his spoil. 23 He who is not with me is against me, and he who does not gather with me scatters."

## Ibid. 12.10

"And everyone who speaks a word against the Son of man will be forgiven; but he who blasphemes against the Holy Spirit will not be forgiven."

## Ibid. 6.43–45

43 "For no good tree bears bad fruit, nor again does a bad tree bear good fruit; 44 for each tree is known by its own fruit. For figs are not gathered from thorns, nor are

grapes picked from a bramble bush. 45 The good man out of the good treasure of his heart produces good, and the evil man out of his evil treasure produces evil; for out of the abundance of the heart his mouth speaks."

---

w Greek *Beelzebul.*
x Some texts read *not.*

## COMMENTARY

25 *a house divided* "A house in which there is division [controversy] in the end will be laid waste."[1]

27 *by whom do your sons cast them out* "Exorcism was widespread in antiquity and although more references to demons and exorcism are to be found in Babylonian material, we do have early examples of Jewish exorcism in Palestinian sources. In the Apocryphal Book of Tobit the angel Raphael teaches Tobias how to ban the evil spirit."[2] R. Joḥanan b. Zakkai said: "Has an evil spirit ever entered into you? Have you never seen a person into whom an evil spirit had entered? What should be done with one so affected? Take roots of herbs, burn them under him, and surround him with water, whereupon the spirit will flee."[3]

29 *strong man* Allusion to the Messiah, who will vanquish Satan. This is similar to "And Beliar shall be bound by him and he shall give power to his children to tread upon the evil spirits,"[4] and "For no man takes spoil from a mighty man."[5]

30 *he who does not gather with me scatters* The language is reminiscent of Pss. Sol., "And he [the Messiah] shall gather together a holy people, whom he shall lead in righteousness,"[6] and "He [the wicked] never ceases to scatter."[7]

32 *he who even speaks against the Holy Spirit will not be forgiven* "Five shall have no forgiveness . . . and he who has on his hands the sin of profaning the Name."[8]

34 *for out of the abundance of the heart the mouth speaks* "If the heart has not revealed it [a secret] to the mouth, to whom can the mouth reveal it?"[9]

36 *on the day of judgment*, etc. "Even words of no importance, casual utterances spoken by man, even his idle talk with his wife are written upon his tablet and read to him on his deathbed." "Keep your tongue from idle words lest they cause your throat to thirst [in Hell?]."[10]

37 *by your words you shall be justified* A similar comment is: "his intention is recognized through his deeds."[11]

## NOTES

1. *DER* 5, Sifre Num. 42; Gen. R. 38.
2. Tob. 6.7, 16, 17; 8.2–3; Cf. also Josephus, *Ant.* VIII.2.5.
3. *PRK* 4 (40a–b).
4. Test. Levi 18.12.
5. Pss. Sol. 5.4. Cf. Isa. 49.24; Rev. 20.2–3; En. 10.4–5; 21.1–2; 62.5 f.; 69.27.
6. Pss. Sol. 12.28.

7. Ibid. 4.13.

8. *ARN* 39. Cf. M. Avot. 4.5, "R. Johanan b. Baroqah said: 'He who profanes the Name of Heaven in secret, they exact the penalty from him openly. Ignorant and willful are all one in regard to profaning the Name.' "

9. *Mid. Ps.* 9.2 (40b); Koh. R. 12.9; Gen. R. 84.8. For a better reading, see *Mid. Ps.* 28.4 (115b). The word "abundance" does not seem to fit. A possible solution is that the original was the Aram. *debaliba befuma*, lit., "what is in the heart is in the mouth." What is here could have been the result of a dittography of *deba* of *debaliba* and was read *rov*, "abundance," *debaliba*, "which is in the heart," and confusing a *resh* with a *dalet*. See Lachs, "Some Semitic Passages and their Jewish Background."

10. B. Yom. 77a. Cf. Jer. 2.25.

11. B. Ḥul. 13a.

# 87. *Warning About Seeking Signs*

## MATT. 12.38–42

38 Then some of the scribes and Pharisees said to him, "Teacher, we wish to see a sign from you." 39 But he answered them, "An evil and adulterous generation seeks for a sign; but no sign shall be given to it except the sign of the prophet Jonah. 40 For as Jonah was three days and three nights in the belly of the whale, so will the Son of man be three days and three nights in the heart of the earth. 41 The men of Nineveh will arise at the judgment with this generation and condemn it; for they repented at the preaching of Jonah, and behold, something greater than Jonah is here. 42 The queen of the South will arise at the judgment with this generation and condemn it; for she came from the ends of the earth to hear the wisdom of Solomon, and behold, something greater than Solomon is here."

## LUKE 11.29–32

29 When the crowds were increasing, he began to say, "This generation is an evil generation; it seeks a sign, but no sign shall be given to it except the sign of Jonah. 30 For as Jonah became a sign to the men of Nineveh, so will the Son of man be to this generation. 32 The men of Nineveh will arise at the judgment with this generation and condemn it; for they repented at the preaching of Jonah, and behold, something greater than Jonah is here. 31 The queen of the South will arise at the judgment with the men of this generation and condemn them; for she came from the ends of the earth to hear the wisdom of Solomon, and behold, something greater than Solomon is here."

### COMMENTARY

38 *we wish to see a sign from you* Authenticating signs were commonplace in the ancient world and among Jews from the days of Moses (see Exod. 4.1 ff). In the talmudic literature the Rabbis speculated about authenticating signs in connection with the coming of the Messiah. A typical expression is "The Son of David will not come until . . . a fish is sought for an invalid and cannot be procured . . . even the pettiest kingdom ceases to have power over

Israel . . . there are no conceited men in Israel . . . all judges and officers are gone from Israel."[1] In Luke the "sign of Jonah" is his preaching, in Matt. it is developed into a prophecy of resurrection.

39 *evil and adulterous generation*  Cf. Isa. 57.3–4.[2]

41 *the men of Nineveh . . . condemn it*  Because they repented and Israel did not.[3]

42 *queen of the South*  I.e., the Queen of Sheba. In Arabic legend she is called Bilkis. The South, i.e., Sheba, which is in Arabia.[4]

### NOTES

1. B. Sanh. 98a. Cf. B. BM 59b; B. Sanh 93b; *PR* 36 (162a); Exod. R. 9.
2. See also Pss. Sol. 89.11, M. Sot. 9.9.
3. See above p. 194, n. 2.
4. See Manson, *SJ*, p. 91. On Sheba see M. Sanh. 10.3; B. BB 15b. See Josephus, *Ant*. VIII.6.5–6.

## 88. *The Return of the Evil Spirit*

### MATT. 12.43–45

43 "When the unclean spirit has gone out of a man, he passes through waterless places, seeking rest, but finds none. 44 Then he says, 'I will return to my house from which I came. And when he comes he finds it empty, swept and put in order. 45 Then he goes and brings with him other spirits more evil than himself and they enter and dwell there, and the last state of that man becomes worse than the first. So shall it be also with this evil generation."

### LUKE 11.24–26

24 "When the unclean spirit has gone out of a man, he passes through waterless places seeking rest; and finding none he says, 'I will return to my house from which I came.' 25 And when he comes he finds it swept and put in order. 26 Then he goes and brings seven other spirits more evil than himself, and they enter and dwell there; and the last state of that man becomes worse than the first."

### COMMENTARY

43 *waterless places*  Demons are said to inhabit the wilderness, especially dry places, and ruins.[1]

44 *I will return to my house*  This language is typical of demonic speech. E.g., ". . . he heard Satan say, 'Alas for this man [i.e., himself] whom R. Meir has driven from his house. "[2] And "the angel [demon] of poverty was following a certain man but could not prevail over him. . . . He then heard the angel [demon] exclaiming, 'Alas he has driven this person [me] out of his house.' "[3]

## NOTES

1. See Lev. 16.10; Isa. 13.21, 34.14; Bar. 4.35; B. Ber. 3b; Rev. 18.2. See above p. 50.
2. B. Git. 52a.
3. B. Ḥul. 105b. See also the Josephus passage above p. 163f.

# 89. *Jesus' True Relatives*

## MATT. 12.46–50

46 While he was still speaking to the people, behold, his mother and his brothers stood outside, asking to speak to him.ʸ 48 But he replied to the man who told him, "Who is my mother, and who are my brothers?" 49 And stretching out his hand toward his disciples, he said, "Here are my mother and my brothers! 50 For whoever does the will of my Father in heaven is my brother, and sister, and mother."

## MARK 3.31–35

31 And his mother and his brothers came; and standing outside they sent to him and called him. 32 And a crowd was sitting about him; and they said to him, "Your mother and your brothersᶻ are outside, asking for you." 33 And he replied, "Who are my mother and my brothers?" 34 And looking around on those who sat about him, he said, "Here are my mother and my brothers! 35 Whoever does the will of God is my brother, and sister, and mother."

## LUKE 8.19–21

19 Then his mother and his brothers came to him, but they could not reach him for the crowd. 20 And he was told, "Your mother and your brothers are standing outside, desiring to see you." 21 But he said to them, "My mother and my brothers are those who hear the word of God and do it."

---

y Some texts add v. 47, *Someone told him, "Your mother and your brothers are standing outside, asking to speak to you."*
z Some add *and your sisters.*

## COMMENTARY

50 *does the will*   Gr. *poiēsē to thelēma*, which translates the Heb. *oseh raẓon.*[1]

## NOTES

1. E.g., Sifre Deut. 40; Exod. R. 21.

# 90. The Parable of the Sower

## MATT. 13.1–9

1 That same day Jesus went out of the house and sat beside the sea. 2 And great crowds gathered about him, so that he got into a boat and sat there; and the whole crowd stood on the beach. 3 And he told them many things in parables, saying, "A sower went out to sow. 4 And as he sowed, some seeds fell along the path, and the birds came and devoured them. 5 Other seeds fell on rocky ground, where they had not much soil, and immediately they sprang up, since they had no depth of soil, 6 but when the sun rose they were scorched; and since they had no root they withered away. 7 Other seeds fell upon thorns, and the thorns grew up and choked them. 8 Other seeds fell on good soil and brought forth grain, some a hundredfold, some sixty, some thirty. 9 He who has ears[a] let him hear."

## MARK 4.1–9

1 Again he began to teach beside the sea. And a very large crowd gathered about him, so that he got into a boat and sat in it on the sea; and the whole crowd was beside the sea on the land. 2 And he taught them many things in parables, and in his teaching he said to them: 3 "Listen! A sower went out to sow. 4 And as he sowed, some seed fell along the path, and the birds came and devoured it. 5 Other seed fell on rocky ground, where it had not much soil, and immediately it sprang up, since it had no depth of soil; 6 and when the sun rose it was scorched, and since it had no root it withered away 7 Other seed fell among thorns and the thorns grew up and choked it, and it yielded no grain. 8 And other seeds fell into good soil and brought forth grain, growing up and increasing and yielding thirtyfold and sixtyfold and a hundredfold." 9 And he said, "He who has ears to hear, let him hear."

## LUKE 8.4–8

4 And when a great crowd came together and people from the town after town came to him, he said in a parable: 5 "A sower went out to sow his seed; and as he sowed, some fell along the path, and was trodden under foot, and the birds of the air devoured it. 6 And some fell on the rock; and as it grew up, it withered away, because it had no moisture. 7 And some fell among thorns; and the thorns grew with it and choked it. 8 And some fell into good soil and grew and yielded a hundredfold." As he said this, he called out, "He who has ears to hear, let him hear."

---

a Some add *to hear*.

## COMMENTARY

2 *and sat there.* See above to Matt. 5.1 (p 67f).[1]
*the whole crowd.* Jews and/or Gentiles.[2]
3 *And he told them many things in parables.* The Heb. *mashal* was the most

common literary vehicle employed to convey moral instruction. (see Prov. 1.6) Although "parable" is the correct translation of *mashal* it included other literary and rhetorical figures, viz., metaphor, simile, and allegory.[3]

*A sower went out to sow* While there are no rabbinic parallels to this parable, note the following: "As the farmer sows over the ground many seeds, and plants a multitude of plants, but in the season not all that have been planted take root, so also those who have sowed in the world, not all shall be saved."[4]

4 *some seed fell along the path*, etc. Some have suggested that this implies that sowing in Palestine preceded plowing.[5]

## NOTES

1. J. D. Kingsburg, *The Parables of Jesus in Matthew 13* (Richmond, Va., 1969), p. 23, explains the Matthean emphasis on Jesus sitting as referring to one worthy of special honor by extension to the teacher and cites Rev. 7.9–12, where God is pictured sitting on his throne (*kathēmai*) with a great crowd (*ochlos*) of worshipers standing (*histemi*) before him.

2. Kingsburg, op. cit., p. 25, following Trilling, *Das wahre Israel*, pp. 130–138, argues for Jews. Others claim that *ochlos* means a number of Jews and Gentiles or even Gentiles exclusively: McNeile, *Matt.*, pp. 47 ff., 232 ff.; Jeremias, *Jesus: Promise to the Nations* (London 1958), pp. 34 ff.; Lohmeyer, *Matt.*, pp. 257 ff.; Davies, *SSM*, pp. 327 ff.

3. On the *mashal*, the parable, see Bacher, *Terminologie*, p. 121. Cf. B. Er. 21b; Lam. R. 1.1; Koh. R. 2.12; B. Sanh. 38b; M. Sot. 9.15. Also cf. R. E. Brown, "Parables and Allegory Reconsidered," *NT* 5 (1962): 36–45.

4. 2 Esd. 8.41. Cf. B. Gerhardsson, "The Parable of the Sower and Its Interpretation," *NTS* 14 (1967–68): 165–193.

5. Cf. M. Shab. 7.2; B. ibid. 73b; M. Ber. 7.2. See also Jub. 11.11. For an explanation of this parable assuming "sowing before plowing," see Jeremias, *PJ*, pp. 9 ff. Contra: K. D. White, "The Parable of the Sower," *JTS* 45 (1965): 300–307; J. Drury, "The Sower, the Vineyard and the Place of Allegory in the Interpretation of Mark's Parables," *JTS* 24 (1973): 367–379.

# 91. *The Reason for Speaking in Parables*

## MATT. 13.10–15

10 Then the disciples came and said to him, "Why do you speak to them in parables?" 11 And he answered them, "To you it has been given to know the secrets of the kingdom of heaven, but to them it has not been given. 12 For to him who has will more be given and he will have abundance; but from him who has not, even what he has will be taken away. 13 This is why I speak to them in parables, because seeing they do not see, and hearing they do not hear, nor do they understand. 14 With them indeed is fulfilled the prophecy of Isaiah which says:

'You shall indeed hear but never understand
and you shall indeed see but never perceive.

15 For this people's heart has grown dull,
and their ears are heavy of hearing,
and their eyes they have closed,
lest they should perceive with their eyes,
and hear with their ears,
and understand with their heart,
and turn for me to heal them.' "

## MARK 4.10–12

10 And when he was alone, those who were about him with the twelve asked him concerning the parables. 11 And he said to them, "To you has been given the secret of the kingdom of God, but for those outside everything is in parables; 12 so that they may indeed see but not perceive, and may indeed hear but not understand; lest they should turn again, and be forgiven."

## LUKE 8.9–10

9 And when his disciples asked him what this parable meant, 10 he said, "To you it has been given to know the secrets of the kingdom of God; but for others they are in parables, so that seeing they may not see, and hearing they may not understand."

## COMMENTARY

12 *For to him who has*, etc.    Note the following passages in the same vein:

R. Zera, or as some say R. Ḥinnana b. Papa, further said: 'Observe how the character of the Holy One, blessed be He, differs from that of flesh and blood. A mortal can put something into an empty vessel but not into a full one, but the Holy One, blessed be He, is not so, He puts more into a full vessel but not into an empty one.'[1]

A matron asked R. Jose b. Ḥalafta: "What is the meaning of the verse *He giveth wisdom to the wise* [Dan. 11.21]? The text should have stated He giveth wisdom to them that are not wise and knowledge to them that know not understanding." He answered her: "I will explain it with a parable. If two persons came to borrow money from you, one rich and the other poor, to whom would you lend, the richer or the poor?" She replied: "To the rich man!" "Why?" he asked; to which she answered: "Because he has the wherewithal to repay me; but if the poor man loses my money from where can he repay me?" He said to her: "Do your ears hear what you have uttered with your mouth? If the Holy One, blessed be He, gave wisdom to fools, they would sit and meditate upon it [Torah] in privies, theaters, and bathhouses; but the Holy One, blessed be He, gave wisdom to the wise, who sit and meditate upon it in Synagogues and Houses of Study, hence He giveth wisdom to the wise and knowledge to them that know understanding."[2]

*him who has not*, etc. In rabbinic sources the following is of note:

R. Issi and R. Hoshaya in the name of R. Ḥiyya the Elder said four things: "The Holy One, blessed be He, said to him [the serpent]: 'I made you that you should be king over all cattle and beasts, but you would not have it, therefore more cursed are you, etc.; I made you that you should be upright like man but you would not, hence, upon your belly shall you go; I made you that you should eat of the food of man but you would not, hence, the earth shall you eat; you wanted to kill Adam and take his wife, therefore I will put enmity between you and the woman.' Thus what he desired was not given to him, and what he possessed was taken from him. And we find the same in the case of Cain, Korah, Gehazi, Absalom, Adonijah, Uzziah, and Haman: what they desired was not given to them, and what they possessed was taken from them."[3]

13 *because seeing they do not see*, etc.   "It is taught: R. Jose says: 'Alas that they see but do not know what they see, they stand but they do not know on what they stand."[4] Also, "*Now Jacob saw that there was corn in Egypt.* Was Jacob in Egypt that the text says *Now Jacob saw that there was corn in Egypt*? Did he not say to his sons, *Behold, I heard that there is corn in Egypt* [Gen. 42.2]? Since the day that Joseph was stolen, however, the Holy Spirit departed from him [Jacob], so that he saw yet did not see, heard yet did not hear."[5]

14 *You shall indeed hear*, etc.   Isa. (LXX) 6.9 ff.[6]

### NOTES

1. B. Ber. 40a; B. Suk. 46a.
2. Koh. R. 1.7.
3. Gen. R. 20.5. See also T. Sot. 4.17–19 (p. 301); B.ibid. 9b.
4. B. Ḥag. 12b.
5. Gen. R. 91.6.
6. See Stendahl, *SSMUOT*, pp. 129 ff.; C. C. Torrey, *Documents of the Primitive Church* (New York 1941), pp. 60–68.

## 92. *The Blessedness of the Disciples*

### MATT. 13.16–17

16 "Blessed are your eyes, for they see, and your ears for they hear. 17 Truly, I say to you, many prophets and righteous men longed to see what you see, and did not see it, and to hear what you hear, and did not hear it."

### LUKE 10.23–24

23 Then turning to the disciples he said privately, "Blessed are the eyes which see what you see! 24 For I tell you that many prophets and kings desired to see what you see, and did not see it, and to hear what you hear, and did not hear it."

## COMMENTARY

16 *Blessed are your eyes* This expression is found frequently in the Psalms of Solomon.[1]

17 *Many prophets and righteous men* There is an interesting parallel to this in the following: *"This is my God and I will glorify Him* [Exod. 15.2]. R. Eliezer says: 'Whence can you say that that which a maidservant saw at the Sea Isaiah and Ezekiel and all the prophets never saw? It says about them [the prophets], *And by the ministry of the prophets have I used similitudes* [Hos. 12.11].' "[2]

### NOTES

1. Pss. Sol. 4.23, 5.16, 6.1, 17.44, 50. In rabbinic literature, cf. B. Ḥag. 14b, "Happy are you, and happy is the one who bore you, and happy are my eyes that have seen this."
2. *Mek.* Exod. 15.2.

## 93. *The Interpretation of the Parable of theSower*

### MATT. 13.18–23

18 "Hear then the parable of the sower. 19 When anyone hears the word of the kingdom and does not understand it, the evil one comes and snatches away what is sown in his heart; this is what was sown along the path. 20 As for what was sown on rocky ground, this is he who hears the word and immediately receives it with joy; 21 yet he has no root in himself, but endures it for a while, and when tribulation or persecution arises on account of the word, immediately he falls away.[b] 22 As for what was sown among thorns, this is he who hears the word, but the cares of the world and the delight in riches choke the word and it proves unfruitful. 23 As for what was sown on good soil, this is he who hears the word and understands it, he indeed bears fruit, and yields in one case a hundredfold, in another sixty, and in another thirty."

### MARK 4.13–20

13 And he said to them, "Do you not understand this parable? How then will you understand all the parables? 14 The sower sows the word. 15 And these are the ones along the path, where the word is sown; when they hear, Satan immediately comes and takes away the word which is sown in them. 16 And these in like manner are the ones sown upon rocky ground, who, when they hear the word, immediately receive it with joy; 17 and they have no root in themselves, but endure for a while; then, when tribulation or persecution arises on account of the word, immediately they fall away.[b] 18 And others are the ones sown among thorns; they are those who hear the word, 19 but the cares of the world, and the delight in riches, and the desire for other things, enter in and choke the word, and it proves unfruitful. 20 But those that were sown upon the good soil are the ones who hear the word and accept it and bear fruit, thirtyfold, and sixtyfold and a hundredfold."

## LUKE 8.11–15

11 "Now the parable is this: The seed is the word of God. 12 The ones along the path are those who have heard; then the devil comes and takes away the word from their hearts, that they may not believe and be saved. 13 And the ones on the rock are those who, when they hear the word, receive it with joy; but these have no root, they believe for a while and in time of temptation fall away. 14 And as for what fell among the thorns, they are those who hear, but as they go on their way they are choked by the cares and riches and pleasures of life, and their fruit does not mature. 15 And as for that in the good soil, they are those who, hearing the word, hold it fast in an honest and good heart, and bring forth fruit with patience."

---

b Or *stumble(s)*.

### COMMENTARY

21 *no root in himself* Cf. "The children of the ungodly shall not bring forth many branches: but are as unclean roots upon a hard rock,"[1] and "Her children shall not take root, and her branches shall bring forth no fruit."[2] "But the multiplying brood of the ungodly shall not thrive, nor take deep rooting from bastard slips, nor lay any fast foundation. For though they flourish in branches for a time, yet standing not fast, they shall be shaken with the wind, and through the force of the winds they shall be rooted out."[3]
　　See above pp. 151.

### NOTES

1. Sira 40.15.
2. Ibid. 23–25.
3. Wisd. Sol. 4.3–5.

# 94. *The Purpose of the Parables*

## MATT. 13.12

"For to him who has will more be given, and he will have abundance; but from him who has not, even what he has will be taken away."

## MARK 4.21–25

21 And he said to them, "Is a lamp brought in to be put under a bushel, or under a bed, and not on a stand? 22 For there is nothing hid, except to be made manifest; nor is anything secret, except to come to light. 23 If any man has ears to hear, let him hear." 24 And he said to them, "Take heed what you hear; the measure you give will be the measure you get, and still more will be given you. 25 For to him who has will more be given; and from him who has not, even what he has will be taken away."

LUKE 8.16–18

16 "No one after lighting a lamp covers it with a vessel, or puts it under a bed, but puts it on a stand, that those who enter may see the light. 17 For nothing is hid that shall not be made manifest, nor anything secret that shall not be known and come to light. 18 Take heed then how you hear; for to him who has will more be given, and from him who has not, even what he thinks that he has will be taken away."
See above Sec. 91 (p. 218f).

# 95. *The Parable of the Seed Growing Secretly*

MARK 4.26–29

26 And he said, "The kingdom of God is as if a man should scatter seed upon the ground, 27 and should sleep and rise night and day, and the seed should sprout and grow, he knows not how. 28 The earth produces of itself, first the blade, then the ear, then the full grain in the ear. 29 But when the grain is ripe, at once he puts in the sickle, because the harvest has come."

## COMMENTARY

No rabbinic parallels to this section, but it has a Semitic ring since it mentions "night" before "day" in v. 27.

# 96. *The Parable of the Weeds*

MATT. 13.24–30

24 Another parable he put before them saying, "The kingdom of heaven may be compared to a man who sowed good seeds in his field; 25 but while men were sleeping, his enemy came and sowed weeds among the wheat, and went away. 26 So when the plants came up and bore grain, then the weeds appeared also. 27 And the servants[c] of the householder came and said to him, 'Sir, did you not sow good seed in your field? How then has it weeds?'28 He said to them, 'An enemy has done this.' The servants[c] said to him, 'Then do you want us to go and gather them?' 29 But he said, 'No, lest in gathering the weeds you root up both the wheat along with them. 30 Let both grow together until the harvest; and at harvest time I will tell the reapers, Gather the weeds first and bind them in bundles to be burned, but gather the wheat into my barn.' "

---

c Or *slaves*.

## COMMENTARY

There are no rabbinic parallels to this passage.

25 *weeds* Gr. *zizanion*, "darnel" *(Lolium temulentum)*. Heb. *zun*, Aram. *zuna*.[1] Darnel closely resembles wheat, and since it cannot readily be distinguished from wheat, it is left in the field until harvest time. The Rabbis looked upon darnel as a degenerative form of wheat, the product of sexual excesses that took place in the plant world before the Flood. The Rabbis fancifully derive its meaning from *z-n-h*, which means "to commit fornication."[2]

27 *householder* Gr. *oikodespotēs*, Heb. *ba'al habayit*.[3]

29 *lest in gathering the weeds*, etc. Reminiscent of the comment, "Whence can be derived the proverbial saying that together with the thorn the cabbage is smitten?"[4]

## NOTES

1. E.g., M. Kil. 1.1; M. Ter. 2.6.
2. See Gen. R. 28.8; Jeremias, *PJ*, pp. 81–85.
3. E.g., M. Pe'ah 4.1, 5.7.
4. B. BQ 92a.

# 97. *The Parable of the Mustard Seed*

## MATT. 13.31–32

31 Another parable he put to them saying, "The kingdom of heaven is like a grain of mustard seed which a man took and sowed in his field; 32 it is the smallest of all seeds, but when it has grown it is the greatest of shrubs and becomes a tree, so that the birds of the air come and make nests in its branches."

## MARK 4.30–32

30 And he said, "With what can we compare the kingdom of God, or what parable shall we use for it? 31 It is like a grain of mustard seed, which, when sown upon the ground, is the smallest of all the seeds on earth; 32 yet when it is sown it grows up and becomes the greatest of all shrubs, and puts forth large branches, so that the bird of the air can make nests in its shade.

## LUKE 13.18–19

18 He said therefore, "What is the kingdom of God like? And to what shall I compare it? 19 It is like a grain of mustard seed which a man took and sowed in his garden; and it grew and became a tree, and the birds of the air made nests in its branches."

## COMMENTARY

There is no direct parallel to this passage in rabbinic sources, but there is one which may throw some light on its meaning. On the verse *I went down into the garden of nuts* [Cant. 6.11], a rabbi commented, "Just as if you have a sack of nuts you can still put in it plenty of sesame grains and mustard seeds, so many proselytes have come and added themselves to Israel, as it is written, *Who has counted the dust of Jacob?* [Num. 23.10]."[1] The mustard tree in the NT parable attracts proselytes who come as birds who make their nest in the branches (the shadow of the Almighty?).[2] To be sure, the imagery is not precise, but the bird/tree metaphor is found frequently in the MT for a great empire, and perhaps the analogue is God's kingdom.[3]

31 *a mustard seed . . . and sowed in his field*  Mark reads *upon the ground.* Matt.'s *in his field* and Luke's *in his garden* are adaptations of the Marcan version. Matthew most likely knew of the rabbinic regulation prohibiting the planting of mustard seeds in a garden,[4] hence "in his field," but it was not known to Luke, as evidenced by his reading.

32 *the smallest of all seeds*  The mustard seed is used frequently in rabbinic sources to describe something of minute size.[5]

*but when it has grown it is the greatest of the shrubs and becomes a tree.*  "It was taught: R. Joseph [MS reads R. Jose] related: 'It once happened to a man at Shihin to whom his father had left three twigs of mustard that one of them split and was found to contain nine kab of mustard, and its timber sufficed to cover a potter's hut.' "[6]

## NOTES

1. Cant. R. 6.1.
2. Jeremias, *PJ*, p. 147; Manson, *TJ*, p. 133; Dodd, *Parables*, pp. 153 ff.; Kingsbury, *The Parables of Jesus in Matthew 13*, p. 82.
3. Note the allegory in Judg. 9.15; Isa. 51.16; Ezek. 17.23; 31.6; Dan. 4.20–21, 1.12.
4. M. Kil. 3.2.
5. E.g., TJ Ber. 5, 8d (36); Lev. R. 31; M. Nid. 5.2. On the mustard seed, see C. H. Hunzinger, *TDNT*, s.v. *sinapi* (7: 287–291).
6. B. Ket. 111b.

# 98. *The Parable of the Leaven*

## MATT. 13.33

He told them another parable. "The kingdom of heaven is like leaven which a woman took and hid in three measures of meal, till it was all leavened."

## LUKE 13.20–21

20 And again he said, "To what shall I compare the kingdom of God? 21 It is like leaven which a woman took and hid in three measures of meal, till it was all leavened."

## COMMENTARY

This parable, as with others, is enigmatic. It is similar to the preceding parable of the mustard seed where the smallest of seeds produces a tall and leafy tree. Here the small quantity of leaven causes the rising of the dough into a large loaf. Together with the small start which ends with great results is the idea that "a process has been started which *must* go on to its inevitable end."[1]

33 *measures* Gr. *saton* = Heb. *se'ah*, a dry measure as well as a liquid measure. According to Josephus, 1 *se'ah* = 1 ½ Roman *modius*, i.e., about 1 ½ pecks.[2] In rabbinic sources *se'ah* indicates a variety of measures, one example is 5 Jerusalem *se'ah* = 6 desert *se'ah*.[3]

### NOTES

1. Manson, *SJ*, p. 123.
2. *Ant.* IX.4.5; cf. Jerome to Matt. ad loc.
3. See M. Men. 7.1; cf. also B. Men. 77a; Targ. O. Exod. 16.36.

## 99. *Jesus' Use of Parables*

### MATT. 13.34–35

34 All this Jesus said to the crowds in parables; indeed he said nothing to them without a parable. 35 This was to fulfill what was spoken by the prophet;[d] "I will open my mouth in parables, I will utter what has been hidden since the foundation of the world."

### MARK 4.33–34

33 With many such parables he spoke the word to them, as they were able to hear it; 34 he did not speak to them without a parable, but privately to his own disciples he explained everything.

---

d Some texts read *the prophet Isaiah.*

## COMMENTARY

35 *I will open my mouth*, etc.   Ps. 78.2. The first half of the verse agrees with the LXX and MT; the second half differs from the LXX and the later Greek versions as well as from the MT.

*the prophet*   Psalm 78 is attributed to Asaph. Asaph was not a prophet but is called a seer in 2 Chron. 29.30. The term "prophet" is often used loosely to include anyone who is divinely inspired, e.g., Kohelet,[2] and the Sages, too, were termed prophets. "R. Abdimi of Haifa said: 'Since the day when the

Temple was destroyed, prophecy has been taken from the prophets and given to the wise.' "[3] Asaph is included in the list of ten who authored the Book of Psalms.[4]

## NOTES

1. On this verse see Stendahl, *SSMUOT*, p. 116.
2. See Koh. R. 1.1.
3. B. BB 12a.
4. B. BB 14–15 and parallels.

## 100. *The Interpretation of the Parable of the Weeds*

### M A T T .  1 3 . 3 6 – 4 3

36 Then he left the crowds and went into the house. And his disciples came to him, saying, "Explain to us the parable of the weeds of the field." 37 He answered, "He who sows the good seed is the Son of man; 38 the field is the world, and the good seed means the sons of the kingdom; the weeds are the sons of the evil one, 39 and the enemy who sowed them is the devil; the harvest is the close of the age, and the reapers are angels. 40 Just as the weeds are gathered and burned with fire, so will it be at the close of the age. 41 The Son of man will send his angels, and they will gather out of his kingdom all causes of sin and all evil doers, 42 and throw them into the furnace of fire; there men will weep and gnash their teeth. 43 Then the righteous will shine like the sun in the kingdom of their Father. He who has ears, let him hear."

## COMMENTARY

38 *the field is the world.* In rabbinic sources it is the garden, not the field, which represents the world.[1] This representation of the *cosmos* agrees more with a universal outlook, as in Matt. 28.18–20, than with the early view of the Mission (Matt. 10. 5 ff.), where the field is only Israel.[2]

*sons of the kingdom* See Matt. 8.12 (above p. 155f).

*sons of the evil one* I.e., the devil. See John 8.44, 1 John 3.10.

39 *the close of the age* The earliest reference to the end of time is Dan. 12.4, "until the end of time," Heb. *ad et qez*: ibid. 12.13, "at the end of days," Heb *qez hayamin*. The expression *aharit hayamin*, Gen. 49.1, is correctly translated "latter days," not "end of days." In the Targum, however, it is understood precisely that way, *besof yomaya*, "the end of days." The end of time comes into prominence in the intertestamental period,[3] and in rabbinic literature.[4]

40 *Just as the weeds are gathered and burned with fire*, etc. The closest parallel in rabbinic literature is that God, who is compared to the owner of a vineyard, removes the thorns from it, the thorns representing the wicked.[5]

41 *The Son of man will send his angels* See Matt. 25.31, n. 2 (below p. 393).[6]

42 *furnace of fire* In the gospels this expression occurs only here and in

Matt. 13.50; cf. Rev. 1,15; 9.2. In the intertestamental literature it also appears: "And then shall the pit of torment appear, and over against it the place of refreshment; the furnace of Gehinnom shall be made manifest, and over against it the Paradise of delight."[7] Again, "their names shall be blotted out of the book of life and out of the holy books . . . and they shall cry and make lamentations in a place that is a chaotic wilderness and in the fire shall they burn."[8]

*gnash their teeth* A favorite phrase of Matt. expressing despair. See above p. 156.[9]

43 *then the righteous will shine like the sun.* Cf. Matt. 17.2. This is a relatively common description of the righteous in the future.[10]

*He who has ears let him hear* Cf. Ezek. 3.27, *But when I speak with you, I will open your mouth, and you shall say to them, "Thus says the Lord God, he that will hear, let him hear, and he that will refuse to hear, let him refuse; for they are a rebellious house.*

## NOTES

1. E.g., Koh. R. 5.11.
2. See Manson, *SJ*, p. 194.
3. See Asmp. Mos. 12.4; 4 Ezra 7.113; Apoc. Bar. 27.15, 30.3; 29.8; 54.21.
4. E.g., B. Sanh. 99a, 97b; *DE* 10.
5. B. BM 83b.
6. For further references in the intertestamental literature, see *SB*, 1:973.
7. 4 Ezra 7.31.
8. En. 108.35.
9. In rabbinic literature see Koh. R. 1.5.
10. Dan. 12.3; En. 37.7, 104.2; Sifre Deut. 10; Gen. R. 12; Koh. R. 1.7; B. Sanh. 100a. See below p. 260.

# 101. *The Parable of the Hidden Treasure and of the Pearl*

## MATT. 13.44–45

44 "The kingdom of heaven is like treasure hidden in a field which a man found and covered up; then in his joy he goes and sells all that[e] he has and buys that field. 45 Again, the kingdon of heaven is like a merchant in search of fine pearls, 46 who, on finding one pearl of great value, went and sold all that he had and bought it."

---

e Some texts read *what*.

## COMMENTARY

There are no parallels in rabbinic literature to either of these "companion parables," so called because they are similar in style and in import. They may have originally been separately circulated. It is not reasonable to see a contrast between the rich merchant and a poor day laborer who finds the treasure in the field.[1] This is unlikely, for were he a poor day laborer he most probably would not have had the purchase price of the field.

Concerning finding a treasure in a field, there is an interesting question discussed in rabbinic sources whether the buyer of the field is entitled to any treasure found within.[2]

**44** *treasure hidden*   Gr. *thēsauros kekrummenos*, Heb. *mamonet genuzah*.[3]

**45** *Again*   Heb. *shuv;* Aram. *tu*, frequently used when citing another illustration or proof.

### NOTES

1. Jeremias, *PJ*, p. 119.
2. See TJ BM 2.5, 8c; *PRK* 9 (74b); Lev. R. 27.1; *Tan.B. Emor* 9 (45a); M. BB 4.8.
3. E.g., B. Pes. 119a.

## 102. *The Parable of the Net*

### MATT. 13.47–50

47 "Again, the kingdom of heaven is like a net which was thrown into the sea and gathered fish of every kind; 48 when it was full, men drew it ashore and sat down and sorted the good into vessels but threw away the bad. 49 So it will be at the close of the age. The angels will come out and separate the evil from the righteous, 50 and throw them into the furnace of fire, there men will weep and gnash their teeth."

### COMMENTARY

There is no rabbinic parallel to this section. The imagery of men compared with fish and the net spread to catch them is found.[1] The point of this parable, as with most, is subject to varied interpretations. E. R. Goodenough makes the interesting observation: "That the Israelites especially those faithful to the Law, are little fishes swimming in the Torah, where alone they can live, must have been a very old conception. It was proverbial in the time of Akiba early in the second century after Christ. . . . Jesus had proverbially compared the pious man to a fish who can survive only in his native element, that of Jewish legalism, and . . . this comparison had come over into Christianity with other Christian heritages from Judaism . . . with the necessity of reinterpretation."[2]

**48** *but threw away the bad*   The rotten or dead ones, or perhaps those prohibited by the dietary laws of Lev. 11.9–12.

**50** *furnace of fire*, etc.   See above p. 227.

## NOTES

1. See, e.g., B. Ḥul. 63b; B. AZ 3b, 4a. On the net see Jeremias, *PJ*, p. 85.
2. E. R. Goodenough, *Jewish Symbols in the Greco-Roman Period* (New York, 1956), 6:33.

# 103. The Parable of the Householder

## MATT. 13.51-52

51 "Have you understood all this?" They said to him, "Yes." 52 And he said to them, "Therefore every scribe who has been trained for the kingdom of heaven is like a householder who brings out of his treasure what is new and what is old."

## COMMENTARY

52 *every scribe who has been trained*, etc. Perhaps every scribe who is expert (late Heb. *baqi*) in matters of the kingdom of heaven. There are parallels—expert in the inner teachings of the Torah,[1] expert in the mysteries of Torah,[2] expert in medicine,[3] and expert in *halakhah*.[4]

*treasure* The best parallel is Akiba, who was called "a full treasure."[5]

*what is new and what is old* Vague as to what is referred to. Perhaps similar to R. Ḥisda's explanation of Cant. 7.14. "*new and old*—The old is the Written Law, the new the words of the Scribes."[6] It may be that old and new in this saying means the old is the Law of Moses; the new is the new interpretation given by Jesus.[7]

## NOTES

1. See Dalman, *Words*, pp. 105–6.
2. Cf. B. Qid. 10b; TJ Ket. 5, 29d (56).
3. B. Yom. 49a.
4. B. Git. 86b.
5. Ibid. 67a.
6. B. Er. 21b.
7. See Manson, *SJ*, p. 198.

# 104. Jesus' True Relatives

## LUKE 8.19-21

19 Then his mother and his brothers came to him, but they could not reach him for the crowd. 20 And he was told, "Your mother and your brothers are standing outside, desiring to see you." 21 But he said to them, "My mother and my brothers are those who hear the word of God and do it."

See above Sec. 89 (p. 216).

# 105. *The Stilling of the Storm*

### Matt. 8.18

Now when Jesus saw great crowds around him, he gave orders to go over to the other side.

### Ibid 8.23–27

23 And when he got into the boat, his disciples followed him. 24 And behold there arose a great storm on the sea, so that the boat was being swamped by the waves; but he was asleep. 25 And they went and woke him, saying, "Save, Lord; we are perishing." 26 And he said to them, "Why are you afraid, O men of little faith?" Then he rose and rebuked the winds and the sea; and there was a great calm. 27 And the men marveled, saying, "What sort of man is this, that even winds and sea obey him?"

### Mark 4.35–41

35 On that day, when evening had come, he said to them, "Let us go across to the other side." 36 And leaving the crowd, they took him with them, just as he was, in the boat. And the other boats were with him. 37 And a great storm of wind arose, and the waves beat into the boat, so that the boat was already filling. 38 But he was in the stern, asleep on the cushion; and they woke him and said to him, "Teacher, do you not care if we perish?" 39 And he awoke and rebuked the wind, and said to the sea, "Peace! Be still!" And the wind ceased, and there was a great calm. 40 He said to them, "Why are you afraid? Have you no faith?"f 41 And they were filled with awe, and said to one another, "Who is this, that even wind and sea obey him?"

### Luke 8.22–25

22 One day he got into a boat with his disciples, and he said to them, "Let us go across to the other side of the lake." So they set out, 23 and as they sailed he fell asleep. And a storm of wind came down on the lake, and they were filling with water, and were in danger. 24 And they went and woke him, saying, "Master, Master, we are perishing!" And he awoke and rebuked the wind and the raging waves; and they ceased, and there was a calm. 25 He said to them, "Where is your faith?" And they were afraid, and they marveled, saying to one another, "Who then is this, that he commands even wind and water, and they obey him?"

---

f  Some texts read *Why are you so very afraid? Why have you no faith?* Others *Why are you so very afraid? Have you no faith?*
See above Sec. 50 (p. 160).

# 106. *The Gerasene Demoniac*

## MATT. 8.28–34

28 And when he came to the other side, to the country of the Gadarenes, two demoniacs met him, coming out of the tombs, so fierce that no one could pass that way. 29 And behold, they cried out, "What have you to do with us, O Son of God? Have you come here to torment us before the time?" 30 Now a herd of many swine was feeding at some distance from them. 31 And the demons begged him, "If you cast us out, send us away into the herd of swine." 32 And he said to them, "Go." So they came out and went into the swine; and behold, the whole herd rushed down the steep bank into the sea, and perished in the waters. 33 The herdsmen fled, and going into the city they told everything, and what had happened to the demoniacs. 34 And behold, all the city came out to meet Jesus; and when they saw him, they begged him to leave their neighborhood.

## MARK 5.1–20

1 They came to the other side of the sea, to the country of the Gerasenes.ʰ 2 And when he had come out of the boat, there met him out of the tombs a man with an unclean spirit, 3 who lived among the tombs; and no one could bind him any more, even with a chain; 4 for he had often been bound with fetters and chains, but the chains he wrenched apart, and the fetters he broke in pieces; and no one had the strength to subdue him. 5 Night and day among the tombs and on the mountains he was always crying out, and bruising himself with stones. 6 And when he saw Jesus from afar, he ran and worshiped him; 7 and crying out with a loud voice, he said, "What have you to do with me, Jesus, Son of the Most High God? I adjure you by God, do not torment me." 8 For he had said to him, "Come out of the man, you unclean spirit!" 9 And Jesusⁱ asked him, "What is your name?" He replied, "My name is Legion; for we are many." 10 And he begged him eagerly not to send them out of the country. 11 Now a great herd of swine was feeding there on the hillside; 12 and they begged him, "Send us to the swine, let us enter them." 13 So he gave them leave. And the unclean spirits came out, and entered the swine; and the herd, numbering about two thousand, rushed down the steep bank into the sea, and were drowned in the sea. 14 The herdsmen fled and told it in the city and in the country. And people came to see what it was that had happened. 15 And they came to Jesus, and saw the demoniac sitting there, clothed and in his right mind, the man who had the legion; and they were afraid. 16 And those who had seen it told what had happened to the demoniac and to the swine. 17 And they began to beg Jesusⁱ to depart from their neighborhood. 18 And as he was getting into the boat, the man who had been possessed with demons begged him that he might be with him. 19 But he refused, and said to him, "Go home to your friends, and tell them how much the Lord has done for you, and how he has had mercy on you." 20 And he went away and began to proclaim in the Decapolis how much Jesus had done for him; and all men marveled.

## LUKE 8.26–39

26 Then they arrived at the country of the Gerasenes,ᵏ which is opposite Galilee. 27 And as he stepped out on land, there met him a man from the city who had demons;

for a long time he had worn no clothes, and he lived not in a house but among the tombs. 28 When he saw Jesus, he cried out and fell down before him, and said with a loud voice, "What have you to do with me, Jesus, Son of the Most High God? I beseech you, do not torment me." 29 For he had commanded the unclean spirit to come out of the man. (For many a time it had seized him; he was kept under guard, and bound with chains and fetters, but he broke the bonds and was driven by the demon into the desert.) 30 Jesus then asked him, "What is your name?" And he said, "Legion," for many demons had entered him. 31 And they begged him not to command them to depart into the abyss. 32 Now a large herd of swine was feeding on the hillside; and they begged him to let them enter these. So he gave them leave. 33 Then the demons came out of the man and entered the swine, and the herd rushed down the steep bank into the lake and were drowned. 34 When the herdsmen saw what had happened, they fled, and told it in the city and in the country. 35 Then people went out to see what had happened, and they came to Jesus, and found the man from whom the demons had gone, sitting at the feet of Jesus, clothed and in his right mind; and they were afraid. 36 And those who had seen it told them how he who had been possessed with demons was healed. 37 Then all the people of the surrounding country of the Gerasenes[l] asked him to depart from them; for they were seized with great fear; so he got into the boat and returned. 38 The man from whom the demons had gone begged that he might be with him; but he sent him away, saying, 39 "Return to your home, and declare how much God has done for you." And he went away, proclaiming throughout the whole city how much Jesus had done for him.

---

g  Some read *Geresenes*, others *Gergesenes*.
h  Some read *Gadarenes*, others *Gergesenes*, others *Gergustenes*.
i  Greek *he*.
j  Greek *him*.
k  Others *Gaderenes*, others *Gergesenes*.
l  Some read *Gergesenes*, others *Gadarenes*.
See above Sec. 51 (p. 161).

## 107. *Jairus' Daughter and the Woman with the Hemorrhage*

### MATT. 9.18–26

18 While he was thus speaking to them, behold, a ruler came in and knelt before him, saying, "My daughter has just died; but come and lay your hand on her, and she will live." 19 And Jesus rose and followed him, with his disciples. 20 And behold, a woman who had suffered from a hemorrhage for twelve years came up behind him and touched the fringe of his garment. 21 For she said to herself, "If I only touch his garment I shall be made well." 22 Jesus turned, and seeing her he said, "Take heart, daughter; your faith has made you well." And instantly the woman was made well. 23 And when Jesus came to the ruler's house, and saw the flute players, and the crowd making a tumult, 24 he said, "Depart; for the girl is not dead but sleeping." And they laughed at him. 25 But when the crowd had been put outside, he went in and took her

by the hand, and the girl arose. 26 And the report of this went through all that district.

## MARK 5.21–43

21 And when Jesus had crossed again in the boat to the other side, a great crowd gathered about him; and he was beside the sea. 22 Then came one of the rulers of the synagogue, Jairus by name; and seeing him, he fell at his feet, 23 and besought him, saying, "My little daughter is at the point of death. Come and lay your hands on her, so that she may be made well, and live." 24 And he went with him, And a great crowd followed him and pressed round him. 25 And there was a woman who had a flow of blood for twelve years, 26 and who had suffered much under many physicians, and had spent all that she had, and was no better but rather grew worse. 27 She had heard the reports about Jesus, and came up behind him in the crowd and touched his garment. 28 For she said, "If I touch even his garments, I shall be made well." 29 And immediately the hemorrhage ceased; and she felt in her body that she was healed of her disease. 30 And Jesus, perceiving in himself that power had gone forth from him, immediately turned about in the crowd, and said, "Who touched my garments?" 31 And his disciples said to him, "You see the crowd pressing around you, and yet you say, 'Who touched me?' " 32 And he looked around to see who had done it. 33 But the woman, knowing what had been done to her, came in fear and trembling and fell down before him, and told him the whole truth. 34 And he said to her, "Daughter, your faith has made you well; go in peace, and be healed of your disease." 35 While he was still speaking, there came from the ruler's house some who said, "Your daughter is dead. Why trouble the Teacher any further? 36 But ignoring[m] what they said, Jesus said to the ruler of the synagogue, "Do not fear, only believe." 37 And he allowed no one to follow him except Peter and James and John the brother of James. 38 When they came to the house of the ruler of the synagogue, he saw a tumult, and people weeping and wailing loudly. 39 And when he had entered, he said to them, "Why do you make a tumult and weep? The child is not dead but sleeping." 40 And they laughed at him. But he put them all outside, and took the child's father and mother and those who were with him, and went in where the child was. 41 Taking her by the hand he said to her, "Talitha cumi"; which means "Little girl, I say to you, arise." 42 And immediately the girl got up and walked; for she was twelve years old. And immediately they were overcome with amazement. 43 And he strictly charged them that no one should know this, and told them to give her something to eat.

## LUKE 8.40–56

40 Now when Jesus returned, the crowd welcomed him, for they were all waiting for him. 41 And there came a man named Jairus, who was a ruler of the synagogue; and falling at Jesus' feet he besought him to come to his house, 42 for he had an only daughter, about twelve years of age, and she was dying. As he went, the people pressed round him. 43 And a woman who had had a flow of blood for twelve years[n] and could not be healed by anyone, 44 came up behind him, and touched the fringe of his garment; and immediately her flow of blood ceased. 45 And Jesus said, "Who was it that touched me? When all denied it, Peter and those who were with him[o] said, "Master, the multitudes surround you and press upon you!" 46 But Jesus said,

"Someone touched me; for I perceive that power has gone forth from me." 47 And when the woman saw that she was not hidden, she came trembling, and falling down before him declared in the presence of all the people why she had touched him, and how she had been immediately healed. 48 And he said to her, "Daughter, your faith has made you well; go in peace." 49 While he was still speaking, a man from the ruler's house came and said, "Your daughter is dead; do not trouble the Teacher anymore." 50 But Jesus on hearing this answered him. "Do not fear; only believe, and she shall be well." 51 And when he came to the house, he permitted no one to enter with him, except Peter and John and James, and the father and mother of the maiden. 52 And all were weeping and bewailing her; but he said, "Do not weep; for she is not dead but sleeping." 53 And they laughed at him, knowing that she was dead. 54 But taking her by the hand he called, saying, "Child, arise." 55 And her spirit returned, and she got up at once; and he directed that something should be given her to eat. 56 And her parents were amazed; but he charged them to tell no one what had happened.

---

m Or *overhearing*, others *hearing*.
n Some texts add *and had spent all her living upon physicians*.
o Some omit *and those who were with him*.
See above Sec. 55 (p. 170).

# 108. *Jesus Rejected in Nazareth*

## MATT. 13.53–58

53 And when Jesus had finished these parables, he went away from there, 54 and coming to his own country he taught them in their synagogue, so that they were astonished, and said, "Where did this man get this wisdom and these mighty works? 55 Is not this the carpenter's son? Is not his mother called Mary? And are not his brothers James and Joseph and Simon and Judas? 56 And are not all his sisters with us? Where then did this man get all this? 57 And they took offenseᴾ at him. But Jesus said to them, "A prophet is not without honor except in his own country and in his own house." 58 And he did not do many mighty works there, because of their unbelief.

## MARK 6.1–6

1 He went away from there and came to his own country; and his disciples followed him. 2 And on the sabbath he began to teach in the synagogue; and many who heard him were astonished, saying, "Where did this man get all this? What is the wisdom given to him? What mighty works are wrought by his hands! 3 Is not this the carpenter, the son of Mary and brother of James and Joses and Judas and Simon, and are not his sisters here with us?" And they took offenseᴾ at him. 4 And Jesus said to them, "A prophet is not without honor, except in his own country, and among his own kin, and in his own house." 5 And he could do no mighty work there, except that

he laid his hands upon a few sick people and healed them. 6 And he marveled because of their unbelief.

_____

p Or *stumbled.*
See above Sec. 10 (p. 54).

## 109. *The Sending Out of the Twelve*

### MATT. 9.35; 10.1, 9–11, 14

9.35 And Jesus went about all the cities and villages, teaching in their synagogues and preaching the gospel of the kingdom, and healing every disease and infirmity. 10.1 And he called to him his twelve disciples and gave them authority over unclean spirits, to cast them out, and to heal every disease and every infirmity. 9 "Take no gold, nor silver, nor copper in your belts, 10 no bag for your journey, nor two tunics, nor sandals, nor a staff; for the laborer deserves his food. 11 And whatever town or village you enter, find out who is worthy in it, and stay with him until you depart. 14 And if anyone will not receive you or listen to your words, shake off the dust from your feet as you leave that house or town."

### MARK 6.6–13

6 And he went about among the villages teaching. 7 And he called to him the twelve, and began to send them out two by two, and gave them authority over the unclean spirits. 8 He charged them to take nothing for their journey except a staff; no bread, no bag, no money in their belts; 9 but to wear sandals and not put on two tunics. 10 And he said to them, "Where you enter a house, stay there until you leave the place. 11 And if any place will not receive you and they refuse to hear you, when you leave, shake off the dust that is on your feet for a testimony against them." 12 So they went out and preached that men should repent. 13 And they cast out many demons, and anointed with oil many that were sick and healed them.

### LUKE 9.1–6

1 And he called the twelve together and gave them power and authority over all demons and to cure diseases, 2 and he sent them out to preach the kingdom of God and to heal. 3 And he said to them, "Take nothing for your journey, no staff, nor bag, nor bread, nor money; and do not have two tunics. 4 And whatever house you enter, stay there, and from there depart. 5 And wherever they do not receive you, when you leave that town shake off the dust from your feet as a testimony against them." 6 And they departed and went through the villages, preaching the gospel and healing everywhere.
See above Sec. 58 (p. 175).

# 110. Herod Thinks Jesus Is John

## MATT. 14.1–2

1 At that time Herod the tetrarch heard about the fame of Jesus; 2 and he said to his servants, "This is John the Baptist, he has been raised from the dead; that is why these powers are at work in him."

## MARK 6.14–16

14 King Herod heard of it; for Jesus'q name had become known. Somer said, "John the baptizer has been raised from the dead; that is why these powers are at work in him." 15 But others said, "It is Elijah." And others said, "It is one of the prophets of old." 16 But when Herod heard of it he said, "John, whom I beheaded, has been raised."

## LUKE 9.7–9

7 Now Herod the tetrarch heard of all that was done, and he was perplexed, because it was said by some that John had been raised from the dead, 8 by some that Elijah had appeared and by others that one of the old prophets had risen. 9 Herod said, "John I beheaded; but who is this about whom I hear such things?" And he sought to see him.

---

q Greek *his*.
r Other ancient authorities read *he*.

### COMMENTARY

1 *Herod the tetrarch*  This is Herod Antipas, younger brother of Archelaus, son of Herod and his Samaritan wife Malthace, who was tetrarch of Galilee and Perea, 4 B.C.E.–39 C.E.[1] In Mark 6.14, "King Herod."

2 *raised from the dead*  The idea that the dead will live again is generally assigned to messianic or some future time but there are exceptions to this general rule; and biblically the Elijah and Elisha stories stand as examples of the dead rising.[2]

*that is why these powers are at work in him*  "John did no miracles (Jo. x.41), but he had risen, and was *therefore* invested with the powers. . . . These powers operate . . . so as to produce miracles."[3] It appears not that Herod thought Jesus to be John but that John was working through Jesus. Dalman suggests that the Aramaic was misunderstood, *gevurata mitabden bē*, "mighty deeds are *done by* him."[4]

### NOTES

1. Cf. Josephus, *Ant.* XVIII.7; *BJ* II.ff.
2. Cf. also Lev. R. 10.4; B. AZ 10b; B. Meg. 7b.

3. McNeile, *Matt.*, p. 208.
4. *Words*, p. 201.

# *111. The Death of John the Baptist*

## MATT 14.3–12

3 For Herod had seized John and bound him and put him in prison, for the sake of Herodias, his brother Philip's wife,ˢ 4 because John said to him, "It is not lawful for you to have her." 5 And though he wanted to put him to death, he feared the people, because they held him to be a prophet. 6 But when Herod's birthday came, the daughter of Herodias danced before the company, and pleased Herod, 7 so that he promised with an oath to give her whatever she might ask. 8 Prompted by her mother, she said, "Give me the head of John the Baptist here on a platter." 9 And the king was sorry; but because of his oaths and his guests he commanded it to be given; 10 he sent and had John beheaded in the prison, 11 and his head was brought on a platter and given to the girl, and she brought it to her mother. 12 And his disciples came and took the body and buried it; and they went and told Jesus.

## MARK 6.17–29

17 For Herod had sent and seized John, and bound him in prison for the sake of Herodias, his brother Philip's wife; because he had married her. 18 For John had said to Herod, "It is not lawful for you to have your brother's wife." 19 And Herodias had a grudge against him, and wanted to kill him. But she could not, 20 for Herod feared John, knowing that he was a righteous and holy man, and kept him safe. When he heard him, he was much perplexed; and yet he heard him gladly. 21 But an opportunity came when Herod on his birthday gave a banquet for his courtiers and officers and the leading men of Galilee. 22 For when Herodias' daughter came in and danced, she pleased Herod and his guests; and the king said to the girl, "Ask me for whatever you wish, and I will grant it." 23 And he vowed to her, "Whatever you ask me, I will give you, even half of my kingdom." 24 And she went out, and said to her mother, "What shall I ask?" And she said, "The head of John the baptizer." 25 And she came in immediately with haste to the king, and asked, saying, "I want you to give me at once the head of John the Baptist on a platter." 26 And the king was exceedingly sorry; because of his oaths and his guests he did not want to break his word to her. 27 And immediately the king sent a soldier of the guard and gave orders to bring his head. He went and beheaded him in the prison, 28 and brought his head on a platter and gave it to the girl; and the girl gave it to her mother. 29 When the disciples heard of it, they came and took his body, and laid it in a tomb.

---

s Some read *his brother's wife*.

## COMMENTARY

3 *and put him in prison* In the fortress of Machaerus on the E of the Dead Sea (see above p. 189). One wonders just where Herod celebrated his birthday. Was it in or near the fortress?

*for the sake of Herodias*, etc.   There is a conflict between the NT account of the *dramatis personae* of this narrative and the account in Josephus who relates that Philip was married to Salome, the daughter of Herod son of Mariamne and her mother was Herodias, the daughter of Aristobulus son of Herod, and they had no children.[1] The question is, was Herodias's first husband Herod II or Philip? Josephus records only one marriage of Philip, and that was to Salome the daughter of Herodias. Philip died in 34. "Josephus condemns Herodias for having transgressed the laws of the Judaeans in divorcing her husband and marrying his brother while her husband was still alive. It is strange that Josephus could condemn Herodias but not Antipas since penta-teuchal law is directed to the man. Josephus also states that some Judaeans thought that the destruction of Antipas' army was a punishment by God for having slain John called the Baptist."[2]

4 *It is not lawful*   A violation of Lev. 18.16.[3] Actually Antipas was married to a Nabatean princess and divorced her to marry Herodias.[4] "Like her brother Agrippa she [Herodias] was ambitious. She left her husband Herod, a commoner, and married Herod Antipas because he was a tetrarch. She probably thought that should there be children through her marriage they would be descendents of the Hasmonean family. . . . John's taunting her as an adulteress, as not being the legal wife of the tetrarch, would make the children no descendents of the Hasmoneans but would brand them as illegitimate children in the eyes of the Judaeans, and that this enraged her."[5]

10 *he sent and had John beheaded in the prison* This, as his marriage to Herodias, is done illegally without a trial. Beheading was one of the captial punishments used by the Jews but only after a trial and conviction.[6]

11 *and his head was brought on a platter*   This is unknown in Jewish literature outside of one example. According to the Midrash, Memukhan told the king that he should have the head of the disobedient Vashti brought in on a platter.[7] This is particularly interesting since the Marcan parallel to this passage, 6.23, has Herod swearing, *Whatever you ask me I will give you even half my kingdom*, and this is right out of Esther (5.4, 7.2).[8]

## NOTES

1. Josephus, *Ant.* XVIII.5.4.
2. Zeitlin, *RFJS*, 2:147.
3. Cf. Sifra Lev. 20.21; M. Ker. 1.1; *Leqah Tov*, Lev. 20.21 II p. 17a.
4. *Ant.* loc. cit.
5. Zeitlin, "The Duration of Jesus' Ministry," *JQR* 55 (1965): 187.
6. See M. Sanh. 7.1, 3. McNeile, *Matt.*, p. 211, is in error in stating that Jewish law did not sanction beheading. Cf. Josephus, *Ant.* XVII.10.6.
7. See Esther R. to 1.19, also ibid. to 1.21.
8. Cf. McNeile, loc. cit.

# 112. The Return of the Twelve and the Feeding of the Five Thousand

## MATT. 14.13–21

13 Now when Jesus heard this, he withdrew from there in a boat to a lonely place apart. But when the crowds heard it, they followed them on foot from the towns. 14 As he went ashore he saw a great throng; and he had compassion on them, and healed their sick. 15 When it was evening, the disciples came to him and said, "This is a lonely place, and the day is now over; send the crowds away to go into the villages to buy food for themselves." 16 Jesus said, "They need not go away; you give them something to eat." 17 They said to him, "We have only five loaves here and two fish." 18 And he said, "Bring them here to me." 19 Then he ordered the crowds to sit down on the grass, and taking the five loaves and the two fish he looked up to heaven and blessed, and broke and gave the loaves to the disciples, and the disciples gave them to the crowds. 20 And they ate and were satisfied. And they took up twelve baskets full of broken pieces left over. 21 And those who ate were about five thousand men, besides women and children.

## MARK 6.30–44

30 The apostles returned to Jesus, and told him all that they had done and taught. 31 And he said to them, "Come away by yourselves to a lonely place, and rest a while." For many were coming and going, and they had no leisure even to eat. 32 And they went away in the boat to a lonely place by themselves. 33 Now many saw them going, and knew them, and they ran there on foot from all the towns, and got there ahead of them. 34 As he landed he saw a great throng, and he had compassion on them, because they were like sheep without a shepherd; and he began to teach them many things. 35 And when it grew late, his disciples came to him and said, "This is a lonely place, and the hour is now late; 36 send them away, to go into the country and villages round about and buy themselves something to eat." 37 But he answered them, "You give them something to eat." And they said to him, "Shall we go and buy two hundred denarii worth of bread, and give it to them to eat?" 38 And he said to them, "How many loaves have you? Go and see," and when they found out, they said, "Five, and two fish." 39 Then he commanded them all to sit down by companies upon the green grass. 40 So they sat down in groups, by hundreds and by fifties, 41 And taking the five loaves and the two fish he looked up to heaven, and blessed, and broke the loaves, and gave them to the disciples to set before the people; and he divided the two fish among them all. 42 And they all ate and were satisfied. 43 And they took up twelve baskets full of broken pieces and of the fish. 44 And those who ate the loaves were five thousand men.

## LUKE 9.10–17

10 On their return the apostles told him what they had done. And he took them and withdrew apart to a city called Bethsaida. 11 When the crowds learned it, they followed him; and he welcomed them and spoke to them of the kingdom of God, and cured those who had need of healing. 12 Now the day began to wear away; and the

twelve came and said to him, "Send the crowd away, to go into the villages and country round about, to lodge and get provisions; for we are here in a lonely place." 13 But he said to them, "You give them something to eat." They said, "We have no more than five loaves and two fish—unless we are to go and buy food for all these people." 14 For there were about five thousand men. And he said to his disciples, "Make them sit down in companies, about fifty each." 15 And they did so, and made them all sit down. 16 And taking the five loaves and the two fish he looked up to heaven, and blessed and broke them, and gave them to the disciples to set before the crowd. 17 And all ate and were satisfied. And they took up what was left over, twelve baskets of broken pieces.

## COMMENTARY

This story is of the same genre as the story of Elisha and the oil of 2 Kings 4.7 ff. and the story of the barley, ibid. 42–44,[1] but modeled on the Last Supper.[2]

19 *looked up to heaven*    a reverential pose. Cf. Gen. (LXX) 5.5, Deut. 4.19, Job 22.26, 2 Macc. 7.28.

*blessed and broke*    Jesus here follows the rabbinic procedure at table, which consists of reciting a blessing over the bread, "Blessed art Thou, O Lord our God, king of the universe, who brings forth bread from the earth." This is then followed by the breaking of the bread and distributing the pieces to the assemblage.[3]

20 *And they ate and were satisfied*    The phrase is from Deut. 8.10, *and you shall eat and be satisfied and bless the Lord your God*, and is the basis for grace after meals, called *birkat hamazon*. What is surprising is that it does not add "and they blessed," which is both the continuation of the biblical quotation and the source for the grace after meals.[4]

*twelve baskets*    The Gr. *kophinos*, Lat. *cophinus* is a wicker basket. According to Juvenal the Jews carried their kosher food with them in this type of basket.[5]

Mark 6.39 *to sit down by companies*    So too Luke 9.14. The Gr. *sumposia* more than likely translates the Heb. *ḥavurot*, "companies" or "groups," the most notable of which were those who ate the paschal meal together in *ḥavurot*.[6] This is the most appealing explanation of the term if indeed this passage is modeled on the Last Supper.

Mark 6.40 *So they sat down in groups*    The Gr. verb *anapiptō* in late Greek means "to recline at table." What has puzzled the commentators is that Mark has changed the terminology from *sumposia* in v. 39 to *prasiai prasiai* here, translated "in groups" or better "in rows" (NEB); *prasiai* actually means "gardenbeds." Luke omits this. A possible explanation of the two terms is that gathering in *sumposia* had reference to the selection of the members of a given group; *prasiai* refers to how they were to be seated, i.e., in straight lines perhaps to facilitate the distribution of the food.[7]

## NOTES

1. Cf. also 1 Kings 17.9–16. Daube, *NTRJ*, pp. 36 ff., sees in this story Ruth 2.14, which is highly fanciful.
2. See John 6.4.
3. M. Ber. 8.7; B. Ber. 35a, 46a; TJ ibid. 8, 11a (41); B. Ḥul. 7b; B. RH 29b.
4. See B. Yom. 39b, B. Shab. 21b.
5. *Sat.* III.114, *Judaeis quorum cophinus faenumque supellex.* Also see ibid. VI.542.
6. See M. Pes. 7.13.
7. The passage in Cant. R. 8.13, cited by J. Moffatt, *Expos. T.* 7 (1914): 89–90, and expanded by Derrett, *SNT*, 1:1–3, does not seem to be on point here.

# 113. *Walking on the Water*

## MATT. 14.22–33

22 Then he made the disciples get into the boat and go before him to the other side, while he dismissed the crowds. 23 And after he had dismissed the crowds, he went up into the hills by himself to pray. When evening came, he was alone, 24 but the boat by this time was many furlongs distant from the land,[t] beaten by the waves; for the wind was against them. 25 And in the fourth watch of the night he came to them, walking on the sea. 26 But when the disciples saw him walking on the sea, they were terrified, saying, "It is a ghost!" And they cried out for fear. 27 But immediately he spoke to them saying, "Take heart, it is I, have no fear." 28 And Peter answered him, "Lord, if it is you, bid me come to you on the water." 29 He said, "Come." So Peter got out of the boat and walked on the water and came to Jesus; 30 but when he saw the wind,[u] he was afraid, and beginning to sink he cried out, "Lord, save me." 31 Jesus immediately reached out his hand and caught him, saying to him, "O man of little faith, why did you doubt?" 32 And when they got into the boat, the wind ceased. 33 And those in the boat worshiped him, saying, "Truly you are the Son of God."

## MARK 6.45–52

45 Immediately he made his disciples get into the boat and go before him to the other side, to Bethsaida, where he dismissed the crowd. 46 And after he had taken leave of them, he went into the hills to pray. 47 And when evening came, the boat was out on the sea, and he was alone on the land. And he saw that they were distressed in rowing, for the wind was against them. 48 And about the fourth watch of the night he came to them, walking on the sea. He meant to pass by them, 49 but when they saw him walking on the sea, they thought it was a ghost, and cried out; 50 for they all saw him[v] and were terrified. But immediately he spoke to them and said, "Take heart, it is I; have no fear." 51 And he got into the boat with them and the wind ceased. And they were utterly astounded, 52 for they did not understand about the loaves, but their hearts were hardened.

---

t  Some omit *many furlongs distant from the land* and insert *out on the sea.*

u Some read *strong wind*, others *very strong wind*.
v Some omit *for they saw him* and put *all* at the end of v. 49.

## COMMENTARY

25  *the fourth watch of the night*  The hours of 3:00–6:00 a.m. According to Jewish usage there were three watches at night, although there is a discussion in the Talmud whether there were three or four.[1] Four watches reflect Roman usage. Mark 13.35 calls them evening, midnight, cock crowing, and morning.[2]

*walking on the water*  There are examples in the MT which speak of God walking on the water, and perhaps the inclusion of this incident is to indicate the divine character of Jesus.[3] It may also represent him as a second Moses (at the Red Sea) or a second Elisha who floated an axe head.[4]

26  *a ghost*  An example of a "ghost" in the MT is the spirit of Samuel raised from the dead by the Witch of En-Dor.[5] Seeing strange phenomena on the waters is recorded in several passages in rabbinic literature.[6]

## NOTES

1. Three watches, see Judg. 7.19, Luke 12.38. See also 1 Kings 11.11; Ps. 89(90).4, 129(130).6; Lam. 2.19; M. Ber. 1.1; T. ibid. 1.1 (p. 1); B. ibid. 3a; TJ ibid., 1, 2d (9); M. Mid. 1.2.
2. Cf. also Mark 6.48 and cf. Acts 12.4; Josephus, *Ant.* V.6.5, XVII.8.6.
3. Cf. Job 9.8, 38.16; Sira 24.5.
4. 2 Kings 6.6.
5. 1 Sam. 28.1 ff.
6. E.g., B. BB 73a–74b; B. Meg. 3a; B. Sanh. 44a.

# *114. Healings at Gennesaret*

## Matt. 14.34–36

34 And when they had crossed over, they came to land at Gennesaret. 35 And when the men of that place recognized him, they sent round to all that region and brought to him all that were sick, 36 and besought him that they might only touch the fringe of his garment; and as many as touched it were made well.

## Mark 6.53–56

53 And when they had crossed over, they came to land at Gennesaret, and moored to the shore. 54 And when they got out of the boat, immediately the people recognized him, 55 and ran about the whole neighborhood and began to bring sick people on their pallets to any place where they heard he was. 56 And wherever he came, in villages, cities, or country, they laid the sick in the marketplaces, and besought him that they might touch even the fringe of his garment; and as many as touched it were made well.

COMMENTARY

36 *touch the fringe of his garment*    See above p. 172.

# 115. *Ceremonial Purification*

## MATT. 15.1–20

1 Then the Pharisees and the scribes came to Jesus from Jerusalem and said, 2 "Why do your disciples transgress the tradition of the elders? For they do not wash their hands when they eat. 3 He answered them, "And why do you transgress the commandment of God for the sake of your tradition? 4 For God commanded, 'Honor your father and your mother,' and 'He who speaks evil of father or mother, let him surely die.' 5 But you say, 'If anyone tells his father or his mother, What you would have gained from me is given to God,[w] he need not honor his father.' 6 So, for the sake of your tradition, you have made void the word[x] of God. 7 You hypocrites! Well did Isaiah prophesy of you, when he said,

8 'This people honors me with their lips
  but their heart is far from me;
9 in vain do they worship me,
  teaching as doctrines the precepts of men.' "

10 And he called the people to him and said to them, "Hear and understand: 11 not what goes into the mouth defiles a man, but what comes out of the mouth, this defiles a man." 12 Then the disciples came and said to him, "Do you know that the Pharisees were offended when they heard this saying?" 13 He answered, "Every plant which my heavenly Father has not planted will be rooted up. 14 Let them alone; they are blind guides. And if a blind man leads a blind man, both will fall into a pit." 15 But Peter said to him, "Explain the parable to us." 16 And he said, "Are you also still without understanding? 17 Do you not see that whatever goes into a mouth passes into the stomach, and so passes on?[y] 18 But what comes out of the mouth proceeds from the heart, and this defiles a man. 19 For out of the heart come evil thoughts, murder, adultery, fornication, theft, false witness, slander. 20 These are what defile a man; but to eat with unwashed hands does not defile a man."

## MARK 7.1–23

1 Now when the Pharisees gathered together to him, with some of the scribes, who had come from Jerusalem, 2 they saw that some of his disciples ate with hands defiled, that is unwashed. 3 (For the Pharisees, and all the Jews, do not eat unless they wash[z] their hands, observing the tradition of the elders; 4 and when they come from the marketplace, they do not eat unless they purify[a] themselves; and there are many other traditions which they observe, the washing of cups and pots and vessels of bronze.)[b] 5 And the Pharisees and the scribes asked him, "Why do your disciples not live[c] according to the tradition of the elders, but eat with hands defiled?" 6 And he said to them, "Well did Isaiah prophesy of you hypocrites, as it is written,

'This people honors me with their lips,
but their heart is far from me,
7 in vain do they worship me,
teaching as doctrines the precepts of men.'

8 You leave the commandment of God, and hold fast the tradition of men." 9 And he said to them "You have a fine way of rejecting the commandment of God, in order to keep your tradition! 10 For Moses said, 'Honor your father and your mother'; and 'He who speaks evil of father or mother, let him surely die.'; 11 but you say, 'If a man tells his father or his mother, What you would have gained from me is Corban' (that is, given to God,)ʷ 12 then you no longer permit him to do anything for his father or mother, 13 thus making void the word of God through your tradition which you hand on. And many such things you do." 14 And he called the people to him again, and said to them, "Hear me, all of you, and understand: 15 there is nothing outside of man which by going into him can defile him; but the things which come out of a man are what defile him."ᵈ 17 And when he had entered the house and left the people, his disciples asked him about the parable. 18 And he said to them, "Then are you also without understanding? Do you not see that whatever goes into a man from the outside cannot defile him, 19 since it enters, not his heart but his stomach, and so passes on?ᵉ (Thus he declared all foods clean.) 20 And he said, "What comes out of a man is what defiles a man. 21 For from within, out of the heart of man, come evil thoughts, fornication, theft, murder, adultery, 22 coveting, wickedness, deceit, licentiousness, an evil eye, slander, pride, foolishness. 23 All these evil things come from within, and they defile a man."

---

w  Or *an offering*.
x  Other ancient authorities read *law*.
y  Or *is evacuated*.
z  Or *carefully wash*, or *frequently wash*.
a  Text *baptize*.
b  Some add *and beds*.
c  Greek *walk*.
d  Some add v. 16, *If any man has ears to hear, let him hear*.
e  Or *is evacuated*.

## COMMENTARY

1 *the Pharisees and the scribes came . . . from Jerusalem*  The scholars of Jerusalem were highly respected for their learning and dialectics and argumentation.[1]

2 *tradition of the elders*  This expression goes back to *divrē zeqenim* or *miẓvot zeqenim*, "the words of the elders" or "the commandments of the elders," or even perhaps to *divrē soferim*, "the words of the scribes," and these terms are always used to differentiate these teachings, part of the Oral Law, and the commands of the Torah, which are the Written Law.[2]

*tradition*  Gr. *paradosis* could also go back to Heb. *mesoret*, since the verb *m-s-r* means "to hand over."[3]

*they do not wash their hands*, etc. The earliest reference to this practice in Jewish sources is the Mishnah.[4] Montefiore and others follow Büchler, who maintained "that in the age of Jesus the law that the hands must be ritually washed before meals was only incumbent upon priests. A few 'pietists' voluntarily elected to live, so far as outward purity was concerned, as if they were priests. But laymen generally, and even Rabbis and their disciples, had no obligation to wash their hands before meals. The first allusion to the rule being made obligatory upon laymen is hardly earlier than the age of Rabbi Akiba—that is about A.D. 100."[5] S. Zeitlin, however, argues, "A few years before the destruction of the Temple, the schools of Shammai and Hillel adopted the 'Eighteen Measures' which put every Jew in a state of ritual uncleanliness, and therefore every Jew would have to undergo Tebilah (bodily immersion) which would be very impracticable. Therefore the rabbis declared that it was not necessary to undergo *Tebilah*, but that it was sufficient to wash the hands. . . . The disciples of Jesus ate without washing their hands, that is, they denied the tradition of the Pharisees and their decrees in which they declared that every Jew was in a state of impurity and hence before eating had to wash his hands. For this the Pharisees reproached Jesus."[6] This is the best explanation of this passage. Zeitlin did, however, point out that following this development, this passage must have been written by the evangelist after the destruction of the Temple and projected back to Jesus and his disciples.

4 *Honor your father and your mother* Exod. 20.12, Deut. 5.10. Cf. Lev. 9.3, 20.9; Deut. 27.16; Exod. 21.16.[7] The force of "honor your father, etc." juxtaposed with the oath of benefit, can be understood only if one realizes that the Rabbis interpreted "honor" as meaning providing the father and mother with the physical necessities and does not mean honor or respect as this term is understood in English.[8]

5 *What you would have gained . . . given to God* The translation does not convey the true meaning of this passage. The expression "given to God", in the Greek is *dōron*, which translates the Heb. *qorban*, "a sacrifice," as in Mark 7.11, which frequently, in tannaitic literature, means an "oath."[9] The text then should read, "If anyone tells his father or his mother, Qorban (a vow!) what you would have gained from me, (you shall not have that benefit), he does not honor his father." "According to the Pharisees, a vow must be kept since it is written in the Bible that a man should not break his word (Deut. 23.24; Num. 30.3). But if a man took a vow against biblical precept he must keep his vow and not observe the precept (See T. Ned. 1.6 *ibid.* 4) for which undoubtedly, according to them, he will be punished for not observing the precept. . . . According to Jesus no vow can be taken against a biblical precept."[10] Zeitlin goes on and points out, "However, to avoid a clash between two commandments in the Bible, namely 'honor thy father and thy mother' and 'he shall not break his word' if a man took a vow not to honor his father and mother, the Pharisees introduced a legal fiction by which he could

absolve his vow. This is called in the Talmud *hafarat nedarim*. Thus according to the Pharisees, if a man takes a vow against a biblical precept his vow can be absolved. (See M. Ned. 11.)"[11]

8 *This people honors me*, etc.   Isa. (LXX) 29.13.[12]

14 *the blind*, etc.   Cf. Luke 6.39.[13]

20 *These are what defile a man*, etc.   Although not directly on point, the following comment is noteworthy: "R. Joḥanan b. Zakkai said: 'It is not a dead body which defiles or that water makes clean, but it is a command of the King of kings.' "[14]

### NOTES

1. See Lam. R. 1.1 (44a).
2. Cf., e.g., TJ Ber. 1, 3b (47); B. Er. 13a; 21b; *Tan. Naso*, 29.
3. Cf. Josephus, *Ant.* XIII.29.7; M. Avot 1.1.
4. See M. Ber. 8.2–4.
5. Montefiore, *SG*, 1:135 ff.
6. S. Zeitlin, "The Pharisees and the Gospels," in *Essays and Studies in Memory of Linda R. Miller*, p. 261. See also idem, "Les Dix-Huit Mesures," *REJ* 67 (1915): 22-36. See, however, L. Finkelstein, *The Pharisees* (Philadelphia, 1940), pp. 277 ff.; B. Gaertner, *The Temple and the Community in Qumran and the New Testament* (Cambridge University Press, 1965), pp. 12 ff. Note also C. E. Carlston, "The Things That Defile (Mark VII.15) and the Law in Matthew and Mark," *NTS* 15 (1968–69): 75-96; J. Neusner, *The Idea of Purity in Ancient Judaism* (Leiden, 1973).
7. McNeile, *Matt.*, p. 223, notes that "*kakologein* 'to curse', 'to speak evil of' (RV), is not strictly the converse of 'to honor' but has the force of *atimazein;* Cf. Deut. xxvii.16 *maqleh* with Driver's note."
8. Cf. B. Qid. 31b.
9. E.g., M. BQ 9.10; M. Ned. 1.1; T. ibid. 1.1 (p. 275). On the oaths/vows, see above pp. 000 ff. and S. Belkin, "The Dissolution of Vows and the Problem of Antisocial Oaths in the Gospels and Contemporary Jewish Literature," *JBL* 55 (1936): 227-234.
10. Zeitlin, *The Pharisees and the Gospels*, p. 265.
11. Ibid. Note also M. Ned. 9.1.
12. See Stendahl, *SSMUOT*, pp. 56 ff., 171, 173.
13. B. BQ 52b.
14. *PRK* 5 (40b).

## 116. *The Syrophoenician Woman*

### MATT 15.21–28

21 And Jesus went away from there and withdrew to the district of Tyre and Sidon. 22 And behold, a Canaanite woman from that region came out and cried, "Have mercy on me, O Lord, Son of David; my daughter is severely possessed by a demon." 23 But he did not answer her a word. And his disciples came and begged him, saying, "Send her away, for she is crying after us." 24 He answered, "I was sent only to the lost sheep of the house of Israel." 25 But she came and knelt before him, saying, "Lord, help me." 26 And he answered, "It is not fair to take the children's bread and

throw it to the dogs." 27 She said, "Yes, Lord, yet even the dogs eat the crumbs that fall from their master's table." 28 Then Jesus answered her, "O woman, great is your faith! Be it done for you as you desire," And her daughter was healed instantly.

## MARK 7.24–30

24 And from there he arose and went away to the region of Tyre and Sidon.[f] And he entered a house and would not have anyone know it; yet he could not be hid. 25 But immediately a woman whose little daughter was possessed by an unclean spirit, heard of him, and came and fell down at his feet. 26 Now the woman was a Greek, a Syrophoenician[g] by birth. And she begged him to cast the demon out of her daughter. 27 And he said to her, "Let the children first be fed, for it is not right to take the children's bread and throw it to the dogs." 28 But she answered him, "Yes, Lord; yet even the dogs under the table eat the children's crumbs." 29 And he said to her, "For this saying you may go your way; the demon has left your daughter." 30 And she went home, and found the child lying in bed, and the demon gone.

---

f  Some texts omit *and Sidon*.
g  Some texts read *Tyrophoenician*, or *Phoenician*, or *a Syrian*, or *a Phoenician by birth*.

## COMMENTARY

22 *a Canaanite woman*  This expression occurs only here in the NT. There were, of course, no Canaanites at the time of Jesus. In early rabbinic sources it is a common term for a non-Jew, originating presumably from the distinction in Exod. 21 between the Hebrew slave and the Canaanite slave.[1] It is also used for a person outside of Palestine[2]—note that she "was a Greek, a Syrophoenician by birth" in Mark 7.26. The term "Canaanite" is also used for a Phoenician merchant.[3]

*my daughter is severely possessed by a demon*  It is not clear in Matt. whether the daughter is with her or at home. In Mark 7.30 it is clearly the latter.[4]

23 *But he did not answer her a word.*  Appears to be Semitic, Heb. *lo anah lah davar.*

*Send her away*, etc.  There is a difficulty in this part of the passage. The meaning is, "Get rid of her, for she is bothersome." But Jesus's response, "*I was sent*, etc., is a non-sequitur. If he refuses to grant her request, why not chase her away? Jesus's response seems to lack any real meaning if we understand the statement of the disciples as meaning "drive her away." We suggest that this is not what the disciples had in mind; on the contrary, they were asking Jesus to fulfill her request and cure her daughter. This may be explained in one of two ways: with slight emendation one could read *auton* for *auten*, not meaning "send *her* away" but "send *it* away," i.e., release the demon which is afflicting her daughter, or else, with no emendation, the verb *apoluō* is to be understood in the sense of "to free from bond or sickness," and means "release her (the daughter) from the grasp of the demon of illness."[5] If either suggestion is correct, the clear sense of Jesus' response is established.[6]

24 *the lost sheep of the house of Israel*   See Matt. 10.5 ff. (above p. 179).

27 *the dogs*   Do the dogs represent the Gentiles, perhaps renegade Jews,[7] or idols?[8]

## NOTES

1. See *Mek.* Exod. 21.26; M. Qid. 1.3.
2. See B. Sot. 35a.
3. See Zech. 14.21; Sifre Deut. 306, Yal. 1.942.
4. On healing from a distance, see above p. 155.
5. In the literature it is found only in the passive. See Tob. 3.6; 2 Macc. 12.45, Josephus, *Ant.* II.65, and here it means "release (her daughter) from the grasp of the demon of illness."
6. For this emendation and discussion of the passage, see Lachs, "Hebrew Elements," 39–40. See also T. A. Burkill, "The Historical Development of the Story of the Syrophoenician Woman Mk. 7.24–31," *NT* 9 (1967): 161–177.
7. See above p. 138 f. Cf. *Mid. Ps.* 4.8 (p. 24b). Philo, *Quod Omn. Prob.* IX.62 calls some persecutors of the Jews "dogs." Perhaps relevant is that Ignatius, *Eph.* VII.1 calls heretics *kynes lyssontes.*
8. See, e.g., B. AZ 54b. On this passage see Burkill, op. cit.; Fiebig, *Jüdische Wundergeschichten des neutestamentlichen Zeitalters* (Tübingen, 1911), pp. 19–22, where R. Joshua b. Levi compares the righteous to the guests invited to the king's table, and the wicked heathen to the dogs who obtain the crumbs that fall therefrom.

# 117. The Healing of the Many Sick Persons

## MATT. 15.29–31

29 And Jesus went on from there and passed along the Sea of Galilee. And he went up into the hills, and sat down there. 30 And great crowds came to him, bringing with them the lame, the maimed, the blind, the dumb, and many others, and they put them at his feet, and he healed them, 31 so that the crowd wondered, when they saw the dumb speaking; the maimed whole, the lame walking, and the blind seeing; and they glorified the God of Israel.

## MARK 7.31–37 (The Healing of the Deaf Mute)

31 Soon after this he returned from the region of Tyre and went through Sidon to the sea of Galilee, through the region of the Decapolis. 32 And they brought to him a man who was deaf and had an impediment in his speech; and they besought him to lay his hand upon him. 33 And taking him aside from the multitude privately, he put his fingers into his ears, and he spat and touched his tongue; 34 and looking up to heaven, he sighed, and said to him, "Ephphatha," that is, "Be opened." 35 And his ears were opened, his tongue was released, and he spoke plainly. 36 And he charged them to tell no one; but the more he charged them, the more zealously they proclaimed it. 37 And they were astonished beyond measure, saying, "He has done all things well; he even makes the deaf hear and the dumb speak."

## COMMENTARY

30 *and they put them*, etc.   Gr. *erripsan autous* translates the Heb *hishlikh otam*, "abandoned them or left them." See below Sec. 243 (p. 423).

Mark, v. 33 *he put his fingers into his ears*   The placing of the finger on a part of the body to heal it is found in the following: "Rabbi [Judah the Prince] had suffered from a toothache for thirteen years. The prophet Elijah came to him in the form of R. Ḥiyya the Elder. He said to him, 'How are you, sir?' He answered, 'A tooth bothers me.' The other said, 'Show me.' When he showed him, he put his finger on the tooth and it was cured."[1]

*and he spat and touched his tongue* Spittle was believed to have magical and curative powers;[2] it was also deemed effective against a spell but condemned by some Rabbis.[3]

34 *Ephphatha* Aram. *itpataḥ*.[4]

### NOTES

1. TJ Ket. 12, 35a (43); parallels: TJ Kil. 9, 32b (36); For other examples of healing by touching, see above pp. 62, 152.
2. B. BB 126b; TJ Shab. 14, 14d (18); TJ AZ 2, 40d (19); B. Shab. 108b; M. Ned. 9.7; TJ Sot. 1, 16d (p. 37).
3. Lev. R. 9.8; T. Sanh. 12.10 (p. 433). See also B. Sanh. 101a. Vespasian was said to have been healed by saliva, Tacitus, *Hist.* IV.81; Suetonius, *Vesp.* 7. See Dibelius, *FTG*, pp. 83 ff. On rabbinic condemnation, see B. Pes. 111a; B. Shab. 110a. Cf. also Josephus, *Ant.* VIII.2.5; T. Shab. 7.23 (p. 119); J. Guttman, "Ueber zwei dogmengeschichtliche Mischnastellen," *MGWJ* 42 (1898): 301.
4. See Zimmermann, *Aramaic Origin*, p. 10; Lev. R. 22; Koh. R. 5.8; Num. R. 18; B. Pes. 42a.

# 118. *The Feeding of the Four Thousand*

## MATT. 15.32–39

32 Then Jesus called his disciples to him and said, "I have compassion on the crowd, because they have been with me now three days, and have nothing to eat; and I am unwilling to send them away hungry, lest they faint on the way." 33 And the disciples said to him, "Where are we to get bread enough in the desert to feed so great a crowd?" 34 And Jesus said to them, "How many loaves have you?" They said, "Seven, and a few small fish." 35 And commanding the crowd to sit down on the ground, 36 he took the seven loaves and the fish, and having given thanks he broke them and gave them to the disciples, and the disciples gave them to the crowds. 37 And they all ate and were satisfied; and they took up seven baskets full of the broken pieces left over. 38 Those who ate were four thousand men, besides women and children. 39 And sending away the crowds, he got into the boat and went to the region of Magadan.

## MARK 8.1–10

1 In those days when again a great crowd had gathered, and they had nothing to eat he called his disciples to him, and said to them, 2 "I have compassion on the crowd, because they have been with me now three days, and have nothing to eat; 3 and if I send them away hungry to their homes, they will faint on the way; and some of them have come a long way." 4 And his disciples answered him, "How can one feed these men with bread here in the desert?" 5 And he asked them, "How many loaves have you?" They said, "Seven." 6 And he commanded the crowd to sit down on the ground; and he took the seven loaves, and having given thanks he broke them and gave them to his disciples to set before the people; and they set them before the crowd. 7 And they had a few small fish; and having blessed them, he commanded that these also should be set before them. 8 And they ate and were satisfied; and they took up the broken pieces left over, seven baskets full. 9 And there were about four thousand people. 10 And he sent them away; and immediately he got into the boat with his disciples, and went to the district of Dalmanutha.h

---

h Some texts read *Melegada*, or *Magdala*, or *Magedan*.

### COMMENTARY

39 *Magadan*   The location of Magadan is uncertain but it is on the Sea of Galilee. Some MSS and RSV read Magadan or Magdala; in Mark 8.10 the best MSS read Dalmanutha. Magdala is on the W. shore of the Sea of Galilee, probably Tarichea, a flourishing city and center of the fishing industry.[1]

7 *a few small fish . . . blessed them*   Mark, not fully conversant with rabbinic law, did not realize that having blessed the bread, all food eaten at the meal was covered by the blessing over the bread and that a special blessing over the fish was superfluous.

### NOTES

1. See Josephus, *BJ* II.21.8, III.20.7. See Jeremias, "Zum Problem des Ur-Markus," *ZNW* 25 (1936): 281–282; Finegan, *Light from the Ancient Past*, suggests that both Magadan and Dalmanutha might go back to Magdo Numa or Nunarta, "Magdol of fish." In the Talmud (B. Pes. 46a) Magdala is located near Tiberias and is called Migdal Nunya ("fish tower").

# 119. *The Pharisees Seek a Sign*

## MATT. 16.1–4

1 And the Pharisees and Sadducees came, and to test him they asked him to show them a sign from heaven. 2 He answered them,i "When it is evening, you say, 'It will be fair weather; for the sky is red.' 3 And in the morning, 'It will be stormy today, for

the sky is red and threatening.' You know how to interpret the appearance of the sky, but you cannot interpret the signs of the times. 4 An evil and adulterous generation seeks for a sign, but no sign shall be given to it except the sign of Jonah." So he left them and departed.

### IBID. 12.38–39

38 Then some of the scribes and Pharisees said to him, "Teacher, we wish to see a sign from you." 39 But he answered them, "An evil and adulterous generation seeks for a sign; but no sign shall be given to it except the sign of the prophet Jonah."

### MARK 8.11–13

11 The Pharisees came and began to argue with him, seeking from him a sign from heaven, to test him. 12 And he sighed deeply in his spirit, and said, "Why does this generation seek a sign? Truly, I say to you, no sign shall be given to this generation." 13 And he left them, and getting into the boat again he departed to the other side.

### LUKE 11.29, 16; 12.54–56

29 When the crowds were increasing, he began to say, 11.16 while others, to try him, sought from him a sign from heaven. 12.54 He also said to the multitudes "When you see a cloud rising in the west, you say at once, 'A shower is coming'; and so it happens. 55 And when you see the south wind blowing, you say, 'There will be scorching heat'; and it happens. 56 You hypocrites! You know how to interpret the appearance of earth and sky; but why do you not know how to interpret the present time?" 11.29 "This generation is an evil generation; it seeks a sign, but no sign shall be given to it except the sign of Jonah."

---

i   In some texts the following words to the end of v. 3 are omitted

## COMMENTARY

1 *a sign from heaven*   This is found frequently in rabbinic literature.[1] The term "heaven" means "God." See above p. 72. Here there is a play on words. The Pharisees and the Sadducees are asking an authenticating sign from him, from God (Heaven), presumably to prove whether he is a prophet (cf. Deut. 18.17) He, on the other hand, purposely challenges them with charges of reading the signs of the sky (heaven) but not understanding the signs of the times, i.e., the will of Heaven (God).

2 *the sky is red*   B. BB 84a speaks of the redness of the sky but does not mention that it is a weather indicator.

Luke, v. 54   See 1 Kings 18.44, *Behold, a little cloud like a man's hand is rising out of the sea (west). And he said, "Go up, say to Ahab: Prepare your chariot and go down lest the rain stay you."*

NOTES

1. E.g., Sifre Deut. 83 175; B. Yev. 90b; TJ Sanh. 2, 30c (38).

## 120. A Discourse on Leaven

### MATT. 16.5–12

5 When the disciples reached the other side, they had forgotten to bring any bread. 6 Jesus said to them, "Take heed and beware of the leaven of the Pharisees and Sadducees." 7 And they discussed it among themselves, saying, "We brought no bread." 8 But Jesus, aware of this, said, "O men of little faith, why do you discuss among yourselves the fact that you have no bread? 9 Do you not yet perceive? Do you not remember the five loaves of the five thousand, and how many baskets you gathered? 10 Or the seven loaves of the four thousand, and how many baskets you gathered? 11 How is it that you fail to perceive that I did not speak about bread? Beware of the leaven of the Pharisees and Sadducees." 12 Then they understood that he did not tell them to beware of the leaven of bread but of the teaching of the Pharisees and Sadducees.

### MARK 8.14–21

14 Now they had forgotten to bring bread; and they had only one loaf with them in the boat. 15 And he cautioned them, saying, "Take heed, beware of the leaven of the Pharisees and the leaven of Herod."j 16 And they discussed it with one another, saying, "We have no bread." 17 And being aware of it, Jesus said to them, "Why do you discuss the fact that you have no bread? Do you not yet perceive or understand? Are your hearts hardened? 18 Having eyes do you not see, and having ears do you not hear? And do you not remember? 19 When I broke the five loaves for the five thousand, how many baskets full of broken pieces did you take up?" They said to him, "Twelve." 20 "And the seven for the four thousand, how many baskets of broken pieces did you take up?" And they said, to him, "Seven." 21 And he said to them "Do you not yet understand?"

### LUKE 12.1

In the meantime, when so many thousands of the multitude had gathered together that they trod upon one another, he began to say to his disciples first, "Beware of the leaven of the Pharisees, which is hypocrisy."

---

j Others *the Herodians*.

### COMMENTARY

6 *the leaven of the Pharisees and Sadducees* "Leaven," which is putrefaction, is used in rabbinic literature in a metaphorical sense for sin or corruption and

here as a teaching to be avoided. It is also used to represent the evil inclination (*yezer hara*).[1] Matt. 13.20 is the only place where "leaven" is used in a positive sense.[2]

## NOTES

1. E.g., B. Ber. 17a; Gen. R. 34; Yal. Ruth 601. It is unlikely that the *SB* citation of TJ Ḥag. 2, 76c (37) and paralleled by *PRK* 16 (121a) is a good parallel to this passage, since the better reading, contained in Lam. R., Introduction 2, p. 29b, is *me'or* for *se'or*.

2. Cf. also 1 Cor. 5.6; Gal. 5.9. In classical sources leaven is bad; see Aulus Gellius X.15 when the Flamen Dialis was forbidden to touch leaven. See also Juvenal, *Sat.* III. 188.

## 121. The Blind Man of Bethsaida

### MARK 8.22–26

22 And they came to Bethsaida. And some people brought to him a blind man, and begged him to touch him. 23 And he took the blind man by the hand, and led him out of the village; and when he had spit on his eyes and laid his hands upon him, he asked him, "Do you see anything?" 24 And he looked up and said, "I see men; but they look like trees, walking." 25 Then again he laid his hands upon his eyes; and he looked intently and was restored, and saw everything clearly. 26 And he sent him away to his home, saying, "Do not even enter the village."k

---

k Some texts add *nor tell it to any in the village.*

### COMMENTARY

25 *and he laid his hands upon his eyes*   On healing by touching, see above pp. 62, 152.

## 122. The Confession at Caesarea Philippi First Prediction of the Passion

### MATT. 16.13–23

13 Now when Jesus came into the district of Caesarea Philippi he asked his disciples, "Who do men say that the Son of man is?"l 14 And they said, "Some say John the Baptist, others say Elijah, and others Jeremiah or one of the prophets." 15 He said to them, "But who do you say that I am?" 16 Simon Peter replied, "You are the Christ, the Son of the living God." 17 And Jesus answered him, "Blessed are you, Simon Bar-Jona! For flesh and blood has not revealed this to you, but my Father who is in heaven. 18 And I tell you, you are Peter,m and on this rockn I will build my church, and the powers of deatho shall not prevail against it. 19 I will give you the keys of the

kingdom of heaven, and whatever you bind on earth shall be bound in heaven, and what you loose on earth shall be loosed in heaven." 20 Then he strictly charged the disciples to tell no one that he was the Christ. 21 From that time Jesus[p] began to show his disciples that he must go to Jerusalem and suffer many things from the elders and chief priests and scribes, and be killed, and on the third day be raised. 22 And Peter took him and began to rebuke him, saying, "God forbid, Lord! This shall never happen to you." 23 But he turned and said to Peter, "Get behind me, Satan! You are a hindrance[q] to me; for you are not on the side of God, but of men."

## MARK 8.27–33

27 And Jesus went on with his disciples, to the villages of Caesarea Philippi; and on the way he asked his disciples, "Who do men say that I am?" 28 And they told him, "John the Baptist"; and others, "Elijah" and others "One of the prophets." 29 And he asked them, "But who do you say that I am?" Peter answered him, "You are the Christ." 30 And he charged them to tell no one about him. 31 And he began to teach them that the Son of man must suffer many things and be rejected by the elders and the chief priests and the scribes, and be killed, and after three days rise again. 32 And he said this plainly. And Peter took him, and began to rebuke him. 33 But turning and seeing his disciples, he rebuked Peter, and said, "Get behind me, Satan! For you are not on the side of God, but of men."

## LUKE 9.18–22

18 Now it happened that as he was praying alone the disciples were with him;[r] and he asked them, "Who do the people say that I am?" 19 And they answered, "John the Baptist; but others say, Elijah; and others that one of the prophets has risen." 20 And he said to them, "But who do you say that I am?" And Peter answered, "The Christ of God." 21 But he charged and commanded them to tell this to no one, 22 saying, "The Son of man must suffer many things, and be rejected by the elders and the chief priests and scribes, and be killed, and on the third day be raised."

---

l  Some read *Who do men say that I the Son of man am?*
m  Greek *Petros*.
n  Greek *petra*.
o  Greek *the gates of Hades*.
p  Some add *the Christ*.
q  Greek *stumbling block*.
r  Some read *met him*.

## COMMENTARY

13 *Caesarea Philippi*  Formerly Paneas. A city on the SW slope of Mount Hermon. In the NT mentioned only here and in Mark 8.27. After Herod's death in 4 B.C.E. it was included in the tetrarchy of Philip, who enlarged and beautified the city and called it Caesarea Philippi in honor of Tiberius Caesar and himself.[1]

14 *Elijah*  Precursor of the Messiah, see above p. 36, below p. 260 f.

*Jeremiah*  In some sources also considered to be the precursor of the Messiah, perhaps because he lived at the time of the destruction of the First Temple and this was to be his role, predicting the redemption.[2]

17 *Bar-Jona*  Assumed to be a mistake for "ben (bar) Joḥanan;" cf. John 1.42, 21.15.[3]

*flesh and blood*  I.e., a mortal, common in rabbinic literature differentiating man from God. See above p. 142.

18 *you are Peter.*  On this name see above p. 58.

*on this rock (petra) I will build my church.*  An interesting parallel is the following:

> *For from the top of the rocks I see him* [Num. 23.9]. There was a king who desired to build and lay foundations. He dug constantly deeper but found only a swamp. At last he dug and found a *petra*. He said, "On this spot I shall build and lay foundations." So the Holy One, blessed be He, desired to create the world, but sitting and meditating upon the generations of Enoch and of the Flood, He said, "How shall I create the world, seeing that those wicked men will only provoke Me?" But as soon as God perceived that there would rise an Abraham, He said, "Behold, I have found a *petra* upon which to build and to lay foundations of the world." Therefore he called Abraham Rock, as it is said, *look to the rock from which you were hewn* . . . [Isa. 51.1–2][4]

*powers of death*  The reading "gates of Sheol [Hell]" goes back to Isa. 38.10.

19 *keys of the kingdom*  Possessing the keys is to possess the authority over that which the keys open. It is of note that the earliest use of this imagery is Isa. 22.22, which involves the house of David, *And I will place on his shoulder the key of the house of David; he shall open and none shall shut, and he shall shut and none shall open.* This is interesting not only because it involves the house (kingdom) of David but because the language of authority, "open-shut," is not dissimilar to "bind and loosen" here in Matt.[5] The authority of Peter is to be over the Church, and this authority is represented by the keys. If the Temple institutionally is the model for the Church, then the tradition that the priests relinquish their authority and return the keys to the Temple of God is applicable: "Moreover, you priests, take the keys of the sanctuary and cast them into the height of heaven, and give them to the Lord and say, 'Guard your house yourself, for behold, we are found to be false stewards' " (2 Bar. 10.18). Similar thoughts in rabbinic literature: "It says *Open thy doors, O Lebanon, that the fire may devour thy cedars* [Zech. 11.1]. This refers to the high priests who were in the Temple, who took their keys in their hands and threw them up to the sky, saying to the Holy One, blessed be He, 'Master of the Universe, here are Thy keys which Thou didst hand over to us, for we have not been trustworthy custodians to do the King's work and to eat of the King's table.' "[6]

19 *bind . . . loose*  These are undoubtedly translations of either the Aram.

*asar* and *share* or the Heb. *asar* and *hitir.* They mean to forbid and/or to permit some act which is determined by the application of the *halakhah.*[7]

21 *chief priests*   See above p. 9.

*On the third day be raised.*   This tradition in a rabbinic passage that the dead rise from the grave on the third day is based on an interpretation of Hos. 6.2, *After two days he will revive us, on the third day he will raise us up, that we may live before him.*[8]

23 *Get behind me, Satan.*   On this expression see above to Matt. 4.10. This probably is not directed to Peter but to himself and to his *yezer hara*, which is the analogue of the Satan.

### NOTES

1. See Josephus, *Ant.* XVIII.2.1; *BJ* II.9.1.
2. See Ginzberg, *Legends*, 4:234. Unfortunately some references in the index are missing in the notes.
3. See Dalman, *Gramm.*, p. 97.
4. Yal. I.766, cited by S. Schechter, *Studies in Judaism*, Second Series, pp. 118–119; Taylor, *Sayings of the Fathers*, p. 160. For other notables being a "keystone" or "beam" in a building, see Gen. R. 66 (Abraham). For other examples see *SB*, 1:732. It is unlikely that the *petra* theme is related to the *even shetiyah*, the foundation stone which was in the Holy of Holies in the Temple and considered to be the navel of the world. See Ginzberg, *Legends*, 5:14–15, nn. 38–39.
5. Cf. also Rev. 3.7.
6. *ARN* 4 and parallels.
7. See, e.g., M. Ter. 5.4. For other rabbinic examples, see *SB*, 1:739. For a discussion of these terms and a comparison of this passage with John. 20.23, see H. J. Cadbury, "The Meaning of John 20.23; Matt. 26.19 and Matt. 18.18," *JBL* 58 (1939): 231–234; J. R. Mantey, "The Mistranslation of the Perfect Tense in John 20.23; Matt. 16.19; Matt. 18.18," *JBL* 58 (1939): 243–249.
8. See *PRE* 51 (123b).

# 123. *Conditions of Discipleship*

## MATT. 16.24–28

24 Then Jesus told his disciples, "If any man would come after me, let him deny himself and take up his cross and follow me. 25 For whoever would save his life will lose it, and whoever loses his life for my sake will find it. 26 For what will it profit a man, if he gains the whole world and forfeits his life? Or what shall a man give in return for his life? 27 For the Son of man is to come with his angels in the glory of his Father, and then he will repay every man for what he has done. 28 Truly, I say to you, there are some standing here who will not taste death before they see the Son of man coming in his kingdom."

## MARK 8.34–9.1

34 And he called to him the multitude with his disciples, and said to them, "If any man would come after me, let him deny himself and take up his cross and follow me.

35 For whoever would save his life will lose it; and whoever loses his life for my sake and the gospel's will save it.⁵ 36 For what does it profit a man, to gain the whole world and forfeit his life? 37 For what can a man give in return for his life? 38 For whoever is ashamed of me and of my words in this adulterous and sinful generation, of him will the Son of man also be ashamed, when he comes in the glory of his Father with the holy angels." 9.1 And he said to them "Truly, I say to you, there are some standing here who will not taste death before they see the kingdom of God come with power."

## Luke 9.23–27

23 And he said to all, "If any man would come after me, let him deny himself and take up his cross daily and follow me, 24 For whoever would save his life will lose it; and whoever loses his life for my sake, he will save it. 25 For what does it profit a man if he gain the whole world and loses or forfeits himself? 26 For whoever is ashamed of me and of my words, of him will the Son of man be ashamed when he comes in his glory and the glory of the Father and of the holy angels. 27 But I tell you truly, there are some standing here who will not taste of death before they see the kingdom of God."

---

s  Some texts read *whoever loses his life for the gospel's sake will save it.*

### COMMENTARY

24 *come after me*   I.e., become my disciple. See above p. 66.
*take up his cross*   See above p. 187.
26 *what will it profit a man* . . . Similar to the question in Koh. 1.3.
27 *and he will repay*   Cf. Ps. 62.12.
28 *taste death*   A common expression in rabbinic literature.[1]
Luke 9.23 *daily* Gr. *hemeron*, perhaps from the *Heb. hayom* and means "today."

### NOTES

1.  E.g., 4 Ezra 6.26; Gen. R. 9.2; B. Yoma 78b; Targ. J. Deut. 32.1 (Aram.).

# 124. The Transfiguration

## Matt. 17.1–8

1 And after six days Jesus took with him Peter and James and John his brother, and led them up a high mountain apart. 2 And he was transfigured before them, and his face shone like the sun, and his garments became white as light. 3 And behold, there appeared to them Moses and Elijah, talking with him. 4 And Peter said to Jesus, "Lord, it is well that we are here; if you wish, I will make three booths here, one for you, and one for Moses, and one for Elijah." 5 He was still speaking, when lo, a

bright cloud overshadowed them, and a voice from the cloud said, "This is my beloved Son,ᵗ with whom I am well pleased; listen to him." 6 When the disciples heard this, they fell on their faces, and were filled with awe. 7 But Jesus came and touched them saying, "Rise, and have no fear." 8 And when they lifted up their eyes, they saw no one but Jesus only.

## MARK 9.2–8

2 And after six days Jesus took with him Peter and James and John, and led them up a high mountain apart by themselves; and he was transfigured before them, 3 and his garments became glistening, intensely white,ᵘ as no fuller on earth could bleach them. 4 And there appeared to them Elijah with Moses; and they were talking to Jesus. 5 And Peter said to Jesus, "Master,ᵛ it is well that we are here; let us make three booths, one for you, and one for Moses, and one for Elijah." 6 For he did not know what to say, for they were exceedingly afraid. 7 And a cloud overshadowed them and a voice came out of the cloud, "This is my beloved Son;ʷ listen to him." 8 And suddenly looking around they no longer saw anyone with them but Jesus only.

## LUKE 9.28–36

28 Now about eight days after these sayings he took with him Peter and John and James, and went up on the mountain to pray. 29 And as he was praying, the appearance of his countenance was altered, and his raiment became dazzling white. 30 And behold, two men talked with him, Moses and Elijah, 31 who appeared in glory and spoke of his departure, which he was to accomplish at Jerusalem. 32 Now Peter and those who were with him were heavy with sleep but kept awake, and they saw his glory and the two men who stood with him. 33 And as the men were parting from him, Peter said to Jesus, "Master, it is well that we are here; let us make three booths, one for you and one for Moses and one for Elijah"—not knowing what he said. 34 And as he said this, a cloud came and overshadowed them; and they were afraid as they entered the cloud. 35 And a voice came out of the cloud, saying, "This is my Son, my Chosen;ʷ listen to him!" 36 And when the voice had spoken, Jesus was found alone. And they kept silent and told no one in those days anything of what they had seen.

---

t  Or *my Son, my* (or *the*) *Beloved.*
u  Some read *white as snow.*
v  Or *Rabbi.*
w  Some read *My Beloved*; others *My Beloved with whom I am well pleased.*

## COMMENTARY

1 *after six days*  It appears that these six days hark back to Exod. 24.16, *The glory of the Lord settled on Mount Sinai, and the clouds covered it six days; and on the seventh day He called Moses out of the midst of the clouds,* and are intended to parallel the Theophany at Sinai. It is also possible that this passage may be connected with the foregoing," . . . there are those standing here who will not

taste death before they see the kingdom of God come with power," because of the reference to Elijah, the forerunner of the kingdom, and his appearance in the Transfiguration.[1]

2 *transfigured*   Changed form, perhaps into a luminous figure.[2]

*face shone like the sun*   This is a common motif. The faces of the righteous beam with light, which is the glory and splendor of God, called *ziv ha-Shekhinah*. This shining countenance is particularly significant since Moses when descending Mount Sinai, is described as having a radiant face (Exod. 34.30).[3]

*and his garments became white as light*   Shining garments are likewise a common motif in rabbinic and apocryphal sources and are also the result of reflecting the splendor of God and marking the individuals as elect.[4]

*high mountain*   Not identified but the proper place for a theophany and a motif present both in the Moses narrative (Exod. 24.34) and the Elijah story (1 Kings 18.20; 19.8, 11).

5 *a bright cloud overshadowed them*   The verb *episkiazo* derives from either the Heb. *zalal* or the Aram. *tallel* and fits both the imagery of the booths *(sukkot)* and the clouds of Glory representing the *Shekhinah*.[5] Cf. also Exod. 24.15–18.

*This is my beloved*   See above p. 47.

## NOTES

1. See B. W. Bacon, "After Six Days: A New Clue for Gospel Critics," *HTR* 8 (1915): 94 ff.; W. A. Heider, *Amer. Journal of Phil.* 45 (1924): 228.

2. Not as *SB*, who cites passages dealing not with transfiguration but with those who did not die, which is not the same thing.

3. See Apoc. Bar. 51.3; 5.10; En. 37.7; 51.5; 4 Ezra 7.97, 125; Slav. En. 66.7; Sifre Deut. 10; Koh. R. 1.7; 1.3; Deut. R. 11 (Moses).

4. En. 62.15; 16; 2 En. 22.8; Rev. 4.4, 7.9, 3.5; Koh. R. 1.7; *PR* 37 (163b); Num. R. 15.

5. This idea is well documented by Daube, *NTRJ*, pp. 27 ff.

# 125. *The Coming of Elijah*

## MATT. 17.9–13

9 And as they were coming down the mountain, Jesus commanded them, "Tell no one the vision, until the Son of man is risen from the dead." 10 And the disciples asked him, "Then why do the scribes say that first Elijah must come?" 11 He replied, "Elijah does come, and he is to restore all things; 12 but I tell you that Elijah has already come, and they did not know him, but did to him whatever they pleased. So, also the Son of man will suffer at their hands." 13 Then the disciples understood that he was speaking to them of John the Baptist.

## MARK 9.9–13

9 And as they were coming down the mountain, he charged them to tell no one what they had seen, until the Son of man should have risen from the dead. 10 So they kept the matter to themselves, questioning what the rising from the dead meant. 11 And they asked him, "Why do the scribes say that first Elijah must come?" 12 And he said to them, "Elijah does come first to restore all things; and how is it written of the Son of man, that he should suffer many things and be treated with contempt? 13 But I tell you that Elijah has come, and they did to him whatever they pleased, as it is written of him."

### COMMENTARY

The translation of Elijah (2 Kings 2.1–12) gave rise to the concept of Elijah redivivus, which finds first expression in Mal. 4.5–6, where he is to *turn the hearts of the fathers to their children and the hearts of the children to their fathers*, and this will be *before the great and terrible day of the Lord comes*. According to another source he is said to come "to restore Israel."[1] In rabbinic literature there is abundant material about Elijah as precursor of the Messiah.[2] Although some contemporaries of Jesus thought that he was Elijah (Matt. 16.14, Luke 9.8), more considered John the Baptist to be Elijah, but he apparently disavowed the role (see John 1.21).

### NOTES

1. Sira 48.10.
2. See M. Eduy. 8.7 et al.

## 126. *Healing of the Epileptic Boy*

### MATT. 17.14–20

14 And when they came to the crowd, a man came up to him and kneeling before him said, 15 "Lord, have mercy on my son, for he is an epileptic and suffers terribly; for often he falls into the fire, and often into the water. 16 And I brought him to your disciples, and they could not heal him." 17 And Jesus answered, "O faithless and perverse generation, how long am I to be with you? How long am I to bear with you? Bring him here to me." 18 And Jesus rebuked him, and the demon came out of him, and the boy was cured instantly. 19 Then the disciples came to Jesus privately and said, "Why could we not cast it out?" 20 He said to them, "Because of your little faith. For truly, I say to you, if you have faith as a grain of mustard seed you will say to this mountain, 'Move hence to yonder place,' and it will move; and nothing will be impossible to you."[x]

## MARK 9.14-29

14 And when they came to the disciples, they saw a great crowd about them, and the scribes arguing with them. 15 And immediately all the crowd, when they saw him, were greatly amazed, and ran up to him and greeted him. 16 And he asked them, "What are you discussing with them?" 17 And one of the crowd answered him, "Teacher, I brought my son to you, for he has a dumb spirit; 18 and wherever it seizes him, it dashes him down; and he foams and grinds his teeth and becomes rigid; and I asked your disciples to cast it out, and they were not able." 19 And he answered them, "O faithless generation, how long am I to be with you? How long am I to bear with you? Bring him to me." 20 And they brought the boy to him; and when the spirit saw him, immediately it convulsed the boy, and he fell on the ground and rolled about, foaming at the mouth. 21 And Jesus[y] asked his father, "How long has he had this?" And he said, "From childhood. 22 And it has often cast him into the fire and into the water, to destroy him; but if you can do anything, have pity on us and help us." 23 And Jesus said to him, "If you can! All things are possible to him who believes." 24 Immediately the father of the child cried out[z] and said, "I believe; help my unbelief!" 25 And when Jesus saw that a crowd came running together, he rebuked the unclean spirit, saying to it, "You dumb and deaf spirit, I command you, come out of him, and never enter him again." 26 And after crying out and convulsing him terribly, it came out, and the boy was like a corpse; so that most of them said, "He is dead." 27 But Jesus took him by the hand and lifted him up, and he arose. 28 And when he had gone home, his disciples asked him privately, "Why could we not cast it out?" 29 And he said to them, "This kind cannot be driven out by anything but prayer."[a]

## LUKE 9.37-43a; 17.6

37 On the next day, when they had come down from the mountain, a great crowd met him. 38 And behold, a man from the crowd cried, "Teacher, I beg you to look upon my son, for he is my only child; 39 and behold, a spirit seizes him, and he suddenly cries out; it convulses him till he foams, and shatters him, and will hardly leave him. 40 And I begged your disciples to cast it out, but they could not." 41 Jesus answered, "O faithless and perverse generation, how long am I to be with you and bear with you? Bring your son here." 42 While he was coming, the demon tore him and convulsed him. But Jesus rebuked the unclean spirit, and healed the boy, and gave him back to his father. 43 And all were astonished at the majesty of God. 17.6 And the Lord said, "If you had faith as a grain of mustard seed, you could say to this sycamine tree, 'Be rooted up, and be planted in the sea,' and it would obey you."

---

x  Other ancient authorities insert v. 21, *But this kind never comes out except by prayer and fasting.*
y  Greek *he.*
z  Other ancient authorities add *with tears.*
a  Other ancient authorities add *and fasting.*

## COMMENTARY

15 *epileptic*   Gr. *selēniazetai*, lit. "moonstruck." See Ps. 121.6 and above to Matt. 4.24.[1]

16 *and they could not heal him*   Is this a parallel to Gehazi's inability to revive the dead boy in 2 Kings 4.31?

17 *O faithless and perverse generation*   Reminiscent of Deut. 32.5.

20 *say to this mountain, Move,* etc.   Cf. 1 Cor. 13.2. For the feat of removing a mountain from its place, the rabbinic expression is *oqer harim,* and it is used to express the idea of doing the near impossible, as here.[2] Miraculously moving a tree from its place, Luke 17.6, is mentioned in rabbinic literature: "May this carob tree be moved, and it was."[3]

## NOTES

1. See Targ. and LXX to Ps. 121.6. Cf. also B. Pes. 111a and 112b; B. Ket. 60b, B. Git. 70a.

2. E.g., B. Sanh. 4a; B. Sot. 9b; B. BB 3b; Lev. R. 8.2.

3. B. BM 58b.

# *127. The Second Prediction of the Passion*

## MATT. 17.22–23

22 As they were gathering[b] in Galilee, Jesus said to them, "The son of man is to be delivered into the hands of men, 23 and they will kill him, and he will be raised on the third day." And they were greatly distressed.

## MARK 9.30–32

30 They went on from there and passed through Galilee. And he would not have anyone know it; 31 for he was teaching his disciples, saying to them, "The Son of man will be delivered into the hands of men, and they will kill him; and when he is killed, after three days he will rise." 32 But they did not understand the saying, and they were afraid to ask him.

## LUKE 9.43b–45

43b But while they were all marveling at everything he did, he said to his disciples, 44 "Let these words sink into your ears; for the Son of man is to be delivered into the hands of men." 45 But they did not understand this saying, and it was concealed from them, that they should not perceive it; and they were afraid to ask him about this saying.

---

b Others *abode;* others *were returning.*

COMMENTARY

23 *on the third day*    See below p. 437.

# 128. *The Temple Tax*

## MATT. 17.24–27

24 And when they came to Capernaum, the collectors of the half-shekel tax went up to Peter and said, "Does not your teacher pay the tax?" 25 He said, "Yes." And when he came home, Jesus spoke to him first, saying, "What do you think, Simon? From whom do kings of the earth take toll or tribute? From their sons or from others?" 26 And when he said, "From others," Jesus said to him, "Then the sons are free. 27 However, not to give offense to them, go to the sea and cast a hook, and take the first fish that comes up, and when you open its mouth you will find a shekel; take that and give it to them for me and for yourself."

## COMMENTARY

24 *the half-shekel*    Called in Gr. of NT *didrachma.* This was to be given by all males over the age of twenty (Exod. 30.13, 38.26). In Neh, 10.32–33 it was designated as a third of a shekel but later it was a half. They were collected in the six weeks before Passover.[1] This half-shekel was, during the Roman period, collected from Jews all over the world.[2] After the destruction of the Temple, Vespasian ordered Jews, despite the destruction of the Temple, to continue to pay it annually to the treasury of Jupiter Capitolinus. The tax collector went from town to town to collect this tax.[3]

26 *Then the sons are free*    This interchange between Jesus and Peter about the payment of the tax is reminiscent of the following:

> R. Johanan said in the name of R. Simeon b. Yohai: "What is the meaning of the verse, *For I the Lord love justice, I hate robbery and wrong* [Isa. 61.8]? This can be understood by a parable of a mortal king who was passing by a customs house. He said to his servants, 'Pay the tax to the tax collectors.' They said to him, 'Do not all the taxes belong to you?' He said to them, 'All travelers should learn from me that they do not escape paying the tax.' So too the Holy One, blessed be He, said, '*I the Lord . . . hate robbery and wrong,* My children should learn from me and avoid theft.' "[4]

27 *take the first fish . . . you will find a shekel*    There is a parallel story in the Talmud and Midrash where a pearl is found in a fish.[5]

*give it to them for me and for yourself*    The Gr. *stater* = *istira* or *itztara.* 1 *stater* = 1 sela = 4 denarii = 2 didrachma, which was enough for two persons. One question remains: Jesus is the son in the parabolic question addressed to Peter, but why should Peter be exempt?[6]

## NOTES

1. Cf. M. Sheq. 1.1. See Josephus, *Ant.* III.8.2.
2. Josephus, *Ant.* XVIII.9.1. On the use of the half-shekel tax, see M. Sheq. esp. chaps. 3, 4. See below pp. 347, 359 n. 9.
3. Josephus, *BJ* VII.6.6; Suetonius, *Domit.* 12.
4. B. Suk. 30a.
5. B. Shab. 119a–b. Cf. also Gen. R. 11.
6. See J. Rendel Harris, "Cod. Ev. 561—Codex·Algerinae Peckover," *JBL* 6 (1886): 79–89.

# *129. The Dispute About Greatness*

## MATT. 18.1–5

1 At that time the disciples came to Jesus, saying, "Who is the greatest in the kingdom of heaven?" 2 And calling to him a child, he put him in the midst of them, 3 and said, "Truly, I say to you, unless you turn and become like children, you will never enter the kingdom of heaven. 4 Whoever humbles himself like this child, he is the greatest in the kingdom of heaven. 5 Whoever receives one such child in my name receives me."

## MARK 9.33–37; 10.15

33 And they came to Capernaum; and when he was in the house he asked them, "What were you discussing on the way?" 34 But they were silent; for on the way they had discussed with one another who was the greatest. 35 And he sat down and called the twelve; and he said to them, "If anyone would be first, he must be last of all and servant of all." 36 And he took a child, and put him in the midst of them; and taking him in his arms, he said to them, 10.15 "Truly, I say to you, whoever does not receive the kingdom of God like a child shall not enter it. 9.37 Whoever receives one such child in my name receives me; and whoever receives me, receives not me but him who sent me."

## LUKE 9.46–48; 18.17

46 And an argument arose among them as to which of them was the greatest. 47 But when Jesus perceived the thought of their hearts, he took a child and put him by his side, 48 and said to them, 18.17 "Truly, I say to you, whoever does not receive the kingdom of God like a child shall not enter it." 9.48 "Whoever receives this child in my name receives me, and whoever receives me receives him who sent me; for he who is least among you all is the one who is great."

## COMMENTARY

To be like a child is to be innocent, not to be humble. The former can be amply illustrated in rabbinic literature, the latter cannot. A possible explanation of this unlikely combination of ideas is that v. 3 deals with the answer to the question of who may enter the kingdom of heaven, and that is to repent, i.e., "turn," Heb. *shuv*, or *ḥazor*, "return" or "turn (back)" and to be like children, i.e., pure from sin.[1] Verse 4 brings up the question not of who may enter the kingdom but of who is the greatest, and the antecedent seems not to be a child but the "servant" of Mark 9.35, "If anyone would be first, he must be last of all and *servant* of all." One wonders if there is a confusion here in this conflated tradition between *pais* and *paidion*.[2]

1 *Who is the greatest*, etc. See above p. 89.

4 *Whoever humbles himself* Cf. "He who makes himself small in this world for the sake of the Torah will be great in the world-to-come; he who makes himself a slave in this world for the sake of the Torah shall be free in the world-to-come."[3]

## NOTES

1. The Heb. expression *ketinoq ben yomo*, "like a child one day old," is used to describe a wholly moral person, e.g., *PRK* 6 (61b).
2. See above p. 155.
3. B. BM 85b.

# 130. *The Strange Exorcist*

## Mark 9.38–41

38 John said to him, "Teacher, we saw a man casting out demons in your name,[c] and we forbade him, because he was not following us." 39 But Jesus said, "Do not forbid him; for no one who does a mighty work in my name will be able soon after to speak evil of me. 40 For he that is not against us is for us. 41 For truly, I say to you, whoever gives you a cup of water to drink because you bear the name of Christ, will by no means lose his reward."

## Luke 9.49–50

49 John answered, "Master, we saw a man casting out demons in your name, and we forbade him, because he does not follow us." 50 But Jesus said to him, "Do not forbid him; for he that is not against you is for you."

---

c Some texts add *who does not follow us*.

## COMMENTARY

38 *John* I.e., the son of Zebedee brother of James.

*because he was not following us* Perhaps they were Jewish exorcists; cf. Matt. 12.22; Acts 19.13. Possibly the meaning is "he did not follow you," i.e., he was not one of your disciples along with us who were give authority over unclean spirits. Cf. Matt. 10.1.[1]

39 *no one who does a mighty work*, etc.[2]

Luke 9.50 *for he that is not against you is for you*  This contradicts Luke 11.23 (Matt. 12.30), "He who is not with me is against me."[3]

## NOTES

1. Fitzmyer, *Luke*, p. 821.
2. SB, 2:19, cites B. BQ 80b and B. BB 12b, which are not at all on point except for the fact that both passages contain the word *bimberab*, which is the translation of the Gr. *tache*, "soon."
3. A forced explanation to reconcile this contradiction is offered by Plummer, *Luke*, p. 259, "for he that is not against you is for you:" "The saying, He that is not with me is against me (xi.23 . . . Mt.xii.30) should be compared with this. There Christ gives a test by which His disciple is to try *himself*: if he cannot see that he is on Christ's side, he is against Him. Here He gives a test by which His disciple is to try *others*: if he cannot see that they are against Christ's cause, he is to consider them as for it."

# 131. On Temptations

## MATT. 18.6–9

6 "But whoever causes one of these little ones who believe in me to sin,[d] it would be better for him to have a great millstone fastened round his neck and to be drowned in the depth of the sea. 7 Woe to the world for temptations to sin![e] For it is necessary that temptations come, but woe to the man by whom the temptation comes! 8 And if your hand or foot causes you to sin,[d] cut it off and throw it from you; it is better for you to enter life maimed or lame than with two hands or two feet to be thrown into the eternal fire. 9 And if your eye causes you to sin,[d] pluck it out and throw it from you; it is better for you to enter life with one eye than with two to be thrown into the hell[f] of fire."

## MARK 9.42–48

42 "Whoever causes one of these little ones who believe in me to sin,[d] it would be better for him if a great millstone were hung round his neck and he were thrown into the sea. 43 And if your hand causes you to sin,[d] cut it off; it is better for you to enter life maimed than with two hands to go to hell,[f] to the unquenchable fire.[g] 45 And if your foot causes you to sin,[d] cut it off; it is better for you to enter life lame than with two feet to be thrown into hell.[fg] 47 And if your eye causes you to sin,[d] pluck it out; it is better for you to enter the kingdom of God with one eye than with two eyes to be thrown into hell,[f] 48 where their worm does not die and the fire is not quenched."

## LUKE 17.1–2

1 And he said to his disciples, "Temptations to sin[e] are sure to come; but woe to him by whom they come! 2 It would be better for him if a millstone were hung round his

neck and he were cast into the sea, than that he should cause one of these little ones to sin."d

---

d Greek *causes . . . to stumble.*
e Greek *stumbling blocks.*
f Greek *Gehenna.*
g Vv. 44 and 46 (which are identical with v. 48) are omitted by the best ancient authorities.

## COMMENTARY

6 *it would be better* This is similar to the statement "It would be better for a man that he throw himself into a fiery furnace than that he should openly put his neighbor to shame."[1]

8 *and if . . . your foot causes you to sin,* etc. See above to Matt. 5.29 ff (p. 97).

## NOTES

1. B. Ket. 67b. For the metaphor of a millstone on one's neck, see B. Qid. 29a. Cf. W. Bacher, *Die Agada der palästinischen Amoräer,* 3 vols. (Strasburg, 1892-99) Vol. I p. 235.

# 132. Concerning Salt

## MATT. 5.13

"You are the salt of the earth; but if salt has lost its taste, how can its saltness be restored? It is no longer good for anything except to be thrown out and trodden underfoot by men."

## MARK 9.49–50

49 "For everyone will be salted with fire.h 50 Salt is good; but if the salt has lost its saltness, how will you season it? Have salt in yourselves, and be at peace with one another."

## LUKE 14.34–35

34 "Salt is good; but if salt has lost its taste, how shall its saltness be restored? 35 It is fit neither for the land nor for the dunghill; men throw it away. He who has ears to hear, let him hear."

---

h Some texts add *and every sacrifice will be salted with salt.*
See above sec. 20 (p. 81 ff).

# 133. *The Lost Sheep*

## MATT. 18.10–14

10 "See that you do not despise one of these little ones; for I tell you that in heaven their angels always behold the face of my Father who is in heaven.[i] 12 What do you think? If a man has a hundred sheep, and one of them has gone astray, does he not leave the ninety-nine on the hills and go in search of the one that went astray? 13 And if he finds it, truly, I say to you, he rejoices over it more than over the ninety-nine that never went astray. 14 So it is not the will of my[j] Father who is in heaven that one of these little ones should perish."

## LUKE 15.3–7

3 So he told them this parable. 4 "What man of you, having a hundred sheep, if he has lost one of them, does not leave the ninety-nine in the wilderness, and go after the one which is lost, until he finds it? 5 And when he has found it, he lays it on his shoulders, rejoicing. 6 And when he comes home, he calls together his friends and his neighbors, saying to them, 'Rejoice with me, for I have found my sheep which was lost.' 7 Even so, I tell you, there will be more joy in heaven over one sinner who repents than over ninety-nine righteous persons who need no repentance."

---

i   Other ancient authorities add v. 11, *For the Son of man came to save the lost.*
j   Other ancient authorities read *your.*

## COMMENTARY

10 *their angels*, etc.   Who these angels are is not clear. One possibility is that it refers to "guardian angels," a concept as old as the Bible, e.g., *He shall give his angels charge over you to keep you in all your ways.*[1] Another is that these angels are guardians of the righteous, individually and/or collectively.[2] A third, which is more likely, is the idea that each person, "each stalk in earth has an angelic star [Heb. *mazal*] in heaven."[3] This is probably originally a Persian concept later incorporated in rabbinic literature.[4]

*always behold the face of my Father*   As in 2 Kings 25.19, "to behold the face of" means "to have direct access to." This expression as to angels is generally restricted to the *malakhē hasharet*, the Ministering Angels.

12 *ninety-nine . . . hundred*   This is used in rabbinic sources to express "one of many."[5]

14 *that one of these little ones should perish.*   "In this verse Jesus is referring not to children but to "humble believers', the little ones of the community, but not the little in age."[6]

## NOTES

1. Ps. 91.11 Personal or guardian angels are relatively common in rabbinic

sources. See T. Shab. 17.2 f. (p. 136); T. AZ 1, 17 f. (p. 461); B. Shab. 119b; *Tan. Mishpatim*. 19.

2. Cf. Dan 10.13, 20; 11.1; 2 Macc. 11b.

3. Gen. R. 10.6.

4. Cf. "Every single flower is appropriate to an angel" (*Bundahish* XXVII.24). For the use of *mazal* in this sense, see, e.g., B. Shab. 146a, 53b; B. Meg. 3b.

5. Cf., e.g., M. Peah 4.1; TJ Shab. 14, 14c (42).

6. Montefiore, *RLGT*, p. 261.

# 134. On Reproving One's Brother

## Matt. 18.15–20

15 "If your brother sins against you, go and tell him his fault, between you and him alone. If he listens to you, you have gained your brother. 16 But if he does not listen, take one or two others along with you, that every word may be confirmed by the evidence of two or three witnesses. 17 If he refuses to listen to them, tell it to the church; and if he refuses to listen even to the church, let him be to you as a Gentile and a tax collector. 18 Truly, I say to you, whatever you bind on earth will be bound in heaven. 19 Again I say to you, if two of you agree about anything they ask, it will be done for them by my Father in heaven. 20 For where two or three are gathered in my name there am I in the midst of them."

## Luke 17.3

3 "Take heed to yourself; if your brother sins, rebuke him, and if he repents, forgive him."

## COMMENTARY

15 . . . *go and tell him his fault* Gr. *elegxein* is the Heb. *hokhi'ah*," to rebuke." This passage goes back to Lev. 19.17, *You shall surely rebuke* (RSV—reason with) *your brother*.[1]

16 *two or three witnesses* Following the principle that any trial involving evidence must be attested to by at least two witnesses whose testimony agrees.[2]

*Gentile and a tax collector* On Gentile, Gr. *ethnikos*, see above p. 109 f. On Jesus and tax collectors, see above p. 167 f.

17 *the church* Matthew is the only gospel writer who uses this term, here and in 16.18.[3] The Gr. *ekklesia* is the Heb. *qahal, kenesset*; Aram. *kenishta*.

18 *bind . . . loose* On this expression see above p. 256 f. Here, however, it seems to mean to have the power of excommunication.[4]

19 *if two of you agree*, etc. This must have reference to the decision of the petit court of three judges where the decision is arrived at by the agreement of at least two of the judges.[5] There is a tradition that when a court renders a just decision God Himself (the Shekhinah) abides with them.[6]

20 *For where two or three are gathered in my name* This concept is well attested to in rabbinic literature.

> R. Hananya the son of Teradyon said: "If two sit together and interchange no words of Torah, they are a meeting of scoffers, concerning whom it is said, *The godly man sits not in the seat of the scoffers;* but if two sit together and interchange the words of the Torah, the Shekhinah abides between them, as it is said, *Then they that feared the Lord spoke one with the other, and the Lord hearkened and heard, and a book of remembrance was written before Him, for them that feared the Lord, and that thought upon His name.*"[7]

> R. Halafta the son of Dosa of the village of Hananya said: "When ten people sit together and occupy themselves with the Torah, the Shekhinah abides among them . . . And whence can it be shown that the same applies to three? Because it is said *He judgeth among the judges* [the minimum number of judges being three], hence can it be shown that the same applies to two? Because it is said, *Then they that feared the Lord,* etc."[8]

### NOTES

1. See *ARN* 29; B. Tam. 62a; B. Shab. 119b; Sifre Deut. 1; Sifra Lev 19.17.
2. Num. 35.30, Deut. 17.6, 19.15; Sifre Num. 161; M. Sot. 1.1 et al.
3. On the term see K. L. Schmidt, *ekklēsia*, *TDNT*, 3:518 ff.
4. Cf. this usage in B. Hul. 132b; B. AZ 25a.
5. M. Sanh. 1.1.
6. See B. Sanh. 7a. Cf. also B. Ber. 6a.
7. M. Avot 3.3.
8. Ibid. 3.7. See also *ARN* 8; B. Sanh. 39a; B. Ber. 5b.

# 135. *On Reconciliation*

## MATT. 18.21–22

21 Then Peter came up and said to him, "Lord, how often shall my brother sin against me, and I forgive him? As many as seven times?" 22 Jesus said to him, "I do not say to you seven times, but seventy times seven."[k]

## LUKE 17.4

"and if he sins against you seven times in the day, and turns to you seven times, and says 'I repent,' you must forgive him."

---

k Or seventy-seven times.

### COMMENTARY

These verses serve as an introduction to the parable which follows (vv. 23–25), which concludes with the admonition to forgive one's brother.[1]

22 *seventy (seven) times*   Perhaps based on Gen. 4.24.[2]

### NOTES

1. On forgiveness and reconciliation, see above Matt. 5.24. (p. 90), 6.14 (p. 117). Also Abrahams, *Studies I*, chaps. 19, 20. Cf. also M. Yom. 8.9; B. ibid. 87a; TJ ibid. 8, 45c (19).

2. See LXX ad loc. as well as Targ. O and J. and Test. Benj. 7. Cf. also E. J. Goodspeed, *Problems of New Testament Translation* (Chicago, 1945), pp. 29–31.

## 136.   *The Parable of the Unmerciful Servant*

### MATT. 18.23–35

23 "Therefore the kingdom of heaven may be compared to a king who wished to settle accounts with his servants. 24 When he began the reckoning, one was brought to him who owed him ten thousand talents; 25 and as he could not pay, his lord ordered him to be sold, with his wife and children and all that he had, and payment to be made. 26 So the servant fell on his knees, imploring him, 'Lord, have patience with me, and I will pay for everything.' 27 And out of pity for him the lord of that servant released him and forgave him the debt. 28 But that same servant, as he went out, came upon one of his fellow servants who owed him a hundred denarii; and seizing him by the throat he said, 'Pay what you owe.' 29 So his fellow servant fell down and besought him, 'Have patience with me, and I will pay you.' 30 He refused and went and put him in prison till he should pay the debt. 31 When his fellow servants saw what had taken place, they were greatly distressed, and they went and reported to their lord all that had taken place. 32 Then his lord summoned him and said to him, 'You wicked servant! I forgave you all that debt because you besought me; 33 and should not you have had mercy on your fellow servant, as I had mercy on you?[1] 34 And in anger his lord delivered him to the jailers,[1] till he should pay all his debt. 35 So also my heavenly Father will do to every one of you, if you do not forgive your brother from your heart."

---

1  Greek *torturers*.

### COMMENTARY

23 *Therefore*   Manson argues that *therefore* does not fit and does not follow logically from v. 21, hence he concludes that it is by Matthew himself.[1] Abrahams, on the other hand, sees a connection particularly because of v. 32, "because thou besought me," being an illustration of the injunction "until seventy times seven" of v. 22.[2]

*a king*   Lit. "a certain king"; Gr. *anthrōpō basilei*, "a man king," i.e., a king of flesh and blood, Heb. *melekh basar va'dam*.   McNeile points out (*Matt.*, p. 269) that *basileus (ei)* has been added or substituted for *oikodespotēs* or Heb. *ba'al habayit* because it is more common in the parables of Jesus, citing Chrysostom ad loc. This is unlikely. The amount of *ten thousand talents* is more likely a transaction between a king and a governor than between a householder and one of his servants.

25 *ordered him to be sold, with his wife and children* There are biblical passages for the selling of children into slavery for the insolvency of their father (2 Kings 4.1, Neh. 5.5, Isa. 50.1), but this was not the rabbinic law at the time of Jesus. The commentators cite both Josephus and rabbinic sources as parallels and as support, but they all fail because the passages cited deal with theft, not with debt.[3] Even in the case of theft the wife could not be taken.[4]

28 *and seizing him by the throat* Although there is an interesting parallel in the Mishnah of one creditor seizing his debtor by the throat in the street for non-payment of the debt, the entire procedure and setting in this parable is Roman. According to Roman law the creditor was permitted to take the debtor forcibly before the authorities; this was called *manus iniectio*.[5]

32 *You wicked servant* Aram. *avda bisha.* This expression is common in rabbinic parables.[6]

## NOTES

1. Manson, *SJ*, p. 213.

2. *Studies I*, p. 163.

3. Examples of this can be found in *SB*, 1:797, who cite Exod. 22.2, Jos. *Ant.* XVI.1.1, *Mek.* Exod. 22.3, all of which deal with theft, not debt.

4. M. Sot. 3.8. Manson, *SJ*, p. 212, comments, "The word 'debt' literally means loans (RS mg). This may perhaps mean that the debtor had been working with capital lent for that purpose by his master Cf. 25.14. His deficiency could then be regarded as embezzlement." This is too far afield. Cf. B. Qid. 22a; T. Sot. 2.9 (p. 259); M. Git. 4.9.

5. See M. BB 10.8 Cf. Plautus, *Poen.* III.5.45. On imprisonment for debt, see A. Deissmann, *Light from the Ancient East*, 2d ed. (New York, 1927), p. 270.

6. E.g., B. BB 4a; Gen. R. 6, 84; Lam. R., Intro. #23, p. 35b.

# II. LUKE'S SPECIAL SECTION

LUKE 9.51–18.14

---

## 137. Jesus in the Samaritan Villages

LUKE 9.51–56

51 When the days drew near for him to be received up, he set his face to go to Jerusalem. And he sent messengers ahead of him, 52 who went and entered a village of the Samaritans, to make ready for him; 53 but the people would not receive him, because his face was set toward Jerusalem. 54 And when his disciples James and John saw it, they said, "Lord, do you want us to bid fire come down from heaven and consume them?ᵐ 55 But he turned and rebuked them,ⁿ 56 And they went on to another village.

---

m Some add *even as Elijah did.*

n Some texts add *and he said, "You do not know what manner of spirit you are of"*; Others *"You do not know what manner of spirit you are of; for the Son of man came not to destroy men's lives but to save them."*

### COMMENTARY

Jesus was to go up to Jerusalem and went by way of Samaria, which was the quickest route from Galilee. It was the one taken by pilgrims when going up to Jerusalem for the festivals.[1] Jerusalem was an anathema to the Samaritans; therefore it is likely that this was the reason they refused hospitality. It is interesting that there was a Samaritan village called Kefar Bish, "an evil village," so called because the inhabitants would not extend hospitality to strangers.[2]

51 *set his face*   A Semitism found both in the MT and in rabbinic sources.[3]

53 *his face was set toward*   Another Semitism.[4]

54 *James and John . . . consume them*   James and John were perhaps the most bellicose of the disciples and are called Sons of Thunder. The addition in some texts of "even as Elijah did" is a gloss with 2 Kings 1.9 ff. in mind.

55 *another village*   It is not clear whether this means another Samaritan village nearby or one which had no Samaritan inhabitants.

### NOTES

1. Josephus, *Ant.* XX.6.1, *Vita* 269.
2. TJ AZ 5.4, 44d; Lam. R. 2.2 (53b). On the Samaritans and the Jews, see

Schürer, *GJV*, 219–23: J. Montgomery, *The Samaritans* (1907); A. S. Halkin, "Samaritan Polemics Against Jews," *PAAJR* 7 (1935–36): 13–59.
   3. E.g., Gen. 31.21; Jer. 42.15, 17; Isa. 50.7; 2 Kings 12.18 (and Targ. ad loc.); Num. R. 20. Cf. also Ezek. 6.2, 13.17; 14.8
   4. Cf. 2 Sam. 17.11.

# 138. *The Nature of Discipleship*

### MATT. 8.19–22

19 And a scribe came up and said to him, "Teacher, I will follow you wherever you go." 20 And Jesus said to him, "Foxes have holes, and birds of the air have nests; but the Son of man has nowhere to lay his head." 21 Another of the disciples said to him, "Lord, let me first go and bury my father." 22 But Jesus said to him, "Follow me, and leave the dead to bury their own dead."

### LUKE 9.57–62

57 And as they were going along the road, a man said to him, "I will follow you wherever you go." 58 And Jesus said to him, "Foxes have holes, and birds of the air have nests; but the Son of man has nowhere to lay his head." 59 To another he said, "Follow me." But he said, "Lord, let me first go and bury my father." 60 But he said to him, "Leave the dead to bury their own dead; but as for you go and proclaim the kingdom of God," 61 Another said, "I will follow you, Lord; but let me first say farewell to those at my home." 62 Jesus said to him, "No one who puts his hand to the plow and looks back is fit for the kingdom of God."
See above Sec. 49 (p. 158).

# 139. *The Sending Out of the Seventy*

### MATT. 9.37–38; 10.7–16

9.37 Then he said to his disciples, "The harvest is plentiful, but the laborers are few; 38 pray therefore the Lord of the harvest to send out laborers into his harvest. 10.16 Lo, I send you out as sheep in the midst of wolves; so be wise as serpents and innocent as doves. 9 Take no gold, nor silver, nor copper in your belts, 10a no bag for your journey, nor two tunics, nor sandals, nor a staff . . . 11 and whatever town or village you enter, find out who is worthy in it, and stay with him until you depart. 12 As you enter the house, salute it. 13 And if the house is worthy, let your peace come upon it; but if it is not worthy, let your peace return to you, 10b . . . for the laborer deserves his food. 7 And preach as you go, saying, 'The kingdom of heaven is at hand.' 8 Heal the sick, raise the dead, cleanse lepers, cast out demons. You received without pay, give without pay. 14 And if anyone will not receive you or listen to your words, shake off the dust from your feet as you leave that house or town. 15 Truly, I say to you, it shall be more tolerable on the day of judgment for the land of Sodom and Gomorrah than for that town."

### Ibid. 11.21–23

11.21 "Woe to you, Chorazin! woe to you, Bethsaida! for if the mighty works done in you had been done in Tyre and Sidon, they would have repented long ago in sackcloth and ashes. 22 But I tell you, it shall be more tolerable on the day of judgment for Tyre and Sidon than for you. 23 And you, Capernaum, will you be exalted to heaven? You shall be brought down to Hades."

### Ibid. 10.40

He who receives you receives me, and he who receives me receives him who sent me.

### Luke 10.1–16

1 After this the Lord appointed seventy° others, and sent them on ahead of him, two by two, into every town and place where he himself was about to come. 2 And he said to them, "The harvest is plentiful, but the laborers are few; pray therefore the Lord of the harvest to sent out laborers into his harvest. 3 Go your way; behold, I send you out as lambs in the midst of wolves. 4 Carry no purse, no bag, no sandals; and salute no one on the road. 5 Whatever house you enter, first say, 'Peace be to this house!' 6 And if a son of peace is there, your peace shall rest upon him; but if not, it shall return to you. 7 And remain in the same house, eating and drinking what they provide, for the laborer deserves his wages; do not go from house to house. 8 Whenever you enter a town and they receive you, eat what is set before you; 9 heal the sick in it and say to them, 'The kingdom of God has come near to you,' 10 But whenever you enter a town and they do not receive you, go into its streets and say, 11 'Even the dust of your town that clings to our feet, we wipe off against you; nevertheless know this, that the kingdom of God has come near.' 12 I tell you, it shall be more tolerable on that day for Sodom than for that town. 13 Woe to you, Chorazin! woe to you, Bethsaida! for if the mighty works done in you had been done in Tyre and Sidon, they would have repented long ago, sitting in sackcloth and ashes. 14 But it shall be more tolerable in the judgment for Tyre and Sidon than for you. 15 And you, Capernaum, will you be exalted to heaven? You shall be brought down to Hades. 16 He who hears you hears me, and he who rejects you rejects me, and he who rejects me rejects him who sent me."

---

o Some texts read *seventy-two.*
See above Sec. 58 (p. 175).

## 140. *The Return of the Seventy*

### Luke 10.17–20

17 The seventyᴾ returned with joy, saying, "Lord, even the demons are subject to us in your name!" 18 And he said to them, "I saw Satan fall like lightening from heaven. 19 Behold, I have given you authority to tread upon serpents and scorpions, and over all the power of the enemy; and nothing shall hurt you. 20 Nevertheless do not

rejoice in this, that the spirits are subject to you; but rejoice that your names are written in heaven."

––––––––––––––––––

p  Some texts read *seventy-two*.

## COMMENTARY

17 *even the demons are subject to us in your name*  On exorcism by use of Jesus' name, see Luke 9.49 ff., Acts. 19.13, and above p. 178.

18 *I saw Satan fall like lightening from heaven*  On Satan as tempter, see above p. 50. Satan, according to the MT, has access to Heaven if not a member of the celestial society.[1] According to another view he had been cast out of heaven at the beginning of creation.[2] Before the messianic age Satan is to be vanquished by God,[3] or by an angel,[4] or by the Messiah.[5]

19 *Behold, I have given you authority to tread upon serpents and scorpions*  Cf. Ps. 91.13, *You shall tread upon the lion and the adder; the young lion and the serpent shall you trample under foot.*[6]

*and nothing shall hurt you*  Those who perform *mizvot* are protected from harm.[7]

20 *spirits are subject to you*  I.e., evil spirits.

*your names are written in heaven*  This imagery has a variety of functions in rabbinic thought; here it refers to the Book of the Righteous destined to be rewarded in the future, either here on earth or in a life of the world-to-come.[8]

## NOTES

1. Job 1.6 ff.; Zech. 3.1 ff.; En. 40.7.
2. See Charles, *Revelation* 1.323.
3. Test. Dan. 5; Test. Zeb 9; Test. Asher 7; Sifra, Lev. 26.6.
4. Test. Levi. 3; En. 54.4.
5. En. 55.4, 69.27; *PR* 36 (161a).
6. The Satan is often identified with the serpent. See 2 En. 31.3; Adam and Eve 14–16; B. Sot. 9b; B. Sanh. 29a.
7. B. Pes. 8b; En. 47.3; 104.1; Jub. 30.30; 36.10.
8. Cf. Pss. 69.29, 87.4–6; Exod. 32.32; Dan. 21.1; Phil. 4.3; Heb. 12.23; Rev. 3.5, 13.8, 17.8; Targ. J. Exod. 32.32; Gen. R. 24.3; *Mid. Ps.* 18.3 (68b); B. RH 16b; TJ ibid. 1.3, 57a (49); *PRK* 25 (157b).

# *141. Jesus' Gratitude to the Father*

## Matt. 11.25–27

25 At that time Jesus declared, "I thank thee, Father, Lord of heaven and earth, that thou hast hidden these things from the wise and understanding and revealed them to babes; 26 yea, Father, for such was thy gracious will.q 27 All things have been delivered to me by my father; and no one knows the Son except the Father, and no one knows the Father except the Son and anyone to whom the Son chooses to reveal him."

## LUKE 10.21–22

21 In that same hour he rejoiced in the Holy Spirit and said, "I thank thee, Father, Lord of heaven and earth, that thou hast hidden these things from the wise and understanding and revealed them to babes; yea, Father, for such was thy gracious will.q 22 All things have been delivered to me by my father; and no one knows who the Son is except the Father, or who the Father is except the Son and anyone to whom the Son chooses to reveal him."

---

q Or *so it was well-pleasing before thee.*

### COMMENTARY

5 *Lord of heaven and earth* Similar to the frequent expression in rabbinic Heb. *ribono shel olam*, "Lord of the world."[1]

*thou hast hidden these things from the wise and understanding and revealed them to babes.* One is reminded of the passage cited above, "R. Johanan said: 'From the time of the destruction of the Temple prophecy was taken from prophets and given to fools and children,' "[2] which is most likely a polemic against Christians.

26 *for such was thy gracious will.* Probably not to be related to the rabbinic formula "May it be thy will," used in prayer, since this is always in the future.[3]

### NOTES

1. See, e.g., B. BB. 9b.
2. B. BB. 12b. This is followed by an example of prophecy from the mouth of a child. See also B. Ber. 56a. See above p. 147.
3. As was suggested by *SB*, 1:607.

## 142. *The Blessedness of the Disciples*

### MATT. 13.16–17

16 "But blessed are your eyes, for they see, and your ears, for they hear. 17 Truly, I say to you, many prophets and righteous men longed to see what you see, and did not see it, and to hear what you hear, and did not hear it."

### LUKE 10.23–24

23 Then turning to the disciples he said privately, "Blessed are the eyes which see what you see! 24 For I tell you that many prophets and kings desired to see what you see, and did not see it, and to hear what you hear, and did not hear it.
See above Sec. 92 (p. 220).

# 143. The Lawyer's Question

## MATT. 22.34–40

34 But when the Pharisees heard that he had silenced the Sadducees, they came together. 35 And one of them, a lawyer, asked him a question, to test him. 36 "Teacher, which is the great commandment in the law?" 37 And he said to him, "You shall love the Lord your God with all your heart, and with all your soul, and with all your mind. 38 This is the first and great commandment. 39 And a second is like it, You shall love your neighbor as yourself. 40 On these two commandments depend all the law and the prophets."

## MARK 12.28–31

28 And one of the scribes came up and heard them disputing with one another, and seeing that he answered them well, asked him, "Which commandment is the first of all? 29 Jesus answered, "The first is 'Hear, O Israel: The Lord our God, the Lord is one; 30 and you shall love the Lord your God with all your heart, and with all your soul, and with all your mind, and with all your strength.' 31 The second is this, 'You shall love your neighbor as yourself.' There is no other commandment greater than these."

## LUKE 10.25–28

25 And behold, a lawyer stood up to put him to the test, saying, "Teacher, what shall I do to inherit eternal life?" 26 He said to him, "What is written in the law? How do you read?" 27 And he answered, "You shall love the Lord your God with all your heart, and with all your soul, and with all your strength, and with all your mind; and your neighbor as yourself." 28 And he said to him, "You have answered right; do this and you will live."

## COMMENTARY

35 *a lawyer* Gr. *nomikos*   Unusual in Matt.; frequent in Luke; Mark reads "scribe," Heb. *sofer*. A play on *nomikos* is found in the description of R. Jose b. Halafta, of whom it was stated, *nemuqo imo*, "his information as to the Law is ever with him."[1] In Josephus, Nomikos is used as a proper name; one Josedros son of Nomikos is mentioned.[2] Nomikos is also explained as being a Sadducean lawyer.[3] Abrahams suggests that he might have been a Gentile lawyer who had recently become a proselyte or contemplated becoming one and that this formulation of a question of what is the greatest commandment was derived from a catechismal formula.[4]

37 *You shall love*, etc.   Deut. 6.5. Mark adds "Hear, O Israel," ibid. 6.4, which is probably part of the original.[5] The text of Deut. 6.5 as well as 2 Kings 33.25, where the same language appears, varies in the LXX.[6] The *Shema*, Deut. 6.4 ff., was of greatest importance: it is called "The acceptance of the yoke of the kingdom of heaven."[7] Akiba died with its words on his lips.[8]

*greatest of the commandments*  "Thou shalt love thy neighbor as thyself (Lev. 19.18). R. Akiba said that this is the greatest principle in the Torah *(zeh klal gadol batorah).* Ben Azzai said that *This is the book of the generations of man* (Gen. 5.1) is a greater principle than that *(klal gadol mizeh)*."[9] The combination of Deut. 6.4 and Lev. 19.18 is already found in the Test. of Iss. 5.2 and in the Test. of Dan. 5.3. It is reasonable to assume that this combination was commonplace in rabbinic teachings, since it combines the love of God with the love of man, "Beloved is man who was created in the image of God."[10] Also, the negative golden rule (see above p. 143) is cited in connection with Lev. 19.18 in the Targum.[11] Hillel's comment on the negative golden rule is significant, "This is the whole Law, the rest is commentary."[12]

*depend all the law and the prophets*  "Depend" is the Heb. *talah*, "to hang."[13]

"The Marcan conclusion asserts that no other commandment can take precedence of these two. That is, these two stand in a class by themselves. Mt.'s conclusion says something different, that these two commandments are the fundamental principles upon which all other commandments in Scripture are based. Mt. thus tacitly excludes the possibility of a clash between the two great commandments and the rest, whereas Mk. reckons with such a possibility and declares how it is to be decided. The Marcan version is the more original of the two; the Matthaean alteration is dictated by Jewish-Christian reverence for the law."[14]

## NOTES

1. See Krauss, *GLL*, s.v. *nimuqo* (p. 361); Bacher, *Die Agada der Tannaiten*, 3 vols. (Strasburg, 1884-90), vol. II, p. 155.
2. Josephus, *BJ* II.21.7.
3. J. Mann, "Jesus and the Sadducean Priests: Luke 10.25–37," *JQR* 6 (1916): 419.
4. Abrahams, *Studies I*, p. 19.
5. Daube, *NTRJ*, p. 248.
6. Chajas, *Markus-Studien*, p. 67, quoted by Abrahams, loc. cit., argues that the LXX to Deut. 6.5 was influenced by rabbinic exegesis.
7. M. Ber. 2.2, 5.
8. B. Ber. 61b.
9. Sifra, Lev. 19.18.
10. M. Avot 3.14; Gen. R. 34; *ARN II*, p. 118; Gen. R. 24.
11. See also Sifra, ad loc.
12. *ARN II* 39, p. 118. Cf. also B. Mak. 23b–24a.
13. See Sifra 19.2; M. Ḥag. 1.8; T. ibid. 1.9 (p. 233); T. Er. 11.23 (p. 154).
14. Manson, *SJ*, p. 227.

# 144. *The Parable of the Good Samaritan*

## LUKE 10.29–37

29 But he, desiring to justify himself, said to Jesus, "And who is my neighbor?" 30 Jesus replied, "A man was going down from Jerusalem to Jericho, and he fell among robbers, who stripped him and beat him, and departed, leaving him half-dead. 31

Now by chance a priest was going down that road; and when he saw him he passed by on the other side. 32 So likewise a Levite, when he came to the place and saw him, passed by on the other side. 33 But a Samaritan, as he journeyed, came to where he was and when he saw him, he had compassion, 34 and went to him and bound up his wounds, pouring on oil and wine; then he set him on his own beast and brought him to an inn, and took care of him. 35 And the next day he took out two denarii and gave them to the innkeeper, saying, 'Take care of him; and whatever more you spend I will repay you when I come back.' 36 Which of these three, do you think, proved neighbor to the man who fell among the robbers?" 37 He said, "The one who showed mercy on him." And Jesus said to him, "Go and do likewise."

## COMMENTARY

29 *And who is my neighbor* Cf. Lev. 19.18. *Love your neighbor as yourself* in Lev. means fellow Jew. What is the definition here? Does it broaden the definition to include the non-Jew? See above Matt. 5.43 (p. 107).

30 *a man* Gr. *anthrōpos tis*, lit. "a certain man," possibly Jesus himself. The use of the third person here might reflect Heb./Aram. *hahu gavra; oto ha-ish* used euphemistically by a speaker or writer when telling of a misfortune.[1]

*going down from Jerusalem to Jericho* This road was infamous in antiquity for its rocky and desert terrain and for the presence of brigands.[2] Jerome records that in his day bands of marauding Arabs traveled this road.[3]

31 *a priest . . . likewise a Levite*, etc. I.e., the elite who should have known the ethical teaching of Lev. 19.18 and should have put it into practice. Another possibility is that they passed by so as not to become ritually impure by contact with the dead. There is evidence that priests and Levites resided in Jericho.[4]

33 *But a Samaritan*, etc. This reading has been challenged by several scholars suggesting that the companion term with "priest and Levite" would have been "Israelite," i.e., a noncleric, and that Luke changed the reading for his Gentile audience, emphasizing the merit of the Gentile benefactor.[5] Manson, although recognizing the difficulty, rejects "Israelite" as being the original and suggests instead *am ha-arez*.[6]

34 *oil and wine* Both were considered curatives.[7]

## NOTES

1. On this type of euphemism, see, e.g., Exod. 1.10, Num. 16.14, Gen. R. 1.12. See S. T. Lachs, "A Rabbinic Comment on Exodus 1.10," *Shiv'im. Essays and Studies in Honor of Ira Eisenstein* (New York, 1977), pp. 91 ff.

2. See Josephus, *BJ*, IV.8.2–3.

3. Jerome, *De Locis Heb.*, s.v. "Adummim." Cf. 2 Chron. 28.5–15; Strabo, *Geog.* XVI.2, 41 states that Pompey destroyed strongholds of brigands near Jericho.

4. See B. Ta'an 27a.

5. See J. Mann, op. cit., pp. 415–422; J. Halevy, *REJ* 4, 219–255; Abrahams, *Studies II*, pp. 33–40.

6. Manson, *SJ*, p. 262.

7. See M. Shab. 19.2.

# 145. *Mary and Martha*

## LUKE 10.38–42

38 Now as they went on their way, he entered a village; and a woman named Martha received him into her house. 39 And she had a sister called Mary, who sat at the Lord's feet and listened to his teaching. 40 But Martha was distracted with much serving; and she went to him and said, "Lord, do you not care that my sister has left me to serve alone? Tell her to help me." 41 But the Lord answered her, "Martha, Martha, you are anxious and troubled about many things; 42 one thing is needful.ʳ Mary has chosen the good portion, which shall not be taken away from her."

---

r Some texts read *few things are needful*, or *only one*.

## COMMENTARY

38 *Martha*  Heb. fem. of *mar*, "madam, lady, mistress," found in the Talmud most frequently as Martha daughter of Boetheus.[1] There are conjectures that Martha is the Aram. equivalent of Miriam.[2] It is also a man's name.[3]

39 *who sat at the Lord's feet . . . teaching*  Sitting at the feet of a teacher has rabbinic parallels, e.g., "Let thy house be a place of meeting for the Wise, and dust thyself with the dust of their feet, and drink their words with thirst."[4]

42 *one thing is needful*  I.e., to hear teaching, and all else is secondary.[5]

*Mary has chosen a good portion*  Most likely a Semitism. Gr. *meris* = Heb. *ḥeleq;*[6] "to choose a good portion," Heb. *levarer ḥeleq yafeh.*[7]

## NOTES

1. E.g., B. Yev. 9.4; Sifre Deut. 281.
2. This is on the basis of Lam. R. 1.16 (57a).
3. E.g., B. Pes. 103a.
4. M. Avot 1.4.
5. E.g., M. Avot 2.8, 3.2.
6. TJ Ber. 4, 7d (32); B. ibid. 28b.
7. B. Qid. 42a.

# 146. *The Lord's Prayer*

## MATT. 6.9–13

9 "Pray then like this:
Our Father who art in heaven,
Hallowed be thy name.
10 Thy kingdom come,
Thy will be done,

On earth as it is in heaven.
11 Give us this day our daily bread,[s]
12 And forgive us our debts,
As we also have forgiven our debtors;
13 And lead us not into temptation,
But deliver us from evil."[tu]

### LUKE 11.1–4

1 He was praying in a certain place, and when he ceased, one of his disciples said to him, "Lord, teach us to pray, as John taught his disciples." 2 And he said to them, "When you pray, say:
Father[v]
hallowed be thy name.
Thy kingdom come.
3 Give us each day our daily bread;[s]
4 and forgive us our sins
for we ourselves forgive everyone
who is indebted to us;
and lead us not into temptation."

---

s  Or *our bread for the morrow.*
t  Or *the evil one.*
u  Some texts add *for thine is the kingdom and the power and the glory forever. Amen.*
v  Some add *Our Father who art in Heaven.*
See above Sec. 30 (p. 117).

## 147. *The Friend at Midnight*

### LUKE 11.5–8

5 And he said to them, "Which of you who has a friend will go to him at midnight and say to him, 'Friend, lend me three loaves; 6 for a friend of mine has arrived on a journey, and I have nothing to set before him'; 7 and he will answer from within, 'Do not bother me; the door is now shut, and my children are with me in bed; I cannot get up and give you anything'? 8 I tell you, though he will not get up and give him anything because he is his friend, yet because of his importunity he will rise and give him whatever he needs.

### COMMENTARY

There are no rabbinic parallels to this passage.

For a bibliography on this passage, see Derrett, *SNT* III, "The Friend at Midnight," p. 37 n. 1.

# 148. *The Answer to Prayer*

## MATT. 7.7–11

7 "Ask and it will be given you; seek, and you will find; knock, and it will be opened to you. 8 For every one who asks receives, and he who seeks finds, and to him who knocks it will be opened. 9 Or what man of you, if his son asks him for a loaf, will give him a stone? 10 Or if he asks for a fish, will give him a serpent? 11 If you then, who are evil, know how to give good gifts to your children, how much more will your Father who is in heaven give good things to those who ask him?"

## LUKE 11.9–13

9 "And I tell you, Ask, and it will be given you; seek, and you will find; knock, and it will be opened to you. 10 For every one who asks receives, and he who seeks finds, and to him who knocks it will be opened. 11 What father among you, if his son asks for<sup>w</sup> a fish, will instead of a fish give him a serpent; 12 or if he asks for an egg, will give him a scorpion? 13 If you then, who are evil, know how to give good gifts to your children, how much more will the heavenly Father give the Holy Spirit to those who ask him?"

---

w Some add *a loaf, will give him a stone; or if he asks for.*
See above Sec. 38 (p. 140).

# 149. *Beelzebub*

## MATT. 12.22–30

22 Then a blind and dumb demoniac was brought to him, and he healed him so that the dumb man spoke and saw. 23 And all the people were amazed, and said, "Can this be the Son of David?" 24 But when the Pharisees heard it they said, "It is only by Beelzebub,<sup>x</sup> the prince of demons, that this man casts out demons." 25 Knowing their thoughts, he said to them, "Every kingdom divided against itself is laid waste, and no city or house divided against itself will stand; 26 and if Satan casts out Satan, he is divided against himself; how then will his kingdom stand? 27 And if I cast out demons by Beelzebub<sup>x</sup> by whom do your sons cast them out? Therefore they shall be your judges. 28 But if it is by the Spirit of God that I cast out demons, then the kingdom of God has come upon you. 29 Or how can one enter a strong man's house and plunder his goods, unless he first binds the strong man? Then indeed he may plunder his house. 30 He who is not with me is against me, and he who does not gather with me scatters."

## MARK 2.22–27

22 And the scribes who came down from Jerusalem said, "He is possessed by Beelzebub,<sup>x</sup> and by the prince of demons he casts out the demons." 23 And he called

them to him, and said to them in parables, "How can Satan cast out Satan? 24 If a kingdom is divided against itself, that kingdom cannot stand. 25 And if a house is divided against itself, that house will not be able to stand. 26 And if Satan has risen up against himself and is divided, he cannot stand, but is coming to an end. 27 But no one can enter a strong man's house and plunder his goods, unless he first binds the strong man; then indeed he may plunder his house."

## LUKE 11.14-23

14 Now he was casting out a demon that was dumb; when the demon had gone out, the dumb man spoke, and the people marveled. 15 But some of them said, "He casts out demons by Beelzebub,ˣ the prince of demons;" 16 while others, to try him, sought from him a sign from heaven. 17 But he, knowing their thoughts, said to them, "Every kingdom divided against itself is laid waste, and house falls upon house. 18 And if Satan also is divided against himself, how will his kingdom stand? For you say that I cast out demons by Beelzebub.ˣ 19 And if I cast out demons by Beelzebub,ˣ by whom do your sons cast them out? Therefore they shall be your judges. 20 But if it is by the finger of God that I cast out demons, then the kingdom of God has come upon you. 21 When a strong man, fully armed, guards his own palace, his goods are in peace; 22 but when one stronger than he assails him and overcomes him, he takes away his armor in which he trusted, and divides his spoil. 23 He who is not with me is against me, and he who does not gather with me scatters."

---

x  Greek *Beelzebul*.
See above Sec. 85 (p. 210).

# 150. *The Return of the Evil Spirit*

## MATT. 12.43-45

43 "When the unclean spirit has gone out of a man, he passes through waterless places seeking rest, but he finds none. 44 Then he says, 'I will return to my house from which I came.' And when he comes he finds it empty, swept, and put in order. 45 Then he goes and brings with him seven other spirits more evil than himself, and they enter and dwell there; and the last state of that man becomes worse than the first. So shall it be also with this evil generation."

## LUKE 11.24-26

24 "When the unclean spirit has gone out of a man, he passes through waterless places seeking rest; and finding none he says, 'I will return to my house from which I came.' 25 And when he comes he finds it swept and put in order. 26 Then he goes and brings seven other spirits more evil than himself, and they enter and dwell there; and the last state of that man becomes worse than the first."
See above Sec. 88 (p. 215).

# 151. *The Blessedness of Mary*

## Luke 11.27–28

27 As he said this, a woman in the crowd raised her voice and said to him, "Blessed is the womb that bore you, and the breasts that you sucked!" 28 But he said, "Blessed rather are those who hear the word of God and keep it."

## COMMENTARY

"Physical relationship to the Master is not the highest relationship. Most blessed are they who listen to the word of God, which he teaches, and perform it. However correct this may be, there is a certain deprecation of the most sacred of human relationships which is out of harmony with Jewish feelings."[1]

27 *Blessed is the womb that bore you* Aside from the well-known statements in this vein about famous rabbis cited above p. 70, one striking parallel is "Blessed is the womb from which he came forth," which is said of the Messiah.[2]

28 *Blessed rather are those who hear the word of God and keep it* Cf. Luke. 6.46; Matt. 7.21; Luke. 4.7; Matt. 7.34–37.

## NOTES

1. Montefiore, *SG*, 2:476.
2. *PRK* 22 (149a); See also B. Pes. 23b; TJ Kil. 1, 27b (14).

# 152. *The Sign for this Generation*

## Matt. 12.38–42

38 Then some of the scribes and Pharisees said to him, "Teacher, we wish to see a sign from you." 39 But he answered them, "An evil and adulterous generation seeks for a sign; but no sign shall be given to it except the sign of the prophet Jonah. 40 For as Jonah was three days and three nights in the belly of the whale, so will the Son of man be three days and three nights in the heart of the earth. 42 The queen of the South will arise at the judgment with this generation and condemn it; for she came from the ends of the earth to hear the wisdom of Solomon, and behold, something greater than Solomon is here. 41 The men of Nineveh will arise at the judgment with this generation and condemn it; for they repented at the preaching of Jonah, and behold, something greater than Jonah is here."

## Luke 11.29–32

29 When the crowds were increasing he began to say, "This generation is an evil generation; it seeks a sign, but no sign shall be given to it except the sign of Jonah. 30

For as Jonah became a sign to the men of Nineveh, so will the Son of man be to this generation. 31 The queen of the South will arise at the judgement with the men of this generation and condemn them; for she came from the ends of the earth to hear the wisdom of Solomon, and behold, something greater than Solomon is here. 32 The men of Nineveh will arise at the judgment with this generation and condemn it; for they repented at the preaching of Jonah, and behold, something greater than Jonah is here."

See above Sec. 87 (p. 214).

# 153. Concerning Light

## MATT. 5.15

"Nor do men light a lamp and put it under a bushel but on a stand, and it gives light to all in the house."

## IBID. 6.22–23

22 "The eye is the lamp of the body. So, if your eye is sound, your whole body will be full of light; 23 but if your eye is not sound, your whole body will be full of darkness. If then the light in you is darkness, how great is the darkness!"

## LUKE 11.33–36

33 "No one after lighting a lamp puts it in a cellar or under a bushel, but on a stand, that those who enter may see the light. 34 Your eye is the lamp of your body; when your eye is sound, your whole body is full of light; but when it is not sound, your body is full of darkness. 35 Therefore be careful lest the light in you be darkness. 36 If then your whole body is full of light, having no part dark, it will be wholly bright, as when a lamp with its rays gives you light."

See above Secs. 20, 33 (pp. 81, 127).

# 154. Discourse Against the Pharisees

## MATT. 23.4, 6, 7, 13, 23, 25–27, 29–31, 34–36

25 "Woe to you, scribes and Pharisees, hypocrites! for you cleanse the outside of the cup and of the plate, but inside they are full of extortion and rapacity. 26 You blind Pharisee! first cleanse the inside of the cup and of the plate, that the outside also may be clean."

23 "Woe to you scribes and Pharisees, hypocrites! for you tithe mint and dill and cummin, and have neglected the weightier matters of the law, justice and mercy and faith; these you ought to have done without neglecting the others. 6 And they love the place of honor at feasts and the best seats in the synagogues, and salutations in the marketplaces, and being called rabbi by men." 27 "Woe to you, scribes and Pharisees,

hypocrites! for you are like whitewashed tombs, which outwardly appear beautiful, but within they are full of dead men's bones and all uncleanness. 4 They bind heavy burdens, hard to bear,ʸ and lay them on men's shoulders; but they themselves will not move them with their finger."

29 "Woe to you, scribes and Pharisees, hypocrites! for you build the tombs of the prophets and adorn the monuments of the righteous, 30 saying, 'If we had lived in the days of our fathers, we would not have taken part with them in shedding the blood of the prophets.' 31 Thus you witness against yourselves, that you are sons of those who murdered the prophets."

34 "Therefore I send you prophets and wise men and scribes, some of whom you will kill and crucify, and some you will scourge in your synagogues and persecute from town to town, 35 that upon you may come all the righteous blood shed on earth, from the blood of innocent Abel to the blood of Zechariah the son of Barachiah, whom you murdered between the sanctuary and the altar. 36 Truly, I say to you all this will come upon this generation."

13 "But woe to you, scribes and Pharisees, hypocrites! because you shut the kingdom of heaven against men; for you neither enter yourselves, nor allow those who would enter to go in."

## Luke 11:37 — 12:1

37 While he was speaking, a Pharisee asked him to dine with him: so he went in and sat at table. 38 The Pharisee was astonished to see that he did not first wash before dinner. 39 And the Lord said to him, "Now you Pharisees cleanse the outside of the cup and of the dish, but inside you are full of extortion and wickedness. 40 You fools! Did not he who made the outside make the inside also? 41 But give for alms those things which are within; and behold, everything is clean for you." 42 "But woe to you Pharisees! for you tithe mint and rue and every herb, and neglect justice and the love of God; these you ought to have done, without neglecting the others." 43 "Woe to you Pharisees! for you love the best seats in the synagogues and salutations in the marketplaces." 44 "Woe to you! for you are like graves which are not seen, and men walk over them without knowing it."

45 One of the lawyers answered him, "Teacher, in saying this you reproach us also." 46 And he said, "Woe to you lawyers also! for you load men with burdens hard to bear, and you yourselves do not touch the burdens with one of your fingers. 47 Woe to you! for you build the tombs of the prophets whom your fathers killed. 48 So you are witnesses and consent to the deeds of your fathers; for they killed them, and you build their tombs.

49 "Therefore also the Wisdom of God said, 'I will send them prophets and apostles, some of whom they will kill and persecute,' 50 that the blood of all the prophets, shed from the foundation of the world, may be required of this generation, 51 from the blood of Abel to the blood of Zechariah, who perished between the altar and the sanctuary. Yet, I tell you, it shall be required of this generation. 52 Woe to you lawyers! for you have taken away the key of knowledge; you did not enter yourselves, and you hindered those who were entering."

53 As he went away from there, the scribes and the Pharisees began to press him hard, and to provoke him to speak of many things, 54 lying in wait for him, to catch at something he might say.

12:1 In the meantime, when so many thousands of the multitude had gathered together that they trod upon one another, he began to say to his disciples first, "Beware of the leaven of the Pharisees, which is hypocrisy."

---

y Some omit *hard to bear*.
See below Sec. 210 (p. 363)

## 155. *Exhortation to Fearless Confession*

### MATT. 10.26–33

26 "So have no fear of them; for nothing is covered that will not be revealed, or hidden that will not be known. 27 What I tell you in the dark, utter in the light; and what you hear whispered, proclaim upon the housetops. 28 And do not fear those who kill the body but cannot kill the soul; rather fear him who can destroy both soul and body in hell.ᶻ 29 Are not two sparrows sold for a penny? And not one of them will fall to the ground without your Father's will. 30 But even the hairs of your head are all numbered. 31 Fear not, therefore, you are of more value than many sparrows. 32 So everyone who acknowledges me before men, I also will acknowledge before my Father who is in heaven; 33 but whoever denies me before men, I also will deny before my Father who is in heaven.

### IBID. 12.32

"And whoever says a word against the Son of man will be forgiven; but whoever speaks against the Holy Spirit will not be forgiven, either in this age or in the age to come."

### IBID. 10.19–20

19 "When they deliver you up, do not be anxious how you are to speak or what you are to say for what you are to say will be given to you in that hour; 20 for it is not you who speak, but the Spirit of your Father speaking through you."

### LUKE 12.2–12

2 "Nothing is covered up that will not be revealed, or hidden that will not be known. 3 Whatever you have said in the dark shall be heard in the light, and what you have whispered in private rooms shall be proclaimed upon the housetops. 4 I tell you, my friends, do not fear those who kill the body, and after that have no more that they can do. 5 But I will warn you whom to fear; fear him who, after he has killed, has the power to cast into hell:ᶻ yes, I tell you, fear him! 6 Are not five sparrows sold for two pennies? And not one of them is forgotten before God. 7 Why even the hairs of your head are all numbered. Fear not; you are of more value than many sparrows. 8 And I tell you, every one who acknowledges me before men, the Son of man also will acknowledge before the angels of God; 9 but he who denies me before men will be denied before the angels of God. 10 And everyone who speaks a word against the Son

of man will be forgiven; but he who blasphemes against the Holy Spirit will not be forgiven. 11 And when they bring you before the synagogues and the rulers and the authorities, do not be anxious how or what you are to answer or what you are to say; 12 for the Holy Spirit will teach you in that very hour what you ought to say."

---

z  Greek *Gehenna*.
See above Secs. 60 (p. 184), 62 (p. 187), 59 (p. 182).

# *156. The Parable of the Rich Fool*

## Luke 12.13–21

13 One of the multitude said to him, "Teacher, bid my brother divide the inheritance with me." 14 But he said to him, "Man, who made me a judge or divider over you?" 15 And he said to them, "Take heed, and beware of all covetousness; for a man's life does not consist in the abundance of his possessions." 16 And he told them a parable, saying, "The land of a rich man brought forth plentifully; 17 and he thought to himself, 'What shall I do, for I have nowhere to store my crops?' 18 And he said, 'I will do this: I will pull down my barns, and build larger ones; and there I will store all my grain and my goods. 19 And I will say to my soul, Soul, you have ample goods laid up for many years; take your ease, eat, drink, be merry.' 20 But God said to him, 'Fool! This night your soul is required of you; and the things you have prepared, whose will they be?' 21 So is he who lays up treasures for himself, and is not rich toward God."

## COMMENTARY

14 *who made me a judge, etc.*  Cf. Exod. 2.14.

15 *and beware of all covetousness*  Rabbinic teaching does not eschew the material things of life, but it does not make of them the ultimate goal of man's existence. Man possesses an insatiable appetite, hence the statement, "Man's nature is such that he is never satisfied."[1] There are many admonitions about the evil of covetousness and avarice, e.g., "A rich man is compared to a mouse lying on dinars."[2]

16 *And he told them a parable*  There is no rabbinic parallel, but the spirit of this passage seems to be contained in the comment: "There is a man who is rich through his diligence and self-denial, and this is the reward allotted to him: when he says, 'I shall enjoy my goods!' he does not know how much time will pass until he leaves them to others and dies."[3]

19 *I will say to my soul*  Heb. *lenafshi*, i.e. "to myself."[4]

20 *the things you have prepared, whose will they be?*[5]

## NOTES

1. B. Sanh. 29b.
2. Ibid. Cf. also Sira 2.1–11; Ps. 49.16–20; Job 31.24 ff.

3. Sira 11.18 ff.
4. B. Ta'an 11a
5. E.g., TJ Shab. 14, 14c (3); Cf. also Ps. 30.6; 49.6; Koh. 2.18–23; Job 27.17–22.

# 157. Anxiety About Material Things

## MATT. 6.25–33

25 "Therefore I tell you, do not be anxious about your life, what you shall eat or what you shall drink, nor about your body, what you shall put on. Is not life more than food, and the body more than clothing? 26 Look at the birds of the air; they neither sow nor reap nor gather into barns, and yet your heavenly Father feeds them. Are you not of more value than they? 27 And which of you by being anxious can add one cubit to his span of life?[a] 28 And why are you anxious about clothing? Consider the lilies of the field, how they grow; they neither toil nor spin; 29 yet I tell you, even Solomon in all his glory was not arrayed like one of these. 30 But if God so clothes the grass of the field, which today is alive and tomorrow is thrown into the oven, will he not much more clothe you, O men of little faith? 31 Therefore do not be anxious, saying, 'What shall we eat?' or 'What shall we drink?' or 'What shall we wear?' 32 For the Gentiles seek all these things; and your heavenly Father knows that you need them all. 33 But seek first his kingdom and his righteousness, and all these things shall be yours as well."

## IBID. 6.19–21

19 "Do not lay up for yourselves treasures on earth, where moth and rust[b] consume and where thieves break in and steal, 20 but lay up for yourselves treasures in heaven, where neither moth nor rust[b] consumes and where thieves do not break in and steal; 21 for where your treasure is, there will your heart be also."

## LUKE 12.22–34

22 And he said to his disciples, "Therefore, I tell you, do not be anxious about your life, what you shall eat, nor about your body, what you shall put on. 23 For life is more than food, and the body more than clothing. 24 Consider the ravens: they neither sow nor reap, they have neither storehouse nor barn, and yet God feeds them. Of how much more value are you than the birds? 25 And which of you by being anxious can add a cubit to his span of life?[a] 26 If then you are not able to do as small a thing as that, why are you anxious about the rest? 27 Consider the lilies, how they grow; they neither toil nor spin,[c] yet I tell you, even Solomon in all his glory was not arrayed like one of these. 28 But if God so clothes the grass which is alive in the field today and tomorrow is thrown into the oven, how much more will he clothe you, O men of little faith? 29 And do not seek what you are to eat and what you are to drink, nor be of anxious mind. 30 For all the nations of the world seek these things; and your Father knows that you need them. 31 Instead, seek his[d] kingdom, and these things shall be yours as well. 32 Fear not, little flock, for it is your Father's good pleasure to give you the kingdom. 33 Sell your possessions, and give alms; provide yourselves with purses that do not grow old, with a treasure in the heavens that does not fail,

where no thief approaches and no moth destroys. 34 For where your treasure is, there will your heart be also."

---

a  Or *to his stature.*
b  Or *worm.*
c  Some read *consider the lilies; they neither spin nor weave.*
d  Some read *God's.*
See above Secs. 35 (p. 130), 32 (p. 125).

# 158. *Watchfulness and Faithfulness*

## MATT 24.43–51

43 "But know this, that if the householder had known in what part of the night the thief was coming, he would have watched and would not have let his house be broken into. 44 Therefore you also must be ready; for the Son of man is coming at an hour you do not expect. 45 Who then is the faithful and wise servant, whom his master has set over his household, to give them their food at the proper time? 46 Blessed is that servant whom his master when he comes will find so doing. 47 Truly, I say to you, he will set him over all his possessions. 48 But if that wicked servant says to himself, 'My master is delayed,' 49 and begins to beat his fellow servants, and eats and drinks with the drunken, 50 the master of that servant will come on a day when he does not expect him and at an hour he does not know, 51 and will punishᶜ him, and put him with the hypocrites; there men will weep and gnash their teeth."

## LUKE 12.35–46

35 "Let your loins be girded and your lamps burning, 36 and be like men who are waiting for their master to come home from the marriage feast, so that they may open to him at once when he comes and knocks. 37 Blessed are those servants whom the master finds awake when he comes; truly, I say to you, he will gird himself and have them sit at table and come and serve them. 38 If he comes in the second watch, or in the third, and finds them so, blessed are those servants! 39 But know this, that if the householder had known at what hour the thief was coming, he would have been awake andᶠ would not have left his house to be broken into. 40 You also must be ready; for the Son of man is coming at an hour you do not expect." 41 Peter said, "Lord, are you telling this parable for us or for all?" 42 And the Lord said, "Who then is the faithful and wise steward, whom his master will set over his household, to give them their portion of food at the proper time? 43 Blessed is that servant whom his master when he comes will find so doing. 44 Truly I tell you, he will set him over all his possessions. 45 But if that servant says to himself. 'My master is delayed in coming,' and begins to beat the menservants and the maidservants, and to eat and drink and get drunk, 46 the master of that servant will come on a day when he does not expect him and at an hour he does not know, and will punish him, and put him with the unfaithful."

---

e  Or *cut him in pieces.*
f  Some omit *would have been awake and.*

## COMMENTARY

The point of this section, as in the preceding, is that no one knows when the Messiah will come and that man must be ready at all times. The rabbinic formulation of the thought is: "Three things come unexpectedly: the Messiah, the discovery of treasure, and the scorpion."[1] There is no rabbinic parallel to this section.

46 *and will punish him.* Gr. *dichotomēsei*, used in the LXX for Heb. *shasaf*; the meaning is "to cut in pieces,"[2] and it is unlikely that this is the meaning here. Note the parallel "and put him with the hypocrites," lit., "to place his portion [Heb. *ḥeleq*] with."[3] Manson has pointed out the Aram. *nattaḥ* means "to take away" or "separate," which makes good sense here. The confusion arose since the Heb. *nittaḥ* means "to cut in pieces."[4]

*gnash their teeth*  A favorite expression with Matt.[5]

## NOTES

1. B. Sanh. 97a.
2. Cf. 2 Sam. 12.31; 1 Chron. 20.3; Sus. 59; Amos (LXX) 1.3.
3. Cf., e.g., TJ Ber. 4, 7d = B. ibid. 28b.
4. Manson, *SJ*, p. 118.
5. Cf. Matt. 13.42; 22.13, 25, 30; 8.13.

# 159. *The Servant's Wages*

## LUKE 12.47-48

47 "And that servant who knew his master's will, but did not make ready or act according to his will, shall receive a severe beating. 48 But he who did not know, and did what deserved a beating, shall receive a light beating. Everyone to whom much is given, of him will much be required; and of him to whom men commit much they will demand the more."

## COMMENTARY

47 *And that servant who knew his master's will*  The punishment is determined by whether the servant acted willfully or out of ignorance. This distinction is made in the MT, i.e., whether one committed an offense with "a high hand," i.e., willfully, or not.[1] In rabbinic literature this is treated extensively, and ignorance is defined so that it includes forgetfulness at the moment of commission: "A great rule they laid down concerning the Sabbath. Whosoever forgetful of the principle of the Sabbath, committed

many acts of works on many Sabbaths, is liable only to one sin-offering; but if mindful of the principle of the Sabbath he yet committed many acts of works on many Sabbaths, he is liable for every Sabbath [which he profaned]."[2] Another source reads, "It is better to sin unknowingly than to sin willfully."[3]

## NOTES

1. E.g., Num. 15.30.
2. M. Shab. 7.1.
3. T. Sot. 15.10 (p. 322); B. BB 6b; B. Shab. 148b; B. Beẓ. 30a; Deut. R. 7; see Matt. 21.31 (p. 353).

## 160. *Interpreting the Present Time*

### M A T T . 1 0 . 3 4 – 3 6

34 "Do not think that I have come to bring peace on earth; I have not come to bring peace, but a sword. 35 For I have come to set a man against his father, and a daughter against her mother, and a daughter-in-law against her mother-in-law; 36 and a man's foes will be those of his own household."

### I B I D 1 6 . 2 – 3

2 He answered them,[g] "When it is evening you say, 'It will be fair weather, for the sky is red.' 3 And in the morning, 'It will be stormy today, for the sky is red and threatening!' You know how to interpret the appearance of the sky, but you cannot interpret the signs of the times."

### L U K E 1 2 . 4 9 – 5 6

49 "I came to cast fire upon the earth; and would that it were already kindled! 50 I have a baptism to be baptized with; and how I am constrained until it is accomplished! 51 Do you think that I have come to give peace on earth! No, I tell you, but rather division; 52 for henceforth in one house there will be five divided, three against two and two against three; 53 they will be divided, father against son, and son against father, mother against daughter and daughter against her mother, mother-in-law against her daughter-in-law and daughter-in-law against her mother-in-law." 54 He also said to the multitudes, "When you see a cloud rising in the west, you say at once, 'A shower is coming'; and so it happens. 55 And when you see the south wind blowing you say, 'There will be scorching heat'; and it happens. 56 You hypocrites! You know how to interpret the appearance of earth and sky; but why do you not know how to interpret the present time?"

---

g Some ancient authorities omit from here to the end of v. 3.
See above Secs. 61 (p. 186) 119 (p. 251).

# 161. *Agreement with One's Accuser*

## MATT. 5.25–26

25 "Make friends quickly with your accuser, while you are going with him to court, lest your accuser hand you over to the judge, and the judge to the guard, and you be put in prison; 26 truly, I say to you, you will never get out till you have paid the last penny."

## LUKE 12.57–59

57 "And why do you not judge for yourselves what is right? 58 As you go with your accuser before the magistrate, make an effort to settle with him on the way, lest he drag you to the judge, and the judge hand you over to the officer, and the officer put you in prison. 59 I tell you you will never get out till you have paid the very last copper."

See above Sec. 22 (p. 90).

# 162. *Repentance or Destruction*

## LUKE 13.1–9

1 There were some present at that very time who told him of the Galileans whose blood Pilate had mingled with their sacrifices. 2 And he answered them, "Do you think that these Galileans were worse sinners than all the other Galileans, because they suffered this? 3 I tell you, No; but unless you repent you will all likewise perish. 4 Or those eighteen upon whom the tower in Siloam fell and killed them, do you think that they were worse offenders than all the others who dwelt in Jerusalem? 5 I tell you, No; but unless you repent you will all likewise perish." 6 And he told this parable: "A man had a fig tree planted in his vineyard; and he came seeking fruit on it and found none. 7 And he said to the vine dresser, 'Lo, these three years I have come seeking fruit on this fig tree, and I find none. Cut it down; why should it use up the ground?' 8 And he answered him, 'Let it alone, sir, this year also, till I dig around it and put on manure. 9 And if it bears fruit next year, well and good; but if not you can cut it down.' "

## COMMENTARY

This section consists of three parts: a massacre of Galileans by Pilate, an accident at the tower of Siloam, and a parable, all of which are cited to exhort the hearer to repentance.

1 *the Galileans whose blood Pilate had mingled with their sacrifices* This event is not recorded elsewhere. It must have taken place, however, in Jerusalem when these Galileans came up to the Temple to offer their sacrifices, and they were slaughtered by Pilate's troops. Pilate's cruelty is well known from the

sources of antiquity.[1] "The question at once arises whether this tale of Pilate's outburst is fact or fiction; and this goes with the further question why the story was brought to Jesus. Two answers may be given to this latter question. Either the story was told in the hope that it would rouse Jesus to lead a revolt against Rome, or in the hope that in his indignation He would say something about Pilate which might be used in evidence against him on a charge of sedition. In the latter case the story did not even need to be true so long as it achieved its object. Those who came and told it would be, of course, enemies of Jesus. In the former case the tellers of the tale would presumably be ardent patriots."[2]

4 *those eighteen upon whom the tower of Siloam fell and killed them*   This accident is likewise not recorded elsewhere. The tower of Siloam was located at the juncture of the south and east walls of the city. It is conjectured that the collapse was caused by the building operations carried on by Pilate to improve the water supply of Jerusalem.[3]

6 *And he told this parable*   Although this parable deals with a fig tree which did not produce figs, there is no other connection between this and the miracle in Matt. 20.18–22, Mark 11.11–14, 20–25, which is lacking in Luke. There is, however, a striking parallel to this parable in the Syriac *Story of Aḥikar:* "I answered and said to him, 'My son, thou hast been to me like that palm tree that stood by a river, and cast all its fruit into the river, and when its lord came to cut it down, it said to him, 'Let me alone this year, and I will bring thee forth carobs.' And its lord said unto it, 'Thou hast not been industrious in what is thine own, and how wilt thou be industrious in what is not thine own.' "[4]

### NOTES

1. See Josephus, *Ant.* XVIII 3.1; XVII.9.3; XX.5.3; *BJ* II.3.3; 9.4, and below p. 000 n. 3.
2. Manson, *SJ*, p. 273.
3. See Josephus, *Ant.* XVIII.60; *BJ* II.175. Manson, *SJ*, p. 274.
4. *Story of Aḥikar* 35 (Syriac) in Charles, *Apocrypha and Pseudepigrapha*, 2:775. Perhaps the Syriac is influenced by the NT.

## 163. *The Healing of the Woman with a Spirit of Infirmity*

### LUKE 13.10–17

10 Now he was teaching in one of the synagogues on the sabbath. 11 And there was a woman who had a spirit of infirmity for eighteen years; she was bent over and could not fully straighten herself. 12 And when Jesus saw her, he called her and said to her, "Woman, you are freed from your infirmity." 13 And he laid his hands upon her, and immediately she was made straight, and she praised God. 14 But the ruler of the synagogue, indignant because Jesus had healed on the sabbath, said to the people,

"There are six days on which work ought to be done; come on those days and be healed, and not on the sabbath day." 15 Then the Lord answered him, "You hypocrites! Does not each of you on the sabbath untie his ox or his ass from the manager, and lead it away to water it? 16 And ought not this woman, a daughter of Abraham whom Satan bound for eighteen years, be loosed from this bond on the sabbath day?" 17 As he said this, all his adversaries were put to shame; and all the people rejoiced at all the glorious things that were done by him.

## COMMENTARY

This story is unique to Luke but is one of the healing-on-the Sabbath stories, cf. Matt. 12.11–12, Luke 14.5. The question addressed here is whether it is permitted to heal on the Sabbath, especially when there is no emergency.

15 *Then the Lord answered* "The argument which Jesus employs is scarcely sound. The ox must be watered every day, or it would suffer greatly. Cruelty to animals was abhorrent to the Rabbis. But the woman, who had been rheumatic for eighteen years, could well have waited another day. Unsound arguments of this kind would have been speedily detected by the trained Rabbis."[1] It is of note that Jesus' argument is a *qal v'homer* (see above p. 142), but Luke omits the traditional formula.

*untie his ox . . . to water it*   The rules on the care of animals especially on the Sabbath are detailed in the Mishnah and Talmud, and involve both the tying and untying of knots and the watering of cattle.[2]

16 *a daughter of Abraham*   A term frequently used for a Jewess.[3]

## NOTES

1. Montefiore, *SG*, 2:501. See Manson, *SJ*, p. 190.
2. See specifically M. Shab. 5.1–4; 2.2; 15.1–2; B. ibid. 113a; M. Er. 1–4; B. ibid. 20b–21a.
3. See, e.g., B. Git. 89a; B. Ket. 72b; B. Suk. 49b; B. Pes. 110b; B. Sanh. 94b.

# *164. The Parables of the Mustard Seed and the Leaven*

## MATT. 13.31–33

31 Another parable he put before them, saying, "The kingdom of heaven is like a grain of mustard seed which a man took and sowed in his field; 32 it is the smallest of all seeds, but when it has grown it is the greatest of shrubs and becomes a tree, so that the birds of the air come and make nests in its branches." 33 He told them another parable. "The kingdom of heaven is like leaven which a woman took and hid in three measures of meal, till it was all leavened."

## MARK 4.30–32

30 And he said, "With what can we compare the kingdom of God, or what parable shall we use for it? 31 It is like a grain of mustard seed, which, when sown upon the

ground, is the smallest of all the seeds on earth; 32 yet when it is sown it grows up and becomes the greatest of all shrubs, and puts forth large branches, so that the birds of the air can make nests in its shade."

## Luke 13.18–21

18 He said therefore, "What is the kingdom of God like? And to what shall I compare it? 19 It is like a grain of mustard seed which a man took and sowed in his garden; and it grew and became a tree, and the birds of the air made nests in its branches." 20 And again he said, "To what shall I compare the kingdom of God? 21 It is like leaven which a woman took and hid in three measures of meal, till it was all leavened." See above Secs. 97, 98 (pp. 224, 225).

# 165. Exclusion from the Kingdom

## Matt. 7.13–14

13 "Enter by the narrow gate; for the gate is wide and the way is easy,[h] that leads to destruction, and those who enter by it are many. 14 For the gate is narrow and the way is hard, that leads to life, and those who find it are few."

## Ibid. 25.10–12

10 "And the door was shut. 11 Afterwards the other maidens came also saying, 'Lord, Lord, open to us.' 12 But he replied, 'Truly, I say to you, I do not know you.' "

## Ibid. 7.22–23

22 "On that day many will say to me, 'Lord, Lord, did we not prophesy in your name, and cast out demons in your name, and do many mighty works in your name? 23 And then will I declare to them, 'I never knew you; depart from me, you evildoers.' "

## Ibid. 8.11–12

11 "I tell you, many will come from east and west and sit at table with Abraham, Isaac, and Jacob in the kingdom of heaven, 12 while the sons of the kingdom will be thrown into the outer darkness; there men will weep and gnash their teeth."

## Ibid. 19.30

"But many that are first will be last, and the last first."

## Ibid. 20.16

"So that the last will be first and the first last."

## MARK 10.31

"But many that are first will be last, and the last first."

## LUKE 13.22–30

22 He went on his way through towns and villages, teaching, and journeying toward Jerusalem. 23 And someone said to him, "Lord, will those who are saved be few?" And he said to them, 24 "Strive to enter by the narrow door; for many, I tell you, will seek to enter and will not be able. 25 When once a householder has risen up and shut the door, you will begin to stand outside and to knock at the door, saying, 'Lord, open to us.' He will answer you, 'I do not know where you come from.' 26 Then you will begin to say, 'We ate and drank in your presence, and you taught in our streets.' 27 But he will say, 'I tell you I do not know where you come from; depart from me, all you workers of iniquity.' 28 There you will weep and gnash your teeth, when you see Abraham and Isaac and Jacob and all the prophets in the kingdom of God and you yourselves thrust out. 29 And men will come from east and west, and from north and south, and sit at table in the kingdom of God. 30 And behold, some are last who will be first, and some are first who will be last."

---

h Some read *for the way is wide and easy.*
See above Secs. 40 (p. 145), 46 (p. 154).

## *166. The Departure from Galilee*

### LUKE 13.31–33

31 At that very hour some Pharisees came, and said to him, "Get away from here, for Herod wants to kill you." 32 And he said to them, "Go and tell that fox, 'Behold, I cast out demons and perform cures today and tomorrow, and the third day I finish my course. 33 Nevertheless I must go on my way today and tomorrow and the day following; for it cannot be that a prophet should perish from Jerusalem.' "

### COMMENTARY

31 *some Pharisees came*   Who they were is uncertain. Perhaps they were those friendly to Jesus or they were sent by Herod to convince Jesus to leave his realm. Jesus was either in Galilee or in Perea.

32 *Go tell that fox*   In rabbinic sources the epithet "fox" or the figure of the fox in parables connotes one who is inferior, as when comparing a fox and a lion; or it describes one who is sly and double-dealing.[1]

*today and tomorrow and the third day*   Perhaps from the Heb. *hayom, mahar, umaharataim—hayom* and *mahar,* i.e., "today and tomorrow," meaning a short time; *maharataim,* "the third day," means "and following this short period either I finish my work here or I am finished."[2]

33 *I must go on my way*   Either "I must leave this area" or it is a euphemism for dying, cf. 1 Kings 2.2.

*For it cannot be . . . from Jerusalem*   A very difficult verse. The Gr. *hoti ouk endechetai* can be understood as "it is not appropriate that," and the meaning is that if a prophet is to die it is fitting that it happen in Jerusalem.

## NOTES

1. See Cant. R. 2.15, 102a; B. Ber. 61b; TJ Shev. 9, 39a (11); B. BQ 117a; TJ Shab. 12c (44), B. Ḥag. 14a; M. Avot 4.15.
2. See, E.g., *Mid. Ps.* 12.1 (52b).

## 167. The Lament Over Jerusalem

### MATT. 23.37–39

37 "O Jerusalem, Jerusalem, killing the prophets and stoning those who are sent to you! How often would I have gathered your children together as a hen gathers her brood under her wings, and you would not! 38 Behold, your house is forsaken and desolate![i] 39 For I tell you, you will not see me again, until you say, 'Blessed be he who comes in the name of the Lord.' "

### LUKE 13.34–35

34 "O Jerusalem, Jerusalem, killing the prophets and stoning those who are sent to you! How often would I have gathered your children together as a hen gathers her brood under her wings, and you would not! 35 Behold, your house is forsaken! And I tell you, you will not see me until you say, 'Blessed be he who comes in the name of the Lord.' "

---

i  Some texts omit *and desolate.*
See below Sec. 211 (p. 374).

## 168. The Healing of a Man with Dropsy

### LUKE 14.1–6

1 One sabbath when he went to dine at the house of a ruler who belonged to the Pharisees, they were watching him. 2 And behold, there was a man before him who had dropsy. 3 And Jesus spoke to the lawyers and Pharisees, saying, "Is it lawful to heal on the sabbath or not?" 4 But they were silent. Then he took him and healed him, and let him go. 5 And he said to them, "Which of you having an ass[j] or an ox that has fallen into a well, will not immediately pull him out on a sabbath day?" 6 And they could not reply to this.

---

j  Some read *a son or an ox.*

## COMMENTARY

This passage is one of the Sabbath-healing stories; cf. Matt. 12.11–12, Luke 13.10–17. On the question about healing on the Sabbath and Jesus' answer, see above Sec. 70 (p. 199).

2 *dropsy* Gr. *hudrōpikos*. In rabbinic literature *idrophiqos* or *hidroqan*.[1] Dropsy is a condition in which there is an inordinate amount of fluid in the tissues or cavities of the body. It is a term which appears frequently in medical works from Hippocrates onwards.[2]

## NOTES

1. Cf. Lev. R. 15.2; B. Ber. 25a, 62b; B. Er. 41b; B. Shab. 33a.
2. See J. Preuss, *Biblisch-Talmudische Medizin* (Berlin, 1923), pp. 190–191.

# 169. On Humility

## Luke 14.7–14

7 Now he told a parable to those who were invited, when he marked how they chose the places of honor, saying to them, 8 "When you are invited by anyone to a marriage feast, do not sit down in a place of honor, lest a more eminent man than you be invited by him; 9 and he who invited you both will come and say to you, 'Give place to this man,' and then you will begin with shame to take the lowest place. 10 But when you are invited, go and sit in the lowest place, so that when your host comes he may say to you, 'Friend, go up higher'; then you will be honored in the presence of all who sit at table with you. 11 For everyone who exalts himself will be humbled, and he who humbles himself will be exalted." 12 He said also to the man who had invited him, "When you give a dinner or a banquet, do not invite your friends or your brothers or your kinsmen or rich neighbors, lest they also invite you in return, and you be repaid. 13 But when you give a feast, invite the poor, the maimed, the lame, the blind, 14 and you will be blessed, because they cannot repay you. You will be repaid at the resurrection of the just."

## COMMENTARY

7 *Now he told a parable*, etc. In its present form the parabolic element seems to be secondary to the instruction on etiquette at a banquet. It most probably was a parable similar to the Laborers in the Vineyard (Matt. 20.1–16) and the Sons of Zebedee (Mark 10.35–45). "Greatness in the Kingdom, whether in its present manifestation or in its final consummation, is determined not by our opinion of our deserts but by God's judgement. And we know from other sayings how God will determine the question of precedence. He will be greatest who is servant of all. One thing is certain. Greatness in the Kingdom will not be attained by standing on one's dignity."[1]

8 *When you are invited*, etc.     There is a striking parallel in rabbinic literature: "R. Simeon b. Azzai said: 'Stay two or three seats below your place [i.e., where you feel you should sit], and sit there until they say to you, 'Come up!' Do not begin by going up because they may say to you, 'Go down!' It is better that they say to you, 'Go up,' than that they say to you, 'Go down!' "[2]

*a place of honor*   There were set rules about the seating of guests and serving of gifts to be observed by the master of the banquet, called in Greek *architriklinos*, and these rules were observed by Jews as well as by Greeks and Romans.[3] It is difficult to ascertain which were the most honorable places at a banquet because there were various customs in vogue—Persian, Greek, and Roman as well as Jewish. The Talmud states that where there were three couches the middle one was for the worthiest, the left for the second, and the right for the third.[4] Among the Greeks the usual custom was for a couch to serve two persons, but both Greeks and Romans frequently had as many as four to one couch.[5]

Similar in spirit to this passage is Prov. 25.6: *Do not put yourself forward in the king's presence or stand in the place of the great; for it is better to be told, "Come up here," than to be put lower in the presence of the prince.*[6]

11 *For everyone who exalts himself*, etc.   A favorite and oft-quoted statement of the gospel tradition.[7]

### NOTES

1. Manson, *SJ*, p. 278.
2. Lev. R. 1.5. Theophrastus, *Characters* 21.2 states that one of the characteristics of a vain person is that when invited to a banquet he tries to find himself a seat of honor next to the host.
3. See M. Ber. 7; T. ibid. 4–7 (pp. 9–16).
4. See below p. 372 n.19.
5. See A. C. Bouquet, *Everyday Life in New Testament Times* (1954), pp. 69–74; Plato, *Sym.* 175A; W. A. Becker, *Charicles*, Sc. VI, Exc. 1; idem, *Gallus* Sc. 9, Exc. 1.2.
6. See also Sira 3.17–20.
7. Cf. Matt. 18.4, 23.12; Luke 18.14. An independent version of this parable in some MSS after Matt. 20.28. Still another in a papyrus frag. from Oxyrhynchus (Grenfell and Hunt, *New Sayings of Jesus*, p. 18; James, *Apoc. NT*, p. 26).

## *170. The Parable of the Great Supper*

### MATT. 22.1–10

1 And again Jesus spoke to them in parables saying, 2 "The kingdom of heaven may be compared to a king who gave a marriage feast for his son, 3 and sent his servants to call those who were invited to the marriage feast; but they would not come. 4 Again he sent other servants saying, 'Tell those who are invited, Behold, I have made ready my dinner, my oxen and my fat calves are killed, and everything is ready; come to the marriage feast.' 5 But they made light of it and went off, one to his farm, another to

his business, 6 while the rest seized his servants, treated them shamefully, and killed them. 7 The king was angry, and he sent his troops and destroyed those murderers and burned their city. 8 Then he said to his servants, 'The wedding is ready, but those invited were not worthy. 9 Go therefore to the thoroughfares, and invite to the marriage feast as many as you find.' 10 And those servants went out into the streets and gathered all whom they found, both bad and good; so the wedding hall was filled with guests."

## LUKE 14.15-24

15 When one of those who sat at table with him heard this, he said to him, "Blessed is he who shall eat bread in the kingdom of God!" 16 But he said to him, "A man once gave a great banquet, and invited many; 17 and at the time for the banquet he sent his servant to say to those who had been invited, 'Come; for all is now ready.' 18 But they all alike began to make excuses. The first said to him, 'I have bought a field, and I must go out and see it; I pray you, have me excused.' 19 And another said, 'I have bought five yoke of oxen, and I go to examine them; I pray you, have me excused.' 20 And another said, 'I have married a wife, and therefore I cannot come.' 21 So the servant came and reported this to his master. Then the householder in anger said to his servant, 'Go out quickly to the streets and lanes of the city, and bring in the poor and maimed and blind and lame.' 22 And the servant said, 'Sir, what you commanded has been done, and still there is room.' 23 And the master said to the servant, 'Go out to the highways and hedges, and compel people to come in, that my house may be filled. 24 For I tell you, none of those men who were invited shall taste my banquet.' " See below Sec. 205 (p. 356).

# 171. The Cost of Discipleship

## MATT. 10.37-38

37 "He who loves father or mother more than me is not worthy of me; and he who loves son or daughter more than me is not worthy of me; 38 and he who does not take his cross and follow me is not worthy of me."

## LUKE 14.25-35

25 Now great multitudes accompanied him; and he turned and said to them, 26 "If anyone comes to me and does not hate his own father and mother and wife and children and brothers and sisters, yes, and even his own life, he cannot be my disciple. 27 Whoever does not bear his own cross and come after me, cannot be my disciple. 28 For which of you, desiring to build a tower, does not first sit down and count the cost, whether he has enough to complete it? 29 Otherwise, when he had laid a foundation, and is not able to finish, all who see it begin to mock him, 30 saying, 'This man began to build, and was not able to finish.' 31 Or what king, going to encounter another king in war, will not sit down first and take counsel whether he is able with ten thousand to meet him who comes against him with twenty thousand?

32 And if not, while the other is yet a great way off, he sends an embassy and asks terms of peace. 33 So therefore, whoever of you does not renounce all that he has cannot be my disciple. 34 Salt is good; but if salt has lost its taste, how shall its saltness be restored? 35 It is fit neither for the land nor for the dunghill; men throw it away. He who has ears to hear, let him hear."

## COMMENTARY

Luke v. 26 *If anyone comes*, etc.   See above to Matt. 16.24–28 (p. 257).

28 *For which of you*, etc.   There are no rabbinic parallels to these two illustrations. The thrust is to contemplate the cost of an endeavor on which you are about to embark, here becoming a disciple. In this vein cf. "Who is wise? He who can anticipate the future."[1]

34 *Salt is good*,etc.   See above Sec. 20 (p. 81).

## NOTES

1. B. Tem. 32a.

# 172. *The Lost Sheep and the Lost Coin*

### MATT. 18.12–14

12 "What do you think? If a man has a hundred sheep, and one of them has gone astray, does he not leave the ninety-nine on the hills and go in search of the one that went astray? 13 And if he finds it, truly, I say to you, he rejoices over it more than over the ninety-nine that never went astray. 14 So it is not the will of my Father who is in heaven that one of these little ones should perish."

### LUKE 15.1–10

1 Now the tax collectors and sinners were all drawing near to hear him. 2 And the Pharisees and the scribes murmured, saying, "This man receives sinners and eats with them." 3 So he told them this parable: 4 "What man of you, having a hundred sheep, if he has lost one of them, does not leave the ninety-nine in the wilderness, and go after the one which is lost, until he finds it? 5 And when he has found it, he lays it on his shoulders, rejoicing. 6 And when he comes home, he calls together his friends and his neighbors, saying to them, 'Rejoice with me, for I have found my sheep which was lost.' 7 Even so, I tell you, there will be more joy in heaven over one sinner who repents than over ninety-nine righteous persons who need no repentance. 8 Or what woman, having ten silver coins, if she loses one coin, does not light a lamp and sweep the house and seek diligently until she finds it? 9 And when she has found it, she calls together her friends and neighbors, saying, 'Rejoice with me, for I have found the coin which I had lost.' 10 Even so, I tell you, there is joy before the angels of God over one sinner who repents."

On the Lost Sheep see above Sec. 133 (p. 269).

## COMMENTARY

The point of both parables is the importance of outreach to sinners to bring them back to the straight and narrow path. "The scribes and Pharisees doubted the wisdom and propriety of such familiar friendship with publicans and sinners. . . . an old Rabbincal rule from Mekhilta on Exod. 18.1 [reads] 'Let not a man associate with the wicked, not even to bring him nigh to the Law.' This no doubt, represents the strictest attitude taken by the sharpest critics of Jesus. Whether every Pharisee would have maintained this rule in full strictness is another question. Jesus' reply to those who did criticise Him is given in the parables."[1]

Luke v. 8 *Or what woman*, etc.   Note: "If a man loses a coin in his house he kindles many lights, and seeks till he finds it. If for something which affords only an hour's life in this world, a man kindles many lights, and searches till he finds it, how much more should you dig as for hidden treasure after the words of the Law, which gives both life in this world and in the world-to-come."[2]

## NOTES

1. Manson, *SJ*, p. 283.
2. Cant. R. 1.9.

# 173. *The Prodigal Son*

## Luke 15.11–32

11 And he said, "There was a man who had two sons; 12 and the younger of them said to his father, 'Father, give me the share of property that falls to me.' And he divided his living between them. 13 Not many days later, the younger son gathered all he had and took his journey into a far country, and there he squandered his property in loose living. 14 And when he had spent everything, a great famine arose in that country, and he began to be in want. 15 So he went and joined himself to one of the citizens of that country, who sent him into his fields to feed swine. 16 And he would gladly have fed on[k] the pods that the swine ate; and no one gave him anything. 17 But when he came to himself he said, 'How many of my father's hired servants have bread enough to spare, but I perish here with hunger! 18 I will arise and go to my father, and I will say to him, "Father, I have sinned against heaven and before you; 19 I am no longer worthy to be called your son; treat me as one of your hired servants." ' 20 And he arose and came to his father. But while he was yet at a distance, his father saw him and had compassion, and ran and embraced him and kissed him. 21 And the son said to him, 'Father, I have sinned against heaven and before you; I am no longer worthy to be called your son.'[l] 22 But the father said to his servants, 'Bring quickly the best robe, and put it on him; and put a ring on his hand, and shoes on his feet; 23 and bring the fatted calf and kill it, and let us eat and make merry; 24

for this my son was dead, and is alive again; he was lost, and is found.' And they began to make merry. 25 Now his elder son was in the field; and as he came and drew near to the house, he heard music and dancing. 26 And he called one of the servants and asked what this meant. 27 And he said to him, 'Your brother has come, and your father has killed the fatted calf, because he has received him safe and sound.' 28 But he was angry and refused to go in. His father came out and entreated him, 29 but he answered his father, 'Lo, these many years I have served you, and I never disobeyed your command; yet you never gave me a kid, that I might make merry with my friends. 30 But when this son of yours came, who has devoured your living with harlots, you killed for him the fatted calf!' 31 And he said to him, 'Son, you are always with me, and all that is mine is yours. 32 It is fitting to make merry and be glad, for this your brother was dead, and is alive; he was lost, and is found.' "

---

k  Others *filled his belly;* still others *filled his belly and fed on.*
l  Others add *treat me as one of your hired servants*

## COMMENTARY

The Parable of the Prodigal Son, or the Two Sons, most likely goes back to Jewish sources, but no exact parallel survives. Some parallel phrases have been traced to *Aḥikar* and some of the ideas to Philo.[1] More cogent proof is the fact that in a Genizah fragment the Gaon R. Aḥa quotes Sanh. 99a, not extant in toto in our texts, in which R. Abbahu cites a parable of "a king who had two sons, one who went in the proper way, the other who went out to 'evil culture.' "[2] Abrahams comments, "This looks like a reminiscence of Luke's Parable, and it may have been removed from the Talmud text by scribes more cognizant than Abbahu was of the source of the story."[3] Ginzberg comments, "The source for the Parable . . . is not known to me. Obviously R. Aḥa must have had it in his text of the Talmud. . . . In any event, it is the short, original form of the New Testament parable of the prodigal son."[4]

12 *give me the share of property that falls to me*  This phrase is common in the papyri and means either privileges to which one is entitled or obligations which one is bound to meet. The same phrase occurs in Aramaic with similar meanings.[5] It is not completely clear how this request and the father's compliance conform to Jewish law and usage. According to the MT, Deut. 21.15–17, Num. 27.8–11, sons inherit property following a set procedure. In the rabbinic period the Sages introduced the will or deed of gift *inter vivos*, the details of which are contained in the Mishnah, BB, chap. 8. If the owner wished to dispose of his property by gift it generally took effect at his death and was used to circumvent the biblical requirement of "automatic inheritance." During the lifetime of the donor he generally held the property but could not, according to the law, dispose of it. The beneficiary might have use of it but could not dispose of it because of the donor's life interest. Here the

younger son requests immediate possession of what would normally have come to him only at the death of the father. This could have been done legally; the younger son receives his inheritance immediately and the remainder was now to become the sole inheritance of the elder brother, presumably on the death of the father. Most likely this was common practice, but was not considered to be advisable, as attested by Ben Sira: "To son or wife, to brother or friend, give no power over thyself while thou livest; and give not thy goods to another so as to have to ask for them again. . . . For it is better that thy children ask of thee than that thou shouldst look to the hand of thy sons. . . . When the days of thy life are ended, in the day of death, distribute thine inheritance."[6]

13 *far country*  Possibly Heb. *medinat hayam*, "a country across the sea."[7]

15 *to feed swine*  The lowest and most degrading of all occupations. "Cursed is the man who rears swine."[8]

16 *pods*  Seed pods of the carob tree *(ceratonia siliqua)* used to feed animals. In Heb. usage the carob is food of the poor. "When Israelites are reduced to eating carob-pods, they repent."[9]

17 *when he came to himself*  I.e., came to his senses or repented. Probably a Semitism, *hazar bo*, but also idiomatic in Greek as well as in Latin. Note that the Palestinian Rabbis had a saying, "When a son [abroad] goes barefoot [through poverty] he remembers the comfort of his father's house."[10]

18 *I have sinned against heaven and before you*  The meaning is "against God and you." It is strange that Luke would use "Heaven" for "God," although it was regularly used by Jews for the Deity; see above p. 72. Manson suggests, "The Greek words translated 'I have sinned against heaven' may mean either 'I have sinned heaven-high,' i.e. I have heaped transgression upon transgression till the sum of my sins is monstrous (cf. Ezra 9.6) or 'I have sinned against God, heaven being the common-Jewish periphrasis for God. . . . The latter interpretation is preferable."[11] The phrase "before you" means "in your estimation"; see above p. 17.

19 *I am no longer worthy to be called your son*  The father-son relationship between God and man is found frequently in the MT and in rabbinic literature. In one passage the question arises as to whether Israel can lose the name "son of God" through unacceptable behavior or whether that relationship is unaffected by it. R. Judah b. Ilai argues that they lose the name, R. Meir maintains that they do not.[12]

20 *ran and embraced him and kissed him*  For this sequence of acts see Gen. 33.4.[13]

As stated above, there is no direct rabbinic parallel to this parable, but the following captures some of the same feeling:

> A king's son fell into evil courses. The king sent his tutor to him with the message "Repent *[hazor]*, my son [or come to yourself, as in Luke 15.16]." But the son sent to his father to say, "How can I [lit. with what face can I

return [or repent]? I am ashamed [to come] before thee." Then the father sent to him to say, "Can a son be ashamed to return to his father? If you return, do you not return to your father?" So God sent Jeremiah to the Israelites who had sinned against him. He said to Jeremiah, "Tell My sons to return [repent]." They replied, "How can we [with what face can we] return to God?" Then God said to them, "My sons, if you return, is it not to your Father that you return?"[14]

**22** *put a ring* Lit., "give," which reflects a Semitic background to the Greek, for in Heb. the verb "give" is often used for "put."

### NOTES

1. See G. Friedlander, *The Grace of God* (1910).
2. L. Ginzberg, *Geonica* (New York, 1909), 2:377.
3. Abrahams, *Studies I*, p. 92.
4. Ginzberg, op cit., p. 351.
5. See A. E. Cowley, *The Aramaic Papyri of the Fifth Century* (Oxford: Clarendon Press, 1923), no. 28. Cf. Gen. R. 98.
6. Sira 33.19–23.
7. E.g., M. Yev. 2.9; 4.6; 10.1, 4.
8. B. BQ 82b. Cf. also TJ Ter. 8, 46b (62); Gen. R. 63.8.
9. Lev. R. 13.3; *PR* 42 (177a); Cant. R. 1.4; B. Hag. 9b. Note also Isa. 1.20, reading *haruv*, "carob," for *herev*, "sword," in *these* sources.
10. Lam. R. 1.7 (53b).
11. Manson, *SJ*, p. 288.
12. B. Qid. 36a. See also Sifre Deut. 96.
13. See also Acts 20.37.
14. Deut. R. 2.24.

# 174. The Unjust Steward

## LUKE 16.1–13

1 He also said to the disciples, "There was a rich man who had a steward, and charges were brought to him that this man was wasting his goods. 2 And he called him and said to him, 'What is this that I hear about you? Turn in the account of your stewardship, for you can no longer be steward.' 3 And the steward said to himself, 'What shall I do, since my master is taking the stewardship away from me? I am not strong enough to dig, and I am ashamed to beg. 4 I have decided what to do, so that people may receive me into their houses when I am put out of the stewardship.' 5 So, summoning his master's debtors one by one, he said to the first, 'How much do you owe my master?' 6 He said, 'A hundred measures of oil.' And he said to him, 'Take your bill, and sit down quickly and write fifty.' 7 Then he said to another, 'And how much do you owe?' He said, 'A hundred measures of wheat.' He said to him, 'Take your bill, and write eighty.' 8 The master commended the dishonest steward for his prudence; for the sons of this world[m] are wiser in their own generation than the sons of light. 9 And I tell you, make friends for yourselves by means of unrighteous

mammon, so that when it fails they may receive you into the eternal habitations. 10 He who is faithful in a very little is faithful also in much; and he who is dishonest in a very little is dishonest also in much. 11 If then you have not been faithful in the unrighteous mammon, who will entrust to you the true riches? 12 And if you have not been faithful in that which is another's, who will give you that which is your own? 13 No servant can serve two masters; for either he will hate the one and love the other, or he will be devoted to the one and despise the other. You cannot serve God and mammon."

m Greek *age*.

## COMMENTARY

This difficult and confused parable has no parallel in rabbinic sources, although certain phrases can be traced to Semitic origins. The basic difference between the central thought of the parable and the attitude of the Rabbis is that here money is by definition evil and the Rabbis differentiate between the mammon of deceit and the mammon of truth. That you cannot serve mammon and God, see above p. 129.[1]

1 *steward* Gr. *oikonomos*; in rabbinic sources *iqonomos, inqolomos*. Perhaps the Roman *dispensator* or *villicus*.[2]

6 *measures* Gr. *batous*. Only here in the NT. It goes back to the Heb. *bat*, as does *koros* (v. 7), which is the Heb. *kor*. A *bat* was a liquid measure, an *ephah* was for solids.[3] "From estimates of the contents of two 8th cent. jar fragments of which have been found with the letters *bt* in archaic Hebrew characters, it is thought that the bath contained 21–23 liters or ca 5½ Amer. gals."[4]

7 *hundred measures of wheat* Dry measure, *kor-homer* or 10 *ephahs*.[5]

8 *sons of this world . . . sons of light* Cf. Luke 20.34. Manson states that there is no rabbinic equivalent for "sons of this world."[6] Perhaps the expression *ben haolam hezeh*, "son of this world," could be contrasted with "sons of light," meaning angels. Cf. "Every spirit of light [angel]."[7]

9 *they may receive you* "They" is used for "God" frequently in rabbinic sources to avoid the use of the name of God.[8]

*unrighteous mammon* Mammon of deceit,[9] contrasted with mammon of truth.

10 *He who is faithful in a very little*, etc. This motif is found in the rabbinic tales about the rise of Moses and of David. See below p. 341.

13 *No servant can serve two masters* See above Sec. 34 (p. 129).

## NOTES

1. E.g., T. BM 9.14 (p. 392); T. BB 3.5 (p. 402); also *gizbar* B. BB 7a; B. Shab. 31a; Exod. R. 51.
2. Plummer, *Luke*, p. 381.

3. See Sym. and Aq. and Th. Isa. 5.15 on *bat*, where LXX reads *keramion*, "earthenware jar." See also Josephus, *Ant.* VIII.2.9. Cf. Krauss, *TA*, 2:396. Cf. TJ Er. 1, 19a (58); cf. Ez. 45.11, 14.

4. *IDB*, s. v. "Bath."

5. Ezek. 45.11; cf. 1 Kings 4.22, 5.11; 2 Chron. 27.5; T. BM 5.9 (p. 382); Josephus, *Ant.* VIII.2.9.

6. Manson, *SJ*, p. 292. See however, *Mid. Prov.* 13.25 (37a) et al.

7. En. 61.12; 108.11. Cf. also John 12.36; 1 Thess. 5.5; Eph. 5.8.

8. E.g., M. Sot. 1.7; M. Qid. 1.10; T. Ta'an 4.9 (p. 220); M. Avot 4.5; 3.8; 4.4.

9. Cf. En. 63.10; Targ. 1 Sam. 12.3; Targ. Hos. 5.11; Targ. Isa. 33.15.

# 175. *The Hypocrisy of the Pharisees*

## LUKE 16.14–15

14 The Pharisees, who were lovers of money, heard all this, and they scoffed at him. 15 But he said to them, "You are those who justify yourselves before men, but God knows your hearts; for what is exalted among men is an abomination in the sight of God."

## COMMENTARY

14 *The Pharisees, who were lovers of money*  The Pharisees were not known for their love of money or of material possessions, nor is the subject of this brief section the love of money but about the sin of pride. Manson suggests that it would be more fitting to read "Sadducees" than "Pharisees," since they "held the great vested interests," and the passages in the Psalms of Solomon which describe the Sadducees speak of their insatiable love of wealth and of their pride and insolence.[1] He likewise calls attention to the fact that there might be a play on the name Sadducee which is connected with the root *ẓdq* = "to be righteous," and the same root is used to translate "justify yourselves" in the Palestinian Aramaic version of these verses, and the meaning might be "You are the people who by taking the name Sadducee make public claim to be the party of righteousness but God looks deeper than party labels, and knows that the name does not correspond to any real righteousness within."[2]

15 *for what is exalted among men is an abomination in the sight of God*  Pride is an abomination in the sight of God, for pride is frequently identified with idolatry, cf. 1 Kings 11.5, Dan. 11.31. Note the parallel in rabbinic literature: "All who are lofty of heart [i.e., proud] are called 'abomination,' as it is said, *Everyone who is lofty of heart is an abomination to the Lord* [Prov. 16.5]. Idolatry is called 'abomination,' as it is said, *and thou shalt not bring an abomination* [i.e., an idol] *into thine house* [Deut. 7.26]. As idolatry pollutes the land and causes the Shekhinah to withdraw from it, so also does pride."[3]

NOTES

1. Manson, *SJ*, p. 295.
2. Ibid.
3. *Mek.* Exod. 20.18, cited by Manson, loc. cit.

## 176. *About the Law and About Divorce*

### MATT. 11.12–13

12 "From the days of John the Baptist until now the kingdom of heaven has suffered violence,[n] and men of violence take it by force. 13 For all the prophets and the law prophesied until John."

### IBID. 5.18

"For truly, I say to you, til heaven and earth pass away, not an iota, not a dot, will pass from the law until all is accomplished."

### IBID. 5.32

"But I say to you that everyone who divorces his wife, except on the ground of unchastity, makes her an adulteress; and whoever marries a divorced woman commits adultery."

### LUKE 16.16–18

16 "The law and the prophets were until John; since then the good news of the kingdom of God is preached, and everyone enters it violently. 17 But it is easier for heaven and earth to pass away, than for one dot of the law to become void. 18 Everyone who divorces his wife and marries another commits adultery, and he who marries a woman divorced from her husband commits adultery."

---

n Or *has been coming violently.*
See above Secs. 65 (p. 191), 24 (p. 98).

## 177. *The Rich Man and Lazarus*

### LUKE 16.19–31

19 "There was a rich man who was clothed in purple and fine linen and who feasted sumptuously every day. 20 And at his gate lay a poor man named Lazarus, full of sores, 21 who desired to be fed with what fell from the rich man's table; moreover the dogs came and licked his sores. 22 The poor man died and was carried by the angels to Abraham's bosom. The rich man also died and was buried; 23 and in Hades, being

in torment, he lifted up his eyes, and saw Abraham far off and Lazarus in his bosom. 24 And he called out, 'Father Abraham, have mercy upon me, and send Lazarus to dip the end of his finger in water and cool my tongue; for I am in anguish in this flame.' 25 But Abraham said, 'Son, remember that you in your lifetime received your good things, and Lazarus in like manner evil things; but now he is comforted here, and you are in anguish. 26 And besides all this, between us and you a great chasm has been fixed, in order that those who would pass from here to you may not be able, and none may cross from there to us.' 27 And he said, 'Then I beg you, father, to send him to my father's house, 28 for I have five brothers, so that he may warn them, lest they also come into this place of torment.' 29 But Abraham said, 'They have Moses and the prophets; let them hear them.' 30 And he said, 'No, father Abraham; but if someone goes to them from the dead, they will repent.' 31 He said to him, 'If they do not hear Moses and the prophets, neither will they be convinced if someone should rise from the dead.' "

## COMMENTARY

There are many parallels in world literature involving a rich man and a poor man and their respective places in the world beyond.[1] In Jewish sources the following two are of interest.

> Two godly men lived in Ashkelon. They ate together, drank together, and studied the Law together. One of them died and kindness was not shown to him [i.e., nobody attended his funeral]. The son of Ma'yan, a tax-collector, died and the whole city stopped work to show him kindness. The [surviving] pious man began to complain; he said, "Alas that no [evil] comes upon the haters of Israel [i.e., the wicked in Israel]."
> In a dream he saw a vision, and one said to him, "Do not despise the children of your Lord [i.e., the Israelites]. The one [the pious] had committed one sin and departed [this life] in it [i.e., his funeral cancelled it], and the other [the wealthy publican] had performed one good deed and departed [this life] in it [i.e., his spendid funeral cancelled it]. What sin had the one committed? Far be it that he had ever committed a [serious] sin. But once he put on the *tephillin* for the head before the *tephillin* for the hand. And what good deed had the other performed? Far be it that he had ever done a [really fine] deed. But once he had arranged a meal for the *bouleutai* [municipal councillors] of the city and they did not come. And he said, "Let the poor eat that it be not wasted." Others say, He once went through the marketplace, and he dropped a loaf, and a poor man picked it up, and he said nothing so as not to make him blush or shame. After some days the pious man saw in a dream his companion walking in the Garden [Paradise] under trees and by wells of water; and he saw the tax-collector, and his tongue sought to drink at the brink of a river; he tried to reach the water, but he could not.[2]

> Consider two wicked men who associated with one another in this world. One of them repented of his evil deeds before his death, while the other did not, with the result that the former stands in the company of the righteous,

while his fellow stands in the company of the wicked. And beholding him he says, "Woe is me . . . is there then favor shown here? We both of us committed robberies, we both of us committed murders together, yet he stands in the company of the righteous and I in the company of the wicked!" And they reply to him and say, "You fool! You were despicable after your death and lay for three days, and did not they drag you to your grave with ropes? . . . And your associate understood and repented of his evil ways, and you, you also had the opportunity of repenting and you did not take it." He thereupon says to them, "Permit me to go and repent!" And they answer him and say, "You fool! Do you know that this world is like the Sabbath, and the world whence you have come is like the eve of the Sabbath? If a man does not prepare his meal on the eve of the Sabbath, what shall he eat on the Sabbath?"[3]

19 *a rich man*   Perhaps a Sadducee.[4]

*purple*   A cloth dyed with a costly dye. Heb. *tekhelet*, on which see above p. 172.

*fine linen*   Gr. *bussos* = Heb. *buz* expensive cloth[5] used to contrast the life style of the rich man with that of Lazarus.

20 *Lazarus*   Gr. form of the Heb. Eliezer, which is shortened in Palestinian usage to Lazar, meaning "the one whom God helps."[6]

21 *who desired to be fed*, etc.   "There are those whose life is no life: he who depends on the table of another [for food], he who is ruled by his wife, and he whose body is burdened with sufferings."[7]

22 *the poor man died and was carried by the angels*   As a rule the soul of the departed is taken by the Angel of Death (sometimes identified with Satan). Worthies are escorted by Gabriel and Michael, e.g., Moses.[8] "For the latter ends of men do show their righteousness (or unrighteousness) when they meet the angels of the Lord and of Satan. For when the soul departs troubled, it is tormented by the evil spirit which also it served in lust and evil works. But if he is peaceful with joy he meets the angel of peace and he leads him into eternal life."[9]

*Abraham's bosom*   Gr. *kolpos*. In Heb. *ḥeq* means both bosom and lap; perhaps the latter meaning is applicable here. This expression is most often used in rabbinic sources for martyrs who find rest in Abraham's bosom.[10] It could mean either at a banquet (cf. John 13.23) or in fellowship.

*the rich man also died . . . being in torment*   If he were a Sadducee, as suggested, he did not believe in a hereafter and is now aware of the error of his disbelief.[11]

24 *Father Abraham*   This indicates that the rich man was a Jew.[12]

*and send Lazarus to dip the end of his finger in water*, etc.   This motif is similar to the one in the rabbinic parallel cited above. The theme of the "thirsty dead" is common in folklore.[13] Waters are one of the dominant characteristics of Paradise.[14] The thirst of the wicked in Gehinnom cannot be slaked, and this is one of their punishments.[15]

25 *you in your lifetime received your good things*    "Blessed is the man who takes his portion with the humble! Woe unto him who takes his portion with the wicked! For the wicked take what is theirs, and then go out of the world, as it is said, *And yet a little while, and the wicked shall not be . . . But the meek shall inherit the earth; and shall delight themselves in the abundance of peace* [Ps. 37.10–11]. Thus the Holy One, blessed be He, declared: 'The wicked have but a single hour. They eat what is theirs in this world; then they pass away and go down into Gehinnom—they, their retainers, and anyone who had anything to do with them!'"[16]

26 *great chasm*    Cf. "Then I asked regarding it, and regarding all the hollow places: Why is one separated from the other? And he answered me and said unto me: These three have been made that the spirits of the dead might be separated. And such a division has been made for the spirits of the righteous, in which there is the bright spring of water. And such has been made for sinners when they die and are buried in the earth and judgment has not been executed on them in their lifetime."[17]

28 *to warn them*    Lit. "to testify," i.e., that there is punishment in the world-to-come.[18]

29 *they have Moses and the prophets*    If the rich man is a Sadducee, Moses and the prophets are his only authority.[19]

30 *if one goes to them from the dead*    There are several passages which tell of the dead contacting the living, generally through dreams.[20]

## NOTES

1. See H. Gressmann, "Vom reichen Mann und armen Lazarus: eine literargeschichtliche Studie," *Abhandlungen der königlichen preussischen Akademie der Wissenschaften* (Phil.-Hist. Kl.7, 1918).
2. TJ Sanh. 6.9, 23c (32); TJ Ḥag. 2.2, 77d (36).
3. Ruth R. 3.3.
4. See Manson, *SJ*, pp. 296 ff.
5. See Krauss, *TA*, 1:537. E.g., Gen. R. 20.12; B. BM 29b.
6. E.g. TJ Ta'an. 2.1, 65b (3); TJ Meg. 2, 73a (25); TJ MQ 1, 80b (22).
7. B. Beẓ. 32b.
8. Deut. R. 1. See also Num. R. 11; B. Ket. 104a; *PR* 2 (5a); Sifre Deut. 357; Koh. R. 12.13; Targ. Cant. 4.12.
9. Test. Asher 6.4–6.
10. See B. Git. 57b; *PR* 43 (180b); B. Qid. 72a; Lam. R. 1. 85. Cf. P. Haupt, "Abraham's Bosom," *AJP* 42 (1921): 162–167.
11. Cf. above and see En. 103.5–8.
12. See Gen. R. 48.9 and B. Er. 19a for, e.g., of "Abraham our Father."
13. Cf. Isa. 5.13; for the literature see T. H. Gaster, *The Holy and the Profane* (New York, 1955), pp. 171–245; idem, *Thespis* (New York, 1950), p. 188.
14. Cf. En. 22.9.
15. Cf. 4 Ezra 8.59; *Mid Ps.* 11.6 (51a).
16. *Mid. Ps.* 28.3 (115a). Cf. also TJ Ḥag. 2, 77d (38).
17. En. 22.8–9.
18. Cf. Lev. R. 2.9; *SER* 7 (35); *SOR* 21; B. BB 15b.

19. See Manson, *SJ*, p. 301.
20. E.g., Koh. R. 9.10; B. MQ 28a.

# 178. On Causing Sin

## MATT. 18.6–7

6 "But whoever causes one of these little ones who believe in me to sin,[o] it would be better for him to have a great millstone fastened round his neck and to be drowned in the depth of the sea. 7. Woe to the world for temptations to sin! For it is necessary that the temptations come, but woe to the man by whom the temptation comes!"

## MARK 9.42

"Whoever causes one of these little ones who believe in me to sin,[o] it would be better for him if a great millstone were hung round his neck and he were thrown into the sea."

## LUKE 17.1–2

1 And he said to his disciples, "Temptations to sin[p] are sure to come; but woe to him by whom they come! 2 It would be better for him if a millstone were hung round his neck and he were cast into the sea, than that he should cause one of these little ones to sin."[o]

o  Or *stumble*.
p  Or *stumbling-blocks*.
See above Sec. 131 (p. 269).

# 179. On Forgiveness

## MATT. 18.15

"If your brother sins against you, go and tell him his fault, between you and him alone. If he listens to you, you have gained your brother."

## IBID. 18.21–22

21 Then Peter came up and said to him, "Lord, how often shall my brother sin against me, and I forgive him? As many as seven times?" 22 Jesus said to him, "I do not say to you seven times, but seventy times seven."[q]

## Luke 17.3–4

3 "Take heed to yourselves; if your brother sins, rebuke him, and if he repents, forgive him; 4 and if he sins against you seven times in the day, and turns to you seven times, and says, 'I repent,' you must forgive him."

---

q Or *seventy-seven times*.
See above Secs. 134 (p. 270), 135 (p. 271).

# 180. On Faith

## MATT. 17.20

He said to them, "Because of your little faith. For truly, I say to you, if you have faith as a grain of mustard seed, you will say to this mountain, 'Move hence to yonder place,' and it will move; and nothing will be impossible to you."

## LUKE 17.5–6

5 The apostles said to the Lord, "Increase our faith!" 6 And the Lord said, "If you had faith as a grain of mustard seed, you could say to this sycamine tree, 'Be rooted up, and be planted in the sea,' and it would obey you."
See above Sec. 126 (p. 261).

# 181. The Servant's Wages

## LUKE 17.7–10

7 "Will any one of you, who has a servant plowing or keeping sheep, say to him when he has come in from the field, 'Come at once and sit down at table'? 8 Will he not rather say to him, 'Prepare supper for me, and gird yourself and serve me, till I eat and drink; and afterward you shall eat and drink'? 9 Does he thank the servant because he did what was commanded? 10 So you also, when you have done all that is commanded you, say, 'We are unworthy servants; we have only done what was our duty.' "

### COMMENTARY

The point of this passage is clear. Whatever is demanded of man by God is to be performed precisely because he is God's servant, and a servant, because of his position, must do all that the master imposes upon him, even though the master is not sensitive or considerate or the task is not appealing. Man should not expect anything in return for performing what it is his duty to do. Cf., e.g., "R. Johanan b. Zakkai said, 'If you have studied much Torah, do not claim merit for yourself, for for this were you created."[1] See also the statement of Antignos of Socho, above p. 131. In rabbinic literature treatment of one's slave is not the same as described here. "When R. Johanan ate meat he also gave his slave to eat, and when he drank he also gave his slaves, etc."[2]

## NOTES

1. M. Avot 2.8.
2. TJ BQ 8.5, 6c (2).

# 182. *The Healing of Ten Lepers*

## LUKE 17.11–19

11 On the way to Jerusalem he was passing along Samaria and Galilee. 12 And as he entered a village, he was met by ten lepers, who stood at a distance 13 and lifted up their voices and said, "Jesus, Master, have mercy on us." 14 When he saw them he said to them, "Go and show yourselves to the priests." And as they went they were cleansed. 15 Then one of them, when he saw that he was healed, turned back, praising God with a loud voice; 16 and he fell on his face at Jesus' feet, giving him thanks. Now he was a Samaritan. 17 Then said Jesus, "Were not ten cleansed? Where are the nine? 18 Was no one found to return and give praise to God except this foreigner?" 19 And he said to him, "Rise and go your way; your faith has made you well."

## COMMENTARY

A healing story similar to Mark 1.40–45, Matt. 8.1–4, Luke 5.12–16. The difference is the non-Jewish element, i.e., the thankful Samaritan who is introduced to emphasize the universal aspect of the preaching or as an example of an anti-Jewish bias.[1]

12 *who stood at a distance* By not approaching them to heal them the story is paralleled by Elisha's long-distance healing of Naaman the Syrian.[2]
14 *Go and show yourselves to the priests* Cf. Matt. 8.4. Luke seems to have slipped up. Why should the Samaritan present himself to the priest in Jerusalem?
19 *Rise go your way* Cf. Luke 7.50, 8.48.

## NOTES

1. See Montefiore, *SG*, p. 544.
2. 2 Kings 5.1 ff.

# 183. On the Kingdom of God

## LUKE 17.20–21

20 Being asked by the Pharisees when the kingdom of God was coming, he answered them, "The kingdom of God is not coming with signs to be observed; 21 nor will they say, 'Lo, here it is! or There!' for behold, the kingdom of God is in the midst of[r] you."

---

r *within.*

### COMMENTARY

There are no rabbinic parallels.

20 *when the kingdom of God was coming*   The more common phraseology in rabbinic sources is: "When is the Son of David or the Messiah to come?"[1]

*with signs to be observed*   I.e., there are no observable signs, hence it is foolhardy to calculate the "coming of the end." Similar warnings are frequent in rabbinic sources.[2]

21 *the kingdom of God is in the midst of you*   This is enigmatic, and the ambiguity stems from the Gr. *entos*, translated "in the midst" (RV text) and "within" (RV m).

"The ambiguity may be illustrated by a Rabbinical discussion . . . on the meaning of the text in Exod. 17.7 'Is the Lord among us *(bekirbenu)* or not?' One Rabbi explains thus: The Israelites in asking this question meant to say, 'If He (God) provides us with food, like a king who dwells in a city (i.e. in the midst of his people), so that the city lacks for nothing, then we will serve Him; if not, we will rebel against Him.' The majority of the Rabbis, however, gave a different interpretation. The question meant: 'If we think our thoughts and He knows what we think (i.e. if He is literally within us and knows the secrets of each individual), then we will serve Him; if not, we will rebel against Him.' (Pesikta 28a)."[3]

### NOTES

1. Cf. Targ. Mic. 4.8.
2. E.g., B. Sanh. 97a; *Aggadat Shir* 6.10.
3. Manson, *SJ*, p. 303.

# 184. The Day of the Son of Man

## MATT. 24.26–27

26 "So, if they say to you, 'Lo, he is in the wilderness,' do not go out; if they say, 'Lo, he is in the inner rooms,' do not believe it. 27 For as the lightning comes from the east and shines as far as the west, so will be the coming of the Son of man."

## I B I D  24.37–39

37 "As were the days of Noah, so will be the coming of the Son of man. 38 For as in those days before the flood they were eating and drinking, marrying and giving in marriage, until the day when Noah entered the ark, 39 and they did not know until the flood came and swept them all away, so will be the coming of the Son of man."

## I B I D  10.39

"He who finds his life will lose it, and he who loses his life for my sake will find it."

## I B I D  24.40–41

"Then two men will be in the field; one is taken and one is left. 41 Two women will be grinding at the mill; one is taken and one is left."

## I B I D  24.28

"Wherever the body is, there the eagles[s] will be gathered together."

## L U K E  17.22–37

22 And he said to the disciples, "The days are coming when you will desire to see one of the days of the Son of man, and you will not see it. 23 And they will say to you, 'Lo, there!' or 'Lo, here!' Do not go, do not follow them. 24 For as the lightning flashes and lights up the sky from one side to the other, so will the Son of man be in his day.[t] 25 But first he must suffer many things and be rejected by this generation. 26 As it was in the days of Noah, so will it be in the days of the Son of Man. 27 They ate, they drank, they married, they were given in marriage, until the day when Noah entered the ark, and the flood came and destroyed them all. 28 Likewise as it was in the days of Lot—they ate, they drank, they bought, they sold, they planted, they built, 29 but on the day when Lot went out from Sodom fire and brimstone rained from heaven and destroyed them all—30 So will it be on the day when the Son of man is revealed. 31 On that day, let him who is on the housetop, with his goods in the house, not come down to take them away; and likewise let him who is in the field not turn back. 32 Remember Lot's wife. 33 Whoever seeks to gain his life will lose it, but whoever loses his life will preserve it. 34 I tell you, in that night there will be two men in one bed; one will be taken and the other left. 35 There will be two women grinding together; one will be taken and the other left."[u] 37 And they said to him, "Where, Lord?" He said to them, "Where the body is, there the eagles[s] will be gathered together."

---

s  Or *vultures*.
t  Some omit *in his day*.
u  Some add v. 36, *Two men will be in the field; one will be taken and the other left.*

## COMMENTARY

**26** *Lo, he is in the wilderness . . . inner rooms*  The sense of this verse is clear, i.e., outside and inside, but the contrasting words "wilderness" and "rooms" are a bit peculiar. See, however, Deut. 32.25, *In the open* [Heb. *miḥuz*] *the sword shall bereave, and in the chambers* [Heb. *umeḥadarim*, lit. in the rooms] *shall be terror.* The Aramaic for *miḥuz,* "in the open," is *mibra,* and it was apparently misread as *midbara,* "wilderness."[1]

**27** *For as the lightning comes*  The Messiah is often described as coming on a cloud together with flashing lightning which illumines the entire world.[2]

*from the east . . . as far as the west*  I.e., the whole world, cf. Matt. 8.11. Luke explains it as "from one side to the other," presumably for a Gentile audience.[3]

There are several suggestions as to the meaning of this passage: "The Advent of the Messiah will be as little unnoticed by men as carcases are unnoticed by eagles. . . . Or as the eagles swoop down upon the carcases, so will false Messiahs appear before the End. Or as the eagles swoop down upon the carcases, so when the world has become steeped in wickedness, will the Son of man come down on to it."[4]

Both in Matt. and in Luke there is a variant reading to "eagles," i.e., "vultures." Both readings may go back to the Heb. *nesher.* There is also an interesting variant between the Matthean and Lucan texts. Matt. reads *ptoma,* "a carcass," while Luke reads *soma,* "a body." The reason may be that vultures eat carrion, *ptoma,* while eagles swoop down and eat only live creatures, hence *soma.*[5]

**37** *As were the days of Noah*  This does not seem to refer to the wickedness of the people before the flood but that they were unaware that the flood was coming.

**38** *eating and drinking . . . giving in marriage*  I.e., living normal lives without care.

**39** *until the flood*  I.e., that the generation of the flood did not believe that the flood would actually come and destroy them. According to the midrash they attempted to destroy the ark constructed by Noah as being an affront to them.[6]

**40** *Then two men will be in the field; one is taken and one is left*  The idea expressed here, of one being taken and another, left seems to have been overlooked by the commentators. The background of this section is the Roman practice of impressing people into governmental service (*angaria*). See above p. 105. The Matthean reading is probably closer to the original since men working in the field and women grinding at the mill form a better couplet than the Lucan reading—men in the bed and women grinding at the mill.

**28** *Wherever the body is there the eagles will be gathered together*  A proverbial saying, Cf. Job (LXX) 39.30, *His young ones suck up blood, and where the slain are, there he is.*

Luke, v. 25    *But first he must suffer,* etc.    Cf. Luke 9.22. On the *ḥevle ha-mashi'aḥ* and its meaning, see below p. 380. On the suffering of the Messiah and the interpretation of the "suffering Servant" passages from Isaiah, see above p. 43 n. 4.

29  *on the day when Lot went out of Sodom*    Gen. 19.1 ff.

33  *Whoever seeks to gain his life will lose it*    See above p. 187.

## NOTES

1. See Lachs, "Some Synoptic Passages." In light of this explanation of the verse, Manson's comment, *SJ*, p. 142, "the Messiah is in the wilderness—the mobilisation place of rebellions—don't go to join him; he is in the inner chambers—the places of intrigues and plots—put no trust in all that" is to be discounted. It is, however, of note that Josephus mentions rebels who led people into the wilderness promising them deliverance (*BJ* II.13.5; cf. Acts 21.37–38).

2. See Apoc. Bar. 53.1 ff; *Aggadat Shir.* 6.10; *PR* 36 (162a), 15 (71b); Lam. R. 2.8 (99b); *PRK* 12 (47b).

3. McNeile, *Matt.*, p. 351.

4. Montefiore, *SG*, 2:313.

5. See Aristotle, *Hist. Anim.* VI.5–6; Pliny, *NH* X.3–8, X.6.19.

6. See Gen. R. 32.7; Sifre Deut. 337.

# 185. *The Parable of the Unjust Judge*

## LUKE 18.1–8

1 And he told them a parable, to the effect that they ought always to pray and not lose heart. 2 He said, "In a certain city there was a judge who neither feared God nor regarded man; 3 and there was a widow in that city who kept coming to him and saying, 'Vindicate me against my adversary.' 4 For a while he refused; but afterward he said to himself, 'Though I neither fear God nor regard man, 5 yet because this widow bothers me, I will vindicate her, or she will wear me out by her continual coming.' " 6 And the Lord said, "Hear what the unrighteous judge says. 7 And will not God vindicate his elect, who cry to him day and night? Will he delay long over them? 8 I tell you, he will vindicate them speedily. Nevertheless when the Son of man comes, will he find faith on earth?"

## COMMENTARY

1 *pray without losing heart*    The Gr. verb *ekkakeō* means "to become tired, to despair." The point of the injunction and of the parable is that God answers prayer. It does, however, require the forbearance of the supplicant. He should not give up hope of an answer. There is also a nuance of *ekkakeō* which implies "without ceasing" (cf. 1 Thess. 5.17), and this had influenced some to cite passages as to the number of times a day one is to pray, e.g., "R.

Johanan stated, 'Would that man could pray the whole day long, for no prayer does harm.' "[1] This misses the point of the passage. What is applicable is "A man has a patron, if he bothers him too much, he [the patron] says, 'I will forget him, he bothers me.' But God is not so; however much you importune Him, He receives you."[2]

2 *who neither feared God nor regarded man*   Not a person apt to be compassionate.[3]

3 *a widow*   A classic example of a defenseless person. Cf. Exod. 22.22 ff., Ps. 68.5.

5 *She will wear me out*   Gr. *hupōpiazē me*, lit., "she will give me a black eye." One suggestion to explain this difficult expression is that it is a translation of *tashehir panai*, "she will blacken my face," meaning she will embarrass me.[4]

7 *And will not God vindicate his elect*   The elect are most likely Israel. Cf., e.g., Isa. 42.1, 43.2, 65.9, 15, 23; Ps. 105.6. God, unlike the weary and bored judge, hears the cry of the defenseless.[5]

## NOTES

1. TJ Ber. 1.2, 3b (14).
2. TJ Ber. 9.1, (11) 13b. Cf. also *Mid. Ps.* 4 (20b), 55 (147a).
3. It is not necessary to assume that the judge is a Gentile, as suggested by Plummer, *Luke*, p. 411.
4. Derrett, *SNT*, 1:43–45. He cites as evidence on p. 44 n. 1. TJ Ḥag. 2, 77d. and on p. 46 Gen. R. 22.6; 1 En. 62.10, 60.11; 4 Ezra 7.125–6. His citation of MT passages is baseless, for not one of them refers to shame.
5. Among the many passages illustrative of God's compassion, note particularly Sira 35.12–20.

## 186. *The Parable of the Pharisee and the Tax Collector*

### LUKE 18.9–14

9 He also told this parable to some who trusted in themselves that they were righteous and despised others; 10 "Two men went up into the temple to pray, one a Pharisee and the other a tax collector. 11 The Pharisee stood and prayed thus with himself, 'God, I thank thee that I am not like other men, extortioners, unjust, adulterers, or even like this tax collector. 12 I fast twice a week, I give tithes of all that I get.' 13 But the tax collector, standing far off, would not even lift up his eyes to heaven, but beat his breast, saying, 'God, be merciful to me a sinner!' 14 I tell you, this man went down to his house justified rather than the other; for every one who exalts himself will be humbled, but he who humbles himself will be exalted."

## COMMENTARY

9 *some who trusted in themselves*   Those who were self-centered and whose self-confidence led to smugness and the despising of others. Several of Hillel

the Elder's statements are on this theme: "Do not separate yourself from the community; trust not in yourself until the day of your death, judge not your fellowman until you have come into his place."[1]

10 *went up into the temple to pray*  More than likely they went to the synagogue to pray. See above p. 115.

11 *The Pharisee stood and prayed thus with himself*  On the posture in prayer, see above p. 115. The expression "with himself" is presumably a translation of Heb. *beno uven azmo*.

*God I thank thee*, etc.   Note similar private prayers:

> R. Neḥunya b. Haqaneh when he came out of the Bet Midrash used to say: "I give thanks before Thee, O Lord my God and God of my fathers, that thou hast placed my portion with those who sit in the House of Study and not with those who sit at street corners, for I and they rise early, I to words of Torah, but they to vain matters; I and they labor, but I labor and receive a reward, whereas they labor and receive no reward; I and they hasten, I to the life of the world-to-come, but they to the pit of destruction."[2]

> It was a favorite saying of the Rabbis of Yavneh: "I am a creature of God and my neighbor is also his creature; my work is in the city and his is in the field; I rise early to my work and he rises early to his. As he cannot excel in my work, so I cannot excel in his work. But perhaps you say, I do great things and he does small things. We have learned that it matters not whether a man does much or little, if only he directs his heart to Heaven."[3]

12 *I fast twice a week*  A private fast, and it is more than is required by law.[4]

## NOTES

1. M. Avot 2.4.
2. B. Ber. 28b.
3. Ibid. 17a.
4. See *Tan.B. Vayera* 43b; B. Git. 56a.

# THE JUDEAN SECTION

MATTHEW 19–27 = MARK 10–15 = LUKE 18.15–23.56

## *A. Journey to Jerusalem*

### 187. *Marriage and Divorce*

#### MATT. 19.1–12

1 Now when Jesus had finished these sayings, he went away from Galilee and entered
the region of Judea beyond the Jordan; 2 and large crowds followed him, and he
healed them there. 3 And Pharisees came up to him and tested him by asking, "Is it
lawful to divorce one's wife for any cause?" 4 He answered, "Have you not read that
he who made them from the beginning made them male and female, 5 and said. 'For
this reason a man shall leave his father and mother and be joined to his wife, and the
two shall become one.?'[v] 6 So they are no longer two but one.[v] What therefore God
has joined together, let no man put asunder." 7 They said to him, "Why then did
Moses command one to give a certificate of divorce, and to put her away?" 8 He said
to them, "For your hardness of heart Moses allowed you to divorce your wives, but
from the beginning it was not so. 9 And I say to you; whoever divorces his wife,
except for unchastity,[w] and marries another, commits adultery."[x] 10 The disciples
said to him, "If such is the case of a man with his wife, it is not expedient to marry."
11 But he said to them, "Not all men can receive this precept, but only those to whom
it is given. 12 For there are eunuchs who have been so from birth, and there are
eunuchs who have been made eunuchs by men, and there are eunuchs who have
made themselves eunuchs for the sake of the kingdom of heaven. He who is able to
receive this, let him receive it."

#### MARK 10.1–12

1 And he left there and went to the region of Judea and beyond the Jordan, and
crowds gathered to him again and again; as his custom was, he taught them. 2 And
Pharisees came up and in order to test him asked, "Is it lawful for a man to divorce his
wife?" 3 He answered them, "What did Moses command you? 4 They said, "Moses
allowed a man to write a certificate of divorce, and to put her away." 5 But Jesus said
to them, "For your hardness of heart he wrote you this commandment. 6 But from
the beginning of creation, 'God made them male and female.' 7 'For this reason a man
shall leave his father and mother and be joined to his wife,[y] 8 and the two shall
become one.'[v] So they are no longer two but one.'[v] 9 What therefore God has joined
together, let not man put asunder." 10 And in the house the disciples asked him again
about this matter. 11 And he said to them, "Whoever divorces his wife and marries

another, commits adultery against her; 12 and if she divorces her husband and marries another, she commits adultery."

---

v  Greek *one flesh.*
w  Other ancient authorities after *unchastity* read *makes her commit adultery.*
x  Other ancient authorities insert *and he who marries a divorced woman commits adultery.*
y  Some texts omit *and be joined to his wife.*

## COMMENTARY

This section presents Jesus' view of marriage and divorce, which goes back to two MT passages on marriage, the creation story, specifically Gen. 2.24; the other, on divorce, involves the interpretation or applicability of Deut. 24.1. There is internal evidence indicating that this presentation reflects teachings of the early church which have been conflated with the original, which did not condone divorce at all, irrespective of Deut. 24.1, for if the argument is that they have become one, etc., divorce is a non-sequitur.[1]

4 *male and female*  Gen. 1.27b.
5 *For this reason a man shall leave*,etc.  Gen. 2.24.
6 *What therefore God has joined together*, etc.  It is true that there are many passages in rabbinic literature which speak of "marriages made in heaven," i.e., determined by God, but there is no idea whatsoever that marriage is a sacrament in the sense that it may never be terminated, for it was always viewed as a contract which could be dissolved.[2]

11 *Not all men can receive this precept*  This together with the argument from the creation story indicates that Jesus' attitude toward divorce was negative in the absolute. His attitude toward marriage itself was less than enthusiastic. The rabbinic emphasis is that marriage is the natural and normal state. "R. Eliezer said, 'Any Jew who does not have a wife is not a man, as it is written, *Male and female He created them, and He blessed them and named them Man when they were created* [Gen. 5.2].' "[3]

12 *For there are eunuchs who have been so from birth*, etc.  The best analysis of this passage is that of Manson:

> There are those for whom marriage in the full sense is an impossibility for physical reasons: either because they are "eunuchs from their mother's womb," i.e. sexually impotent from birth, or because they have been "made eunuchs by men," i.e. rendered sexually impotent by a surgical operation. This distinction is recognized by the rabbinical treatment of the subject.[4] There is yet a third class—those who have "made themselves eunuchs for the kingdom of heaven's sake." Does this mean that they have voluntarily submitted to an operation whereby they become sexually impotent, or does it mean simply that they have voluntarily embraced a life of celibacy? The following considerations favour the latter alternative:

(1) The whole sentiment of Judaism was against castration. The eunuch was disqualified for membership of the community (Deut. 23.1). A Jew would not understand how this operation could serve the ends of the Kingdom of God.

(2) The word "eunuch" and the abstract noun derived from it appears in early Christian literature with the sense, unknown to classical or Hellenistic Greek of "celibate" and "celibacy" respectively. The classic example is Clement of Alexandria's definition (*Paed.* III.4, (26): "The true eunuch is not he who cannot but he who will not indulge himself."

(3) There is no evidence that Jesus had any sympathy with asceticism for asceticism's sake. He requires—and makes—the greatest sacrifices for the sake of the Kingdom. If the Kingdom requires the sacrifice of the happiness of marriage, the sacrifice it to be made. Self-mutilation cannot add anything to the fullness of such sacrifice.

(4) The literal sense is inappropriate here as it is in Mk. 9.43–48 and Mt. 5.29f.

(5) Jesus, John the Baptist, Paul, and probably some of the Twelve were unmarried; others of the Twelve sacrificed their homelife for the sake of the Kingdom. But that was all. There is no word of any becoming eunuchs in the literal sense of the word.[5]

## NOTES

1. On divorce, see above pp. 98 ff. See A. Isaksson, *Marriage and Ministry in the New Temple* (Lund, 1965) and the review by J. D. M. Derrett, *JBL* 85 (1966): 98 ff.

2. On marriages made in heaven, see *PRK* 2 (11b), which indicates that God determines who shall marry whom but it does not carry with it the idea of the indissolubility of that marriage. Cf. also B. MQ 18b. There is a passage which also speaks of divorce as a divine institution: TJ Qid. 1, 58c (17). See also Gen. R. 18.3. Schechter, *Fragments of a Zadokite Work* 7.2, wrongly assumes that this passage is one against divorce. It is against polygamy, not divorce. See Charles ad loc., p. 810.

3. There must be both male and female to be called man, B. Yev. 63a. Montefiore, *RLGT* on v. 12 is correct in pointing out that the Ben Azzai story, B. Yev. 63b, is not applicable here.

4. In rabbinic literature the term for one who has been born a eunuch is *seris ḥamma,* i.e., a eunuch from the time he sees the sun, and is one born without testicles, cf. M. Yev. 8.4; one made a eunuch by man is called *seris adam,* ibid.

5. Manson, *SJ*, pp. 215–216. See Bauer in the *Heinrici Festschrift*, pp. 234–244, as cited by Manson. It is not clear whether Paul was unmarried; 1 Cor. 7.7 might mean that he was widowed.

# 188. *Blessing of the Children*

## MATT. 19.13–14; 18.3; 19.15

13 Then children were brought to him that he might lay his hands on them and pray. The disciples rebuked the people; 14 but Jesus said, "Let the children come to me, and do not hinder them; for to such belongs the kingdom of heaven. 18.3 Truly I say

to you, unless you turn and become children, you will never enter the kingdom of heaven." 19.15 And he laid his hands on them and went away.

## MARK 10.13–16

13 And they were bringing children to him, that he might touch them; and the disciples rebuked them. 14 But when Jesus saw it he was indignant, and said to them, "Let the children come to me, do not hinder them; for to such belongs the kingdom of God. 15 Truly, I say to you, whoever does not receive the kingdom of God like a child shall not enter it." 16 And he took them in his arms and blessed them, laying his hands upon them.

## LUKE 18.15–17

15 Now they were bringing even infants to him that he might touch them; and when the disciples saw it they rebuked them. 16 But Jesus called them to him, saying, "Let the children come to me, and do not hinder them; for to such belongs the kingdom of God. 17 Truly, I say to you, whoever does not receive the kingdom of God like a child shall not enter it."

### COMMENTARY

13 *lay his hands on them*, etc.    As an act accompanying a blessing, see Gen. 48.14.[1]

14 *for to such belongs the kingdom of heaven*    See above to Matt. 18.14 (p. 269).

16 *Let the children come to me*    This indicates that they were, as in the other gospels, capable of coming on their own and did not have to be carried, otherwise it would have read "Let them bring them to me."

Mt. 18.v.3 *turn*    Heb. *ḥazar*, "return/repent."

Luke, v. 15 *infants*    The Greek *brephos* does mean a very young child, an infant. Luke's version, as the other gospels here, goes back to a Heb. original, *tinoqot*, which means both "infants" and "young children." The later meaning makes better sense here.

### NOTES

1. On the subject of laying on of hands, see Daube, *NTRJ*, pp.224 ff.

## 189. The Rich Young Man

### MATT. 19.16–30

16 And behold, one came up to him, saying, "Teacher, what good deed must I do, to have eternal life?" 17 And he said to him, "Why do you ask me about what is good? One there is who is good. If you would enter life, keep the commandments." 18 He said to him, "Which?" And Jesus said "You shall not kill, You shall not commit

adultery, You shall not steal, You shall not bear false witness, 19 Honor your father and mother, and, You shall love your neighbor as yourself." 20 The young man said to him, "All these I have observed; what do I still lack?" 21 Jesus said to him, "If you would be perfect, go, sell what you possess and give it to the poor, and you will have treasure in heaven; and come, follow me." 22 When the young man heard this he went away sorrowful; for he had great possessions. 23 And Jesus said to his disciples, "Truly, I say to you, it will be hard for a rich man to enter the kingdom of heaven. 24 Again, I tell you, it is easier for a camel to go through the eye of a needle than for a rich man to enter the kingdom of God." 25 When the disciples heard this they were greatly astonished, saying, "Who then can be saved?" 26 But Jesus looked at them and said to them, "With men this is impossible, but with God all things are possible." 27 Then Peter said in reply, "Lo, we have left everything and followed you. What then shall we have?" 28 Jesus said to them, "Truly, I say to you, in the new world when the Son of man shall sit on his glorious throne, you who have followed me will also sit on twelve thrones, judging the twelve tribes of Israel. 29 And everyone who has left houses or brothers or sisters or father or mother or children or lands, for my name's sake, will receive a hundredfold[z] and inherit eternal life. 30 But many that are first will be last, and the last first."

## MARK 10.17–31

17 And as he was setting out on his journey, a man ran up and knelt before him, and asked him, "Good Teacher, what must I do to inherit eternal life?" 18 And Jesus said to him, "Why do you call me good? No one is good but God alone. 19 You know the commandments: 'Do not kill, Do not commit adultery, Do not steal, Do not bear false witness. Do not defraud, Honor your father and mother.' " 20 And he said to him, "Teacher, all these I have observed from my youth." 21 And Jesus looking upon him loved him, and said, to him, "You lack one thing; go, sell what you have, and give it to the poor, and you will have treasure in heaven; and come, follow me." 22 At that saying his countenance fell, and he went away sorrowful, for he had great possessions. 23 And Jesus looked around and said to his disciples, "How hard it will be for those who have riches to enter the kingdom of God!" 24 And the disciples were amazed at his words. But Jesus said to them again, "Children, how hard it is[a] to enter the kingdom of God! 25 It is easier for a camel to go through the eye of a needle than for a rich man to enter the kingdom of God." 26 And they were exceedingly astonished and said to him,[b] "Then who can be saved?" 27 Jesus looked at them and said, "With men it is impossible, but not with God; for all things are possible with God." 28 Peter began to say to him, "Lo, we have left everything and followed you." 29 Jesus said, "Truly, I say to you, there is no one who has left house or brothers or sisters or mother or father or children or lands, for my sake and for the gospel, 30 who will not receive a hundredfold now in this time, houses and brothers and sisters and mothers and children and lands, with persecutions, and in the age to come eternal life. 31 But many that are first will be last, and the last first."

## LUKE 18.18–30; 22.28–30; 13.30

18 And a ruler asked him, "Good Teacher, what shall I do to inherit eternal life? 19 And Jesus said to him, "Why do you call me good? No one is good but God alone. 20

You know the commandments: 'Do not commit adultery, Do not kill, Do no bear false witness, Honor your father and mother.' " 21 And he said, "All these I have observed from my youth." 22 And when Jesus heard it, he said to him, "One thing you still lack. Sell all that you have and distribute to the poor, and you will have treasure in heaven; and come, follow me." 23 But when he heard this he became sad, for he was very rich. 24 Jesus looking at him said, "How hard it is for those who have riches to enter the kingdom of God! 25 For it is easier for a camel to go through the eye of a needle than for a rich man to enter the kingdom of God." 26 Those who heard it said, "Then who can be saved?" 27 But he said, "What is impossible with men is possible with God." 28 And Peter said, "Lo, we have left our homes and followed you." 29 And he said to them, "Truly, I say to you, 22.28 You are those who have continued with me in my trials; 22.29 as my Father appointed a kingdom for me, so do I appoint for you 30 that you may eat and drink at my table in my kingdom and sit on thrones judging the twelve tribes of Israel." 18.29b . . . there is no man who has left house or wife or brothers or parents or children, for the sake of the kingdom of God, 30 who will not receive manifold more in this time, and in the age to come eternal life. 13.30 And behold, some are last who will be first, and some are first who will be last."

---

z  Others *manifold*.
a  Some add *for those who trust in riches*.
b  Some read *to one another*.

## COMMENTARY

16  *What good deed must I do to have eternal life?*  "Eternal life," Heb. *ḥayyē olam (haba)*, opposite of *ḥayyē sha'ah*. A similar question was asked of R. Eliezer:

> Our Rabbis taught, "When R. Eliezer fell ill his disciples came to visit him. They said to him, 'Rabbi, teach us the paths of life that we may merit the life of the world-to-come.' He said to them, 'Be careful about the honor of your colleagues; restrain your sons from studying Greek learning [lit. logic] and place them between the knees of the Sages, and when you pray know before whom you stand, and thereby you will merit the life of the world-to-come.' "[1]

17  *Why do you ask me about what is good? One there is who is good.*  The meaning is that God is the only one called good, and His will is embodied in the Torah, which is also called good; therefore go and observe the commands of the Good One in the work called good, the Torah. ". . . and 'good' only means Torah, as it is said, *and I give you good doctrine, forsake not My Torah* [Prov. 28.1]."[2] The Matthean text, is inferior to that of Mark and Luke, where the young man addresses Jesus as "Good Teacher" and hence the correct text: "Why do you call me good, etc."[3]

18  *You shall not kill*  Exod. 20.14, Deut. 5.17.

*You shall not steal*  Exod. 20.15, Deut. 5.17.

*You shall not bear false witness*  Exod. 20.16, Deut. 5.18.

19 *Honor your father and mother*  Exod. 20.12, Lev. 19.3, Deut. 5.16.

*Love your neighbor*  Lev. 19.18, Matt. 22.39, Rom. 13.8, James 2.8–9.

20 *What do I still lack?*  Similar to the question: What more is my obligation that I might do it.[4]

21 *If you would be perfect*  Presumably what Jesus meant is expressed in the rabbinic phrase *zaddiq gamur*, "a completely righteous man," i.e., one who observes all of the *mizvot*.[5]

*sell what you possess and give to the poor*  The implication here is not that the young man should help the poor with charity but that he should divest himself of his possessions. This is contrary to rabbinic teaching, which states that a man should not give away more than one fifth of his possessions during his lifetime lest he become a public charge.[6] It is true, however, that there were those who, in a gesture of unusual charity, gave away all they had.[7]

24 *It is easier for a camel to go through the eye of a needle*, etc.  This is an obvious folksaying to illustrate a nearly impossible task or something extraordinary. In the Talmud we find a similar expression," an elephant passing through a needle's eye"[8] refering to an impossible dream or over-subtle dialectics.[9]

30 *many that are first will be last, and the last first*  This probably belongs to the beginning of the next chapter. In a rabbinic source the expression is that those who are above, i.e., on top, because of their wealth will in the next world be beneath, and those in this world who are beneath will be on top in the next world.[10]

Mark 10.21 *loved him*  better "pitied him." The root *r-ḥ-m* in Aram. means "love"; in Heb., "pity." Nineham, sensing the difficulty in translating the Gr. *agapaō*, suggests, "Here we should perhaps think rather of some definite outward gesture or affection—caressed him or put his arms about him."[11] Translating "he pitied" would solve the problem.

## NOTES

1. Heb. *hayye ha'olam haba*, B. Ber. 28b.

2. M. Avot 6.3. Cf. also B. AZ 19b; B. Ber. 5a. God is called "Good:" e.g., ". . . For rain and good tidings he should say, 'Blessed is He the Good and the Doer of good' " (M. Ber. 9.2). See also TJ Hag. 2, (77c) (5); B. Men. 53b; PR 35 (161a).

3. Abrahams, *Studies II*, p. 186, correctly points out the error of Plummer (p. 422) that "There is no instance in the whole Talmud of a Rabbi being addressed as *good master*, the title was absolutely unknown among Jews." Abrahams, quoting Dalman, *Words*, p. 337, cites an example, i.e., "Good greeting to the good teacher from the good Lord of whose goodness doeth good to his people" (B. Ta'an. 24b).

4. B. Sot. 22b.

5. E.g., B. RH 16b; B. Ber. 7b; 61b; B. Er. 21b; B. Git. 68b.

6. Cf. B. Ket, 50a and parallels. See also Montefiore, *RLGT*, p. 281. The passage in B. Ber. 61b cited by *SB*, 1:817 is applicable only insofar as it shows that it is difficult for some to part with their material possessions, which are dearer to them than their lives, but not as a religious dictum.

7. See, e.g., B. Ta'an. 24a.

8. B. Ber. 55b, B. BM 38b.

9. On this proverb see L. Dukes, *Rabbinische Blumenlese* (1844), pp. 119, 212; A. Cohen, *Ancient Jewish Proverbs* (1911), pp. 113–114. See also Abrahams, *Studies II*, p. 208, where he cites a contrasting passage from a difficult text, *PR* 15 (70a), "The Holy One said: Open for Me a door as big as a needle's eye and I will open for you a door through which may enter tents and (?)." Cf. also Cant. R. 5.2. One suggestion is that it may be *kirka'ot* of Isa. 66.20, where the meaning is probably "dromedaries." "If this be so the parallel, or rather contrast is striking. The repentant sinner opens a needle's eye to God, and God opens a gate in which tents and camels might camp. The figure almost seems employed as a foil to the Gospel passage quoted." Others have explained that in Syriac/Aram., "camel" could be a misreading of "rope."

10. B. BB 10a.

11. Nineham, *Mark*, p. 275, citing Dibelius, *FTG*, p. 50 n. 1.

# 190. *The Parable of the Laborers in the Vineyard*

## MATT. 20.1–16

1 "For the kingdom of heaven is like a householder who went out early in the morning to hire laborers for his vineyard. 2 After agreeing with the laborers for a denarius a day, he sent them into his vineyard. 3 And going out about the third hour he saw others standing idle in the market place; 4 and to them he said, 'You go into the vineyard too, and whatever is right I will give you.' So they went. 5 Going out again about the sixth hour and the ninth hour, he did the same. 6 And about the eleventh hour he went out and found others standing and he said to them, 'Why do you stand here idle all day?' 7 They said to him, 'Because no one has hired us.' He said to them, 'You go into the vineyard too.' 8 And when evening came, the owner of the vineyard said to his steward, 'Call the laborers and pay them their wages, beginning with the last, up to the first.' 9 And when those hired about the eleventh hour came, each of them received a denarius, 10 Now when the first came, they thought they would receive more; but each of them also received a denarius. 11 And on receiving it they grumbled at the householder, 12 saying, 'These last worked only one hour, and you have made them equal to us who have borne the burden of the day and the scorching heat.' 13 But he replied to one of them, 'Friend, I am doing you no wrong; did you not agree with me for a denarius? 14 Take what belongs to you, and go; I choose to give to this last as I give to you. 15 Am I not allowed to do what I choose with what belongs to me? Or do you begrudge my generosity?c 16 So the last will be first, and the first last.'"

---

c Or *is your eye evil because I am good.*

## COMMENTARY

This parable, as with the others, must be studied from two points of view: as an independent or original parable, and as a parable within the context of NT teaching. The interpretation of this parable is as varied as its commentators.

Some see it, within its NT context, as concentrating on the element of time;[1] others, Jeremias, for example, seeks a *Sitz im Leben* at the harvest season when the householder is desperate and those who are hired late are as important to him as those who are hired at the earlier hours.[2] Still others see in this parable the emphasis on God's grace and not the merit of man; it is the personal, subjective will of the householder to pay his employees according to his own desires.[3] Manson comments, "In its present context this parable stands in sharp contrast to what has gone before. The promise of special pre-eminence to the Twelve is balanced by a strong affirmation of equality of reward in the Kingdom. The Twelve who have laboured with Jesus from the beginning of his ministry will receive neither more nor less than any other disciple; and they may not expect or claim more."[4] There are three passages in rabbinic sources which are of note here; but not one combines both the form and message of this parable. First, one could point to the well-known statement "Some obtain and enter the Kingdom in an hour, while others reach it only after a lifetime."[5] The idea here is parallel to that of the parable but not its form. The other two are closer to its form, but their application is completely different.

When R. Bun bar R. Ḥiyya died, R. Ze'ira came in and delivered a eulogy over him: "*Sweet is the sleep of the laborer whether he has eaten little or much*. It is not written here 'sleep,' but whether he has eaten little or much. To what can R. Bun bar R. Ḥiyya be compared? To a king who hired many laborers and there was there one who was more skilled in his work, more [than others]. What did the king do? He walked up and down with him. At evening the laborers came to get their wages and he gave him the same wages as he gave to them. Whereupon they murmured and said, 'We labored the whole day long and this one worked but two hours and he gave him the same as he gave us.' The king said to them, 'This one did in two hours more than you did in the entire day.' Similarly, R. Bun labored in the study of Torah for twenty-eight years and learned what a diligent scholar could learn in a hundred years."[6]

. . . to what can this be compared? To a king who hired two laborers, one of them worked a whole day and received a dinar, and one worked one hour and received a dinar. Which one was more beloved to him [the king]? The one who worked one hour and received a dinar. Similarly, Moses our teacher served Israel for one hundred and twenty years, and Samuel served for fifty-two years, and the two of them were equal before the Omnipresent, as it is said, *Then the Lord said to me, "Though Moses and Samuel stood before Me . . ."* [Jer. 15.1], and likewise it is written, *Moses and Aaron were among His priests, Samuel also was among those who called upon His name* [Ps. 99.6], and similar to these verses it is said, *sweet is the sleep of the laborer whether he has eaten little or much* [Koh. 5.11].[7]

2 *a denarius a day* This seems to have been standard for a day's wages. The Israelites considered that they were entitled to the silver and gold which

they took from the Egyptians by calculating a denarius a day for their period of slavery.[8] Again, the angel Raphael in Tobit receives a drachma a day, the drachma equaling a dinar.[9]

3 *the third hour* 9:00 A.M.

*others standing idle* "Idle" here is the Heb. *batel* and suggests the "idle workman," Heb. *po'el batel*, a term used to express one to whom one pays "minimum wage."[10]

15 *do you begrudge my generosity* Lit. "evil eye," the Heb. idiom "to be niggardly," on which see above to Matt. 6.23 (p. 127).

## NOTES

1. E.g., Dodd, *Parables of the Kingdom*, pp. 94–95.
2. Jeremias, *PJ*, pp. 35–36.
3. Montefiore, *SG*, 2:278.
4. Manson, *SJ*, p. 218.
5. B. AZ 17a.
6. TJ Ber. 2.8, 5c. Parallels: Koh. R. 5.11; Cant. R. 6.2. In these two parallels the reading is "a king had a vineyard." McNeile, *Matt.*, p. 285, cites this passage but mistranslates it. He notes that it comes from TJ Ber. but he leaves out sections in his translation, sections which indicate that his source was either Koh. R. or Cant. R.
7. M. Semahot, ed. Higger, chap. 3, pp. 220–221. See also his Introduction, p. 6, for an extensive list of parallels to this parable.
8. Gen. R. 61. See F. C. Grant, *The Economic Background of the Gospels*, pp. 68–69; Klausner, *JN*, p. 187.
9. Tob. 5.14.
10. See M. BM 5.4; B. ibid. 68a–b, 76a–b; M. Bekh. 4.6; T. ibid. 3.9 (p. 537); B. ibid. 29a–b. On the *po'el batel* and its implications, see Derrett, *SNT*, 1:59–61, citing among others J. H. Heinemann, "Payment of a Po'el Batel," *JJS* 1 (1949): 178–181; idem, "The Status of the Labourer in Jewish Law and Society in the Tannaitic Period," *HUCA* 25 (1954): 263–325.

# *191. The Third Prediction of the Passion*

## MATT. 20.17–19

17 And as Jesus was going up to Jerusalem he took the twelve disciples aside, and on the way he said to them, 18 "Behold, we are going up to Jerusalem; and the Son of man will be delivered to the chief priests and scribes, and they will condemn him to death, 19 and deliver him to the Gentiles to be mocked and scourged and crucified, and will be raised on the third day."

## MARK 10.32–34

32 And they were on the road, going up to Jerusalem, and Jesus was walking ahead of them; and they were amazed, and those who followed were afraid. And taking the twelve again, he began to tell them what was to happen to him, 33 saying, "Behold, we are going up to Jerusalem; and the Son of man will be delivered to the chief priests

and the scribes, and they will condemn him to death, and deliver him to the Gentiles; 34 and they will mock him, and spit upon him, and scourge him, and kill him; and after three days he will rise."

## LUKE 18.31–34

31 And taking the twelve, he said to them, "Behold, we are going up to Jerusalem, and everything that is written of the Son of man by the prophets will be accomplished. 32 For he will be delivered to the Gentiles, and will be mocked and shamefully treated and spit upon; 33 they will scourge him and kill him, and on the third day he will rise." 34 But they understood none of these things; this saying was hid from them, and they did not grasp what was said.


## COMMENTARY

There are many passages in rabbinic literature which describe the sufferings preceding the advent of the Messiah, called *hevle hamashiah*. One cluster of such passages is in *PR*, chaps. 34–37, and one is relevant here. It should be noted, however, that it deals with the Messiah son of Joseph (Ephraim), who will precede the coming of the Messiah son of David. It is relatively atypical, since *hevle hamashiah* describes the sufferings preceding the advent of the Messiah, not the sufferings of the Messiah himself. The actual sufferings of the Messiah are mentioned only in late compilations. It should also be noted that nowhere is it recorded that his death is an atonement or a ransom for others.[1]

It is taught, moreover, that in the month of Nisan the Patriarchs will arise and say to the Messiah: "Ephraim, our true Messiah, even though we are thy forebears, thou art greater than we because thou didst suffer for the iniquities of our children, and terrible ordeals befell thee, such ordeals as did not befall earlier generations or later ones; for the sake of Israel thou didst become a laughingstock and a derision among the nations of the earth; and didst sit in darkness, in thick darkness, and thine eyes saw no light and thy skin cleaved to thy bones, and thy body was as dry as a piece of wood; and thine eyes grew dim from fasting, and thy strength was dried up like a potsherd—all these afflictions on account of the iniquities of our children benefit by that goodness which the Holy One, blessed be He, will bestow in abundance upon Israel. Yet it may be because of the anguish which thou didst greatly suffer on their account—for thine enemies put thee in prison—that thou are displeased with them." He will reply: "O Patriarchs, all that I have done, I have done only for your sake and for the sake of your children, that they will benefit from that goodness which the Holy One, blessed be He, will bestow in abundance upon them, upon Israel." The Patriarchs will say to him: "Ephraim, our true Messiah, be content with what thou hast done, for thou hast made content the mind of thy Maker and our minds also."[2]

## NOTES

1. See Montefiore, *RLGT*, p. 305.
2. *PR* 37, (62b). Cf. also "Sufferings are divided into three parts, of which one has been alloted to all the generations of the world, one to the age of the [Hadrianic] persecutions, and one part to the Messiah, as it is written, *He was wounded for our transgressions.*" *Mid. Sam.*, 19, 29b.

# 192. *Jesus and the Sons of Zebedee*

## Matt. 20.20–28

20 Then the mother of the sons of Zebedee came up to him, with her sons, and kneeling before him she asked him for something. 21 And he said to her, "What do you want?" She said to him, "Command that these two sons of mine may sit, one at your right hand and one at your left, in your kingdom." 22 But Jesus answered, "You do not know what you are asking. Are you able to drink the cup that I am to drink?" They said to him, "We are able." 23 He said to them, "You will drink my cup, but to sit at my right hand and at my left is not mine to grant, but it is for those for whom it has been prepared by my Father." 24 And when the ten heard it, they were indignant at the two brothers. 25 But Jesus called them to him and said, "You know that the rulers of the Gentiles lord it over them, and their great men exercise authority over them. 26 It shall not be so among you; but whoever would be great among you must be your servant, 27 and whoever would be first among you must be your slave; 28 even as the Son of man came not to be served but to serve, and to give his life as a ransom for many."

## Mark 10.35–45

35 And James and John, the sons of Zebedee, came forward to him, and said to him, "Teacher, we want you to do for us whatever we ask of you." 36 And he said to them, "What do you want me to do for you?" 37 And they said to him, "Grant us to sit, one at your right hand and one at your left, in your glory." 38 But Jesus said to them, "You do not know what you are asking. Are you able to drink the cup that I drink, or to be baptized with the baptism with which I am baptized?" 39 And they said to him, "We are able." And Jesus said to them, "The cup that I drink you will drink; and with the baptism with which I am baptized, you will be baptized; 40 but to sit at my right hand or at my left is not mine to grant, but it is for those for whom it has been prepared." 41 And when the ten heard it, they began to be indignant at James and John. 42 And Jesus called them to him and said to them, "You know that those who are supposed to rule over the Gentiles lord it over them, and their great men exercise authority over them. 43 But it shall not be so among you; but whoever would be great among you must be your servant, 44 and whoever would be first among you must be slave of all. 45 For the Son of man also came not to be served but to serve, and to give his life as a ransom for many."

## LUKE 22.24–27

24 A dispute also arose among them, which of them was to be regarded as the greatest. 25 And he said to them, "The kings of the Gentiles exercise lordship over them; and those in authority over them are called benefactors. 26 But not so with you; rather let the greatest among you become as the youngest and the leader as one who serves. 27 For which is greater, one who sits at table, or one who serves? Is it not the one who sits at table? But I am among you as one who serves."

### COMMENTARY

21 *one at your right hand, and one at your left*  As a matter of etiquette position was important. The most important person was always in the middle, the next most important was to his right, and the third in importance was to his left. This was true both at table as well as in walking and standing.[1]

22. *to drink the cup*  i.e.," to experience what I will experience." This imagery is found frequently in the MT.[2] In the Martyrdom of Isaiah, the prophet says, "for me alone hath God mingled the cup."[3]

26 *whoever would be great among you must be your servant*[4]

### NOTES

1. See M. Yom. 3.9; B. ibid. 37a; T. Sanh. 8.1 (p. 427); *Mid. Ps.* 18 (79b).
2. E.g., Ps. 74.9; Isa. 51.17; Jer. 32.1 ff.; Ezek. 33.31; Lam. 2.13.
3. Mart. Isa. 5.13.
4. Cf. B. Hor. 10a; B. Ta'an. 10b; Sifre Deut. 324; Montefiore, *RLGT*, p.299, is correct in pointing out that *SB's* citation of B. Qid. 32b is not applicable.

# 193. *The Healing of Bartimaeus*

## MATT. 20.29–34

29 And as they went out of Jericho, a great crowd followed him. 30 And behold, two blind men sitting by the roadside, when they heard that Jesus was passing by, cried out, "ᵈHave mercy on us, Son of David!" 31 The crowd rebuked them, telling them to be silent; but they cried out the more, "Lord, have mercy on us, Son of David!" 32 And Jesus stopped and called them, saying, "What do you want me to do for you?" 33 They said to him, "Lord, let our eyes be opened." 34 And Jesus in pity touched their eyes, and immediately they received their sight and followed him.

## MARK 10.46–52

46 And they came to Jericho; and as he was leaving Jericho with his disciples and a great multitude, Bartimaeus, a blind beggar, the son of Timaeus, was sitting by the

roadside. 47 And when he heard that it was Jesus of Nazareth, he began to cry out and say, "Jesus, Son of David, have mercy on me!" 48 And many rebuked him, telling him to be silent; but he cried out all the more, "Son of David, have mercy on me!" 49 And Jesus stopped and said, "Call him." And they called the blind man, saying to him, "Take heart; rise, he is calling you." 50 And throwing off his mantle he sprang up and came to Jesus. 51 And Jesus said to him, "What do you want me to do for you?" And the blind man said to him, "Master,$^e$ let me receive my sight." 52 And Jesus said to him, "Go your way; your faith has made you well." And immediately he received his sight and followed him on the way.

## LUKE 18.35–43

35 As he drew near to Jericho, a blind man was sitting by the roadside begging; 36 and hearing a multitude going by he inquired what this meant. 37 They told him, "Jesus of Nazareth is passing by." 38 And he cried "Jesus, Son of David, have mercy on me!" 39 And those who were in front rebuked him, telling him to be silent; but he cried out all the more, "Son of David, have mercy on me!" 40 And Jesus stopped, and commanded him to be brought to him; and when he came near, he asked him, 41 "What do you want me to do for you?" He said, "Lord, let me receive my sight." 42 And Jesus said to him, "Receive your sight; your faith has made you well." 43 And immediately he received his sight and followed him, glorifying God; and all the people, when they saw it, gave praise to God.

------------------------

d Some add *Lord*.
e Or *Rabbi*.
See above Sec. 56 (p. 173).

# 194. *Zacchaeus*

## LUKE 19.1–10

1 He entered Jericho and was passing through. 2 And there was a man named Zacchaeus; he was a chief tax collector, and rich. 3 And he sought to see who Jesus was, but could not, on account of the crowd, and because he was small of stature. 4 So he ran on ahead and climbed up into a sycamore tree to see him, for he was to pass that way. 5 And when Jesus came to the place, he looked up and said to him, "Zacchaeus, make haste and come down; for I must stay at your house today." 6 So he made haste and came down and received him joyfully. 7 And when they saw it they all murmured. "He has gone in to be the guest of a man who is a sinner." 8 And Zacchaeus stood and said to the Lord, "Behold, Lord, the half of my goods I give to the poor; and if I have defrauded any one of anything, I restore it fourfold." 9 And Jesus said to him, "Today salvation has come to this house, since he also is a son of Abraham. 10 For the Son of man came to seek and to save that which was lost."

## COMMENTARY

2 *And there was a man named Zacchaeus* This seems to be a recast of the Matthew-Levi story of Matt. 9.9–13, Luke. 5.7–32, Mark 2.13.17.

*Zacchaeus* This name in Gr. is found in 2 Macc. 10.19. In MT Ez. 2.9; Neh. 7.14 *zakkai*, lit. "the innocent." It is the name of the famous Patriarch R. Joḥanan b. Zakkai, who lived at the time of the destruction of the Temple in 70 c.e. It is interesting that there is a record of a Zacchaeus in Jericho who might have come from the same family.[1]

*chief tax collector and rich* Many have conjectured that his wealth came from the fact that Jericho was the eastern center of trade and that the nearby areas were particularly fertile, noted for their palm and balsam groves.[2]

5 *Zacchaeus. . . come down* Some say that Jesus was told of the man in the tree, others argue that he knew it through divine inspiration, still others say that he simply looked in that direction and saw him there.

7 *sinner* I.e., a tax-collector. See above pp. 109–110.

8 *if I have defrauded . . . fourfold* He considers that he has acquired his wealth illegally and applies the law of theft to his ill-gotten gains. Cf. Exod. 22. 1 ff.[3]

9 *Son of Abraham* A relatively common designation for a Jew.[4]

10 *to seek and save* See Ezek. 34.16.

## NOTES

1. See Schürer, *GJV*, 1:478.
2. Josephus, *Ant.* XV.4.2; *BJ* IV.8.23.
3. See B. BQ 62a; B. Sanh. 25b, 26b.
4. See, e.g., M. BM 8.1; B. BQ 32b; Gen. R. 53.12; M. Avot. 5.19.

# 195. The Parable of the Talents

### MATT. 25.14–30

14 "For it will be as when a man going on a journey called his servants and entrusted to them his property; 15 to one he gave five talents, to another two, to another one, to each according to his ability. Then he went away. 16 He who had received the five talents went at once and traded with them; and he made five talents more. 17 So, also, he who had the two talents made two talents more. 18 But he who had received the one talent went and dug in the ground and hid his master's money. 19 Now after a long time the master of those servants came and settled accounts with them. 20 And he who had received the five talents came forward, bringing five talents more, saying, 'Master, you delivered to me five talents; here I have made five talents more.' 21 His master said to him, 'Well done, good and faithful servant; you have been faithful over a little, I will set you over much; enter into the joy of your master.' 22 And he also who had the two talents came forward, saying, 'Master, you delivered to me two talents; here I have made two talents more.' 23 His master said to him, 'Well done,

good and faithful servant; you have been faithful over a little, I will set you over much; enter into the joy of your master.' 24 He also who had received the one talent came forward, saying, 'Master, I knew you to be a hard man, reaping where you did not sow, and gathering where you did not winnow; 25 so I was afraid, and I went and hid your talent in the ground. Here you have what is yours.' 26 But his master answered him, 'You wicked and slothful servant! You knew that I reap where I have not sowed, and gather where I have not winnowed? 27 Then you ought to have invested my money with the bankers, and at my coming I should have received what was my own with interest. 28 So take the talent from him, and give it to him who has the ten talents.' 29 For to everyone who has will more be given, and he will have abundance; but from him who has not, even what he has will be taken away. 30 And cast the worthless servant into the outer darkness; there men will weep and gnash their teeth."

## Luke 19.11–27

11 As they heard these things, he proceeded to tell a parable, because he was near to Jerusalem, and because they supposed that the kingdom of God was to appear immediately. 12 He said therefore, "A nobleman went into a far country to receive kingly power[f] and then return. 13 Calling ten of his servants, he gave them ten pounds and said to them, 'Trade with these till I come.' 14 But his citizens hated him and sent an embassy after him, saying, 'We do not want this man to reign over us.' 15 When he returned, having received the kingly power, he commanded these servants, to whom he had given the money, to be called to him, that he might know what they had gained by trading. 16 The first came before him, saying, 'Lord, your pound has made ten pounds more.' 17 And he said to him, 'Well done, good servant! Because you have been faithful in a very little, you shall have authority over ten cities.' 18 And the second came, saying, 'Lord, your pound has made five pounds.' 19 And he said to him, 'And you are to be over five cities.' 20 Then another came, saying, 'Lord, here is your pound, which I have kept laid away in a napkin; 21 for I was afraid of you, because you are a severe man; you take up what you did not lay down, and reap what you did not sow.' 22 He said to him, 'I will condemn you out of your own mouth, you wicked servant! You knew that I was a severe man, taking up what I did not lay down and reaping what I did not sow? 23 Why then did you not put my money into the bank, and at my coming I should have collected it with interest?' 24 And he said to those who stood by, 'Take the pound from him, and give it to him who has the ten pounds.' 25 (and they said to him, 'Lord, he has ten pounds!') 26 'I tell you that to everyone who has will more be given, but from him who has not, even what he has will be taken away. 27 But as for these enemies of mine, who did not want me to reign over them, bring them here and slay them before me.' "

---

f  Gr. *a kingdom.*

## COMMENTARY

Although it appears that the Parable of the Talents in Matt. and the Parable of the Pounds in Luke are variations of one original parable, the differences are so great as to cast doubt on this conjecture. It is more reasonable to assume that they stem from different sources.

The Matthean parable points up the lesson of service to God. "Man himself, all that he has, and all that he can produce, all belong to God. The purpose of man's existence is to serve God, and apart from such service his life is meaningless and worthless. The reward of such service is opportunity for further and larger service and the worst punishment for failure to serve is to be deprived of the opportunity to serve at all."[1]

The Lucan parable may well be based on an historical account. Herod the Great in his will divided his kingdom, but the Roman government had to confirm the bequests. One son, Archelaus went to Rome, and Augustus gave him one half of Herod's kingdom, despite the objections of the Jews, who sent an embassy to fight his appointment over the territory and his position as ethnarch. The rest of the kingdom was divided between Philip and Antipas, each becoming a tetrarch.[2] The elements of this incident might be reflected in the Lucan parable (see below).

There is no rabbinic parallel to the Matthean parable, but the following is similar in style and content: "A king has two servants, one who fears and loves the king, one who only fears him. The king goes away and apparently leaves his palace and estate to these two servants to deal with. The one who only fears the king does nothing, and the gardens and grounds become waste and desolate; the one who loves the king plants trees and flowers and fruit. Then the king returns, he is pleased with the one servant and angry with the other." The point of the parable, however, is the difference of the reward of the servant who loves from the reward of the servant who only fears. He who loves God will enjoy both this world and the world-to-come. The idolater has only this world.[3]

18 *dug in the ground and hid his master's money* Burying money or valuables or any entrusted property in the ground was considered the safest way of keeping a bailment and hence being free of responsibility.[4]

21 *good and faithful servant* Heb. *tov v'ne'eman*.[5]

*faithful over little . . . set you over much* This motif is found frequently in rabbinic literature. E.g., "God does not give greatness to a man till he has proved him in a small matter, only then does He promote him to a great post. Two were proved and found faithful and God promoted them to greatness. He tested David with sheep.. . . and God said, 'You were found faithful with the sheep, I will give you My sheep that you should feed them,' and so with Moses, who fed his father-in-law's sheep. To him God said the same."[6]

*enter into the joy of your master.* Heb. *simḥah (rabbah)*; Aram. *ḥedva, ḥedvata*. The Gr. *chara* can mean a feast or holiday celebration, for it seems to equal Heb. *mishteh*, "a feast."[7]

27 *bankers* Gr. *trapezitai*, Heb. sing. *shulḥani*.[8]

29 *outer darkness.* A favorite phrase of Matt. on which see above p. 156.

Luke 13 *Calling ten of his servants*, etc. Archelaus before setting out to go to Rome entrusted his castle and treasuries to his officers.[9]

*trade* the Gr. *pragmateusasthe* also has the meaning of "to engage in state business," and therefore this might be a conflated reading.[10]

*ten pounds* Lit. "ten *mina*." 1 *mina* = 100 *dinars*. Perhaps there is a Semitic wordplay here: *manot*, "minas," and *medinot*, "cities"; or even an indication that there is a conflated parable here, and that in one the nobleman gave his servants authority over ten *manot*, which was read *medinot*.

14 *but his citizens hated him*, etc. Perhaps the Jews who sent their embassy to Augustus objecting to Archelaus' confirmation.[10]

20 *laid away in a napkin* Gr. *soundarion*, Lat. *sudarium*, perhaps "wrapped in the fold of a garment."[12]

21 *take up what you did not lay down*.[13]

27 *enemies of mine . . . slay them*. This is not recorded of Archelaus but certainly the author could have had him in mind.

## NOTES

1. Manson, *SJ*, p. 245.
2. Josephus, *Ant.* XVII.8–9, *BJ* II.6.
3. Yal. Deut. 837, cited by Montefiore, *RLGT*, pp. 331–332. Cf. also M. Sem., ed. Higger, p. 221.
4. B. BM 42b; M. BB 4.8. See *SB*, 1:970 f.
5. E.g., B. Ber 16b.
6. *Tan. Shemot* 14; Exod. R. 2.
7. Cf. Deut. R. 9.1; Lev. R. 28.2; B. Git. 68b. See also Esther 9.17.
8. E.g., B. BM 43a, M. BM 3.11 ff.
9. Josephus, *BJ* II.18.
10. Manson, *SJ*, p. 313.
11. Ibid.
12. Cf. John 11.44; 20.7; Acts 19.12; B. Ket. 67b; M. BM 3.10; Lev. R. 6.3.
13. Only here in Luke, perhaps from a current proverb; it does not fit the following, which is from agriculture.

# B. The Days in Jerusalem

M A T T H E W   2 1 – 2 5   =   M A R K   1 1 – 1 3   =   L U K E   1 9 . 2 8 – 2 1 . 3 8

# 196. The Entry into Jerusalem

M A T T .   2 1 . 1 – 9

1 And when they drew near to Jerusalem and came to Bethphage, to the Mount of Olives, then Jesus sent two disciples, 2 saying to them, "Go into the village opposite you, and immediately you will find an ass tied, and a colt with her; untie them and

bring them to me. 3 If anyone says anything to you, you shall say, 'The Lord has need of them,' and he will send them immediately." 4 This took place to fulfill what was spoken by the prophet, saying,

> 5 "Tell the daughter of Zion, behold, your
> king is coming to you, humble, and mounted
> on an ass, and on a colt, the foal of the ass."

6 The disciples went and did as Jesus had directed them; 7 they brought the ass and the colt, and put their garments on them<sup>g</sup> and he sat thereon. 8 Most of the crowd spread their garments on the road, and others cut branches from the tree and spread them on the road. 9 And the crowds that went before him and that followed him shouted, "Hosanna to the Son of David! Blessed be he who comes in the name of the Lord! Hosanna in the highest!"

## MARK 11.1–10

1 And when they drew near to Jerusalem, to Bethphage and Bethany, at the Mount of Olives, he sent two of his disciples, 2 and said to them, "Go into the village opposite you, and immediately as you enter it you will find a colt tied, on which no one has ever sat; untie it and bring it. 3 If anyone says to you, 'Why are you doing this?' say, 'The Lord has need of it and will send it back here immediately.' " 4 And they went away, and found a colt tied at the door out in the open street; and they untied it. 5 And those who stood there said to them, "What are you doing, untying the colt?" 6 And they told them what Jesus said; and they let them go. 7 And they brought the colt to Jesus, and threw their garments on it; and he sat upon it. 8 And many spread their garments on the road, and others spread leafy branches which they had cut from the fields. 9 And those who went before and those who followed cried out, "Hosanna! Blessed be he who comes in the name of the Lord! 10 Blessed be the kingdom of our father David that is coming! Hosanna in the highest!"

## LUKE 19.28–38

28 And when he had said this, he went on ahead, going up to Jerusalem. 29 When he drew near to Bethphage and Bethany, at the mount that is called Olivet, he sent two of the disciples, 30 saying, "Go into the village opposite, where on entering you will find a colt tied, on which no one has ever yet sat; untie it and bring it here. 31 If anyone asks you, 'Why are you untying it?' you shall say this, 'The Lord has need of it.' " 32 So those who were sent went away and found it as he had told them. 33 And as they were untying the colt, its owners said to them, "Why are you untying the colt?" 34 And they said, "The Lord has need of it." 35 And they brought it to Jesus, and throwing their garments on the colt they set Jesus upon it. 36 And as he rode along, they spread their garments on the road. 37 As he was now drawing near at the descent of the Mount of Olives, the whole multitude of the disciples began to rejoice and praise God with a loud voice for all the mighty works that they had seen, 38 saying, "Blessed be the King who comes in the name of the Lord! Peace in the heaven and glory in the highest!"

---

g  Some read *on the colt*; others omit.

## COMMENTARY

1 *Bethphage* Aram. *bait pagi*, lit., "house of unripe figs." A village near Jerusalem and Bethany, probably E of the latter; considered in the Talmud as an extension of Jerusalem as regards the halakhah.[1] Mark 11.1 (Western text) reads Bethany, other MSS of Mark read both Bethany and Bethphage.

*Mount of Olives* Heb. *har hazeitim, ma'aleh hazeitim*,[2] part of the range of mountains which runs N–S through central and southern Israel. It is also called Mount Scopus.[3] Zech. 14.4 is a prophecy on the destruction of Jerusalem when the mountain (Mount of Olives) would be split in two before the coming of the Lord. This is significant because Matt. 24.3, Mark 13.3–4, Luke 21.5 ff. contain the words of Zech. 14.1–5. Furthermore, because Matt. 24.32–51 contains the parables of watchfulness before the Day of Judgment, it may well have been delivered on the Mount of Olives.[4] There is also a tradition that the Messiah will appear on the Mount of Olives.[5]

2 *an ass tied, and a colt with her* The ass and the colt mentioned in Zech. 9.9 are widely interpreted in rabbinic literature as referring to the animal of the Messiah.[6]

3 *to fulfill what was spoken* On this formula see above p. 6.

5 *Tell the daughter of Zion*, etc. The citation here seems to be a composite—*Tell the daughter of Zion* is from Isa. 62.11, the beginning of Zech. 9.9 reads *Rejoice greatly, O daughter of Zion, Shout aloud, O daughter of Jerusalem*, and most probably quoting from memory, the evangelist confused the two texts. The parallelism of the MT, i.e., *humble and riding on an ass, on the colt, the foal of an ass*, was misunderstood by the translator, who translated the *vav* of *ve'al* literally as "and" instead of omitting it or translating it as "even"; as a result two animals were requested![7]

8 *Most of the crowd spread their garments on the road* Reminiscent of 2 Kings 9.13, *Then in haste every man of them took his garment, and put it under him on the bare steps, and they proclaimed, "Jehu is king."* Reference to this practice can be found in rabbinic literature. When Moses, according to legend, was proclaimed king of Kush, the people took off their garments and spread them out on the ground.[8] Of Naqdimon b. Gorion it is related that when he went from his house to the House of Study they would spread out woolen garments under him.[9] Mention is made of spreading carpeting from homes to the graves of the Davidic kings;[10] and of spreading a carpet for the high priest from his house to the Temple.[11]

*others cut branches from the trees and spread them on the road* Similarly when Mordecai came out of the king's gate, the streets were strewn with myrtle.[12]

9 *Hosanna to the Son of David* Hosanna Heb. *hoshana, hosha-na*, or *hoshi'a-na*, meaning "save us, we beseech thee," Ps. 118.25.[13] Matthew understood this as a greeting, hence the dative "To the Son of David."[14] On the festival of Sukkot the people of Jerusalem would cry out Hosanna while marching and carrying the branches of palm, myrtle and willow. On the seventh day the

willow sprigs were beaten against the altar.[15] The willow is even called *hoshana*.[16] The simplest and perhaps best reading is John 12.13, *So they took branches of palm trees and went out to meet him, crying, 'Hosanna! Blessed be he who comes in the name of the Lord, even the King of Israel,'* which has the correct and logical order of the verses, i.e., Ps. 118.25 followed by 118.26. Luke 19.38, apparently because he was writing for Gentiles, omits the palm branches and the hosanna and reads, *Blessed is the King who comes in the name of the Lord! Peace in heaven and glory in the highest!* Mark 11.8–10 has a bit of the two, *Hosanna. Blessed is he who comes in the name of the Lord. Blessed be the kingdom of our father David that is coming, Hosanna in the highest.*"[17]

*Blessed be he who comes in the name of the Lord* Ps. 118.26.[18]

*Hosanna in the highest* This is meaningful only through the Lucan reading. It means "let the angels on high praise, etc." Cf. Ps. 148.1, *Praise the Lord from the Heavens, praise him in the heights,* and Targum ad loc., where the heavenly beings and the hosts of angels are called upon to praise God.

Luke, 34 *owners* Probably there was only one, and the Gr. is a translation of the Heb. *be'alav;* the plural of *ba'al* is regularly used in the singular third person.

## NOTES

1. See M. Men. 11.2; T. ibid. 11.1 (p. 529), 7.3 (p. 521); B. ibid. 78b. See also B. Sot. 45a, B. Sanh. 14b.
2. 2 Sam. 15.30.
3. Cf. Josephus, *BJ* II.19.4; *Vita* IV.1.
4. See *IDB*, s.v. "Mount of Olives."
5. Cf. B. Men. 11b; Josephus, *BJ* II.13.5; *Ant.* XX.8.6.
6. E.g., Gen. R. 98.9; B. Sanh. 98a, 99a; Koh. R. 1.9.
7. See Stendahl, *SSMUOT*, pp. 118 ff.
8. Yal. Exod. 168.
9. B. Ket. 66b.
10. Lam. R., Intro. #25, p. 29.
11. Ibid. 1.16, p. 86.
12. See Targ. Esther 1.5.
13. Cf. 2 Sam. 14.4; Ps. 20.10.
14. Montefiore, *SG*, 2:280.
15. See M. Suk. 3.9, 4.5.
16. B. Suk. 30b, 31a, 37a–b, 46b.
17. A. Wünsche, "Neue Beiträge zur Erläuterungen der Evangelien aus Talmud und Midrasch," (Göttingen, 1878) p. 241, suggests that there has been a confusion in the Synoptic tradition between Passover and Sukkot. A. Geiger, *Wiss. Zeit. Jud. Theol.*, 1836, p. 417, notes that Easter week in the Syrian Church is called Shabeta de Osha'ana, i.e., Hosanna week, found in the Chronicle Bar Hebraeus. Brascomb (*Mark*, p. 199) has suggested Sukkot as the time for the entrance into Jerusalem. Burkitt (*Jesus: An Historical Outline* [London and Glasgow, 1932], pp. 42–43) has opted for Hanukkah (Sukkot in Kislev). On Hosanna in the Gospels, see E. Werner, "Hosanna in the Gospels," *JBL* 65 (1946): 97–122; J. S. Kennard, Jr., "Hosanna and the Purpose of Jesus," *JBL* 67 (1948): 171–176; *JTS*, 1916.
18. This verse with messianic import, see B. Pes. 119a, *Mid. Ps.* 118.24 (242a).

# 197. *Prediction of the Destruction of Jerusalem*

## LUKE 19.39–44

39 And some of the Pharisees in the multitude said to him, "Teacher, rebuke your disciples." 40 He answered, "I tell you, if these were silent, the very stones would cry out." 41 And when he drew near and saw the city he wept over it, 42 saying, "Would that even today, you knew the things that make for peace! But now they are hid from your eyes. 43 For the days shall come upon you, when your enemies will cast up a bank about you and surround you, and hem you in on every side. 44 and dash you to the ground, you and your children within you, and they will not leave one stone upon another in you; because you did not know the time of your visitation."

### COMMENTARY

There are no rabbinic parallels to this section.

40 *the very stones would cry out* Cf. Hab. 2.11, *For the stone will cry out from the wall, and the beam from the woodwork respond.* This verse is used similarly in rabbinic sources.[1]

42 *the things that make for peace* Apparently a homiletic play on the name Jerusalem, i.e., "city of peace."[2]

*But now they are hid from your eyes* This expression means that you have no answers.[3]

44 *they will not leave one stone upon another* Referring to the destruction of the Temple and Jerusalem.[4]

### NOTES

1. Cf., e.g., *Mid. Ps.* 73.4 (108a), B. Ḥag. 16a, B. Ta'an 11a.
2. Cf. Gen. R. 56.
3. Ibid. 32.7.
4. See B. Yom. 9a, T. Men. 13.22 (pp. 533–534), B. Shab. 119b.

# 198. *Jesus in the Temple*

## MATT. 21.10–17

10 And when he entered Jerusalem, all the city was stirred, saying, "Who is this?" 11 And the crowds said, "This is the prophet Jesus from Nazareth of Galilee." 12 And Jesus entered the temple of God[h] and drove out all who sold and bought in the temple, and he overturned the tables of the money-changers and the seats of those who sold pigeons. 13 He said to them, "It is written, 'My house shall be called a house of prayer': but you make it a den of robbers." 14 And the blind and the lame came to him in the temple, and he healed them. 15 But when the chief priests and scribes saw the wonderful things that he did, and the children crying out in the temple, "Hosanna to the Son of David!" they were indignant; 16 and they said to him, "Do you hear

what they are saying?" And Jesus said to them, "Yes; have you ever read, 'Out of the mouth of babes and sucklings thou hast brought perfect praise?' " 17 and leaving them, he went out of the city to Bethany and lodged there.

## MARK 11.11

And he entered Jerusalem and went into the temple; and when he had looked round at everything, as it was already late, he went out to Bethany with the twelve.

## LUKE 19.45–46

45 And he entered the temple and began to drive out those who sold, 46 saying to them, "It is written, 'My house shall be a house of prayer'; but you have made it a den of robbers."

---

h Other ancient authorities omit *of God*.

## COMMENTARY

12 *money-changers* Gr. *kollubistēs*, Heb. *shulḥani*, "one who sits at a table" (*shulḥan*). For their fee called in Gr. *kollubos* which is used both in Heb. and Aram., *kolbon*. These money-changers were fulfilling a real need. The biblical law, Exod. 30.11 ff., requires all adult males to pay a half sheqel to the Sanctuary, which in NT times was to be paid in Tyrian silver coins. One month before the Passover, on the 15th of Adar (see above p. 264), the money-changers set up their tables in the provinces for the collections,[1] then ten days later, when the Jews would be arriving in Jerusalem, especially those from foreign countries, the money-changers set up in the Temple courts. Jesus himself, it is recorded, paid the half-sheqel for himself and for Peter (Matt. 17.24 ff.), and therefore we may presume that he did not object to this practice. What then was his objection? He must have objected to the charge of the *kollubos*, which he thought to be unfair or excessive. The amount of the *kollubos* was one twenty-fourth of a sheqel, which hardly sounds excessive, and there is no unanimity as to what happened to this *kollubos*, "To what use were the kolbons turned? R. Meir says: 'They were added to the fund of the sheqalim'; R. Lazer says: 'For providing free-will burnt offerings [*nedavah*].' R. Simeon of Shizur (Saijur) says: 'They provided them with gold-plates and covering for the Holy of Holies'; Ben Azzai says: 'The bankers took them as their own profit'; and some say that they were used for the expense of keeping the roads in repair."[2] It is likely that the collectors were priests.

*the seats of those who sold pigeons* These vendors provided the doves for sacrificial offerings. Here we do have evidence of abuse, as a result of profiteering in the sale of doves. "Once in Jerusalem a pair of doves cost a golden dinar.[3] Rabban Simeon ben Gamaliel said: 'By this Temple! I will not have the night pass before they cost but a [silver] dinar.' He went into the court and taught: 'If a woman suffered five miscarriages that were not in doubt or five issues that were not in doubt, she need bring out one offering, and she may eat of the animal offering and she is not obligated to offer the other offering [for the other four].' And the same day the price of a pair of doves stood at a quarter dinar each."[4]

13 *My house shall be called a house of prayer* Isa. 56.7, which adds *For all people*.

*a den of robbers* Jer. 7.11.[5]

14 *And the blind and the lame came to him in the temple* There was no prohibition excluding the blind and the lame from the Temple, as some have maintained.[6] The mishnah "All are subject to the command to appear before the Lord [at the Festivals] except for the deaf mute, the imbecile, the minor, one of the doubtful sex, one of double sex, women, slaves that have not been freed, a man that is lame or blind or sick or aged, and one that cannot go up to Jerusalem on his feet" is not applicable to prove that "the blind and the lame were excluded from the Temple."[7] This mishnah merely states that those mentioned are not *obligated* to attend the Temple at Festival time to fulfill the biblical command of Deut. 16.6. It does not mean that they were excluded from the Temple.[8]

15 *children crying out in the temple, Hosanna* Only here in Matt. In Luke 19.39–44 the incident takes place on the road; the Pharisees told Jesus to rebuke his disciples, who were shouting, "Blessed be the king, etc." (v. 38), to which Jesus responded that if these were silent the very stones would cry out. This appears to be closer to the original. The Matthean version involves *banim*, "children," which was read for *avanim*, "stones." Children would not have behaved in such a manner in the Temple.

16 *Out of the mouth of babes*, etc. Ps. 8.3, according to the LXX against the MT,[9] reading "praise," not "strength." The implication here is that Jesus sees in this a revelation from God not coming from flesh and blood.[10] Little children, however, were taught the *Hallel*, which contains the Hosanna.[11]

17 *Bethany* Derivation uncertain. Some see it as "house of Ananiah" or "house of the poor." In Jth 1.9 it appears as Baitane or Batane. In the Talmud it is Bet Hini, which may refer to the late-season green figs of the region of Bethany and Bethphage.[12] It is a small village 1⅝ miles E of Jerusalem on the E slope of the Mount of Olives, today El Aziriyeh.[13]

## NOTES

1. M. Sheq. 1.3.
2. TJ Sheq. 1.8, 46b (end); B. Men. 108a. On the money-changers, see S. Krauss, *TA* (Leipzig 1911), 2:411; Abrahams, *Studies I*, pp. 82–89.
3. Equaling 25 silver dinars. For a discussion of this passage, see L. Finkelstein, *Akiba: Scholar, Saint and Martyr* (New York, 1936), pp. 51 ff.
4. M. Ker. 1.7. Other excesses see B. Pes. 57a, TJ Ḥag. 2.3.

5. On this verse see Stendahl, *SSMUOT*, pp. 66 ff. Note below p. 350 that Mark 11.17 cites Isa. 56.7, *My house shall be called a house of prayer for all the nations*. This has a universal ring to it, while the reading in Matt. and Luke which omits *for all the nations* restricts the Temple to Israel. On this complex problem see Stendahl, op. cit., pp. 66 ff.

6. Manson, *SJ*, pp. 220–221.

7. M. Ḥag. 1.1.

8. The citation from 2 Sam. 5.8 (RV m) is hardly applicable because of the different time period.

9. See Stendahl, op. cit., pp. 67, 134.

10. Cf. Matt. 16.17, as Manson, *SJ*, p. 221.

11. T. Sot. 6.2 ff. (p. 303).

12. B. Pes. 53a, B. BM 88a; see above p. 344.

13. Bethany is not mentioned in the MT, unless it be identified with Ananiah of Neh. 11.32. See IDB, s.v. "Bethany."

# 199. The Cursing of the Fig Tree

## MATT. 21.18–19

18 In the morning, as he was returning to the city, he was hungry. 19 And seeing a fig tree by the wayside he went to it and found nothing on it but leaves only. And he said to it, "May no fruit ever come from you again!" And the fig tree withered at once.

## MARK 11.12–14

12 On the following day, when they came from Bethany, he was hungry. 13 And seeing in the distance a fig tree in leaf, he went to see if he could find anything on it. When he came to it, he found nothing but leaves, for it was not the season for figs. 14 And he said to it, "May no one ever eat fruit from you again." And his disciples heard it.

### COMMENTARY

There are no rabbinic parallels to this section.

# 200. The Cleansing of the Temple

## MATT. 21.12–13

12 And Jesus entered the temple of God[i] and drove out all who sold and bought in the temple, and he overturned the tables of the money-changers and the seats of those who sold pigeons. 13 He said to them, "It is written, 'My house shall be called a house of prayer,' but you make it a den of robbers."

## MARK 11.15–19

15 And they came to Jerusalem. And he entered the temple and began to drive out those who sold and those who bought in the temple, and he overturned the tables of the money-changers and the seats of those who sold pigeons; 16 and he would not allow anyone to carry anything through the temple. 17 And he taught, and said to them, "Is it not written, 'My house shall be called a house of prayer for all the nations'? But you have made it a den of robbers." 18 And the chief priests and the scribes heard it and sought a way to destroy him; for they feared him, because all the multitude was astonished at his teaching. 19 And when evening came theyʲ went out of the city.

## LUKE 19.45–48

45 And he entered the temple and began to drive out those who sold, 46 saying to them, "It is written, 'My house shall be a house of prayer'; but you have made it a den of robbers." 47 And he was teaching daily in the temple. The chief priests and the scribes and the principal men of the people sought to destroy him; 48 but they did not find anything they could do, for all the people hung upon his words.

---

i  Some omit *of God*.
j  Some read *he*.
 See above Sec. 198 (p. 346).

### COMMENTARY

Mark 11.16 *he would not allow anyone*, etc.  This is found only here in Mark. Perhaps it is a scribal addition. According to Josephus, no one was allowed to carry a vessel into the Temple.[1] Other restrictions were that one might not enter the Temple Mount with his staff or his sandal or his wallet or with the dust upon his feet, nor might he make of it a short-path, still less might he spit there.[2]

### NOTES

 1. *Contra Ap*. II.8.
 2. M. Ber. 9.5.

## 201. *The Meaning of the Withered Fig Tree*

### MATT. 21.20–22

20 When the disciples saw it they marveled, saying, "How did the fig tree wither at once?" 21 And Jesus answered them, "Truly, I say to you, if you have faith, and never doubt, you will not only do what has been done to the fig tree, but even if you say to this mountain, 'Be taken up and cast into the sea,' it will be done. 22 And whatever you ask in prayer, you will receive, if you have faith."

## IBID 6.14

14 "For if you forgive men their trespasses, your heavenly Father also will forgive you."

## MARK 11.20–25

20 As they passed by in the morning, they saw the fig tree withered away to its roots. 21 And Peter remembered and said to him, "Master,k look! The fig tree which you cursed has withered." 22 And Jesus answered them, "Have faith in God. 23 Truly, I say to you, whoever says to this mountain, 'Be taken up and cast into the sea,' and does not doubt in his heart, but believes that what he says will come to pass, it will be done for him. 24 Therefore I tell you, whatever you ask in prayer, believe that you will receive it, and you will. 25 And whenever you stand praying, forgive, if you have anything against anyone; so that your Father also who is heaven may forgive you your trespasses."l

---

k Or *Rabbi*.
l Other ancient authorities add v. 26, *But if you do not forgive, neither will your Father who is in heaven forgive your trespasses.*

### COMMENTARY

21 *even if you say to this mountain.* See above Matt. 17.20 (p. 263).

# 202. *The Question About Authority*

## MATT. 21.23–27

23 And when he entered the temple, the chief priests and the elders of the people came up to him as he was teaching, and said, "By what authority are you doing these things, and who gave you this authority?" 24 Jesus answered them, "I also will ask you a question; and if you tell me the answer, then I also will tell you by what authority I do these things. 25 The baptism of John, whence was it? From heaven or from men?" And they argued with one another, "If we say, 'From heaven,' he will say to us, 'Why then did you not believe him?' 26 But if we say, 'From men,' we are afraid of the multitude; for all hold that John was a prophet." 27 So they answered Jesus, "We do not know." And he said to them, "Neither will I tell you by what authority I do these things."

## MARK 11.27–33

27 And they came again to Jerusalem. And as he was walking in the temple, the chief priests and the scribes and the elders came to him, 28 and they said to him, "By what authority are you doing these things, or who gave you this authority to do them?" 29 Jesus said to them, "I will ask you a question: answer me, and I will tell you by what

authority I do these things. 30 Was the baptism of John from heaven or from men? Answer me." 31 And they argued with one another, "If we say, 'From heaven,' he will say, 'Why then did you not believe him?' 32 But shall we say, 'From men'?"—they were afraid of the people, for all held that John was a real prophet. 33 So they answered Jesus, "We do not know." And Jesus said to them, "Neither will I tell you by what authority I do these things."

### LUKE 20.1–8

1 One day, as he was teaching the people in the temple and preaching the gospel, the chief priests and the scribes with the elders came up 2 and said to him, "Tell us by what authority you do these things, or who it is that gave you this authority." 3 He answered them, "I also will ask you a question; now tell me, 4 Was the baptism of John from heaven or from men?" 5 And they discussed it with one another, saying, "If we say, 'From heaven,' he will say, 'Why did you not believe him?' 6 But if we say, 'From men,' all the people will stone us; for they are convinced that John was a prophet." 7 So they answered that they did not know whence it was. 8 And Jesus said to them, "Neither will I tell you by what authority I do these things."

### COMMENTARY

23 *authority* Gr. *exousia*. Heb. *reshut*. It is doubtful that *exousia* is used here as in Matt. 7.27, *For he taught them as one who had authority*. If that is what is meant here, then the question should have been, "By whose authority do you *teach* these things," not "*do* these things."[1] What is referred to is the performance of miraculous cures, etc., and the question has awkwardly been attached to the phrase "as he was teaching" and making it the antecedent. This is borne out by Jesus' question about the authority of John's baptism from heaven, i.e., God, or from men, which then parallels Jesus' activity, not his teaching.[2]

24 *I also will ask you a question* The counter-question, especially as a means of avoiding answering a question already asked, is found frequently in rabbinic literature.[3]

### NOTES

1. Contra: Daube, *NTRJ*, p. 217.
2. On divine *reshut*, "authority," see TJ Sanh. 6.12, 23d (bot.).
3. E.g., *PR* 10 (40a); B. Ta'an. 7a; B. Sanh. 65b.

## 203. *The Parable of the Two Sons*

### MATT. 21.28–32

28 "What do you think? A man had two sons; and he went to the first and said, 'Son, go and work in the vineyard today.' 29 And he answered 'I will not'; but afterward he repented and went. 30 And he went to the second and said the same; and he

answered, 'I go sir,' but did not go. 31 Which of the two did the will of the father?" They said "The first." Jesus said to them, "Truly, I say to you, the tax collectors and the harlots go into the kingdom of God before you. 32 For John came to you in the way of righteousness and you did not believe him; and even when you saw it, you did not afterward repent and believe him."m

---

m Some read *even when you did not see it, you afterward repented;* others *when you saw it you afterward repented.*

### COMMENTARY

There are no rabbinic parallels to this parable unique to Matthew. The parable itself is textually difficult and exists in three different recensions.[1] There is, however, a similar parable of the same genre:

> . . . a parable of a king who had a field and he desired to turn it over to a tenant farmer. He called to the first and said to him, "Will you take this field?" He said to him, "I don't have the strength, it is too hard for me." So it was with the second, the third, and the fourth, they too did not accept it from him. He called to the fifth and said to him, "Will you take this field?" He said to him, "Yes!" The owner said, "On condition that you work it according to the Law?" He said, "Yes." When the tenant farmer entered [the field], he left it unworked. With whom should the king be angry? On those who said that they were unable to accept it or on the one who took it upon himself and having taken it upon himself left it unworked? Should he not be angry with the latter?[2]

### NOTES

1. For good analyses of the textual problems, see Manson, *SJ*, p. 222, and Derrett *SNT*, 1:78 ff.
2. Exod. R. 27. A bit more remote as a parallel, see B. BQ 79b. See also Jellinek, *BHM*, 5:91.

## 204. *The Parable of the Wicked Tenants*

### MATT. 21.33–46

33 "Hear another parable. There was a householder who planted a vineyard and set a hedge around it, and dug a wine press in it, and built a tower, and let it out to tenants, and went into another country. 34 When the season of fruit drew near, he sent his servants to the tenants, to get his fruit; 35 and the tenants took his servants and beat one, killed another, and stoned another. 36 Again he sent other servants, more than the first; and they did the same to them. 37 Afterward he sent his son to them, saying, 'They will respect my son.' 38 But when the tenants saw the son they said to themselves, 'This is the heir; come, let us kill him and have his inheritance.' 39 And they took him and cast him out of the vineyard, and killed him. 40 When therefore

the owner of the vineyard comes, what will he do to those tenants?" 41 They said to him, "He will put those wretches to a miserable death, and let out the vineyard to other tenants who will give him the fruits in their seasons." 42 Jesus said to them, 'Have you never read in the scriptures:

> 'The very stone which the builders rejected has
> become the head of the corner; this was the Lord's
> doing, and it is marvelous in our eyes'?

43 Therefore I tell you, the kingdon of God will be taken away from you and given to a nation producing the fruits of it."[n] 45 When the chief priests and the Pharisees heard his parables, they perceived that he was speaking about them. 46 But when they tried to arrest him, they feared the multitudes, because they held him to be a prophet.

## Mark 12.1–12

1 And he began to speak to them in parables. "A man planted a vineyard, and set a hedge around it, and dug a pit for the wine press, and built a tower, and let it out to tenants, and went into another country. 2 When the time came, he sent a servant to the tenants, to get from them some of the fruit of the vineyard. 3 And they took him and beat him, and sent him away empty-handed. 4 Again he sent to them another servant, and they wounded him in the head, and treated him shamefully. 5 And he sent another, and him they killed; and so with many others, some they beat and some they killed. 6 He had still one other, a beloved son; finally he sent him to them, saying, 'They will respect my son.' 7 But those tenants said to one another, 'This is the heir; come, let us kill him, and the inheritance will be ours.' 8 And they took him and killed him, and cast him out of the vineyard. 9 What will the owner of the vineyard do? He will come and destroy the tenants, and give the vineyard to others. 10 Have you not read this scripture:

> 'The very stone which the builders rejected
> has become the head of the corner;
> 11 this was the Lord's doing, and
> it is marvelous in our eyes'?"

12 And they tried to arrest him, but feared the multitude, for they perceived that he had told the parable against them; so they left him and went away.

## Luke 20.9–19

9 And he began to tell the people this parable: "A man planted a vineyard and let it out to tenants, and went into another country for a long while. 10 When the time came, he sent a servant to the tenants, that they should give him some of the fruit of the vineyard; but the tenants beat him, and sent him away empty-handed. 11 And he sent another servant; him also they beat and treated shamefully, and sent him away empty-handed. 12 And he sent yet a third; this one they wounded and cast out. 13 Then the owner of the vineyard said, 'What shall I do? I will send my beloved son; it may be they will respect him,' 14 But when the tenants saw him, they said to themselves, 'This is the heir; let us kill him, that the inheritance may be ours.' 15 And they cast him out of the vineyard and killed him. What then will the owner of the vineyard do to them? 16 He will come and destroy those tenants, and give the

vineyard to others." When they heard this, they said, "God forbid!" 17 But he looked at them and said, "What then is this that is written,
>'The very stone which the builders rejected
>has become the head of the corner'?

18 Everyone who falls on that stone will be broken to pieces; but when it falls on anyone it will crush him." 19 The scribes and the chief priests tried to lay hands on him at that very hour, but they feared the people; for they perceived that he had told this parable against them.

---

n Other ancient authorities add v. 44, *And he who falls on this stone will be broken to pieces; but when it falls on anyone, it will crush him.*

## COMMENTARY

33 *A householder who planted a vineyard* The background of this verse is the Song of the Vineyard of Isa. 5.1–7. There is no rabbinic parallel to the parable itself.[1]

34 *When the season of fruit drew near* Some say after three years, since vines in this area produce grapes only after three years;[2] but following Lev. 19.23, 25, assuming that it was new planting, it would be after four years.[3]

*tenants* Gr. *geōrgoi*, Heb. *arisim*, i.e., tenant farmers, sharecroppers.[4]

38 *come, let us kill him* Reminiscent of Gen. (LXX) 37.18, 28, but to see in it a Joseph typology is unlikely.[5]

*and have his inheritance* It is extremely doubtful that the principle of adverse possession is involved here.[6] What is more probable is that the householder was a proselyte for when a proselyte died intestate, his property became ownerless and went to the first claimant.[7] Here the tenant had the first opportunity to claim by occupation.[8]

42 *The very stone*, etc. Ps. 118.2. In one late passage the Messiah is compared to a stone.[9]

## NOTES

1. Lev. R. 5.8 and B. Sanh. 107a cited by A. Feldman, *The Parables and Similes of the Rabbis* (Cambridge, 1924), p. 42, n.2 are not applicable.
2. Lagrange, *Marc*, p. 306.
3. Cf. Derrett, *LNT*, p. 290.
4. On the *arisim* and the interpretation of this verse, see Derrett, "The Stone That the Builders Rejected," *Studia Evangelica* 5 (Berlin, 1968), p. 181 n. 1; H. J. Cadbury in F. J. Foakes Jackson and Kirsopp Lake, *The Beginnings of Christianity*, pt. I, *The Acts of the Apostles*, 5 vols. (London, 1922–39), 5:373 ff.
5. See C. E. Carlston, *The Parables of The Triple Tradition* (Philadelphia: Fortress Press, 1975), p. 180, n.a.
6. See Derrett, *LNT* p. 300.
7. See B. Qid. 17b.
8. See Jeremias, *PJ* p. 76.
9. See Esther R. 3.6

# 205. *The Parable of the Marriage Feast*

## MATT. 22.1–14

1 And again Jesus spoke to them in parables, saying, 2 "The kingdom of heaven may be compared to a king who gave a marriage feast for his son, 3 and sent his servants to call those who were invited to the marriage feast; but they would not come. 4 Again he sent other servants, saying, 'Tell those who are invited, Behold, I have made ready my dinner, my oxen and my fat calves are killed, and everything is ready; come to the marriage feast.' 5 But they made light of it and went off, one to his farm, another to his business, 6 while the rest seized his servants, treated them shamefully, and killed them. 7 The king was angry, and he sent his troops and destroyed those murderers and burned their city. 8 Then he said to his servants, 'The wedding is ready, but those invited were not worthy. 9 Go therefore to the thoroughfares, and invite to the marriage feast as many as you find.' 10 And those servants went out into the streets and gathered all whom they found, both bad and good; so the wedding hall was filled with guests. 11 But when the king came in to look at the guests, he saw there a man who had no wedding garment; 12 and he said to him, 'Friend, how did you get in here without a wedding garment?' And he was speechless. 13 Then the king said to the attendants, 'Bind him hand and foot and cast him into the outer darkness; there men will weep and gnash their teeth.' 14 For many are called, but few are chosen."

## LUKE 14.16–24

16 But he said to him, "A man once gave a great banquet, and invited many; 17 and at the time for the banquet he sent his servant to say to those who had been invited, 'Come; for all is now ready.' 18 But they all alike began to make excuses. The first said to him, 'I have bought a field, and I must go out and see it; I pray you, have me excused.' 19 And another said, 'I have bought five yoke of oxen, and I go to examine them; I pray you, have me excused.' 20 And another said, 'I have married a wife, and therefore I cannot come.' 21 So the servant came and reported this to his master. Then the householder in anger said to his servant, 'Go quickly to the streets and lanes of the city, and bring in the poor and maimed and blind and lame.' 22 And the servant said, 'Sir, what you have commanded has been done, and still there is room.' 23 And the master said to the servant, 'Go out to the highways and hedges and compel people to come in, that my house may be filled. 24 For I tell you, none of those men who were invited shall taste my banquet.' "

## COMMENTARY

This section seems to be a composite from many sources, which would account for the overlap of material and themes. Matt. 22.1–10 is paralleled by Luke 14.26–24, but vv. 11–14 are peculiar to Matt.[1] There are many parables in rabbinic literature of a king making a wedding for his son, but they do not serve as parallels to this material except for one which is relevant, but only to the theme of the wedding garment.

R. Johanan b. Zakkai said: "A parable of a king who invited his servants to a banquet but did not specify to them the time. The clever ones among them adorned themselves and sat at the entrance of the king's house. They said: 'Does the king's house lack anything?' The foolish among them went to their work, for they said: 'Can there be a banquet without preparation?' Suddenly the king asked for his servants. The clever among them entered before him as they were adorned, but the foolish among them entered before him dirty as they were. The king rejoiced to greet the clever ones but was angry with the foolish ones. He said: 'These who have adorned themselves for the banquet, let them be seated and eat and drink, but these who have not adorned themselves for the banquet, let them stand and merely observe.' " The son-in-law of R. Meir said in the name of R. Meir: "But the foolish would appear like attendants, let both sit down, but let the clean servants eat and drink, while the dirty ones shall go hungry and thirst."[2]

4 *everything is ready*  On the banquet with its messianic overtones, see above p. 80 n. 37.

13 *bind him hand and foot*  Cf. I En. 10.4, where the angel Raphael is commanded by God to bind the rebellious Azazel "hand and foot" and cast him into the darkness.

14 *many are called, but few are chosen*  Dalman reads it as an Aram. adage, *saggi'in zeminin, za'irin behirin?*[3] A similar idea is expressed in "many have been created, but few shall be saved,"[4] and "There are more who perish than shall be saved."[5]

## NOTES

1. On the textual problems of this passage, see Manson, *SJ*, pp. 224–226.
2. B. Shab. 153a and Koh. R. 9.8, 3.8.
3. *Words*, 1:97.
4. 4 Ezra 8.3.
5. Ibid. 9.15. See also Apoc. Bar. (Syr.) 44.15.

# 206. Concerning Tribute to Caesar

## MATT. 22.15–22

15 Then the Pharisees went and took counsel how to entangle him in his talk. 16 And they sent their disciples to him, along with the Herodians, saying, "Teacher, we know that you are true, and teach the way of God truthfully, and care for no man; for you do not regard the position of men. 17 Tell us, then, what you think. Is it lawful to pay taxes to Caesar, or not?" 18 But Jesus, aware of their malice, said, "Why put me to the test, you hypocrites? 19 Show me the money for the tax." And they brought him a coin.[o] 20 And Jesus said to them, "Whose likeness and inscription is this?" 21 They said, "Caesar's." Then he said to them, "Render therefore to Caesar the things that are Caesar's and to God the things that are God's." 22 When they heard it, they marveled; and they left him and went away.

## MARK 12.13–17

13 And they sent to him some of the Pharisees and some of the Herodians, to entrap him in his talk. 14 And they came and said to him, "Teacher, we know that you are true, and care for no man; for you do not regard the position of men, but truly teach the ways of God. Is it lawful to pay taxes to Caesar, or not? 15 Should we pay them, or should we not?" But knowing their hypocrisy, he said to them, "Why put me to the test? Bring me a coin,° and let me look at it." 16 And they brought one. And he said to them, "Whose likeness and inscription is this?" They said to him, "Caesar's." 17 Jesus said to them, "Render to Caesar the things that are Caesar's and to God the things that are God's." And they were amazed at him.

## LUKE 20.20–26

20 So they watched him, and sent spies, who pretended to be sincere, that they might take hold of what he said, so as to deliver him up to the authority and jurisdiction of the governor. 21 They asked him, "Teacher, we know that you speak and teach rightly, and show no partiality, but truly teach the way of God. 22 Is it lawful for us to give tribute to Caesar, or not?" 23 But he perceived their craftiness, and said to them, 24 "Show me a coin.° Whose likeness and inscription has it?" They said, "Caesar's." 25 He said to them, "Then render to Caesar the things that are Caesar's, and to God the things that are God's." 26 And they were not able in the presence of the people to catch him by what he said; but marveling at his answer they were silent.

---

o  Greek *a denarius*.

### COMMENTARY

16 *Herodians*  The term is not found in Luke or John and identification is difficult, probably followers of Herod Antipas.[1]

17 *taxes*  Gr. *kēnsos* (also Mark, but Luke reads *phoros*) appears also in Aram. and late Heb. *kenas*. In Gr. it was a poll tax and had to be paid in Roman coin which had the figure of the Caesar struck on it. In Jesus time this would apply in Judea, which was under Roman rule, but not in Galilee, which was ruled by Antipas. It is this tax which Judas of Galilee fought against.[2]

21 *Caesar*  The image of the Caesar was a point of irritation to the Jews, especially when it threatened to invade the Temple precincts, as in the days of Caius Caligula (became Caesar in 37 C.E.), who demanded that the Jews set up his statues in the Temple, under penalty of death.[3] Jews on several instances were willing to die rather than to permit this.[4] Petronius, the emissary of Caius, gave in and the danger was averted. Petronius was spared the consequences of his act by the death of the emperor in 41.[5] As to the emperor's image on the coin, this did not raise such violent objections on the part of the Jews, although they most assuredly found both his image and the tax itself objectionable. Only the most scrupulously pious avoided looking on

the images on coins. It is related that R. Nahum b. Simlai was known for his holiness because "he never looked upon the form on a coin."[6] Jews were dutybound to respect the government even though it was foreign, as long as it did not interfere with their religious practices.[7] The dictum is *dina demalkhuta dina*, "the law of the government is law."[8]

Although the Roman taxes were oppressive at the time of Jesus, the Jew was dutybound to pay them provided they were not arbitrarily imposed by the local tax farmer.[9] T. Reinach pointed out that the procurators respected Jewish sensitivities in this regard and struck coins which bore no figures of humans.[10]

*Render to Caesar*, etc.[11]

## NOTES

1. This is the view of E. Bickerman, "Les Hérodiens," *RB* 47 (1938): 184–197. For a selective bibliography on the Herodians, see *IDB*, s.v. "Herodians."

2. See *Ant.* XVIII.1.1; *BJ* II.8.1.

3. Josephus, *BJ* X.1.

4. Ibid. II.9.3.

5. For further details on this confrontation, see Philo, *Leg. ad Gaium* 32.24.

6. B. Pes. 104a and parallels.

7. See *Tan.B. Gen. Noaḥ* 10 (33a).

8. B. BQ 113b; B. BB 54a; B. Git. 10b; B. Ned. 28a.

9. See B. BQ 113a; B. Ned. 28a; M. Sem. 2.9, ed. Higger, p. 107. On the tax of 15 shekels imposed after the destruction of the Temple, see *Mek.* Exod. 19.1; TJ Shek. 3.2, 47c (33); M. Avot 3.7.

10. T. Reinach, *Jewish Coins*, ed. Hill, p. 41. Abrahams, *Studies I*, pp. 62–66.

11. See B. AZ 6b.

## 207. *Concerning Resurrection*

### MATT. 22.23–33

23 The same day Sadducees came to him, who say that there is no resurrection; and they asked him a question, 24 saying, "Teacher, Moses said, 'If a man dies, having no children, his brother must marry the widow, and raise up children for his brother.' 25 Now there were seven brothers among us; the first married, and died, and having no children left his wife to his brother. 26 So too the second and third, down to the seventh. 27 After them all, the woman died. 28 In the resurrection, therefore, to which of the seven will she be the wife? For they all had her." 29 But Jesus answered them, "You are wrong, because you know neither the scriptures nor the power of God. 30 For in the resurrection they neither marry nor are given in marriage but are like angelsᴾ in heaven. 31 And as for the resurrection of the dead, have you not read what was said to you by God, 32 'I am the God of Abraham and the God of Isaac, and the God of Jacob'? He is not the God of the dead, but of the living." 33 And when the crowd heard it, they were astounded at his teaching.

## Mark 12.18–27

18 And Sadducees came to him, who say that there is no resurrection; and they asked him a question, saying, 19 "Teacher, Moses wrote for us that if a man's brother dies and leaves a wife, but leaves no child, the man[q] must take the wife and raise up children for his brother. 20 There were seven brothers; the first took a wife, and when he died left no children; 21 and the second took her, and died, leaving no children; and the third likewise; 22 and the seven left no children. Last of all the woman also died. 23. In the resurrection[r] whose wife will she be? For the seven had her as wife." 24 Jesus said to them, "Is not this why you are wrong, that you know neither the scriptures nor the power of God? 25 For when they rise from the dead, they neither marry nor are given in marriage, but are like the angels in heaven. 26 And as for the dead being raised, have you not read in the book of Moses, in the passage about the bush, how God said to him, 'I am the God of Abraham and the God of Isaac and the God of Jacob'? 27 He is not the God of the dead but of the living; you are quite wrong."

## Luke 20.27–40

27 There came to him some Sadducees, those who say that there is no resurrection, 28 and they asked him a question, saying, "Teacher, Moses wrote for us that if a man's brother dies, having a wife but no children, the man[q] must take the wife and raise up children for his brother. 29 Now there were seven brothers; the first took a wife, and died without children; 30 and the second 31 and the third took her, and likewise all seven left no children and died. 32 Afterward the woman also died. 33 In the resurrection, therefore, whose wife will the woman be? For the seven had her as a wife." 34 And Jesus said to them, "The sons of this age marry and are given in marriage; 35 but those who are accounted worthy to attain to that age and to the resurrection from the dead neither marry nor are given in marriage, 36 for they cannot die anymore, because they are equal to angels and are the sons of God, being the sons of the resurrection. 37 But that the dead are raised even Moses showed, in the passage about the bush, where he calls the Lord the God of Abraham, and the God of Isaac, and the God of Jacob. 38 Now he is not the God of the dead, but of the living; for all live to him." 39 And some of the scribes answered, "Teacher, you have spoken well." 40 For they no longer dared to ask him any question.

---

p  Other ancient authorities add *of God.*
q  Or *his brother.*
r  Some add *when they shall arise.*

## COMMENTARY

23  *Sadducees*  On this group and their doctrines, see above pp. 40 f.[1]

24  *If a man dies*, etc.  The law of the levirate marriage, Deut. 25.5 ff. See also Gen. 38.8.[2]

25  *there were seven brothers*  In the tannaitic period a woman who had been widowed several times was not permitted to remarry, since she was consid-

ered to be dangerous and was called *qatlanit,* "a killer," and another marriage was deemed inadvisable. According to R. Judah the Prince, twice was enough to establish the presumption; according to R. Simeon b. Gamaliel, three established the presumption and a fourth was prohibited.[3]

29 *You are wrong, because you know neither the scriptures nor the power of God* Similar expression in the Talmud, "You know how to read the Scriptures but you do not know how to expound them."[4]

30 *For in the resurrection they neither marry,* etc. There is no parallel, but in the same spirit: "In the world-to-come there is no eating and drinking, or procreation and childbearing or trade or business or enmity and strife, but the righteous sit with crowns on their heads and enjoy the radiance of the Shekhinah."[5]

*like angels in heaven* Cf. "for you shall become companions of the hosts of heaven,"[6] and "they shall respectively be transformed, the latter into the splendor of the angels, and the former shall yet more waste away."[7]

32 *I am the God of Abraham and the God of Isaac,* etc. Exod. 3.6. There is no such treatment of this verse in rabbinic sources, but the exposition is in the rabbinic tradition.[8]

## NOTES

1. On resurrection and the Sadducees, see also Acts. 4.1–2, 23.6–10, S. T. Lachs, "The Pharisees and Sadducees on Angels: A Reexamination of Acts XXIII.8," *Gratz College Annual of Jewish Studies* 6 (1977): 35 ff.

2. On the levirate marriage, see Sifre Deut. 288. On the interpretation of this law by the Pharisees and the Sadducees, see Meg. Ta'an. 4 and Sifre Deut. 237; B. Ket. 46a; M. Yev. 12.6; C. M. Burrows, "The Marriage of Boaz and Ruth," *JBL* 59 (1940): 22–33, 445–454.

3. T. Shab. 15.8 (p. 133); B. Yev. 64b. See also L. Epstein, *Marriage Laws in the Bible and Talmud* (Cambridge, Mass, 1942), pp. 77–144.

4. TJ Ber. 4, 4d (2). It is also possible that the Gr. *ten dunamin tou theou,* rather than understood as "power," should be understood as "a spiritual being," and this is supported by its usage in a similar way in the papyri. See *BAG,* s.v. *dunamis* (6). This fits well with the next verse, which compares the deceased to the angels.

5. B. Ber. 17a. Cf. also *ARN* 1. See Montefiore's criticism of *SB's* citations on this subject ad loc., *RLGT,* p. 312.

6. En. 104.6.

7. 2 Bar. 51.4. See also *PR* 43 (179 a); Gen. R. 8.11; B. Ḥag. 16a; *PRK* 6 (57a); *PR* 16 (80a), Num. R. 21.

8. For a cluster of passages attempting to prove resurrection from biblical texts, see B.Sanh. 90b. See particularly B. Ber. 19b.

## 208. *The Greatest Commandment*

### MATT. 22.34–40

34 But when the Pharisees heard that he had silenced the Sadducees, they came together. 35 And one of them, a lawyer, asked him a question, to test him. 36 "Teacher, which is the great commandment in the law?" 37 And he said to him, "You

shall love the Lord your God with all your heart, and with all your soul, and with all your mind. 38 This is the great and first commandment. 39 And a second is like it, You shall love your neighbor as yourself. 40 On these two commandments depend all the law and the prophets."

## MARK 12.28–34

28 And one of the scribes came up and heard them disputing with one another, and seeing that he answered them well, asked him, "Which commandment is the first of all?" 29 Jesus answered, "The first is, 'Hear, O Israel: The Lord our God, the Lord is one; 30 and you shall love the Lord your God with all your heart, and with all your soul, and with all your mind, and with all your strength.' 31 The second is this, 'You shall love your neighbor as yourself.' There is no other commandment greater than these." 32 And the scribe said to him, "You are right, Teacher; you have truly said that he is one, and there is no other but he; 33 and to love him with all the heart, and with all the understanding, and with all the strength, and to love one's neighbor as oneself, is much more than all whole burnt offerings and sacrifices." 34 And when Jesus saw that he answered wisely, he said to him, "You are not far from the kingdom of God." And after that no one dared to ask him any question.

## LUKE 10.25–28

25 And behold, a lawyer stood up to put him to the test, saying, "Teacher, what shall I do to inherit eternal life?" 26 He said to him, "What is written in the Law? How do you read?" 27 And he answered, "You shall love the Lord your God with all your heart, and with all your soul, and with all your strength, and with all your mind; and your neighbor as yourself." 28 And he said to him, "You have answered right; do this, and you will live."
See above Sec. 143 (p. 280).

# 209. *About David's Son*

## MATT. 22.41–46

41 Now when the Pharisees were gathered together, Jesus asked them a question, 42 saying, "What do you think of the Christ? Whose son is he?" They said to him, "The son of David." 43 He said to them, "How is it then that David, inspired by the Spirit,⁵ calls him Lord, saying,

> 44 'The Lord said to my Lord,
> Sit at my right hand,
> till I put thy enemies under thy feet'?

45 If David thus calls him Lord, how is he his son?" 46 And no one was able to answer him a word, nor from that day did any one dare to ask him any more questions.

## MARK 12.35–37a

35 And as Jesus taught in the temple, he said, "How can the scribes say that the Christ is the son of David? 36 David himself, inspired by the Holy Spirit[t] declared,
'The Lord said to my Lord,
Sit at my right hand,
till I put thy enemies under thy feet.'
37 David himself calls him Lord; so how is he his son?"

## LUKE 20.41–44

41 But he said to them, "How can they say that the Christ is David's son? 42 For David himself says in the Book of Psalms,
'The Lord said to my Lord,
Sit at my right hand,
43 till I make thy enemies a stool for thy feet.'
44 David thus calls him Lord; so how is he his son?"

---

s  Or *David in the Spirit*.
t  Or *himself in the Holy Spirit*.

### COMMENTARY

43 *inspired by the Spirit*  I.e., the spirit which inspired the authors to compose their works. The prophets and others, such as David, all composed their books through the *ruaḥ haqodesh*.[1] This is a rabbinic term indicating a canonical book.[2]

*The Lord said to my Lord*  Ps. 110. See also ibid. 8.7.[3]

45 *If David thus calls him Lord, how is he his son?*  This passage appears to assume that Jesus was not David's progeny.

### NOTES

1. On David and the Holy Spirit, see B. Ar. 15b.
2. Bacher, *Exeg. Term.*, 2:202 ff.
3. See Stendahl, *SSMUOT*, pp. 77 ff., for the dependence of the Synoptics on the LXX.

## 210. *Woes against the Pharisees*

### MATT. 23.1–36

1 Then said Jesus to the crowds and to his disciples, 2 "The scribes and the Pharisees sit on Moses' seat; 3 so practice and observe whatever they tell you, but not what they do; for they preach, but do not practice. 4 They bind heavy burdens, hard to bear,[u]

and lay them on men's shoulders; but they themselves will not move them with their finger. 5 They do all their deeds to be seen by men; for they make their phylacteries broad and their fringes long, 6 and they love the place of honor at feasts and the best seats in the synagogues, 7 and salutations in the market places, and being called rabbi by men. 8 But you are not to be called rabbi, for you have one teacher, and you are all brethren. 9 And call no man your father on earth, for you have one Father, who is in heaven. 10 Neither be called masters, for you have one master, the Christ. 11 He who is greatest among you shall be your servant; 12 whoever exalts himself will be humbled, and whoever humbles himself, will be exalted.

13 "But woe to you, scribes and Pharisees, hypocrites! because you shut the kingdom of heaven against men; for you neither enter yourselves, nor allow those who would enter to go in.ᵛ

15 "Woe to you, scribes and Pharisees, hypocrites! for you traverse sea and land to make a single proselyte, and when he becomes a proselyte, you make him twice as much of a child of hellʷ as yourselves.

16 "Woe to you, blind guides, who say, 'If anyone swears by the temple, it is nothing; but if anyone swears by the gold of the temple, he is bound by his oath.' 17 You blind fools! For which is greater, the gold or the temple that has made the gold sacred? 18 And you say, 'If anyone swears by the altar, it is nothing; but if anyone swears by the gift that is on the altar, he is bound by his oath.' 19 You blind men! For which is greater, the gift or the altar that makes the gift sacred? 20 So he who swears by the altar swears by it and by everything on it; 21 and he who swears by the temple, swears by it and by him who dwells in it; 22 and he who swears by heaven, swears by the throne of God, swears by it and by him who sits upon it.

23 "Woe to you, scribes and Pharisees, hypocrites! for you tithe mint and dill and cummin, and have neglected the weightier matters of the law, justice and mercy and faith; these you ought to have done, without neglecting the others.

24 "You blind guides, straining out a gnat and swallowing a camel!

25 "Woe to you, scribes and Pharisees, hypocrites! for you cleanse the outside of the cup and of the plate, but inside they are full of extortion and rapacity. 26 You blind Pharisees! first cleanse the inside of the cup and of the plate, that the outside also may be clean.

27 "Woe to you, scribes and Pharisees, hypocrites! for you are like whitewashed tombs, which outwardly appear beautiful, but within they are full of dead men's bones and all uncleanness. 28 So you also outwardly appear righteous to men, but within you are full of hypocrisy and iniquity.

29 "Woe to you, scribes and Pharisees, hypocrites! for you build the tombs of the prophets and adorn the monuments of the righteous, 30 saying, 'If we had lived in the days of our fathers, we would not have taken part with them in shedding the blood of the prophets.' 31 Thus you witness against yourselves, that you are sons of those who murdered the prophets. 32 Fill up, then, the measure of your fathers. 33 You serpents, you brood of vipers, how are you to escape being sentenced to hell?ʷ 34 Therefore I send you prophets and wise men and scribes, some of whom you will kill and crucify, and some you will scourge in your synagogues and persecute from town to town, 35 that upon you may come all the righteous blood shed on the earth, from the blood of innocent Abel to the blood of Zechariah the son of Barachiah, whom you murdered between the sanctuary and the altar. 36 Truly, I say to you, all this will come upon this generation."

## MARK 12.37b–40

37b And the great throng heard him gladly. 38 And in his teaching he said, "Beware of the scribes, who like to go about in long robes, and to have salutations in the market places 39 and the best seats in the synagogues and the places of honor at feasts, 40 who devour widows' houses and for a pretense make long prayers. They will receive the greater condemnation."

## LUKE 20.45–47, 11.39–42, 44, 46–52

45 And in the hearing of all the people he said to his disciples,. . . 11.46 And he said, "Woe you lawyers also! For you load men with burdens hard to bear, and you yourselves do not touch the burdens with one of your fingers. 20.46 Beware of the scribes, who like to go about in long robes, and love salutations in the market places and the best seats in the synagogues and the places of honor at feasts, . . . 11.52 Woe to you lawyers! for you have taken away the key of knowledge; you did not enter yourselves, and you hindered those who were entering. 20.47 . . . who devour widows' houses and for a pretense make long prayers. They will receive the greater condemnation. 11.42 But woe to you Pharisees! for you tithe mint and rue and every herb and neglect justice and the love of God; these you ought to have done without neglecting the others.

11.39 Now you Pharisees cleanse the outside of the cup and of the dish, but inside you are full of extortion and wickedness. 40 You fools! Did not he who made the outside make the inside also? 41 But give for alms those things which are within; and behold, everything is clean for you.

44 Woe to you! for you are like graves which are not seen and men walk over them with out knowing it.

47 Woe to you! for you build the tombs of the prophets whom your fathers killed. 48 So you are witnesses and consent to the deeds of your fathers; for they killed them, and you build their tombs. 49 Therefore also the Wisdom of God said, 'I will send them prophets and apostles, some of whom they will kill and persecute,' 50 that the blood of all the prophets, shed from the foundation of the world, may be required of this generation, 51 from the blood of Abel to the blood of Zechariah, who perished between the altar and the sanctuary. Yes, I tell you, it will be required of this generation."

---

u  Other ancient authorities omit *hard to bear*.

v  Other authorities add here No.14 (or after v. 12., *Woe to you, scribes and Pharisees, hypocrites! for you devour widows' houses and for a pretense you make long prayers; therefore you will receive the greater condemnation*.

w  Greek *Gehenna*.

## COMMENTARY

2 *Moses' seat*  I.e., carrying on the tradition. This expression in Heb. is *qatedra de moshe*.[1] It was also a special seat in the ancient synagogues: "The first 'Seat of Moses' was unearthed at Hammath-by-Tiberias, and was

followed by another at Chorazin. We know that whereas the congregation sat on the stone benches that are still found along the side walls of many ancient synagogues, or else on mats on the floor, 'the elders' sat 'with their faces to the people and their backs to the Holy (i.e. to Jerusalem).' It was evidently for the most distinguished among 'the elders' that the stone chair found near the south wall of the Hammath synagogue was reserved. This was no doubt 'the Seat of Moses.' "[2]

3 *so practice*, etc.   This is based on Deut. 17.10, which is the biblical basis for rabbinic authority replacing that of the priests.[3]

*what they tell you to do*   The idea is that "they say and do not."[4]

4 *bind heavy burdens*   Referring to *issurim*, prohibitions, or the enactment of *gezerot*, severe decrees.

*they themselves will not move them with their finger.*   "Move" here means "remove" (cf. Rev. 2.5, 6.14). The meaning is that they would not lift a finger to remove the oppressive ordinances.[5]

5 *to be seen by men*   I.e., for personal aggrandizement, and there is a plethora of statements warning against this evil.

> He who makes worldly use of the crown [of Torah] shall pass away.[6]

> A man must not say, "I will study so as to be called a wise man, or Rabbi, or an elder, or to have a seat in the Academy," but he must study out of love, and the honor will come of itself.[7]

*make broad their phylacteries*   I.e., the *tephillin*, which are never referred to as phylacteries, protective amulets, in *early* rabbinic tradition, but there seems to be evidence that they were treated as such by many in all segments of society.[8]

Many explanations have been offered to explain the phrase "to make broad their phylacteries."[9] The best explanation is that it does not refer to the boxes which contain the parchments on which the biblical passages are written but to the straps, for as Abrahams commented, "it can hardly refer to the boxes, which were cubical. One hardly widens a cube."[10] "The tephillah of the arm (box and strap alike) was invisible. But the head tephillah was displayed, hence its greater importance in Rabbinic eyes. The head tephillah is bound over the brow, the box overhanging the centre of the forehead, and a knob at the middle of the neck, the two ends of the strap hanging over the shoulders in front. There was, however, another method of dealing with the ends of the strap, viz. to tie them around twice or thrice not to leave the ends loose. This method referred to in Men. 35b would explain Mt.'s verb *platunousin*."[11] It is strange that Abrahams did not note the fact that S[1] and S[2] have "the thongs of their frontlets"! Garland's suggestion, "Because of the clear example of the abuse of wearing the tephillin in J. Ber. 2.3 it seems that this refers to the length of time the tephillin were worn beyond the normal requirements,"[12] is not appealing on two counts: first, the verb does not mean to lengthen time, and second, shortening the time would not obviate the abuse. It has been suggested that to broaden the phylacteries is paralleled by the Marcan "and for a pretense make long prayers," the reason being that *tephillin* also means "prayers" and that there was a double meaning of the Aram. "long/broaden."[13]

*make fringes long*   Lit. "make their borders long." Apparently referring to the *zizit*, Num. 15.38 ff.[14] Fringes and *tephillin* are paired in the statement that an *am ha-arez* was anyone who did not put on *tephillin* or did not wear fringes on his garment (B. Sota 22a), and presumably anyone who did fulfill them both but with ostentation came under justifiable criticism. The *tallit* was the outer garment worn by all Jews, but the *tallit* of the scholar, the distinguished men of the community, and rabbis, was of finer quality.[15] The *tallit* of the scholar extended to within a handbreadth of the length of the bottom of his undergarment.[16] The *tallit* was worn in a variety of ways, occasionally doubled, and sometimes with the ends thrown over the shoulders.[17] Perhaps it is not the fringes which they lengthened but the *tallit* itself. This then could harmonize this reading with Mk. 12.38, *who like to go about in long robes*.

6 *place of honor at feasts*   There was a protocol as to seating at a meal. In the court seating was according to wisdom; at table (lit., reclining) according to age.[18] The order of seating was set out in detail: "When there are two couches, the more important guest reclines first and the other above him; when there are three, the chief guest reclines in the middle couch, the next in importance above him, and the third below him."[19]

*and the best seats in the synagogues*   The best seats in the synagogue were on the platform facing the congregation, and the backs were against the wall on which the Ark of the Torah scrolls stood. These were occupied by the *zeqenim*, i.e., the scholars.[20]

7 *and salutations in the market places*   There was a protocol about greeting, i.e., that the greeting was to be initiated by one of lower rank in learning of the Law.[21] There are many examples of the learned who, as a matter of humility, did not stand on this dignity and chose to initiate the greeting, as in the case of R. Johanan b. Zakkai, the Patriarch. He was always the first to greet even the Gentile in the marketplace.[22] It is possible that *and salutations in the market place* is the Matthean parallel of the Marcan *to be called of men, Rabbi*. Matt. retains both because of v. 8.[23]

8 *Rabbi*   There is a disagreement among scholars whether the title *rabbi* in the NT is anachronistic. Zeitlin has argued convincingly that the title *rabbi* was not used by Jews until the destruction of the Temple: "The word rabbi which is found in this chapter may therfore throw light on the authenticity of the entire chapter. Jesus was usually addressed as *didaskale* (teacher). Even when the Pharisees and the Scholars of the Law addressed him they always called him Teacher not Rabbi (Matt. 22.35–36; Mk. 12.14, 32; Lk. 20.21, 28, 39). We therefore expect that the Pharisees and the Scholars of the Law,

when they asked Jesus questions in the Law, would have addressed him as Rabbi, if such a title had been in vogue."[24]

*and you are all brethren* This phrase seems to go better in the following verse, where it could be parallel to *neither be called masters*, the meaning being "we are equals and there is no lordship of man over man," similar to the comment: "Shemayah said . . . 'hate lordship [Heb. *harabbanut*]' ".[25] *Rabbanut* is connected with the titles *rabbi* and *rav*.[26]

9 *Father* This is a bit enigmatic. Beside the use of *av* (Heb.) or *abba* (Aram.) as *pater familias*, it is restricted to (a) the Patriarchs Abraham, Isaac, and Jacob; (b) a teacher, as in M. Avot, e.g., Hillel, Shammai, the other pairs *(zugot)*; R. Ishmael and R. Akiba were called *Avot haolam*.[27]

10 *master* *moreh* or *mori*, essentially the same as v. 8, perhaps a translation of *rabbi* for Gentile Christians.[28]

11 *He who is greatest among you shall be your servant* Perhaps one of the most meaningful examples of this dictum is a story involving the Patriarch R. Gamaliel II which is based on the principle of *imitatio dei*.

> Once R. Eliezer and R. Joshua and R. Zadoq were reclining at table at the wedding of the son of Rabban Gamaliel. Rabban Gamaliel filled [lit. mixed] R. Eliezer's cup and he refused to accept it from him. R. Joshua, however, accepted it. R. Eliezer said to R. Joshua: "What is this, Joshua? We are reclining at table and R. Gamaliel is standing and serving [us]?" R. Joshua said: "Let him serve. Abraham, the greatest in the world, served the Ministering Angels, thinking that they were idolatrous Arabs, as it is written, *And he raised his eyes and saw* [Gen. 18.2]. Now it is logical— Abraham, who was the greatest in the world, served the Ministering Angels, thinking that they were idolatrous Arabs, should not R. Gamaliel serve us [who are scholars]?" R Zadok said to them: "You have left the honor of God and are occupied with the honor of mortals! If He who spoke and the world came into being causes the wind to blow, brings up mist and clouds, and causes the rains to fall and causes vegetation to grow, and sets a table for everyone, should not Rabban Gamaliel serve us?"[29]

12 *whoever exalts himself*, etc. An exact rabbinic parallel is "He who humbles himself God will exalt, he who exalts himself God will humble."[30]

13 *But woe to you, scribes and Pharisees, hypocrites!* The Rabbis themselves vehemently decried most of all those things which Jesus is said to condemn. E.g., "The hypocrites will fall into hell."[31] "Four classes of men never receive the face of the Shekinah: mockers, hypocrites, liars, and slanderers."[32]

*you shut the kingdom of heaven against men* The point of reference is vague. He could be referring to excluding the Judeo-Christians from the synagogue, or perhaps to excluding the potential proselyte who would be dissuaded from becoming a Jew because of the strict requirements of the Law.

14 *for you devour widows' houses* Omitted in the best MSS. This does not fairly characterize Pharisaic teaching or practice. It is purely polemical, and a

similar charge is directed by the Pharisees against their opponents.[33] To be sure, there were those who probably took advantage of the helpless widow. From the biblical period through the rabbinic era the law specifically enjoins one from oppressing them. "He who robs the widow and the orphan is as if he has robbed God Himself."[34] It should be noted that some passages in the Talmud where *perushim* is found do not refer to Pharisees, but to some who deviate from the halakhic rule. Among them are those who cause *makkat perushim*, "the wound of the *perushim*," presumed by some to refer to those who, under pretext of strict observance of the letter of the Law, cause injury or withhold benevolence from the deserving. E.g., he who advises heirs to evade paying alimentation to the widow,[35] "his friends under the pretext of benevolence have deprived him of benefit of the poor-law."[36] Josephus calls attention to the fact that a certain Pharisaic faction has a great influence over women.[37] The rabbinic law, following the biblical tradition, sought to protect the widow from the unscrupulous.[38]

15 *you cross land and sea to make one proselyte* During the Hellenistic period down to the time of the destruction of the Temple, the Jews were relatively active in proselytizing. They attracted those who no longer could accept idolatrous myths and who were revolted by the gross immorality which was widespread in the Roman empire. They were particularly attracted by the moral values of Judaism and were impressed by its lifestyle. The synagogues, especially in the Diaspora, had coteries of Gentiles who worshiped with the Jews and lived by the moral precepts taught there. These were called the *yerai Adonai*, "God Fearers," Gr. *sebomenoi*, Lat. *metuentes*, but they were not proselytes. Proselytes, on the other hand, were those who were formally converted and took up membership in the Jewish people. This required instruction in the principles of Judaism, if a male to be circumcised, to undergo the ritual immersion, and during the days of the Temple to bring a sacrifice.[39]

*you make him twice as much a child of hell* The point here is not that proselytism is bad, but that the new convert, as is often the case, will be more zealous than those born into the culture and will go beyond the Pharisees in their insistence on the observance of the minutiae of the Law.

*a child of hell* The opposite of "son of the kingdom," Matt. 8.12, 18.3. The expression is relatively rare in rabbinic literature.[40]

16 *blind guides* See above Matt. 15.14. It should be noted that in this "woe" the Pharisees and Sadducees are not mentioned and perhaps this was not originally in this list.

*If anyone swears by the temple*, etc. "The rule of the Palestinian Halacha was that all the ordinary uncertain formulas introduced with terms such as . . . *Yerushalayim she'aini . . . hahechal she'aini . . . hamizbe'ah she'aini* ('By Jerusalem 'that I shall not . . . or 'by the Temple' that I shall not . . . or 'by the Altar' that I shall not . . . ") etc. are not binding. A man is bound by an oath only when it contains the word *shebu'a* or His name (or His attributes); an oath by any other holy object does not bind the man. An exception was made only for the word *qorban* because people were in the habit of dedicating objects to the Temple by using this word, and TP (Ned. I.4, 37a) concluded that when a man says *qorban*, we take him to mean *keqorban*, 'As a Qorban' and he is bound."[41] Matt. 23.16 is in accord with Pharisaic procedure: "For when a person, in *ordinary speech* [emphasis added], swears by the gold of the Temple or by the gift of the Altar we regard him as if he said 'keqorban.' It seems to me that the Jews used to vow and swear not only by 'qorban,' which comprises sacrifices as well as the 'gold (treasury) of the Temple' (Josephus *BJ* II.9.4.175; Matt. 27.6) but also by *zehab hahekhal* or *hon hamiqdash* which is equivalent to qorban."[42] This still does not explain which gold is meant, and whether there is proof that they did indeed swear by "the gold of the Temple." Perhaps the matter can be clarified and harmonized with the following verse by reading *zevah*, "a sacrifice," for *zahav*, "gold," for gold in this context occurs nowhere in Jewish sources.[43]

18 *If anyone swears by the altar*, etc.   Same form and logic as in v. 16. The altar, as the Temple, gives holiness to the sacrifice. Cf. "The altar makes holy whatever is prescribed as its due."[44]

20 *So he who swears by the altar*, etc.   "This verse goes with 21 f. The object of the two latter verses is to show that the mere fact that the name of God is not mentioned in taking an oath counts for nothing. The substitution of something else for the Divine name is an evasion, for all the time it is God that is mentioned. That being so, it may be suspected that there is something wrong with v.20. What we should expect is: 'He therefore that sweareth by the altar, sweareth by it, and by Him to whom offering is made thereon!' or something to the same effect."[45]

22 *and he who swears by heaven*, etc.   See above p. 102.

23 *for you tithe mint and dill and cummin*   Tithing goes back to Deut. 14.22–23, Num. 18.12, Lev. 27.30. All of these mentioned are subject to tithing.[46] The leaf of mint may be referred to in M. Sheb. 7.1. Biblically, only grain, wine, and oil are subject to the law of the tithe; rabbinically, vegetables and greens are also included. Here Matt. is contrasting the minutiae of the law with the essentials, i.e., justice, mercy, and faith, which are the weightier matters, perhaps a reference to Mic. 6.8[47] The weightier matters here are not the light and weightier commandments of Matt. 19.24, but the important and the trifling.[48]

24 *straining out a gnat and swallowing a camel*   Both are unclean,[49] but the point is the hyperbolic comparison of their respective sizes. Straining out a gnat goes back to the practice of straining wine through a cloth or wicker basket.[50] According to another passage,[51] an insect called *yabchush* was removed from wine in this fashion, and it was believed that it was generated in the dregs of the wine and in the pulp of the pressed grapes in the wine press.[52]

25 *for you cleanse the outside of the cup*, etc.   The question arises here

whether one is to interpret this passage literally or metaphorically. Most prefer the latter, i.e., the inner man vs. the man seen by society.[53]

27 *for you are like whitewashed tombs*, etc.   There have been many suggestions to explain this verse which is intended to illustrate hypocrisy, and they all miss the mark.[54] "Tomb" here, Gr. *taphos*, is probably a variant of *taphē*, meaning a funerary urn containing the ashes of the deceased.[55] Whitewash seems not to be appropriate to the sense of the passage.[56] Whitewashing does not in itself indicate any real beautification, nor is the deletion of the word *kekoniameno* advisable. The solution may lie in the word *konia*, meaning "dust" or "powder." It was a common practice to mix powdered marble and lime to form a mixture which was then applied to structures and objects made of limestone. The purpose of this was not only to give support and to fill in the porous surface so that the decorations could be added, but it also gave a sheen and "rich look" to the plain limestone. It is noteworthy that the majority of the ossuaries in Palestine in the first Christian century were made of limestone.[57]

*but within they are full of dead men's bones and all uncleanness*   There is a striking parallel to this imagery in the Talmud. The autocratic Patriarch Rabban Gamaliel II of Yavneh, ca. 80, decreed that "a disciple whose character does not correspond to his exterior [lit. whose inside is not as his outside] may not enter the Academy." He was removed from his office by the Rabbis because of his constant harassment of the learned and venerable Rabbi Joshua ben Ḥananiah. After he was deposed the Rabbis permitted all who wished to attend the proceedings to come without restriction, and according to the Talmud between four and seven hundred benches had to be added to accommodate the influx. On seeing this Rabban Gamaliel became alarmed and said, "Perhaps, God forbid, I withheld Torah from Israel!" Subsequently, he was shown in a dream white casks (urns) full of ashes [suggesting that those he had kept out were, in fact, not worthy of admission] (B. Ber. 28a). This event described corresponds to the time of the writing of Matt. The imagery of the cask or urn, white on the outside and containing ashes, possibly of the dead, together with the phrase "whose outside is not as his inside" indicates hypocrisy or duplicity.[58]

32 *fill up the measure of your fathers*   I.e., be as wicked as they were, cf. Gen. 15.16, and a similar usage in B. Ar. 15a, Targ. J. Gen. 15.16.

33 *You serpents*   See above p. 42.

34 *prophets, wise men and scribes*   These could refer to those of the biblical period or perhaps contemporaries, and prophets could include men like John the Baptist, who were persecuted.[59]

*scourge in your synagogues*   Origin in Deut. 25.2 ff. The number of lashes is fixed at forty (39). For the details about the punishment of lashing, see M. Makkot.

35 *the blood of innocent Abel to the blood of Zechariah the son of Barachiah*   Abel was not a prophet but is an example of the pious.[60] Abel and Zechariah were

probably chosen as setting up a range extending from the earliest biblical murder, mentioned in Genesis, to the last, recounted in Chronicles, the last book of the MT. Concerning the identification of this Zechariah there is no unanimous opinion. Most are agreed that reference is to the Zechariah of 2 Chron. 24.20–22, but there he is called son of Jehoiada. Perhaps Barachiah is a corruption of Jehoiadah. Luke has simply Zechariah. Others understand it variously as referring to Zechariah the father of John the Baptist; Zechariah the prophet, son of Berechah and grandson of Iddo (Zech. 1.1, 7) of priestly family (Neh. 12.14, 16); Zechariah son of Barris, murdered in the Temple by two zealots in 67 (*BJ* IV.5.4).[61]

## NOTES

1. *Qatedra de Moshe.* The idea is expressed in the statement, "Every council of three in Israel is like the council of Moses" (B. RH 25a); the expression itself is found in several passages, e.g., B. Pes. 7b; Esther R. 1.2.

2. E. L. Sukenik, *Ancient Synagogues in Palestine and Greece*, pp. 50 ff.; Bacher, *Ag. Pal. Amor.*, 3:138. Cf. also *REJ* 34 (1897): 299.

3. See Sifre Deut. 154; B. RH. 25a–b.

4. See Sifra Lev. 26.3; Lev. R. 35.7.

5. Note McNeile's baseless comment, *Matt.*, p. 330, "The Scribes would not move a finger to ease the burdens which their rulers imposed. The school of Hillel indeed tended to laxity, but in the time of Jesus they were a minority." This conclusion is faulty, just the opposite was the case; cf. B. AZ. 36a, "One does not institute a decree on the community unless the community is able to bear it." Also TB. Hor. 3b. See Urbach, *The Sages*, pp. 391–393; Moore, *Judaism*, 1:263.

6. M. Avot 1.13.

7. TJ Shev. 4.2, 35b, B. Ned. 62a.

8. The *tephillin* contain Exod. 13.1–10, 11–16; Deut. 6.4–9, 11.13–20. See Garland, p. 56, who leaves out Exod. 11–16. They were worn every day except Sabbaths and Festivals. See *Letter of Aristeas* 158; Josephus, *Ant.* IV.2.12 ff.

9. Cf. also C. F. Burney, *The Aramaic Origin of the Fourth Gospel*, p. 10; Abrahams, *Studies II*, pp. 203–205; Manson, *SJ*, pp. 230–31; G. G. Fox, "The Matthean Misrepresentation of Tephillin," *JNES* 1 (1942): 373–375; Tigay, "On the Term Phylacteries (Matt. 23.5)," *HTR* 72 (1979): 45–52.

10. Abrahams, *Studies II*, p. 205.

11. Ibid.

12. Garland, op. cit., p. 56 n. 84.

13. Manson, *SJ*, p. 230.

14. On the *talit* in the time of Jesus, see Y. Yadin *Cave of Letters*, 1:204 ff.

15. Cf. B. BB 98a, Gen. R. 36.6.

16. B. BB 57b.

17. B. Shab. 147a, B. Men. 41a.

18. B. BB 120a.

19. T. Ber. 5.5 (12); *SB*, Excur. #4. Cf. TJ Ta'an 4, 68a (51), B. Ber. 46b.

20. See T. Meg. 4.21 (p. 227). B. BB 12a, cited by *SB*, is not applicable since it does not mention synagogues but only "seating," which traditionally refers to the law courts. See Rashi ad loc. See also TJ Pe'ah 8, 21b (44); *ARN* 25; B. Ta'an. 21b.

21. TJ Ber. 2, 4b (24). "A man must greet a superior in the knowledge of the Law."

22. B. Ber. 17a.

23. Manson, *SJ*, p. 231.

24. Zeitlin, *Who Crucified Jesus*, p. 139. Other studies: *Contra:* H. Shanks, "Is the Title Rabbi Anachronistic in the Gospels?" *JQR* 53 (1963): 317–345; idem, "Origin of the Title Rabbi," *JQR* 59 (1969): 152–157; S. Zeitlin, "A Reply," *JQR* 53 (1963): 345–349; Dalman, *Words*, pp. 331–340; Davies, *SSM*, pp. 297–298; J. Donaldson, "The Title Rabbi in the Gospels: Some Reflections on the Evidence of the Gospels," *JQR* 63 (1973): 288–290. For a discussion of these positions, see Garland, op. cit., pp. 58–60.

25. M. Avot 1.10. See Manson, *SJ*, p. 231.

26. M. Eduy. 1.4. Cf Urbach, *The Sages: Their Concepts and Beliefs* (Jerusalem, 1975) pp. 186–190. See also Gal. 1.14; Josephus, *Ant.* XVIII.297, 408 hence the title *rabbi*, a teacher. See Targ. 2 Kings 2.12, 5.13, 6.21, 13.14; 1 Sam. 24.12. See also J. Townsend, "Matthew XXIII.9" *JTS* 12 (1961): 56–59, who offers four alternatives; and K. Kohler, "Abba Father Title of Spiritual Leader and Saint," *JQR* 13 (1900–1901): 567–580.

27. See, e.g., M. Eduy. 1.4, TJ RH 1, 56d (21); TJ Sheq. 3, 47b (22).

28. The term *kathegetes*, "teacher," occurs only here in the NT. Garland, op. cit., p. 60, makes the interesting comment that it alludes to the *kathedra* of Moses in v. 2 by homonymy. Note that in Sifre Deut. 34 disciples are called "sons," the teacher *(rav)* is called "father." *(av)*.

29. Sifre Deut. 38; *Mek.* Exod. 18.12, B. Qid. 32b; M. Avot 6.5; B. Ber. 7b, 47b; B. Ket. 96a; *DEZ* 8.

30. B. Er. 13b; see also *DEZ* 9, B. Sanh. 17a, *ARN* 11.

31. B. Sot. 41b.

32. Ibid. 42a Cf. also B. Yom. 86b.

33. Cf. Ps. Sol. 4, Asmp. Moses 7.6.

34. Exod. R. 30.8.

35. TJ Sot. 3.4; B. ibid. 22b. On these *perushim*, see E. Rifkin, *A Hidden Revolution* (Nashville, Tenn.: Abingdon, 1978), pp. 168 ff.

36. Ibid.

37. Josephus, *Ant.* XVII.2.4.

38. See Abrahams, *Studies I*, pp. 79–81.

39. See B. Yev. 46b, 47a; B. Shab. 31a. On Jewish proselytism, see B. J. Bamberger, *Proselytism in the Talmudic Period;* W. Braude, *Jewish Proselytizing in the First Five Centuries of the Common Era: The Age of the Tannaim and Amoraim;* S. Lieberman, *Greek in Jewish Palestine*, pp. 68–90; N. J. McEleney, "Conversion, Circumcision and the Law," *NTS* 20 (1975): 319–341.

40. See, e.g., B. RH. 17a; B. Ber. 10a.

41. Lieberman, *Greek in Jewish Palestine*, p. 134.

42. Ibid. On the basis of his assumption Lieberman attempts to explain an obscure passage in S. Schechter, *Documents of Jewish Sectaries* 6.15.

43. *SB*'s citation of B. Ned. 14b is not relevant.

44. M. Zev. 9. Swearing by the altar; e.g., B. Pes. 118b, Lam R. 2.10; Esther R. 1.9; Koh. R. 9.2; M. Men. 12.1.

45. Manson, *SJ*, p. 235.

46. M. M.Sh. 4.5; Dem. 2.1.

47. Cf. T. Sot. 14.3 (p. 320); Hos. 6.6.

48. See Manson, *SJ*, p. 236; Garland, p. 137. On tithing, see L. Finkelstein, *JBL* 44 (1930): 32 ff.

49. Lev. 11.4, 41 ff.

50. B. Shab. 20a.

51. B. Hul. 67a.

52. Some see a wordplay as well, i.e., *gamla*, "camel," and *kamla*, targumic translation of "mosquitoes" of Exod. 8.12 (16 ff.). *SB* citation of B. Ber. 63a is farfetched.

53. See J. Neusner, "First Cleanse the Inside: Halakhic Background of a Controversial Saying," *NTS* 22 (1976): 486–495; H. Maccoby, "The Washing of Cups" *JSNT* 14 (1982): 3–15.

54. For a list of suggestions see Garland, op. cit. pp. 163 ff.

55. Cf. Sophocles, *Electra* 1210. In the Oxy. P. 736.13 (1st cent. c.e.) the term is used for "mummy."

56. McNeile, *Matt.*, p. 339. "Some have suggested that it should be deleted as a piece of antiquarianism."

57. Cf. J. Finegan, *The Archaeology of the New Testament* (Princeton University Press, 1969), pp. 216–217 and bibliography cited.

58. For this suggestion and proof, see S. T. Lachs, "On Matthew 23.27–28," *HTR* 68 (1975): 385–388.

59. See Manson, *SJ*, p. 239. He has difficulty with the order of these three, arguing: "Rabbinical Judaism would almost certainly have given the order: prophets, scribes, wise men." Not necessarily so, since "the wise" could have meant the authors of the wisdom literature, who then were followed by the *soferim*, i.e., the scribes.

60. See Test. Iss. 7.1–7.

61. See the literature for these suggestions in Manson, *SJ*, pp. 103–104. See S. H. Blank, "The Death of Zechariah in Rabbinic Literature," *HUCA* 12-13 (1937-38): 327–346.

## 211. *The Lament Over Jerusalem*

### MATT. 23.37–39

37 "O Jerusalem, Jerusalem, killing the prophets and stoning those who are sent to you! How often would I have gathered your children together as a hen gathers her brood under her wings, and you would not! 38 Behold, your house is forsaken and desolate.ˣ 39 For I tell you, you will not see me again, until you say, 'Blessed be he who comes in the name of the Lord.' "

### LUKE 13.34–35

34 "O Jerusalem, Jerusalem, killing the prophets and stoning those who are sent to you! How often would I have gathered your children together as a hen gathers her brood under her wings, and you would not! 35 Behold, your house is forsaken! And I tell you, you will not see me until you say, 'Blessed be he who comes in the name of the Lord."

---

x  Some omit *desolate*.

### COMMENTARY

37 *as a hen gathers her brood*, etc.  This imagery of protection is found in the following: "The hen, when her chicks are young, gathers them together and places them under her wings and warms them and digs up the earth before them. But when they grow bigger, if one of them wants to come near

to her as she pecks him on the head and says to him, 'Dig in your own dirt!' "[1] Coming under the wings (of God) is common in the MT, e.g., Ps. 17.8, 36.8, 57.2, 61.5; Deut. 32.11; Ruth 2.12. In rabbinic literature the imagery is used for proselytes who "come under the wings of the Shekhinah."[2]

39 *Blessed be he who comes in the name of the Lord.* Ps. 118.26.

### NOTES

1. Lev. R. 25.
2. See, e.g., Lev. R. 2.

## 212. *The Widow's Gift*

### MARK 12.41–44

41 And he sat down opposite the treasury, and watched the multitude putting money into the treasury. Many rich people put in large sums. 42 And a poor widow came, and put in two copper coins, which make a penny. 43 And he called his disciples to him, and said to them, "Truly, I say to you, this poor widow has put in more than all those who are contributing to the treasury. 44 For they all contributed out of their abundance; but she out of her poverty has put in everything she had, her whole living."

### LUKE 21.1–4

1 He looked up and saw the rich putting their gifts into the treasury; 2 and he saw a poor widow put in two copper coins. 3 And he said, "Truly I tell you, this poor widow has put in more than all of them; 4 for they all contributed out of their abundance, but she out of poverty put in all the living that she had."

### COMMENTARY

The importance of this passage is best summed up in the rabbinic saying, "It does not matter whether your offering be much or little, so long as your heart is directed to Heaven."[1] A close parallel to the widow's mite is the following, based on Lev. 2.1: "There is a story of a woman who brought a handful of meal as an offering. A priest despised it and said, 'See what they offer! What is in it that one could eat, what is in it that can be sacrificed?' It was shown to him in a dream 'Do not despise her; it is as if she has sacrificed herself [Heb. *nafshah*] as the sacrifice." If in regard to one who does not sacrifice himself, the text uses the term *nefesh* [soul], how much more if one who does!"[2] Another in the same vein: "What is the peculiarity of the meal offering that *nefesh* is used [Lev. 2.1]? Who brings the meal offering? The poor. 'I reckon it,' says God, 'as if he has offered himself before Me.' "[3] And a third: "God prefers the one handful of a free-will offering of the poor to the heap of incense which is offered by the high priest."[4]

42 *two copper coins, which make a penny* Gr. *lepton*, the smallest Greek copper coin, and *kodpantes* is the Greek term for the smallest Roman copper coin, *quadrans* (which equals two leptons or a dilepton). This would be the Heb. *perutah*, a small coin, one eighth of the *as* (*issur*).[5]

43 *to the treasury* Gr. *gazophulakeion*, Aram. *gaza*.[6] The sources treating of the Temple treasury often use this term in the plural.[7] In this passage, where it is in the singular, probably means one of the thirteen receptacles in the form of trumpets in the Temple used for charitable contributions.[8]

## NOTES

1. M. Men. 13.11.
2. Lev. R. 3.5.
3. Yal. Lev. 447.
4. Koh. R. 4.6. For others see B. BB 10a; Num. R. 14; B. Pes. 118a.
5. See M. Shev. 6.1; M. BM 4.7; M. Qid. 1.1.
6. B. Ḥul. 139a, which refers to the "Lord's treasury," i.e., the Temple.
7. *BAG*, s.v. *gazophulakeion*.
8. M. Sheq. 6.5. See above pp. 000 ff.

## 213. *Prediction of the Destruction of the Temple*

### MATT. 24.1–3

1 Jesus left the temple and was going away, when his disciples came to point out to him the buildings of the temple. 2 But he answered them, "You see all these, do you not? Truly, I say to you, there will not be left here one stone upon another, that will not be thrown down." 3 As he sat on the Mount of Olives the disciples came to him privately, saying. "Tell us when will this be, and what will be the sign of your coming and of the close of the age?'

### MARK 13.1–4

1 And as he came out of the temple, one of his disciples said to him, 'Look, Teacher, what wonderful stones and what wonderful buildings!" 2 And Jesus said to him, "Do you see these great buildings? There will not be left here one stone upon another, that will not be thrown down."[y] 3 And as he sat on the Mount of Olives opposite the temple, Peter and James and John and Andrew asked him privately, 4 "Tell us, when will this be, and what will be the sign when these things are all to be accomplished?"

### LUKE 21.5–7

5 And as some spoke of the temple, how it was adorned with noble stones and offerings, he said, 6 "As for these things which you see, the days will come when there shall not be left here[z] one stone upon another that will not be thrown down." 7

And they asked him, "Teacher, when will this be, and what will be the sign when is this about to take place?"

---

y  Some add *and after three days another will be raised without hand.*

z  Some omit *here*, others *one stone upon another here.*

## COMMENTARY

1 *the buildings of the temple*  Herod's temple was of striking beauty. "They say that he who has not seen the building of Herod has never seen a beautiful building in all his days."[1] Josephus, too, describes it similarly[2] and gives the measurements of its stones as $25 \times 8 \times 12$ cubits.[3]

3 *when will this be . . . ?* This type of question is met frequently in the literature from Daniel through rabbinic sources.[4]

## NOTES

1. B. Suk. 51a, B. BB 4a.
2. Josephus, *BJ* V. 5.
3. *Ant.* XV.11.3.
4. E.g., Dan. 8.13, 12.6; Test. Levi 10; Apoc. Bar. 59.8; 4 Ezra 4.33, 35; B. Sanh. 96b; *PR* 1 (4b).

# THE SYNOPTIC APOCALYPSE

MATTHEW 24.4–36, MARK 13.5–37, LUKE 21.8–36

## 214. Ia The Signs of the Parousia

### MATT. 24.4–8

4 And Jesus answered them, "Take heed, that no one leads you astray. 5 For many will come in my name, saying, 'I am the Christ,' and they will lead many astray. 6 And you will hear of wars and rumors of wars; see that you are not alarmed; for this must take place, but the end is not yet. 7 For nation will rise against nation, and kingdom against kingdom, and there will be famines and earthquakes in various places: 8 all this is but the beginning of the sufferings."

### MARK 13.5–9

5 And Jesus began to say to them, "Take heed that no one leads you astray. 6 Many will come in my name, saying, 'I am he!' and they will lead many astray. 7 And when you hear of wars and rumors of wars, do not be alarmed; this must take place, but the end is not yet. 8 For nation will rise against nation, and kingdom against kingdom; there will be earthquakes in various places, there will be famines; this is but the beginning of the sufferings."

### LUKE 21.8–11

8 And he said, "Take heed that you are not led astray; for many will come in my name, saying, 'I am he!' and 'The time is at hand!' Do not go after them. 9 And when you hear of wars and tumults, do not be terrified; for this must take place, but the end will not be at once." 10 Then he said to them, "Nation will rise against nation, and kingdom against kingdom; 11 there will be great earthquakes, and in various places famines and pestilences; and there will be terrors and great signs from heaven."

## COMMENTARY

5 *For many will come in my name*, etc.   There are no specific serious claims recorded in Jewish sources until Bar Kokhba (ca. 132), but there were several deceptive claims made which deceived the populace.[1]

6 *but the end is not yet*   This refers not to the messianic era but to the end of this present time, Heb. *olam hazeh*.[2]

7 *For nation will rise against nation*   Throughout the apocalyptic literature universal fighting is considered to be a sign that the end is approaching. "When you see the kingdoms fighting against one another look and expect the foot of the Messiah."[3]

*famines and earthquakes*  In the MT these are manifestations of divine punishment. See Isa. 8.21 (hunger), 13.13 (earthquake), 14.30 (famine). Cf. also "sword . . . famine . . . earthquake . . . and fire";[4] "illness and pain, frost, fear, famine, death, sword, captivity."[5]

8 *the beginning of the sufferings*  This refers to the "sufferings or pangs of the Messiah," Heb. *ḥevlē hamashi'aḥ*. The biblical material abounds with passages describing the troubles, woes, breakdown of family, and the general moral decline which will precede the coming great age and time of the redemption.[6] These are argmented in the apocryphal literature[7] as well as in rabbinic sources.[8]

## NOTES

1. See Acts 5.36 ff., 8.9, 21, 38; *Didache* 14.3 ff.; Sib. Or. 2.165, 3.63.
2. Cf. Dan. 12.4.
3. Gen. R. 42.4. See also Sib. Or. 3.538, 635 ff., 660, 5.361 ff.; 4 Ezra 13.29–31; B. Sanh. 97a.
4. Apoc. Bar. 2.3 ff.
5. Jub. 23.13. See *JE*, s.v. "Eschatology."
6. Dan. 12.1; Hos. 13.13; Joel 2.10 ff.; Mic. 7.1–6; Zech. 14.6 ff.
7. Cf. Jub. 23.29; Sib. Or. 2.154 ff., 3.796 ff.; En. 99.4 ff., 100 ff. 2 Ezra 5–6; Apoc. Bar. 25–27, 48.31 ff.
8. Cf. B. Shab. 118a; B. Pes. 118a; B. Sanh. 96b–97a, 98b; *Mek.* Exod. 16.29; M. Sot. 9.15; *DEZ* 10.

# 215. Ib The Beginnings of the Troubles

## MATT. 24.9–14; 10.17–21

9a "Then they will deliver you up to tribulation, . . . 10.17 Beware of men; for they will deliver you up to councils, and flog you in their synagogues, 18 and you will be dragged before governors and kings for my sake, to bear testimony before them and the Gentiles. 19 When they deliver you up, do not be anxious how you are to speak or what you are to say; for what you are to say will be given to you in that hour; 20 for it is not you who speak, but the Spirit of your Father speaking through you. 21 Brother will deliver up brother to death, and the father his child, and children will rise against parents and have them put to death; 9b . . . and put you to death; and you will be hated by all nations for my name's sake. 10 And then many will fall away,[a] and betray one another, and hate one another. 11 And many false prophets will rise and lead many astray. 12 And because wickedness is multiplied, most men's love will grow cold. 13 But he who endures to the end will be saved. 14 And this gospel of the kingdom will be preached throughout the whole world, as a testimony to all nations; and then the end will come."

## MARK 13.9–13

9 "But take heed to yourselves; for they will deliver you up to councils; and you will be beaten in synagogues; and you will stand before governors and kings for my sake,

to bear testimony before them. 10 And the gospel must first be preached to all nations. 11 And when they bring you to trial and deliver you up, do not be anxious beforehand what you are to say; but say whatever is given you in that hour, for it is not you who speak, but the Holy Spirit. 12 And brother will deliver up brother to death, and the father his child, and children will rise against parents and have them put to death; 13 and you will be hated by all for my name's sake. But he who endures to the end will be saved."

## LUKE 21.12–19

12 "But before all this they will lay their hands on you and persecute you, delivering you up to the synagogues and prisons, and you will be brought before kings and governors for my name's sake. 13 This will be a time for you to bear testimony. 14 Settle it therefore in your minds, not to meditate beforehand how to answer; 15 for I will give you a mouth and wisdom, which none of your adversaries will be able to withstand or contradict. 16 You will be delivered up even by parents and brothers and kinsmen and friends, and some of you will put to death; 17 you will be hated by all for my name's sake. 18 But not a hair of your head will perish. 19 By your endurance you will gain your lives."

---

a  Or *stumble*.

## COMMENTARY

10 *and hate one another*  I.e., persecution of the Christians; and hatred will be rampant, and this is a sign of the coming of the end.[1]

11 *false prophets*  Apparently Christians. Josephus speaks of many false prophets in Jerusalem at the time of the siege who tried to delude the people.[2] *wickedness is multiplied*  Also a sign of the end.[3]

> Behold, the days come when the inhabitants of the earth shall be seized with great panic and the way of truth shall be hidden, and the land of faith be barren. And iniquity shall be increased above that which thou thyself now seest or that thou hast heard of long ago.[4]

> With the footprints of the Messiah [*iqve hamashi'ah*] presumption shall increase and earth reach its height . . . and the empire shall fall into heresy, and there shall be none to utter reproof. The council-chamber shall be given to fornication. . . . The wisdom of the Scribes shall become insipid, and they that shun sin shall be deemed contemptible, and truth shall nowhere be found.[5]

13 *He who endures to the end*  See above p. 183.[6]

14 *the gospel of the kingdom*, etc.[7]

## NOTES

1. Cf. 4 Ezra. 6.18 ff.; Apoc. Bar. 40.30, 70.2 ff.; B. Sanh. 97a; M. Sot. 9.5.
2. *BJ* VI.5.2. See also Apoc. Bar. 48 ff.; Rev. 19.20.

3. Cf. 4 Ezra. 4.51 ff., 5.2, 10; En. 91.7; Lam. R. 2.13 (101a); *Mid. Ps.* 92.10

4. 4 Ezra. 5.1 ff. Cf. En. 91.7.

5. M. Sot. 9.15.

6. Cf. also 4 Ezra, 6.18 ff., 13.16; Apoc. Bar. 25.1 ff., 28; Lam. R. 2.13 (100b); B. Sanh. 97b.

7. B. Sanh. 38a, 97a, 98b; B. Yev. 62a.

# 216. IIa The Desolating Sacrilege

## MATT. 24.15–22

15 "So when you see the desolating sacrilege spoken by the prophet Daniel, standing in the holy place (let the reader understand), 16 then let those who are in Judea flee to the mountains; 17 let him who is on the housetop not go down to take what is in his house; 18 and let him who is in the field not turn back to take his mantle. 19 And alas for those who are with child and for those who give suck in those days! 20 Pray that your flight may not be in winter or on a sabbath. 21 For then there will be great tribulation, such as has not been from the beginning of the world until now, no, and never will be. 22 And if those days had not been shortened, no human being would be saved; but for the sake of the elect those days will be shortened."

## MARK 13.14–20

14 "But when you see the desolating sacrilege set up where it ought not to be (let the reader understand), then let those who are in Judea flee to the mountains; 15 let him who is on the housetop not go down, nor enter his house, to take anything away; 16 and let him who is in the field not turn back to take his mantle. 17 And alas for those who are with child and for those who give suck in those days! 18 Pray that it may not happen in winter. 19 For in those days there will be such tribulation as has not been from the beginning of the creation which God created until now, and never will be. 20 And if the Lord had not shortened the days, no human being would be saved; but for the sake of the elect, whom he chose, he shortened the days."

## LUKE 21.20–24

20 "But when you see Jerusalem surrounded by armies, then know that its desolation has come near. 21 Then let those who are in Judea flee to the mountains, and let those who are inside the city depart, and let not those who are out in the country enter it, 22 for these are the days of vengeance, to fulfill all that is written. 23 Alas for those who are with child and for those who give suck in those days! For great distress shall be upon the earth and wrath upon this people; 24 they will fall by the edge of the sword, and be led captive among all nations; and Jerusalem will be trodden down by the Gentiles, until the times of the Gentiles are fulfilled.

## COMMENTARY

15 *desolating sacrilege* The origin of this phrase is Dan. 9.27, 11.31, 12.11,8.13.[1] It refers to the altar to Zeus Olympius which was erected by

Antiochus IV on the site of the altar in the Temple.[2] The problem, however, is what does it mean here in its NT context? Several suggestions have been offered. Some say that it was the desecration of the Temple by some Zealots just before the siege of Jerusalem.[3] Others suggest some action on the part of the Romans, such as Pilate's bringing into the city of Jerusalem standards bearing the image of Caesar or Caligula's attempt to set up his statue in the Temple.[4] Jerome says that it was the erection of Vespasian's equestrian statue in the Holy of the Holies. Chrysostom mentions the statue of Titus on the site of the ruined Temple. It has also been identified with the Antichrist.[5] Still another is that since it states in Mark "a holy place," it could have referred to the setting up of a statue to Claudius in the synagogue at Dor, 7 miles N of Caesarea, by the Syrian rabble during the reign of Agrippa I.[6] Apparently Luke did not understand that "desolating sacrilege" was a specific term.

16 *flee to the mountains* To the caves which abound in the hills of Judea where they could seek refuge.[7]

19 *for those who are with child* For whom flight is especially dangerous.[8]

20 *not in winter* Flight in the cold of winter would add to the misery. At the destruction of the First Temple God lengthened the days so that it occurred in the summer and not in winter![9]

*not on the sabbath* As not to violate the Sabbath.[10] According to some, this is one of the Judeo-Christian passages in Matthew, indicating that in Matthew's day, some early Christians were observing the Sabbath.[11]

21 *tribulation* See Dan. 12.1.[12]

22 *the days will be shortened* Does this refer to the period of the rule of the Antichrist (i.e., the fixed periods in Dan. 8.14, 9.24–27, 12.7, 11 ff.), or that the days themselves are made shorter?[13]

## NOTES

1. On the meaning of these difficult grammatical forms, see H. L. Ginsberg, *Studies in Daniel* ad loc.

2. See 1 Macc. 1.54, 59; 6.7, where the same expression is used. See also M. Ta'an. 4.6; TJ ibid. 4, 68c (67); B ibid. 28b.

3. Josephus, *BJ* IV.3.6–8; 6.3.

4. Josephus, *Ant.* XVIII.8.8.

5. Stretter, *Matthäus* p. 492, McNeile, *Matt.*, p. 348; Loisy, *Luc*, 2:420; Klostermann, *Das Markusevangelium* pp. 151 et al.

6. Bacon, *Gospel of Mark*, pp. 93, 99.

7. Cf. 1 Macc. 2.28, Ezra 7.16, *Leqaḥ Tov* Num. 24.1 (129b), Ruth R. 2.14.

8. See TJ Kil. 9, 32b (35), TJ Ket. 12, 35a (48).

9. See Lam. R. 1.14 (56a).

10. 1 Macc. 2.31–38.

11. Montefiore, *SG*, 2:312.

12. See also 1 Macc. 9.27, Asmp. Mos. 8.1.

13. Lam. R. 2.7 (99a); TB Ket. 111a; B. BM 85; Lev. R. 21.9; Targ. J. I Gen. 28.10.

# 217. IIb The Culmination of the Troubles

### MATT. 24.23–25

23 "Then if anyone says to you, 'Lo, here is the Christ!'" or "There he is!' do not believe it. 24 For false Christs and false prophets will arise and show great signs and wonders, so as to lead astray, if possible, even the elect. 25 Lo, I have told you beforehand."

### MARK 13.21–23

21 "And then if anyone says to you, 'Look, here is the Christ!' or 'Look, there he is!' do not believe it. 22 False Christs and false prophets will arise and show signs and wonders, to lead astray, if possible, the elect. 23 But take heed; I have told you all things beforehand.

### COMMENTARY

**24** *signs and wonders* Heb. *otot u'moftim*. These are the stock-in-trade of false prophets. E.g., Deut. 13.2–3: *If a prophet arises among you, or a dreamer of dreams, and gives you a sign or a wonder, and the sign or wonder which he tells you comes to pass, and if he says, "Let us go after other gods, which you have not known, and let us serve them," you shall not listen to the words of that prophet or to that dreamer of dreams; for the Lord your God is testing you.*

# 218. IIc The Day of the Son of Man

### MATT. 24.26–28

26 "So, if they say to you, 'Lo, he is in the wilderness,' do not go out; if they say, 'Lo, he is in the inner rooms,' do not believe it. 27 For as the lightning comes from the east and shines as far as the west, so will be the coming of the Son of man. 28 Wherever the body is, there the eagles[b] will be gathered together."

### LUKE 17.23–24, 37

23 "And they will say to you, 'Lo there! or 'Lo, here!' Do not go; do not follow them. 24 For as the lightning flashes and lights up the sky from one side to the other, so will the Son of man be in his day.[c] 37 Where the body is, there the eagles[a] will be gathered together."

---

b Or *vultures*.
c Some omit *in his day*.
See above Sec. 184 (p. 319).

# 219. IIIa The Parousia of the Son of Man

## MATT. 24.29–31

29 "Immediately after the tribulation of those days, the sun will be darkened, and the moon will not give its light, and the stars will fall from heaven, and the powers of the heavens will be shaken; 30 then will appear the sign of the Son of man in heaven, and then all the tribes of the earth will mourn, and they will see the Son of man coming on the clouds of heaven with power and great glory; 31 and he will send out his angels with a loud trumpet call, and they will gather his elect from the four winds, from one end of heaven to the other."

## MARK 13.24–27

24 "But in those days, after that tribulation, the sun will be darkened, and the moon will not give its light, 25 and the stars will be falling from heaven, and the powers in the heavens will be shaken. 26 And then they will see the Son of man coming in clouds with great power and glory. 27 And then he will send out the angels, and gather his elect from the four winds, from the ends of the earth to the ends of heaven."

## LUKE 21.25–28

25 "And there will be signs in the sun and moon and stars, and upon the earth distress of nations in perplexity at the roaring of the sea and the waves, 26 man fainting with fear and with foreboding of what is coming on the world; for the powers of the heavens will be shaken. 27 And then they will see the Son of man coming in a cloud with power and great glory. 28 Now when these things begin to take place, look up and raise your heads, because your redemption is drawing near."

## COMMENTARY

29 *the sun . . . and the moon*, etc.   The normal functioning of the heavenly bodies will cease, and this will indicate the coming of the end time.[1]

*powers of heaven*   Gr. *ai dunameis tōn ouranōn*, trans. of Heb. *ẓeva hashamayim*.[2]

30 *tribes of the earth*   Based on Zech. 12.10–12.[3]

*sign of the Son of man*   Probably does not refer to a separate sign but to the appearance of the Son of man himself.[4]

*coming on the clouds of heaven*   Dan. 7.13 and Rev. 1.7.[5]

31 *his angels*   See above Matt. 16.27.[6]

*with a loud trumpet blast*   Also a feature of the eschatological picture of Isa. 27.13.

*they will gather his elect*   I.e, the gathering of the exiles.[7]

## NOTES

1. This is found frequently in the MT, e.g., Isa. 13.10, 24.23, 34.4; Joel 3.4, 4.15. In the intertestamental literature see 4 Esd. 5.4, En. 80.4–7, Test. Levi 4.1, Asmp.

Mos. 10.5, Sib. Or. 3.976 f. In the NT, 2 Pet. 3.12, Rev. 6.12 ff. In rabbinic sources see B. Sanh. 91b, B. Pes. 68a, B. Suk. 29a.

2. Cf. Isa. (LXX) 34.4, Targ. Ps. 96.11 *ḥailē shemaya*.

3. See Stendahl, *SSMUOT*, pp. 212 ff.

4. See Isa. 60.1. Cf. *PR* 36 (161a, 162a).

5. See also En. 90.37, 46.1; 4 Esd. 13.1; B. Sanh. 98a; *Tan.B. Toledot* 20 (70b).

6. See also En. 61.1, 5.

7. Cf. Zech. 9.14, Ps. Sol. 9.1, 4; 4 Esd. 6.23; TJ Ta'an. 2, 65d (8); *Shemoneh Esreh*, Tenth Benediction *(teqa beshofar)*, Singer, *APB*, p. 48.

# 220. IIIb *The Parable of the Fig Tree*

## MATT. 24.32–33

32 "From the fig tree learn its lesson: as soon as its branch becomes tender and puts forth its leaves, you know that summer is near. 33 So, also, when you see all these things, you know that he is near, at the very gates."

## MARK 13.28–29

29 "From the fig tree learn its lesson: as soon as its branches becomes tender and puts forth its leaves, you know that summer is near. 29 So also, when you see these things taking place,you know that he is near, at the very gates."

## LUKE 21.29–31

29 And he told them a parable: "Look at the fig tree, and all the trees; 30 as soon as they come out in leaf, you see for yourselves and know that the summer is already near. 31 So also, when you see these things taking place, you know that the kingdom of God is near."

### COMMENTARY

32 *fig tree* This is either an independent parable or it might be related to the fig tree incident recorded above Matt. 21.19 (p. 349).[1] What may underlie this parable is the play on the Heb. *qeẓ*, "end", and *qayiẓ*, "summer fruit," as in Amos 7.2.[2] Some have maintained that "any tree would have served as an illustration."[3] Others have argued that it had to be the fig tree since it puts out its leaves first, long before the vines.[4]

### NOTES

1. See Wellhausen, *Marcus*, 2nd ed., ad loc.

2. See Mic. 7.1; 2 Sam. 16.1; Isa. 28.4

3. McNeile, p. 354.

4. Carlston, *Parables of the Triple Tradition*, p. 192 n. 5. Carlston cites Cant. 2.11 ff. and points out in n. 7 that "in addition, the dry fig tree is a sign of desolation,

judgment etc. (Is. 34.4; Jer. 8.13. Hos. 2.12; Joel 1.7, 12; Hab. 3.17; Hag. 2.19). The budding of the fig tree is a sign of God's blessing (Joel 2.22, Zech. 3.10)."

## 221. IIIc The Time of the Parousia

### MATT. 24.34–36

34 "Truly, I say to you, this generation will not pass away till all these things take place. 35 Heaven and earth will pass away, but my words will not pass away. 36 But of that day and hour no one knows, not even the angels of heaven, nor the Son,[d] but the Father only."

### MARK 13.30–32

30 "Truly, I say to you, this generation will not pass away before all these things take place. 31 Heaven and earth will pass away, but my words will not pass away. 32 But of that day or that hour no one knows, not even the angels in heaven, nor the Son, but only the Father."

### LUKE 21.32–33

32 "Truly, I say to you, this generation will not pass away till all has taken place. 33 Heaven and earth will pass away, but my words will not pass away."

---

d Other ancient authorities omit *nor the Son.*

#### COMMENTARY

34 *this generation will not pass away,* etc.   See above to Matt. 16.28 (p. 258).
35 *Heaven and earth will pass away*   See above p. 88.[1]

#### NOTES

1. See also B. Sanh. 99a, 38b; Deut. R. 1.

## 222. Mark's Ending to the Discourse

### MATT. 25.14–15b

14 "For it will be as when a man going on a journey called his servants and entrusted to them his property; 15b . . . to each according to his ability. Then he went away."

### IBID. 25.42

"Watch therefore, for you do not know on what day your Lord is coming."

### I B I D . 2 5 . 1 3

"Watch therefore, for you know neither the day nor the hour."

### M A R K 1 3 . 3 3 – 3 7

33 "Take heed, watch;[e] for you do not know when the time will come. 34 It is like a man going on a journey, when he leaves home and puts his servants in charge, each with his work, and commands the doorkeeper to be on the watch. 35 Watch therefore—for you do not know when the master of the house will come, in the evening, or at midnight, or at cockcrow, or in the morning—36 lest he come suddenly and find you asleep. 37 And what I say to you I say to all: Watch."

### L U K E 1 9 . 1 2 – 1 3

12 He said therefore, "A noblemen went into a far country to receive kingly power[f] and then return. 13 Calling ten of his servants, he gave them ten pounds."

### I B I D . 1 2 . 4 0

"You also must be ready; for the Son of man is coming at an hour you do not expect."

### I B I D . 1 2 . 3 8

"If he comes in the second watch or in the third, and finds them so, blessed are those servants!"

---

e Some add *and pray.*
f Greek *kingdom.*
  See below Secs. 225 (p. 389), 231 (p. 397), and above Sec. 158 (p. 293).

## 223. *Luke's Ending to the Discourse*

### L U K E 2 1 . 3 4 – 3 6

34 "But take heed to yourself lest your hearts be weighed down with dissipation and drunkenness and cares of this life, and that day come upon you suddenly like a snare; 35 for it will come upon all who dwell upon the face of the whole earth. 36 But watch at all times, praying that you may have strength to escape all these things that will take place, and to stand before the Son of man."

### COMMENTARY

34 *your hearts be weighed down* Cf. Isa. 24.17 ff.
36 *to stand before* Either for judgment or as disciples. Cf. Ps. 1.5.

## 224. *The Need for Watchfulness*

### MATT. 24.37–41

37 "As were the days of Noah, so will be the coming of the Son of man. 38 For as in those days before the flood they were eating and drinking, marrying and giving in marriage, until the day when Noah entered the ark, 39 and they did not know until the flood came and swept them all away, so will be the coming of the Son of man. 40 Then two men will be in the field ; one is taken and one is left. 41 Two women will be grinding at the mill; one is taken and one is left."

### LUKE 17.26–27, 34–35

26 "As it was in the days of Noah, so will it be in the days of the Son of man. 27 They ate, they drank, they married, they were given in marriage, until the day when Noah entered the ark, and the flood came and destroyed them all. 34 I tell you, in that night there will be two men in one bed; one will be taken and the other left. 35 There will be two women grinding together; one will be taken and the other left."
See above Sec. 184 (p. 319).

## 225. *The Watchful Householder*

### MATT. 24.42–44

42 "Watch therefore, for you do not know on what day your Lord is coming. 43 But know this, that if the householder had known in what part of the night the thief was coming, he would have watched and would not have let his house be broken into. 44 Therefore you also must be ready; for the Son of man is coming at an hour you do not expect."

### LUKE 12.39–40

39 "But know this, that if the householder had known at what hour the thief was coming, he would have been awake andg would not have left his house to be broken into. 40 You also must be ready; for the Son of man is coming at an hour you do not expect."

---

g Some texts omit *would have been awake and.*

### COMMENTARY

42 *for you do not know on what day*, etc.   There is, however, a tradition that the Messiah or Elijah will come on the fourteenth of Nisan but not on a Sabbath nor on a holiday.[1]

NOTES

1. See TJ Pes. 3.6, 30b (39); B. ibid. 13a; B. Er. 43a; Exod. R. 18.12.

## 226. *The Faithful Wise Servant*

### MATT. 24.45–51

45 "Who then is the faithful and wise servant, whom his master has set over his household, to give them their food at the proper time? 46 Blessed is that servant whom his master when he comes will find so doing. 47 Truly, I say to you, he will set him over all his possessions. 48 But if that wicked servant says to himself, 'My master is delayed,' 49 and begins to beat his fellow servants, and eats and drinks with the drunken, 50 the master of that servant will come on a day when he does not expect him and at an hour he does not know. 51 And will punish him,[h] and put him with the hypocrites; there men will weep and gnash their teeth."

### LUKE 12.42–46

42 "Who then is the faithful and wise steward, whom his master will set over his household, to give them their portion of food at the proper time? 43 Blessed is that servant whom his master when he comes will find so doing. 44 Truly, I tell you, he will set him over all his possessions. 45 But if that servant says to himself, 'My master delayed in coming,' and begins to beat the menservants and the maidservants, and to eat and drink and get drunk, 46 the master of that servant will come on a day when he does not expect him and at an hour he does not know, and will punish him,[h] and put him with the unfaithful."

---

h Or *cut him in pieces.*
See above Sec. 158 (p. 293).

## 227. *The Parable of the Ten Maidens*

### MATT. 25.1–13

1 "Then the kingdom of heaven shall be compared to ten maidens who took their lamps and went to meet the bridegroom.[i] 2 Five of them were foolish, and five were wise. 3 For when the foolish took their lamps, they took no oil with them; 4 but the wise took flasks of oil with their lamps. 5 As the bridegroom was delayed, they all slumbered and slept. 6 But at midnight there was a cry, 'Behold the bridegroom! Come out to meet him.' 7 Then all those maidens rose and trimmed their lamps. 8 And the foolish said to the wise, 'Give us some of your oil, for our lamps are going out,' 9 But the wise replied, 'Perhaps there will not be enough for us and for you; go rather to the dealer and buy for yourself.' 10 And while they went to buy, the

bridegroom came, and those who were ready went in with him to the marriage feast; and the door was shut. 11 Afterward the other maidens came also, saying, 'Lord, Lord, open to us.' 12 But he replied, 'Truly, I say to you, I do not know you.' 13 Watch therefore, for you know neither the day nor the hour."

---

i  Some add *and the bride*.

## COMMENTARY

There is no parallel to this section, but Luke 12.35–36 is similar in import, "Let your loins be girded and your lamps burning, and be like men who are waiting for their master to come home from the marriage feast," etc. This is a crisis parable dealing with the Parousia.[1] There is no rabbinic parallel, but the passage from B. Shab. 153 cited above in connection with Matt. 22.2–14 (p. 357) is instructive in that reference is made to the wise and foolish guests.[2]

6 *Behold the bridegroom*  If the bridegroom is God, then this motif is relatively common in rabbinic sources. Perhaps the best illustration is the one in which Moses wakens Israel saying, "The Bridegroom is coming."[3]

12 *I do not know you*  See above p. 150.

## NOTES

1. See Jeremias, *PJ*, pp. 51, 175. His citation of *Mek.* Exod. 19.17, where Deut. 33.21 is interpreted "like a bridegroom who goes forth to meet the bride," is off the mark and has no relationship to any part of this NT parable. See also F. C. Burkitt, "The Parable of the Ten Virgins," *JTS* 30 (1929): 267–270, who argues from an old Latin version that the original reading was "to meet the bridegroom and the bride."

2. See also Koh. R. 9.8.

3. *PRE* 41.

4. See also B. BQ 80b; Koh. R. 11.9.

# 228. *The Parable of the Talents*

## MATT. 25.14–30

14 "For it will be as when a man going on a journey called his servants and entrusted to them his property; 15 to one he gave five talents, to another two, to another one, to each according to his ability. Then he went away. 16 He who received the five talents went at once and traded with them; and he made five talents more. 17 So too, he who had the two talents made two talents more. 18 But he who had received the one talent, went and dug in the ground and hid his master's money. 19 Now after a long time the master of those servants came and settled accounts with them. 20 And he who had received the five talents came forward, bringing five talents more, saying, 'Master, you delivered to me five talents; here I have made five talents more.' 21 His

master said to him, 'Well done, good and faithful servant; you have been faithful over a little, I will set you over much; enter into the joy of your master.' 22 And he also who had the two talents came forward, saying, 'Master, you delivered to me two talents; here I have made two talents more.' 23 His master said to him, 'Well done, good and faithful servant; you have been faithful over a little, I will set you over much; enter into the joy of your master.' 24 He also who had received the one talent came forward, saying 'Master, I knew you to be a hard man, reaping where you did not sow, and gathering where you did not winnow; 25 so I was afraid, and I went and hid your talent in the ground. Here you have what is yours.' 26 But his master answered him, 'You wicked and slothful servant! You knew that I reap where I have not sowed, and gather where I have not winnowed? 27 Then you ought to have invested my money with the bankers, and at my coming I should have received what was my own with interest. 28 So take the talent from him, and give it to him who has the ten talents.' 29 For to everyone who has will more be given, and he will have abundance; but from him who has not, even what he has will be taken away 30 And cast the worthless servant into the outer darkenss; there men will weep and gnash their teeth."

## LUKE 19.12–27

12 He said therefore, "A nobleman went into a far country to receive kingly power and then return. 13 Calling ten of his servants, he gave them ten pounds,ʲ and said to them. 'Trade with these till I come.' 14 But his citizens hated him and sent an embassy after him, saying, 'We do not want this man to reign over us.' 15 When he returned, having received the kingly power, he commanded these servants to whom he had given the money, to be called to him,that he might know what they had gained by trading. 16 The first came before him, saying, 'Lord, your pound has made ten pounds more.' 17 And he said to him, 'Well done, good servant! Because you have been faithful in a very little, you shall have authority over ten cities.' 18 And the second came, saying, 'Lord, your pound has made five pounds.' 19 And he said to him, 'And you are to be over five cities.' 20 Then another came, saying, 'Lord, here is your pound, which I kept laid away in a napkin; 21 for I was afraid of you, because you are a severe man; you take up what you did not lay down, and reap what you did not sow.' 22 He said to him, 'I will condemn you out of your own mouth, you wicked servant! You knew that I was a severe man, taking up what I did not lay down and reaping what I did not sow? 23 Why then did you not put my money into the bank, and at my coming I should have collected it with interest?' 24 And he said to those who stood by, 'Take the pound from him, and give it to him who has the ten pounds.' 25 (And they said to him, 'Lord, he has ten pounds!') 26 I tell you, that to everyone who has will more be given, but from him who has not, even what he has will be taken away. 27 But as for these enemies of mine, who did not want me to reign over them, bring them here and slay them before me.'

---

ʲ The mina, rendered here by pound.
See above Sec. 195 (p. 339).

## 229. *The Last Judgment*

### MATT. 25.31–46

31 "When the Son of man comes in his glory, and all the angels with him, then he will sit on his glorious throne. 32 Before him will be gathered all the nations, and he will separate them one from another as a shepherd separates the sheep from the goats, 33 and he will place the sheep at his right hand, but the goats at the left. 34 Then the King will say to those at his right hand, 'Come, O blessed of my Father, inherit the kingdom prepared for you from the foundation of the world; 35 for I was hungry and you gave me food, I was thirsty and you gave me drink, I was a stranger and you welcomed me, 36 I was naked and you clothed me, I was sick and you visited me, I was in prison and you came to me.' 37 Then the righteous will answer him, 'Lord, when did we see thee hungry and feed thee, or thirsty and give thee drink? 38 And when did we see thee a stranger and welcome thee or naked and clothe thee? 39 and when did we see thee sick or in prison and visit thee?' 40 And the King will answer them, 'Truly, I say to you, as you did it to one of the least of these my brethren, you did it to me.' 41 Then he will say to those at his left hand, 'Depart from me, you cursed, into the eternal fire prepared for the devil and his angels; 42 for I was hungry and you gave me no food, I was thirsty and you gave me no drink. 43 I was a stranger and you did not welcome me, naked and you did not clothe me, sick and in prison and you did not visit me.' 44 Then they also will answer, 'Lord, when did we see thee hungry or thirsty or a stranger or naked or sick or in prison, and did not minister to thee?' 45 Then he will answer them, 'Truly, I say to you, as you did it not to one of the least of these, you did it not to me.' 46 And they will go away into eternal punishment, but the righteous into eternal life."

### COMMENTARY

Matthew's description of the Last Judgment contains a confused *dramatis personae*. It starts with the Son of man with his angels surrounding him, then the king is introduced, who seems to be part of a separate parable, and the moral involving either the Son of man or the king, God. Finally the sheep and the goats, representing the righteous and the wicked respectively, could be either Israel and the nations or the good Gentiles and the bad Gentiles.[1]

31 *When the Son of man comes . . . sit on his glorious throne* The Son of man (Messiah) sitting on the throne of judgment is reminiscent of a similar description in Enoch: "And thus the Lord commanded the kings and the mighty and the exalted and those who dwell on the earth and said, 'Open your eyes and lift up your horns if you are able to recognize the Elect One,' And the Lord of Spirits seated him on the throne of His glory . . . and he will deliver them to the angels for punishment to execute vengeance on them because they have oppressed His children and his Elect."[2]

32 *Before him will be gathered all the nations*, etc. There are many passages which describe God sitting in judgment of his creatures; some refer to an

annual judgment, i.e., on Rosh Hashannah, others "in the time to come" or at judgment day.[3]

33 *right hand . . . at the left hand*  The preferred are on the right, the rejected on the left; the two, right and left, have positive and negative meanings respectively in most languages.[4] Another division of people at the last judgment is described as follows: "We have learned in a *baraita:* The School of Shammai says: On the day of judgment there will be three classes, one consisting of the perfectly righteous, one of the perfectly wicked, and one of the intermediates. The first are immediately inscribed and sealed for a perfect life; and the third are likewise immediately sealed for Gehinom . . . the intermediate descend to Gehinom and cry out."[5]

34 *inherit the kingdom*  See above p. 74.[6]

*from the foundation of the world* Heb. *yesod olam*, things created before the creation of the world, i.e., Heaven and Hell.[7]

35 *I was hungry and you gave me food*, etc.   All of the deeds mentioned here are acts of kindness (Heb. *gemilut ḥasadim):* feeding the hungry, giving drink to the thirsty, hospitality, clothing the naked, visiting the sick, burying the dead, and freeing the captives.[8] He who performs any one of them is considered praiseworthy, and it is as if he has done them to God himself. "He who receives his fellow man kindly, it is as if he has received the Shekhinah."[9] "He who visits the sick will be saved from Gehinom."[10] This line of reasoning is based on the notion that man is created in the image of God, and that by serving man with concern and compassion, man serves God. This is not the same as the doctrine of *Imitatio Dei*, which is the very opposite.[11]

Very much on point here is the following: "In the future world man will be asked, 'What was your occupation?' If he replies, 'I fed the hungry,' then they will reply, 'This is the gate of the Lord. He who feeds the hungry let him enter.' So with giving drink to the thirsty, clothing the naked, with those who look after the orphans, and those generally who do deeds of loving-kindness. All these are gates of the Lord, and those who do such deeds shall enter within them."[12]

*the devil and his angels*.[13]   See above p. 227.

## NOTES

1. Cf. B. AZ 2b.

2. En. 61.6. See also 63.12, 62.10.

3. E.g., B. RH 16b–17a. Cf. J. Townsend, "I Corinthians 3.5 and the School of Shammai," *HTR* 61 (1968): 500-504. See also 1 Cor. 3.15.

4. Cf. B. Hor. 12a; M. Shev. 6.15; *Mid. Ps.* 18.29 (79a); B. Shab. 63a, 88b; Lam. R. 1.9 (90); Num. R. 22; Cf. Test. Benj. 10.4.

5. T. Sanh. 13.3 (p.434).

6. Cf. also B. Yom. 72b; Targ. Lam. 1.3; B. Ber. 51a.

7. *SB*, 1:981.

8. See Isa. 58.7; Job 22.7; Prov. 25.21; Exod. 18.7; Tob. 4.16; Sira 2.35; Test. Joseph 1; B. Suk. 49b; M. Avot 1.2. Cf. Deut. 22.2; Judg. 19.18.

9. B. Shab. 127a; B. Shev. 35b; *Mid. Ps.* 18.29 (78b); Gen. R. 48.9; *MHG* Gen., p. 292; *Yal.* Gen. 82.

10. B. Ned. 40a.

11. As Montefiore, *RLGT*, pp. 338–339.

12. *Mid. Ps.* 118.19 (243b).

13. See Exod. R. 20; T. Shab. 17.2 (p. 136); Test. Asher 6; Slav. En. 29.4; Jub. 10.7–11.

## 230. A Summary of the Days Spent in Jerusalem

### LUKE 21.37–38

37 And every day he was teaching in the temple, but at night he went out and lodged on the mount called Olivet. 38 And early in the morning all the people came to him in the temple to hear him.

### COMMENTARY

37 *lodged on the mount called Olivet*   See above p. 344. Note that in Mark 11.19 he lodged in Bethany, not on Mount Olivet.

# THE PASSION NARRATIVE

MATTHEW 26–27 = MARK 14–15 = LUKE 22–23

## 231. The Conspiracy of the Jews

### MATT. 26.1–5

1 When Jesus had finished all these sayings, he said to his disciples, 2 "You know that after two days the Passover is coming, and the Son of man will be delivered up to be crucified." 3 Then the chief priests and the elders of the people gathered in the palace of the high priest, who was called Caiaphas, 4 and took counsel together in order to arrest Jesus by stealth and kill him. 5 But they said, "Not during the feast, lest there be a tumult among the people."

### MARK 14.1–2

1 It was now two days before the Passover and the feast of Unleavened Bread. And the chief priests and the scribes were seeking how to arrest him by stealth, and kill him; 2 for they said "Not during the feast, lest there be a tumult of the people."

### LUKE 22.1–2

1 Now the feast of Unleavened Bread drew near, which is called the Passover. 2 And the chief priests and the scribes were seeking how to put him to death; for they feared the people.

### COMMENTARY

It has been assumed, because of the centrality of the Passion, Death, and Resurrection to Christianity, that this section of the gospel is the oldest. It contains more problems historical, legal, and religious than the rest of the gospel material. "It was not the aim of the individual evangelists to give in their descriptions an exact account of the actual events, as seen in the light of history, nor were they in any position to give such an account had it been their intention to do so. What they intended, and what they did, was to present the significance of Jesus' death, as contemplated in the light of religious faith."[1]

1 *all these sayings* "All (in this summary only) is emphatic. The whole teaching of Jesus contained in the five discourses is now concluded."[2]
2 *after two days* Speaking on Wednesday and meaning Friday.[3]

397

*The Passover is coming* Gr. *pascha*, Heb. *pesaḥ*, Aram. *pisha*. Technically *ḥag hapesaḥ* refers to the Festival of Pesaḥ (Passover), which falls on the fourteenth of the month of Nisan, when the paschal lamb was slaughtered and eaten later that evening.[4] Starting on the fifteenth of Nisan (i.e., the night of the fourteenth day) is an independent holiday lasting seven days called *ḥag ḥamazot*, the Festival of Unleavened Bread,[5] and the term *Pesaḥ* had in the course of time become attached to this latter holiday.[6] In the Synoptics there is little question that *ḥag ḥamazot* is meant;[7] that the description of the Last Supper is a description of the Seder which is celebrated on the fifteenth of Nisan.[8] In the Gospel of John, the Last Supper is a non-festive meal and took place on the fourteenth of Nisan, the night of the thirteenth. There is theological import to both dates. In the Synoptics the Festival of Unleavened Bread is the Festival of Redemption and the redemptive element is the interpretation of the crucifixion. John sees Jesus as the *Angus Dei*, the Lamb of God, the paschal lamb which was sacrificed on the fourteenth of Nisan.[9]

*to be crucified* Crucifixion was a Roman, not a Jewish, mode of execution. Jews had four, viz., stoning, burning, decapitation, and strangulation.[10] That Jesus was crucified shows that he was tried and sentenced and executed under Roman law for a political crime. Had Jesus been guilty of blasphemy, Pilate would probably have had to ratify the sentence, but it would have been by stoning, as prescribed by Lev. 24.10–15.[11]

3 *gathered in the palace of the high priest* Gr. *aulē*, Heb. *ḥazer*, a courtyard, an *atrium*, not strictly a palace. This was not the place where the Sanhedrin was to assemble according to Jewish law. The members of the court were to sit in a place called *lishkat hagazit*, the Chamber of Hewn Stones.[12] It should be noted that in Mark 14.1 it appears as an informal meeting, but in Matt. it is turned into a formal session of the court. The meeting here might have been for reasons of secrecy.[13]

*called Caiaphas* Probably from *qipa'ai, qai'if*, "a soothsayer."[14] His name was Joseph, and he was appointed high priest by Valerius Gratus (Gratian) ca. 18 C.E.[15] Mark does not name him. He served for eighteen years until he was removed from office by the procurator Vitellius (ca. 36–37).[16] This was the longest tenure of any high priest from Herod to the fall of Jerusalem; during this period there were twenty-eight.[17] The office was frequently sold to the Aaronid who paid the highest price to the Roman governor, for from 6 to 36 C.E. the high priestly garments were kept by him.[18] Note the comment of R. Judah b. Ilai, "Because one gives money for the high priesthood they change every twelve months."[19] From the length of his tenure it is apparent that Caiaphas was a political favorite of the Roman authorities.

4 *and took counsel together* "This conspiracy was spear-headed by the priestly caste who were for the most part pro-Roman collaborationists. What is remarkable is that the Pharisees, except for Mt. 27.62, are significantly absent in the narratives whereas in Jesus' Galilean ministry they represent his strongest opposition."[20]

5 *Not during the feast* The Roman authorities always worried about

insurrection during the festival periods when the masses of Jews assembled in Jerusalem. This was especially true of the Passover, which emphasizes the message of freedom and redemption from Egyptian servitude. Also, the procurator had his residence at Caesarea on the coast but at the festival took up residence in Jerusalem.

## NOTES

1. P. Winter, *On the Trial of Jesus*, (Berlin, 1961), p. 51.
2. Green, *Matt.*, p. 209.
3. McNeile, *Matt.*, p. 372, struggles unnecessarily with the meaning of "after two days."
4. See Exod. 12.1 ff., Deut. 16.1; Num. 9.1–14.
5. Exod. 12.15, Deut. 16.1–8; Ezek. 45.21–25. See also Josephus, *Ant.* XVIII.2.2.
6. In the first sense see M. Pes. 2.8, 3.7; in the second, ibid. 2.2, 3, 4, 5, "*pesaḥ dorot noheg kol shiv'ah.*"
7. See below p. 403.
8. See below pp. 405 f.
9. See Zeitlin, *Who Crucified Jesus*, pp. 103 ff.
10. M. Sanh. 7. On these modes of execution see Winter, op. cit., pp. 62ff. E. Stauffer, *Jerusalem und Rom im Zeitalter Jesu Christi* (Bern, 1957), pp. 123–27, argues without foundation that crucifixion was a method of execution among Jews. For a refutation of this thesis, see Winter, *Trial*, pp. 62 ff. The bodies of executed criminals were in fact hanged and removed before a nightfall, Deut. 21.22–23. The Gr. *stauroō*, Heb. *talah*, "to hang," cf. Est. 7.9, 8.13, and is used in Polybius for crucifixion (I.86. 4).
11. See M. Sanh 7.4 Cf. O. Cullmann, *The State in the New Testament* (London, 1957), p. 42.
12. See Josephus, *BJ* II.16.3, VI.6.3, V.144; M. Sanh. 11.2; M. Mid. 5.4; T. Sanh. 7.1 (p. 425); TJ ibid. 1.4 (19a); B. Shab. 15a; B. RH 31a; B. Sanh. 12a; 41a; 88b; B.AZ 8b. Further on the Sanhedrin, see below p. 419 f.
13. Montefiore, *SG*, 2:328.
14. See Dalman, *Gramm.* 161.2.
15. Josephus, *Ant.* XVIII.2.2, 4.2.
16. See also ibid. XIX.8.1. On the problem of Caiaphas and Annas, see below p. 419 n. 4. See M. Smallwood, "High Priests and Politics in Roman Palestine," *JTS* 13 (1962): 22–29.
17. See Josephus, *Ant.* VIII.2.2.
18. Ibid. XV.11.4, XVIII.4.3, XX.1.1.
19. B. Yom. 8b.
20. J. Townsend, *A Liturgical Interpretation of Our Lord's Passion in Narrative Form* (New York: National Conference of Christians and Jews, 1977), p. 11 n. 9, who also discusses the various views about this omission.

## 232. *The Anointing at Bethany*

### MATT. 26.6–13

6 Now when Jesus was at Bethany in the house of Simon the leper, 7 a woman came up to him with an alabaster jar of very expensive ointment, and she poured it on his head, as he sat at table. 8 But when the disciples saw it, they were indignant, saying,

"Why this waste? 9 For this ointment might have been sold for a large sum, and given to the poor." 10 But Jesus, aware of this, said to them, "Why do you trouble the woman? For she has done a beautiful thing to me. 11 For you always have the poor with you, but you will not always have me. 12 In pouring this ointment on my body she has done it to prepare me for burial. 13 Truly, I say to you, wherever this gospel is preached in the whole world, what this woman has done will be told in memory of her."

## MARK 14.3–9

3 And while he was at Bethany in the house of Simon the leper, as he sat at table, a woman came with an alabaster jar of ointment of pure nard, very costly, and she broke the jar and poured it over his head. 4 But there were some who said to themselves indignantly, "Why was the ointment thus wasted? 5 For this ointment might have been sold for more than three hundred denarii, and given to the poor." And they reproached her. 6 But Jesus said, "Let her alone; why do you trouble her? She has done a beautiful thing to me. 7 For you always have the poor with you, and whenever you will, you can do good to them; but you will not always have me. 8 She has done what she could; she has anointed my body beforehand for burying. 9 And truly, I say to you, wherever the gospel is preached in the whole world, what she has done will be told in memory of her."

## COMMENTARY

The reason for the inclusion of the anointing episode is not clear. Mark and Matthew see it as an adumbration of the burial; Luke 7.36–50 treats it simply as an act of kindness on the part of the woman.[1]

6 *Bethany* See above to Matt. 21.17. (p. 348)
*Simon the leper* Is he identical with Simon the Pharisee (Luke 9.36–50, cf. Mark 14.3–9, John 12.1–8)? Some say that the original is the Aram. *garba*, which may mean a "jar merchant," but since the root *g-r-b* means "to scrape," hence "a leper." This is far-fetched. If he had been a leper, possibly he was once cured by Jesus. Some have suggested that he was the husband of Martha or the father of Mary, Martha, and Lazarus because according to John 12.1 ff., the anointing took place in the house of Lazarus.[2]

7 *an alabaster jar of very expensive ointment* Gr. *alabastron murou* = Heb. *ẓeloḥit shel poliaton*, a flask of oil ointment prepared from the leaves of spikenard,[3] a flask of foliatrum, Gr. *fouliaton*, cf. Mark 14.3, which adds *nardou pistikēs*, "nard" = "spikenard."[4] *Muron* is a perfume but could it be myrrh, Heb. *mor*, which is generally rendered in Gr. *smurna?* Myrrh was used in embalming.[5] Alabaster containers were commonly used for precious ointments.[6]

*and she poured it on his head.* It was a custom to anoint one (a guest) at table.[7] At the bath the anointing began with the head.[8] Note that the disciples were angry not at the anointing of Jesus at the table, but that the ointment was costly.[9] Note in John 7.3 Jesus is anointed on his feet.

9 *this ointment might have been sold for a large sum*    Unguents and ointments were indeed costly: A wife could demand one tenth of her dowery income for unguents and perfumes. The daughter of Naqdimon ben Gorion was accustomed to spend four hundred gold denarii for them.[10]

11 *for you always have the poor with you.*    Cf. Deut. 15.11, *for the poor will never cease out of the land*—according to rabbinic interpretation, even in the days of the Messiah.[11]

12 *In pouring out this ointment . . . prepare me for burial*    It was a custom among Jews in preparing the dead for burial that the body be anointed.[12]

13 *what she has done . . . told in memory of her*    Gr. *mnēmosunon*, Heb. *zikaron*, Aram. *dukhrana*.[13]    There were various formulae in rabbinic literature connected with the mentioning of the dead: e.g., "may that man be remembered for good,"[14] and "remembering him for praise."[15]

### NOTES

1. See J. K. Elliott, "The Anomoly of Jesus," *Expos. T.* 85 (1974): 105–107; Daube, *NTRJ* pp. 310–324.
2. See J. Finegan, *Die Ueberlieferung der Leidens- und Auferstehungsgeschichte Jesu. BZNW* (Giessen, 1934), pp. 63 ff., who argues that since Simon is not known from any other source, he is historical.
3. Cant. R. 1.3.
4. Cf. Gen. R. 39.2; B. Sanh. 108a.
5. Cf. Herodotus, II.86; John 19.39, Mark 16.1, Luke 24.1.
6. See Theoc. XV.114; Pliny, *NH* XXXVI.12.
7. Cf. B. Ḥul. 94a.
8. B. Shab. 41a, B. Sota 11b.
9. Cf. T. BB 6.14 (p. 406); TJ M. Sh. 2, 53b; TJ Shab. 9.4, 12a; T. Shab. 3 (4).6 (pp. 113–4).
10. B. Ket. 66b.
11. Cf. B. Shab. 63a. Also M. Ber. 5 (end).
12. See M. Shab. 23.5.
13. See, e.g., Targ. Prov. 10.7, Targ. Ps. 112.6; cf. Neh. 5.17, 13; 14.21, 31.
14. B. BB 21a, B. Shab. 13b; M. Yom. 3.9.
15. Cf., e.g., *Tan. Ha'azinu* 1.

## 233. *The Betrayal by Judas*

### MATT. 26.14–16

14 Then one of the twelve, who was called Judas Iscariot, went to the chief priests, 15 and said, "What will you give me if I deliver him to you?" And they paid him thirty pieces of silver. 16 And from that moment he sought an opportunity to betray him.

### MARK 14.10–11

10 Then Judas Iscariot, who was one of the twelve, went to the chief priests in order to betray him to them. 11 And when they heard it they were glad, and promised to give him money. And he sought an opportunity to betray him.

## LUKE 22.3–6

3 Then Satan entered into Judas called Iscariot, who was of the number of the twelve; 4 he went away and conferred with the chief priests and captains how he might betray him to them. 5 And they were glad and engaged to give him money. 6 So he agreed, and sought an opportunity to betray him to them in the absence of the multitude.

### COMMENTARY

The crucial question here is, why did Judas betray Jesus? It seems to be out of the question to assume that he betrayed the Master merely for thirty pieces of silver. The gospels strangely do not supply an answer to this perplexing problem. One suggestion is that "Judas was a follower of the Apocalyptics and believed that Jesus was the Son of God. But Judas feared lest some disciples were ready that Passover night to declare Jesus the Messiah, the King of the Jews. He, therefore, went to the authorities and told them of these designs, and urged Jesus' arrest. He himself, as John records, led a Roman cohort to arrest Jesus. The cause of Judas' fear lay in the fact that, when Jesus entered Jerusalem, he was hailed as King of the Jews, the Son of David. Indeed the question which was put to Jesus before Pilate was whether he was the Messiah, the King of the Jews; while on the cross were inscribed the words 'Jesus of Nazareth, King of the Jews.' "[1]

14 *Judas Iscariot*   On the name Iscariot, see above p. 179.

15 *thirty pieces of silver*   The amount "thirty" has no antecedent in Jewish sources except for Exod. 21.32, where an ox gores a slave and its owner must pay the master thirty shekels of silver, which is clearly not applicable here. Note that neither Mark nor Luke mentions an amount. Matt. apparently relied homiletically on Zech. 11.12.[2]

*and they paid him*   Gr. *hoi de estēsan autō*, going back to *shaqal* = "to weigh," Zech. 11.12. They did not, however, weigh out the money, but gave him coin.[3]

### NOTES

1. Zeitlin, *Who Crucified Jesus*, p. 162.
2. See below to Matt. 27.3 ff. (p. 422).
3. On *estēsan*, see *BAG*, s.v. *histēmi*.

## 234. *Preparation for the Passover*

### MATT. 26.17–19

17 Now on the first day of Unleavened Bread the disciples came to Jesus saying, "Where will you have us prepare for you to eat the passover?" 18 He said, "Go into the city to such a one, and say to him, 'The Teacher says, My time is at hand; I will

keep the passover at your house with my disciples.' 19 And the disciples did as Jesus had directed them, and they prepared the passover.

## MARK 14.12–16

12 And on the first day of Unleavened Bread, when they sacrificed the passover lamb, his disciples said to him, "Where will you have us go and prepare for you to eat the passover?" 13 And he sent two of his disciples, and said to them, "Go into the city, and a man carrying a jar of water will meet you; follow him, 14 and wherever he enters, say to the householder, 'The Teacher says Where is my guest room, where I am to eat the passover with my disciples?' 15 And he will show you a large upper room furnished and ready; there prepare for us." 16 And the disciples set out and went to the city, and found it as he had told them; and they prepared the passover.

## LUKE 22.7–13

7 Then came the day of Unleavened Bread, on which the passover lamb had to be sacrificed. 8 So Jesus[k] sent Peter and John, saying, "Go and prepare the passover for us, that we may eat it." 9 They said to him, "Where will you have us prepare it?" 10 He said to them, "Behold, when you have entered the city, a man carrying a jar of water will meet you; follow him into the house which he enters, 11 and tell the householder 'The Teacher says to you, Where is the guest room, where I am to eat the passover with my disciples?' 12 And he will show you a large upper room furnished; there make ready." 13 And they went, and found it as he had told them; and they prepared the passover.

--------

k Greek *he*.

## COMMENTARY

17 *Now on the first day of Unleavened Bread . . . to eat the passover* I.e., *ḥag ḥamazot.* As stated above p. 398, Matt. and Mark describe the last supper as the eating of the paschal offering, the Seder, while John saw it as an ordinary meal, i.e., the beginning of the fourteenth of Nisan, the day on which the paschal lamb was slaughtered and which, according to John, coincided with the crucifixion, hence John's use of "The Lamb of God."[1] But this verse is a *crux interpretum* in that the first day of Unleavened Bread, the fifteenth of Nisan, is too late for "the preparation of the passover." If to "prepare the passover" meant to slaughter and roast the animal, this had to be done on the afternoon of the fourteenth of Nisan on the day *before* the first day of Unleavened Bread. The slaughter of the *pesaḥ*, i.e., the sacrifice of the lamb, was done in the Temple court, after which the individuals who had subscribed to a group then repaired to their own homes or rented residences in Jerusalem to celebrate the Passover.[2] Perhaps the text is defective and the original reading was "on the day before the first day of Unleavened Bread."[3] Allen,[4] on the basis of a suggestion of Chwolson, argues that *qama'a*, the Aram. for "first," and *qama* or *qamei*, "before," were confused in Mark and

that the Aram. might have meant "on the day before the *Azuma*," i.e., on the day before the passover. More likely, however, the Synoptic tradition was influenced by a conflated tradition that the last supper was the paschal meal.[5] It is highly unlikely that the disciples waited until nightfall to make arrangements as to where the paschal lamb was to be eaten.[6]

18 *to such a one* Gr. *pros ton deina*, Heb. *peloni almoni*,[7] who was most likely to be a friend or disciple.

*The Teacher says* This would be understood by the man but it is sufficiently enigmatic to retain secrecy. Note that only in Mark and Luke will the man be carrying a water jar and would stand out, since women normally carried water jars, while men carried leather bags.[8]

19 *And the disciples did . . . and they prepared the passover* The disciples probably did two things in Jerusalem: they arranged for the place for the paschal meal and they slaughtered the paschal lamb. There is, however, a problem. According to Jewish law, those who would eat of the lamb had to be present at the slaughter.[9] Note that Matt., who knew more about Jewish law than Mark and Luke, omits the number of the disciples who went to Jerusalem, whereas Mark and Luke record two, and only Luke names them.

## NOTES

1. Zeitlin, *Who Crucified Jesus*, pp. 103 ff.
2. See B. Yom. 12b, B. Meg. 26a.
3. For attempts to explain this crux, see Jeremias, *EWJ*, pp. 26–36, 41–48; Green, *Matt.*, p. 211; Townsend, *Liturgical Interpretation*, p. 13 n. 20.
4. M. Holtzmann, "Auf die Septuaginta zurückgehende Uebersetzungsfehler," *MGWJ* 72 (1928): 537ff.
5. McNeile, *Matt.*, p. 378.
6. Townsend, op. cit., p. 13 n. 21, comments: "In Jesus' day Passover was *largely* [emphasis added] a Temple rite and had to be celebrated in Jerusalem. After A.D. 70 when there was no more Temple, Paschal sacrifices ceased; and the meal was eaten at home." It is highly possible, as suggested by Zeitlin, *RFJS*, 3:233, citing B. Pes. 74a, that the paschal sacrifice continued in Jerusalem until the defeat of Bar Kokhba, when the Jews were forbidden to enter the city.
7. See Aq. Ruth; 1 Sam. 22.2; 2 Kings 6.8.
8. See M. J. Lagrange, *Evangile selon Saint Marc* (Paris, 1966), p. 373.
9. M. Pes. 5.5 ff.

# THE LAST SUPPER

MATTHEW 26.20–29 = MARK 14.17–25 = LUKE 22.14–38

## 235. *The Traitor*

### MATT. 26.20–25

20 When it was evening, he sat at table with the twelve disciples;[l] 21 and as they were eating, he said, "Truly, I say to you, one of you will betray me." 22 And they were very sorrowful, and began to say to him one after another, "Is it I, Lord?" 23 He answered, "He who has dipped his hand in the dish with me, will betray me. 24 The Son of man goes as it is written of him, but woe to that man by whom the Son of man is betrayed! It would have been better for that man if he had not been born." 25 Judas, who betrayed him, said, "Is it I, Master?"[m] He said to him "You have said so."

### MARK 14.17–21

17 And when it was evening he came with the twelve. 18 And as they were at table eating, Jesus said, "Truly, I say to you, one of you will betray me, one who is eating with me." 19 They began to be sorrowful, and to say to him one after another, "Is it I?" 20 He said to them, "It is one of the twelve, one who is dipping bread in the same dish with me. 21 For the Son of man goes, as it is written of him, but woe to that man by whom the Son of man is betrayed! It would have been better for that man if he had not been born."

### LUKE 22.14, 21–23

14 And when the hour came, he sat at table, and the apostles with him. 21"But behold the hand of him who betrays me is with me on the table. 22 For the Son of man goes as it has been determined; but woe to that man by whom he is betrayed." 23 And they began to question one another, which of them it was that would do this.

---

l  Some omit *disciples*.
m  Or *Rabbi*.

### COMMENTARY

20 *When it was evening*  Did he wait for the cover of darkness to ensure secrecy,[1] or did he sit down with his disciples to eat only after nightfall since the Seder meal could, according to the Law, be eaten only after dark?[2]

*he sat at table* Gr. *anekaito*, Luke *anepesen* both mean "he reclined at a meal." This was the posture at the Passover meal, Heb. *hasabah*.[3] This was particularly significant at this meal since in the Greco-Roman world only free men were permitted to recline at table, hence its significance at the Festival of Freedom.

23 *He who has dipped his hand in the dish with me* At the time of Jesus was there a common dish? According to the Mishnah, no.[4] Dipping some vegetables, sometimes meat, generally in vinegar, was a regular custom at a Palestinian meal. On the Passover it was established that one "dips twice."[5] These dippings symbolized the blood of the paschal lamb[6] and the blood of circumcision,[7] and homiletically were connected with the verse *By your blood shall you live, by your blood shall you live.*[8] The formula recited on the first night of Passover is, "on all other nights we dip once, on this night twice."[9] The Babylonian formula is, "on all other nights we do not dip even once, on this night twice."[10] There was an etiquette connected with the dipping.[11] The meaning is "one of you," since all dipped with him.[12] In the Dead Sea Scrolls we find that the Rule of the Community (IQS vi.1–8) states that the food, after preparation, was to be eaten by the men according to rank and position. Fensham argues that "with me" means that Judas did not wait his turn—denied leadership to Jesus and revealed himself a rebel.

24 *Son of Man* See above p. 158.

*It would have been better . . . not been born* Cf. Matt. 18.6, 8 f.; 5.29. "Where then will be the dwelling of the sinners, and where the resting place of those who have denied the Lord of Spirits? It had been good for them if they had not been born."[13]

25 *You have said so* See Matt. 26.64. Here it apparently means "you are correct," but still enigmatic.[14]

## NOTES

1. McNeile, *Matt.*, p. 37.
2. M. Pes. 10.1.
3. Ibid.
4. Ibid. 10.3. Jeremias, *EWJ*, pp. 67 f., objects, stating that the Mishnah refers to a practice in post-70.
5. M. Pes. 10.4.
6. Cf. Exod. 12.21 ff.
7. Ibid. 12.48.
8. Ezek. 16.6. See also *Mek.* Exod. 12.6; Rashi to Exod. 12.6.
9. M. Pes. 10.4.
10. B. Pes. 116a.
11. Cf. B. Ber. 47a, B. Git. 59b; B. Ned. 4.4.
12. See F. C. Fensham, "Judas' Hand in the Bowl and Qumran," *Revue de Qumran* 5 (1964–65): 259–261.
13. En. 38.2. See Sifre Deut. 303, M. Ḥag. 2.1.
14. See T. Kel. (BQ) 1.6. (p. 569), where *amarta*, as here, has an affirmative meaning. See Dalman, *Words*, p. 254; J.H. Thayer, "Su eipas Su legeis in the Answers of Jesus," *JBL* 13 (1894): 40–49; Abrahams, *Studies II*, pp. 1–3.

# 236. *The Meal*

## MATT. 26.26–29

26 Now as they were eating, Jesus took bread, and blessed, and broke it, and gave it to the disciples and said, "Take, eat; this is my body." 27 And he took a cup, and when he had given thanks he gave it to them, saying, "Drink of it, all of you; 28 for this is my blood of the[n] covenant, which is poured out for many for the forgiveness of sins. 29 I tell you I shall not drink again of this fruit of the vine until that day when I drink it new with you in my Father's kingdom."

## MARK 14.22–25

22 And as they were eating, he took bread, and blessed, and broke it, and gave it to them and said, "Take; this is my body." 23 And he took a cup, and when he had given thanks he gave it to them, and they all drank of it. 24 And he said to them, "This is my blood of the[o] covenant, which is poured out for many. 25 Truly, I say to you, I shall not drink again of the fruit of the vine until that day when I drink it new in the kingdom of God."

## LUKE 22.15–20

15 And he said to them, "I have earnestly desired to eat this passover with you before I suffer; 16 for I tell you I shall never eat again[p] until it is fulfilled in the kingdom of God. 17 And he took a cup, and when he had given thanks he said, "Take this, and divide it among yourselves; 18 for I tell you that from now on I shall not drink of the fruit of the vine until the kingdom of God comes." 19 And he took bread, and when he had given thanks he broke it and gave it to them, saying, "This is my body."[q]

---

n Some texts add *new.*
o Some texts add *new.*
p Some texts omit *again.*
q Some texts add v. 19b–20, *which is given for you, Do this in remembrance of me." 20 And likewise the cup after supper, saying, "This cup poured out for you is the new covenant in my blood."*

### COMMENTARY

*Jesus took bread, and blessed, and broke it* The bread is the *maẓah*, unleavened bread. The blessing over the *maẓah* is: "Blessed art Thou, O Lord our God, King of the universe, who brings forth bread from the earth."[1]

26 *this is my body* The bread and the wine are interpreted by the early church symbolically; the bread's representing the body of Jesus may be suggested by the meaning of the *maẓah*, which is called in the Bible *leḥem oni*, "the bread of affliction" (Deut. 16.3), thus adumbrating the Passion.[2]

27 *and he took a cup and when he had given thanks* At the Seder service four cups of wine are drunk, each representing a redemptive word connected with

the Exodus,[3] two before the meal and two after the meal.[4] Before drinking each cup a blessing is recited: "Blessed art Thou, O Lord our God, King of the universe, who creates the fruit of the vine."[5] In connection with the third cup it is stated, "after they have mixed for him the third cup he recites grace [after meals], i.e., he gives thanks for the food. Over a fourth cup he completes the *Hallel*, etc."[6] This seems to be what is meant here, for he says, in the following verse, "I shall not drink again of this fruit of the vine until that day"; i.e., this is the last cup of wine at the Seder and the last cup drunk before the crucifixion.[7]

*for this is my blood of the covenant*, etc.    The idea of a blood covenant is very old. It is connected with the rite of circumcision, Heb. *dam berit*, "the blood of the covenant," which is also connected with the Passover (Exod. 12.48); note also: *And Moses took the blood and threw it upon the people and said, "Behold the blood of the covenant which the Lord made with you in accordance with all these words"* (Exod. 24.8). The expression "my blood of the covenant" seem to emphasize the difference between the Mosaic covenant and the covenant of Jesus. Also, significant in the spirit of Matt.'s favorite phrase "forgiveness of sins" (omitted by Mark) is Lev. 17.11, *For the life of the flesh is in the blood, and I have given it for you upon the altar to make atonement for your souls, for it is the blood that maketh atonement by reason of the life.*[8]

29 *When I drink it new in my Father's kingdom*    Does this refer to the theme of the "wine of paradise"? "What is the significance of the verse *No eye has seen*, etc. [Isa. 64.3]? R. Joshua b. Levi said, 'It refers to the wine pressed in the grape from the six days of creation.' "[9] Or does it refer to the Messianic Banquet?[10]

## NOTES

1. M. Ber. 6.1. It is difficult to ascertain whether there was in Jesus' day an additional blessing specifically for *mazah* which became part of the Passover liturgy. "Blessed art Thou, O Lord our God, king of the universe, who has sanctified us by thy commandments and commanded us concerning the eating of unleavened bread." Cf. B. Pes. 115a, which mentions a blessing over the *mazah;* it could mean either the blessing over the bread or specifically over *mazah*. Townsend, *Liturgical Interpretation*, p. 15 n. 29, is in error in stating: "The words may have been said over the aphikoman. See Pesahim 10:8, 119b; T. Pesahim 10.11." The reason is that the *aphikomen*, the last bit of food eaten at the meal at the time of Jesus, was the paschal lamb, *not* bread *(mazah)*. See B. Pes. 49b, 120a. On the suggested meaning of *aphikomen*, see M. Pes. 10.8; B. ibid., loc. cit. TJ ibid. 10.8, 37d; Krauss, *GLL*, 2:107. On speculation as to the messianic meaning given to *aphikomen* by Melito of Sardis, *Paschal Homily* 66 (467) 86 (642), that *aphikomanos* = "he that cometh," see Townsend, loc. cit.

2. Not as Allen, *Matt.*, p. 276, who connects it with *"broken* bread."

3. M. Pes. 10.1, TJ ibid. 10.1, 37c (1).

4. On whether there was a common cup at the Passover meal, see Jeremias, *EWJ*, pp. 69 ff.

5. M. Ber. 6.1., cf. *Didache* 9.11, "We thank Thee, O our Father, for the Holy Vine of David."

6. M. Pes. 10.7.

7. Cf. Heb. 9.22, *Without the shedding of blood there is no forgiveness of sins.*

8. Daube, *NTRJ*, pp. 330 ff., argues that "the fourth cup will not be taken. . . . it will be postponed till the kingdom is fully established." This does not seem indicated by the passage. It is a comment about wine prompted by the drinking of the fourth cup.

9. Called in Heb. *yayin meshumar.* See B. Sanh. 99b B. Ber. 34b, Targ. Koh.9.7.

10. See above p. 74 n. 37. On the major versions of the words over the bread and wine, see Townsend, op. cit., p. 16 n. 32.

# 237. *Last Words*

## LUKE 22.21–38

# a. *The Betrayal Prophesied*

## LUKE 22.21–23

21 "But behold the hand of him who betrays me is with me on the table. 22 For the Son of man goes as it has been determined; but woe to that man by whom he is betrayed!" 23 And they began to question one another, which of them it was that would do this."
See above Sec. 235 (p. 405).

# b. *Greatness in the Kingdom of God*

## MATT. 20.25–28; 19.28

25 But Jesus called them to him and said, "You know that the rulers of the Gentiles lord it over them, and their great men exercise authority over them. 26 It shall not be so among you; but whoever would be great among you must be your servant, 27 and whoever would be first among you must be your slave; 28 even as the Son of man came not to be served but to serve, and to give his life as a ransom for many." 19.28 Jesus said to them, "Truly I say to you, in the new world, when the Son of man shall sit on his glorious throne, you who have followed me will also sit on twelve thrones, judging the twelve tribes of Israel."
See above Secs. 192 (p. 336), 189 p. (328).

## MARK 10.42–45

42 And Jesus called them to him and said to them, "You know that those who are supposed to rule over the Gentiles lord it over them, and their great men exercise authority over them. 43 But it shall not be so among you; but whoever would be great among you must be your servant, 44 and whoever would be first among you must be

slave of all. 45 For the Son of man also came not to be served but to serve, and to give his life as a ransom for many."
See above Sec. 192 (p. 336).

## LUKE 22.24–30

24 A dispute also arose among them, which of them was to be regarded as the greatest. 25 And he said to them. "The kings of the Gentiles exercise lordship over them; and those in authority over them are called benefactors. 26 But not so with you; rather let the greatest among you become as the youngest, and the leader as one who serves. 27 For which is the greater, one who sits at table, or one who serves? Is it not the one who sits at table? But I am among you as one who serves. 28 You are those who have continued with me in my trials; 29 as my Father appointed a kingdom for me, so do I appoint for you 30 that you may eat and drink at my table in my kingdom and sit on thrones judging the twelve tribes of Israel."

## c. *Peter's Denial Prophesied*

### LUKE 22.31–34

31 "Simon, Simon, behold, Satan demanded to have you,[r] that he might sift you[r] like wheat, 32 but I have prayed for you that your faith may not fail; and when you have turned again, strengthen your brethren." 33 And he said to him, "Lord, I am ready to go with you to prison and to death." 34 He said, "I tell you, Peter, the cock will not crow this day, until you three times deny that you know me."

---

r  The Greek word for *you* here is plural; in v. 32 it is singular.
See below Sec. 238 (p. 411).

### COMMENTARY

31 *Simon, Simon*  The double vocative is relatively common in Luke. Cf. 8.24, 10.41, 13.34. In Heb. usage the repetition of a name is an expression either of affection or of urgency. "*Abraham, Abraham* [Gen. 22.11]. In the school of R. Ḥiyya it was taught: this is an expression of love and an expression of encouragement."[1]

*Satan demanded to have you*  Reminiscent of Job. 1–2, Zech. 3.1 ff. Note: "Fear the Lord and love your neighbor, and even though the spirits of Beliar [i.e., Satan] claim you to afflict you with every evil, they shall not have dominion over you."[2]

### NOTES

1. Gen. R. 56.7. See also Num. R. 14. Exod. R. 2. on *Moses, Moses* of Exod. 3.4. For the repetition of a name in rabbinic sources, see B. Git. 57b; TJ Ber. 2, 5a (16); TJ Shab 8, 11a (35); Lev. R. 25; Koh. R. 5.14.
2. Test. Benj. 3.3

# d. The Two Swords

## LUKE 22.35–38

35 And he said to them, "When I sent you out with no purse or bag or sandals, did you lack anything?" They said, "Nothing." 36 He said to them, "But now, let him who has a purse take it, and likewise a bag. And let him who has no sword sell his mantle and buy one. 37 For I tell you that this scripture must be fulfilled in me, 'And he was reckoned with transgressors'; for what is written about me has its fulfillment." 38 And they said, "Look, Lord, here are two swords." And he said to them, "It is enough."

### COMMENTARY

There are no rabbinic parallels to this section.

37 *And he was reckoned with transgressors* Isa. 53.12

# 238. The Way to Gethsemane; Peter's Denial Prophesied

## MATT. 26.30–35

30 And when they had sung a hymn, they went out to the Mount of Olives. 31 Then Jesus said to them, "You will all fall away because of me this night; for it is written, 'I will strike the shepherd, and the sheep of the flock will be scattered.' 32 But after I am raised up, I will go before you to Galilee." 33 Peter declared to him, "Though they all fall away because of you, I will never fall away." 34 Jesus said to him, "Truly, I say to you, this very night, before the cock crows, you will deny me three times." 35 Peter said to him, "Even if I must die with you I will not deny you." And so said all the disciples.

## MARK 14.26–31

26 And when they had sung a hymn, they went out to the Mount of Olives. 27 And Jesus said to them, "You will all fall away; for it is written, 'I will strike the shepherd, and the sheep will be scattered.' 28 But after I am raised up, I will go before you to Galilee."ˢ 29 Peter said to him, "Even though they all fall away, I will not." 30 And Jesus said to him, "Truly, I say to you, this very night, before the cock crows twice,ᵗ you will deny me three times." 31 But he said vehemently, "If I must die with you, I will not deny you." And they all said the same.

## LUKE 22.39

And he came out, and went as was his custom, to the Mount of Olives; and the disciples followed him.

## IBID. 22.31–34

31 "Simon, Simon, behold, Satan demanded to have you, that he might sift you like wheat, 32 but I have prayed for you that your faith may not fail; and when you have returned again, strengthen your brethren." 33 And he said to him, "Lord, I am ready to go with you to prison and to death." 34 He said, "I tell you, Peter, the cock will not crow this day, until you three times deny that you know me."

---

s   v. 28 omitted in the Fayum Fragment.
t   Some omit *twice*.

### COMMENTARY

30 *And when they had sung a hymn*   So too in Mark 14.26. What is meant here is either Pss. 113–118, which are recited at the Seder, the first two before the meal, and the rest after, or more probably *Hallel Hagadol*, the great Hallel, i.e., Ps. 136.[1]

*Mount of Olives*   See above on Matt. 21.1 (p. 344). See also on Matt. 24.3 (p. 376).

31 *I will strike the shepherd*, etc.   Zech. 13.7. Both the MT and LXX read the imper. "strike!"[2]

34 *Before the cock crows*   There is an interesting tradition that while the Temple stood there were no cocks in the city of Jerusalem.[3] Reference to the cock's crow indicating the break of day is relatively common.[4] As indicating a specific time it called *gallicinium;* the changing of the Roman guard at Antonia fortress was at 3:00 A.M.[5]

35 *Even if I must die with you*, etc.   There is no parallel, but rather close is the phrase: "Whether for life or death we are with you."[6]

### NOTES

1. See M. Pes. 10.5–7.
2. See Stendahl, *SSMUOT*, pp. 80 ff.
3. M. BQ 7.7.
4. E.g, M. Yom. 1.8; M. Tam. 1.2.
5. Cf. Mayo, "St. Peter's Token of the Cock Crow," *JTS* 22 (1921): 367 ff.
6. *PRE* 18 (93a).

# 239. *Jesus in Gethsemane*

## MATT. 26.36–46

36 Then Jesus went with them to a place called Gethsemane, and he said to his disciples, "Sit here, while I go yonder and pray." 37 And taking with him Peter and the two sons of Zebedee, he began to be sorrowful and troubled. 38 Then he said to

them, "My soul is very sorrowful, even to death; remain here, and watch[u] with me." 39 And going a little farther, he fell on his face and prayed, "My Father, if it be possible, let this cup pass from me; nevertheless, not as I will, but as thou wilt." 40 And he came to the disciples and found them sleeping; and said to Peter, "So you could not watch[u] with me one hour? 41 Watch[u] and pray that you may not enter into temptation; the spirit indeed is willing, but the flesh is weak." 42 Again, for the second time, he went away and prayed, "My Father, if this cannot pass unless I drink it, thy will be done." 43 And again he came and found them sleeping, for their eyes were heavy. 44 So, leaving them again, he went away and prayed for the third time, saying the same words. 45 Then he came to the disciples and said to them, "Are you still sleeping and taking your rest? Behold, the hour is at hand, and the Son of man is betrayed into the hands of sinners. 46 Rise, let us be going; see my betrayer is at hand."

### MARK 14.32–42

32 And they went to a place which was called Gethsemane; and he said to his disciples, "Sit here, while I pray." 33 And he took with him Peter and James and John, and began to be greatly distressed and troubled. 34 And he said to them, "My soul is very sorrowful, even to death; remain here, and watch."[u] 35 And going a little farther, he fell on the ground and prayed that, if it were possible, the hour might pass from him. 36 And he said, "Abba, Father, all things are possible to thee; remove this cup from me; yet not what I will but what thou wilt." 37 And he came and found them sleeping, and he said to Peter, "Simon, are you asleep? Could you not watch[u] one hour? 38 Watch[u] and pray that you may not enter into temptation; the spirit indeed is willing, but the flesh is weak." 39 And again he went away and prayed, saying the same words. 40 And again he came and found them sleeping, for their eyes were very heavy; and they did not know what to answer him. 41 And he came the third time, and said to them, "Are you still sleeping and taking your rest? It is enough; the hour has come; the Son of man is betrayed into the hands of sinners. 42 Rise, let us be going; see, my betrayer is at hand."

### LUKE 22.40–46

40 And when he came to the place he said to them, "Pray that you may not enter into temptation." 41 And he withdrew from them about a stone's throw and knelt down and prayed, 42 "Father, if thou art willing, remove this cup from me; nevertheless not my will, but thine, be done." 43 And there appeared to him an angel from heaven, strengthening him. 44 And being in agony he prayed more earnestly; and his sweat became like great drops of blood falling down upon the ground.[v] 45 And when he rose from prayer, he came to the disciples and found them sleeping for sorrow, 46 and he said to them, "Why do you sleep? Rise and pray that you may not enter into temptation."

---

u  Or *keep awake*.
v  Some authorities omit vv. 43–44.

## COMMENTARY

**36** *Gethsemane* Aram. *gat shamni,* "an oil vat." Jerome derives it from *gai shamni,* "fat valleys" (Isa. 28.1), but this is more plausibly explained as a Greek corruption of the original name into *ge samanei,* "oil plots."[1]

**38** *my soul is very sorrowful* Cf. Ps. 42.6.

**39** *this cup* The cup is the symbol of pain and suffering—Ezek. 23.32–34; also destiny or fate—Isa. 51.17, 22; Lam. 4.21; Ps. 11.6.

**43** *found them sleeping, for their eyes were heavy* So, too, Mark. Luke 22.45 reads "sleeping for sorrow," Gr. *apo tēs lupēs.*[2] This, indeed, is an odd expression. Montefiore felt the difficulty and commented, "the cause is a sort of excuse."[3] Plummer explained, "Prolonged sorrow produces wakefulness."[4] Perhaps the solution can be found in a mistranslation of a Semitic original. Two possibilities come to mind. One is that the Heb. *zarah,* which means "sorrow," is often paired with *yegi'ah,* "weariness," and the phrase means "toil (trouble) and weariness," and the translator chose "sorrow" over "toil," i.e., sleep from exhaustion. The second is that the original was the Heb. יגיעה, "weariness," and was misread as *yagon,* יגון , "sorrow."[5]

## NOTES

1. See *IDB,* s.v. "Gethsemane"; Klausner, *JN,* p. 330 n. 5.
2. See Daube, *NTRJ,* p. 334, where he argues without merit: "We may conclude that, though Jesus asked his disciples to stay awake because he wanted to feel they were with him in mind, yet his request had a more specific meaning; they should not let the habhura come to an early close." He bases his argument on M. Pes. 10.8, "if some members of a Passover company doze, the meal may be resumed again, but if they fall into a deep sleep, it may not be resumed again" (p. 333). There is no indication from the NT texts that continuation of the meal was contemplated. Furthermore, the Mishnah has reference to those at table, not those who were outside.
3. Montefiore, SG, 2:609.
4. Plummer, *Luke,* p. 511.
5. See *Mid. Ps.* 2 (13a). Note that *lupē* translates *yagon;* cf. Gen. (LXX) 44.31; Isa. (LXX) 35.10, 51.11.

# 240. Jesus Taken Captive

## MATT. 26.47–56

47 While he was still speaking, Judas came, one of the twelve, and with him a great crowd with swords and clubs, from the chief priests and the elders of the people. 48 Now the betrayer had given them a sign, saying, "The one I shall kiss is the man; seize him." 49 And he came up to Jesus at once and said, "Hail, Master!"ʷ And he kissed him. 50 Jesus said to him, "Friend why are you here?"ˣ Then they came up and laid hands on Jesus and seized him. 51 And behold, one of those who were with Jesus

stretched out his hand and drew his sword, and struck the slave of the high priest, and cut off his ear. 52 Then Jesus said to him, "Put your sword back into its place; for all who take the sword will perish by the sword. 53 Do you think that I cannot appeal to my Father, and he will at once send me more than twelve legions of angels? 54 But how then should the scriptures be fulfilled, that it must be so?" 55 At that hour Jesus said to the crowds, "Have you come out as against a robber, with swords and clubs to capture me? Day after day I sat in the temple teaching and you did not seize me. 56 But all this has taken place, that the scriptures of the prophets might be fulfilled." Then all the disciples forsook him and fled.

## MARK 14.43–52

43 And immediately, while he was still speaking, Judas came, one of the twelve, and with him a crowd with swords and clubs, from the chief priests and the scribes and the elders. 44 Now the betrayer had given them a sign, saying, "The one I shall kiss is the man; seize him and lead him away safely." 45 And when he came, he went up to him at once, and said, "Master!"ʷ And he kissed him. 46 And they laid hands on him and seized him. 47 But one of those who stood by drew his sword, and struck the slave of the high priest and cut off his ear. 48 And Jesus said to them, "Have you come out as against a robber, with swords and clubs to capture me? 49 Day after day I was with you in the temple teaching, and you did not seize me. But let the scriptures be fulfilled." 50 And they all forsook him and fled. 51 And a young man followed him with nothing but a linen cloth about his body; and they seized him, 52 but he left the linen cloth and ran away naked.

## LUKE 22.47–53

47 While he was still speaking, there came a crowd, and the man called Judas, one of the twelve, was leading them. He drew near to Jesus to kiss him; 48 but Jesus said to him, "Judas, would you betray the Son of man with a kiss?" 49 And when those who were about him saw what would follow, they said, "Lord, shall we strike with the sword?" 50 And one of them struck the slave of the high priest and cut off his right ear. 51 But Jesus said. "No more of this!" And he touched his ear and healed him. 52 Then Jesus said to the chief priests and captains of the temple and the elders, who had come out against him, "Have you come out as against a robber, with swords and clubs? 53 When I was with you day after day in the temple, you did not lay hands on me. But this is your hour, and the power of darkness."

---

w Or, *Rabbi.*
x Or, *do that for which you have come.*

## COMMENTARY

The arrest described in this section, in all the Synoptic Gospels, is by the "masses," Gr. *ochlos.* John 18.3, 12, on the other hand, describes an official arrest by both Jews and Gentiles and that Judas brings the official Roman garrison with a tribune and the servants of the Sanhedrin.

48 *The one I shall kiss* The kiss here is a type of salutation and hence here the worst type of hypocrisy. A disciple is not permitted to greet the teacher first, since this would imply equality and hence an insult to the master.[1]

50 *Friend why are you here?* The term "friend" seems out of place and perhaps there is an error in transmission of a Heb. original which read *rasha*, "wicked one," and it was read *re'a*, "friend."[2]

51. *And behold, one of those . . . drew his sword* Is it possible that he was one of the *sicarii*?

52 *for all who take the sword will perish by the sword* There is no rabbinic paralled to this statement. One suggestion is that there is a similarity in the Targ. of Isa. 1.11, "Behold, all you that kindle a fire, that take the sword, go fall into the fire you have kindled, and fall by the sword you have taken, from my word [*memra*] you have this; you shall return to your destruction."[3]

53 *twelve legions of angels* Cf. Ps. 91.11. Angels were frequently described in rabbinic literature as coming in legions.[4]

*But how then*, etc. I.e., the suffering of the Messiah.

55 *Day after day* Gr. *kath'hēmeran* "They could mean 'day by day' (daily) *quotidie, täglich*—and so they are usually rendered—but they could also mean 'in the hours of day-light,' 'in the course of a day,' 'by day' *die, tagsüber*. . . . Jesus reproaches those who have come upon him by night. . . as upon a guerilla-fighter, although he is not a leader of a secret band who would conduct his affairs under the cover of night; he is a preacher, a religious teacher *(didaskōn)* and should not be treated as a political insurgent *(lēstēs)*. . . . A rebel leader may have to be sought out in his haunts by night, but a teacher can be found among his pupils at any time of day."[5] "Jesus was offended not because he was arrested but because they came against him armed with swords. Jesus objected because they took him to be one of the followers of the Fourth Philosophy who sought to effect their ideas by force and were looked upon as 'robbers' as they were designated by Josephus."[6]

*I sat in the Temple* On the posture of the teacher while teaching, see above to Matt. 5.2 (p. 67). Perhaps the meaning of this line is that you should have arrested me when I was sitting in the Temple court since according to a tannaitic tradition sitting in the court of the Temple was forbidden except for the kings of the house of David. By sitting there he indicated that he was the messiah king.[7]

56 *that the scriptures of the prophets might be fulfilled* Perhaps Isa. 53.2, 12.

## NOTES

1. See M. Aberbach, "The Relations between Master and Disciple in the Talmudic Age," *Essays Presented to Chief Rabbi Israel Brodie on the Occasion of his Seventieth Birthday* (London, 1965).

2. See Lachs, "Studies in the Semitic Background," 214–217.

3. H. Kosmala, *NT* 4 (1960): 81–95. Albright-Mann, *Matt.*, citing this article (p. 329) comment, "This is then not simply a proverbial saying, but a scriptural saying with eschatological meaning, God's will is being fulfilled and nothing can hinder it."

4. T. Sot. 3.14 (279); Lev. R. 16.9; B. Ber 32b.

5. Winter, *Trial*, p. 49; Cf. Luke 19.47, 21.37.

6. Zeitlin, *Who Crucified Jesus*, p. 163, also pp. 166–167. Cf also Wilson, pp. 110 f.; K. H. Rengstorf, "lestes," *TDNT*, 4:257–262.

7. See TJ Pes. 5.7 (32d); Yom. 3, (40b); Sot. 7.7 (22a); B. Yom. 25b; *Mid. Ps.* 1.2 (p. 1).

## 241. Jesus Before the Sanhedrin; Peter's Denial

### MATT. 26.57–75

57 Then those who had seized Jesus led him to Caiaphas the high priest, where the scribes and the elders had gathered. 58 But Peter followed him at a distance, as far as the courtyard of the high priest, and going inside he sat with the guards to see the end. 59 Now the chief priests and the whole council sought false testimony against Jesus that they might put him to death, 60 but they found none, though many false witnesses came forward. At last two came forward 61 and said, "This fellow said, 'I am able to destroy the temple of God, and to build it in three days.' " 62 And the high priest stood up and said, "Have you no answer to make? What is it that these men testify against you?" 63 But Jesus was silent. And the high priest said to him, "I adjure you by the living God, tell us if you are the Christ, the Son of God." 64 Jesus said to him, "You have said so. But I tell you, hereafter you will see the Son of man seated at the right hand of Power, and coming on the clouds of heaven." 65 Then the high priest tore his robes, and said, "He has uttered blasphemy. Why do we still need witnesses? You have now heard his blasphemy. 66 What is your judgment?" They answered, "He deserves death." 67 Then they spat in his face, and struck him; and some slapped him, 68 saying, "Prophesy to us, you Christ! Who is it that struck you?" 69 Now Peter was sitting outside in the courtyard. And a maid came up to him, and said, "You also were with Jesus the Galilean." 70 But he denied it before them all, saying, "I do not know what you mean." 71 And when he went out to the porch, another maid saw him, and she said to the bystanders, "This man was with Jesus of Nazareth." 72 And again he denied it with an oath, "I do not know the man." 73 After a little while the bystanders came up and said to Peter, "Certainly you are also one of them, for your accent betrays you." 74 Then he began to invoke a curse on himself and to swear, "I do not know the man." And immediately the cock crowed. 75 And Peter remembered the saying of Jesus, "Before the cock crows, you will deny me three times." And he went out and wept bitterly.

### MARK 14.53–72

53 And they led Jesus to the high priest; and all the chief priests and the elders and the scribes were assembled. 54 And Peter had followed him at a distance, right into the courtyard of the high priest; and he was sitting with the guards, and warming himself at the fire. 55 Now the chief priests and the whole council sought testimony against Jesus, to put him to death; but they found none. 56 For many bore false witness against him, and their witness did not agree. 57 And some stood up and bore false witness against him, saying, 58 "We heard him say, 'I will destroy this temple that is made with hands, and in three days I will build another, not made with hands.' " 59 Yet not even so did their testimony agree. 60 And the high priest stood up in the

midst, and asked Jesus, "Have you no answer to make? What is it that these men testify against you?" 61 But he was silent and made no answer. Again the high priest asked him, "Are you the Christ, the Son of the Blessed?" 62 And Jesus said, "I am; and you will see the Son of man sitting at the right hand of Power, and coming with the clouds of heaven." 63 And the high priest tore his mantle, and said, "Why do we still need witnesses? 64 You have heard his blasphemy. What is your decision?" And they all condemned him as deserving death. 65 And some began to spit on him, and to cover his face, and to strike him, saying to him, "Prophesy!" And the guards received him with blows. 66 And as Peter was below in the courtyard, one of the maids of the high priest came; 67 and seeing Peter warming himself, she looked at him, and said, "You also were with the Nazarene, Jesus." 68 But he denied it, saying, "I neither know nor understand what you mean." And he went out into the gateway.*y* 69 And the maid saw him, and began again to say to the bystanders, "This is one of them." 70 But again he denied it. And after a little while again the bystanders said to Peter, "Certainly, you are one of them; for you are a Galilean." 71 But he began to invoke a curse on himself and to swear, "I do not know this man of whom you speak." 72 And immediately the cock crowed a second time. And Peter remembered how Jesus had said to him, "Before the cock crows twice, you will deny me three times." And he broke down and wept.

## LUKE 22.54–71

54 Then they seized him and led him away, bringing him*z* into the high priest's house. Peter followed at a distance; 55 and when they had kindled a fire in the middle of the courtyard and sat down together, Peter sat among them. 56 Then a maid, seeing him as he sat in the light and gazing at him, said, "This man also was with him." 57 But he denied it saying, "Woman, I do not know him." 58 And a little later someone else saw him and said, "You also are one of them." But Peter said, "Man, I am not." 59 And after an interval of about an hour still another insisted, saying, "Certainly this man also was with him; for he is a Galilean." 60 But Peter said, "Man, I do not know what you are saying." And immediately, while he was still speaking, the cock crowed. 61 And the Lord turned and looked at Peter. And Peter remembered the word of the Lord, how he had said to him, "Before the cock crows today, you will deny me three times." 62 And he want out, and wept bitterly. 63 Now the men who were holding Jesus mocked him and beat him; 64 they also blindfolded him and asked him, "Prophesy! Who is it that struck you?" 65 And they spoke many other words against him, reviling him. 66 When the day came, the assembly of the elders of the people gathered together, both chief priests and scribes; and they led him away to their council, and they said, 67 "If you are the Christ, tell us." But he said to them, "If I tell you, you will not believe; 68 and if I ask you, you will not answer. 69 But from now on the Son of man shall be seated at the right hand of the Power of God." 70 And they all said, "Are you the Son of God?" And he said to them, "You say that I am." 71 And they said, "What further testimony do we need? We have heard it ourselves from his own lips.'

---

y  Some texts add *and the cock crowed*.
z  Some texts omit *bringing him*.

## COMMENTARY

The Synoptic description of the trial of Jesus before the Sanhedrin is very much at variance with its procedures as recorded in early rabbinic sources. This indeed is a serious problem if, in reality, this court was the Great Sanhedrin of seventy-one.[1] To wipe away the problem by stating that rabbinic criminal law was never operative is absurd.[2] Some have suggested a solution sometimes called the "Two Sanhedrin Theory," namely, that there were two bodies, one religious, the other political.[3] The last word is yet to be written on this difficulty.

57 *led him to Caiaphas* According to John 18.13–14, 19–24, Jesus was first brought to Annas, for he was the father-in-law of Caiaphas, who was the high priest for that year (v. 13). In v. 19 Annas is called high priest and Annas sends him to Caiaphas.[4] The locale again is difficult. See above to Matt. 26.3 (p. 398). Although 26.3 ff. has the difficulty of locale, this passage has the added difficulty as to time. According to Jewish sources, the Sanhedrin met only during the day, never at night.[5] Note that Luke does not mention night.[6] Zeitlin, an advocate of the "Two Sanhedrin Theory," i.e., that one was a religious Sanhedrin, the other a political one, wrote: "The later political Sanhedrin had no definite place to hold its sessions, it had no statutory regulations, it could be called into session anytime of the day or night, holiday or Sabbath."[7] It is only a theory but if correct obviates the problem of place and time of meeting.

59 *The whole council* Presumably 71 members of the Sanhedrin.

60 *At last two came forward* The minimum number of witnesses; see Num. 35.30, Deut. 17.6, 19.15. Note that Matt. makes no comment on validating the testimony, whereas Mark, vv. 57, 59, does.[8]

61 *I am able to destroy the temple of God* A most interesting parallel to this passage is one related by Josephus illustrating what was happening in Jerusalem at that time: "A man by the name of Jesus, the son of Ananias, a farmer, standing in the Temple, suddenly began to cry out, 'A voice against Jerusalem and the sanctuary! A voice against all the people.' This Jesus went through the streets of Jerusalem day and night crying out, 'Woe to Jerusalem, woe to Jerusalem' "[9] According to Josephus this happened when Albinus was the procurator, during the Festival of Tabernacles. Some of the leading men arrested this person and severely chastised him. However, in spite of his arrest and punishment, Jesus continued his cry Woe to Jerusalem. Then the leaders began to suspect the man to be under divine inspiration. Therefore they turned him over to the procurator Albinus. He was scourged, but the victim did not shed a tear nor did he beg for mercy. When Albinus asked him why he uttered these cries, he never answered a word. Albinus in the end released him, taking him to be a madman.[10]

62 *high priest* Presumably acting as presiding judge, although at the time of Jesus the high priest did not occupy that position.[11]

*Have you no answer?* The accused had the right to defend himself in court.[12]

*the Son of God* Note Mark. 14.61 reads "the Son of the Blessed." "Blessed" is a substitute for the name of God.

63 *But Jesus was silent* Is this meant to be the fulfillment of Isa. 53.7?[13]

*I adjure you*[14]

64 *You have said* Mark 14.62 says "I am," and Luke 22.70 says "you say that I am," but all versions agree on the reading "You have said so" when Jesus is before Pilate.

*You will see the Son of man seated at the right hand of Power coming on the clouds of heaven* A combination of Dan. 7.13 and possibly Ps. 110.1.[15]

*Power* Gr. *tēs dunameōs* = Heb. *gevera*, Aram. *gevurta*, a substitute for the name of God.[16]

65 *The high priest tore his robes* This was done when one heard blasphemy uttered;[17] the high priest, however, was not allowed to tear his clothes in mourning for the dead.[18] "According to tannaitic law, a man who uses abusive language against God cannot be put to death by a court (TB Jer. 7). At most he would be punished by divine visitation, that is, a person who uses slanderous language against God is liable to premature death, but that punishment rests in the hands of God. Only the man who curses God with the name of God 'cursing God by the name of God' (M. Sanh. VII0, was liable to capital punishment. Jesus did not curse God."[19] Many Jews looked forward to the future world where they would sit in the company of God and enjoy the Divine Glory.[20] Townsend makes the most sensible suggestion: "What seems most likely is that blasphemy entered the Passion tradition when Christians began to apply the title Son of God to Jesus in a metaphysical sense. Since a Jewish High Priest might indeed regard metaphysical sonship as blasphemous, the early Christians simply assumed that he did."[21]

66 *He deserves death* Perhaps the mishnaic *mithayev benafsho.*[22] Is this the pronouncement of the death sentence, or is the death sentence found only in Mark 14.64? Perhaps it means, "we have a case to take to Pilate."[23]

68 *Prophesy to us, you Christ!* One can assume from this that he was considered by some to be a false prophet, as were other messianic pretenders.[24]

73 *Your accent betrays you* The Galileans were distinguishable by their speech. This observation is found several times in rabbinic sources.[25]

## NOTES

1. Winter, *Trial*, pp. 27 ff.; S. Rosenblatt, "The Crucifixion of Jesus from the Standpoint of Pharisaic Law," *JBL* 75 (1956): 317–319.

2. Blinzler, *Trial*, pp. 149–157.

3. A Büchler, *Das Synedrion in Jerusalem and das grosse Beth-Din in der Quaderkammer des Jerusalemischen Tempels* (Jahresbericht der Israelitisch-Theologischen Lehranstalt in

Wien, 1902); Zeitlin, *Who Crucified Jesus*, pp. 55, 72, 74, 156, 163; H. Mantel, *Studies in the History of the Sanhedrin*, Harvard Semitic Series 17 (Cambridge, Mass., 1965), pp. 54–101.

4. On this problem see the literature in Townsend, *Liturgical Interpretation*, p. 19, no. 48.

5. See M. Sanh. 4.1.

6. On this see Catchpole, *Trial*, pp. 183–201; Winter, *Trial*, pp. 27–43; Sloyan, p. 95.

7. Zeitlin, *Who Crucified Jesus*, p. 163.

8. On the interrogation of witnesses, see M. Sanh. 3.6, 4.5; 5.1–4; B. ibid. 30a, 31a, 40b–42a; *Mek.* Exod. 23.4.

9. Josephus *BJ* VI.5.3.

10. Ibid.

11. See Zeitlin, *RFJS*, 1:203 ff.

12. See M. Sanh. 4.3.

13. For a discussion of the problem whether the NT indicates the interpretation of the so-called Suffering Servant chapters of Isaiah, see M. D. Hooker, *Jesus and the Servant* (Greenwich, Conn., 1959), pp. 1–24; R. T. France, "The Servant of the Lord in the Teaching of Jesus," *Tyndale Bulletin* 19 (1968): 26–52.

14. See M. Shev. 4.3, 13.

15. Sloyan, p. 58.

16. See, e.g., Sifre Num. 112; B. Hor. 8a; B. Er. 24b.

17. See 2 Kings 18.37; M. Sanh. 7.5; cf. Acts 14.14.

18. Lev. 10.6, 21.10. See M. Sanh 7.5; B. ibid. 60b; TJ ibid. 7, 25a (65); B. MQ 25b = TJ ibid. 3.7, 83b (6). See Exod. 23.27.

19. Zeitlin, *Who Crucified Jesus*, p. 153.

20. Ibid.

21. Townsend, op. cit., p. 24 n. 66.

22. Cf., e.g., M. Avot 3.1 f; cf. M. Sanh. 6, which is violated here.

23. See Cohen, *Trial*, p. 136; Blinzler, *Trial*, pp. 16 f, 122 n. 1.

24. See TJ Shab. 16, 15d (30); B. Er. 53a–b; B. Meg 24b; Neubauer, *Géographie du Talmud*, pp. 184 f.; Chomsky, op. cit., pp. 215, 304. Cf also Acts. 4.13.

25. Cf. Josephus, *BJ* II. 13.5.

# 242. *Jesus Delivered to Pilate*

## MATT. 27.1–2

1 When morning came, all the chief priests and the elders of the people took counsel against Jesus to put him to death; 2 and they bound him and led him away and delivered him to Pilate, the governor.

## MARK 15.1.

And as soon as it was morning the chief priests, with the elders and scribes, and the whole council held a consultation; and they bound Jesus and led him away and delivered him to Pilate.

## LUKE 22.66, 23.1

22.66 When the day came, the assembly of the elders of the people gathered together, both chief priests and scribes; and they led him away to their council. 23.1 Then the whole company of them arose, and brought him before Pilate.

## COMMENTARY

1 *When morning came*, etc. Some have conjectured that if Pilate was willing to have the trial take place early in the morning, he must have had knowledge of the affair and could have been a party to it from the start.[1]

2 *Pilate the governor* Pontius Pilatus was appointed governor of Judea, from Samaria to the Dead Sea, by Tiberius Caesar, 26–36 C.E. His praenomen is unknown. Pontius, his nomen, indicates that he was of an ancient Samnite family, afterwards Roman gens. Pilatus, "armed with a javelin," was his cognomen. He was summoned to Rome in 36 and was succeeded by Marcellus. Outside of the NT Pilate is mentioned by Tacitus in connection with Jesus.[2] This account was written ca. 115. In Jewish sources he is described as a man lacking in any humanity.[3] In the NT only Luke speaks about Pilate's cruelty. "In addition to the concern of early preachers to persuade Jews that the crucifixion proved Jesus to be the Elect of God expected of old, there enters a new motive (yet early enough to have influenced *all* evangelists in their descriptions of Jesus' trial), namely, the apologetic purpose of convincing Roman officials that the profession of the Christian faith was not subversive of imperial institutions. The manner of Jesus' death known to have been ordered by the representative of Roman rule was a serious obstacle to the propagation of Christianity throughout the provinces of the Empire. Hence the peculiar sort of role assigned to Pilate in all Gospels and in Christian traditions generally."[4]

## NOTES

1. Winter, *Trial*, pp. 65 ff.; Cohn, *Trial*, p. 86.
2. *Ann.* XV.44 In Latin his title would have been *praefectus*. See A. H. M. Jones, *Studies on Roman Government and Law* (New York, 1960), pp. 117 ff.; A. N. Sherwin-White, *Roman Society and Roman Law in the New Testament* (New York: Oxford, 1963), pp. 6–12.
3. Philo, *De legatione ad Gaium* 38; Josephus, *Ant.* XVIII.3.1; *BJ* II.9.2; *Ant.* XVIII.3.2; *BJ* II.9.4; *Ant.* XVIII.4.2.
4. Winter, *Trial*, p. 53.

# 243. *The Death of Judas*

## MATT. 27.3–10

3 When Judas, his betrayer saw that he was condemned, he repented and brought back the thirty pieces of silver to the chief priests and the elders, 4 saying, "I have sinned in betraying innocent blood." They said, "What is that to us? See to it

yourself." 5 And throwing down the pieces of silver in the temple, he departed; and he went and hanged himself. 6 But the chief priests, taking the pieces of silver, said, "It is not lawful to put them into the treasury, since they are blood money." 7 So they took counsel, and bought with them the potter's field, to bury strangers in. 8 Therefore that field has been called the Field of Blood to this day. 9 Then was fulfilled what had been spoken by the prophet Jeremiah, saying, "And they took the thirty pieces of silver, the price of him on whom a price had been set by some of the sons of Israel, 10 and they gave them for the potter's field, as the Lord directed me."

## COMMENTARY

5 *and throwing down the pieces of silver* Cf. Zech. 11.13, *Then the Lord said to me, "Cast [hashlikhehu] it into the treasury"* [Heb. *el hayozer*, "to the potter"]. The reading "treasury," *el haozar*, is as LXX and implied in the Targum. Here in Matt. both traditions are present; see v. 7. The verb in Heb., *lehashlikh*, does not necessarily mean "to throw something down violently," but rather it can mean "to abandon," cf. Gen. 21.15.[1]

*and he went and hanged himself* Cf. 2 Sam. 12.23. "Ahitophel, the treacherous friend of David, and Judas, the treacherous friend of the Son of David, met a similar end."[2] There is a different tradition in Acts, 1.18.[3]

6 *treasury* Gr. *korbanas*, a Grecized form of Heb. *qorban*. It was the fund from which *qorbanot*, "sacrifices," were purchased. Accepting the money was forbidden because of its source, cf. Deut. 23.18.[4]

*they are blood money* Gr. *epei timē haimatos estin*, lit., "price of blood." It is a wordplay, *demē dama; damin* means "price" but could by extension be rendered "money," and the phrase could convey the meaning of "blood money".[5]

7 *to bury strangers* I.e., foreigners. So it is characterized by the pilgrim Antonius Martyr (ca. 560 C.E.). Identified since the fourth cent. as at the E. end of the Valley of Hinnom where pilgrims are interred.

8 *field of Blood* In Gr. transliterated *Akeldamach*; Aram. *haqal dama* in Acts. 1.19. In Matt. translated *agros haimatos*. Klostermann et al. suggest *haqel damakh*, "field of sleeping," i.e., cemetery.[6]

9 *spoken by the prophet Jeremiah* Various traditions are commingled here. There is an allusion to Jer. 32.8–9, where the prophet buys a field for seventeen silver shekels, Jer. 18.2–3, where he visits the potter's house, and Zech. 11.12–13. Jerome (on Matt. 27.9), citing the *Gospel according to the Hebrews*, comments, "I read not long ago in a certain Hebrew book, which a Jew of the Nazarene sect gave me, an apocryphal book of Jeremiah in which I found this [i.e., Matt. 27.9b–10] written word for word.[7]

## NOTES

1. See M. Cohan, "A Technical Term for Expense," *JNES* 27 (1968): 133—135, and Lachs, "The Gospels and Their Semitic Background."
2. McNeile, *Matt.*, p. 407.

3. Cf. F. H. Chase, "On prenes genomenos in Acts 1.18," *Expos. T.* (Jan. 1912): 278 ff.; J. Rendell Harris, "Did Judas Really Commit Suicide?" *AJTh* 4 (1900): 490 ff., thinks that the tradition, for which Matt.'s account is a milder substitute, was derived from the legend of Nadan son of Ahikar. See also idem, XVIII.127–31.

4. Cf. usage of *korbanes* in Josephus, *BJ* II.175.

5. Cf. B. Meg. 14b *damin* has two meanings. Rashi ad loc. differentiates: "*damin* has two meanings, i.e., 'blood' and 'money.' " See Zimmermann, *Aramaic Origin*, p. 78.

6. Klostermann, *Probleme in Aposteltexte*, pp. 6 ff. Since *chi* in the LXX transliterates not only *kaf* but occasionally *ḥeth*, the Greek letters were thought to represent *ḥaqel dama*, a field of blood.

7. See Stendahl, *SSMUOT*, pp. 120–126; Abrahams, *Studies II*, pp. 193–194.

# 244. *The Trial Before Pilate*

## MATT. 27.11–14

11 Now Jesus stood before the governor; and the governor asked him, "Are you the King of the Jews?" Jesus said to him, "You have said so." 12 But when he was accused by the chief priests and elders, he made no answer. 13 Then Pilate said to him, "Do you not hear how many things they testify against you?" 14 But he gave him no answer, not even to a single charge; so that the governor wondered greatly.

## MARK 15.2–5

2 And Pilate asked him, "Are you the King of the Jews?" And he answered him, "You have said so." 3 And the chief priests accused him of many things. 4 And Pilate again asked him, "Have you no answer to make? See how many charges they bring against you." 5 But Jesus made no further answer, so that Pilate wondered.

## LUKE 23.2–5

2 And they began to accuse him, saying, "We found this man perverting our nation, and forbidding us to give tribute to Caesar, and saying that he himself is Christ a king." 3 And Pilate asked him, "Are you the King of the Jews?" And he answered him, "You have said so." 4 And Pilate said to the chief priests and the multitudes, "I find no crime in this man." 5 But they were urgent, saying, "He stirs up the people, teaching throughout all Judea, from Galilee even to this place."

## COMMENTARY

Verses 27.11–14 are a continuation of the narrative of 27.1–2, which is interrupted by the narrative of the death of Judas.

11 *Are you the king of the Jews?* "The king of the Jews" has a double meaning: Do you claim to be a king, i.e., a ruler over them, or are you a Messiah? Both ideas are spelled out in Luke" . . . and saying that he himself is Christ a King."[1] Pilate's question clearly concerns the political implications of

the term. Jesus was executed for political not religious reasons. He was thought to be an instigator of insurrectionist activities (cf. Mark 14.48b, 49), and he was crucified with two revolutionaries (Mark 15.27; cf. Matt. 27.38, Luke 23.52, John 19.18b). The charge was stated explicitly on the *titulus* on the cross.[2] "Jesus of Nazareth was not in any sense of the word a *lēstēs*. He was not revolutionary, prompted by political ambitions for the power of government; he was a teacher who openly proclaimed his teaching. He never announced the coming of his own kingdom but preached the Kingdom of God that comes without observation. Senseless though the arrest, cruel though the sentence was, the oldest of the Gospels preserved the reason for both: Jesus was arrested, accused, condemned, and executed, on a charge of rebellion."[3]

*you have said so*   Mark 14.62 says "I am," and Luke is silent. We have here one of the most enigmatic answers in history. It could mean, "What you have said is correct";[4] "What you have said is correct but you don't understand its implications"; "You say it, but it is not so"; "You are making the accusation, and it will mean nothing were I to deny or answer it."[5]

### NOTES

1. See M. de Jonge, "The Use of the word 'Anointed' in the Time of Jesus," *NT* 8 (1966): 132–146; Catchpole, *Trial*, pp. 86–126, 132.
2. See Suetonius, *Caligula* 32, which states that the crime was to be inscribed on the *titulus*.
3. Winter, *Trial*, p. 50.
4. T. Kel. (BQ) 1.6 (p. 569).
5. See Abrahams, *Studies II*, pp. 1–3. As an evasion see Dodd, op. cit., p. 99 n. 1. For a full discussion of the meaning of the phrase, see Catchpole, "The Answer of Jesus to Caiaphas (Matt. 26.64)," *NTS* 17 (1970–71): 213–226; Cohn, *Trial*, p. 174.

## 245. *Jesus Before Herod*

### LUKE 23.6–16

6 When Pilate heard this, he asked whether the man was a Galilean. 7 And when he learned that he belonged to Herod's jurisdiction, he sent him over to Herod, who was himself in Jerusalem at that time. 8 When Herod saw Jesus, he was very glad, for he had long desired to see him, because he had heard about him, and he was hoping to see some sign done by him. 9 So he questioned him at some length; but he made no answer. 10 The chief priests and the scribes stood by, vehemently accusing him. 11 And Herod with his soldiers treated him with contempt and mocked him; then, arraying him in gorgeous apparel, he sent him back to Pilate. 12 And Herod and Pilate became friends with each other that very day, for before this they had been at enmity with each other. 13 Pilate then called together the chief priests and the rulers and the people, 14 and said to them, "You brought me this man as one who was perverting the people; and after examining him before you, behold, I did not find this man guilty of any of your charges against him; 15 neither did Herod, for he sent him

back to us. Behold, nothing deserving death has been done by him; 16 I will therefore chastise him and release him."

## COMMENTARY

This section is found only in Luke and is considered to be unhistorical by many scholars.[1] "If Jesus appeared before Pilate, was then sent to Herod, and then back to Pilate, he could hardly have been crucified at nine in the morning."[2] The purpose of this section is to emphasize the guilt of the Jews and lessen the responsibility of Pilate. It has been suggested that "Acts IV.24–29 shows that Psalm ii.1, 2 had brought about the belief that Pilate and Herod must have been the kings and the rulers of whom the Psalm speaks."[3]

12 *And Herod and Pilate became friends* A friendship presumably born of their common dislike of the Jews.[4]

## NOTES

1. See, e.g., Dibelius, "Herod und Pilatus," *ZNW* (1915): 113–126; Loisy, *Luc*, p. 547; Verrall, *JTS*, 1909, pp. 321–353; Wilson, *The Execution of Jesus* (New York, 1970), pp. 136–139, 141.
2. Montefiore, *SG*, p. 619.
3. Ibid.
4. Cf. B. Sanh, 105a; *Tan. B. Balaq* 4 (67b), Num. R. 20.

# 246. *The Sentence of Death*

## MATT. 27.15–26

15 Now at the feast the governor was accustomed to release for the crowd any one prisoner whom they wanted. 16 And they had then a notorious prisoner, called Barabbas.[z] 17 So when they had gathered, Pilate said to them, "Whom do you want me to release for you, Barabbas[z] or Jesus who is called Christ?" 18 For he knew that it was out of envy that they had delivered him up. 19 Besides, while he was sitting on the judgment seat, his wife sent word to him, "Have nothing to do with that righteous man, for I have suffered much over him today in a dream." 20 Now the chief priests and the elders persuaded the people to ask for Barabbas and destroy Jesus. 21 The governor again said to them, "Which of the two do you want me to release for you?" And they said, "Barabbas." 22 Pilate said to them, "Then what shall I do with Jesus who is called Christ?" They all said, "Let him be crucified." 23 And he said, "Why, what evil has he done?" But they shouted all the more, "Let him be crucified." 24 So when Pilate saw that he was gaining nothing, but rather that a riot was beginning, he took water and washed his hands before the crowd, saying, "I am innocent of this man's blood;[a] see to it yourselves." 25 And all the people answered, "His blood be on us and on our children!" 26 Then he released for them Barabbas, and having scourged Jesus, delivered him to be crucified.

## MARK 15.6–15

6 Now at the feast he used to release for them any one prisoner whom they asked. 7 And among the rebels in prison, who had committed murder in the insurrection, there was a man called Barabbas. 8 And the crowd came up, and began to ask Pilate to do as he was wont to do for them. 9 And he answered them, "Do you want me to release for you the King of the Jews?" 10 For he perceived that it was out of envy that the chief priests had delivered him up. 11 But the chief priests stirred up the crowd to have him release for them Barrabas instead. 12 And Pilate again said to them, "Then what shall I do with the man whom you call the King of the Jews?" 13 And they cried out again, "Crucify him." 14 And Pilate said to them, "Why, what evil has he done?" But they shouted all the more, "Crucify him." 15 So Pilate, wishing to satisfy the crowd, released for them Barabbas; and having scourged Jesus, he delivered him to be crucified.

## LUKE 23.17–25

17 Now he was obliged to release one man to them at the festival.[b] 18 But they all cried out together, "Away with this man, and release to us Barabbas"—19 a man who had been thrown into prison for an insurrection started in the city, and for murder. 20 Pilate addressed them once more, desiring to release Jesus; 21 but they shouted out, "Crucify, crucify him!" 22 A third time he said to them, "Why, what evil has he done? I have found in him no crime deserving death; I will therefore chastise him and release him." 23 But they were urgent, demanding with loud cries that he should be crucified. And their voices prevailed. 24 So Pilate gave sentence that their demand should be granted. 25 He released the man who had been thrown into prison for insurrection and murder, whom they asked for; but Jesus he delivered up to their will.

---

z Some read *Jesus Barabbas*.
a Some read *this righteous blood*. Others *this righteous man's blood*.
b Some texts omit v. 17.

## COMMENTARY

15 *the governor was accustomed to release*, etc.   There is no evidence outside of the NT to support this practice.[1]

16 *and they had* etc.   I.e., the Romans.

*Barabbas*   Bar Abba (Son of the Father). Cf. Ber. 18b as a proper name. According to the *Gospel According to the Hebrews* he was *filius magistri eorum*, "son of their teacher," "father" equaling "teacher."[2] Origen said that the name in some old MSS was Jesus Barabbas.[3] Then the force of Pilate's question was, which Jesus?[4] Zeitlin suggests that Barabbas was a member of the Fourth Philosophy.[5]

18 *it was out of envy*   In Matt. it is the envy of the crowds, in Mark it is because of the priests, and this seems more probable.

19 *on the judgment seat* Gr. *epi tou bēmatos*, Heb. *bimah*.[6] The *bimah* was an elevated stand or platform for public meetings for speakers, readers, and for holding court.[7] It was probably set up outside of the praetorium owing to the scruples of the Jews (cf. John 18.18). "The Jews did not enter the judgment hall that night on account of eating the Paschal lamb. Therefore Pilate in order to speak to them, had to come from the judgment hall."[8]

*his wife* Christian tradition calls her Procla or Claudia Procula.[9]

*have nothing to do with that righteous man* I.e., with that innocent man. Similar advice is recorded in the Talmud: "The matter came to the hearing of King Shapur [Sapor], who wanted to punish Raba for the deed, but Ifra 'Ormuzd, mother of King Shapur, said to him, Have no quarrels with the Jews . . ."[10]

22 *let him be crucified* On crucifixion see above to Matt. 26.2 (p. 398).

24 *he took water and washed his hands before the crowd* This was to show noncomplicity or innocence in the happening.[11] Jewish sources of note are: Deut. 21.6, describing the law for the expiation of murder where the slayer is unknown, *And the elders of that city nearest to the slain man shall wash their hands over the heifer whose neck was broken in the valley, and they shall testify, "Our hands did not shed this blood."*[12]

*I am innocent of this man's blood* Hebraism *naqi midam ha'ish*. Cf. Num. 5. 31, 2 Kings 3.28, Acts 20.26.

25 *His blood be upon us and upon our children* This has a Hebraic ring.[13]

26 *Then he . . . delivered him to be crucified* Scholars are divided on the question of whether the Jews had the right at that time to inflict the death penalty. Those who take the negative position point to John 18.31, where the Jews say to Pilate, "It is not lawful for us to put anyone to death."[14] Those who maintain that they did have the right point to recorded cases where indeed the Jews did inflict capital punishment, but these cases are termed "unusual" or "exceptional" by those who take the opposite position.[15]

## NOTES

1. Cf. John 18.38; H. Z. Maccoby, "Jesus and Barabbas," *NTS* 16 (1969–70): 55; Brown, *John*, pp. 854 ff.; Wilson, p. 140; Cohn, *Trial*, pp. 166 ff.; Winter, *Trial*, pp. 132–134. Citation of M. Pes. 8.6, which mentions the paschal sacrifice for one who was promised to be released from prison, is not applicable since it does not imply an annual custom. Suggested by C. G. Chavel, "The Releasing of a Prisoner on the Eve of Passover in Ancient Jerusalem," *JBL* 60 (1941): 273–278, *Contra:* Brown, *John*, p. 855. See Townsend, *Liturgical Interpretation*, p. 27 n. 83; Cohn, *Trial*, pp. 164–171; Sloyan, pp. 67 ff.; Maccoby op. cit., pp. 55–60—all regard both the *Privilegium Paschale* and the whole Barabbas incident as fictional.

2. Jerome on Matthew, ad loc.

3. Comm. on Matt, ad loc.

4. See Abrahams, *Studies II*, pp. 201–202.

5. *Who Crucified Jesus*, p. 166. H. A. Riggs, "Barabbas," *JBL* 64 (1945): 417–465, and Maccoby, op. cit., pp. 55–60, argue that Jesus of Nazareth and Jesus Barabbas were the same person.

6. See Jastrow, s.v.בימה, who rejects any connection with the Gr. *bēma*. and relates it to the Heb. *bamah*.

7. See Acts 12.21, 18.12.

8. Zeitlin, op. cit., p. 169.

9. Gos. Nicod. 2; Tacitus, *Ann*. 3.33 f. relates that governors in the provinces might be accompanied by their wives.

10. B. Ta'an. 24b.

11. For this practice among the Greeks and the Romans, see commentaries to Herodotus I.35; Virgil, *Aeneid* 2.719; Sophocles, *Ajax* 654.

12. See also M. Sot. 9.6; Ps. 35(36).6; 72(73).13; B. Git. 36a. Also the *Letter of Aristeas* 306 on the washing of the hands, an indication that no wrong was done.

13. Cf. B. AZ 12b; B. Yom. 21a; Sifra 24.14; B. AZ 30a; *PRE* 10; TJ Ber. 7.6, 11c (61); B. Pes. 111a; B. Meg. 17a.

14. They also cite Josephus, *BJ* II.8.1; TJ Sanh. 50.1, 18a; B. ibid. 41a, *Megillat Ta'anit*, Elul 22 (ed. Lichtenstein, p. 80). Among those advocating this position are Schürer, *GJV* 2:260–263; Kilpatrick, pp. 17–20; Sherwin-White, op. cit., pp. 35–46; Lohse, *synedrion*, *TDNT* 7:865–866; Catchpole, *Trial*, pp. 236–254.

15. These scholars include J. Juster, *Les Juifs dans l'Empire Romain* (Paris, 1914), pp. 128–152; Lietzmann, pp. 251–263; Winter, *Trial*, pp. 110–130; idem, "The Trial of Jesus and the Competence of the Sanhedrin," *NTS* 10 (1963–64): 494–499.

# 247. *The Mocking by the Soldiers*

## MATT. 27.27–31

27 Then the soldiers of the governor took Jesus into the praetorium, and they gathered the whole battalion before him. 28 And they stripped him and put a scarlet robe upon him. 29 and plaiting a crown of thorns they put it on his head, and put a reed in his right hand. And kneeling before him they mocked him, saying, "Hail, King of the Jews!" 30 And they spat on him, and took the reed and struck him on the head. 31 And when they had mocked him, they stripped him of the robe, and put his own clothes on him, and led him away to crucify him.

## MARK 15.16–20

16 And the soldiers led him away inside the palace (that is, the praetorium); and they called together the whole battalion. 17 And they clothed him in a purple cloak, and plaiting a crown of thorns they put in on him, 18 And they began to salute him, "Hail, King of the Jews!" 19 And they struck his head with a reed, and spat upon him, and they knelt down in homage to him, 20 And when they had mocked him, they stripped him of the purple cloak and they put his own clothes on him. And they led him out to crucify him.

## COMMENTARY

27 *praetorium* Originally the headquarters of the praetor or general of the Roman camp. In the Gospels and in Acts it is the official residence of the governor.[1] Although the official residence was in Caesarea, on the festivals

the governor was in Jerusalem.[2] Some have placed it at Herod's palace at the NE corner of the upper city, others in the tower of Antonia at the NW corner of the outer court of the Temple.[3]

29 *a crown of thorns* A similar incident is recorded in Alexandria, where Jews did this to an imbecile in order to insult Agrippa.[4]

### NOTES

1. Cf. Acts 23.35, 15.5; Josephus, *BJ* II.14.8.
2. See above p. 399. Also J. Kregenbuhl, "Das Ort der Verurteilung Jesu," *ZNW* 2 (1902): 15–22.
3. See Brown, *John*, 2:845, who discusses the probable site.
4. Philo, *Flac*, VI.36–39; Plutarch, *Pomp.* XXIV. Cf. also Dio Chrysostom, *De Regno* IV.67.

## 248. *The Road to Golgotha*

### MATT. 27.32

As they were marching out, they came upon a man of Cyrene, Simon by name; this man they compelled to carry his cross.

### MARK 15.21

And they compelled a passer-by, Simon of Cyrene, who was coming in from the country, the father of Alexander and Rufus, to carry his cross.

### LUKE 23.26–32

26 And as they led him away, they seized one Simon of Cyrene, who was coming in from the country, and laid upon him the cross, to carry it behind Jesus. 27 And there followed him a great multitude of the people, and of women who bewailed and lamented him. 28 But Jesus turning to them said, "Daughters of Jerusalem, do not weep for me, but weep for yourselves and for your children. 29 For behold, the days are coming when they will say, 'Blessed are the barren, and the wombs that never bore, and the breasts that never gave suck.' 30 Then they will begin to say to the mountains, 'Fall on us;' and to the hills, 'Cover us.' 31 For if they do this when the wood is green, what will happen when it is dry?" 32 Two others also, who were criminals, were led away to be put to death with him.

### COMMENTARY

32 *Cyrene* A Greek city on the N coast of Africa, capital of Cyrenaica. There were Greek-speaking Jews there who had come from Alexandria.[1] Since Mark 15.21 gives family details, Simon appears to be a real person.[2]

*his cross* The cross-bar (*patibulum*) only, for the upright was stationary at the place of crucifixion.

## NOTES

1. Josephus, *Contra Ap.* II.4; cf. *Ant.* XIV 7.2. Cf. also Acts. 6.9.
2. See Bultmann, *HST*, p. 434; Lietzmann, "Bermerkungen zum Prozess Jesu," *ZNW* 30 (1931): 214 ff.

# 249. *The Crucifixion*

### MATT. 27.33–44

33 And when they came to a place called Golgotha (which means the place of a skull), 34 they offered him wine to drink, mingled with gall; but when he tasted it, he would not drink it. 35 And when they had crucified him, they divided his garments among them by casting lots; 36 then they sat down and kept watch over him there. 37 And over his head they put the charge against him, which read, "This is Jesus the King of the Jews." 38 Then two robbers were crucified with him, one on the right and one on the left. 39 And those who passed by derided him, wagging their heads 40 and saying, "You who would destroy the temple to build it in three days, save yourself! If you are the Son of God, come down[c] from the cross." 41 So also the chief priests, with the scribes and elders, mocked him, saying, 42 "He saved others; he cannot save himself. He is the King of Israel; let him come down now from the cross, and we will believe in him. 43 He trusts in God; let God deliver him now, if he desires him; for he said, 'I am the Son of God.' " 44 And the robbers who were crucified with him also reviled him in the same way.

### MARK 15.22–32

22 And they brought him to the place called Golgotha (which means the place of a skull). 23 And they offered him wine mingled with myrrh; but he did not take it. 24 And they crucified him, and divided his garments among them, casting lots for them, to decide what each should take. 25 And it was the third hour, when they crucified him. 26 And the inscription of the charge against him read, "The King of the Jews." 27 And with him they crucified two robbers, one on his right and one on his left.[d] 29 And those who passed by derided him, wagging their heads, and saying, "Aha! You who could destroy the temple and build it in three days, 30 save yourself, and come down from the cross!" 31 So also the chief priests mocked him to one another with the scribes, saying "He saved others; he cannot save himself. 32 Let the Christ, the King of Israel, come down now from the cross, that we may see and believe." Those who were crucified with him also reviled him.

### LUKE 23.33–43

33 And when they came to the place which is called The Skull, there they crucified him, and the criminals, one on the right and one on the left. 34 And Jesus said, "Father, forgive them; for they know not what they do."[e] And they cast lots to divide his garments. 35 And the people stood by watching; but the rulers scoffed at him saying, "He saved others; let him save himself, if he is the Christ of God, his Chosen One!" 36 The soldiers also mocked him, coming up and offering him vinegar, 37 and

saying, "If you are the King of the Jews, save yourself!" 38 There was also an inscription over him,[f] "This is the King of the Jews." 39 One of the criminals who were hanged railed at him, saying, "Are you not the Christ? Save yourself and us!" 40 But the other rebuked him, saying, "Do you not fear God, since you are under the same sentence of condemnation? 41 And we indeed justly; for we are receiving the due reward of our deeds; but this man has done nothing wrong." 42 And he said, "Jesus, remember me when you come into your kingly power."[g] 43 And he said to him, "Truly, I say to you, today you will be with me in Paradise."

---

c Some texts: *save yourself, if you are the Son of God, and come down.*
d Some texts add v. 28, *And the scripture was fulfilled which says, "He was reckoned with transgressors."*
e Some omit *And Jesus said, "Father forgive them for they know not what they do."*
f Some add *in letters of Greek and Latin and Hebrew.*
g Greek *kingdom.*

## COMMENTARY

33 *Golgotha* Aram. *gulgalta*, "a skull;" Heb. *gulgolet*. In Greek *Golgotha* but in Luke 23.33 *Kranion*; Lat. *Calvaria*. It was outside of Jerusalem but the precise place is unknown.[1]

34 *wine mingled with gall* Gr. *chole*. Mark 15.23 reads "with myrrh." Myrrh and gall are both bitter. Why the change? Montefiore suggests that "in Mk. the object of the offered drink is to remove consciousness, it was a narcotic and was regularly given to Jewish criminals by the Jews. "R. Ḥiyya bar R. Ashi said in the name of R. Ḥisda: 'He who goes out to be executed, they give him a grain of frankincense in a cup of wine so that his mind becomes confused as it is said, *Give strong drink to one who is perishing, and wine to the bitter of soul* (Prov. 31.6).' "[2] In Matthew this humane custom is turned into mockery. In Mark, Jesus knows the object of the drink, and refuses it in order to die with full consciousness; in Matthew he tries it but refuses to drink it because of the odious taste."[3]

These may be references to Ps. 69.21, *They gave me poison for food, and for my thirst they gave me vinegar to drink*; Lam. 3.15, *He has filled me with bitterness he has sated me with wormwood.* Perhaps there is an interchange between Heb. *mor*, Aram *mora*, "myrrh," and Heb. *merara*, "gall."[4]

35 *they divided his garments* Ps. 22.18, *they divided my garments among them, and for my raiment they cast lots.* The condemned were crucified naked, and the executioners were allowed to divide their clothing and property among them.[5]

37 *over his head*, etc. The *titulus* which contained the crime for which the criminal was executed, here as "king of the Jews" a political offense.[6]

38 *two robbers* Gr. *lestai*, i.e., political offenders, see above p. 416; perhaps members of the Fourth Philosophy. Cf. Isa. 53.12, *he was numbered with transgressors.*

43 *He trusts in God*, etc. We find a striking parallel: "For if the righteous

be God's son, He will uphold him, and save him from the hand of his adversaries."[7] This may be a Christian interpolation, but both this passage and the NT verse may both derive from Ps. 22.8, *He committed his cause to the Lord; let Him deliver him, let Him rescue him, for He delights in him.*[8]

## NOTES

1. For some suggestions, see J. Finegan, *Light from the Ancient Past* (1946), pp. 433–438; R. H. Smith, "The Tomb of Jesus," *BA* 30 (1967): 14–90.
2. B. Sanh. 43a; M. Sem. 2.9.
3. *SG*, 2:347–348.
4. *Chole* in the LXX translates *la'anah*, "wormwood" (Prov. 5.4, Lam. 3.15); *mererah*, "gall" (Job 16.13); *merorah*, "gall" (ibid. 20.14); *rosh*, "poison" (Ps. 68[69].21, Deut. 29.17).
5. See Artemidorus Daldianus, *Onirocriticus* 2.61.
6. See Dio Cassius 54.8; Suetonius, *Caligula* 32 and *Domitian* 10. See also Cullmann, *State in the New Testament*, pp. 42 ff. Each passage in the Synoptics and in John 19.19 has a slightly different wording. Winter, *Trial*, pp. 107 ff., sees this as a reflection of different theologies.
7. Wisdom 3.18, 20.
8. Cf. also Ps. 20.6; Lam. 2.15; Isa. 42.1.

## 250. The Death on the Cross

### MATT. 27.45–56

45 Now from the sixth hour there was darkness over all the land[h] until the ninth hour. 46 And about the ninth hour Jesus cried with a loud voice, "Eli, Eli, lama sabachthani?" that is, "My God, My God, why hast thou forsaken me?" 47 And some of the bystanders hearing it said, "This man is calling Elijah." 48 And one of them at once ran and took a sponge, filled it with vinegar, and put it on a reed, and gave it to him to drink. 49 But the others said, "Wait, let us see whether Elijah will come to save him."[i] 50 And Jesus cried again with a loud voice and yielded up his spirit. 51 And behold, the curtain of the temple was torn in two, from top to bottom; and the earth shook, and the rocks were split; 52 the tombs also were opened, and many bodies of the saints who had fallen asleep were raised, 53 and coming out of the tombs after his resurrection they went into the holy city and appeared to many. 54 When the centurion and those who were with him, keeping watch over Jesus, saw the earthquake and what took place, they were filled with awe, and said, "Truly this was a Son of God!" 55 There were also many women there, looking on from afar, who had followed Jesus from Galilee, ministering to him; 56 among whom were Mary Magdalene, and Mary the mother of James and Joseph, and the mother of the sons of Zebedee.

### MARK 15.33–41

33 And when the sixth hour had come, there was darkness over the whole land[h] until the ninth hour. 34 And at the ninth hour Jesus cried with a loud voice, "Eloi, Eloi, lama sabachthani?" which means, "My God, my God, why hast thou forsaken me?"

35 And some of the bystanders hearing it said, "Behold, he is calling Elijah." 36 And one ran and, filling a sponge full of vinegar, put it on a reed and gave it to him to drink, saying, "Wait, let us see whether Elijah will come to take him down." 37 And Jesus uttered a loud cry, and breathed his last. 38 And the curtain of the temple was torn in two, from top to bottom. 39 And when the centurion, who stood facing him, saw that he thus breathed his last, he said, "Truly, this man was a Son of God." 40 There were also women looking on from afar, among whom were Mary Magdalene and Mary the mother of James the younger and of Joses, and Salome, 41 who, when he was in Galilee, followed him, and ministered to him; and also many other women who came up with him to Jerusalem.

## LUKE 23.44–49

44 It was now about the sixth hour, and there was darkness over the whole land[h] until the ninth hour, 45 while the sun's light failed;[j] and the curtain of the temple was torn in two. 46 Then Jesus, crying with a loud voice, said, "Father, into thy hands I commit my spirit!" And having said this he breathed his last. 47 Now when the centurion saw what had taken place, he praised God, and said, "Certainly this man was innocent!" 48 And all the multitudes who assembled to see the sight, when they saw what had taken place, returned home beating their breasts. 49 And all his acquaintances and the women who had followed him from Galilee stood at a distance and saw these things.

----

h  Or *earth*.
i  Some add *and another took a spear and pierced his side, and there came out water and blood*.
j  Some read *the sun was darkened*.

## COMMENTARY

45  *from the sixth hour*, etc.   I.e., from noon to 3:00 P.M.

*there was darkness*   On darkness at time of catastrophy note "The earth quakes before them, the heavens tremble, the sun and the moon are darkened, and the stars withdraw their shining."[1] Rabbinic sources also recount strange occurrences at the death of notable rabbis.[2]

46  *Eli, eli*, etc.   Aram. of Ps. 22.1 (but not quite the same as the Targum, which reads *metul mah* for *lama*).

47  *This man is calling Elijah*   This is because of the sound of the words *eli* (God) and *Eli*(yah) (Elijah), which are similar. Less likely is that it is a gibe—that Elijah should come and save him since he comes to the aid of the distressed.[3] Note that Luke 23.46 reads, "Father, into thy hands I commit my spirit," presumably to soften the dependency of Jesus on God by uttering "Eli, Eli."[4]

48  *took a sponge . . . to drink*   Some see in this the influence of Ps. 69.22.[5]

51  *the curtain of the temple was torn in two*   There were two curtains, an inner and an outer, but here what is meant is the outer, so that it was visible to the populace. There is an interesting story that forty years before the destruction of the Temple the western light dimmed. Among other strange

happenings, the doors of the sanctuary opened on their own accord.[6] It is reported that at the destruction of the Temple Titus slashed the veil with his sword.[7]

*the earth shook* Josephus records that there was indeed an earthquake before the fall of Jerusalem.[8]

52 *the tombs were open*, etc.   That the dead will rise at messianic times is commonplace.

53 *and coming out of the tombs*, etc.   This is clearly a later addition.

56 *Mary Magdalene*   She is mentioned in the Talmud in a Jesus passage.[9]

*Magdalene*   Near Tiberias and mentioned frequently in rabbinic sources.[10]

## NOTES

1. Joel 2.10. Cf. also ibid. 31; 3.4; 4.15; Isa. 13.10, 50.3; Jer. 13.16, 15.9; Amos 8.9.

2. E.g., TJ AZ 3, 42c (1); B. MQ 25b.

3. Albright-Mann, p. 350. See Daube, *NTRJ*, p. 25. Also cf. Guillaume, "Matthew XXVII.46 in Light of the Dead Sea Scroll of Isaiah," *Palestine Exploration Quarterly*, 1951, 78 ff. See 2 Kings 2.12; Targ. 2 Kings 13.14; B. Sanh. 68b.

4. Cf. *Gospel of Peter*, v. 19, "My power, my power why have you forsaken me?" This too might be a softening of the text. See Townsend, *Liturgical Interpretation*, p. 30 n. 104. It is also possible that it is the Heb. *hagevurah*, a substitute for the name of God.

5. See Bultmann, *HST*, p. 273: Klausner, *JN*, p. 353.

6. TJ Yom. 6, 43c (61); B. ibid. 39b; *BJ*.VI.5.3–4.

7. B. Git. 56b.

8. *BJ* VI.5.3–4. Earthquakes at times of catastrophies; see TJ Ber. 9.13c (33), *Mid. Ps.* 18 (71a), *Tan.B. Bereshit* 12 (4b).

9. Cf. B. Shab. 104b and also B.Ḥag. 4b, where she is called a hairdresser and is identified with the mother of Jesus.

10. TJ Shevi'it 9.1, 38d (34); TJ M.Sh. 3.1, 50c (20); TJ Er. 5, 22d (58); Lam. R. 2.2 (64a).

# 251. *The Burial of Jesus*

## MATT. 27.57–61

57 When it was evening, there came a rich man from Arimathea, named Joseph, who also was a disciple of Jesus. 58 He went to Pilate and asked for the body of Jesus. Then Pilate ordered it to be given to him. 59 And Joseph took the body, and wrapped it in a clean linen shroud, 60 and laid it in his own new tomb, which he had hewn in the rock; and he rolled a great stone to the door of the tomb, and departed. 61 Mary Magdalene and the other Mary were there, sitting opposite the tomb.

## MARK 15.42–47

42 And when evening had come, since it was the day of Preparation, that is the day before the sabbath, 43 Joseph of Arimathea, a respected member of the council, who

was also himself looking for the kingdon of God, took courage and went to Pilate, and asked for the body of Jesus. 44 And Pilate wondered if he were already dead; and summoning the centurion, he asked him whether he was already dead.[k] 45 And when he learned from the centurion that he was dead, he granted the body to Joseph. 46 And he bought a linen shroud, and taking him down, wrapped him in the linen shroud, and laid him in a tomb which had been hewn out of the rock; and he rolled a stone against the door of the tomb. 47 Mary Magdalene and Mary the mother of Joses saw where he was laid.

## LUKE 23.50–56

50 Now there was a man named Joseph from the Jewish town of Arimathea. He was a member of the council, a good and righteous man, 51 who had not consented to their purpose and deed, and he was looking for the kingdom of God. 52 This man went to Pilate and asked for the body of Jesus. 53 Then he took it down and wrapped it in a linen shroud, and laid him in a rock-hewn tomb, where no one had ever yet been laid, 54 It was the day of Preparation, and the sabbath was beginning.[l] 55 The women who had come with him from Galilee followed, and saw the tomb, and how his body was laid; 56 then they returned and prepared spices and ointments. On the sabbath they rested according to the commandment.

---

k  Some read *whether he had been some time dead;* others *whether he was dead.*
l  Greek *was dawning.*

## COMMENTARY

57  *When it was evening*   More likely when it was late, almost evening, Gr. *opsias;* sometimes it is difficult to decide whether it refers to the period just before or just after sundown.[1] It was important to bury on the day of death.[2] Furthermore, the body was not to be left unburied, i.e., uncovered.[3]

*Joseph of Arimathea*   Arimathea is probably Haramataim, 10 miles E of Lydda and ca. 10 miles SE of Antipatris. It might be Ramataim Zofim of 1 Sam. 1.[4]

59  *clean linen shrouds*   It is recorded that the Patriarch Gamaliel II decreed that all Jews regardless of their station in life were to be buried in linen shrouds.[5] It is difficult to determine whether this use of linen shrouds was current before the decree of Rabban Gamaliel or because of it.

60  *new tomb*   Not in Jerusalem, as burials were forbidden there.[6]
*rolled a great stone.*[7]

## NOTES

1. See Jth. 13.1 and *BAG,* s.v. *opsias.*
2. B. MQ 28a; Sifre Deut. 221.
3. Sifre Deut. 221; B. Sanh. 47a; M. Sem. 8 (bg.); B. Ber. 18a. Cf. John 19.31–34. See Josephus, *BJ* IV.5.2.
4. See 1 Macc. 11.34; Josephus, *Ant.* XIII.4.9 (Ramatha). See *IDB,* s.v. *Arimathea.*

5. See B. MQ 27b. Cf. also TJ Kil. 9.3 32a (68); TJ Ket. 12.3 35a (8); TJ Ter. 8.10 46b (49).
6. Burials have to be at least 50 cubits from the city. Cf. M. BB 2.9; B. ibid. 100b.
7. See M. Ohol 2.4; B. Ket. 4b; B. Sanh. 47b.

# 252. *The Guard on the Tomb*

## MATT. 27.62–66

62 Next day, that is, after the day of Preparation, the chief priests and the Pharisees gathered before Pilate 63 and said, "Sir, we remember how that imposter said, while he was still alive, 'After three days I will rise again.' 64 Therefore order the tomb to be made secure until the third day, lest his disciples go and steal him away, and tell the people, 'He has risen from the dead,' and the last fraud will be worse than the first." 65 Pilate said to them, "You have a guard[m] of soldiers; go, make it as secure as you can."[n] 66 So they went and made the tomb secure by sealing the stone and setting a guard.

---

m Or *take a guard*.
n Greek *know*.

## COMMENTARY

62 *The day of Preparation* Gr. *paraskeuē* = Friday or the day before a holiday, Heb. *erev*, even more specifically between the hours of three and six.[1] "The historicity of the verses is very questionable; the high priests and Pharisees would not, on a Sabbath and a high festival, take any such action, especially if it brought them into contact with a pagan."[2]

64 *until the third day* "By the third day (on which according to popular belief, dissolution began, and the soul finally departed from proximity to the body) not only would the Deceiver's prediction have proved false, but the Jews in general would know that it had, so that the disciples could not then practice fraud. The whole sentence assumes that the prediction about the third day was widely known. The passage arose as an attempt of Christians to silence the report that the disciples had stolen the body (xxviii.15), by showing that the religious authorities had deliberately, and falsely, set it in motion."[3]

66 *sealing the stone* Reminiscent of Dan. 6.17.

## NOTES

1. Cf. Josephus, *Ant.* XVI.6.2; *Didache* 8.
2. McNeile, *Matt.*, p. 428.
3. Ibid.

# 253. *The Empty Tomb*

## MATT. 28.1–10

1 Now after the sabbath, toward the dawn of the first day of the week, Mary
Magdalene and the other Mary went to see the tomb. 2 And behold, there was a great
earthquake; for an angel of the Lord descended from heaven and came and rolled back
the stone, and sat upon it. 3 His appearance was like lightning, and his raiment white
as snow. 4 And for fear of him the guards trembled and became like dead men. 5 But
the angel said to the women, "Do not be afraid; for I know that you seek Jesus who
was crucified. 6 He is not here; for he has risen, as he said. Come, see the place where
he[o] lay. 7 Then go quickly and tell his disciples that he has risen from the dead, and
behold, he is going before you to Galilee; there you will see him. Lo, I have told you."
8 So they departed quickly from the tomb with fear and great joy, and ran to tell his
disciples. 9 And behold, Jesus met them and said, "Hail!" And they came up and took
hold of his feet and worshiped him. 10 Then Jesus said to them, "Do not be afraid; go
and tell my brethren to go to Galilee, and there they will see me."

## MARK 16.1–8

1 And when the sabbath was past, Mary Magdalene, and Mary the mother of James
and Salome, brought spices, so that they might go and anoint him. 2 And very early
on the first day of the week they went to the tomb when the sun had risen. 3 And they
were saying to one another, "Who will roll away the stone for us from the door of the
tomb?" 4 And looking up, they saw that the stone was rolled back; for it was very
large. 5 And entering the tomb, they saw a young man sitting on the right side,
dressed in a white robe; and they were amazed. 6 And he said to them, "Do not be
amazed; you seek Jesus of Nazareth, who was crucified. He has risen, he is not here;
see the place where they laid him. 7 But go, tell his disciples and Peter that he is going
before you to Galilee; there you will see him, as he told you." 8 And they went out
and fled from the tomb; for trembling and astonishment had come upon them; and
they said nothing to anyone, for they were afraid.

## LUKE 24.1–11

1 But on the first day of the week, at early dawn, they went to the tomb, taking the
spices which they had prepared. 2 And they found the stone rolled away from the
tomb, 3 but when they went in they did not find the body.[p] 4 While they were
perplexed about this, behold, two men stood by them in dazzling apparel; 5 and as
they were frightened and bowed their faces to the ground, the men said to them,
"Why do you seek the living among the dead?[q] 6 Remember how he told you while he
was still in Galilee, 7 that the Son of man must be delivered into the hands of sinful
men, and be crucified and on the third day rise." 8 And they remembered his words,
9 and returning from the tomb they told all this to the eleven and to all the rest. 10
Now it was Mary Magdalene and Joanna and Mary the mother of James and the other
women with them who told this to the apostles; 11 but these words, seemed to them
an idle tale, and they did not believe them.[r]

o Some read *the Lord.*
p Some add *of Jesus*, others add *of the Lord.*
q Some add *He is not here but has risen.*
r Some add v. 12, *But Peter rose and ran to the tomb, stooping and looking in, he saw the linen cloths by themselves, and he went home wondering at what had happened.*

## COMMENTARY

1 *After the Sabbath* Gr. *opse de sabbatōn.* The meaning is probably "late in the Sabbath."[1]

*toward the dawn of the first day* This is parallel to "after the sabbath" and does not mean Sunday morning. The use of *eis mian sabbatōn* is purely Semitic, *be'ehad beshabbat.*[3]

9 *Hail* Gr. *chairete;* in rabbinic literature *heri* or *qiri.*[4]

## NOTES

1. This finds parallels in the papyri. See J.H. Moulton and C. Milligan, *The Vocabulary of the Greek New Testament Illustrated from the Papyri and other non-Literary Sources* (London, 1949), 1.72.

2. See Turner, "The Gospel of Peter," *JTS* 15 (1914): 188f.; Burkitt, "Epphōskein," *JTS* 15 (1914): 538–546; idem, "A Further Note on Epphōskein," *JTS* 16 (1915): 79.

3. Cf. Gen. R. 11; M. Ned. 8.1; M. Ta'an.; n. 3. Albright-Mann, p. 358, are in error.

4. Gen. R. 89; *Tan.B. miqez* 11 (196).

# APPEARANCES OF THE RISEN CHRIST

## The Matthean Narrative

### A. MATT. 28.11–20

## 1. The Bribing of the Soldiers

### MATT. 28.11–15

11 While they were going, behold, some of the guard went into the city and told the chief priests all that had taken place. 12 And when they had assembled with the elders and taken counsel, they gave a sum of money to the soldiers, 13 and said, "Tell people, 'His disciples came by night and stole him away while we were asleep.' 14 And if this comes to the governor's ears, we will satisfy him and keep you out of trouble." 15 So they took the money and did as they were directed; and this story has been spread among the Jews to this day.

### COMMENTARY

"This story, the unhistorical character of which is obvious, is the *sequitur* of xxvii. 62–66. When the Christians said not only that Jesus was risen, but that his tomb was empty, the Jews retorted that, if the tomb were empty, this was due to the body having been stolen by the disciples. The Christian rejoinder is contained in Matthew's story. Both the attack and defence are late; they arose when the situation of the tomb was already forgotten, or when no examination on the spot could be made."[1]

15 *to this day* Presumably many years after the event.

### NOTES

1. Montefiore, *SG*, 1:356.

## 2. The Command to Baptize

### MATT. 28.16–20

16 Now the eleven disciples went to Galilee, to the mountain to which Jesus had directed them. 17 And when they saw him they worshiped him; but some doubted.

18 And Jesus came and said to them, "All authority in heaven and on earth has been given to me. 19 Go therefore and make disciples of all nations, baptizing them in the name of the Father and of the Son and of the Holy Spirit, 20 teaching them to observe all that I have commanded you; and lo, I am with you always, to the close of the age."

## COMMENTARY

Verse 19 and 20 reflect a very late period, perhaps the beginning of the second century, for they speak of universal preachment and of the baptism with the trinitarian formula.[1]

19 *in the name.* Gr. *eis to onoma* = *Heb. leshem,* "for the purpose, to the end," as in the expression "baptizing a slave to *become* a free man."[2]

## NOTES

1. See M. S. Enslin, *Christian Beginnings* (New York, 1938), p. 399.
2. B. Yev. 45b. Cf. also M. Zev. 4.6; B. Yev. 47b; T. AZ 3.12 (p. 464). TJ. Yev. 8.1, 8d (63).

# B. The Lucan Narrative

## LUKE 24.13–53

# 1. The Road to Emmaus

## LUKE 24.13–35

13 That very day two of them were going to a village named Emmaus, about seven miles[s] from Jerusalem, 14 and talking with each other about all these things that had happened. 15 While they were talking and discussing together, Jesus himself drew near and went with them, 16 But their eyes were kept from recognizing him. 17 And he said to them, "What is this conversation which you are holding with each other as you walk?" And they stood still, looking sad. 18 Then one of them, named Cleopas, answered him, "Are you the only visitor to Jerusalem who does not know the things that have happened there in these days?" 19 And he said to them, "What things?" And they said to him, "Concerning Jesus of Nazareth, who was a prophet mighty in deed and word before God and all the people, 20 and how our chief priests and rulers delivered him up to be condemned to death and crucified him. 21 But we had hoped that he was the one to redeem Israel. Yes, and besides all this, it is now the third day since this happened. 22 Moreover, some women of our company amazed us. They were at the tomb early in the morning 23 and did not find his body; and they came back saying that they had even seen a vision of angels who said that he was alive. 24 Some of those who were with us went to the tomb, and found it just as the women had said; but him they did not see." 25 And he said to them, "O foolish men, and slow

of heart to believe all that the prophets have spoken! 26 Was it not necessary that the Christ should suffer these things and enter into his glory?" 27 And beginning with Moses and all the prophets, he interpreted to them in all the scriptures the things concerning himself. 28 So they drew near to the village to which they were going; and he made as though he would go further, 29 but they constrained him, saying "Stay with us, for it is toward evening and the day is now far spent." So he went in to stay with them. 30 When he was at table with them, he took the bread and blessed, and broke it, and gave it to them. 31 And their eyes were opened and they recognized him; and he vanished out of their sight. 32 They said to each other, "Did not our hearts burn within us while he talked to us on the road, while he opened to us the scriptures?" 33 And they rose that same hour and returned to Jerusalem; and they found the eleven gathered together and those who were with them, 34 who said, "The Lord has risen indeed, and has appeared to Simon!" 35 Then they told what had happened on the road, and how he was known to them in the breaking of the bread.

---

s   Greek *sixty stadia.*

## COMMENTARY

13 *Emmaus*   A Judean town mentioned several times in Maccabees,[1] Josephus,[2] and rabbinic sources[3] The identification of the town is not certain. Two popular suggestions are (a) Colonia, more than 4 miles from Jerusalem. Josephus (BJ VII.6.6) states that Vespasian settled eight hundred veterans at "a place called Emmaus thirty stadia from Jerusalem." Perhaps this is the Mozah of Josh. 18.26. (b) Amwas (Necopolis), 22 Roman miles W of Jerusalem on the road to Joppa where Judah Maccabeus defeated Gorgias.[4]

16 *their eyes were kept from seeing*   The Gr. *ekratounto* may go back to *aḥizat enayim.*[5]

19 *a prophet* Gr. *anēr prophētes* = Heb. *ish navi.*[6]

*mighty in deed and word*   There is a similar expression in rabbinic sources, "mighty in Torah and *miẓvot.*"[7]

*before God*   A Semitism; see above p. 17.

26 *Was it not necessary that the Christ should suffer,* etc.   See above p. 322.

32 *Did not our hearts burn within us?*   Cf. Test. Naph. 7.4.

## NOTES

1. 1 Macc. 9.50.
2. *Ant.* XIV.11.2; XVII.10.9; *BJ* II.20.14.
3. E.g., TJ Shevi'it 9.2, 38d (69).
4. 1 Macc. 3.40, 57; 4.1–15. Cf. Josephus, *BJ* III.3.5. For other suggested sites, see *IDB*, s.v. "Emmaus."
5. See M. Sanh. 7.11 on Deut. 18.10; Sifra 19.26; Sifre Deut. 171; B. Sanh. 65b, 67b; TJ ibid. 7.19, 25d.
6. Judg. 6.8; Targ. and LXX. ad loc.
7. B. Sot. 14a.

# 2. *The Appearance of the Risen Christ in Jerusalem*

## LUKE 24.36–49

36 As they were saying this, Jesus himself stood among them.ᵗ 37 But they were startled and frightened, and supposed that they saw a spirit. 38 And he said to them, "Why are you troubled, and why do questionings rise in your hearts? 39 See my hands and my feet, that it is I myself; handle me, and see; for a spirit has not flesh and bones, as you see that I have."ᵘ 41 And while they still disbelieved for joy, and wondered, he said to them, "Have you anything here to eat?" 42 They gave him a piece of broiled fish, 43 and he took it and ate before them. 44 Then he said to them, "These are my words which I spoke to you, while I was still with you, that everything written about me in the law of Moses and the prophets and the psalms must be fulfilled." 45 Then he opened their minds to understand the scriptures 46 and said to them, "Thus it is written that the Christ should suffer and on the third day rise from the dead, 47 and that repentance and forgiveness of sins should be preached in his name to all nations,ᵛ beginning from Jerusalem. 48 You are witnesses of these things. 49 And behold, I send the promise of my Father upon you; but stay in the city, until you are clothed with power from on high."

---

t   Some add *and said to them, "Peace to you"*; others add *and said to them, "It is I; do not be afraid; peace to you"*; still others add *peace to you* before *It is I*.

u   Some texts add v. 40, *and when he had said this, he showed them his hands and his feet.*

v   Or *nations. Beginning from Jerusalem you are witnesses.*

## COMMENTARY

38   *and why do questionings rise in your hearts*   This has a Semitic ring—the combination of "rise" and "heart" (mind)![1]

47   *that repentance and forgiveness of sins . . . beginning from Jerusalem.*   It is a common motif that the beginnings of the messianic age shall first be noticeable in Jerusalem. E.g., "R. Levi said: 'All goodness and blessings and consolation which the Holy One, blessed be He, will give to Israel comes only from Zion.' "[2]

49   *with power from on high*   Gr. *ech hupsous dunamin.*   See Isa. 32. 15, "spirit from on high," *ru'ah mimarom*, rendered in the Targum, "Spirit from his Shekhinah in the height of the Heaven."

## NOTES

1. Cf. Targ. Jer. 3.14 and LXX ad loc.; Targ. Ezek. 11.5. and LXX ad loc., and the Heb. expression *alu bemahshavah*," "came (up) to mind."

2. Lev. R. 24. Parallels: *PR* 41 (173b); *Mid. Ps.* 14 (57a), 20 (88b). Cf also *Aggad. Ber.* 53 (beg.), B. Yom. 54b.

# 3. The Ascension

## LUKE 24.50–53

50 Then he led them out as far as Bethany, and lifting up his hands he blessed them. 51 While he blessed them, he parted from them.<sup>w</sup> 52 And they<sup>x</sup> returned to Jerusalem with great joy, 53 and were continually in the temple blessing God.

---

w Some texts read *he was carried up from them;* others add *and was carried up into heaven.*
x Some texts add *worshiped him and.*

### COMMENTARY

51 *parted from them (and was carried up into heaven)*   R. Abbahu (ca. 300), in a polemical statement, said, "If a man says to you 'I am God,' he is a liar; if he says 'I am the son of man,' in the end people will laugh at him; if he says 'I will go up to heaven,' he says but shall not perform it."[1]

### NOTES

1. TJ Ta'an. 2.1, 65b (59). On this passage see Herford, *CTM* pp. 62 ff.; Lachs, "Rabbi Abbahu and the Minim," 199.

# C. The Longer Ending of Mark

## MARK 16.9–20

9 Now when he rose early on the first day of the week, he appeared first to Mary Magdalene, from whom he had cast out seven demons. 10 She went and told those who had been with him, as they mourned and wept. 11 But when they heard that he was alive and had been seen by her, they would not believe it. 12 After this he appeared in another form to two of them, as they were walking into the country. 13 And they went back and told the rest, but they did not believe them. 14 Afterward he appeared to the eleven themselves as they sat at table; and he upbraided them for their unbelief and hardness of heart, because they had not believed those who saw him after he had risen. 15 And he said to them, "Go into all the world and preach the gospel to the whole creation. 16 He who believes and is baptized will be saved; but he who does not believe will be condemned. 17 And these signs will accompany those who believe: in my name they will cast out demons; they will speak in new tongues; 18 they will pick up serpents, and if they drink any deadly thing, it will not hurt them; they will lay their hands on the sick, and they will recover." 19 So then the Lord Jesus, after he had spoken to them, was taken up into heaven, and sat down at the right hand of God. 20 And they went forth and preached everywhere, while the Lord worked with them and confirmed the message by the signs that attended it. Amen.

## COMMENTARY

There is a consensus among most scholars that the "Longer Ending of Mark" is not part of the original work, and this can be established by both internal and external evidence.[1]

## NOTES

1. See Hort, *The New Testament in the Original Greek*, Appendix to vol. 2, pp. 28–51. Cf also Swete, ciii–cxiii, and Lagrange, *Évangile selon Saint Marc*, pp. 456–68. See, however, Enslin, *Christian Beginnings*, pp. 387–388.

# BIBLIOGRAPHY

Abel, F. M. *Géographie de la Palestine*. Paris, 1933.

Abelson, J. *The Immanence of God in Rabbinical Literature*. London, 1912.

Aberbach, M. "The Change from a Standing to a Sitting Posture by Students after the Death of Rabban Gamaliel" *JQR* 52 (1960) 168–174.

"The Relations between Master and Disciple in the Talmudic Age." In *Essays Presented to Chief Rabbi Israel Brodie on the Occasion of His Seventieth Birthday*. London, 1965.

Aitken, W. E. M. "Beelzebul" *JBL* 21 (1912) 34–53.

Abrahams, I. *Studies in Pharisaism and the Gospels, First and Second Series*. New York: Ktav, 1967.

Albright, W. F. "Zabûl Yam and Thâpit Nahar in the Combat between Baal and the Sea" *JPOS* 16 (1936) 17–20.

Albright, W. F. and C. S. Mann. *Matthew*. Anchor Bible. Garden City: Doubleday, 1971.

Allegro, J. M. "Further Messianic References in Qumran Literature" *JBL* 75 (1956) 174–187.

Allen, W. C. *A Critical and Exegetical Commentary on the Gospel According to Saint Matthew*. ICC. 3rd ed. Edinburgh, 1912.

Amram, D. W. *Jewish Law of Divorce*. Philadelphia, 1886.

Andrews, M. E. "Pierasmos: A Study in Form Criticism" *Anglican Review* 24 (1942) 229–244.

Avi Yonah, M. "The Caesarea Inscription of the Twenty-Four Priestly Courses." In *The Teacher's Yoke: Studies in Memory of Henry Trantham*, eds. E. J. Vardaman, J. L. Garrett Jr. Waco Texas: Baylor University Press, 1964.

"A list of Priestly Courses from Caesarea" *IEJ* 12 (1962) 132–139.

Bacher, W. *Die Agada der Tannaiten*, 3 vols. Strassburg: K. J. Truebner, 1884–90.

"Le Siège de Moïse" *REJ* 34 (1897) 299–301.

*Die Agada der palästinischen Amoräer*, 3 vols. Strassburg: K. J. Truebner, 1892–99.

*Die exegetische Terminologie der jüdischen Traditions-literatur*. Leipzig, 1899.

Bacon, B. W. "After Six Days: A New Clue for Gospel Critics" *HTR* 8 (1915) 94–121.

*The Gospel of Mark: Its Composition and Date*. New Haven, 1925.

Bamberger, B. J. *Proselytism in the Talmudic Period*. Cincinnati: HUC Press, 1939.

*Fallen Angels*. Philadelphia: Jewish Publication Society, 1952.

Bammel, E. "ptochos" *TDNT* 6.881–915.

Bauer, W. *A Greek-English Lexicon of the New Testament and Other Early Christian Literature*, trans. and adapted by W. F. Arndt and F. W. Gingrich. Chicago: University of Chicago Press, 1957.

Baumgartner, W. *Hebräisches und aramäisches Lexikon zum Alten Testament*. Leiden: E. J. Brill, 1967.

Beare, F. W. "The Sabbath Was Made for Man" *JBL* 79 (1960) 131–136.
   *The Earliest Records of Jesus*. London, 1964.
Belkin, S. "The Dissolution of Vows and the Problem of Antisocial Oaths in the Gospels and Contemporary Jewish Literature" *JBL* 55 (1936) 227–234.
   *Philo and the Oral Law*. Cambridge, Mass., 1940.
Becker, W. A. *Gallus*, trans. F. Metcalf. West Strand, 1849.
   *Charicles*, trans. F. Metcalf. 3rd. ed. London, 1866.
Ben Dor, I. "Palestinian Alabaster Vases" *QDAP* 11 (1945) 93–112.
Benko, S. "The Magnificat: A History of the Controversy" *JBL* 86 (1967) 263–275.
Best, E. *The Temptation and the Passion: The Markan Soteriology*. Cambridge, 1965.
Bickerman, E. J. "Les Hérodiens" *RB* (1938) 184–197.
   "The Maxim of Antigonus of Socho" *HTR* 44 (1951) 153–165.
Black, M. *An Aramaic Approach to the Gospels and Acts*, 3rd ed. Oxford: Clarendon Press, 1967.
Blank, S. H. "The Death of Zechariah in Rabbinic Literature" *HUCA* 12–13 (1937–38) 327–246.
Blinzler, J. *The Trial of Jesus*. Westminster, Md.: Newman Press, 1959.
Bornkamm, G., Barth, G., Held, H. J. *Tradition and Interpretation in Matthew*. Philadelphia, 1962.
Bouquet, A. C. *Everyday Life in New Testament Times*. New York: Scribners, 1954.
Box, G. H. "The Gospel Narrative of the Nativity and the Alleged Influence of Heathen Ideas" *ZNW* 6 (1905) 80–101.
Brandt, W. "Der Spruch von *lumen internum*: exegetische Studie" *ZNW* 44 (1913) 97–116.
Braude, W. *Jewish Proselytizing in the First Five Centuries of the Common Era: The Age of the Tannaim and the Amoraim*. Providence: Brown University Press, 1940.
Bright, J. *A History of Israel*. Philadelphia: Westminister Press, 1952.
Brown, F., Driver, S. R., Briggs, C. A. *Hebrew and English Lexicon of the Old Testament*. Boston/New York, 1928.
Brown, R. E. "Parables and Allegory Reconsidered," *NT* 5 (1962) 36–45.
   "The Paternoster as an Eschatological Prayer." In *New Testament Essays*. Milwaukee: Bruce, 1965, 217ff.
   *The Birth of the Messiah*. Garden City, New York: Doubleday, 1977.
Büchler, A. *Das Synedrion in Jerusalem und das grosse Beth-Din in der Quaderkammer des jerusalemischen Tempels*. Jahresbericht der Israelitisch-Theologischen Lehranstalt in Wien. 1902.
   "St. Matthew VI. 1–6 and Other Allied Passages" *JTS* 26 (1909) 266–270.
   *Types of Jewish Palestinian Piety From 70 C.E.: The Ancient Pious Men*. New York: Ktav, 1968.
Bultmann, R. *The History of the Synoptic Tradition*. Oxford: Blackwell, 1968.
Burkill, T. A. "The Historical Development of the Story of the Syrophoenician Woman Mk. 7.24–31" *NT* 9 (1967) 161-177.
Burkitt, F. C. "Epphoskein" *JTS* 15 (1914) 538–546.
   "A Further Note on Epphoskein" *JTS* 16 (1915) 79.
   "The Parable of the Ten Virgins" *JTS* 30 (1929) 267–270.
   *Jesus: An Historical Outline*. London/Glasgow, 1932.
Burney, C. F. *The Poetry of Our Lord*. Oxford: The Clarendon Press, 1925.
Burrows, C. M. "The Marriage of Boaz and Ruth" *JBL* 59 (1940) 22–33; 445–454.

Cadbury, H. J. "The Meaning of John 20.23, Matt. 26.19 and Matt. 18.18" *JBL* 58 (1939) 231–234.

"The Single Eye" *HTR* 45 (1954) 69–74.

Carlston, C. E. "The Things that Defile (Mk. VII.15 and the Law in Matthew and Mark" *NTS* 15 (1968–69) 75–96.

*The Parables of the Triple Tradition.* Philadelphia, 1975.

Catchpole, D. R. "The Answer of Jesus to Caiaphas Matt. 26.64" *NTS* (1970–71) 213–226.

*The Trial of Jesus: A Study in the Gospels and Jewish Historiography from 1770 to the Present.* Leiden: E. J. Brill, 1971.

Charles, R. H. "A Fragment of a Zadokite Work." In *Apocrypha and Pseudepigrapha of the Old Testament*, 2 vols. Oxford: The Clarendon Press, 1913, pp. 785–834.

Chase, F. H. "On 'prēnēs genomenos' in Acts 1.18" *Expos. T.* (Jan. 1912) 278ff.

Chavel, C. G. "The Releasing of a Prisoner on the Eve of Passover in Ancient Jerusalem" *JBL* 60 (1941) 273–278.

Chomsky, W. *Hebrew: The Eternal Language.* Philadelphia: Jewish Publication Society, 1957.

Cohen, A. *Ancient Jewish Proverbs.* London: Murray, 1911.

Cohen, B. "The Rabbinic Law Presupposed by Matthew XII.1 and Luke VI.1" *HTR* 23 (1930) 91–92.

Cohen, M. "A Technical Term for Expense" *JNES* 27 (1968) 133–135.

Cohn, H. *The Trial and Death of Jesus.* New York: Ktav, 1977.

Colpe, O. L. "ho nios toū anthrōpou" *TDNT* 8.400–477.

Conzelmann, H. *The Theology of St Luke*, trans. S. Boswell. New York: Harper, 1961.

Cook, M. J. *Mark's Treatment of the Jewish Leaders.* Supplements to Novum Testamentum 51. Leiden: E. J. Brill, 1978.

Cowley, A. E. *Aramaic Papyri of the Fifth Century.* Oxford: Clarendon Press, 1923.

Cullmann, O. *The State in the New Testament.* London, 1957.

Cutler, A. "Does the Simeon of Luke 2 Refer to Simeon the Son of Hillel?" *JBR* 34 (1966) 29–35.

Dalman, G. *Grammatik des jüdisch-palästinischen Aramäisch nach den Idiomen des palästinischen Talmud, des Onkelostargum und Prophetentargum und der jerusalemischen Targum.* Leipzig, 1905.

*The Words of Jesus: Considered in the Light of Post-Biblical Jewish Writings and the Aramaic Language*, trans. D. M. Kay. Edinburgh, 1909.

Daube, D. "*Echousia* in Mark 2 and 27" *JTS* 39 (1938) 45–59.

"Three Questions of Form in Matthew V" *JTS* 45 (1944) 21–24.

*The New Testament and Rabbinic Judaism.* London: The Athlone Press, 1956.

Davies, W. D. "Knowledge in the Dead Sea Scrolls and Matthew 11.25–30" *HTR* 46 (1953) 117ff.

*The Setting of the Sermon on the Mount.* Cambridge: Cambridge University Press, 1964.

Deissmann, A. *Biblical Studies.* Edinburgh, 1903.

"In Light of Recently Discovered Texts of the Graeco-Roman World" *Expos. T.* 18 (Nov. 1906) 62.

*Light From the Ancient East*, 2nd ed. New York, 1927.

Derrett, J. D. M. "A Review: Marriage and Ministry in the New Temple, by Hugh Isaksson" *JBL* 85 (1966) 98–99.

"The Stone that the Builders Rejected" *Studia Evangelica* 4 (1968) 180–186.

*Studies in the New Testament*, 3 vols. Leiden: E. J. Brill, 1977–.

Descamps, A. *Les justes et la justice dans les évangiles et le christianisme primitif: hormis la doctrine proprement paulinienne*. Louvain: J. Duculot, 1950.

Dibelius, M. *Die urchristliche Ueberlieferung von Johannes dem Täufer*. Göttingen, 1911.

"Herod und Pilatus" *ZNW* 16 (1915) 113–126.

*From Tradition to Gospel*, trans. B. L. Woolf. New York: Scribners, 1938.

Dodd, C. H. *The Parables of the Kingdom*, rev. ed. New York: Scribners, 1961.

Donalson, J. "The Title Rabbi in the Gospels: Some Reflexions on the Evidence of the Gospels" *JQR* 63 (1973) 288–290.

Driver, S. R. and Neubauer, A. *The 53rd Chapter of Isaiah According to Jewish Interpretation: Texts and Translations*, 2 vols. Oxford, 1876.

Drury, J. "The Sower and the Vineyard and the Place of Allegory in the Interpretation of Mark's Parables," *JTS* (1973) 367–379.

Dukes, L. *Rabbinische Blumenlese*. Leipzig: Hahn, 1844.

Dupont, J. *Les Béatitudes*. Bruges, 1958.

*Mariage et divorce dans l'évangile*. Bruges, 1959.

Dupont-Sommer, A. (ed.). *The Essene Writings from Qumran*. Cleveland: Meridian Books, 1961.

Easton, B. S. "The Beelzebul Sections" *JBL* 32 (1913) 57–73.

Ehrman, A. "Judas Iscariot and Abba Saqqara" *JBL* 97 (1978) 572–573.

Elliott, J. K. "The Anomaly of Jesus" *Expos. T.* 85 (1974) 105–107.

Enslin, M. S. *Christian Beginnings*. New York/London: Harper, 1938.

"The Christian Stories of the Nativity" *JBL* 54 (1940) 317–338.

Epstein, A. *Miqadmoniyot Hayehudim*. (Hebrew). Vienna, 1887.

Epstein, L. *Marriage Laws in the Bible and Talmud*. Cambridge, Mass., 1942.

Evans, C. F. *The Lord's Prayer*. London, 1963.

Even Shemuel, J., (Kaufman). *Midrashe Geullah*. (Hebrew). Jerusalem, 1953–54.

Farrer, A. *St. Matthew and St. Mark*. Westminster: Dacre Press, 1954.

Feldman, A. *The Parables and the Similes of the Rabbis*. Cambridge, 1924.

Fensham, F. C. "Judas' Hand in the Bowl and Qumran" *Revue de Qumran* 5 (1964–5) 259–261.

Fenton, J. C. "Inclusio and Chiasmus in Matthew" *Studia Evangelica* 3, 1964.

Fiebig, P. *Jüdische Wundergeschichten des neutestamentlichen Zeitalters*. Tübingen, 1911.

Finegan, J. *Die Ueberliefererung der neutestamentlichen Auferstehungsgeschichte Jesu*. (BZNW 35). Giessen, 1934.

*Light from the Ancient East: The Archeological Background of the Hebrew-Christian Religion*. Princeton: Princeton University Press, 1946.

*Handbook of Biblical Chronology*. Princeton: Princeton University Press, 1964.

*The Archaeology of the New Testament*. Princeton: Princeton University Press, 1969.

Finkel, A. *The Pharisees and the Teacher of Nazareth*. Leiden: E. J. Brill, 1964.

Finkelstein, L. *Akiba Scholar Saint and Martyr*. New York, 1936.

*The Pharisees. The Sociological Background of their Faith*. 2 vols. Philadelphia: Jewish Publication Society, 1940.

*Mabo leMassekhtot Abot ve-Abot d'Rabbi Natan*. (Hebrew). New York 1950.

Fitzmyer, J. *Essays on the Semitic Background of the New Testament*. London: Geoffrey Chapman, 1971.

*The Gospel According to Luke*. Anchor Bible, 2 vols. Garden City, New York: Doubleday, 1981, 1985.

Foakes Jackson, F. J. and K. Lake. *The Beginnings of Christianity*. Part One, *The Acts of the Apostles*, 5 vols. London, 1927–39.

Foerster, W. "diabolos" *TDNT* 2.74–80.

"beelzebul" *TDNT* 1.605–606.

Ford, J. M. "The Son of Man a Euphemism?" *JBL* 87 (1968) 257–267.

Fox, G. G. "The Matthean Misrepresentation of Tephillin" *Journal of Near Eastern Studies* 1 (1942) 373–375.

France, R. T. "The Servant of the Lord in the Teaching of Jesus" *Tyndale Bulletin*, 19 (1968) 26–52.

Friedlander, G. *The Law of Love in the Old and New Testament*. London, 1909.

*The Grace of God*. London, 1910.

*The Jewish Sources of the Sermon on the Mount*. New York: Ktav, 1969.

Gärtner, B. *The Temple and the Community of Qumran and the New Testament*. Cambridge, 1965.

Garland, D. E. *The Intention of Matthew 23*. Leiden: E. J. Brill, 1979.

Gaster, T. H. "Beelzebul" *IDB* 1.374

"Demons" *IDB* 1.817–824.

*Thespis*. New York, 1950.

*The Holy and the Profane*. New York, 1955.

Gerhardsson, B. "The Parable of the Sower and its Interpretation" *NTS* 14 (1967–68) 165–193.

Gils, F. *Jésus prophète d'après les évangiles synoptiques*. Louvain, 1957.

Ginsberg, H. L. *Studies in Daniel*. New York: Jewish Theological Seminary of America, 1948.

Ginzberg, L. "Aram the Dyer" *JE* 1.35

*Geonica*, 2 Vols. New York, 1909.

*Eine unbekannte jüdische Sekte*. New York, 1922.

*The Legends of the Jews*, 7 Vols. Philadelphia, 1938.

*A Commentary on the Palestinian Talmud*. 3 Vols. (Hebrew). New York, 1941.

Ginsburg, C. D. *The Massorah*. London, 1880–1905.

Goodenough, E. R. *Jewish Symbols in the Greco-Roman Period*, 8 vols. New York, 1956.

Goodspeed, E. J. *Problems of New Testament Translation*. Chicago: University of Chicago Press, 1945.

*The Twelve*. Philadelphia, 1957.

Gordon, C. H. "Almah in Is. 7.14" *JBR* 21 (1954) 106.

Graetz, H. *Geschichte der Juden*, 11 Vols. Leipzig, 1853–76.

Grant, F. C. *The Economic Background of the Gospels*. London: Oxford University Press, 1926.

Green, H. B. *The Gospel According to Matthew*. London, 1975.

Greenstone, J. "Jewish Legends About Simon Peter" *Historia Judaica* 12 no. 2 Oct. 1950 89–104.

Grenfell, B. P. *New Sayings of Jesus and Fragment of a Lost Gospel*, Brookline, Mass. 1910.

Gressmann, H. "Vom reichen Mann und armen Lazarus: Eine literarturgeschichtliche Studie" *Abhandlungen der königliche preussischen Akademie der Wissenschaften* Phil. Hist. Kl.7. Berlin, 1918.

Grintz, M. "Hebrew as Spoken and Written Language in the Last Days of the Second Temple" *JBL* 79 (1960), 32–47.

Güdemann, M. *Religionsgeschichtliche Studien.* Leipzig, 1876.

Guillaume, A. "Matthew XXVII 46 in Light of the Dead Sea Scroll of Isaiah" *Palestine Exploration Quarterly* 83 (1951) 78–89.

Guttman, J. "Ueber zwei dogmengeschichtliche Mischnastellen" *MGWJ* 42 (1898) 30ff.

Hadas, M. *Aristeas to Philocrates (The Letter of Aristeas).* New York, 1951.

Halkin, A. S. "Samaritan Polemics Against Jews" *PAAJR* 7 (1935–36) 13–59.

Hare, D. R. A. *The Theme of Jewish Persecution of Christians in the Gospel of St. Matthew. SNTSM* 6. Cambridge, 1967.

Harris, J. R. "Cod. Ev. 561 Codex Algerinae Peckover" *JBL* 6 (1886) 79–89.

"Did Judas Really Commit Suicide?" *AJTh* 4 (1900) 490–513.

Heinemann J. H. "Payment of a Po'el Batel" *Journal of Jewish Studies* 1 (1949) 178–181.

"The Status of the Labourer in Jewish Law and Society in the Talmudic Period" *HUCA* 25 (1954) 263–325.

"The Triennial Lectionary Cycle" *Journal of Jewish Studies* 19 (1968) 41–48.

Herford, R. T. *Christianity in Talmud and Midrash.* New York: Ktav, 1975.

*Pharisaism Its Aim and Method.* London, 1912, revised and enlarged as *The Pharisees.* New York, 1924.

*Talmud and Apocrypha.* London: Soncino Press, 1933.

Hoehner, H. W. *Herod Antipas (SNTSMS).* Cambridge, 1972.

Holtzmann, M. "Auf die Septuaginta zurückgehende Uebersetzungsfehler" *MGWJ* 72 (1928) 537f.

Honeyman, A. M. "The Etymology of Mammon" *Archivum Linguisticum* IV fasc. 1 (1953) 60–65.

"Matthew 5.18 and the Validity of the Law" *NTS* 1 (1954) 141–142.

Hooker, M. D. *Jesus and the Servant.* Greenwich, Conn., 1959.

Hort, F. J. A. and Westcott, B. F. *The New Testament in the Original Greek.* Cambridge, London, 1882.

Houghton, H. P. "On the Temptation of Christ and Zarathustra" *Anglican Review* 26 (1944) 166–175.

Hunzinger, C. H. "Die jüdische Bannpraxis im neutestamentlichen Zeitalter" *Theologische Literaturzeitung* 80 (1955) 144f.

"sinapi" *TDNT* 7. 287–291.

Ingholt, H. "The Surname of Judas Iscariot." In *Studia Orientalia Ioanni Petersen . . . dicata.* Copenhagen, 1953. 159 ff.

Isaksson, A. *Marriage and the Ministry in the New Temple.* Lund, 1965.

Jackson, B. S. "Liability for Mere Intention in Early Jewish Law" *HUCA* 42 (1971) 192–255.

James, M. R. *The Apocryphal New Testament.* Oxford: Clarendon Press, 1924.

Jastrow, M. *A Dictionary of the Targum, the Talmud Babli and Yerushalmi and the Midrashic Literature.* New York/Berlin/London, 1926.

Jellinek, A. *Bet Hamidrasch.* (Hebrew), 6 vols. Jerusalem, 1938.

Jeremias, J. "Adam Qadmon" *TDNT* 1. 141–143.

"pais theou" *TDNT* 5. 617–677.

"Zöllner und Sünder" *ZNW* 30 (1931) 292–300.

"Zum Problem des Ur-Markus" *ZNW* 25 (1936) 280–282.

"Die Lampe unter dem Scheffel" *ZNW* 39 (1940) 237–240.

*Jesus: Promise to the Nations.* London, 1958.

"The Lord's Prayer in Modern Research" *Expos. T.* 71 no. 5 Feb. 1960.

*The Parables of Jesus.* rev. ed. Trans. S. H. Hooke. New York, 1963.

*The Eucharistic Words of Jesus.* New York: Scribners, 1966.

*Jerusalem in the Time of Jesus*, trans. F. H. and C. H. Cave, 3rd ed. London, 1967.

> *The Sermon on the Mount.* (Facet Books. Biblical Series 2), trans. N. Perrin. Philadelphia: Fortress Press, 1963.

Johnson, M. *The Purpose of the Biblical Genealogies.* Cambridge, 1969.

Johnson, S. E. *The Gospel According to St. Mark.* London, 1960.

Jones, A. H. M. *The Herods of Judaea.* Oxford, 1939.

> *Studies in Roman Government and Law.* New York, 1960.

de Jonge, M. "The Use of the Word 'Anointed' in the Time of Jesus" *NT* 8 (1966) 132–148.

Jülicher, A. *Die Gleichnisreden Jesu*, 2 vols. Tübingen, 1910.

Juster, J. *Les Juifs dans l'empire romain*, 2 vols. Paris, 1914.

Kee, A. "The Old Coat and the New Wine: A Parable of Repentance" *NT* 12 (1970) 13–21.

Kee, H. C. "The Terminology of Mark's Exorcism Stories" *NTS* 14 (1967–58) 232–246.

Kennard Jr., J. S. "Hosanna and the Purpose of Jesus" *JBL* 67 (1948) 171–176.

Kilpatrick, G. D. *The Origins of the Gospel According to St. Matthew.* Oxford: Clarendon Press, 1946.

> *The Church and the Law of Nullity of Marriage.* London, 1955.

King, G. B. "The Negative Golden Rule" *Journal of Religion* 8 (1928) 268–279.

Kingsburg, J. D. *The Parables of Jesus in Matthew 13: A Study in Redaction Criticism.* Richmond: John Knox Press, 1969.

Kittel, G. *Theological Dictionary of the New Testament*, ed. G. W. Bromiley. Grand Rapids, Mich., 1964–76.

Klausner, J. *Jesus of Nazareth*, trans. H. Danby. New York: Macmillan, 1943.

Klostermann, E. *Das Markusevangelium*, 2nd ed. Tübingen, 1926.

Knox, W. L. *Some Hellenistic Elements in Primitive Christianity.* London: British Academy, 1944.

Koehler, L. "Hebräische Vokabeln II" *ZAW* 55 (1937) 161–174.

Kohler, K. "Abba Father Title of Spiritual Leader and Saint" *JQR* 13 (1900–01) 567–580.

> "Zu Mat. 5.22" *ZNW* 19 (1920) 91–95.

Kosmala, H. "Das tut zu meinem Gedächtnis" *NT* 4 (1960) 81–94.

Kraeling, C. H. *John the Baptist.* New York: Scribners, 1951.

Krauss, S. *Griechische und lateinische Lehnwörter im Talmud, Midrasch und Targum*, 2 vols. Berlin, 1898–99.

> *Das Leben Jesu nach jüdischen Quellen.* Berlin, 1902.

> *Talmudische Archäologie*, 3 vols. Leipzig, 1910.

> *Synagogale Altertümer.* Berlin/Vienna, 1922.

Kregenbuhl, J. "Das Ort der Verurteilung Jesu" *ZNW* 2 (1902) 15–22.

Lacheman, E. R. "Apropos Is. 7.14" *JBR* 22 (1954) 43.

Lachs, S. T. "A Jesus Passage in the Talmud Re-examined" *JQR* 59 (1969) 244–247.

> "Rabbi Abbahu and the Minim" *JQR* 60 (1970) 197–212.

> "On Matthew VI.12" *Novum Testamentum* 17 (1975) 6–8.

"On Matthew 23.27–28" *HTR* 68 (1975) 385–388.

"John the Baptist and his Audience" *Gratz College Annual of Jewish Studies* 4 (1975) 28–32.

"Evidence for an emendation: Exodus IV.11" *Vetus Testamentum* 24 (1976) 249–250.

"Studies in the Semitic Background to the Gospel of Matthew" *JQR* 67 (1977) 195–217.

"The Pharisees and Sadducees on Angels: A Reexamination of Acts XXIII.8" *Gratz College Annual of Jewish Studies* 6 (1977) 35–42.

"A Rabbinic Comment on Exodus 1.10." In *Shiv'im: Essays and Studies in Honor of Ira Eisenstein*. New York, 1977, 91–95.

"Some Textual Observations on the Sermon on the Mount" *JQR* 69 (1978) 99–111.

"Epiousios: Another Suggestion." In *Jewish Civilization: Essays and Studies*, ed. R. A. Brauner. Philadelphia, 1979, 65–71.

"Hebrew Elements in the Gospels and Acts" *JQR* 71 (1980) 31–43.

"The End of the Blue Thread." In *Jewish Civilization: Essays and Studies*, Vol. II, ed. R. A. Brauner. Philadelphia, 1981, 55ff.

"Rabbinic Sources for New Testament Studies: Use and Misuse" *JQR* 74 (1983) 159–173.

"Rabbinic Miscellany" *Gratz College Anniversary Volume: On the Occasion of the Ninetieth Anniversary of the Founding of the College Anniversary Volume*. Philadelphia, 1986 (in press).

"Semitic Readings in the Synoptic Gospels" (forthcoming).

Ladel, G. E. *Jesus and the Kingdom*. London, 1966.

Lagrange, M-J. *Evangile selon Saint Marc*. Paris, 1966.

Leaney, A. R. C. "Birth Narratives in St. Luke and St. Matthew" *NTS* 8 (1961–62) 161f.

Lidzbarski, M. *Handbuch der nordsemitischen Epigraphik* Weimar: E. Felber, 1898.

Lieberman, S. *Greek in Jewish Palestine*. New York, 1942.

    *Hellenism in Jewish Palestine*. New York, 1950.

    *Tosefta Kifshuta, Seder Zeraim*. New York, 1955.

    *Tosefta Kifshuta, Seder Nashim*. New York, 1955.

Lietzmann, H. "Bemerkungen zum Prozess Jesu" *ZNW* 30 (1931) 211–214.

Lohmeyer, E. *The Lord's Prayer*, English trans. London, 1965.

    *Das Evangelium des Markus*. Göttingen, 1970.

Lohse, E. "synedrion" *TDNT* 7.865–866.

Löw, I. *Die Flora der Juden*. Vienna, 1924–28.

Maccoby, H. Z. "Jesus and Barabbas" *NTS* 16 (1969–70) 55–59.

    "The Washing of Cups" *JSNT* 14 (1982) 3–15.

Mann, J. "Jesus and the Sadducean Priests: Luke 10. 25–37" *JQR* 6 (1916) 415–422.

Mantel, H. *Studies in the History of the Sanhedrin*. Harvard Semitic Series, 17. Cambridge, Mass., 1965.

Mantey, J. R. "The Mistranslation of the Perfect Tense in John 20.23, Matt. 16.19, Matt. 18.18." *JBL* 58 (1939) 234–249.

Marmorstein, A. *Studies in Jewish Theology*, ed. J. J. Rabbinowitz and M. Slew. London, New York, Toronto: Oxford University Press, 1950.

McEleney, N. J. "Conversion, Circumcision and the Law" *NTS* 20 (1974) 319–341.

McNeile, A. M. *The Gospel According to St. Matthew*. London, 1915.

Manson, T. W. *The Sayings of Jesus*. London: SCM Press, 1971.
 *The Teachings of Jesus*. Cambridge, 1931.
Mayo, C. H. "St. Peters' Token of the Cock-Crow" *JTS* 22 (1921) 367–370.
Metzger, B. "How Many times Does *Epiousios* Occur Outside of the Lord's Prayer?" *Expos.T.* 69 no. 2 (Nov. 1957).
 *A Textual Commentary on the Greek New Testament*. New York, 1971.
Montefiore, C. G. *The Synoptic Gospels*, 2 vols. New York: Ktav, 1968.
 *Rabbinic Literature and Gospel Teaching*. New York: Ktav, 1970.
Montgomery, J. *The Samaritans, The Earliest Jewish Sect, Their History, Theology and Literature*. Philadelphia, 1907.
Moore, G. F. "Christian Writers on Judaism" *HTR* 14 (1921) 187–254.
 *Judaisim in the First Centuries of the Christian Era: The Age of the Tannaim*, 2 Vols. Cambridge: Harvard University Press, 1927; Vol. 3 *Notes* 1930.
Moulton, J. H. and G. Milligan. *Vocabulary of the Greek New Testament Illustrated from the Papyri and Other Non-Literary Sources*. London, 1949.
Nestle, E. "Epiousios in Hebrew and Aramaic" *Expos. T.* 21 (1909–1910) 43.
Neubauer, A. *La géographie du Talmud*. Paris, 1868.
Neusner, J. *The Rabbinic Traditions about the Pharisees before 70*, 3 vols. Leiden: E. J. Brill, 1971.
 *The Idea of Purity in Ancient Judaism*. Leiden: E. J. Brill, 1973.
 "First Cleanse the Inside. Halakhic Background of a Controversial Saying" *NTS* 22 (1976) 486–489.
Nineham, D. E. (ed.) *Studies in the Gospels: Essays in Memory of R. H. Lightfoot*. Oxford, 1955.
 *The Gospel of St. Mark*. Pelican Gospel Commentaries. Harmondsworth, 1962.
Nicholson, E. B. *The Gospel According to the Hebrews*. London, 1879.
Noth, N. *Die israelitischen Personennamen*. Stuttgart, 1928.
Olsen, V. N. *The New Testament Logic on Divorce*. Tübingen, 1971.
Perles, F. "Zwei Übersetzungsfehler im Text der Evangelien 1. Mt. 8.22 (= Lc 9.60) 2. Lc.14.35" *ZNW* 19 (1919–20) 96–103.
 "Zur Erklärung von Mt. 7.6" *ZNW* 25 (1926) 163–164.
 "La parabole du sel sourd" *REJ* 82 (1926) 122ff.
Perrins, N. *The Kingdom of God in the Teaching of Jesus*. London, 1963.
Perowne, S. *The Life and Times of Herod the Great*. London, 1956.
Petuchowski, J. J. and Brocke, M. eds. *The Lord's Prayer and the Jewish Liturgy*. New York, 1978.
Philippides, L. *Die 'Goldene Regel' religionsgeschichtlich untersucht*. Leipzig, 1929.
Plummer, A. *The Gospel according to St. Luke* (ICC). Edinburgh, 1908.
 "The Woman that was a Sinner" *Expos. T.* 27 (1915–16) 42–43.
Pope, M. *The Song of Songs*. Anchor Bible. Garden City, New York: Doubleday, 1977.
Preuss, J. *Biblisch-talmudische Medizin*. Berlin, 1923.
Rabinowitz, J. J. "The Sermon on the Mount and the School of Shammai" *HTR* 49 (1956) 79ff.
Rawlinson, A. E. J. *The Gospel According to St. Mark*, 7th ed. London, 1949.
Reinach, T. *Jewish Coins*. London: Lawrence & Bullen, 1903.
Rengstorf, K. H. "lestes" *TDNT* 4. 257–262.
Riggs, H. A. "Barabbas" *JBL* 64 (1945) 417–465.
Rivkin, E. *A Hidden Revolution*. Nashville: Abingdon, 1978.

Rosenblatt, S. "The Crucifixion of Jesus from the Standpoint of Pharisaic Law" *JBL* 75 (1956) 317–319.

Ruger, H. P. "Mit welchem Mass ihr messt, wird euch gemessen werden" *ZNW* 60 (1969) 174–183.

Sanders, J. A. "From Isaiah 61 to Luke 4." In *Christianity, Judaism and Other Graeco-Roman Cults (SJLA* 2), ed. J. Neusner. Leiden: E. J. Brill, 1975.

Sandmel, S. "Parallelomania" *JBL* 81 (1962) 1ff.

*We Jews and Jesus.* New York: Oxford University Press, 1965.

Schechter, S. "The Rabbinical Concept of Holiness" *JQR* 10 (1898) 11f.

"On the Study of the Talmud." In *Studies in Judaism*, Second Series. Philadelphia, 1908 pp. 102–110.

*Some Aspects of Rabbinic Theology.* London, New York, 1910.

*Documents of Jewish Sectaries* Vol. I *Fragments of a Zadokite Work . . . with an English translation, Introduction and Notes.* Cambridge, 1910.

Schlatter, A. *Die Kirche Jerusalems vom Jahre 70–130.* Gütersloh, 1898.

*Der Evangelist Matthäus*, 6th ed. Stuttgart, 1963.

Schmid, J. *Das Evangelium nach Markus*, 4th ed. Regensburg, 1958.

Schnakenburg, R. *God's Rule and the Kingdom*, English trans. London, 1963.

Schmidt, K. L. "ekklesia" *TDNT* 3.501–526.

Schürer, E. *Geschichte des jüdischen Volkes im Zeitalter Jesu Christi*, 3rd–4th ed. 3 vols. Leipzig, 1901–1911.

Shanks, H. "Is the Title Rabbi Anachronistic in the Gospels?" *JQR* 53 (1963) 317–345.

Sherwin-White, A. N. *Roman Society and Roman Law in the New Testament.* New York, Oxford, 1963.

Shubert, K. "The Sermon on the Mount and the Qumran Texts." In *The Scrolls and the New Testament*, ed. K. Stendahl. London, 1958, 118–128.

Simon, M. *Jewish Sects at the Time of Jesus.* Philadelphia, 1973.

Singer, I. *Authorized Prayer Book: Hebrew and English*, 13th ed. London, 1925.

Sloyan, G. *Jesus on Trial.* Philadelphia, 1973.

Smallwood, M. "High Priests and Politics in Roman Palestine" *JTS* 13 (1962) 22–29.

Smith, R. H. "The Tomb of Jesus" *BA* 30 (1967) 14–90.

Smith, M. "Mt. 5.43 'Hate Thine Enemy' " *HTR* 45 (1952) 75ff.

"Zealots and Sicarii, their Origins and Relation" *HTR* 64 (1971) 1–19.

*Jesus the Magician.* San Francisco: Harper Row, 1978.

Sparks, H. F. D. "The Doctrine of Divine Fatherhood in the Gospels" *Studies in the Gospels*, ed. D. Nineham. Oxford, 1955, 241–262.

Stauffer, E. *Jerusalem und Rom im zeitalter Jesu Christi.* Bern 1957.

Stendahl, K. (ed.) *The Scrolls and the New Testament.* London, 1958.

*The School of Matthew and its Use of the Old Testament.* Philadelphia, Fortress Press. 1968.

Strack, H. and Billerbeck, P. *Kommentar zum Neuen Testament*, 6 vols. Munich 1922.

Streeter, B. H. *The Four Gospels: A Study of Origins.* London, 1962.

Sukenik, E. L. "Ancient Synagogues in Palestine and Greece" *JPOS* 8 (1928) 119f.

Swete, H. B. *The Gospel According to St. Mark.* London, 1920.

Taylor, C. *The Sayings of the Fathers.* Cambridge: Cambridge University Press, 1877.

Thayer, J. H. *"Su eipas Su legeis* in the Answers of Jesus" *JBL* 13 (1894) 40–49.

Thompson, S. *Motif-Index of Folk-Literature.* Bloomington Indiana: University of Indiana Press. 1958.

Tigay, J. "On the Term Phylacteries in Matt. 23.5" *HTR* 75 (1982) 245–252.

Torrey, C. C. "Medina and Polis and Luke 5.39" *HTR* 17 (1924) 83–91.

*Documents of the Primitive Church.* New York, 1941.

"The Name Iscariot" *HTR* 36 (1943) 51–62.

*The Four Gospels: A New Translation,* 2nd ed. New York, 1947.

*The Lives of the Prophets.* Philadelphia, SBL 1964.

Townsend, J. "Matthew XXIII.9" *JTS* 12 (1961) 56–59.

"I Corinthians 3.15 and the School of Shammai" *HTR* 61 (1968) 500–504.

*A Liturgical Interpretation of Our Lord's Passion in Narrative Form.* New York: National Conference of Christians and Jews, 1977.

Toy, C. H. *Quotations in the New Testament.* New York: Scribners, 1884.

Turner, C. H. "The Gospel of Peter" *JTS* 14 (1912–13) 161–195.

Urbach, E. E. *The Sages: Their Concepts and Beliefs,* trans. I. Abrahams. Jerusalem, 1975.

Verrall, A. W. "Christ Before Herod" *JTS* 10 (1909) 321–353.

Weiss *Die Schriften des Neuen Testaments überzetzt und . . . erklärt.* Vol. I *Die Drei Ältern Evanglien,* 3rd ed. 1917.

Wellhausen, J. *Das Evangelium Matthäii.* Berlin, 1904.

Werner, E. "Hosanna in the Gospels" *JBL* 65 (1946) 97–122.

White, K. D. "The Parable of the Sower" *JTS* 45 (1965) 300–307.

Wilson, W. R. *The Execution of Jesus.* New York, 1970.

Winter, P. "Luke 2.49 and Targum Yerushalmi" *ZNW* 45 (1954) 145–149.

"Luke 2.49 and Targum Yerushalmi Again" *ZNW* 46 1955 140–144.

"Lukanische Miszellen" *ZNW* 49 (1958) 65–66.

*On the Trial of Jesus.* Berlin, 1961.

"The Trial of Jesus and the Competence of the Sanhedrin" *NTS* 10 (1963–64) 494–499.

Wünsche, A. *Neue Beiträge zur Erläuterungen der Evangelien aus Talmud und Midrasch.* Göttingen, 1878.

Yadin, Y. *The Cave of Letters.* Jerusalem, 1963.

Zeitlin, S. "Les dix-huit Mesures" *REJ* 67 (1915) 22–36.

"The Christ Passage in Josephus" *JQR* 17 (1928) 230–255.

*Josephus on Jesus.* Philadelphia, 1931.

"The Am HaAretz" *JQR* 23 (1931) 45ff.

"The Origin of the Synagogue" *PAAJR* 2 (1930–31) 69–81.

"An Historical Study of the Canonization of Hebrew Scriptures" *PAAJR* 3 (1931–2) 121–158.

"The Pharisees and the Gospels." In *Essays and Studies in Memory of Linda R. Miller,* ed. Israel Davidson. New York, 1938, pp. 235–286.

*Who Crucified Jesus?* New York/London:Harper, 1942.

"Prosbul: A Study in Tannaitic Jurisprudence" *JQR* 37 (1947) 347–362.

"The Liturgy of the First Night of Passover" *JQR* 38 (1948) 431–460.

*The Rise and Fall of the Judaean State,* 3 vols. Philadelphia, 1962–78.

"A Reply" *JQR* 53 (1963) 345–349.

"The Date of the Birth and Crucifixion of Jesus" *JQR* 55 (1964) 1–22.

"The Duration of Jesus' Ministry" *JQR* 55 (1965) 181–200.

Zimmermann, F. *The Aramaic Origin of the Four Gospels.* New York: Ktav, 1979.

Zunz, L. *Die gottesdienstlichen Vorträge der Juden.* Frankfort am Main, 1892.

"Namen der Juden" *Gesammelte Schriften,* vol. 2. Berlin, 1876, pp. 1–83.

# INDEX TO THE COMMENTARY

459